Alexander Pope
Ezra Pound
Craig Raine
Dudley Randall
John Crowe Ransom
Henry Reed
James Reeves
Alastair Reid
Adrienne Rich
John Ridland
Rainer Maria Rilke
Edwin Arlington Robinson
Theodore Roethke
Wendy Rose
Christina Rossetti
Clare Rossini
Run D.M.C.
Kay Ryan
Benjamin Alire Sáenz
Mary Jo Salter

Carl Sandburg
Carole Satyamurti
Gjertrud Schnackenberg
Anne Sexton
William Shakespeare
Percy Bysshe Shelley
Charles Simic
Paul Simon
Louis Simpson
David Slavitt
Christopher Smart
Bessie Smith
Stevie Smith
William Jay Smith
Gary Snyder
Cathy Song
Sor Juana
William Stafford
A. E. Stallings
Jon Stallworthy

Timothy Steele
James Stephens
Wallace Stevens
Anne Stevenson
Michael Stillman
Ruth Stone
Alfonsina Storni
Jonathan Swift
Stephen Tapscott
Henry Taylor
Sara Teasdale
Alfred, Lord Tennyson
Cornelius Ter Maat
Diane Thiel
Dylan Thomas
Chidiock Tichborne
Charles Tomlinson
Jean Toomer
Grace Treasone
Natasha Trethewey

Amy Uyematsu
César Vallejo
Hakuro Wada
Derek Walcott
Arthur Waley
Edmund Waller
Walt Whitman
Richard Wilbur
C. K. Williams
Clarence Williams
William Carlos Williams
William Wordsworth
James Wright
Mary Sidney Wroth
Sir Thomas Wyatt
William Butler Yeats
Chryss Yost

CRITICS

Mark Bauerlein
Roland Barthes
Harold Bloom
Cleanth Brooks
Rita Dove
Judith Farr
Leslie Fiedler
Stanley Fish
Sigmund Freud

Northrop Frye
Sandra Gilbert
Heather Glen
Susan Gubar
Geoffrey Hartman
Thomas Wentworth
    Higginson
Onwuchekwa Jemie
Thomas H. Johnson

Carl Jung
Alfred Kazin
Hugh Kenner
Robert Langbaum
Georg Lukacs
Stephanie Merrim
Brett Millier
Joseph Moldenhauer
Emir Rodríguez Monegal

Marilyn Nelson
Darryl Pinckney
Arnold Rampersad
Alastair Reid
Robert Scholes
Elaine Showalter
Peter Townsend
Richard Wilbur
Cynthia Griffin Wolff

WRITING RESOURCES

An Introduction to
POETRY

An Introduction to
POETRY

Eleventh Edition

X. J. KENNEDY

DANA GIOIA

PEARSON
Longman

New York   Boston   San Francisco
London   Toronto   Sydney   Tokyo   Singapore   Madrid
Mexico City   Munich   Paris   Cape Town   Hong Kong   Montreal

Vice President and Editor-in-Chief: Joseph Terry
Development Manager: Janet Lanphier
Development Editor: Katharine Glynn
Senior Marketing Manager: Melanie Craig
Senior Supplements Editor: Donna Campion
Media Supplements Editor: Nancy Garcia
Production Manager: Joseph Vella
Project Coordination, Text Design, and Electronic Page Makeup: Nesbitt Graphics, Inc.
Cover Design Manager: John Callahan
Cover Designer: Mary McDonnell
Cover Image: Winslow Homer, *Fisherman's Family (The Lookout)*, 1881, bequest of John
    T. Spaulding. Photograph © 2003 Museum of Fine Arts, Boston. All rights reserved.
Photo Researcher: Photosearch, Inc.
Manufacturing Buyer: Roy L. Pickering, Jr.
Printer and Binder: Quebecor World Taunton
Cover Printer: The Lehigh Press, Inc.

For permission to use copyrighted material, grateful acknowledgment is made to the copyright holders on pp. 711–722, which are hereby made part of this copyright page.

Library of Congress Cataloging-in-Publication Data
On file at the Library of Congress.

Please visit our website at http://www.ablongman.com/kennedy

ISBN 0-321-20939-7

1 2 3 4 5 6 7 8 9 10—QWT—07 06 05 04

Contents

3 *Words* 53

6   Figures of Speech   118

7 Song   141

8   *Sound*   165

9   *Rhythm*   188

13 Myth and Narrative 278

21 Lives of the Poets

WRITING

22 Writing About Literature

23 Writing About a Poem

Glossary of Literary Terms   693

16 *Critical Casebook: Latin American Poetry* 345

17 Recognizing Excellence 370

Preface

What is poetry? Pressed for an answer, Robert Frost made a classic reply: "Poetry is the kind of thing poets write." In all likelihood, Frost was not trying merely to evade the question but to chide his questioner into thinking for himself. A trouble with definitions is that they may stop thought. If Frost had said, "Poetry is a rhythmical composition of words expressing an attitude, designed to surprise and delight, and to arouse an emotional response," the questioner might have settled back in his or her chair, content to have learned the truth about poetry. He or she would have learned nothing, or not so much as one might learn by continuing to wonder.

The nature of poetry eludes simple definitions. (In this respect it is rather like jazz. Asked after one of his concerts, "What is jazz?" Louis Armstrong replied, "Man, if you gotta ask, you'll never know.") Definitions will be of little help at first, if we are to know poetry and respond to it. We have to go to it willing to see and hear. For this reason, you are asked in reading this book not to be in any hurry to decide what poetry is, but instead to study poems and to let them grow in your mind.

Confronted with a formal introduction to poetry, you may be wondering, "Who needs it?" and you may well be right. It's unlikely that you have avoided meeting poetry before; and perhaps you already have a friendship, or at least a fair acquaintance, with some of the great English-speaking poets of all time. What this book provides is an introduction to the study of poetry. It tries to help you look at a poem closely, to offer you a wider and more accurate vocabulary with which to express what poems say to you. It will suggest ways to judge for yourself the poems you read. It may set forth some poems new to you.

A frequent objection is that poetry ought not to be studied at all. In this view, a poem is either a series of gorgeous noises to be funneled through one ear and out the other without being allowed to trouble the mind, or an experience so holy that to analyze it in a classroom is as cruel and mechanical as dissecting a hummingbird. To the first view, it might be countered that a good poem has something to say that is well worth listening to. To the second view, it might be argued that poems are much less perishable than hummingbirds, and luckily, we can study them in flight. The risk of a poem's dying from observation is not nearly so great as the risk of not really seeing it at all. It is doubtful that any excellent poem has ever vanished from human memory because people have read it too closely. More likely, poems that vanish are poems that no one reads closely, for no one cares.

That poetry matters to the people who write it has been shown unmistakably by the ordeal of Soviet poet Irina Ratushinskaya. Sentenced to prison for three and a half years, she was given paper and pencil once or twice a month to write letters to her husband and her parents and was not allowed to write anything else. Nevertheless, Ratushinskaya composed more than two hundred poems in her cell, engraving them with a burnt match in a bar of soap, then memorizing the lines. "I would read the poem and read it," she said, "until it was committed to memory—then with one washing of my hands, it would be gone."

Good poetry is something that readers and listeners, too, can care about. In fact, an ancient persuasion of humankind is that the hearing of a poem, as well as the making of a poem, can be a religious act. Poetry, in speech and song, was part of classic Greek drama, which for playwright, actor, and spectator alike was a holy-day ceremony. The Greeks' belief that a poet writes a poem only by supernatural assistance is clear from the invocations to the Muse that begin the *Iliad* and the *Odyssey* and from the opinion of Socrates (in Plato's *Ion*) that a poet has no powers of invention until divinely inspired. Among the ancient Celts, poets were regarded as magicians and priests, and whoever insulted one of them might expect to receive a curse in rime potent enough to afflict him with boils and to curdle the milk of his cows. Such identifications between the poet and the magician are less common these days, although we know that poetry is invoked in the primitive white-magic of children, who bring themselves good luck in a game with the charm "Roll, roll, tootsie-roll! / Roll the marble in the hole!" and who warn against a hex while jumping along a sidewalk "Step on a crack, / Break your mother's back." Whether we attribute the effect of a poem to a divine spirit or to the reactions of our glands and cortexes, we have to take the reading of poetry seriously (not solemnly), if only because few other efforts can repay us so generously, both in wisdom and in joy.

If, as we hope you will do, you sometimes browse in the book for fun, you may be annoyed to see so many questions following the poems. Should you feel this way, try reading with a slip of paper to cover up the questions. You will then—if the Muse should inspire you—have paper in hand to write a poem.

A WORD ABOUT CAREERS

Students tend to agree that to read poets such as Shakespeare, Keats, Emily Dickinson, and Robert Frost is probably good for the spirit, and most even take some pleasure in the experience. But many, not planning to teach English and impatient to begin some other career, wonder if the study of poetry, however enjoyable, isn't a waste of time—or at least, an annoying obstacle.

This objection may seem reasonable at first glance, but it rests on a shaky assumption. Success in a career does *not* depend merely on learning the specialized information and skills required to join a profession. In most careers, according to one senior business executive, people often fail not because they don't understand their jobs, but because they don't understand their co-workers, their clients, or their customers. They don't ever see the world from another person's point of view. Their problem is a failure of imagination.

To leap over the wall of self, to look through another's eyes—this is valuable experience, which literature offers. Although if you are lucky, you may never meet (or have to do business with) anyone *exactly* like the insanely jealous speaker of the poem "Soliloquy of the Spanish Cloister," you will probably learn much about the kind of person he is from Robert Browning's portrait of him. Who knows? Among your fellow students may be a J. Alfred Prufrock (the central character of T. S. Eliot's poem), or someone like John Updike's ex-basketball player.

What is it like to be black, a white may wonder? Perhaps Langston Hughes, Claude McKay, Gwendolyn Brooks, Rita Dove, Dudley Randall, Yusef Komunyakaa, and others have something to tell. What is it like to be a woman? If a man would learn, let him read (for a start) Emily Dickinson, Sylvia Plath, Anne Sexton, Denise Levertov, Adrienne Rich, Anne Bradstreet, Carole Satyamurti, Rhina Espaillat, Sharon Olds, and many more.

Plodding single-mindedly toward careers, some people are like horses wearing blinders. For many, the goals looked fixed and predictable. Competent nurses, accountants, and dental technicians seem always in demand. Others may find that in our society some careers, like waves in the sea, will rise or fall unexpectedly. Think of how many professions we now take for granted which a few years ago didn't even exist: genetic engineering, energy conservation, digital editing, and Website design. Others that once looked like lifetime meal tickets have been cut back and nearly ruined: shoe repairing, commercial fishing, railroading.

In a perpetually changing society, it may be risky to lock yourself on one track to a career, refusing to consider any other. "We are moving," writes John Naisbitt in *Megatrends*, a study of our changing society, "from the specialist, soon obsolete, to the generalist who can adapt." Perhaps the greatest opportunity in your whole life lies in a career that has yet to be invented. If you do change your career as you go along, you will be like most people. According to a U.S. Bureau of Labor Statistics survey conducted in April, 2000, the average person holds over nine jobs between the ages of 18 and 34—often completely changing his or her basic occupation. When for some unforeseen reason you have to make such a change, basic skills—and knowledge of humanity—may be your most valuable credentials.

Literature has much practical knowledge to offer you. An art of words, it can help you become more sensitive to language—both your own and other people's. It can make you aware of the difference between the word that is exactly right and the word that is merely good enough—Mark Twain calls it "the difference between the lightning and the lightning-bug." Read a fine work of literature alertly, and some of its writer's sensitivity to words may grow on you. A Supreme Court Justice, John Paul Stevens, once remarked that the best preparation for law school is to study poetry. Why? George D. Gopen, an English professor with a law degree, says it may be because "no other discipline so closely replicates the central question asked in the study of legal thinking: Here is a text; in how many ways can it have meaning?"

Many careers today, besides law, call for close reading and clear writing—as well as careful listening and thoughtful speech. Lately, college placement directors have reported more demand for graduates who are good readers and writers. The reason is evident: employers need people who can handle words. In a survey conducted by Cornell University, business executives were asked to rank in importance the traits they look for when hiring. Leadership was first, but skill in writing and speaking came in fourth, ahead of both managerial and analytical skills. Times change, but to think cogently and to express yourself well will always be the abilities the world needs.

KEY LITERARY TERMS

Every discipline has its own terminology. This book introduces a large range of critical terms that may help you in both your reading and writing. When these important words and phrases are first defined, they are printed in **boldface.** If you meet a critical term anywhere in this book you don't know or don't recall—what is a *carpe diem* poem or iambic pentameter?—just look it up in the "Glossary of Literary Terms" in the back of the book.

TEXTS AND DATES

Every effort has been made to supply each selection in its most accurate text and (where necessary) in a lively, faithful translation. For the reader who wishes to know when a work was written, at the right of each title appears the date of its first publication in book form. Parentheses around a date indicate the work's date of composition or first magazine publication, given when it was composed much earlier than when it was first published in book form.

A POSSIBLY PUZZLING ASTERISK

Throughout the book you will often notice an asterisk (*) after a poet's byline. This asterisk indicates that there is a short biography of the author in Chapter 21, "Lives of the Poets." This special chapter offers 79 biographies of the poets represented in the anthology by two or more poems. For easy reference we have tucked them into one place. The only exceptions are the more extensive biographical notes on Sor Juana, Pablo Neruda, Jorge Luis Borges, and Octavio Paz, the poets collected in Chapter 16, "Critical Casebook: Latin American Poetry," and Emily Dickinson and Langston Hughes, which appear (with substantial selections of their work) in Chapter 19, "Two Critical Casebooks: Emily Dickinson and Langston Hughes."

But enough housekeeping, let's enjoy ourselves and read some poems.

X. J. K. AND D. G.

To the Instructor

An *Introduction to Poetry*, Eleventh Edition, is a book divided into two parts—poetry and writing. The aim of the book is first to introduce college students to the appreciation and experience of poetry. Second, the book tries to develop the student's ability to think critically and to communicate effectively through writing.

Both editors of this volume are poets. We believe that textbooks should not only be informative and accurate but also lively, accessible, and engaging. Our intent has always been to write a book that students will read eagerly and enjoy.

The new edition of *An Introduction to Poetry* offers a number of compelling features:

- **Great poems old and new**—Over 500 poems mixing classic favorites with exciting contemporary work.
- **Author casebooks**—Two extensive casebooks on Emily Dickinson and Langston Hughes present multiple selections by each author along with reflections by the author, critical articles, and other contextual material.
- **New Casebook on Latin American Poetry**—invites students to experience an important world poetry in a different language and translation. Poems from Sor Juana, Pablo Neruda, Jorge Luis Borges, Octavio Paz, and others illuminate different cultural experiences.
- **Critical coverage**—58 critical excerpts including a comprehensive survey of ten major schools of literary criticism and theory.
- **Writing coverage**—integrated into every chapter with exercises, sample papers, and pragmatic advice. Three complete chapters are devoted to writing about literature and include student drafts and completed papers.
- **New chapter on writing a research paper**—offers helpful advice on such topics as getting started, evaluating and using Internet sources, guarding academic integrity, plagiarism, and acknowledging and documenting sources.
- **Real student writing**—6 student essays by real students provide credible examples on how to write about literature.

All in all, we have tried to create a book to help readers develop sensitivity to language, culture, and identity to lead them beyond the boundaries of their own selves and see the world through the eyes of others. This book is built on the assumption that great literature can enrich and enlarge the lives it touches.

FEATURES IN THIS EDITION

We have revised the eleventh edition of *An Introduction to Poetry* with the simple aim of introducing useful new features and selections without losing the best liked material. We have been guided in this effort by scores of instructors and students who use the book in their classrooms. Teaching is a kind of conversation between instructor and student and between reader and text. By revising *An Introduction to Poetry*, we try to help keep this conversation fresh by mixing the classic with the new and the familiar with the surprising.

CASEBOOKS ON MAJOR POETS

We continue to include two substantial casebooks on major poets. This special chapter presents a variety of material—biographies, photographs, critical commentaries, statements by the authors, and a deep selection of the featured writer's work. Our aim has been to provide everything a student might need to begin an in-depth study of each poet. We present in-depth selections from Emily Dickinson and Langston Hughes with fifteen poems each—supplemented by others elsewhere in the volume—as well as ten critical articles, photographs, facsimiles, letters, and statements.

NEW LATIN AMERICAN POETRY CASEBOOK

Experiencing poetry in a different language and in translation gives students the opportunity to see how poetry represents and illuminates a different cultural experience. A new thematic casebook, "Latin American Poetry," gives students this enriching and challenging experience with voices including Sor Juana, Pablo Neruda, Jorge Luis Borges, and Octavio Paz. Students are also introduced to the role of surrealism in Latin American poetry with an image from Frida Kahlo and words from César Vallejo and Olga Orozco. We feel this important and unique new chapter will not only broaden most students' knowledge of world poetry, but will also recognize the richness of Spanish-language poetry in the literature of the Americas—a very relevant subject to today's multicultural classrooms.

GLOSSARY OF LITERARY TERMS

The comprehensive "Glossary of Literary Terms" at the back of the book has been retained by popular demand from the previous edition. It includes every term highlighted in boldface throughout the text as well as other important terms—over 200 entries in all—providing a clear and accurate definition usually with cross references to related terms. The purpose of the glossary is to provide a single accessible reference for students of all key literary terms.

WRITING MATERIAL

All the main chapters still include a "Writer's Perspective," a "Writing Critically" feature, and "Further Suggestions for Writing." The extremely popular "Writer's

Perspective" provides an author's own comments on his or her work reprinted in the chapter. You will read Adrienne Rich discussing "Aunt Jennifer's Tigers," Gwendolyn Brooks on "We Real Cool," and Anne Sexton on her reinterpretations of fairy tales. Other "Writer's Perspectives" show poets explaining their views on the general topic of the chapter. Ezra Pound discusses poetic imagery, W. B. Yeats talks about poetic symbols, and Rhina Espaillat examines the notion of being a bilingual writer. These selections not only illuminate the poems found in the chapter; they also introduce students to the many ways that writers discuss poetry. Meanwhile "Writing Critically" focuses on the practical issues students face in planning and composing student essays. This feature gives students strategies to begin writing on poetry. Many students feel intimidated by poetry—especially when asked to write about it in critical terms. As its title suggests, "Writing Critically" provides students with some accessible advice on both critical thinking and the writing process. Each "Writing Critically" section also concludes with a specific assignment for a term paper.

We have also reprinted the student essays from the last edition—six complete papers to provide students with models for their own critical writing. Three of the papers are found in Chapter 23, "Writing About Poetry," where they illustrate three different approaches to critical writing—explication, analysis, and comparison. Three papers (written by real students) will be found in earlier chapters. Each focuses on a single poem in the book (Theodore Roethke's "My Papa's Waltz," Elizabeth Bishop's "The Fish," and H. D.'s "Helen"). The papers provide close readings of the poems that emphasize specific elements of their structure and meaning.

New Chapter, "Writing a Research Paper"

A new addition to the writing section is Chapter 24, "Writing a Research Paper." Guiding students through the research process, the chapter covers such topics as getting started, evaluating and using Internet sources, guarding academic integrity, plagiarism, and acknowledging and documenting sources. This chapter also provides extensive guidelines and examples for preparing and formatting papers according to 2003 MLA standards.

New Poems

There are many new selections in the book. A great deal of help came from both instructors and students who use the book. Their suggestions helped confirm the new poems that work best in the classroom while identifying older selections that seemed less valuable and could be retired to make room for new work.

An Introduction to Poetry, Eleventh Edition proudly provides the most extensive selection of poems found in any comparable book in the field—over 500 poems in the new edition. We have added more than 70 new poems to the book—to freshen the selections, update our coverage of contemporary work, and expand our presentation of Asian and Latin American poetry.

The new Latin American poetry casebook includes a pair of poems by Sor Juana, Pablo Neruda, Jorge Luis Borges, and Octavio Paz. Surrealism in Latin American poetry is explored through an image from Frida Kahlo and words from César Vallejo and Olga Orozco. Works from other fine contemporary Latin American poets are included.

Many other fine new poems have been added by writers including Sherman Alexie, W. H. Auden, Connie Bensley, Gwendolyn Brooks, Billy Collins, Wendy Cope, Rita Dove, B. H. Fairchild, Donald Justice, Louis MacNeice, Suiko Matsushita, Robert McDowell, Josephine Miles, John Milton, Rainer Maria Rilke, Gary Snyder, Natasha Trethewey, Amy Uyematsu, and William Carlos Williams. Not only are Dickinson and Hughes presented in depth, but the reader will also find multiple selections by W. H. Auden, William Blake, Gwendolyn Brooks, E. E. Cummings, John Donne, T. S. Eliot, Robert Frost, Thomas Hardy, Gerard Manley Hopkins, John Keats, Edna St. Vincent Millay, Adrienne Rich, William Shakespeare, Wallace Stevens, Alfred, Lord Tennyson, Walt Whitman, William Carlos Williams, William Wordsworth, and William Butler Yeats.

CRITICAL APPROACHES TO LITERATURE

Chapter 25, "Critical Approaches to Literature," has proven so popular in the last few editions that we have kept and slightly updated it in the new edition of *An Introduction to Poetry*. There are two selections for every major critical school—20 selections in all. The critical excerpts have been carefully chosen both to illustrate the major theoretical approaches and to be accessible to beginning students. The critical selections focus on literary works found in the present edition. Taken together with the many commentaries in the casebooks and Writer's Perspectives, *An Introduction to Poetry* now includes a total of 58 critical excerpts. This expanded coverage gives the book both more depth and flexibility for instructors who prefer to incorporate literary theory and criticism into their introductory courses.

OTHER EDITIONS AVAILABLE

Instructors who wish to cover the other major forms of literature may want to know about *Literature: An Introduction to Fiction, Poetry, and Drama*, Ninth Edition, and *An Introduction to Fiction*, Ninth Edition. Each book has writing chapters applicable to its subject, and "Writing About Literature," "Writing a Research Paper," and "Critical Approaches to Literature." There is also a compact edition in paperback of *Literature: An Introduction to Fiction, Poetry, and Drama* for instructors who find the full edition of *Literature* "too much book." Although this compact version offers a slightly abridged table of contents, it still covers the complete range of topics presented in the full edition.

For instructors who want to incorporate media into their class, interactive editions of *Literature*, Ninth Edition and of *Literature*, Fourth Compact Edition come packaged with *The Craft of Literature* CD-ROM. This multi-media CD-ROM offers film footage, audio, photographs, Web links, interactive readings, critical articles, and student papers related to the selections in *Literature*.

RESOURCES FOR STUDENTS AND INSTRUCTORS

FOR STUDENTS

COMPANION WEBSITE TO AN INTRODUCTION TO POETRY, ELEVENTH EDITION

(*http://www.ablongman.com/kennedy*)

The text-specific site includes biographies, bibliographies, and links to sites about many of the authors found in *An Introduction to Poetry*, Eleventh Edition.

HANDBOOK OF LITERARY TERMS

Handbook of Literary Terms by X. J. Kennedy, Dana Gioia, and Mark Bauerlein is a user-friendly primer of over 350 critical terms brought to life with literary examples, pronunciation guides, and scholarly yet accessible explanations. Aimed at undergraduates getting their first taste of serious literary study, the volume will help students engage with the humanities canon and become critical readers and writers ready to experience the insights and joy of great fiction, poetry, and drama.

RESPONDING TO LITERATURE: A WRITER'S JOURNAL

This free journal provides students with their own personal space for writing. Helpful writing prompts for responding to poetry are also included.

LITERATURE TIMELINE

This accessible and visually appealing timeline provides students with a chronological overview of major literary works written throughout history. The timeline also lists the major sociocultural and political events that occurred contemporaneously with these major works of literature, providing students with historical and contextual insights into the impact historical events have had on writers and their works and vice versa.

RESEARCH NAVIGATOR GUIDE FOR ENGLISH

Designed to teach students how to conduct high-quality online research and to document it properly, *Research Navigator* guides provide discipline-specific academic resources in addition to helpful tips on the writing process, online research, and finding and citing valid sources. Free when packaged with any Longman text, *Research Navigator* guides include an access code to Research Navigator™, providing access to thousands of academic journals and periodicals, the New York Times Search by Subject Archive, Link Library, Library Guides, and more.

For Instructors

Instructor's Manual

A separate *Instructor's Manual* is available to instructors. If you have never seen our *Instructor's Manual* before, don't prejudge it. We actually write the manual ourselves, and we work hard to make it as interesting, lively, and informed as the parent text. It offers commentary and teaching ideas for every selection in the book. It also contains additional commentary, debate, qualifications and information—including scores of classroom ideas—from over one hundred teachers and authors. As you will see, our *Instructor's Manual* is no ordinary book.

Teaching Composition with Literature

For instructors who either use *An Introduction to Poetry* in expository writing courses or have a special emphasis on writing in their literature courses, there is an invaluable supplement, *Teaching Composition with Literature: 101 Writing Assignments from College Instructors*. Edited by Dana Gioia and Patricia Wagner, *Teaching Composition with Literature* collects proven writing assignments and classroom exercises from scores of instructors across North America. Each assignment or exercise uses one or more selections in *Literature* as its departure point. A great many instructors have enthusiastically shared their best writing assignments for *Teaching Composition with Literature*.

Video Program

For qualified adopters, an impressive selection of videotapes is available to enrich students' experience of literature. The videos include selections from William Shakespeare, Sylvia Plath, Ezra Pound, and Alice Walker. Contact your Allyn & Bacon/Longman sales representative to see if you qualify.

Teaching Literature On-line, Second Edition

Concise and practical, *Teaching Literature On-line* provides instructors with strategies and advice for incorporating elements of computer technology into the literature classroom. Offering a range of information and examples, this manual provides ideas and activities for enhancing literature courses with the help of technology.

The Longman Electronic Testbank for Literature

This electronic test bank features various objective questions on major works of fiction, short fiction, poetry, and drama. With this user-friendly CD-ROM, instructors simply choose questions from the electronic test bank, then print out the completed test for distribution.

CONTACT US

For examination copies of any of these books, CDs, videos, and programs, please contact your Allyn & Bacon/Longman sales representative, or write to Literature Marketing Manager, Longman Publishers, 1185 Avenue of the Americas, New York, NY 10036. For examination copies only, call (800) 922-0579. To order an examination copy via the Internet: *http://www.ablongman.com* or E-mail: *exam.copies@ablongman.com*.

THANKS

The collaboration necessary to create this new edition goes far beyond the partnership of its two editors. *An Introduction to Poetry* has once again been revised, corrected, and shaped by wisdom and advice from instructors who actually put it to the test—also from a number who, in teaching literature, preferred other textbooks to it, but who generously criticized this book anyway and made suggestions for it. (Some responded to the book in part, focusing their comments on the previous editions of *Literature: An Introduction to Fiction, Poetry, and Drama*.)

Deep thanks to Alvaro Aleman, University of Florida; Jonathan Alexander, University of Southern Colorado; Ann P. Allen, Salisbury State University; Brian Anderson, Central Piedmont Community College; Kimberly Green Angel, Georgia State University; Carmela A. Arnoldt, Glendale Community College; Herman Asarnow, University of Portland; Beverly Bailey, Seminole Community College; Carolyn Baker, San Antonio College; Rosemary Baker, State University of New York at Morrisville; Lee Barnes, Community College of Southern Nevada, Las Vegas; Sandra Barnhill, South Plains College; Bob Baron, Mesa Community College; Ellen Dugan-Barrette, Brescia University; Melinda Barth, El Camino Community College; Robin Barrow, University of Iowa; Joseph Bathanti, Mitchell Community College; Judith Baumel, Adelphi University; Anis Bawarski, University of Kansas; Bruce Beckum, Colorado Mountain College; Elaine Bender, El Camino Community College; Pamela Benson, Tarrant County Junior College; Jennifer Black, McLennan Community College; Brian Blackley, North Carolina State University; Paul Buchanan, Biola University; Andrew Burke, University of Georgia; Jolayne Call, Utah Valley State College; Stasia Callan, Monroe Community College; Uzzie T. Cannon, University of North Carolina at Greensboro; Al Capovilla, Folsom Lake Community College; Eleanor Carducci, Sussex County Community College; Thomas Carper, University of Southern Maine; Jean W. Cash, James Madison University; Michael Cass, Mercer University; Dr. Patricia Cearley, South Plains College; Fred Chancey, Chemeketa Community College; Kitty Chen, Nassau Community College; Edward M. Cifelli, County College of Morris; Marc Cirigliano, Empire State College; Maria Clayton, Middle Tennessee State University; Cheryl Clements, Blinn College; Jerry Coats, Tarrant County Community College; Peggy Cole, Arapahoe Community College; Patricia Connors, University of Memphis; Steve Cooper, California State University, Long Beach; Cynthia Cornell, DePauw University; Ruth Corson, NCTC, Norwalk; James Finn Cotter, Mount St. Mary College; Dessa Crawford, Delaware Community College; Janis Adams Crowe, Furman University; Allison M. Cummings, University of Wisconsin, Madison; Elizabeth Curtin, Salisbury State University; Robert Darling, Keuka College; Denise David, Niagara County Community College; Alan Davis, Moorhead State University; Kathleen De Grave, Pittsburg State University; Apryl Denny, Viterbo University; Fred Dings, University of South Carolina; Dr. Leo Doobad, Stetson University; Dennis Driewald, Laredo Community College; David Driscoll, Benedictine College; John Drury, University of Cincinnati; Victoria Duckworth, Santa Rosa Junior College; Dixie Durman, Chapman University; Janet Eber, County College of Morris; Terry Ehret, Santa Rosa Junior College; George Ellenbogen, Bentley College; Peggy Ellsberg, Barnard College; Toni Empringham, El Camino Community College; Lin Enger, Moorhead State University; Alexina Fagan, Virginia Commonwealth University; Lynn Fauth, Oxnard College; Annie Finch, Miami University; Katie Fischer, Clarke College; Susan Fitzgerald, University of Memphis; Juliann Fleenor, Harper College; Richard Flynn, Georgia Southern University; Deborah Ford, University of Southern Mississippi; James E. Ford, University of Nebraska, Lincoln; Peter Fortunato, Ithaca College; Ray Foster, Scottsdale Community College; Maryanne Garbowsky, County College of Morris; John Gery, University of New Orleans; Mary Frances Gibbons, Richland College; Maggie Gordon, University of Mississippi; Joseph Green, Lower Columbia College; William E. Gruber, Emory University; Huey Guagliardo, Louisana State University; R. S. Gwynn, Lamar University; Steven K. Hale, DeKalb College; Renée Harlow, Southern Connecticut State University; John Harper, Seminole Community College; Iris Rose Hart, Santa Fe Community College; Karen Hatch, California State University, Chico; Jim Hauser, William Patterson College; Jennifer Heller, Johnson County Community College; Mary Piering Hiltbrand, University of Southern Colorado; Jan Hodge, Morningside College; Dr. David E. Hoffman, Averett University; Patricia Hymson, Delaware County Community College; Alan Jacobs, Wheaton College; Kimberlie Johnson, Seminole Community College; Peter Johnson, Providence College; Ted E. Johnston, El Paso Community College; Dr. Cris Karmas, Graceland University; D. S. Koelling, Northwest College; Dennis Kriewald, Laredo Community College; Paul Lake, Arkansas Technical University; Susan Lang, Southern Illinois University; Sherry Little, San Diego State University; Alfred Guy Litton, Texas Woman's University; Heather Lobban-Viravong, Grinnell College; Karen Locke, Lane Community College; Eric Loring, Scottsdale Community College; Gerald Luboff, County College of Morris; Susan Popkin Mach, UCLA; Samuel Maio, California State University, San Jose; Paul Marx, University of New Haven; David Mason, Colorado College; Mike Matthews, Tarrant County Junior College; Janet McCann, Texas A&M; Susan McClure, Indiana University of PA; Kim McCollum-Clark, Millersville University; David McCracken, Texas A&M; Nellie McCrory, Gaston College; Robert McPhillips, Iona College; Dr. Jim McWilliams, Dickinson State University; Elizabeth Meador, Wayne Community College; Bruce Meyer, Toronto; Tom Miller, University of Arizona; Joseph Mills, University of California at Davis; Cindy Milwe, Santa Monica High School; Mary Alice Morgan, Mercer University; Samantha Morgan, University of Tennessee; Bernard Morris, Modesto Junior College; Brian T. Murphy, Burlington Community College; Madeleine Mysko, Johns Hopkins University; Kevin Nebergall, Kirkwood Community College; Eric Nelson, Georgia Southern University; Jeff Newberry, University of West Florida; Marsha Nourse, Dean College; Hillary Nunn, University of Akron; James Obertino, Central Missouri State University; Julia O'Brien, Meredith College; Sally O'Friel, John Carroll University; Elizabeth Oness, Viterbo College; Regina B. Oost, Wesleyan College; Mike Osborne, Central Piedmont Community College; Jim Owen, Columbus State University; Jeannette Palmer, Motlow State Community College; Mark Palmer, Tacoma Community College; Dianne Peich, Delaware County Community College; Betty Jo Peters, Morehead State University; Timothy Peters, Boston University; Norm Peterson, County College of Morris; Louis Phillips, School of Visual Arts; Robert Phillips, University of Houston; Rodney Phillips, New York Public Library; Teresa Point, Emory University; Deborah Prickett, Jacksonville State University; William Provost, University of Georgia; Wyatt Prunty, University of the South, Sewanee; Allen Ramsey, Central Missouri State University; Ron Rash, Tri-County Technical College; Michael W. Raymond, Stetson University; Mary Anne Reiss, Elizabethtown Community College; Barbara Rhodes, Central Missouri State University; Diane Richard-Alludya, Lynn University; Gary Richardson, Mercer University; Fred Robbins, Southern Illinois University; Daniel Robinson, Colorado State University; Dawn Rodrigues, University of Texas, Brownsville; Linda C. Rollins, Motlow State Community College; Laura Ross, Seminole Community College; Jude Roy, Madisonville Community College; M. Runyon, Saddleback College; Mark Sanders, College of the Mainland; Kay Satre, Carroll College; Ben Sattersfield, Mercer University; SueAnn Schatz, University of New Mexico; Roy Scheele, Doane College; Bill Schmidt, Seminole Community College; Beverly Schneller, Millersville University; Meg Schoerke, San Francisco State University; William Scurrah, Pima Community College; Susan Semrow, Northeastern State University; Tom Sexton, University of Alaska, Anchorage; Chenliang Sheng, Northern Kentucky University; Phillip Skaar, Texas A&M; Michael Slaughter, Illinois Central College; Richard Spiese, California State, Long Beach; Lisa S. Starks, Texas A&M; John R. Stephenson, Lake Superior State University; Jack Stewart, East Georgia College; Dabney Stuart, Washington and Lee University; David Sudol, Arizona State University; Stan Sulkes, Raymond Walters College; Gerald Sullivan, Savio Preparatory School; Henry Taylor, American University; Jean Tobin, University of Wisconsin Center, Sheboygan County; Linda Travers, University of Massachusetts, Amherst; Tom Treffinger, Greenville Technical College; Lee Upton, Lafayette College; Rex Veeder, St. Cloud University; Deborah Viles, University of Colorado, Boulder; Joyce Walker, Southern Illinois University-Carbondale; Sue Walker, University of Southern Alabama; Irene Ward, Kansas State University; Penelope Warren, Laredo Community College; Barbara Wenner, University of Cincinnati; Mary Wilder, Mercer University;

Terry Witek, Stetson University; Sallie Wolf, Arapahoe Community College; Beth Rapp Young, University of Alabama; William Zander, Fairleigh Dickinson University; and Tom Zaniello, Northern Kentucky University.

Three distinguished writers made invaluable contributions to the new edition. Michael Palma scrupulously examined and updated every chapter from the previous edition. His deep knowledge of literature and crisp sense of style kept the new edition fresh, informed, and accessible. Diane Thiel of the University of New Mexico, Albuquerque, masterminded the new Latin American poetry casebook. Working with the editors, she drafted the chapter and helped select the poems—providing three superb new translations especially for this edition. Susan Balée co-authored the new chapter on writing a research paper. Ongoing thanks also goes to Mark Bernier of Blinn College in Brenham, Texas, who helped make the writing material exemplary in both quality and practicality, and to John Swensson of De Anza College who provided ongoing excellent practical suggestions from the classroom.

On the publisher's staff, Joseph Terry, Katharine Glynn, Janet Lanphier, and Melanie Craig made many contributions to the development and revisions for the new edition. Joe Vella and Lois Lombardo directed the complex job of managing production of the book from manuscript to the final printed form. Virginia Creeden handled the difficult job of permissions. Shaie Dively supervised the expansion of photographs and artwork in the new edition; Nancy Garcia oversaw work on the Website for the book.

Mary Gioia was involved in every stage of planning, editing, and execution. Not only could the book have not been done without her capable hand and careful eye, but her expert guidance made every chapter better.

Past debts that will never be repaid are outstanding to hundreds of instructors named in prefaces past and to Dorothy M. Kennedy.

X. J. K. AND D. G.

About the Authors

X. J. KENNEDY, after graduation from Seton Hall and Columbia, became a journalist second class in the Navy ("Actually, I was pretty eighth class"). His poems, some published in the *New Yorker*, were first collected in *Nude Descending a Staircase* (1961). Since then he has written six more collections, several widely adopted literature and writing textbooks, and seventeen books for children, including two novels. He has taught at Michigan, North Carolina (Greensboro), California (Irvine), Wellesley, Tufts, and Leeds. Cited in *Bartlett's Familiar Quotations* and reprinted in some 200 anthologies, his verse has brought him a Guggenheim fellowship, a Lamont Award, a *Los Angeles Times* Book Prize, an award from the American Academy and Institute of Arts and Letters, an Aiken-Taylor prize, and the Award for Poetry for Children from the National Council of Teachers of English. He now lives in Lexington, Massachusetts, where he and his wife Dorothy have collaborated on four books and five children.

DANA GIOIA is a poet, critic, and teacher. Born in Los Angeles of Italian and Mexican ancestry, he attended Stanford and Harvard before taking a detour into business. ("Not many poets have a Stanford M.B.A., thank goodness!") After years of writing and reading late in the evenings after work, he quit a vice presidency to write and teach. He has published three collections of poetry, *Daily Horoscope* (1986), *The Gods of Winter* (1991), and *Interrogations at Noon* (2001), which won the American Book Award, an opera libretto, *Nosferatu* (2001), and three critical volumes, including *Can Poetry Matter?* (1992), an influential study of poetry's place in contemporary America. Gioia has taught at Johns Hopkins, Sarah Lawrence, Wesleyan (Connecticut), Mercer, and Colorado College. He is also the co-founder of the summer poetry conference at West Chester University in Pennsylvania and "Teaching Poetry" in Santa Rosa, California. In 2003 he became Chairman of the National Endowment for the Arts. He currently lives in Washington, D.C, with his wife Mary, two sons, and an uncontrollable cat.

(The surname Gioia is pronounced JOY-A. As some of you may have already guessed, *gioia* is the Italian word for *joy*.)

About the Authors

An Introduction to
POETRY

POETRY

Gwendolyn Brooks c. 1950, the year she won the Pulitzer Prize.

To the Muse

Give me leave, Muse, in plain view to array
Your shift and bodice by the light of day.
I would have brought an epic. Be not vexed
Instead to grace a niggling schoolroom text;
Let down your sanction, help me to oblige
Those who would lead fresh devots to your liege,
And at your altar, grant that in a flash
Readers and I know incense from dead ash.

—X. J. K.

1 Reading a Poem

How do you read a poem? The literal-minded might say, "Just let your eye light on it"; but there is more to poetry than meets the eye. What Shakespeare called "the mind's eye" also plays a part. Many a reader who has no trouble understanding and enjoying prose finds poetry difficult. This is to be expected. At first glance, a poem usually will make some sense and give some pleasure, but it may not yield everything at once. Sometimes it only hints at meaning still to come if we will keep after it. Poetry is not to be galloped over like the daily news: a poem differs from most prose in that it is to be read slowly, carefully, and attentively. Not all poems are difficult, of course, and some can be understood and enjoyed on first encounter. But good poems yield more if read twice; and the best poems—after ten, twenty, or a hundred readings—still go on yielding.

Approaching a thing written in lines and surrounded with white space, we need not expect it to be a poem just because it is **verse.** (Any composition in lines of more or less regular rhythm, usually ending in rimes, is verse.) Here, for instance, is a specimen of verse that few will call poetry:

> Thirty days hath September,
> April, June, and November;
> All the rest have thirty-one
> Excepting February alone,
> To which we twenty-eight assign
> Till leap year makes it twenty-nine.

in verse, but not quite poetry

To a higher degree than that classic memory-tickler, poetry appeals to the mind and arouses feelings. Poetry may state facts, but, more important, it makes imaginative statements that we may value even if its facts are incorrect. Coleridge's error in placing a star within the horns of the crescent moon in "The Rime of the Ancient Mariner" does not stop the passage from being good poetry, though it is faulty astronomy. According to one poet, Gerard Manley Hopkins, poetry is "to be heard for its own sake and interest even over and above its interest of meaning." There are other elements in a poem besides plain prose sense: sounds, images, rhythms, figures of speech. These may strike us and please us even before we ask, "But what does it all mean?"

This is a truth not readily grasped by anyone who regards a poem as a kind of puzzle written in secret code with a message slyly concealed. The effect of a poem (one's whole mental and emotional response to it) consists of much more than simply a message. By its musical qualities, by its suggestions, it can work on the reader's unconscious. T. S. Eliot put it well when he said in *The Use of Poetry and the Use of Criticism* that the prose sense of a poem is chiefly useful in keeping the reader's mind "diverted and quiet, while the poem does its work upon him." Eliot went on to liken the meaning of a poem to the bit of meat a burglar brings along to throw to the family dog. What is the work of a poem? To touch us, to stir us, to make us glad, and possibly even to tell us something.

How to set about reading a poem? Here are a few suggestions.

To begin with, read the poem once straight through, with no particular expectations; read open-mindedly. Let yourself experience whatever you find, without worrying just yet about the large general and important ideas the poem contains (if indeed it contains any). Don't dwell on a troublesome word or difficult passage—just push on. Some of the difficulties may seem smaller when you read the poem for a second time; at least, they will have become parts of a whole for you.

On the second reading, read for the exact sense of all the words; if there are words you don't understand, look them up in a dictionary. Dwell on any difficult parts as long as you need to.

If you read the poem silently, sound its words in your mind. (This is a technique that will get you nowhere in a speed-reading course, but it may help the poem to do its work on you.) Better still, read the poem aloud, or hear someone else read it. You may discover meanings you didn't perceive in it before. Even if you are no actor, to decide how to speak a poem can be an excellent method of getting to understand it. Some poems, like bells, seem heavy till heard. Listen while reading the following lines from Alexander Pope's *Dunciad*. Attacking the minor poet James Ralph, who had sung the praises of a mistress named Cynthia, Pope makes the goddess of Dullness exclaim:

"Silence, ye wolves! while Ralph to Cynthia howls,
And makes night hideous—answer him, ye owls!"

When *ye owls* slide together and become *yowls*, poor Ralph's serenade is turned into the nightly outcry of a cat.

Try to **paraphrase** the poem as a whole, or perhaps just the more difficult lines. In paraphrasing, we put into our own words what we understand the poem to say, restating ideas that seem essential, coming out and stating what the poem may only suggest. This may sound like a heartless thing to do to a poem, but good poems can stand it. In fact, to compare a poem to its paraphrase is a good way to see the distance between poetry and prose. In making a paraphrase, we generally work through a poem or a passage line by line. The statement that results may take as many words as the original, if not more. A paraphrase, then, is ampler than a **summary,** a brief condensation of gist, main idea, or story. (Summary of a horror film in *TV Guide:* "Demented biologist, coveting power over New York, swells sewer rats to hippopotamus-size.") Here is a poem worth considering line by line. The poet writes of an island in a lake in the west of Ireland, in a region where he spent many summers as a boy.

William Butler Yeats   (1865–1939)*

THE LAKE ISLE OF INNISFREE   1892

I will arise and go now, and go to Innisfree,
And a small cabin build there, of clay and wattles made;
Nine bean-rows will I have there, a hive for the honey-bee,
And live alone in the bee-loud glade.

And I shall have some peace there, for peace comes dropping slow,   5
Dropping from the veils of the morning to where the cricket sings;
There midnight's all a glimmer, and noon a purple glow,
And evening full of the linnet's wings.

I will arise and go now, for always night and day,
I hear lake water lapping with low sounds by the shore;   10
While I stand on the roadway, or on the pavements gray,
I hear it in the deep heart's core.

Though relatively simple, this poem is far from simple-minded. We need to absorb it slowly and thoughtfully. At the start, for most of us, it raises problems: what are *wattles,* from which the speaker's dream-cabin is to be made? We might guess, but in this case it will help to consult a dictionary: they are "poles interwoven with sticks or branches, formerly used in building as frameworks to support walls or roofs." Evidently, this getaway house will be built in an old-fashioned way: it won't be a prefabricated log cabin or A-frame house, nothing modern or citified. The phrase *bee-loud glade* certainly isn't commonplace language of the sort we find on a cornflakes package, but right away, we can understand it, at least partially: it's a place loud with bees. What is a *glade?* Experience might tell us that it is an open space in woods, but if that word stops us, we can look it up. Although the *linnet* doesn't live in North America, it is a creature with wings—a songbird of the finch family, adds the dictionary. But even if we don't make a special trip to the dictionary to find *linnet,* we probably recognize that the word means "bird," and the line makes sense to us.

*The asterisk indicates a poet who is described in the chapter "Lives of the Poets."

A paraphrase of the whole poem might go something like this (in language easier to forget than that of the original): "I'm going to get up now, go to Innisfree, build a cabin, plant beans, keep bees, and live peacefully by myself amid nature and beautiful light. I want to because I can't forget the sound of that lake water. When I'm in the city, a gray and dingy place, I seem to hear it deep inside me."

These dull remarks, roughly faithful to what Yeats is saying, seem a long way from poetry. Nevertheless, they make certain things clear. For one, they spell out what the poet merely hints at in his choice of the word *gray:* that he finds the city dull and depressing. He stresses the word; instead of saying *gray pavements,* in the usual word order, he turns the phrase around and makes *gray* stand at the end of the line, where it rimes with *day* and so takes extra emphasis. The grayness of the city therefore seems important to the poem, and the paraphrase tries to make its meaning obvious.

Whenever you paraphrase, you stick your neck out. You affirm what the poem gives you to understand. And making a paraphrase can help you see the central thought of the poem, its **theme.** Theme isn't the same as **subject,** the main topic, whatever the poem is "about." In Yeats's poem, the subject is the lake isle of Innisfree, or a wish to retreat to it. But the theme is, "I yearn for an ideal place where I will find perfect peace and happiness." Themes can be stated variously, depending on what you believe most matters in the poem. Taking a different view of the poem, placing more weight on the speaker's wish to escape the city, you might instead state the theme: "This city is getting me down—I want to get back to nature." But after taking a second look at that statement, you might want to sharpen it. After all, this Innisfree seems a special, particular place, where the natural world means more to the poet than just any old trees and birds he might see in a park. Perhaps a stronger statement of theme, one closer to what matters most in the poem, might be: "I want to quit the city for my heaven on earth." That, of course, is saying in an obvious way what Yeats says more subtly, more memorably.

Not all poems clearly assert a proposition, but many do; some even declare their themes in their opening lines: "Gather ye rose-buds while ye may!"—that is, enjoy love before it's too late. This theme, stated in that famous first line of Robert Herrick's "To the Virgins, to Make Much of Time" (page 495), is so familiar that we give it a name: *carpe diem,* Latin for "seize the day." (For the original *carpe diem* poem, see the Latin poet Horace's ode on page 332.) Seizing the joys of the present moment is a favorite argument of poets. You will meet it in more than these two poems in this book.

A paraphrase, of course, never tells *all* that a poem contains, nor will every reader agree that a particular paraphrase is accurate. We all make our own interpretations, and sometimes the total meaning of a poem evades even the poet who wrote it. Asked to explain a passage in one of his poems, Robert Browning replied that when he had written the poem, only God and he knew what it meant; but "Now, only God knows." Still, to analyze a poem *as if* we could be certain of its meaning is, in general, more fruitful than to proceed as if no certainty could ever be had. The latter approach is likely to end in complete subjectivity, the attitude of the reader who says, "Yeats's 'Lake Isle of Innisfree' is really about the lost island of Atlantis. It is because I think it is. How can you prove me wrong?" Interpretations can't be proven "wrong." A more fruitful question might be, "What can we understand from the poem's very words?"

All of us bring personal associations to the poems we read. "The Lake Isle of Innisfree" might give you special pleasure if you have ever vacationed on a small island or on the shore of a lake. Such associations are inevitable, even to be welcomed, as long as they don't interfere with our reading the words on the page. We need to distinguish irrelevant responses from those the poem calls for. The reader who can't stand "The Lake Isle of Innisfree" because she is afraid of bees isn't reading a poem by Yeats, but one of her own invention.

Now and again we meet a poem—perhaps startling and memorable—into which the method of paraphrase won't take us far. Some portion of any deep poem resists explanation, but certain poems resist it almost entirely. Many poems by religious mystics seem closer to dream than waking. So do poems that purport to record drug experiences, such as Coleridge's "Kubla Khan" (page 462), as well as poems that embody some private system of beliefs, such as Blake's "The Sick Rose" (page 454), or the same poet's lines from *Jerusalem*

> For a Tear is an Intellectual thing,
> And a Sigh is the Sword of an Angel King.

So do nonsense poems, translations of primitive folk songs, and surreal poems.[1] Such poetry may move us and give pleasure (although not, perhaps, the pleasure of intellectual understanding). We do it no harm by trying to paraphrase it, though we may fail. Whether logically clear or strangely opaque, good poems appeal to the intelligence and do not shrink from it.

So far, we have taken for granted that poetry differs from prose; yet all our strategies for reading poetry—plowing straight on through and then going back, isolating difficulties, trying to paraphrase, reading aloud, using a dictionary—are no different from those we might employ in unraveling a complicated piece of prose. Poetry, after all, is similar to prose in most respects. At the very least, it is written in the same language. Like prose, poetry shares knowledge with us. It tells us, for instance, of a beautiful island in Lake Gill, County Sligo, Ireland, and of how one man feels toward it. Maybe the poet knows no more about Innisfree than a writer of a travel guidebook knows. And yet Yeats's poem indicates a kind of knowledge that tourist guidebooks do not ordinarily reveal: that the human heart can yearn for peace and happiness, that the lake isle of Innisfree with its "low sounds by the shore" can echo and reecho in memory forever.

---

[1]The French poet André Breton, founder of **Surrealism,** a movement in art and writing, declared that a higher reality exists, which to mortal eyes looks absurd. To mirror that reality, surrealist poets are fond of bizarre and dreamlike objects such as soluble fish and white-haired revolvers.

LYRIC POETRY

Originally, as its Greek name suggests, a *lyric was a poem sung* to the music of a lyre. This earlier meaning—*a poem made for singing*—is still current today, when we use *lyrics* to mean the words of a popular song. But the kind of printed poem we now call a *lyric* is usually something else, for over the past five hundred years the nature of lyric poetry has changed greatly. Ever since the invention of the printing press in the fifteenth century, poets have written less often for singers, more often for readers. In general, this tendency has made lyric poems contain less word-music and (since they can be pondered on a page) more thought—and perhaps more complicated feelings.

Here is a rough definition of a **lyric** as it is written today: *a short poem expressing the thoughts and feelings of a single speaker*. Often a poet will write a lyric in the first person ("I will arise and go now, and go to Innisfree"), but not always. Instead, a lyric might describe an object or recall an experience without the speaker's ever bringing himself or herself into it. (For an example of such a lyric, one in which the poet refrains from saying "I," see William Carlos Williams's "The Red Wheelbarrow" on page 35, Theodore Roethke's "Root Cellar" on page 96, or Gerard Manley Hopkins's "Pied Beauty" on page 101.)

Perhaps because, rightly or wrongly, some people still think of lyrics as lyre-strummings, they expect a lyric to be an outburst of feeling, somewhat resembling a song, at least containing musical elements such as rime, rhythm, or sound effects. Such expectations are fulfilled in "The Lake Isle of Innisfree," that impassioned lyric full of language rich in sound (as you will hear if you'll read it aloud). Many contemporary poets, however, write short poems in which they voice opinions or complicated feelings—poems that no reader would dream of trying to sing. Most people would call such poems lyrics, too; one commentator has argued that a lyric may contain an argument.[2]

But in the sense in which we use it, *lyric* will usually apply to a kind of poem you can easily recognize. Here, for instance, are two lyrics. They differ sharply in subject and theme, but they have traits in common: both are short, and (as you will find) both set forth one speaker's definite, unmistakable feelings.

D. H. Lawrence   (1885–1930)*   — man's memories

PIANO   1918

Softly, in the dusk, a woman is singing to me;
Taking me back down the vista of years, till I see
A child sitting under the piano, in the boom of the tingling strings
And pressing the small, poised feet of a mother who smiles as she sings.

---

[2]Jeffrey Walker, "Aristotle's Lyric," *College English* 51 (January 1989) 5–26.

In spite of myself, the insidious mastery of song   5
Betrays me back, till the heart of me weeps to belong
To the old Sunday evenings at home, with winter outside
And hymns in the cozy parlor, the tinkling piano our guide.

So now it is vain for the singer to burst into clamor
With the great black piano appassionato. The glamor   10
Of childish days is upon me, my manhood is cast
Down in the flood of remembrance, I weep like a child for the past.

QUESTIONS

1. Jot down a brief paraphrase of this poem. In your paraphrase, clearly show what the speaker says is happening at present and also what he finds himself remembering. Make clear which seems the more powerful in its effect on him.
2. What are the speaker's various feelings? What do you understand from the words *insidious* and *betrays*?
3. With what specific details does the poem make the past seem real?
4. What is the subject of Lawrence's poem? How would you state its theme?

Adrienne Rich (b. 1929)* — *memories of certain / proud times*

AUNT JENNIFER'S TIGERS — *always be around* 1951
vs

Aunt Jennifer's tigers prance across a screen,
Bright topaz denizens of a world of green.
They do not fear the men beneath the tree;
They pace in sleek chivalric certainty.

Aunt Jennifer's fingers fluttering through her wool   5
Find even the ivory needle hard to pull.
The <u>massive</u> weight of Uncle's wedding band → *restricts her as a wife*
Sits <u>heavily</u> upon Aunt Jennifer's hand.

When Aunt is dead, her terrified hands will lie
Still ringed with ordeals she was mastered by.   10
The tigers in the panel that she made
Will go on prancing, proud and unafraid.

COMPARE

"Aunt Jennifer's Tigers" with Adrienne Rich's critical comments on the poem reprinted in the "Writer's Perspective" at the end of this chapter.

diction = word choice

enjambment — continuing one idea to next
- emphasize
- reader works for it

NARRATIVE POETRY

Although a lyric sometimes relates an incident, or like "Piano" draws a scene, it does not usually relate a series of events. That happens in a **narrative poem,** one whose main purpose is to tell a story.

In Western literature, narrative poetry dates back to the Babylonian *Epic of Gilgamesh* (composed before 2000 B.C.) and Homer's epics the *Iliad* and the *Odyssey* (composed before 700 B.C.). It may well have originated much earlier. In England and Scotland, storytelling poems have long been popular; in the late Middle Ages, ballads—or storytelling songs—circulated widely. Some, such as "Sir Patrick Spence" and "Bonny Barbara Allan," survive in our day, and folksingers sometimes perform them.

Evidently the art of narrative poetry invites the skills of a writer of fiction: the ability to draw characters and settings briefly, to engage attention, to shape a plot. Needless to say, it calls for all the skills of a poet as well. Here are two narrative poems: one medieval, one modern. How would you paraphrase the stories they tell? How do they hold your attention on their stories?

Anonymous   (traditional Scottish ballad)

Sir Patrick Spence

The king sits in Dumferling toune,
   Drinking the blude-reid wine:
"O whar will I get guid sailor
   To sail this schip of mine?"

Up and spak an eldern knicht,°   *knight*   5
   Sat at the kings richt kne:
"Sir Patrick Spence is the best sailor
   That sails upon the se."

The king has written a braid letter,
   And signed it wi' his hand,   10
And sent it to Sir Patrick Spence,
   Was walking on the sand.

The first line that Sir Patrick red,
   A loud lauch lauchèd he;
The next line that Sir Patrick red,   15
   The teir blinded his ee.

"O wha° is this has don this deid,   *who*
   This ill deid don to me,
To send me out this time o' the yeir,
   To sail upon the se!   20

[handwritten: bringing back a man who had left the world]

"Mak haste, mak haste, my mirry men all,
   Our guid schip sails the morne."
"O say na sae,° my master deir,   *so*
   For I feir a deadlie storme.

"Late late yestreen I saw the new moone,   25
   Wi' the auld moone in hir arme,
And I feir, I feir, my deir master,
   That we will cum to harme."

O our Scots nobles wer richt laith°   *loath*
   To weet° their cork-heild schoone,°   *wet; shoes* 30
Bot lang owre° a' the play wer playd,   *before*
   Their hats they swam aboone.°   *above (their heads)*

O lang, lang may their ladies sit,
   Wi' their fans into their hand,
Or ere° they se Sir Patrick Spence   *long before* 35
   Cum sailing to the land.

O lang, lang may the ladies stand,
   Wi' their gold kems° in their hair,   *combs*
Waiting for their ain° deir lords,   *own*
   For they'll se thame na mair.   40

Haf owre,° haf owre to Aberdour,   *halfway over*
   It's fiftie fadom deip,
And thair lies guid Sir Patrick Spence,
   Wi' the Scots lords at his feit.

SIR PATRICK SPENCE. 9 *braid*: Broad, but broad in what sense? Among guesses are *plain-spoken, official,* and *on wide paper*.

QUESTIONS

1. That the king drinks "blood-red wine" (line 2)—what meaning do you find in that detail? What does it hint, or foreshadow?
2. What do you make of this king and his motives for sending Spence and the Scots lords into an impending storm? Is he a fool, is he cruel and inconsiderate, is he deliberately trying to drown Sir Patrick and his crew, or is it impossible for us to know? Let your answer depend on the poem alone, not on anything you read into it.
3. Comment on this ballad's methods of storytelling. Is the story told too briefly for us to care what happens to Spence and his men, or are there any means by which the poet makes us feel compassion for them? Do you resent the lack of a detailed account of the shipwreck?
4. Lines 25–28—the new moon with the old moon in her arm—has been much admired as poetry. What does this stanza contribute to the story as well?

Robert Frost   (1874–1963)*

"Out, Out—"   1916

The buzz-saw snarled and rattled in the yard
And made dust and dropped stove-length sticks of wood,
Sweet-scented stuff when the breeze drew across it.
And from there those that lifted eyes could count
Five mountain ranges one behind the other   5
Under the sunset far into Vermont.
And the saw snarled and rattled, snarled and rattled,
As it ran light, or had to bear a load.
And nothing happened: day was all but done.
Call it a day, I wish they might have said   10
To please the boy by giving him the half hour
That a boy counts so much when saved from work.
His sister stood beside them in her apron
To tell them "Supper." At the word, the saw,
As if to prove saws knew what supper meant,   15
Leaped out at the boy's hand, or seemed to leap—
He must have given the hand. However it was,
Neither refused the meeting. But the hand!
The boy's first outcry was a rueful laugh,
As he swung toward them holding up the hand   20
Half in appeal, but half as if to keep
The life from spilling. Then the boy saw all—
Since he was old enough to know, big boy
Doing a man's work, though a child at heart—
He saw all spoiled. "Don't let him cut my hand off—   25
The doctor, when he comes. Don't let him, sister!"
So. But the hand was gone already.
The doctor put him in the dark of ether.
He lay and puffed his lips out with his breath.
And then—the watcher at his pulse took fright.   30
No one believed. They listened at his heart.
Little—less—nothing!—and that ended it.
No more to build on there. And they, since they
Were not the one dead, turned to their affairs.

"Out, Out—" The title of this poem echoes the words of Shakespeare's Macbeth on receiving news that his queen is dead: "Out, out, brief candle! / Life's but a walking shadow, a poor player / That struts and frets his hour upon the stage / And then is heard no more. It is a tale / Told by an idiot, full of sound and fury, / Signifying nothing" (*Macbeth* V, v, 23–28).

1. How does Frost make the buzz-saw appear sinister? How does he make it seem, in another way, like a friend?
2. What do you make of the people who surround the boy—the "they" of the poem? Who might they be? Do they seem to you concerned and compassionate, cruel, indifferent, or what?
3. What does Frost's reference to *Macbeth* contribute to your understanding of "'Out, Out—'"? How would you state the theme of Frost's poem?
4. Set this poem side by side with "Sir Patrick Spence." How does "'Out, Out—'" resemble that medieval folk ballad in subject, or differ from it? How is Frost's poem similar or different in its way of telling a story?

DRAMATIC POETRY

A third kind of poetry is **dramatic poetry,** which presents the voice of an imaginary character (or characters) speaking directly, without any additional narration by the author. A dramatic poem, according to T. S. Eliot, does not consist of "what the poet would say in his own person, but only what he can say within the limits of one imaginary character addressing another imaginary character." Strictly speaking, the term *dramatic poetry* describes any verse written for the stage (and until a few centuries ago most playwrights, like Shakespeare and Molière, wrote their plays mainly in verse). But the term most often refers to the **dramatic monologue,** a poem written as a speech made by a character (other than the author) at some decisive moment. A dramatic monologue is usually addressed by the speaker to some other character who remains silent. If the listener replies, the poem becomes a dialogue (such as Thomas Hardy's "The Ruined Maid" on page 68) in which the story unfolds in the conversation between two speakers.

The Victorian poet Robert Browning, who developed the form of the dramatic monologue, liked to put words in the mouths of characters who were conspicuously nasty, weak, reckless, or crazy: see, for instance, Browning's "Soliloquy of the Spanish Cloister" (page 458), in which the speaker is an obsessively proud and jealous monk. The dramatic monologue has been a popular form among American poets, including Edwin Arlington Robinson, Robert Frost, Ezra Pound, Randall Jarrell, and Sylvia Plath. The most famous dramatic monologue ever written is probably Browning's "My Last Duchess," in which the poet creates a Renaissance Italian Duke whose words reveal more about himself than the aristocratic speaker intends.

Robert Browning   (1812–1889)*

MY LAST DUCHESS   1842

Ferrara

That's my last Duchess painted on the wall,
Looking as if she were alive. I call
That piece a wonder, now; Frà Pandolf's hands
Worked busily a day, and there she stands.
Will't please you sit and look at her? I said   5
"Frà Pandolf" by design, for never read
Strangers like you that pictured countenance,
The depth and passion of its earnest glance,
But to myself they turned (since none puts by
The curtain I have drawn for you, but I)   10
And seemed as they would ask me, if they durst,
How such a glance came there; so, not the first
Are you to turn and ask thus. Sir, 'twas not
Her husband's presence only, called that spot
Of joy into the Duchess' cheek; perhaps   15
Frà Pandolf chanced to say, "Her mantle laps
Over my lady's wrist too much," or "Paint
Must never hope to reproduce the faint
Half-flush that dies along her throat." Such stuff
Was courtesy, she thought, and cause enough   20
For calling up that spot of joy. She had
A heart—how shall I say?—too soon made glad,
Too easily impressed; she liked whate'er
She looked on, and her looks went everywhere.
Sir, 'twas all one! My favor at her breast,   25
The dropping of the daylight in the West,
The bough of cherries some officious fool
Broke in the orchard for her, the white mule
She rode with round the terrace—all and each
Would draw from her alike the approving speech,   30
Or blush, at least. She thanked men,—good! but thanked
Somehow—I know not how—as if she ranked
My gift of a nine-hundred-years-old name
With anybody's gift. Who'd stoop to blame
This sort of trifling? Even had you skill   35
In speech—which I have not—to make your will
Quite clear to such an one, and say "Just this
Or that in you disgusts me; here you miss,
Or there exceed the mark"—and if she let
Herself be lessoned so, nor plainly set   40

Her wits to yours, forsooth, and made excuse—
E'en then would be some stooping; and I choose
Never to stoop. Oh, sir, she smiled, no doubt,
Whene'er I passed her; but who passed without
Much the same smile? This grew; I gave commands;   45
Then all smiles stopped together. There she stands
As if alive. Will't please you rise? We'll meet
The company below, then. I repeat,
The Count your master's known munificence
Is ample warrant that no just pretense   50
Of mine for dowry will be disallowed;
Though his fair daughter's self, as I avowed
At starting, is my object. Nay, we'll go
Together down, sir. Notice Neptune, though,
Taming a sea-horse, thought a rarity,   55
Which Claus of Innsbruck cast in bronze for me!

MY LAST DUCHESS. Ferrara, a city in northern Italy, is the scene. Browning may have modeled his speaker after Alonzo, Duke of Ferrara (1533–1598). 3 *Frà Pandolf* and 56 *Claus of Innsbruck*: fictitious names of artists.

QUESTIONS

1. Who is the Duke addressing? What is this person's business in Ferrara?
2. What is the Duke's opinion of his last Duchess's personality? Do we see her character differently?
3. If the Duke was unhappy with the Duchess's behavior, why didn't he make his displeasure known? Cite a specific passage to explain his reticence.
4. How much do we know about the fate of the last Duchess? Would it help our understanding of the poem to know more?
5. Does Browning imply any connection between the Duke's art collection and his attitude toward his wife?

Today, lyrics in the English language seem more plentiful than other kinds of poetry. Although there has recently been a revival of interest in writing narrative poems, they have a far smaller audience today than long verse narratives, such as Henry Wadsworth Longfellow's *Evangeline* and Alfred, Lord Tennyson's *Idylls of the King,* enjoyed in the nineteenth century.

Also more fashionable in former times was a fourth variety of poetry, **didactic poetry:** a poem apparently written to state a message or teach a body of knowledge. In a lyric, a speaker may express sadness; in a didactic poem, he or she may explain that sadness is inherent in life. Poems that impart a body of knowledge, such as Ovid's *Art of Love* and Lucretius's *On the Nature of Things,* are didactic. Such instructive poetry was favored especially by classical Latin poets and by English poets of the eighteenth century. In *The Fleece* (1757), John Dyer celebrated the British woolen industry and included practical advice on raising sheep:

In cold stiff soils the bleaters oft complain
Of gouty ails, by shepherds termed the halt:
Those let the neighboring fold or ready crook
Detain, and pour into their cloven feet
Corrosive drugs, deep-searching arsenic,
Dry alum, verdegris, or vitriol keen.

One might agree with Dr. Johnson's comment on Dyer's effort: "The subject, Sir, cannot be made poetical." But it may be argued that the subject of didactic poetry does not make it any less poetical. Good poems, it seems, can be written about anything under the sun. Like Dyer, John Milton described sick sheep in "Lycidas," a poem few readers have thought unpoetic:

The hungry sheep look up, and are not fed,
But, swoll'n with wind and the rank mist they draw,
Rot inwardly, and foul contagion spread . . .

What makes Milton's lines better poetry than Dyer's is, among other things, a difference in attitude. Sick sheep to Dyer mean the loss of a few shillings and pence; to Milton, whose sheep stand for English Christendom, they mean a moral catastrophe.

WRITER'S PERSPECTIVE

Adrienne Rich

Adrienne Rich on Writing

RECALLING "AUNT JENNIFER'S TIGERS"   1971

I know that my style was formed first by male poets: by the men I was reading as an undergraduate—Frost, Dylan Thomas, Donne, Auden, MacNeice, Stevens, Yeats. What I chiefly learned from them was craft. But poems are like dreams: in them you put what you don't know you know. Looking back at poems I wrote before I was 21, I'm startled because beneath the conscious craft are glimpses of the split I even then experienced between the girl who wrote poems, who defined herself in writing poems, and the girl who was to define herself by her relationships with men. "Aunt Jennifer's Tigers," written while I was a student, looks with deliberate detachment at this split. In writing this poem, composed and apparently cool as it is, I thought I was creating a portrait of an imaginary woman. But this woman suffers from the opposition of her imagination, worked out in tapestry, and her life-style, "ringed with ordeals she was mastered by." It was important to me that Aunt Jennifer was a person as distinct from myself as possible—distanced by the formalism of the poem, by its objective, observant tone—even by putting the woman in a different generation.

In those years formalism was part of the strategy—like asbestos gloves, it allowed me to handle materials I couldn't pick up bare-handed.

From "When We Dead Awaken: Writing as Re-Vision"

WRITING CRITICALLY

Can a Poem Be Paraphrased?

Since the full meaning of a poem is so completely wedded to its exact wording, some people maintain that no poem can be truly paraphrased. As we have discussed earlier in the chapter, however, such an opinion misses the point of paraphrasing. A paraphrase doesn't attempt to recreate the full effect of a poem; it only tries to map out clearly the key images, actions, and ideas. A map is no substitute for a landscape, but a good map often helps us find our way through the landscape without getting lost.

Let's look at an example of a paraphrase written, not by a critic, but by an author about one of his own poems. When an editor asked William Stafford if one of his poems could be paraphrased, Stafford responded by providing his own paraphrase of a short poem. Here is the poem he chose, along with his own restatement in prose of what the poem says.

William Stafford   (1914–1993)*
Ask Me   1975

Some time when the river is ice ask me
mistakes I have made. Ask me whether
what I have done is my life. Others
have come in their slow way into
my thought, and some have tried to help   5
or to hurt—ask me what difference
their strongest love or hate has made.

I will listen to what you say.
You and I can turn and look
at the silent river and wait. We know   10

the current is there, hidden; and there
are comings and goings from miles away
that hold the stillness exactly before us.
What the river says, that is what I say.

William Stafford (1914–1993)*
A Paraphrase of "Ask Me"   1977

I think my poem can be paraphrased—and that any poem can be paraphrased. But
every pass through the material, using other words, would have to be achieved at
certain costs, either in momentum, or nuance, or dangerously explicit (and therefore misleading in tone) adjustments. I'll try one such pass through the poem:

> When it's quiet and cold and we have some chance to interchange
> without hurry, confront me if you like with a challenge about
> whether I think I have made mistakes in my life—and ask me, if
> you want to, whether to me my life is actually the sequence of
> events or exploits others would see. Well, those others tag along in
> my living, and some of them in fact have played significant roles in
> the narrative run of my world; they have intended either helping or
> hurting (but by implication in the way I am saying this you will
> know that neither effort is conclusive). So—ask me how important
> their good or bad intentions have been (both intentions get a
> drastic *leveling* judgment from this cool stating of it all). You, too,
> will be entering that realm of maybe-help-maybe-hurt, by entering
> that far into my life by asking this serious question—so: I will stay
> still and consider. Out there will be the world confronting us both;
> we will both know we are surrounded by mystery, tremendous
> things that do not reveal themselves to us. That river, that world—
> and our lives—all share the depth and stillness of much more sig-
> nificance than our talk, or intentions. There is a steadiness and
> somehow a solace in knowing that what is around us so greatly sur-
> passes our human concerns.

> From "Ask Me"

Writing Assignment

Write a concise, accurate paraphrase of a short poem from "Poems for Further Reading."
Your instructor may suggest a particular poem or poems. Although your paraphrase should
cover the entire poem, it need not mention everything. Try to include the most vital
points and details and try to state the poem's main thought or theme. Be as specific as possible, but explain the poem in your own words without quoting any original passages.

Be prepared to share your paraphrase with the rest of the class and to compare it with
other paraphrases of the same poem. You may then be able to test yourself as a reader of
poetry. What in the poem whizzed by you that other students noticed? What did you
catch that others ignored?

2 *Listening to a Voice*

TONE

In old Western movies, when one hombre taunts another, it is customary for the second to drawl, "Smile when you say that, pardner" or "Mister, I don't like your tone of voice." Sometimes in reading a poem, although we can neither see a face nor hear a voice, we can infer the poet's attitude from other evidence.

Like tone of voice, **tone** in literature often conveys an attitude toward the person addressed. Like the manner of a person, the manner of a poem may be friendly or belligerent toward its reader, condescending or respectful. Again like tone of voice, the tone of a poem may tell us how the speaker feels about himself or herself: cocksure or humble, sad or glad. But usually when we ask, "What is the tone of a poem?" we mean, "What attitude does the poet take toward a theme or a subject?" Is the poet being affectionate, hostile, earnest, playful, sarcastic, or what? We may never be able to know, of course, the poet's personal feelings. All we need know is how to feel when we read the poem.

Strictly speaking, tone isn't an attitude; it is whatever in the poem makes an attitude clear to us: the choice of certain words instead of others, the picking out of certain details. In A. E. Housman's "Loveliest of trees," for example, the poet communicates his admiration for a cherry tree's beauty by singling out for attention its white blossoms; had he wanted to show his dislike for the tree, he might have concentrated on its broken branches, birdlime, or snails. To perceive the tone of a poem rightly, we need to read the poem carefully, paying attention to whatever suggestions we find in it.

Theodore Roethke (1908–1963)*

My Papa's Waltz   1948

The whiskey on your breath
Could make a small boy dizzy;
But I hung on like death:
Such waltzing was not easy.

We romped until the pans   5
Slid from the kitchen shelf;
My mother's countenance
Could not unfrown itself.

The hand that held my wrist
Was battered on one knuckle;   10
At every step you missed
My right ear scraped a buckle.

You beat time on my head
With a palm caked hard by dirt,
Then waltzed me off to bed   15
Still clinging to your shirt.

What is the tone of this poem? Most readers find the speaker's attitude toward his father critical, but nonetheless affectionate. They take this recollection
of childhood to be an odd but happy one. Other readers, however, concentrate
on other details, such as the father's rough manners and drunkenness. One
reader has written that "Roethke expresses his resentment for his father, a
drunken brute with dirty hands and whiskey breath who carelessly hurt the
child's ear and manhandled him." Although this reader accurately noticed some
of the events in the poem and perceived that there was something desperate in
the son's hanging onto the father "like death," he simplifies the tone of the poem
and so misses its humorous side.

While "My Papa's Waltz" contains the dark elements of manhandling and
drunkenness, the tone remains grotesquely comic. The rollicking rhythms of the
poem underscore Roethke's complex humor—half loving and half censuring of
the unwashed, intoxicated father. The humor is further reinforced by playful
rimes such as *dizzy* and *easy*, *knuckle* and *buckle*, as well as the joyful suggestions
of the words *waltz*, *waltzing*, and *romped*. The scene itself is comic, with kitchen
pans falling due to the father's roughhousing while the mother looks on una-
mused. However much the speaker satirizes the overly rambunctious father, he
does not have the boy identify with the soberly disapproving mother. Not all
comedy is comfortable and reassuring. Certainly, this small boy's family life has
its frightening side, but the last line suggests the boy is *still clinging* to his father
with persistent if also complicated love.

Such a poem, though it includes lifelike details that aren't pretty, has a tone
relatively easy to recognize. So does **satiric poetry,** a kind of comic poetry that

generally conveys a message. Usually its tone is one of detached amusement, withering contempt, and implied superiority. In a satiric poem, the poet ridicules some person or persons (or perhaps some kind of human behavior), examining the victim by the light of certain principles and implying that the reader, too, ought to feel contempt for the victim.

Countee Cullen (1903–1946)

FOR A LADY I KNOW   1925

She even thinks that up in heaven
  Her class lies late and snores,
While poor black cherubs rise at seven
  To do celestial chores.

QUESTIONS

1. What is Cullen's message?
2. How would you characterize the tone of this poem? Wrathful? Amused?

In some poems the poet's attitude may be plain enough; while in other poems attitudes may be so mingled that it is hard to describe them tersely without doing injustice to the poem. Does Andrew Marvell in "To His Coy Mistress" (page 512) take a serious or playful attitude toward the fact that he and his lady are destined to be food for worms? No one-word answer will suffice. And what of T. S. Eliot's "The Love Song of J. Alfred Prufrock" (page 473)? In his attitude toward his redemption-seeking hero who wades with trousers rolled, Eliot is seriously funny. Such a mingled tone may be seen in the following poem by the wife of a governor of the Massachusetts Bay Colony and the earliest American poet of note. Anne Bradstreet's first book, *The Tenth Muse Lately Sprung Up in America* (1650), had been published in England without her consent. She wrote these lines to preface a second edition:

Anne Bradstreet (1612?–1672)

THE AUTHOR TO HER BOOK   1678

Thou ill-formed offspring of my feeble brain,
Who after birth did'st by my side remain,
Till snatched from thence by friends, less wise than true,
Who thee abroad exposed to public view;
Made thee in rags, halting, to the press to trudge,   5
Where errors were not lessened, all may judge.
At thy return my blushing was not small,
My rambling brat (in print) should mother call;
I cast thee by as one unfit for light,

Thy visage was so irksome in my sight;   10
Yet being mine own, at length affection would
Thy blemishes amend, if so I could:
I washed thy face, but more defects I saw,
And rubbing off a spot, still made a flaw.
I stretched thy joints to make thee even feet,   15
Yet still thou run'st more hobbling than is meet;
In better dress to trim thee was my mind,
But nought save homespun cloth in the house I find.
In this array, 'mongst vulgars may'st thou roam;
In critics' hands beware thou dost not come;   20
And take thy way where yet thou are not known.
If for thy Father asked, say thou had'st none;
And for thy Mother, she alas is poor,
Which caused her thus to send thee out of door.

In the author's comparison of her book to an illegitimate ragamuffin, we may be struck by the details of scrubbing and dressing a child: details that might well occur to a mother who had scrubbed and dressed many. As she might feel toward such a child, so she feels toward her book. She starts by deploring it but, as the poem goes on, cannot deny it her affection. Humor enters (as in the pun in line 15). She must dress the creature in *homespun cloth*, something both crude and serviceable. By the end of her poem, Bradstreet seems to regard her book-child with tenderness, amusement, and a certain indulgent awareness of its faults. To read this poem is to sense its mingling of several attitudes. A poet can be merry and in earnest at the same time.

Walt Whitman   (1819–1892)*

TO A LOCOMOTIVE IN WINTER   1881

Thee for my recitative,
Thee in the driving storm even as now, the snow, the winter-day
    declining,
Thee in thy panoply,° thy measur'd dual throbbing and thy beat
    convulsive,   *suit of armor*
Thy black cylindric body, golden brass and silvery steel,
Thy ponderous side-bars, parallel and connecting rods, gyrating,   5
    shuttling at thy sides,
Thy metrical, now swelling pant and roar, now tapering in the distance,
Thy great protruding head-light fix'd in front,
Thy long, pale, floating vapor-pennants, tinged with delicate purple,
The dense and murky clouds out-belching from thy smoke-stack,
Thy knitted frame, thy springs and valves, the tremulous twinkle of thy   10
    wheels,

Thy train of cars behind, obedient, merrily following,
Through gale or calm, now swift, now slack, yet steadily careering;
Type of the modern—emblem of motion and power—pulse of the
    continent,
For once come serve the Muse and merge in verse, even as here I see
    thee,
With storm and buffeting gusts of wind and falling snow,   15
By day thy warning ringing bell to sound its notes,
By night thy silent signal lamps to swing.
Fierce-throated beauty!
Roll through my chant with all thy lawless music, thy swinging lamps
    at night,
Thy madly-whistled laughter, echoing, rumbling like an earthquake,   20
    rousing all,
Law of thyself complete, thine own track firmly holding,
(No sweetness debonair of tearful harp or glib piano thine,)
Thy trills of shrieks by rocks and hills return'd,
Launch'd o'er the prairies wide, across the lakes,
To the free skies unpent and glad and strong.   25

Emily Dickinson   (1830–1886)*

I LIKE TO SEE IT LAP THE MILES   (ABOUT 1862)[1]

I like to see it lap the Miles –
And lick the Valleys up –
And stop to feed itself at Tanks –
And then – prodigious step

Around a Pile of Mountains –   5
And supercilious peer
In Shanties – by the sides of Roads –
And then a Quarry pare

To fit its Ribs
And crawl between   10
Complaining all the while
In horrid – hooting stanza –
Then chase itself down Hill –

And neigh like Boanerges –
Then – punctual as a Star   15
Stop – docile and omnipotent
At its own stable door –

[1]Parentheses around a date that follows a poem title indicate the poem's date of composition, when it
was composed much earlier than its first publication date.

QUESTIONS

1. What differences in tone do you find between Whitman's and Dickinson's poems? Point out in each poem whatever contributes to these differences.
2. *Boanerges* in Dickinson's last stanza means "sons of thunder," a name given by Jesus to the disciples John and James (see Mark 3:17). How far should the reader work out the particulars of this comparison? Does it make the tone of the poem serious?
3. In Whitman's opening line, what is a *recitative?* What other specialized terms from the vocabulary of music and poetry does each poem contain? How do they help underscore Whitman's theme?
4. Poets and songwriters probably have regarded the locomotive with more affection than they have shown most other machines. Why do you suppose this is so? Can you think of any other poems or songs as examples?
5. What do these two poems tell you about locomotives that you would not be likely to find in a technical book on railroading?
6. Are the subjects of the two poems identical? Discuss.

Benjamin Alire Sáenz   (b. 1954)

TO THE DESERT   1995

I came to you one rainless August night.
You taught me how to live without the rain.
You are thirst and thirst is all I know.
You are sand, wind, sun, and burning sky,
The hottest blue. You blow a breeze and brand   5
Your breath into my mouth. You reach—then *bend*
Your force, to break, blow, burn, and make me new.
You wrap your name tight around my ribs
And keep me warm. I was born for you.
Above, below, by you, by you surrounded.   10
I wake to you at dawn. Never break your
Knot. Reach, rise, blow, *Sálvame, mi dios,*
Trágame, mi tierra. Salva, traga, Break me,
I am bread. I will be the water for your thirst.

TO THE DESERT. 5–6 *bend . . . make me new*: quoted from John Donne's "Batter my heart" (page 57). 12–13 *Sálvame, mi dios . . . traga*: Spanish for "Save me, my god, / Take me, my land. Save me, take me." (*Trágame* literally means "swallow me.")

QUESTIONS

1. How does the speaker feel about the land being described? What words in the poem suggest or convey those feelings?
2. What effect does the speaker's sudden switch into Spanish create? What is the tone of the Spanish?
3. Of what kind of language do the last few lines of the poem remind you?

Weldon Kees (1914–1955)

For My Daughter   1940

Looking into my daughter's eyes I read
Beneath the innocence of morning flesh
Concealed, hintings of death she does not heed.
Coldest of winds have blown this hair, and mesh
Of seaweed snarled these miniatures of hands;   5
The night's slow poison, tolerant and bland,
Has moved her blood. Parched years that I have seen
That may be hers appear: foul, lingering
Death in certain war, the slim legs green.
Or, fed on hate, she relishes the sting   10
Of others' agony; perhaps the cruel
Bride of a syphilitic or a fool.
These speculations sour in the sun.
I have no daughter. I desire none.

Questions

1. How does the last line of this sonnet affect the meaning of the poem?
2. "For My Daughter" was first published in 1940. What considerations might a potential American parent have felt at that time? Are these historical concerns mirrored in the poem?
3. Donald Justice has said that "Kees is one of the bitterest poets in history." Is bitterness the only attitude the speaker reveals in this poem?

The Person in the Poem

The tone of a poem, we said, is like tone of voice in that both communicate feelings. Still, this comparison raises a question: when we read a poem, whose "voice" speaks to us?

"The poet's" is one possible answer; and in the case of many a poem that answer may be right. Reading Anne Bradstreet's "The Author to Her Book," we can be reasonably sure that the poet speaks of her very own book, and of her own experiences. In order to read a poem, we seldom need to read a poet's biography; but in truth there are certain poems whose full effect depends upon our knowing at least a fact or two of the poet's life. Here is one such poem.

Natasha Trethewey   (b. 1966)

WHITE LIES   2000

The lies I could tell,
when I was growing up
light-bright, near-white,
high-yellow, red-boned
in a black place,   5
were just white lies.

I could easily tell the white folks
that we lived uptown,
not in that pink and green
shanty-fied shotgun section   10
along the tracks. I could act
like my homemade dresses
came straight out the window
of Maison Blanche. I could even
keep quiet, quiet as kept,   15
like the time a white girl said
(squeezing my hand), *Now
we have three of us in this class.*

But I paid for it every time
Mama found out.   20
She laid her hands on me,
then washed out my mouth
with Ivory soap. *This
is to purify*, she said,
and cleanse your lying tongue.   25
Believing her, I swallowed suds
thinking they'd work
from the inside out.

Through its pattern of vivid color imagery, Trethewey's poem tells of a black child light enough to "pass for white" in a society that was still extremely race-sensitive. But knowing the author's family background gives us a deeper insight into the levels of meaning in the poem. Trethewey was born in Mississippi in 1966, at a time when her parents' interracial marriage was a criminal act in that state. On her birth certificate, her mother's race was given as "colored"; in the box intended to record the race of her father—who was white and had been born in Nova Scotia—appeared the word "Canadian" (although her parents divorced before she began grade school, she remained extremely close to both of them). Trethewey has said of her birth certificate: "Something is left out of the official record that way. The irony isn't lost on me. Even in documenting myself as a person there is a little fiction." "White Lies" succeeds admirably on its own, but these biographical details allow us to read it as an even more complex meditation on issues of racial definition and personal identity in America.

Most of us can tell the difference between a person we meet in life and a person we meet in a work of art—unlike the moviegoer in the Philippines who, watching a villain in an exciting film, pulled out a revolver and peppered the screen. And yet, in reading poems, we are liable to temptation.

When the poet says "I," we may want to assume that he or she is making a personal statement. But reflect: do all poems have to be personal? Here is a brief poem inscribed on the tombstone of an infant in Burial Hill cemetery, Plymouth, Massachusetts:

> Since I have been so quickly done for,
> I wonder what I was begun for.

We do not know who wrote those lines, but it is clear that the poet was not a short-lived infant writing from personal experience. In other poems, the speaker is obviously a **persona,** or fictitious character: not the poet, but the poet's creation. As a grown man, William Blake, a skilled professional engraver, wrote a poem in the voice of a boy, an illiterate chimney sweeper. (The poem appears later in this chapter.)

Let's consider a poem spoken not by a poet, but by a persona—in this case a mysterious one. Edwin Arlington Robinson's "Luke Havergal" is a dramatic monologue, but the identity of the speaker is never clearly stated. Upon first reading the poem in Robinson's *The Children of the Night* (1897), President Theodore Roosevelt was so moved that he wrote a review of the book that made the author famous. Roosevelt, however, admitted that he found the musically seductive poem difficult. "I am not sure I understand 'Luke Havergal,'" he wrote, "but I am entirely sure I like it." Possibly what most puzzled our twenty-sixth president was who was speaking in the poem. How much does Robinson let us know about the voice and the person it addresses?

Edwin Arlington Robinson (1869–1935)*

Luke Havergal 1897

Go to the western gate, Luke Havergal,
There where the vines cling crimson on the wall,
And in the twilight wait for what will come.
The leaves will whisper there of her, and some,
Like flying words, will strike you as they fall;   5
But go, and if you listen she will call.
Go to the western gate, Luke Havergal—
Luke Havergal.

No, there is not a dawn in eastern skies
To rift the fiery night that's in your eyes;   10

But there, where western glooms are gathering,
The dark will end the dark, if anything:
God slays Himself with every leaf that flies,
And hell is more than half of paradise.
No, there is not a dawn in eastern skies—   15
In eastern skies.

Out of a grave I come to tell you this,
Out of a grave I come to quench the kiss
That flames upon your forehead with a glow
That blinds you to the way that you must go.   20
Yes, there is yet one way to where she is,
Bitter, but one that faith may never miss.
Out of a grave I come to tell you this—
To tell you this.

There is the western gate, Luke Havergal,   25
There are the crimson leaves upon the wall.
Go, for the winds are tearing them away,—
Nor think to riddle the dead words they say,
Nor any more to feel them as they fall;
But go, and if you trust her she will call.   30
There is the western gate, Luke Havergal—
Luke Havergal.

QUESTIONS

1. Who is the speaker of the poem? What specific details does the author reveal about the speaker?
2. What does the speaker ask Luke Havergal to do?
3. What do you understand "the western gate" to be?
4. Would you advise Luke Havergal to follow the speaker's advice? Why or why not?

No literary law decrees that the speaker in a poem even has to be human. Good poems have been uttered by clouds, pebbles, clocks, and cats. Here is a poem spoken by a hawk, a dramatic monologue that expresses the animal's thoughts and attitudes in a way consciously designed to emphasize how different its worldview is from a human perspective.

Ted Hughes   (1930–1998)

HAWK ROOSTING   1960

I sit in the top of the wood, my eyes closed.
Inaction, no falsifying dream
Between my hooked head and hooked feet:
Or in sleep rehearse perfect kills and eat.

The convenience of the high trees!
The air's buoyancy and the sun's ray
Are of advantage to me;
And the earth's face upward for my inspection.

My feet are locked upon the rough bark.
It took the whole of Creation   10
To produce my foot, my each feather:
Now I hold Creation in my foot

Or fly up, and revolve it all slowly—
I kill where I please because it is all mine.
There is no sophistry in my body: 15
My manners are tearing off heads—

The allotment of death.
For the one path of my flight is direct
Through the bones of the living.
No arguments assert my right: 20

The sun is behind me.
Nothing has changed since I began.
My eye has permitted no change.
I am going to keep things like this.

QUESTIONS

1. Find three observations the hawk makes about its world that a human would probably not make. What do these remarks tell us about the bird's character?
2. In what ways does Ted Hughes create an unrealistic portrayal of the hawk's true
   mental powers? What statements in the poem would an actual hawk be unlikely to
   make? Do these passages add anything to the poem's impact? What would be lost if
   they were omitted?

In a famous definition, William Wordsworth calls poetry "the spontaneous
overflow of powerful feelings . . . recollected in tranquillity." But in the case of the
following poem, Wordsworth's feelings weren't all his; they didn't just overflow
spontaneously; and the process of tranquil recollection had to go on for years.

William Wordsworth   (1770–1850)*

I WANDERED LONELY AS A CLOUD   1807

I wandered lonely as a cloud
    That floats on high o'er vales and hills,
When all at once I saw a crowd,
    A host, of golden daffodils,
Beside the lake, beneath the trees,   5
Fluttering and dancing in the breeze.

Continuous as the stars that shine
   And twinkle on the milky way,
They stretched in never-ending line
   Along the margin of a bay: 10
Ten thousand saw I at a glance,
Tossing their heads in sprightly dance.

The waves beside them danced; but they
   Out-did the sparkling waves in glee;
A poet could not but be gay,   15
   In such a jocund company;
I gazed—and gazed—but little thought
What wealth the show to me had brought:

For oft, when on my couch I lie
   In vacant or in pensive mood,
They flash upon that inward eye   20
   Which is the bliss of solitude;
And then my heart with pleasure fills,
And dances with the daffodils.

Between the first printing of the poem in 1807 and the version of 1815 given here, Wordsworth made several deliberate improvements. He changed *dancing* to *golden* in line 4, *Along* to *Beside* in line 5, *Ten thousand* to *Fluttering and* in line 6, *laughing* to *jocund* in line 16, and he added a whole stanza (the second). In fact, the writing of the poem was unspontaneous enough for Wordsworth, at a loss for lines 21–22, to take them from his wife Mary. It is likely that the experience of daffodil-watching was not entirely his to begin with but was derived in part from the recollections his sister Dorothy Wordsworth had set down in her journal of April 15, 1802, two years before he first drafted his poem.

Dorothy Wordsworth   (1771–1855)

JOURNAL ENTRY   1802

When we were in the woods beyond Gowbarrow Park we saw a few daffodils close to the water-side. We fancied that the lake had floated the seeds ashore, and that the little colony had so sprung up. But as we went along there were more and yet more; and at last, under the boughs of the trees, we saw that there was a long belt of them along the shore, about the breadth of a country turnpike road. I never saw daffodils so beautiful. They grew among the mossy stones about and about them; some rested their heads upon these stones as on a pillow for weariness; and the rest tossed and reeled and danced, and seemed as if they verily laughed with the wind, that flew upon them over the Lake; they looked so gay, ever glancing, ever changing. This wind blew directly over the Lake to them. There was here and there a little knot, and a few stragglers a few yards higher up;

but they were so few as not to disturb the simplicity, unity, and life of that one busy highway.

Notice that Wordsworth's poem echoes a few of his sister's observations. Weaving poetry out of their mutual memories, Wordsworth has offered the experience as if altogether his own, made himself lonely, and left Dorothy out. The point is not that Wordsworth is a liar or a plagiarist but that, like any other good poet, he has transformed ordinary life into art. A process of interpreting, shaping, and ordering had to intervene between the experience of looking at daffodils and the finished poem.

We need not deny that a poet's experience can contribute to a poem nor that the emotion in the poem can indeed be the poet's. Still, to write a good poem one has to do more than live and feel. It seems a pity that, as Randall Jarrell has said, a cardinal may write verses worse than his youngest choirboy's. But writing poetry takes skill and imagination—qualities that extensive travel and wide experience do not necessarily give. For much of her life, Emily Dickinson seldom strayed from her family's house and grounds in Amherst, Massachusetts; yet her rimed life studies of a snake, a bee, and a hummingbird contain more poetry than we find in any firsthand description (so far) of the surface of the moon.

James Stephens   (1882–1950)*

A GLASS OF BEER   1918

The lanky hank of a she in the inn over there
Nearly killed me for asking the loan of a glass of beer;
May the devil grip the whey-faced slut by the hair,
And beat bad manners out of her skin for a year.

That parboiled ape, with the toughest jaw you will see   5
On virtue's path, and a voice that would rasp the dead,
Came roaring and raging the minute she looked at me,
And threw me out of the house on the back of my head!

If I asked her master he'd give me a cask a day;
But she, with the beer at hand, not a gill° would arrange!   *quarter-pint*   10
May she marry a ghost and bear him a kitten, and may
The High King of Glory permit her to get the mange.

QUESTIONS

1. Who do you take to be the speaker? Is it the poet? The speaker may be angry, but what is the tone of this poem?
2. Would you agree with a commentator who said, "To berate anyone in truly memorable language is practically a lost art in America"? How well does the speaker (an Irishman) succeed? Which of his epithets and curses strike you as particularly imaginative?

Anne Sexton (1928–1974)*

HER KIND   1960

I have gone out, a possessed witch,
haunting the black air, braver at night;
dreaming evil, I have done my hitch
over the plain houses, light by light:
lonely thing, twelve-fingered, out of mind.   5
A woman like that is not a woman, quite.
I have been her kind.

I have found the warm caves in the woods,
filled them with skillets, carvings, shelves,
closets, silks, innumerable goods;   10
fixed the suppers for the worms and the elves:
whining, rearranging the disaligned.
A woman like that is misunderstood.
I have been her kind.

I have ridden in your cart, driver,   15
waved my nude arms at villages going by,
learning the last bright routes, survivor
where your flames still bite my thigh
and my ribs crack where your wheels wind.
A woman like that is not ashamed to die.   20
I have been her kind.

QUESTIONS

1. Who is the speaker of this poem? What do we know about her?
2. What does the speaker mean by ending each stanza with the statement, "I have been her kind?"
3. Who are the figures with whom the speaker identifies? What do these figures tell us about the speaker's state of mind?

EXPERIMENT: *Reading with and without Biography*

Read the following poem and state what you understand from it. Then consider the circumstances in which it probably came to be written. (Some information is offered in a note on page 52.) Does the meaning of the poem change? To what extent does an appreciation of the poem need the support of biography?

William Carlos Williams (1883–1963)*

THE RED WHEELBARROW   1923

so much depends
upon

a red wheel
barrow

glazed with rain   5
water

beside the white
chickens.

IRONY

To see a distinction between the poet and the words of a fictitious character—between Robert Browning and "My Last Duchess"—is to be aware of **irony:** a manner of speaking that implies a discrepancy. If the mask says one thing and we sense that the writer is in fact saying something else, the writer has adopted an **ironic point of view.** No finer illustration exists in English than Jonathan Swift's "A Modest Proposal," an essay in which Swift speaks as an earnest, humorless citizen who sets forth his reasonable plan to aid the Irish poor. The plan is so monstrous no sane reader can assent to it: the poor are to sell their children as meat for the tables of their landlords. From behind his false face, Swift is actually recommending not cannibalism but love and Christian charity.

A poem is often made complicated and more interesting by another kind of irony. **Verbal irony** occurs whenever words say one thing but mean something else, usually the opposite. The word *love* means *hate* here: "I just *love* to stay home and do my hair on a Saturday night!" If the verbal irony is conspicuously bitter, heavy-handed, and mocking, it is **sarcasm:** "Oh, he's the biggest spender in the world, all right!" (The sarcasm, if that statement were spoken, would be underscored by the speaker's tone of voice.) A famous instance of sarcasm is Mark Antony's line in his oration over the body of slain Julius Caesar: "Brutus is an honorable man." Antony repeats this line until the enraged populace begins shouting exactly what he means to call Brutus and the other conspirators: traitors, villains, murderers. We had best be alert for irony on the printed page, for if we miss it, our interpretations of a poem may go wild.

Robert Creeley (b. 1926)

Oh No   1959

If you wander far enough
you will come to it
and when you get there
they will give you a place to sit

for yourself only, in a nice chair,   5
and all your friends will be there
with smiles on their faces
and they will likewise all have places.

This poem is rich in verbal irony. The title helps point out that between the speaker's words and attitude lie deep differences. In line 2, what is *it*? Old age? The wandering suggests a conventional metaphor: the journey of life. Is *it* literally a rest home for "senior citizens," or perhaps some naïve popular concept of heaven (such as we meet in comic strips: harps, angels with hoops for halos) in which the saved all sit around in a ring, smugly congratulating one another? We can't be sure, but the speaker's attitude toward this final sitting-place is definite. It is a place for the selfish, as we infer from the phrase *for yourself only*. And *smiles on their faces* may hint that the smiles are unchanging and forced. There is a difference between saying "They had smiles on their faces" and "They smiled": the latter suggests that the smiles came from within. The word *nice* is to be regarded with distrust. If we see through this speaker, as Creeley implies we can do, we realize that, while pretending to be sweet-talking us into a seat, actually he is revealing the horror of a little hell. And the title is the poet's reaction to it (or the speaker's unironic, straightforward one): "Oh no! Not *that!*"

Dramatic irony, like verbal irony, contains an element of contrast, but it usually refers to a situation in a play wherein a character whose knowledge is limited says, does, or encounters something of greater significance than he or she knows. We, the spectators, realize the meaning of this speech or action, for the playwright has afforded us superior knowledge. In Sophocles' *King Oedipus*, when Oedipus vows to punish whomever has brought down a plague upon the city of Thebes, we know—as he does not—that the man he would punish is himself. (Referring to such a situation that precedes the downfall of a hero in a tragedy, some critics speak of **tragic irony** instead of dramatic irony.) Superior knowledge can be enjoyed not only by spectators in a theater but by readers of poetry as well. In *Paradise Lost*, we know in advance that Adam will fall into temptation, and we recognize his overconfidence when he neglects a warning. The situation of Oedipus also contains **cosmic irony,** or **irony of fate:** some Fate with a grim sense of humor seems cruelly to trick a human being. Cosmic irony clearly exists in poems in which fate or the Fates are personified and seen as hostile, as in Thomas Hardy's "The Convergence of the Twain" (page 486); and it may be said to occur also in Robinson's "Richard Cory" (page 146). Obviously it is a twist of fate for the most envied man in town to kill himself.

To sum up: the effect of irony depends on the reader's noticing some incongruity or discrepancy between two things. In *verbal irony*, there is a contrast between the speaker's words and meaning; in an *ironic point of view*, between the writer's attitude and what is spoken by a fictitious character; in *dramatic irony*, between the limited knowledge of a character and the fuller knowledge of the reader or spectator; in *cosmic irony*, between a character's aspiration and the treatment he or she receives at the hands of Fate. Although, in the work of an inept poet, irony can be crude and obvious sarcasm, it is invaluable to a poet of more complicated mind, who imagines more than one perspective.

W. H. Auden   (1907–1973)*

The Unknown Citizen   1940

(To JS/07/M/378
This Marble Monument
Is Erected by the State)

He was found by the Bureau of Statistics to be
One against whom there was no official complaint,
And all the reports on his conduct agree
That, in the modern sense of an old-fashioned word, he was a saint,
For in everything he did he served the Greater Community.   5
Except for the War till the day he retired
He worked in a factory and never got fired,
But satisfied his employers, Fudge Motors Inc.
Yet he wasn't a scab or odd in his views,
For his Union reports that he paid his dues,   10
(Our report on his Union shows it was sound)
And our Social Psychology workers found
That he was popular with his mates and liked a drink.
The Press are convinced that he bought a paper every day
And that his reactions to advertisements were normal in every way. 15
Policies taken out in his name prove that he was fully insured,
And his Health-card shows he was once in hospital but left it cured.
Both Producers Research and High-Grade Living declare
He was fully sensible to the advantages of the Installment Plan
And had everything necessary to the Modern Man,   20
A phonograph, a radio, a car and a frigidaire.
Our researchers into Public Opinion are content
That he held the proper opinions for the time of year;
When there was peace, he was for peace; when there was war, he went.
He was married and added five children to the population,   25
Which our Eugenist says was the right number for a parent of his
        generation,
And our teachers report that he never interfered with their education.

Was he free? Was he happy? The question is absurd:
Had anything been wrong, we should certainly have heard.

QUESTIONS

1. Read the three-line epitaph at the beginning of the poem as carefully as you read what follows. How does the epitaph help establish the voice by which the rest of the poem is spoken?
2. Who is speaking?
3. What ironic discrepancies do you find between the speaker's attitude toward the subject and that of the poet himself? By what is the poet's attitude made clear?
4. In the phrase "The Unknown Soldier" (of which "The Unknown Citizen" reminds us), what does the word *unknown* mean? What does it mean in the title of Auden's poem?
5. What tendencies in our civilization does Auden satirize?
6. How would you expect the speaker to define a Modern Man, if a CD player, a radio, a car, and a refrigerator are "everything" a Modern Man needs?

Sharon Olds   (b. 1942)*

RITES OF PASSAGE   1983

As the guests arrive at my son's party
they gather in the living room—
short men, men in first grade
with smooth jaws and chins.
Hands in pockets, they stand around   5
jostling, jockeying for place, small fights
breaking out and calming. One says to another
How old are you? Six. I'm seven. So?
They eye each other, seeing themselves
tiny in the other's pupils. They clear their   10
throats a lot, a room of small bankers,
they fold their arms and frown. *I could beat you
up*, a seven says to a six,
the dark cake, round and heavy as a
turret, behind them on the table. My son,   15
freckles like specks of nutmeg on his cheeks,
chest narrow as the balsa keel of a
model boat, long hands
cool and thin as the day they guided him
out of me, speaks up as a host   20
for the sake of the group.
We could easily kill a two-year-old,
he says in his clear voice. The other
men agree, they clear their throats
like Generals, they relax and get down to   25
playing war, celebrating my son's life.

Questions

1. What is ironic about the way the speaker describes the first-grade boys at her son's birthday party?
2. What other irony does the author underscore in the last two lines?
3. Does this mother sentimentalize her own son by seeing him as better than the other little boys?

John Betjeman (1906–1984)

In Westminster Abbey   1940

Let me take this other glove off
   As the *vox humana* swells,
And the beauteous fields of Eden
   Bask beneath the Abbey bells.
Here, where England's statesmen lie,   5
Listen to a lady's cry.

Gracious Lord, oh bomb the Germans.
   Spare their women for Thy Sake,
And if that is not too easy
   We will pardon Thy Mistake.   10
But, gracious Lord, whate'er shall be,
Don't let anyone bomb me.

Keep our Empire undismembered,
   Guide our Forces by Thy Hand,
Gallant blacks from far Jamaica,   15
   Honduras and Togoland;
Protect them Lord in all their fights,
And, even more, protect the whites.

Think of what our Nation stands for:
   Books from Boots' and country lanes,   20
Free speech, free passes, class distinction,
   Democracy and proper drains.
Lord, put beneath Thy special care
One-eighty-nine Cadogan Square.

Although dear Lord I am a sinner,   25
   I have done no major crime;
Now I'll come to Evening Service
   Whensoever I have the time.
So, Lord, reserve for me a crown,
And do not let my shares° go down.   *stocks* 30

I will labor for Thy Kingdom,
    Help our lads to win the war,
Send white feathers to the cowards,
    Join the Women's Army Corps,
Then wash the Steps around Thy Throne   35
In the Eternal Safety Zone.

Now I feel a little better,
    What a treat to hear Thy Word,
Where the bones of leading statesmen
    Have so often been interred.   40
And now, dear Lord, I cannot wait
Because I have a luncheon date.

IN WESTMINSTER ABBEY. First printed during World War II. 2 *vox humana*: an organ stop that makes tones similar to those of the human voice. 20 *Boots'*: a chain of pharmacies whose branches had lending libraries.

QUESTIONS

1. Who is the speaker? What do we know about her lifestyle? About her prejudices?
2. Point out some of the places in which she contradicts herself.
3. How would you describe the speaker's attitude toward religion?
4. Through the medium of irony, what positive points do you believe Betjeman makes?

Sarah N. Cleghorn   (1876–1959)

THE GOLF LINKS   1917

The golf links lie so near the mill
    That almost every day
The laboring children can look out
    And see the men at play.

QUESTIONS

1. Is this brief poem satiric? Does it contain any verbal irony or is the poet making a matter-of-fact statement in words that mean just what they say?
2. What other kind of irony is present in the poem?
3. Sarah N. Cleghorn's poem dates from before the enactment of legislation against child labor. Is it still a good poem, or is it hopelessly dated?
4. How would you state its theme?
5. Would you call this poem lyric, narrative, or didactic?

Josephine Miles   (1911–1985)

CIVILIAN   1966

The largest stock of armaments allows me
A reason not to kill.
Defense Department does the blasting for me
As soundly as I will.

Indeed, can cover a much wider area   5
Than I will ever score
With a single rifle sent me on approval
From a Sears Roebuck store.

Only the psycho, meaning sick in spirit,
Would aim his personal shot   10
At anybody; he is sick in spirit
As I am not.

QUESTIONS

1. For what reasons does the speaker adopt a position of personal nonviolence?
2. What type of irony is demonstrated in this poem? Explain.

Connie Bensley   (b. 1929)

THE COVETOUS CAT   1994

Because the common is remote
they walk along hand in hand.

On the path ahead of them
some bird-lover has scattered bread

and in the middle of it a plump cat crouches   5
chewing at the crusts.

Cats don't really like bread, the man remarks,
he only wants it because it's someone else's.

Like you, she thinks,
withdrawing her hand slightly.   10

QUESTIONS

1. What is ironic about the man's remark?
2. Is there any hint earlier in the poem about the nature of the couple's relationship?

Point out the kinds of irony that occur in the following poem.

Thomas Hardy   (1840–1928)*

THE WORKBOX   1914

"See, here's the workbox, little wife,
   That I made of polished oak."
He was a joiner,° of village life;   *carpenter*
   She came of borough folk.

He holds the present up to her   5
   As with a smile she nears
And answers to the profferer,
    "'Twill last all my sewing years!"

"I warrant it will. And longer too.
   'Tis a scantling that I got   10
Off poor John Wayward's coffin, who
   Died of they knew not what.

"The shingled pattern that seems to cease
   Against your box's rim
Continues right on in the piece   15
   That's underground with him.

"And while I worked it made me think
   Of timber's varied doom:
One inch where people eat and drink,
   The next inch in a tomb.   20

"But why do you look so white, my dear,
   And turn aside your face?
You knew not that good lad, I fear,
   Though he came from your native place?"

"How could I know that good young man,   25
   Though he came from my native town,
When he must have left far earlier than
   I was a woman grown?"

"Ah, no. I should have understood!
   It shocked you that I gave   30
To you one end of a piece of wood
   Whose other is in a grave?"

"Don't, dear, despise my intellect,
   Mere accidental things
Of that sort never have effect   35
   On my imaginings."

Yet still her lips were limp and wan,
    Her face still held aside,
As if she had known not only John,
    But known of what he died.   40

FOR REVIEW AND FURTHER STUDY

William Blake   (1757–1827)*

THE CHIMNEY SWEEPER   1789

When my mother died I was very young,
And my father sold me while yet my tongue
Could scarcely cry "'weep! 'weep! 'weep! 'weep!"
So your chimneys I sweep, and in soot I sleep.

There's little Tom Dacre, who cried when his head,   5
That curled like a lamb's back, was shaved: so I said
"Hush, Tom! never mind it, for when your head's bare
You know that the soot cannot spoil your white hair."

And so he was quiet, and that very night,
As Tom was a-sleeping, he had such a sight!   10
That thousands of sweepers, Dick, Joe, Ned, and Jack,
Were all of them locked up in coffins of black.

And by came an Angel who had a bright key,
And he opened the coffins and set them all free;
Then down a green plain leaping, laughing, they run,   15
And wash in a river, and shine in the sun.

Then naked and white, all their bags left behind,
They rise upon clouds and sport in the wind;
And the Angel told Tom, if he'd be a good boy,
He'd have God for his father, and never want° joy.   lack 20

And so Tom awoke; and we rose in the dark,
And got with our bags and our brushes to work.
Though the morning was cold, Tom was happy and warm;
So if all do their duty they need not fear harm.

QUESTIONS

1. What does Blake's poem reveal about conditions of life in the London of his day?
2. What does this poem have in common with "The Golf Links" (page 40)?
3. Sum up your impressions of the speaker's character. What does he say and do that
    displays it to us?
4. What pun do you find in line 3? Is its effect comic or serious?
5. In Tom Dacre's dream (lines 11–20), what wishes come true? Do you understand
    them to be the wishes of the chimney sweepers, of the poet, or of both?

6. In the last line, what is ironic in the speaker's assurance that the dutiful *need not fear harm?* What irony is there in his urging all to *do their duty?* (Who have failed in their duty to *him?*)
7. What is the tone of Blake's poem? Angry? Hopeful? Sorrowful? Compassionate? (Don't feel obliged to sum it up in a single word.)

Robert McDowell (b. 1953)

AT HOME WITH DOLLFACE   2002

I stepped down into the little cardboard town.
All day and night we were posing.
I did not need to water or cut
Our plastic lawn, and I gave up shaving because
In my beloved's world no hair or green thing grew.   5
My teeth were exquisitely white,
My body fat absolutely zero.
We dressed from wardrobes without end,
And drove our pink convertible to the river each day.

One might think that we yearned for some controversy,   10
A little spice mixed into the bland stew of our days.
In fact, we were deliriously happy, content with our clothes
And gadgets, determined to look out
At the world's woe through the wise eyes of toys.

QUESTIONS

1. Who is the speaker in this poem?
2. What seems to be the author's attitude toward what he describes? How does his tone help to provide an answer?

William Stafford (1914–1993)*

AT THE UN-NATIONAL MONUMENT ALONG THE CANADIAN BORDER   1977

This is the field where the battle did not happen,
where the unknown soldier did not die.
This is the field where grass joined hands,
where no monument stands,
and the only heroic thing is the sky.   5

Birds fly here without any sound,
unfolding their wings across the open.
No people killed—or were killed—on this ground
hallowed by neglect and an air so tame
that people celebrate it by forgetting its name.   10

QUESTIONS

1. What nonevent does this poem celebrate? What is the speaker's attitude toward it?
2. The speaker describes an empty field. What is odd about the way in which he describes it?
3. What words does the speaker appear to use ironically?

H. L. Hix   (b. 1960)

I LOVE THE WORLD, AS DOES ANY DANCER   2000

I love the world, as does any dancer,
with the tips of my toes. I love the world
more than I love my wife, for it contains
more crannies and crevasses, it tenders
more textures to my twenty digits' touch.   5
Lush grass underfoot after April rain,
a pile of petals fallen from a rose,
sun-seared sidewalk in summer, sand, fresh-turned
garden dirt, and, yes, her hummocked ankle
rubbed by the ball of my foot as she sleeps.   10

QUESTIONS

1. This poem describes parts of the world by the way they feel to the speaker's feet. How does that unusual perspective affect the tone of the poem?
2. If you revised the poem to be about the sense of sight rather than touch (for example, "I love the world, as does any painter/with my eyes . . ."), would that shift change the poem's personality?

EXERCISE: *Telling Tone*

Here are two radically different poems on a similar subject. Try stating the theme of each poem in your own words. How is tone (the speaker's attitude) different in the two poems?

Richard Lovelace   (1618–1658)

TO LUCASTA   1649

On Going to the Wars

Tell me not, Sweet, I am unkind
    That from the nunnery
Of thy chaste breast and quiet mind,
    To war and arms I fly.

True, a new mistress now I chase,
    The first foe in the field;
And with a stronger faith embrace
    A sword, a horse, a shield.

Yet this inconstancy is such
    As you too shall adore;
I could not love thee, Dear, so much,
    Loved I not Honor more.

Wilfred Owen   (1893–1918)*

DULCE ET DECORUM EST   1920

Bent double, like old beggars under sacks,
Knock-kneed, coughing like hags, we cursed through sludge,
Till on the haunting flares we turned our backs
And towards our distant rest began to trudge.
Men marched asleep. Many had lost their boots
But limped on, blood-shod. All went lame; all blind;
Drunk with fatigue; deaf even to the hoots
Of tired, outstripped Five-Nines that dropped behind.

Gas! Gas! Quick, boys!—An ecstasy of fumbling,
Fitting the clumsy helmets just in time;
But someone still was yelling out and stumbling
And flound'ring like a man in fire or lime . . .
Dim, through the misty panes and thick green light,
As under a green sea, I saw him drowning.

In all my dreams, before my helpless sight,
He plunges at me, guttering, choking, drowning.

If in some smothering dreams you too could pace
Behind the wagon that we flung him in,
And watch the white eyes writhing in his face,
His hanging face, like a devil's sick of sin;
If you could hear, at every jolt, the blood
Come gargling from the froth-corrupted lungs,
Obscene as cancer, bitter as the cud
Of vile, incurable sores on innocent tongues,—
My friend, you would not tell with such high zest
To children ardent for some desperate glory,
The old Lie: Dulce et decorum est
Pro patria mori.

DULCE ET DECORUM EST. 8 *Five-Nines:* German howitzers often used to shoot poison gas shells 17 *you too:* Some manuscript versions of this poem carry the dedication "To Jessie Pope" (a writer of patriotic verse) or "To a certain Poetess." 27–28 *Dulce et . . . mori:* a quotation from the Latin poet Horace, "It is sweet and fitting to die for one's country."

Wilfred Owen

Wilfred Owen was only twenty-one years old when World War I broke out in 1914. Twice wounded in battle, he was rapidly promoted and eventually became a company commander. The shocking violence of modern war summoned up his poetic genius, and in a two-year period he grew from a negligible minor poet into the most important English-language poet of World War I. Owen, however, did not live to see his talent recognized. He was killed one week before the end of the war; he was twenty-five years old. Owen published only four poems during his lifetime. Shortly before his death he drafted a few lines of prose for the preface of a book of poems. (For a short biography of Owen, consult "Lives of the Poets.")

Wilfred Owen on Writing

WAR POETRY (1917?)

This book is not about heroes. English poetry is not yet fit to speak of them.

Nor is it about deeds, or lands, nor anything about glory, honour, might, majesty, dominion, or power, except War.

Above all I am not concerned with Poetry.

My subject is War, and the pity of War.

The Poetry is in the pity.

Yet these elegies are to this generation in no sense consolatory. They may be to the next. All a poet can do today is warn. That is why the true Poets must be truthful.

From Collected Poems

Paying Attention to the Obvious

If tone is a speaker's attitude toward his or her material, then to understand the tone of a poem, we need mostly just to listen—as we might listen to a real conversation. The key is to hear not only *what* is being said but also *how* it is being said. Does the speaker sound noticeably surprised, angry, nostalgic, tender, or expectant? A common mistake in analyzing poetry is to discuss subtle points of interpretation before you fully understand the *obvious* features of a poem. In critical writing it almost never hurts to begin by asking obvious questions:

1. Does the speaker reveal any obvious emotion or attitude about the subject or the setting of the poem? (When D. H. Lawrence, for example, ends his poem "Piano" on page 10 by saying, "I weep like a child for the past," he makes his nostalgic and tender tone explicit.)

2. If there is an implied listener or listeners to the poem, how does the speaker address them? Is there anything obviously unusual about the tone? (In Betjeman's "In Westminster Abbey," for example, the speaker addresses God with astonishing egocentricity and snooty nonchalance.)

3. Is there any obvious difference between the reaction of the speaker to what is happening in the poem and your own honest reaction? If the gap between the two reactions is large (as it is in Robert Browning's "My Last Duchess," for instance), what does it suggest?

4. If the difference between your honest reaction and the speaker's is enormous, is the poem in some way ironic?

WRITING ASSIGNMENT

Using any poetry selection from this chapter, analyze the speaker's attitude toward the poem's main subject. Support your argument by examining the author's choice of specific words and images to create the particular tone used to convey the speaker's attitudes. (Possible subjects might include Wilfred Owen's attitude toward war in "Dulce et Decorum Est," the tone and imagery of Weldon Kees's "For My Daughter," Ted Hughes's view of the workings of nature in "Hawk Roosting," or Anne Bradstreet's attitude toward her own poetry in "The Author to Her Book.")

Here is an example of an essay written for this assignment by Kim Larsen, a student of Karen Locke at Lane Community College in Eugene, Oregon.

Kim Larsen

Professor Locke

English 110

21 November 20xx

Word Choice, Tone, and Point of View in Roethke's

"My Papa's Waltz"

Some readers may find Theodore Roethke's "My Papa's Waltz" a reminiscence of a happy childhood scene. I believe, however, that the poem depicts a more painful and complicated series of emotions. By examining the choice of words that Roethke uses to convey the tone of his scene, I will demonstrate that beneath the seemingly comic situation of the poem is a darker story. The true point of view of "My Papa's Waltz" is that of a resentful adult reliving his fear of a domineering parent.

The first clue that the dance may not have been a mutually enjoyable experience is in the title itself. The author did not title the poem "Our Waltz" or "Waltzing with My Papa," either of which would set an initial tone for readers to expect a shared, loving sentiment. It does not even have a neutral title, such as "The Waltz." The title specifically implies that the waltz was exclusively the father's. Since a waltz normally involves two people, it can be reasoned that the father dances his waltz without regard for his young partner.

Examining each stanza of the poem offers numerous examples where the choice of words sustains the tone implied in the title. The first line, "The whiskey on your breath," conjures up an olfactory image that most would find unpleasant. The small boy finds it so overpowering he is made "dizzy." This stanza contains the only simile in the poem, "I hung on like death" (3), which creates a ghastly and stark visual image. There are innumerable choices of similes to portray hanging on: a vine, an infant, an animal cub, all of which would have illustrated a lighthearted romp. The choice of "death" was purposefully used to convey an intended image. The first stanza ends by stating the "waltzing was not easy." The definitions of easy, as found in Webster's New Collegiate Dictionary, include "free from pain, annoyance or anxiety," and "not difficult to endure or undergo" ("Easy"). Obviously the speaker did not find those qualities in the waltz.

Further evidence of this harsh and oppressive scene is brought to mind by reckless disregard for "the pans / Slid from the kitchen shelf" (5-6), which the reader can almost hear crashing on the floor in loud cacophony, and the "mother's countenance," which "[c]ould not unfrown itself" (8). If this was only a silly, playful romp between father and son, even a stern, fastidious mother might be expected to at least make an unsuccessful attempt to suppress a grin. Instead, the reader gets a visual image of a silent, unhappy woman, afraid, probably due to past experience, to interfere in the domestic destruction around her. Once more, this detail suggests a domineering father who controls the family.

The third stanza relates the father's "battered" hand holding the boy's wrist. The tactile image of holding a wrist suggests dragging or forcing an unwilling person, not holding hands as would be expected with a mutual dance partner. Further disregard for the son's feelings is displayed by the lines "At every step you missed / My right ear scraped a buckle" (11-12). In each missed step, probably due to his drunkenness, the father causes the boy physical pain.

The tone continues in the final stanza as the speaker recalls "You beat time on my head / With a palm caked hard by dirt" (13-14). The visual and tactile image of a dirt-hardened hand beating on a child's head as if it were a drum is distinctly unpleasant. The last lines "Then waltzed me off to bed / Still clinging to your shirt" (15-16) are the most ambiguous in the poem. It can be reasoned, as X. J. Kennedy and Dana Gioia do, that the lines suggest "the boy is still clinging to his father with persistent if also complicated love" (22). On the other hand, if one notices the earlier dark images, the conclusion could describe a boy clinging out of fear, the physical fear of being dropped by one who is drunk and the emotional fear of not being loved and nurtured as a child needs to be by his father.

It can also be argued that the poem's rollicking rhythm contributes to a sense of fun, and in truth, the poem can be read in that fashion. On the other hand, it can be read in such a way as to deemphasize the rhythm, as the author himself does in his recording of "My Papa's Waltz" (Roethke, Reads). The joyful, rollicking rhythm can be seen as ironic. By reminding readers of a waltzing tempo, it is highlighting the discrepancy of what a waltz should be and the bleak, frightening picture painted in the words.

While "My Papa's Waltz" can be read as a roughhouse comedy, by examining Roethke's title and choice of words closely to interpret the meaning of their images and sounds, it is also plausible to hear an entirely different tone. I believe "My Papa's Waltz" employs the voice of an embittered adult remembering a harsh scene in which both he and his mother were powerless in the presence of a drunk and domineering father.

Works Cited

"Easy." <u>Merriam-Webster's Collegiate Dictionary</u>. 11th ed.
2003.

Kennedy, X. J., and Dana Gioia, eds. <u>An Introduction to
Poetry</u>. 11th ed. New York: Longman, 2005. 22.

Roethke, Theodore. "My Papa's Waltz." <u>An Introduction to
Poetry</u>. Ed. X. J. Kennedy and Dana Gioia. 11th ed. New
York: Longman, 2005. 22.

---. <u>Theodore Roethke Reads His Poetry</u>. Audiocassette.
Caedmon, 1972.

INFORMATION FOR EXPERIMENT: *Reading with and without Biography*

THE RED WHEELBARROW (page 35). Dr. Williams's poem reportedly contains a personal experience: he was gazing from the window of the house where one of his patients, a small girl, lay suspended between life and death. (This account, from the director of the public library in Williams's native Rutherford, N.J., is given by Geri M. Rhodes in "The Paterson Metaphor in William Carlos Williams's *Paterson*," master's essay, Tufts U, 1965.)

FURTHER SUGGESTIONS FOR WRITING

1. Do you think Wilfred Owen's "Dulce et Decorum Est" fulfills his intentions as stated in "War Poetry"? Write a brief essay comparing Owen's poem to his goals as a writer. Cite specific instances of where the poem meets or fails to meet his criteria.
2. In a paragraph, sum up your initial reactions to "The Red Wheelbarrow." Then, taking another look at the poem in light of information noted above, write a second paragraph summing up your further reactions.
3. Write a short essay titled "What Thomas Hardy Leaves Unsaid in 'The Workbox.'"
4. Write a verbal profile or short character sketch of the speaker of John Betjeman's "In Westminster Abbey."
5. In a brief essay, consider the tone of two poems on a similar subject. Compare and contrast Walt Whitman and Emily Dickinson as locomotive-fanciers; or, in the poems by Richard Lovelace and Wilfred Owen, compare and contrast attitudes toward war. (For advice on writing about poetry by the method of comparison and contrast, see "Writing About a Poem.")
6. Rewrite Ted Hughes's "Hawk Roosting" from the perspective of either a pigeon or a turkey. Use either prose or verse for your version.

3 Words

LITERAL MEANING: WHAT A POEM SAYS FIRST

Although successful as a painter, Edgar Degas found poetry discouragingly hard to write. To his friend, the poet Stéphane Mallarmé, he complained, "What a business! My whole day gone on a blasted sonnet, without getting an inch further . . . and it isn't ideas I'm short of . . . I'm full of them, I've got too many . . . "

"But Degas," said Mallarmé, "you can't make a poem with ideas—you make it with *words!*" [1]

Like the celebrated painter, some people assume that all it takes to make a poem is a bright idea. Poems state ideas, to be sure, and sometimes the ideas are invaluable; and yet the most impressive idea in the world will not make a poem, unless its words are selected and arranged with loving art. Some poets take great pains to find the right word. Unable to fill a two-syllable gap in an unfinished line that went, "The seal's wide—gaze toward Paradise," Hart Crane paged through an unabridged dictionary. When he reached S, he found the object of his quest in *spindrift:* "spray skimmed from the sea by a strong wind." The word is exact and memorable. Any word can be the right word, however, if artfully chosen and placed. It may be a word as ordinary as *from.* Consider the difference between "The sedge is withered *on* the lake" (a misquotation of a line by Keats) and "The sedge is withered *from* the lake" (what Keats in fact wrote). Keats's original line suggests, as the altered line doesn't, that because the sedge (a growth of grasslike plants) has withered *from* the lake, it has withdrawn mysteriously.

In reading a poem, some people assume that its words can be skipped over rapidly, and they try to leap at once to the poem's general theme. It is as if they fear being thought clods unless they can find huge ideas in the poem (whether or

[1]Paul Valéry, *Degas . . . Manet . . . Morisot,* translated by David Paul (New York: Pantheon, 1960) 62.

not there are any). Such readers often ignore the literal meanings of words: the ordinary, matter-of-fact sense to be found in a dictionary. (As you will see in the next chapter, "Saying and Suggesting," words possess not only dictionary meanings—denotations—but also many associations and suggestions—connotations.) Consider the following poem and see what you make of it.

William Carlos Williams   (1883–1963)*

This Is Just to Say   1934

I have eaten
the plums
that were in
the icebox

and which   5
you were probably
saving
for breakfast

Forgive me
they were delicious   10
so sweet
and so cold

Some readers distrust a poem so simple and candid. They think, "What's wrong with me? There has to be more to it than this!" But poems seldom are puzzles in need of solutions. We can begin by accepting the poet's statements, without suspecting the poet of trying to hoodwink us. On later reflection, of course, we might possibly decide that the poet is playfully teasing or being ironic; but Williams gives us no reason to think that. There seems no need to look beyond the literal sense of his words, no profit in speculating that the plums symbolize worldly joys and that the icebox stands for the universe. Clearly, a reader who held such a grand theory would have overlooked (in eagerness to find a significant idea) the plain truth that the poet makes clear to us: that ice-cold plums are a joy to taste.

To be sure, Williams's small poem is simpler than most poems are; and yet in reading any poem, no matter how complicated, you will do well to reach slowly and reluctantly for a theory to explain it by. To find the general theme of a poem, you first need to pay attention to its words. Recall Yeats's "The Lake Isle of Innisfree" (page 7), a poem that makes a statement—crudely summed up, "I yearn to leave the city and retreat to a place of ideal peace and happiness." And yet before we can realize this theme, we have to notice details: nine bean rows, a glade loud with bees, "lake water lapping with low sounds by the shore," the gray of a pavement. These details and not some abstract remark make clear what the poem is saying: that the city is drab, while the island hideaway is sublimely beautiful.

Poets often strive for words that point to physical details and solid objects. They may do so even when speaking of an abstract idea:

> Beauty is but a flower
> Which wrinkles will devour;
> Brightness falls from the air,
> Queens have died young and fair,
> Dust hath closed Helen's eye.
> I am sick, I must die:
>   Lord, have mercy on us!

In these lines by Thomas Nashe, the abstraction *beauty* has grown petals that shrivel. Brightness may be a general name for light, but Nashe succeeds in giving it the weight of a falling body.

If a poem says *daffodils* instead of *plant life*, *diaper years* instead of *infancy*, we call its **diction,** or choice of words, **concrete** rather than **abstract.** Concrete words refer to what we can immediately perceive with our senses: *dog, actor, chemical,* or particular individuals who belong to those general classes: *Bonzo the fox terrier, Clint Eastwood, hydrogen sulfate.* Abstract words express ideas or concepts: *love, time, truth.* In abstracting, we leave out some characteristics found in each individual, and instead observe a quality common to many. The word *beauty,* for instance, denotes what may be observed in numerous persons, places, and things.

Ezra Pound gave a famous piece of advice to his fellow poets: "Go in fear of abstractions." This is not to say that a poet cannot employ abstract words, nor that all poems have to be about physical things. Much of T. S. Eliot's *Four Quartets* is concerned with time, eternity, history, language, reality, and other things that cannot be physically handled. But Eliot, however high he may soar for a larger view, keeps returning to earth. He makes us aware of *things.*

Marianne Moore   (1887–1972)*

SILENCE   1924

> My father used to say,
> "Superior people never make long visits,
> have to be shown Longfellow's grave
> or the glass flowers at Harvard.
> Self-reliant like the cat—   5
> that takes its prey to privacy,
> the mouse's limp tail hanging like a shoelace from its mouth—
> they sometimes enjoy solitude,

and can be robbed of speech
by speech which has delighted them.   10
The deepest feeling always shows itself in silence;
not in silence, but restraint."
Nor was he insincere in saying, "Make my house your inn."
Inns are not residences.

QUESTIONS

1. Almost all of "Silence" consists of quotation. What are some possible reasons why the speaker prefers using another person's words?
2. What are the words the father uses to describe people he admires?
3. The poem makes an important distinction between two similar words (lines 13–14). Explain the distinction Moore implies.
4. Why is "Silence" an appropriate title for this poem?

Robert Graves   (1895–1985)*

DOWN, WANTON, DOWN!   1933

Down, wanton, down! Have you no shame
That at the whisper of Love's name,
Or Beauty's, presto! up you raise
Your angry head and stand at gaze?

Poor bombard-captain, sworn to reach   5
The ravelin and effect a breach—
Indifferent what you storm or why,
So be that in the breach you die!

Love may be blind, but Love at least
Knows what is man and what mere beast;   10
Or Beauty wayward, but requires
More delicacy from her squires.

Tell me, my witless, whose one boast
Could be your staunchness at the post,
When were you made a man of parts   15
To think fine and profess the arts?

Will many-gifted Beauty come
Bowing to your bald rule of thumb,
Or Love swear loyalty to your crown?
Be gone, have done! Down, wanton, down!   20

DOWN, WANTON, DOWN! 5 *bombard-captain*: officer in charge of a bombard, an early type of cannon that hurled stones. 6 *ravelin*: fortification with two faces that meet in a protruding angle. *effect a breach*: break an opening through (a fortification). 15 *man of parts*: man of talent or ability.

1. How do you define a *wanton?*
2. What wanton does the poet address?
3. Explain the comparison drawn in the second stanza.
4. In line 14, how many meanings do you find in *staunchness at the post?*
5. Explain any other puns you find in lines 15–19.
6. Do you take this to be a cynical poem making fun of Love and Beauty, or is Graves making fun of stupid, animal lust?

John Donne (1572–1631)*

BATTER MY HEART, THREE-PERSONED GOD, FOR YOU   (ABOUT 1610)

Batter my heart, three-personed God, for You
As yet but knock, breathe, shine, and seek to mend.
That I may rise and stand, o'erthrow me, and bend
Your force to break, blow, burn, and make me new.
I, like an usurped town to another due,   5
Labor to admit You, but Oh! to no end.
Reason, Your viceroy in me, me should defend,
But is captived, and proves weak or untrue.
Yet dearly I love You, and would be lovèd fain,
But am betrothed unto Your enemy;   10
Divorce me, untie or break that knot again;
Take me to You, imprison me, for I,
Except You enthrall me, never shall be free,
Nor ever chaste, except You ravish me.

QUESTIONS

1. In the last line of this sonnet, to what does Donne compare the onslaught of God's love? Do you think the poem is weakened by the poet's comparing a spiritual experience to something so grossly carnal? Discuss.
2. Explain the seeming contradiction in the last line: in what sense can a ravished person be *chaste?* Explain the seeming contradictions in lines 3–4 and 12–13: how can a person thrown down and destroyed be enabled to *rise and stand;* an imprisoned person be *free?*
3. In lines 5–6 the speaker compares himself to a *usurped town* trying to throw off its conqueror by admitting an army of liberation. Who is the "usurper" in this comparison?
4. Explain the comparison of *Reason* to a *viceroy* (lines 7–8).
5. Sum up in your own words the message of Donne's poem. In stating its theme, did you have to read the poem for literal meanings, figurative comparisons, or both?

THE VALUE OF A DICTIONARY

> Use the dictionary. It's better than the critics.
> —Elizabeth Bishop to her students

If a poet troubles to seek out the best words available, the least we can do is to find out what the words mean. The dictionary is a firm ally in reading poems; if the poems are more than a century old, it is indispensable. Meanings change. When the Elizabethan poet George Gascoigne wrote, "O Abraham's brats, O brood of blessed seed," the word *brats* implied neither irritation nor contempt. When in the seventeenth century Andrew Marvell imagined two lovers' "vegetable love," he referred to a vegetative or growing love, not one resembling a lettuce. And when Queen Anne, in a famous anecdote, called the just-completed Saint Paul's Cathedral "awful, artificial, and amusing," its architect, Sir Christopher Wren, was overwhelmed with joy and gratidue, for what she had told him was that it was awe-inspiring, artful, and stimulating to contemplate (or *muse* upon).

In reading poetry, there is nothing to be done about the inevitable tendency of language to change except to watch out for it. If you suspect that a word has shifted in meaning over the years, most standard desk dictionaries will be helpful, an unabridged dictionary more helpful still, and most helpful of all the *Oxford English Dictionary* (OED), which gives, for each definition, successive examples of the word's written use through the past thousand years. You need not feel a grim obligation to keep interrupting a poem in order to rummage in the dictionary; but if the poem is worth reading very closely, you may wish any aid you can find.

One of the valuable services of poetry is to recall for us the concrete, physical sense that certain words once had, but since have lost. As the English critic H. Coombes has remarked in *Literature and Criticism*,

> We use a word like *powerful* without feeling that it is really "powerfull."
> We do not seem today to taste the full flavor of words as we feel that
> Falstaff (and Shakespeare, and probably his audience) tasted them
> when he was applauding the virtues of "good sherris-sack," which makes
> the brain "apprehensive, quick, forgetive, full of nimble, fiery, and de-
> lectable shapes." And being less aware of the life and substantiality of
> words, we are probably less aware of the things . . . that these words
> stand for.

"Every word which is used to express a moral or intellectual fact," said Emerson in his study *Nature*, "if traced to its root, is found to be borrowed from some material appearance. *Right* means straight; *wrong* means twisted. *Spirit* primarily means wind; *transgression*, the crossing of a line; *supercilious*, the raising of an eyebrow." Browse in a dictionary and you will discover such original concretenesses. These are revealed in your dictionary's etymologies, or brief notes on the derivation of words, given in most dictionaries near the beginning of an entry on a word; in some dictionaries, at the end of the entry. Look up *squirrel*, for instance, and you will find it comes from two Greek words meaning "shadow-tail." For another example of a common word that originally contained a poetic metaphor, look up the origin of *daisy*.

EXPERIMENT: *Using the Dictionary*

The following short poem seems very simple and straightforward, but much of its total effect depends on the reader knowing the literal meanings of several words. The most crucial word is in the title—*aftermath*. Most readers today will assume that they know what that word means, but in this poem Longfellow uses it in both its current sense and its original, more literal meaning. Read the poem twice—first without a dictionary, then a second time after looking up the meanings of *aftermath*, *fledged*, *rowen*, and *mead*. How does knowing the exact meanings of these words add to both your literal and critical reading of the poem?

Henry Wadsworth Longfellow   (1807–1882)

AFTERMATH   1873

When the summer fields are mown,
When the birds are fledged and flown,
   And the dry leaves strew the path;
With the falling of the snow,
With the cawing of the crow,   5
Once again the fields we mow
   And gather in the aftermath.

Not the sweet, new grass with flowers
In this harvesting of ours;
   Not the upland clover bloom;   10
But the rowen mixed with weeds,
Tangled tufts from marsh and meads,
Where the poppy drops its seeds
   In the silence and the gloom.

QUESTIONS

1. How does the etymology and meaning of *aftermath* help explain this poem? (Look the word up in your dictionary.)
2. What is the meaning of *fledged* (line 2) and *rowen* (line 11)?
3. Once you understand the literal meaning of the poem, do you think that Longfellow intended any further significance to it?

John Clare (1793–1864)

Mouse's Nest   (ABOUT 1835)

I found a ball of grass among the hay
And progged it as I passed and went away;
And when I looked I fancied something stirred,
And turned again and hoped to catch the bird—
When out an old mouse bolted in the wheats   5
With all her young ones hanging at her teats;
She looked so odd and so grotesque to me,
I ran and wondered what the thing could be,
And pushed the knapweed bunches where I stood;
Then the mouse hurried from the craking° brood.   *crying*   10
The young ones squeaked, and as I went away
She found her nest again among the hay.
The water o'er the pebbles scarce could run
And broad old cesspools glittered in the sun.

QUESTIONS

1. "To prog" (*progged*, line 2) means "to poke about for food, to forage." In what ways does this word fit more exactly here than *prodded, touched,* or *searched?*
2. Is *craking* (line 10) better than *crying*? Which word better fits the poem? Why?
3. What connections do you find between the last two lines and the rest of the poem? To what are water that *scarce could run* and *broad old cesspools* (lines 13 and 14) likened?

An **allusion** is an indirect reference to any person, place, or thing—fictitious, historical, or actual. Sometimes, to understand an allusion in a poem, we have to find out something we didn't know before. But usually the poet asks of us only common knowledge. When, in his poem "To Helen," Edgar Allan Poe refers to "the glory that was Greece / And the grandeur that was Rome," he assumes that we have heard of those places. He also expects that we will understand his allusion to the cultural achievements of those ancient nations and perhaps even catch the subtle contrast between those two similar words *glory* and *grandeur*, with its suggestion that, for all its merits, Roman civilization was also more pompous than Greek.

Allusions not only enrich the meaning of a poem, they also save space. In "The Love Song of J. Alfred Prufrock" (page 473), T. S. Eliot, by giving a brief introductory quotation from the speech of a damned soul in Dante's *Inferno,* is able to suggest that his poem will be the confession of a soul in torment, who sees no chance of escape.

Often in reading a poem, you will meet a name you don't recognize, on which the meaning of a line (or perhaps a whole poem) seems to depend. In this book, most such unfamiliar references and allusions are glossed or footnoted, but when you venture out on your own in reading poems, you may find yourself needlessly perplexed unless you look up such names, the way you look up any other words. Unless the name is one that the poet made up, you will probably find it in one of the larger desk dictionaries, such as *Webster's Collegiate Dictionary* or the *American Heritage Dictionary*. If you don't solve your problem there, try an encyclopedia, a world atlas, *The Houghton Mifflin Dictionary of Biography*, or *Brewer's Dictionary of Phrase & Fable*.

Some allusions are quotations from other poems. In R. S. Gwynn's "1-800," the narrator describes an insomniac watching late-night infomercials:

> Credit cards out, pencil and notepad handy,
>   The insomniac sinks deeply in his chair,
> Begging swift needles in his glass of brandy
>   To knit once more the raveled sleeve of care,
> As with control, remotely, in one hand he
>   Summons bright visions from the midnight air:

In addition to some witty wordplay, like the pun on *remote control*, Gwynn borrows a famous line from Shakespeare's *Macbeth*, "Sleep that knits up the raveled sleave of care," to describe his unsnoozing protagonist. (*To ravel* means the same as *to unravel*—to loosen or disentangle.) Why quote Shakespeare in a poem about watching TV commercials? Partly it is just one poet's delight in replaying another poet's verbal home runs, but well-chosen allusions also pack an extra wallop of meaning into a poem. The line that Gwynn borrows comes from Macbeth's description of a mysterious voice he claims to have heard after murdering Duncan. The voice prophesied that "Macbeth shall sleep no more." Alluding to Shakespeare's line, therefore, Gwynn can summon up all sorts of dark, nocturnal associations that he then turns to satiric ends.

EXERCISE: *Catching Allusions*

From your knowledge, supplemented by a dictionary or other reference work if need be, explain the allusions in the following poems.

J. V. Cunningham   (1911–1985)*

FRIEND, ON THIS SCAFFOLD   1960
THOMAS MORE LIES DEAD

Friend, on this scaffold Thomas More lies dead
Who would not cut the Body from the Head.

Kelly Cherry (b. 1940)

ADVICE TO A FRIEND WHO PAINTS   1975

Consider shy Cezanne,
the lay of the land he loved,
its dumbstruck vanity, polite and brute.
The bather in his sketchy suit.
The skull upon the mute pull of cloth.   5
In your taxing and tearing, tugging at art,
consider shy Cezanne.
His blushing apples.
His love of man.

QUESTIONS

How do you account for the odd combination of images that occur in lines 4–8? What possible connection do a bather, a skull, and an apple share?

Carl Sandburg (1878–1967)*

GRASS   1918

Pile the bodies high at Austerlitz and Waterloo.
Shovel them under and let me work—
       I am the grass; I cover all.

And pile them high at Gettsyburg
And pile them high at Ypres and Verdun.   5
Shovel them under and let me work.

Two years, ten years, and passengers ask the conductor:
       What place is this?
       Where are we now?

       I am the grass.   10
       Let me work.

QUESTIONS

1. What do the five proper nouns in Sandburg's poem have in common?
2. How much does the reader need to understand about the allusions in "Grass" to appreciate their importance to the literal meaning of the poem?

WORD CHOICE AND WORD ORDER

Even if Samuel Johnson's famous *Dictionary* of 1755 had been as thick as Webster's unabridged, an eighteenth-century poet searching through it for words to use would have had a narrower choice. For in English literature of the

neoclassical period or **Augustan age**—that period from about 1660 into the late eighteenth century—many poets subscribed to a belief in **poetic diction:** "A system of words," said Dr. Johnson, "refined from the grossness of domestic use." The system admitted into a serious poem only certain words and subjects, excluding others as violations of **decorum** (propriety). Accordingly, such common words as *rat, cheese, big, sneeze,* and *elbow,* although admissible to satire, were thought inconsistent with the loftiness of tragedy, epic, ode, and elegy. Dr. Johnson's biographer, James Boswell, tells how a poet writing an epic reconsidered the word "rats" and instead wrote "the whiskered vermin race." Johnson himself objected to Lady Macbeth's allusion to her "keen knife," saying that "we do not immediately conceive that any crime of importance is to be committed with a knife; or who does not, at last, from the long habit of connecting a knife with sordid offices, feel aversion rather than terror?" Probably Johnson was here the victim of his age, and Shakespeare was right, but Johnson in one of his assumptions was right too: there are inappropriate words as well as appropriate ones.

Neoclassical poets chose their classical models more often from Roman writers than from Greek, as their diction suggests by the frequency of Latin derivatives. For example, a *net,* according to Dr. Johnson's dictionary, is "any thing reticulated or decussated, at equal distances, with interstices between the intersections." In company with Latinate words often appeared fixed combinations of adjective and noun ("finny prey" for "fish"), poetic names (a song to a lady named Molly might rechristen her Parthenia), and allusions to classical mythology. Neoclassical poetic diction was evidently being abused when, instead of saying "uncork the bottle," a poet could write

> Apply thine engine to the spongy door,
> Set *Bacchus* from his glassy prison free,

in some bad lines ridiculed by Alexander Pope in *Peri Bathous, or The Art of Sinking in Poetry.*

Not all poetic diction is excess baggage. To a reader who knew firsthand both living sheep and the pastoral poems of Virgil—as most readers nowadays do not—such a fixed phrase as "the fleecy care," which seems stilted to us, conveyed pleasurable associations. But "fleecy care" was more than a highfalutin way of saying "sheep"; as one scholar has pointed out, "when they wished, our poets could say 'sheep' as clearly and as often as anybody else. In the first place, 'fleecy' drew attention to wool, and demanded the appropriate visual image of sheep; for aural imagery the poets would refer to 'the bleating kind'; it all depended upon what was happening in the poem."[2]

Other poets have found some special kind of poetic language valuable: Old English poets, with their standard figures of speech ("whale-road" for the sea, "ring-giver" for a ruler); makers of folk ballads who, no less than neoclassicists,

---

[2]Bonamy Dobrée, *English Literature in the Early Eighteenth Century, 1700–1740* (New York: Oxford UP, 1959) 161.

love fixed epithet-noun combinations ("milk-white steed," "blood-red wine," "steel-driving man"); and Edmund Spenser, whose example made popular the adjective ending in *-y* (*fleecy, grassy, milky*).

When Wordsworth, in his Preface to *Lyrical Ballads*, asserted that "the language really spoken by men," especially by humble rustics, is plainer and more emphatic, and conveys "elementary feelings . . . in a state of greater simplicity," he was, in effect, advocating a new poetic diction. Wordsworth's ideas invited freshness into English poetry and, by admitting words that neoclassical poets would have called "low" ("His poor old *ankles* swell"), helped rid poets of the fear of being thought foolish for mentioning a commonplace.

This theory of the superiority of rural diction was, as Coleridge pointed out, hard to adhere to, and, in practice, Wordsworth was occasionally to write a language as Latinate and citified as these lines on yew trees:

> Huge trunks!—and each particular trunk a growth
> Of intertwisted fibers serpentine
> Up-coiling, and inveterately convolved . . .

Language so Latinate sounds pedantic to us, especially the phrase *inveterately convolved*. In fact, some poets, notably Gerard Manley Hopkins, have subscribed to the view that English words derived from Anglo-Saxon (Old English) have more force and flavor than their Latin equivalents. *Kingly*, one may feel, has more power than *regal*. One argument for this view is that so many words of Old English origin—*man, wife, child, house, eat, drink, sleep*—are basic to our living speech. It may be true that a language closer to Old English is particularly fit for rendering abstract notions concretely—as does the memorable title of a medieval work of piety, the *Ayenbite of Inwit* ("again-bite of inner wisdom" or "remorse of conscience"). And yet this view, if accepted at all, must be accepted with reservations. Some words of Latin origin carry meanings both precise and physical. In the King James Bible is the admonition, "See then that ye walk circumspectly, not as fools, but as wise" (Ephesians 5:15). To be *circumspect* (a word from two Latin roots meaning "to look" and "around") is to be watchful on all sides—a meaning altogether lost in a modernized wording of the passage once printed on a subway poster for a Bible society: "Be careful how you live, not thoughtlessly but thoughtfully."

When E. E. Cummings begins a poem, "mr youse needn't be so spry / concernin questions arty," we recognize another kind of diction available to poetry: **vulgate** (speech not much affected by schooling). Handbooks of grammar sometimes distinguish various **levels of diction.** A sort of ladder is imagined, on whose rungs words, phrases, and sentences may be ranked in an ascending order of formality, from the curses of an illiterate thug to the commencement-day address of a doctor of divinity. These levels range from vulgate through **colloquial** (the casual conversation or informal writing of literate people) and **general English** (most literate speech and writing, more studied than colloquial but not pretentious), up to **formal English** (the impersonal language of educated persons, usually only written, possibly spoken on dignified occasions). Recently, however, lexicographers have been shunning such labels. The designation *colloquial* was expelled from *Webster's Third New International Dictionary* on the grounds that "it is impossible to know whether a word out of context is colloquial or not" and that the diction of Americans nowadays is more fluid than the labels suggest. Aware that we are being unscientific, we may find the labels useful. They may help roughly to describe what happens when, as in the following poem, a poet shifts from one level of usage to another.

Robert Herrick   (1591–1674)*

UPON JULIA'S CLOTHES   1648

Whenas in silks my Julia goes,
Then, then, methinks, how sweetly flows
That liquefaction of her clothes.

Next, when I cast mine eyes and see
That brave vibration each way free,   5
O how that glittering taketh me!

Even in so short a poem as "Upon Julia's Clothes," we see how a sudden shift in the level of diction can produce a surprising and memorable effect. One word in each stanza—*liquefaction* in the first, *vibration* in the second—stands out from the standard, but not extravagant, language that surrounds it. Try to imagine the entire poem being written in such formal English, in mostly unfamiliar words of several syllables each: the result, in all likelihood, would be merely an oddity, and a turgid one at that. But by using such terms sparingly, Herrick allows them to take on a greater strength and significance through their contrast with the words that surround them. It is *liquefaction* in particular that strikes the reader: like a great catch by an outfielder, it impresses both for its appropriateness in the situation and for its sheer beauty as a demonstration of superior skill. Once we have read the poem, we realize that the effect would be severely compromised, if not ruined, by the substitution of any other word in its place.

At present, most poetry in English avoids elaborate literary expressions such as "fleecy care" in favor of more colloquial language. In many English-speaking areas, such as Scotland, there has even been a movement to write poems in regional dialects. (A **dialect** is a particular variety of language spoken by an identifiable regional group or social class of persons.) Dialect poets frequently try to capture the freshness and authenticity of the language spoken in their immediate locale.

Most Americans know at least part of one Scottish dialect poem by heart—"Auld Lang Syne," the song commonly sung as the clock strikes twelve on New Year's Eve. Although Robert Burns wrote most of the song's stanzas, the poet claimed to have copied down the famous opening stanza (following) from an old man he heard singing. *Auld* is the Scots word for "old"; *lang syne* means "long since." How different the lines would seem if they were standard English.

> Should auld acquaintance be forgot,
> And never brought to mind?
> Should auld acquaintance be forgot
> And days of auld lang syne?
> And days of auld lang syne, my dear,
> And days of auld lang syne,
> Should auld acquaintance be forgot,
> And days of auld lang syne?

Not only the poet's choice of words makes a poem seem more formal, or less, but also the way the words are arranged into sentences. Compare these lines

> Jack and Jill went up the hill
> To fetch a pail of water.
> Jack fell down and broke his crown
> And Jill came tumbling after.

with Milton's account of a more significant downfall:

> Earth trembled from her entrails, as again
> In pangs, and Nature gave a second groan;
> Sky loured, and, muttering thunder, some sad drops
> Wept at completing of the mortal sin
> Original; while Adam took no thought
> Eating his fill, nor Eve to iterate
> Her former trespass feared, the more to soothe
> Him with her loved society, that now
> As with new wine intoxicated both
> They swim in mirth, and fancy that they feel
> Divinity within them breeding wings
> Wherewith to scorn the Earth.

Not all the words in Milton's lines are bookish: indeed, many of them can be found in nursery rimes. What helps, besides diction, to distinguish this account of the Biblical fall from "Jack and Jill" is that Milton's nonstop sentence seems further removed from usual speech in its length (83 words), in its complexity (subordinate clauses), and in its word order ("with new wine intoxicated both" rather than "both intoxicated with new wine"). Should we think less (or more) highly of Milton for choosing a style so elaborate and formal? No judgment need be passed: both Mother Goose and the author of *Paradise Lost* use language appropriate to their purposes.

Among languages, English is by no means the most flexible. English words must be used in fairly definite and inviolable patterns, and whoever departs too far from them will not be understood. In the sentence "Cain slew Abel," if you change the word order, you change the meaning: "Abel slew Cain." Such inflexibility was not true of Latin, in which a poet could lay down words in almost any sequence and, because their endings (inflections) showed what parts of speech they were, could trust that no reader would mistake a subject for an object or a noun for an adjective. (E. E. Cummings has striven, in certain of his poems, for the freedom of Latin. One such poem, "anyone lived in a pretty how town," appears on page 71.)

The rigidity of English word order invites the poet to defy it and to achieve unusual effects by inverting it. It is customary in English to place adjective in front of noun (*a blue mantle, new pastures*). But an unusual emphasis is achieved when Milton ends "Lycidas" by reversing the pattern:

> At last he rose, and twitched his mantle blue:
> Tomorrow to fresh woods, and pastures new.

Perhaps the inversion in *mantle blue* gives more prominence to the color associated with heaven (and in "Lycidas," heaven is of prime importance). Perhaps the inversion in *pastures new*, stressing the *new*, heightens the sense of a rebirth.

Coleridge offered two "homely definitions of prose and poetry; that is, *prose:* words in their best order; *poetry:* the best words in the best order." If all goes well, a poet may fasten the right word into the right place, and the result may be—as T. S. Eliot said in "Little Gidding"—a "complete consort dancing together."

Kay Ryan (b. 1945)*

BLANDEUR   2000

If it please God,
let less happen.
Even out Earth's
rondure, flatten
Eiger, blanden   5
the Grand Canyon.
Make valleys
slightly higher,
widen fissures
to arable land,   10
remand your
terrible glaciers
and silence
their calving,
halving or doubling   15
all geographical features
toward the mean.
Unlean against our hearts.

Withdraw your grandeur
from these parts.   20

BLANDEUR. 5 *Eiger:* a mountain in the Alps.

QUESTIONS

1. The title of Ryan's poem is a word that she invented. What do you think it means?
   Explain the reasoning behind your theory.
2. Where else does Ryan use a different form of this new word?
3. What other unusual but real words does the author use?

Thomas Hardy   (1840–1928)*

THE RUINED MAID   1901

"O 'Melia, my dear, this does everything crown!
Who could have supposed I should meet you in Town?
And whence such fair garments, such prosperi-ty?"—
"O didn't you know I'd been ruined?" said she.

—"You left us in tatters, without shoes or socks,   5
Tired of digging potatoes, and spudding up docks°;   *spading up dockweed*
And now you've gay bracelets and bright feathers three!"—
"Yes: that's how we dress when we're ruined," said she.

—"At home in the barton° you said 'thee' and 'thou,'   *farmyard*
And 'thik oon,' and 'theäs oon,' and 't'other'; but now   10
Your talking quite fits 'ee for high compa-ny!"—
"Some polish is gained with one's ruin," said she.

—"Your hands were like paws then, your face blue and bleak
But now I'm bewitched by your delicate cheek,
And your little gloves fit as on any la-dy!"—   15
"We never do work when we're ruined," said she.

—"You used to call home-life a hag-ridden dream,
And you'd sigh, and you'd sock°; but at present you seem   *groan*
To know not of megrims° or melancho-ly!"—   *blues*
"True. One's pretty lively when ruined," said she.   20

—"I wish I had feathers, a fine sweeping gown,
And a delicate face, and could strut about Town!"—
"My dear—a raw country girl, such as you be,
Cannot quite expect that. You ain't ruined," said she.

QUESTIONS

1. Where does this dialogue take place? Who are the two speakers?
2. Comment on Hardy's use of the word *ruined*. What is the conventional meaning of the word when applied to a woman? As 'Melia applies it to herself, what is its meaning?
3. Sum up the attitude of each speaker toward the other. What details of the new 'Melia does the first speaker most dwell on? Would you expect Hardy to be so impressed by all these details, or is there, between his view of the characters and their view of themselves, any hint of an ironic discrepancy?
4. In losing her country dialect (*thik oon* and *theäs oon* for *this one* and *that one*), 'Melia is presumed to have gained in sophistication. What does Hardy suggest by her *ain't* in the last line?

Richard Eberhart   (b. 1904)

THE FURY OF AERIAL BOMBARDMENT   1947

You would think the fury of aerial bombardment
Would rouse God to relent; the infinite spaces
Are still silent. He looks on shock-pried faces.
History, even, does not know what is meant.

You would feel that after so many centuries   5
God would give man to repent; yet he can kill
As Cain could, but with multitudinous will,
No farther advanced than in his ancient furies.

Was man made stupid to see his own stupidity?
Is God by definition indifferent, beyond us all?   10
Is the eternal truth man's fighting soul
Wherein the Beast ravens in its own avidity?

Of Van Wettering I speak, and Averill,
Names on a list, whose faces I do not recall
But they are gone to early death, who late in school   15
Distinguished the belt feed lever from the belt holding pawl.

QUESTIONS

1. As a naval officer during World War II, Richard Eberhart was assigned for a time as an instructor in a gunnery school. How has this experience apparently contributed to the diction of his poem?
2. In his *Life of John Dryden*, complaining about a description of a sea fight Dryden had filled with nautical language, Samuel Johnson argued that technical terms should be excluded from poetry. Is this criticism applicable to Eberhart's last line? Can a word succeed for us in a poem, even though we may not be able to define it? (For more evidence, see also the technical terms in Henry Reed's "Naming of Parts," page 533.)

3. Some readers have found a contrast in tone between the first three stanzas of this poem and the last stanza. How would you describe this contrast? What does diction contribute to it?

Wendy Cope   (b. 1945)*

LONELY HEARTS   1986

Can someone make my simple wish come true?
Male biker seeks female for touring fun.
Do you live in North London? Is it you?

Gay vegetarian whose friends are few,
I'm into music, Shakespeare and the sun,   5
Can someone make my simple wish come true?

Executive in search of something new—
Perhaps bisexual woman, arty, young.
Do you live in North London? Is it you?

Successful, straight and solvent? I am too—   10
Attractive Jewish lady with a son.
Can someone make my simple wish come true?

I'm Libran, inexperienced and blue—
Need slim non-smoker, under twenty-one.
Do you live in North London? Is it you?   15

Please write (with photo) to Box 152.
Who knows where it may lead once we've begun?
Can someone make my simple wish come true?
Do you live in North London? Is it you?

LONELY HEARTS. This poem has a double form: the rhetorical, a series of "lonely heart" personal ads from a newspaper, and metrical, a **villanelle,** a fixed form developed by French courtly poets in imitation of Italian folk song. For other villanelles, see Elizabeth Bishop's "One Art" (page 384) and Dylan Thomas's "Do not go gentle into that good night" (page 231). In the villanelle, the first and the third lines are repeated in a set pattern throughout the poem.

QUESTIONS

1. What sort of language does Wendy Cope borrow for this poem?
2. The form of the villanelle requires that the poet end each stanza with one of two repeating lines. What special use does the author make of these mandatory repetitions?
3. How many speakers are there in the poem? Does the author's voice ever enter or is the entire poem spoken by individuals in personal ads?
4. The poem seems to begin satirically. Does the poem ever move beyond the critical, mocking tone typical of satire?

FOR REVIEW AND FURTHER STUDY

E. E. Cummings   (1894–1962)*

ANYONE LIVED IN A PRETTY HOW TOWN   1940

anyone lived in a pretty how town
(with up so floating many bells down)
spring summer autumn winter
he sang his didn't he danced his did.

Women and men(both little and small)   5
cared for anyone not at all
they sowed their isn't they reaped their same
sun moon stars rain

children guessed(but only a few
and down they forgot as up they grew   10
autumn winter spring summer)
that noone loved him more by more

when by now and tree by leaf
she laughed his joy she cried his grief
bird by snow and stir by still   15
anyone's any was all to her

someones married their everyones
laughed their cryings and did their dance
(sleep wake hope and then)they
said their nevers they slept their dream   20

stars rain sun moon
(and only the snow can begin to explain
how children are apt to forget to remember
with up so floating many bells down)

one day anyone died i guess   25
(and noone stooped to kiss his face)
busy folk buried them side by side
little by little and was by was

all by all and deep by deep
and more by more they dream their sleep   30
noone and anyone earth by april
wish by spirit and if by yes.

Women and men(both dong and ding)
summer autumn winter spring
reaped their sowing and went their came   35
sun moon stars rain

1. Summarize the story told in this poem. Who are the characters?
2. Rearrange the words in the two opening lines into the order you would expect them usually to follow. What effect does Cummings obtain by his unconventional word order?
3. Another of Cummings's strategies is to use one part of speech as if it were another; for instance, in line 4, *didn't* and *did* ordinarily are verbs, but here they are used as nouns. What other words in the poem perform functions other than their expected ones?

Billy Collins   (b. 1941)*

THE NAMES   2002

Yesterday, I lay awake in the palm of the night.
A soft rain stole in, unhelped by any breeze,
And when I saw the silver glaze on the windows,
I started with A, with Ackerman, as it happened,
Then Baxter and Calabro,   5
Davis and Eberling, names falling into place
As droplets fell through the dark.

Names printed on the ceiling of the night.
Names slipping around a watery bend.
Twenty-six willows on the banks of a stream.   10

In the morning, I walked out barefoot
Among thousands of flowers
Heavy with dew like the eyes of tears,
And each had a name—
Fiori inscribed on a yellow petal   15
Then Gonzalez and Han, Ishikawa and Jenkins.

Names written in the air
And stitched into the cloth of the day.
A name under a photograph taped to a mailbox.
Monogram on a torn shirt,   20
I see you spelled out on storefront windows
And on the bright unfurled awnings of this city.
I say the syllables as I turn a corner—
Kelly and Lee,
Medina, Nardella, and O'Connor.   25

When I peer into the woods,
I see a thick tangle where letters are hidden
As in a puzzle concocted for children.
Parker and Quigley in the twigs of an ash,

Rizzo, Schubert, Torres, and Upton,   30
Secrets in the boughs of an ancient maple.

Names written in the pale sky.
Names rising in the updraft amid buildings.
Names silent in stone
Or cried out behind a door.   35
Names blown over the earth and out to sea.

In the evening—weakening light, the last swallows.
A boy on a lake lifts his oars.
A woman by a window puts a match to a candle,
And the names are outlined on the rose clouds—   40
Vanacore and Wallace,
(let X stand, if it can, for the ones unfound)
Then Young and Ziminsky, the final jolt of Z.

Names etched on the head of a pin.
One name spanning a bridge, another undergoing a tunnel.   45
A blue name needled into the skin.
Names of citizens, workers, mothers and fathers,
The bright-eyed daughter, the quick son.
Alphabet of names in a green field.
Names in the small tracks of birds.   50
Names lifted from a hat
Or balanced on the tip of the tongue.
Names wheeled into the dim warehouse of memory.
So many names, there is barely room on the walls of the heart.

THE NAMES. This poem originally appeared in the *New York Times* on September 11, 2002. On that same day its author, the Poet Laureate of the United States, read the poem before a joint session of Congress specially convened in New York City to mark the one-year anniversary of the attack on the World Trade Center.

QUESTIONS

1. Occasional poetry—verse written to commemorate a public or historical occasion—is generally held in low esteem because such poems tend to be self-important and overwritten. Does Collins avoid these pitfalls?
2. Discuss the level of diction in "The Names." Is it appropriate to the subject? Explain.

Read the following poems and see what kinds of diction and word order you find in them. Which poems are least formal in their language and which most formal? Is there any use of vulgate English? Any dialect? What does each poem achieve that its own kind of English makes possible?

Anonymous   (American oral verse)

CARNATION MILK   (ABOUT 1900?)

Carnation Milk is the best in the land;
Here I sit with a can in my hand—
No tits to pull, no hay to pitch,
You just punch a hole in the son of a bitch.

CARNATION MILK. "This quatrain is imagined as the caption under a picture of a rugged-looking cowboy seated upon a bale of hay," notes William Harmon in his *Oxford Book of American Light Verse* (New York: Oxford UP, 1979). Possibly the first to print this work was David Ogilvy (1911–1999), who quotes it in his *Confessions of an Advertising Man* (New York: Atheneum, 1963).

William Wordsworth   (1770–1850)*

MY HEART LEAPS UP WHEN I BEHOLD   1807

My heart leaps up when I behold
   A rainbow in the sky:
So was it when my life began;
So is it now I am a man;
So be it when I shall grow old,   5
   Or let me die!
The Child is father of the Man;
And I could wish my days to be
Bound each to each by natural piety.

William Wordsworth   (1770–1850)*

MUTABILITY   1822

From low to high doth dissolution climb,
And sink from high to low, along a scale
Of awful notes, whose concord shall not fail;
A musical but melancholy chime,
Which they can hear who meddle not with crime,   5
Nor avarice, nor over-anxious care.
Truth fails not; but her outward forms that bear
The longest date do melt like frosty rime,°   *frozen dew*
That in the morning whitened hill and plain
And is no more; drop like the tower sublime   10

Of yesterday, which royally did wear
His crown of weeds, but could not even sustain
Some casual shout that broke the silent air,
Or the unimaginable touch of Time.

Anonymous

SCOTTSBORO   1936

Paper come out—done strewed de news
Seven po' chillun moanin' deat' house blues,
Seven po' chillun moanin' deat' house blues.
Seven nappy° heads wit' big shiny eye   *frizzy*
All boun' in jail and framed to die,   5
All boun' in jail and framed to die.

Messin' white woman—snake lyin' tale
Hang and burn and jail wit' no bail.
Dat hang and burn and jail wit' no bail.
Worse ol' crime in white folks' lan'   10
Black skin coverin' po' workin' man,
Black skin coverin' po' workin' man.

Judge and jury—all in de stan'
Lawd, biggety name for same lynchin' ban',
Lawd, biggety name for same lynchin' ban'.   15
White folks and nigger in great co't house
Like cat down cellar wit' nohole mouse.
Like cat down cellar wit' nohole mouse.

SCOTTSBORO. This folk blues, collected by Lawrence Gellert in *Negro Songs of Protest* (New York: Carl Fischer, 1936), is a comment on the Scottsboro case. In 1931 nine black youths were arrested near Scottsboro, Alabama, and charged with the rape of two white women. Though eventually, after several trials, they were found not guilty, some of them at the time this song was composed had been convicted and sentenced to death.

Lewis Carroll
[Charles Lutwidge Dodgson]   (1832–1898)

JABBERWOCKY   1871

'Twas brillig, and the slithy toves
    Did gyre and gimble in the wabe:
All mimsy were the borogoves,
    And the mome raths outgrabe.

"Beware the Jabberwock, my son!   5
    The jaws that bite, the claws that catch!
Beware the Jubjub bird, and shun
    The frumious Bandersnatch!"

He took his vorpal sword in hand;
    Long time the manxome foe he sought— 10
So rested he by the Tumtum tree
    And stood awhile in thought.

And, as in uffish thought he stood,
    The Jabberwock, with eyes of flame,
Came whiffling through the tulgey wood, 15
    And burbled as it came!

One, two! One, two! And through and through
    The vorpal blade went snicker-snack!
He left it dead, and with its head
    He went galumphing back. 20

"And hast thou slain the Jabberwock?
    Come to my arms, my beamish boy!
O frabjous day! Callooh, Callay!"
    He chortled in his joy.

'Twas brillig, and the slithy toves 25
    Did gyre and gimble in the wabe:
All mimsy were the borogoves,
    And the mome raths outgrabe.

JABBERWOCKY. Fussy about pronunciation, Carroll in his preface to *The Hunting of the Snark* declares: "The first 'o' in 'borogoves' is pronounced like the 'o' in 'borrow.' I have heard people try to give it the sound of the 'o' in 'worry.' Such is Human Perversity." *Toves*, he adds, rimes with *groves*.

QUESTIONS

1. Look up *chortled* (line 24) in your dictionary and find out its definition and origin.
2. In *Through the Looking Glass*, Alice seeks the aid of Humpty Dumpty to decipher the meaning of this nonsense poem. "*Brillig*," he explains, "means four o'clock in the afternoon—the time when you begin *broiling* things for dinner." Does *brillig* sound like any other familiar word?
3. "*Slithy*," the explanation goes on, "means 'lithe and slimy.' 'Lithe' is the same as 'active.' You see it's like a portmanteau—there are two meanings packed up into one word." *Mimsy* is supposed to pack together both "flimsy" and "miserable." In the rest of the poem, what other portmanteau—or packed suitcase—words can you find?

Lewis Carroll

Lewis Carroll on Writing

HUMPTY DUMPTY EXPLICATES "JABBERWOCKY"   1871

"You seem very clever at explaining words, sir," said Alice. "Would you kindly tell me the meaning of the poem called 'Jabberwocky'?"

"Let's hear it," said Humpty Dumpty. "I can explain all the poems that ever were invented—and a good many that haven't been invented just yet."

This sounded very hopeful, so Alice repeated the first verse:

> " 'Twas brillig, and the slithy toves
>   Did gyre and gimble in the wabe:
> All mimsy were the borogoves,
>   And the mome raths outgrabe."

"That's enough to begin with," Humpty Dumpty interrupted: "there are plenty of hard words there. *'Brillig'* means four o'clock in the afternoon—the time when you begin *broiling* things for dinner."

"That'll do very well," said Alice. "And *'slithy'*?"

"Well, *'slithy'* means 'lithe and slimy.' 'Lithe' is the same as 'active.' You see, it's like a portmanteau—there are two meanings packed up in one word."

"I see it now," Alice remarked thoughtfully. "And what are *'toves'*?"

"Well, *'toves'* are something like badgers—they're something like lizards—and they're something like corkscrews."

"They must be very curious-looking creatures."

"They are that," said Humpty Dumpty, "also they make their nests under sundials—also they live on cheese."

"And what's to *'gyre'* and to *'gimble'*?"

"To '*gyre*' is to go round and round like a gyroscope. To '*gimble*' is to make holes like a gimlet."

"And '*the wabe*' is the grass plot round a sundial, I suppose?" said Alice, surprised at her own ingenuity.

"Of course it is. It's called '*wabe*,' you know, because it goes a long way before it, and a long way behind it."

"And a long way beyond it on each side," Alice added.

"Exactly so. Well, then, '*mimsy*' is flimsy and miserable (there's another portmanteau for you). And a '*borogove*' is a thin, shabby-looking bird with its feathers sticking out all round—something like a live mop."

"And then '*mome raths*'?" said Alice. "I'm afraid I'm giving you a great deal of trouble."

"Well, a '*rath*' is a sort of green pig: but '*mome*' I'm not certain about. I think it's short for 'from home'—meaning that they'd lost their way, you know."

"And what does '*outgrabe*' mean?"

"Well, '*outgribing*' is something between bellowing and whistling, with a kind of sneeze in the middle; however, you'll hear it done, maybe—down in the wood yonder—and when you've once heard it you'll be *quite* content. Who's been repeating all that hard stuff to you?"

"I read it in a book," said Alice.

From *Through the Looking Glass*

HUMPTY DUMPTY EXPLICATES "JABBERWOCKY." This celebrated passage is the origin of the term **portmanteau word,** an artificial word that combines parts of other words to express some combination of their qualities. (*Brunch*, for example, is a meal that combines aspects of both breakfast and lunch.) A portmanteau is a large suitcase that opens up into two separate compartments.

◄══ WRITING CRITICALLY ══►

How Much Difference Does a Word Make?

Although a poem may contain images and ideas, it is made up of words. Language is the medium of poetry, and the exact wording of a successful poem is the chief source of its power. Writers labor mightily to shape each word and phrase to create particular expressive effects. Changing a single word sometimes ruins a poem's effect, just as changing one number in a combination lock's sequence makes all the other numbers useless.

Before writing about the language of a poem, recruit your intuition into working with your intellect. As you read the poem, ask yourself if there is some particular word or combination of words that gives you particular pleasure or especially intrigues you. Don't worry about why the word or words impress you. Don't even worry about the meaning. Just underline the word or phrase in your book. Then let your analytical powers go to work. Try to determine what makes this part of the poem so intriguing to you. How does it relate to the other lines? What does it contribute to the effect of the poem? In writing about the poem, let that word or phrase be your key into the poem. Often by understanding how a single key word operates in the context of a poem, we gain a special sense of what the whole poem means.

Writing Assignment

In no more than two pages, analyze how a single word or phrase contributes to a poem's total impact. Begin by choosing from any poem in this chapter a line or two that you particularly like. Then, select a key word or phrase and explore how they help shape the poem's total meaning. As part of your analysis rewrite the line by substituting a synonym in place of a single important word. Discuss what is lost by the substitution. A possible topic might be Robert Herrick's line from "Upon Julia's Clothes," "the liquefaction of her clothes." What does the beautiful but unusual word *liquefaction* add to the poem that a synonym would not? Other interesting poems to analyze include Wendy Cope's "Lonely Hearts," Robert Graves's "Down, Wanton, Down," Kay Ryan's "Blandeur," and William Wordsworth's "Mutability."

Further Suggestions for Writing

1. Choosing a poem that strikes you as particularly inventive or unusual in its language, such as E. E. Cummings's "anyone lived in a pretty how town" (page 71), Gerard Manley Hopkins's "The Windhover" (page 497), or Wendy Cope's "Lonely Hearts" (page 70), write a brief analysis of it. Concentrate on the diction of the poem and word order. For what possible purposes does the poet depart from standard English or incorporate unusual vocabulary? (For pointers on writing about poetry by the method of analysis, see "Writing About a Poem.")
2. In a short essay, set forth the pleasures of browsing in a dictionary. As you browse, see if you can discover any "found poems."
3. "Printing poetry in dialect, such as 'Scottsboro,' insults the literacy of a people." Think about this critical charge and comment on it.

4 Saying and Suggesting

To write so clearly that they might bring "all things as near the mathematical plainness" as possible—that was the goal of scientists, according to Bishop Thomas Sprat, who lived in the seventeenth century. Such an effort would seem bound to fail, because words, unlike numbers, are ambiguous indicators. Although it may have troubled Bishop Sprat, the tendency of a word to have multiplicity of meaning rather than mathematical plainness opens broad avenues to poetry.

Every word has at least one **denotation:** a meaning as defined in a dictionary. But the English language has many a common word with so many denotations that a reader may need to think twice to see what it means in a specific context. The noun *field*, for instance, can denote a piece of ground, a sports arena, the scene of a battle, part of a flag, a profession, and a number system in mathematics. Further, the word can be used as a verb ("he fielded a grounder") or an adjective ("field trip," "field glasses").

A word also has **connotations:** overtones or suggestions of additional meaning that it gains from all the contexts in which we have met it in the past. The word *skeleton*, according to a dictionary, denotes "the bony framework of a human being or other vertebrate animal, which supports the flesh and protects the organs." But by its associations, the word can rouse thoughts of war, of disease and death, or (possibly) of one's plans to go to medical school. Think, too, of the difference between "Old Doc Jones" and "Theodore E. Jones, M.D." In the mind's eye, the former appears in his shirtsleeves; the latter has a gold nameplate on his door. That some words denote the same thing but have sharply different connotations is pointed out in this anonymous Victorian jingle:

> Here's a little ditty that you really ought to know:
> Horses "sweat" and men "perspire," but ladies only "glow."

The terms *druggist*, *pharmacist*, and *apothecary* all denote the same occupation, but apothecaries lay claim to special distinction.

Poets aren't the only people who care about the connotations of language. Advertisers know that connotations make money. Nowadays many automobile dealers advertise their secondhand cars not as "used" but as "pre-owned," as if fearing that "used car" would connote an old heap with soiled upholstery and mysterious engine troubles. "Pre-owned," however, suggests that the previous owner has taken the trouble of breaking in the car for you. Not long ago prune-packers, alarmed by a slump in sales, sponsored a survey to determine the connotations of prunes in the public consciousness. Asked, "What do you think of when you hear the word *prunes?*" most people replied, "dried up," "wrinkled," or "constipated." Dismayed, the packers hired an advertising agency to create a new image for prunes, in hopes of inducing new connotations. Soon, advertisements began to show prunes in brightly colored settings, in the company of bikinied bathing beauties.

In imaginative writing, connotations are as crucial as they are in advertising. Consider this sentence: "A new brand of journalism is being born, or spawned" (Dwight Macdonald writing in the *New York Review of Books*). The last word, by its associations with fish and crustaceans, suggests that this new journalism is scarcely the product of human beings. And what do we make of Romeo's assertion that Juliet "is the sun"? Surely even a lovesick boy cannot mean that his sweetheart is "the incandescent body of gases about which the earth and other planets revolve" (a dictionary definition). He means, of course, that he thrives in her sight, that he feels warm in her presence or even at the thought of her, that she illumines his world and is the center of his universe. Because in the mind of the hearer these and other suggestions are brought into play, Romeo's statement, literally absurd, makes excellent sense.

Here is a famous poem that groups together things with similar connotations: certain ships and their cargoes. (A *quinquireme*, by the way, was an ancient Assyrian vessel propelled by sails and oars.)

John Masefield (1878–1967)

CARGOES   1902

Quinquireme of Nineveh from distant Ophir,
Rowing home to haven in sunny Palestine,
With a cargo of ivory,
And apes and peacocks,
Sandalwood, cedarwood, and sweet white wine.   5

Stately Spanish galleon coming from the Isthmus,
Dipping through the Tropics by the palm-green shores,
With a cargo of diamonds,

Emeralds, amethysts,
Topazes, and cinnamon, and gold moidores.°   *Portuguese coins*   10

Dirty British coaster with a salt-caked smoke stack,
Butting through the Channel in the mad March days,
With a cargo of Tyne coal,
Road-rails, pig-lead,
Firewood, iron-ware, and cheap tin trays.   15

To us, as well as to the poet's original readers, the place-names in the first
two stanzas suggest the exotic and faraway. Ophir, a vanished place, may have
been in Arabia; according to the Bible, King Solomon sent expeditions there for
its celebrated pure gold, also for ivory, apes, peacocks, and other luxury items.
(See I Kings 9–10.) In his final stanza, Masefield groups commonplace things
(mostly heavy and metallic), whose suggestions of crudeness, cheapness, and ugliness he deliberately contrasts with those of the precious stuffs he has listed earlier. For British readers, the Tyne is a stodgy and familiar river; the English
Channel in March, choppy and likely to upset a stomach. The quinquireme is
rowing, the galleon is *dipping,* but the dirty British freighter is *butting,* aggressively
pushing. Conceivably, the poet could have described firewood and even coal as
beautiful, but evidently he wants them to convey sharply different suggestions
here, to go along with the rest of the coaster's cargo. In drawing such a sharp
contrast between past and present, Masefield does more than merely draw up
bills-of-lading. Perhaps he even implies a wry and unfavorable comment on life
in the present day. His meaning lies not so much in the dictionary definitions of
his words ("*moidores:* Portuguese gold coins formerly worth approximately five
pounds sterling") as in their rich and vivid connotations.

William Blake   (1757–1827)*

LONDON   1794

I wander through each chartered street,
Near where the chartered Thames does flow,
And mark in every face I meet
Marks of weakness, marks of woe.

In every cry of every man,   5
In every infant's cry of fear,
In every voice, in every ban,
The mind-forged manacles I hear.

How the chimney-sweeper's cry
Every black'ning church appalls   10

And the hapless soldier's sigh
Runs in blood down palace walls.

But most through midnight streets I hear
How the youthful harlot's curse
Blasts the new born infant's tear   15
And blights with plagues the marriage hearse.

Here are only a few of the possible meanings of three of Blake's words:

chartered (lines 1, 2)

> DENOTATIONS: Established by a charter (a written grant or a certificate of in-
> corporation); leased or hired.
> CONNOTATIONS: Defined, limited, restricted, channeled, mapped, bound by
> law; bought and sold (like a slave or an inanimate object); Magna Carta;
> charters given to crown colonies by the King.
> OTHER WORDS IN THE POEM WITH SIMILAR CONNOTATIONS: *Ban*, which can
> denote (1) a legal prohibition; (2) a churchman's curse or malediction;
> (3) in medieval times, an order summoning a king's vassals to fight for
> him. *Manacles*, or shackles, restrain movement. *Chimney-sweeper, soldier,*
> and *harlot* are all hirelings.
> INTERPRETATION OF THE LINES: The street has had mapped out for it the di-
> rection in which it must go; the Thames has had laid down to it the course
> it must follow. Street and river are channeled, imprisoned, enslaved (like
> every inhabitant of London).

black'ning (line 10)

> DENOTATION: Becoming black.
> CONNOTATIONS: The darkening of something once light, the defilement of
> something once clean, the deepening of guilt, the gathering of darkness at
> the approach of night.
> OTHER WORDS IN THE POEM WITH SIMILAR CONNOTATIONS: Objects becoming
> marked or smudged (*marks of weakness, marks of woe* in the faces of
> passers-by; bloodied walls of a palace; marriage blighted with plagues); the
> word *appalls* (denoting not only "to overcome with horror" but "to make
> pale" and also "to cast a pall or shroud over"); *midnight streets.*
> INTERPRETATION OF THE LINE: Literally, every London church grows black
> from soot and hires a chimney-sweeper (a small boy) to help clean it. But
> Blake suggests too that by profiting from the suffering of the child laborer,
> the church is soiling its original purity.

Blasts, blights (lines 15, 16)

> DENOTATIONS: Both *blast* and *blight* mean "to cause to wither" or "to ruin and
> destroy." Both are terms from horticulture. Frost *blasts* a bud and kills it;
> disease *blights* a growing plant.

CONNOTATIONS: Sickness and death; gardens shriveled and dying; gusts of wind and the ravages of insects; things blown to pieces or rotted and warped.

OTHER WORDS IN THE POEM WITH SIMILAR CONNOTATIONS: Faces marked with weakness and woe; the child becomes a chimney-sweep; the soldier killed by war; blackening church and bloodied palace; young girl turned harlot; wedding carriage transformed into a hearse.

INTERPRETATION OF THE LINES: Literally, the harlot spreads the plague of syphilis, which, carried into marriage, can cause a baby to be born blind. In a larger and more meaningful sense, Blake sees the prostitution of even one young girl corrupting the entire institution of matrimony and endangering every child.

Some of these connotations are more to the point than others; the reader of a poem nearly always has the problem of distinguishing relevant associations from irrelevant ones. We need to read a poem in its entirety and, when a word leaves us in doubt, look for other things in the poem to corroborate or refute what we think it means. Relatively simple and direct in its statement, Blake's account of his stroll through the city at night becomes an indictment of a whole social and religious order. The indictment could hardly be this effective if it were "mathematically plain," its every word restricted to one denotation clearly spelled out.

Wallace Stevens (1879–1955)*

DISILLUSIONMENT OF TEN O'CLOCK 1923

The houses are haunted
By white night-gowns.
None are green,
Or purple with green rings,
Or green with yellow rings,   5
Or yellow with blue rings.
None of them are strange,
With socks of lace
And beaded ceintures.
People are not going   10
To dream of baboons and periwinkles.
Only, here and there, an old sailor,
Drunk and asleep in his boots,
Catches tigers
In red weather.   15

1. What are *beaded ceintures*? What does the phrase suggest?
2. What contrast does Stevens draw between the people who live in these houses and the old sailor? What do the connotations of *white night-gowns* and *sailor* add to this contrast?
3. What is lacking in these people who wear white night-gowns? Why should the poet's view of them be a "disillusionment"?

Gwendolyn Brooks   (1917–2000)*

THE INDEPENDENT MAN   1945

Now who could take you off to tiny life
In one room or in two rooms or in three
And cork you smartly, like the flask of wine
You are? Not any woman. Not a wife.
You'd let her twirl you, give her a good glee   5
Showing your leaping ruby to a friend.
Though twirling would be meek. Since not a cork
Could you allow, for being made so free.

A woman would be wise to think it well
If once a week you only rang the bell.   10

QUESTIONS

1. The poem is addressed to its title character. What can we infer about his personality from the details in lines 1–8?
2. In the last two lines, the poet doesn't explain why "a woman would be wise . . . ," etc. Has she told us enough so that we can supply the explanation ourselves?

Timothy Steele   (b. 1948)*

EPITAPH   1979

Here lies Sir Tact, a diplomatic fellow
Whose silence was not golden, but just yellow.

QUESTIONS

1. To what famous saying does the poet allude?
2. What are the connotations of *golden*? Of *yellow*?

Geoffrey Hill (b. 1932)

MERLIN   1959

I will consider the outnumbering dead:
For they are the husks of what was rich seed.
Now, should they come together to be fed,
They would outstrip the locusts' covering tide.

Arthur, Elaine, Mordred; they are all gone   5
Among the raftered galleries of bone.
By the long barrows of Logres they are made one,
And over their city stands the pinnacled corn.

MERLIN. In medieval legend, Merlin was a powerful magician and a seer, an aide of King Arthur. 5 *Elaine:* in Arthurian romance, the beloved of Sir Launcelot. *Mordred:* Arthur's treacherous nephew by whose hand the king died. 7 *barrows:* earthworks for burial of the dead. *Logres:* name of an ancient British kingdom, according to the twelfth-century historian Geoffrey of Monmouth, who gathered the legends of King Arthur.

QUESTIONS

1. What does the title "Merlin" contribute to this poem? Do you prefer to read the poem as though it is Merlin who speaks to us—or the poet?
2. Line 4 alludes to the plague of locusts that God sent upon Egypt (Exodus 10): "For they covered the face of the whole earth, so that the land was darkened . . ." With this allusion in mind, explain the comparison of the dead to locusts.
3. Why are the suggestions inherent in the names of *Arthur*, *Elaine*, and *Mordred* more valuable to this poem than those we might find in the names of other dead persons called, say, Gus, Tessie, and Butch?
4. Explain the phrase in line 6: *the raftered galleries of bone.*
5. In the last line, what *city* does the poet refer to? Does he mean some particular city, or is he making a comparison?
6. What is interesting in the adjective *pinnacled*? How can it be applied to corn?

Walter de la Mare (1873–1956)

THE LISTENERS   1912

"Is there anybody there?" said the Traveller,
    Knocking on the moonlit door;
And his horse in the silence champed the grasses
    Of the forest's ferny floor:
And a bird flew up out of the turret,   5
    Above the Traveller's head:
And he smote upon the door again a second time;
    "Is there anybody there?" he said.

But no one descended to the Traveller;
    No head from the leaf-fringed sill   10
Leaned over and looked into his gray eyes,
    Where he stood perplexed and still.
But only a host of phantom listeners
    That dwelt in the lone house then
Stood listening in the quiet of the moonlight   15
    To that voice from the world of men:
Stood thronging the faint moonbeams on the dark stair
    That goes down to the empty hall,
Hearkening in an air stirred and shaken
    By the lonely Traveller's call.   20
And he felt in his heart their strangeness,
    Their stillness answering his cry,
While his horse moved, cropping the dark turf,
    'Neath the starred and leafy sky;
For he suddenly smote on the door, even   25
    Louder, and lifted his head:—
"Tell them I came, and no one answered,
    That I kept my word," he said.
Never the least stir made the listeners,
    Though every word he spake   30
Fell echoing through the shadowiness of the still house
    From the one man left awake:
Ay, they heard his foot upon the stirrup,
    And the sound of iron on stone,
And how the silence surged softly backward,   35
    When the plunging hoofs were gone.

QUESTIONS

1. Before you had read this poem, what suggestions did its title bring to mind?
2. Now that you have read the poem, what do you make of these "listeners"? Who or what do you imagine them to be?
3. Why is *the moonlit door* (in line 2) a phrase more valuable to this poem than if the poet had written simply "the door"?
4. What does *turret* (in line 5) suggest?
5. Reconstruct some earlier events that might have preceded the Traveller's visit. Who might this Traveller be? Who are the unnamed persons—"them" (line 27)—for whom the Traveller leaves a message? What promise has he kept? (The poet doesn't tell us; we can only guess.)
6. Do you think this poem any the worse for the fact that its setting, characters, and action are so mysterious? What does "The Listeners" gain from not telling us all?

Robert Frost   (1874–1963)*

FIRE AND ICE   1923

Some say the world will end in fire,
Some say in ice.
From what I've tasted of desire
I hold with those who favor fire.
But if it had to perish twice,   5
I think I know enough of hate
To say that for destruction ice
Is also great
And would suffice.

QUESTIONS

1. To whom does Frost refer in line 1? In line 2?
2. What connotations of *fire* and *ice* contribute to the richness of Frost's comparison?

Clare Rossini   (b. 1954)

FINAL LOVE NOTE   1997

For months we've been together, hardly wanton,
Never touching. Yet your shade commingled
With my clothes strewn on the floor, and your wind
Moaned over me at night, never tiring
As human lovers do. My lifted garden,   5
Pure-green, wooden-hearted, all your leaves moved
Summer-long, then suddenly caught fire.
In winter I endured your silences,
My sight tangled in your black network
Which trapped whatever moon was on the rise.   10

This summer, the slugs ate the yellow hearts
Right out of my lilies, while you, elm, died on—

Dying as you have for years, leafless branches
Subdividing your shade. Slowly the sun
Found more of my roof, the attic grew hotter.   15
Some nights, the heat would not leave my bed
Until two or three, while I tossed and turned
In my abandonment.

              This morning,
I hear the chain saw cry out ecstatically.
My heart beats. Then a dull thunder shakes the house.   20

Your many arms are falling. And I must live
More with sky now, that garish blue stretch
Or drafty ceiling harshly lit by stars.

QUESTIONS

1. What do the images of the opening lines suggest about the speaker's feelings toward
   the elm tree?
2. A factual summary of this poem might state merely that "the speaker misses the
   shade of a dying elm tree that had to be cut down." What does that summary not suggest about the full effect of the poem?
3. Does the poem become more or less effective because of the equation of the tree with a
   lost lover? Defend your opinion with lines from the poem that you especially like or
   dislike.

Alfred, Lord Tennyson   (1809–1892)*

TEARS, IDLE TEARS   1847

    Tears, idle tears, I know not what they mean,
Tears from the depth of some divine despair
Rise in the heart, and gather to the eyes,
In looking on the happy autumn-fields,
And thinking of the days that are no more.   5

    Fresh as the first beam glittering on a sail,
That brings our friends up from the underworld,
Sad as the last which reddens over one
That sinks with all we love below the verge;
So sad, so fresh, the days that are no more.   10

    Ah, sad and strange as in dark summer dawns
The earliest pipe of half-awakened birds
To dying ears, when unto dying eyes
The casement slowly grows a glimmering square;
So sad, so strange, the days that are no more.   15

    Dear as remembered kisses after death,
And sweet as those by hopeless fancy feigned
On lips that are for others; deep as love,
Deep as first love, and wild with all regret;
O Death in Life, the days that are no more!   20

Richard Wilbur   (b. 1921)*

LOVE CALLS US TO THE THINGS   1956
OF THIS WORLD

The eyes open to a cry of pulleys,
And spirited from sleep, the astounded soul
Hangs for a moment bodiless and simple
As false dawn.
             Outside the open window
The morning air is all awash with angels.   5

    Some are in bed-sheets, some are in blouses,
Some are in smocks: but truly there they are.
Now they are rising together in calm swells
Of halcyon feeling, filling whatever they wear
With the deep joy of their impersonal breathing;   10

    Now they are flying in place, conveying
The terrible speed of their omnipresence, moving
And staying like white water; and now of a sudden
They swoon down into so rapt a quiet
That nobody seems to be there.
                  The soul shrinks   15

    From all that it is about to remember,
From the punctual rape of every blessèd day,
And cries,
       "Oh, let there be nothing on earth but laundry,
Nothing but rosy hands in the rising steam
And clear dances done in the sight of heaven."   20

    Yet, as the sun acknowledges
With a warm look the world's hunks and colors,
The soul descends once more in bitter love
To accept the waking body, saying now
In a changed voice as the man yawns and rises,   25

    "Bring them down from their ruddy gallows;
Let there be clean linen for the backs of thieves;
Let lovers go fresh and sweet to be undone,
And the heaviest nuns walk in a pure floating
Of dark habits,
           keeping their difficult balance."   30

LOVE CALLS US TO THE THINGS OF THIS WORLD. Wilbur claimed that his title was taken from St. Augustine, but in a recent interview he admitted that neither he nor any critic has ever been able to locate the quotation again. Whatever its source, however, the title establishes the poem's central idea that love allows us to return from the divine world of the spirit to the imperfect world of our everyday lives. Wilbur's own comments on the poem are printed following.

QUESTIONS

1. What are the *angels* in line 5? Why does this metaphor seem appropriate to the situation?
2. What is "the punctual rape of every blessed day?" Who is being raped? Who or what commits the rape? Why would Wilbur choose this particular word with all its violent associations?
3. Who or what does the soul love in line 23, and why is that love bitter?
4. Is it merely obesity that make the nuns' balance "difficult" in the two final lines of the poem? What other "balance" does Wilbur's poem suggest?
5. The soul has two speeches in the poem. How do they differ in tone and imagery?
6. The spiritual world is traditionally considered invisible. What concrete images does Wilbur use to express its special character?

WRITER'S PERSPECTIVE

Richard Wilbur

Richard Wilbur on Writing

CONCERNING "LOVE CALLS US   1966
TO THE THINGS OF THIS WORLD"

If I understand this poem rightly, it has a free and organic rhythm: that is to say, its movement arises naturally from the emotion, and from the things and actions described. At the same time, the lines are metrical and disposed in stanzas. The subject matter is both exalted and vulgar. There is, I should think, sufficient description to satisfy an Imagist, but there is also a certain amount of statement; my hope is that the statement seems to grow inevitably out of the situation described. The language of the poem is at one moment elevated and at the next colloquial or slangy: for example, the imposing word "omnipresence" occurs not far from the undignified word "hunks." A critic would find in this poem certain patterns of sound, but those patterns of sound do not constitute an abstract music; they are meant, at any rate, to be inseparable from what is being said, a subordinate aspect of the poem's meaning.

The title of the poem is a quotation from St. Augustine: "Love Calls Us to the Things of This World." You must imagine the poem as occurring at perhaps seven-thirty in the morning; the scene is a bedroom high up in a city apartment building; outside the bedroom window, the first laundry of the day is being yanked across the sky, and one has been awakened by the squeaking pulleys of the laundry-line.

From "On My Own Work"

⊸▸◤WRITING CRITICALLY◥◂⊸

The Ways a Poem Suggests

If we open the front door and find a friend standing there in hysterical tears, the person does not need to say "I'm miserable." We see that already. In a like manner, poems suggest some messages so clearly through imagery, tone, and diction that they do not need to declare them overtly. Poetry is a special way of speaking that requires a special way of listening. Poetry does not merely speak to the analytical parts of our minds but to the wholeness of our humanity. A good poem invites us to become fully alive and respond with our intuition, imagination, emotions, and intelligence. It even speaks to our physical bodies through sound, rhythm, and sensory imagery.

Since poems speak to us so completely, they often convey their meaning indirectly. An image may express something so clearly that the poem does not need to repeat it explicitly. In this sense, poems operate no differently from daily life.

In writing about a poem, listen carefully to everything it is telling you. Before beginning your essay, jot down a few key observations both about what the poem tells us and what we might want to know but aren't told. Note anything important to the story or situation of the poem that we have to infer for ourselves. When journalists write a news story, they always try to cover the "five W's" in their opening paragraph—*who, what, where, when, why.* These may be worthwhile questions to ask about a poem. If one or more of them is missing, how does that affect our understanding of the poem?

1. *Who?* Who is the speaker or central figure of the poem? (In Blake's "London," for instance, the speaker is also the protagonist who witnesses the hellish horror of the city.)
2. *What?* What is being seen or presented? Does the poem ever suddenly change its subject? (In Stevens's "Disillusionment at Ten O'Clock," for example, there are essentially two scenes—one dull and proper, the other wild and disreputable. What does that obvious shift suggest about Stevens's meaning?)
3. *Where?* Where is the poem set? Does the setting so clearly suggest something important that the rest of the poem does not need to repeat the message. (The setting of De la Mare's "The Listeners" goes a long way toward creating the mood that the poet wants to evoke.)

4. *When?* When does the poem take place? If a poet explicitly states a time of day or time of year, it is very likely that the *when* of the poem is important. (The fact that Stevens's poem takes place at 10:00 P.M. rather than 2:00 A.M. tells us a great deal about the people it describes.)

5. *Why?* If the poem describes some dramatic action but does not tell us *why* it is being performed, perhaps the author wants us to ponder the situation carefully. (De la Mare's "The Listeners" gains extra mystery by leaving us in the dark about the people involved, and Tennyson's "Tears, Idle Tears" becomes more evocative by not being explicit about why the speaker weeps.)

You don't have to answer all the questions, but it will help to ask them. Remember, it is almost as important to know what a poem doesn't tell us as what it does.

WRITING ASSIGNMENT

In a short essay (750–1000 words) explain why the speaker in Alfred, Lord Tennyson's "Tears, Idle Tears" (page 89) is weeping. Although the speaker claims not to know what the tears mean, the poem's language and imagery suggest some compelling reasons. Support your theory with specific examples. Be sure to differentiate between evidence that the poem explicitly provides and where an idea or event is only suggested. Feel free to extrapolate slightly beyond the limits of the poem, but *state clearly* where your interpretation goes beyond the literal meaning of the words and where it sticks closely to the text.

FURTHER SUGGESTIONS FOR WRITING

1. In a short essay, analyze a poem full of words that radiate suggestions. Looking into "Poems for Further Reading," you might consider T. S. Eliot's "The Love Song of J. Alfred Prufrock," John Keats's "To Autumn," Sylvia Plath's "Daddy," or many others. Focus on particular words: explain their connotations and show how these suggestions are part of the poem's meaning. (For guidelines on writing about poetry by the method of analysis, see "Writing About a Poem.")

2. In a current newspaper or magazine, select an advertisement that tries to surround a product with an aura. A new car, for instance, might be described in terms of some powerful jungle cat ("purring power, ready to spring"). Likely hunting-grounds for such ads are magazines that cater to the affluent (*New Yorker*, *Vogue*, and others). Clip or photocopy the ad and circle words in it that seem especially suggestive. Then, in an accompanying paper, unfold the suggestions in these words and try to explain the ad's appeal. How is the purpose of connotative language used in advertising copy different from that of such language when used in poetry?

5 Imagery

Ezra Pound (1885–1972)*

IN A STATION OF THE METRO   1916

The apparition of these faces in the crowd;
Petals on a wet, black bough.

Pound said he wrote this poem to convey an experience: emerging one day from a train in the Paris subway (*Métro*), he beheld "suddenly a beautiful face, and then another and another." Originally he had described his impression in a poem thirty lines long. In this final version, each line contains an image, which, like a picture, may take the place of a thousand words.

Though the term **image** suggests a thing seen, when speaking of images in poetry, we generally mean *a word or sequence of words that refers to any sensory experience*. Often this experience is a sight (**visual imagery,** as in Pound's poem), but it may be a sound (**auditory imagery**) or a touch (**tactile imagery,** as a perception of roughness or smoothness). It may be an odor or a taste or perhaps a bodily sensation such as pain, the prickling of gooseflesh, the quenching of thirst, or—as in the following brief poem—the perception of something cold.

Taniguchi Buson (1716–1783)*

THE PIERCING CHILL I FEEL   (ABOUT 1760)

The piercing chill I feel:
   my dead wife's comb, in our bedroom,
     under my heel . . .
         —*Translated by Harold G. Henderson*

As in this haiku (in Japanese, a poem of about seventeen syllables) an image can convey a flash of understanding. Had he wished, the poet might have spoken of the dead woman, of the contrast between her death and his memory of her, of his feelings toward death in general. But such a discussion would be quite different from the poem he actually wrote. Striking his bare foot against the comb, now cold and motionless but associated with the living wife (perhaps worn in her hair), the widower feels a shock as if he had touched the woman's corpse. A literal, physical sense of death is conveyed; the abstraction "death" is understood through the senses. To render the abstract in concrete terms is what poets often try to do; in this attempt, an image can be valuable.

An image may occur in a single word, a phrase, a sentence, or, as in this case, an entire short poem. To speak of the **imagery** of a poem—all its images taken together—is often more useful than to speak of separate images. To divide Buson's haiku into five images—*chill, wife, comb, bedroom, heel*—is possible, for any noun that refers to a visible object or a sensation is an image, but this is to draw distinctions that in themselves mean little and to disassemble a single experience.

Does an image cause a reader to experience a sense impression? Not quite. Reading the word *petals*, no one literally sees petals; but the occasion is given for imagining them. The image asks to be seen with the mind's eye. And although "In a Station of the Metro" records what Ezra Pound saw, it is of course not necessary for a poet actually to have lived through a sensory experience in order to write of it. Keats may never have seen a newly discovered planet through a telescope, despite the image in his sonnet on Chapman's Homer (page 503).

It is tempting to think of imagery as mere decoration, particularly when we read Keats, who fills his poems with an abundance of sights, sounds, odors, and tastes. But a successful image is not just a dab of paint or a flashy bauble. When Keats opens "The Eve of St. Agnes" with what have been called the coldest lines in literature, he evokes by a series of images a setting and a mood:

> St. Agnes' eve—Ah, bitter chill it was!
> The owl, for all his feathers, was a-cold;
> The hare limped trembling through the frozen grass,
> And silent was the flock in woolly fold:
> Numb were the Beadsman's fingers, while he told
> His rosary, and while his frosted breath,
> Like pious incense from a censer old,
> Seemed taking flight for heaven, without a death, . . .

Indeed, some literary critics look for much of the meaning of a poem in its imagery, wherein they expect to see the mind of the poet more truly revealed than in whatever the poet explicitly claims to believe. Though Shakespeare's Theseus (in A *Midsummer Night's Dream*) accuses poets of being concerned with "airy nothings," poets are usually very much concerned with what is in front of them. This concern is of use to us. Perhaps, as Alan Watts has remarked, Americans are not the materialists they are sometimes accused of being. How could anyone taking a look at an American city think that its inhabitants deeply cherish material things? Involved in our personal hopes and apprehensions, anticipating the future so hard that much of the time we see the present through a film of thought across our eyes, perhaps we need a poet occasionally to remind us that even the coffee we absentmindedly sip comes in (as Yeats put it) a "heavy spillable cup."

T. S. Eliot (1888–1965)*

THE WINTER EVENING SETTLES DOWN   1917

The winter evening settles down
With smell of steaks in passageways.
Six o'clock.
The burnt-out ends of smoky days.
And now a gusty shower wraps   5
The grimy scraps
Of withered leaves about your feet
And newspapers from vacant lots;
The showers beat
On broken blinds and chimney-pots,   10
And at the corner of the street
A lonely cab-horse steams and stamps.

And then the lighting of the lamps.

QUESTIONS

1. What mood is evoked by the images in Eliot's poem?
2. What kind of city neighborhood has the poet chosen to describe? How can you tell?

Theodore Roethke (1908–1963)*

ROOT CELLAR   1948

Nothing would sleep in that cellar, dank as a ditch,
Bulbs broke out of boxes hunting for chinks in the dark,
Shoots dangled and drooped,
Lolling obscenely from mildewed crates,
Hung down long yellow evil necks, like tropical snakes.   5
And what a congress of stinks!—
Roots ripe as old bait,
Pulpy stems, rank, silo-rich,
Leaf-mold, manure, lime, piled against slippery planks.

Nothing would give up life: 10
Even the dirt kept breathing a small breath.

QUESTIONS

1. As a boy growing up in Saginaw, Michigan, Theodore Roethke spent much of his
    time in a large commercial greenhouse run by his family. What details in his poem
    show more than a passing acquaintance with growing things?
2. What varieties of image does "Root Cellar" contain? Point out examples.
3. What do you understand to be Roethke's attitude toward the root cellar? Does he
    view it as a disgusting chamber of horrors? Pay special attention to the last two lines.

Elizabeth Bishop (1911–1979)*

THE FISH   1946

I caught a tremendous fish
and held him beside the boat
half out of water, with my hook
fast in a corner of his mouth.
He didn't fight.   5
He hadn't fought at all.
He hung a grunting weight,
battered and venerable
and homely. Here and there
his brown skin hung in strips   10
like ancient wall-paper,
and its pattern of darker brown
was like wall-paper:
shapes like full-blown roses
stained and lost through age.   15
He was speckled with barnacles,
fine rosettes of lime,
and infested
with tiny white sea-lice,
and underneath two or three   20
rags of green weed hung down.
While his gills were breathing in
the terrible oxygen
—the frightening gills,
fresh and crisp with blood,   25
that can cut so badly—
I thought of the coarse white flesh
packed in like feathers,
the big bones and the little bones,
the dramatic reds and blacks   30

of his shiny entrails,
and the pink swim-bladder
like a big peony.
I looked into his eyes
which were far larger than mine   35
but shallower, and yellowed,
the irises backed and packed
with tarnished tinfoil
seen through the lenses
of old scratched isinglass.   40
They shifted a little, but not
to return my stare.
—It was more like the tipping
of an object toward the light.
I admired his sullen face,   45
the mechanism of his jaw,
and then I saw
that from his lower lip
—if you could call it a lip—
grim, wet, and weapon-like,   50
hung five old pieces of fish-line,
or four and a wire leader
with the swivel still attached,
with all their five big hooks
grown firmly in his mouth.   55
A green line, frayed at the end
where he broke it, two heavier lines,
and a fine black thread
still crimped from the strain and snap
when it broke and he got away.   60
Like medals with their ribbons
frayed and wavering,
a five-haired beard of wisdom
trailing from his aching jaw.
I stared and stared   65
and victory filled up
the little rented boat,
from the pool of bilge
where oil had spread a rainbow
around the rusted engine   70
to the bailer rusted orange,
the sun-cracked thwarts,
the oarlocks on their strings,
the gunnels—until everything
was rainbow, rainbow, rainbow!   75
And I let the fish go.

QUESTIONS

1. How many abstract words does this poem contain? What proportion of the poem is imagery?
2. What is the speaker's attitude toward the fish? Comment in particular on lines 61–64.
3. What attitude do the images of the rainbow of oil (line 69), the orange bailer (bailing bucket, line 71), the *sun-cracked thwarts* (line 72) convey? Does the poet expect us to feel mournful because the boat is in such sorry condition?
4. What is meant by *rainbow, rainbow, rainbow*?
5. How do these images prepare us for the conclusion? Why does the speaker let the fish go?

Anne Stevenson   (b. 1933)*

THE VICTORY   1974

I thought you were my victory
though you cut me like a knife
when I brought you out of my body
into your life.

Tiny antagonist, gory,   5
blue as a bruise. The stains
of your cloud of glory
bled from my veins.

How can you dare, blind thing,
blank insect eyes?   10
You barb the air. You sting
with bladed cries.

Snail! Scary knot of desires!
Hungry snarl! Small son.
Why do I have to love you?   15
How have you won?

QUESTIONS

1. Newborn babies are often described as "little angels" or "bundles of joy." How does the speaker of "The Victory" describe her son?
2. Why does the speaker describe the child as an "antagonist" (line 5)?
3. Why is the poem titled "The Victory"?
4. Why is the infant compared to a knife in both lines 2 and 12?

Charles Simic (b. 1938)*

FORK 1969

This strange thing must have crept
Right out of hell.
It resembles a bird's foot
Worn around the cannibal's neck.

As you hold it in your hand,   5
As you stab with it into a piece of meat,
It is possible to imagine the rest of the bird:
Its head which like your fist
Is large, bald, beakless, and blind.

QUESTIONS

1. The title image of this poem is an ordinary and everyday object. What happens to it
   in the first two lines?
2. How does the word *crept* in line 1 change our sense of the fork? How does the author
   develop this new sense later in the poem?

Emily Dickinson (1830–1886)*

A ROUTE OF EVANESCENCE (1879)

A Route of Evanescence
With a revolving Wheel –
A Resonance of Emerald –
A Rush of Cochineal° –   *red dye*
And every Blossom on the Bush   5
Adjusts its tumbled Head –
The mail from Tunis, probably,
An easy Morning's Ride –

A ROUTE OF EVANESCENCE. Dickinson titled this poem "A Humming-bird" in an 1880 letter to a
friend. 1 *Evanescence*; ornithologist's term for the luminous sheen of certain birds' feathers. 7 *Tunis*:
capital city of Tunisia, North Africa.

QUESTIONS

What is the subject of this poem? How can you tell?

Jean Toomer   (1894–1967)

REAPERS   1923

Black reapers with the sound of steel on stones
Are sharpening scythes. I see them place the hones
In their hip-pockets as a thing that's done,
And start their silent swinging, one by one.
Black horses drive a mower through the weeds,   5
And there, a field rat, startled, squealing bleeds,
His belly close to ground. I see the blade,
Blood-stained, continue cutting weeds and shade.

QUESTIONS

1. Imagine the scene Jean Toomer describes. Which particulars most vividly strike the mind's eye?
2. What kind of image is *silent swinging?*
3. Read the poem aloud. Notice especially the effect of the words *sound of steel on stones* and *field rat, startled, squealing bleeds.* What interesting sounds are present in the very words that contain these images?
4. What feelings do you get from this poem as a whole? Would you agree with someone who said, "This poem gives us a sense of happy, carefree life down on the farm, close to nature"? Exactly what in "Reapers" makes you feel the way you do? Besides appealing to our auditory and visual imagination, what do the images contribute?

Gerard Manley Hopkins   (1844–1889)*

PIED BEAUTY   (1877)

Glory be to God for dappled things—
   For skies of couple-color as a brinded° cow;   *streaked*
     For rose-moles all in stipple upon trout that swim;
Fresh-firecoal chestnut-falls; finches' wings;
   Landscape plotted and pieced—fold, fallow, and plow;   5
     And áll trádes, their gear and tackle and trim.°   *equipment*

All things counter, original, spare, strange;
   Whatever is fickle, freckled (who know how?)
     With swift, slow; sweet, sour; adazzle, dim;
He fathers-forth whose beauty is past change: 10
           Praise him.

QUESTIONS

1. What does the word *pied* mean? (Hint: what does a Pied Piper look like?)
2. According to Hopkins, what do *skies, cow, trout, ripe chestnuts, finches' wings,* and *landscapes* all have in common? What landscapes can the poet have in mind? (Have

you ever seen any *dappled* landscape while looking down from an airplane, or from a mountain or high hill?)

3. What do you make of line 6: what can carpenters' saws and ditch-diggers' spades possibly have in common with the dappled things in lines 2–4?

4. Does Hopkins refer only to contrasts that meet the eye? What other kinds of variation interest him?

5. Try to state in your own words the theme of this poem. How essential to our understanding of this theme are Hopkins's images?

About Haiku

Arakida Moritake (1473–1549)

The falling flower

The falling flower
I saw drift back to the branch
Was a butterfly.

—Translated by Babette Deutsch

Haiku means "beginning-verse" in Japanese—perhaps because the form may have originated in a game. Players, given a haiku, were supposed to extend its three lines into a longer poem. Haiku (the word can also be plural) consist mainly of imagery, but as we saw in Buson's lines about the cold comb, their imagery is not always only pictorial; it can also involve any of the five senses. Haiku are so short that they depend on imagery to trigger associations and responses in the reader. A haiku in Japanese is rimeless; its seventeen syllables are traditionally arranged in three lines, usually following a pattern of five, seven, and five syllables. English haiku frequently ignore such a pattern, being rimed or unrimed as the poet prefers. What English haiku do try to preserve is the powerful way Japanese haiku capture the intensity of a particular moment, usually by linking two concrete images. There is little room for abstract thoughts or general observations. The following attempt, though containing seventeen syllables, is far from haiku in spirit:

Now that our love is gone
I feel within my soul
a nagging distress.

Unlike the author of those lines, haiku poets look out upon a literal world, seldom looking inward to *discuss* their feelings. Japanese haiku tend to be seasonal in subject, but because they are so highly compressed, they usually just *imply* a season: a blossom indicates spring; a crow on a branch, autumn; snow, winter. Not just pretty little sketches of nature (as some Westerners think), haiku assume a view of the universe in which observer and nature are not separated.

Haiku emerged in sixteenth-century Japan and soon developed into a deeply esteemed form. Even today, Japanese soldiers, stockbrokers, scientists, schoolchildren, and even the emperor still find occasion to pen haiku. Soon after the form first captured the attention of Western poets at the end of the nineteenth century, it became immensely influential for modern poets such as Ezra Pound, William Carlos Williams, and H. D., as a model for the kind of verse they wanted to write—concise, direct, and imagistic.

The Japanese consider the poems of the "Three Masters"—Basho, Buson, and Issa—to be the pinnacle of the classical haiku. Each poet had his own personality: Basho, the ascetic seeker of Zen enlightenment; Buson, the worldly artist; Issa, the sensitive master of wit and pathos. Here are free translations of poems from each of the "Three Masters."

Matsuo Basho   (1644–1694)*

HEAT-LIGHTNING STREAK

Heat-lightning streak—
through darkness pierces
the heron's shriek.

IN THE OLD STONE POOL

In the old stone pool
a frogjump:
splishhhhh.
　　—Translations by X. J. Kennedy

Taniguchi Buson   (1716–1783)*

ON THE ONE-TON TEMPLE BELL

On the one-ton temple bell
a moonmoth, folded into sleep,
sits still.
—Translated by X. J. Kennedy

I GO

I go,
you stay;
two autumns.
—Translated by Robert Hass

Kobayashi Issa   (1763–1827)*

ONLY ONE GUY

only one guy and
only one fly trying to
make the guest room do.
—Translated by Cid Corman

CRICKET

Cricket, be
careful! I'm rolling
over!
—Translated by Robert Bly

Japanese immigrants brought the tradition of haiku-writing to the United States, often forming local clubs to pursue their shared literary interests. During World War II, when Japanese Americans were unjustly considered "enemy aliens" and confined to federal internment camps, these poets continued to write in their bleak new surroundings. Today these haiku provide a vivid picture of the deprivations suffered by the poets, their families, and their fellow internees.

Suiko Matsushita

Rain shower from mountain
quietly soaking
barbed wire fence

Cosmos in bloom
as if no war
were taking place
—*Translations by Violet Kazue de Cristoro*

Neiji Ozawa

War forced us from California
No ripples this day
on desert lake

The war—this year
New Year midnight bell
ringing in the desert
—*Translations by Violet Kazue de Cristoro*

Hakuro Wada

Even the croaking of frogs
comes from outside the barbed wire fence
this is our life
—*Translated by Violet Kazue de Cristoro*

If you care to try your hand at haiku-writing, here are a few suggestions: make every word matter. Include few adjectives, shun needless conjunctions. Set your poem in the present. ("Haiku," said Basho, "is simply what is happening in this place at this moment.") Like many writers of haiku, you may wish to confine your poem to what can be seen, heard, smelled, tasted, or touched. Mere sensory reports, however, will be meaningless unless they make the reader feel something.

Here are seven more recent haiku written in English. (Don't expect them all to observe a strict arrangement of seventeen syllables, however.) Haiku, in any language, is an art of few words, many suggestions. A haiku starts us thinking and telling. "So the reader," Raymond Roseliep wrote, "keeps getting on where the poet got off."

Making jazz swing in
Seventeen syllables AIN'T
No square poet's job.
    —Etheridge Knight

Visitor's Room—
everything bolted down
except my brother.
    — Lee Gurga

broken bowl
the pieces
still rocking.
    —Penny Harter

Born Again
she speaks excitedly
of death.
    —Jennifer Brutschy

The Lazy Man's Haiku

out in the night
a wheelbarrowful
of moonlight.
       —John Ridland

Last Haiku

No, wait a minute,
I can't be old already:
I'm just about to.
       —Connie Bensley

Learning to Shave
(Father Teaching Son)

   A nick on the jaw
The razor's edge of manhood
   Along the bloodline.
      — Adelle Foley

For Review and Further Study

John Keats   (1795–1821)*

Bright star! would I were   (1819)
steadfast as thou art

Bright star! would I were steadfast as thou art—
   Not in lone splendor hung aloft the night,
And watching, with eternal lids apart,
   Like Nature's patient, sleepless Eremite,°   *hermit*
The moving waters at their priest-like task   5
   Of pure ablution round earth's human shores,
Or gazing on the new soft-fallen mask
   Of snow upon the mountains and the moors—
No—yet still steadfast, still unchangeable,
   Pillowed upon my fair love's ripening breast,   10
To feel for ever its soft fall and swell,
   Awake for ever in a sweet unrest,
Still, still to hear her tender-taken breath,
And so live ever—or else swoon to death.

Questions

1. Stars are conventional symbols for love and a loved one. (Love, Shakespeare tells us in a sonnet, "is the star to every wandering bark.") In this sonnet, why is it not possible for the star to have this meaning? How does Keats use it?
2. What seems concrete and particular in the speaker's observations?
3. Suppose Keats had said *slow and easy* instead of *tender-taken* in line 13. What would have been lost?

EXPERIMENT: *Writing with Images*

Taking the following poems as examples from which to start rather than as models to be slavishly copied, try to compose a brief poem that consists largely of imagery.

Walt Whitman   (1819–1892)*

THE RUNNER   1867

On a flat road runs the well-train'd runner;
He is lean and sinewy, with muscular legs;
He is thinly clothed—he leans forward as he runs,
With lightly closed fists, and arms partially rais'd.

T. E. Hulme   (1883–1917)

IMAGE   (ABOUT 1910)

Old houses were scaffolding once
          and workmen whistling.

Chana Bloch   (b. 1940)

TIRED SEX   1998

We're trying to strike a match in a matchbook
that has lain all winter under the woodpile:
damp sulphur
on sodden cardboard.
I catch myself yawning. Through the window   5
I watch that sparrow the cat
keeps batting around.

Like turning the pages of a book the teacher assigned—

You ought to read it, she said.
It's great literature.   10

Robert Bly   (b. 1926)*

DRIVING TO TOWN LATE TO MAIL A LETTER   1962

It is a cold and snowy night. The main street is deserted.
The only things moving are swirls of snow.
As I lift the mailbox door, I feel its cold iron.
There is a privacy I love in this snowy night.
Driving around, I will waste more time.   5

Gary Snyder   (b. 1930)

PIUTE CREEK   1965

One granite ridge
A tree, would be enough
Or even a rock, a small creek,
A bark shred in a pool.
Hill beyond hill, folded and twisted   5
Tough trees crammed
In thin stone fractures
A huge moon on it all, is too much.
The mind wanders. A million
Summers, night air still and the rocks   10
Warm.   Sky over endless mountains.
All the junk that goes with being human
Drops away, hard rock wavers
Even the heavy present seems to fail
This bubble of a heart.   15
Words and books
Like a small creek off a high ledge
Gone in the dry air.

A clear, attentive mind
Has no meaning but that   20
Which sees is truly seen.
No one loves rock, yet we are here.
Night chills. A flick
In the moonlight
Slips into Juniper shadow: 25
Back there unseen
Cold proud eyes
Of Cougar or Coyote
Watch me rise and go.

H. D. [Hilda Doolittle]   (1886–1961)*

HEAT   1916

O wind, rend open the heat,
cut apart the heat,
rend it to tatters.

Fruit cannot drop
through this thick air—
fruit cannot fall into heat   5
that presses up and blunts
the points of pears
and rounds the grapes.

Cut the heat—   10
plough through it,
turning it on either side
of your path.

Louise Glück   (b. 1943)

MOCK ORANGE   1985

It is not the moon, I tell you.
It is these flowers
lighting the yard.

I hate them.
I hate them as I hate sex,   5
the man's mouth
sealing my mouth, the man's
paralyzing body—

and the cry that always escapes,
the low, humiliating   10
premise of union—

In my mind tonight
I hear the question and pursuing answer
fused in one sound
that mounts and mounts and then   15
is split into the old selves,
the tired antagonisms. Do you see?
We were made fools of.
And the scent of mock orange
drifts through the window.   20

How can I rest?
How can I be content
when there is still
that odor in the world?

MOCK ORANGE. The mock orange is a flowering shrub with especially fragrant white blossoms and
fruit that resemble those of an orange tree.

Billy Collins (b. 1941)*

EMBRACE   1988

You know the parlor trick.
Wrap your arms around your own body
and from the back it looks like
someone is embracing you,
her hands grasping your shirt,   5
her fingernails teasing your neck.

From the front it is another story.
You never looked so alone,
your crossed elbows and screwy grin.
You could be waiting for a tailor   10
to fit you for a straitjacket,
one that would hold you really tight.

John Haines (b. 1924)

WINTER NEWS   1966

They say the wells
are freezing
at Northway where
the cold begins.

Oil tins bang   5
as evening comes on,
and clouds of
steaming breath drift
in the street.

Men go out to feed   10
the stiffening dogs,

the voice of the snowman
calls the white-
haired children home.

1. Which of the images in this poem strike you as the most vivid? To which senses do Haines's images appeal?
2. Why are the children described as "white-haired"?

Stevie Smith (1902–1971)*

NOT WAVING BUT DROWNING   1957

Nobody heard him, the dead man,
But still he lay moaning:
I was much further out than you thought
And not waving but drowning.

Poor chap, he always loved larking   5
And now he's dead
It must have been too cold for him his heart gave way,
They said.

Oh, no no no, it was too cold always
(Still the dead one lay moaning)   10
I was much too far out all my life
And not waving but drowning.

Ezra Pound

Ezra Pound on Writing

THE IMAGE   1913

An "Image" is that which presents an intellectual and emotional complex in an instant of time. I use the term "complex" rather in the technical sense employed by the newer psychologists, such as Hart, though we might not agree absolutely in our application.

It is the presentation of such a "complex" instantaneously which gives that sense of sudden liberation; that sense of freedom from time limits and space limits; that sense of sudden growth, which we experience in the presence of the greatest works of art.

It is better to present one Image in a lifetime than to produce voluminous works.

All this, however, some may consider open to debate. The immediate necessity is to tabulate A LIST OF DON'TS for those beginning to write verses. I can not put all of them into Mosaic negative.

Use no superfluous word, no adjective which does not reveal something.

Don't use such an expression as "dim lands *of peace.*" It dulls the image. It mixes an abstraction with the concrete. It comes from the writer's not realizing that the natural object is always the *adequate* symbol.

Go in fear of abstractions. Do not retell in mediocre verse what has already been done in good prose. Don't think any intelligent person is going to be deceived when you try to shirk all the difficulties of the unspeakably difficult art of good prose by chopping your composition into line lengths.

From "A Few Don'ts"

Analyzing Images

To help you analyze how the imagery of a poem works, here is a simple exercise: Make a short list of the poem's key images. Be sure to write down the images in the order they appear in the poem, because the sequence of images is often as important as the images themselves. (For example, a poem whose images move from *sunlight* to *darkness* might well signify something different from one that begins with *darkness* and concludes with *sunlight*.) Remember that not all images are visual. Images can draw on any or all of the five senses. In jotting down images, don't omit key adjectives or other qualifying words. Those words are often your best clues to a poem's tone or perspective. (T. E. Hulme's image of "whistling" workmen on page 106, for instance, implies something happier than "sweating" workmen would.)

Let's try this method on a short poem. An initial list of images in Robert Bly's "Driving to Town Late to Mail a Letter" (page 107) might look something like this:

> cold and snowy night
> deserted main street
> mailbox door—cold iron
> snowy night (speaker *loves* its privacy)
> speaker drives around (to waste time)

Did we forget anything? Yes, the title! Always look to a poem's title for guidance. Bly's title, for instance, contains several crucial images. Let's add them to the top of the list:

> driving (to town)
> late night
> a letter (to be mailed)

Looking at our list, we see how the images provide an outline of the poem's story. We also see how Bly begins the poem without allowing us initially to understand how his speaker views the situation. Is driving to town late on a snowy evening a positive, negative, or neutral experience? By noting where (in line 4) the speaker reveals a subjective response to an image ("There is a privacy I love in this snowy night"), we also begin to grasp the overall emotional structure of the poem. We might also note on our list how the poem begins and ends with the same image (driving), but uses it for different effects at the two places. At the beginning the speaker is driving for the practical purpose of mailing a letter but at the end merely for the pure pleasure of it.

After adding a few notes on our list to capture these insights, we are ready to begin writing our paper. Without realizing it, we have already worked out a rough outline—all on a single sheet of paper or a few inches of computer screen.

WRITING ASSIGNMENT

Examining any poem in this chapter (or in "Poems for Further Reading"), demonstrate how its imagery helps communicate its general theme. Be specific in noting how each key image contributes to the poem's total effect. Feel free to consult criticism on the poem but make sure to credit any observation you borrow exactly from a critical source. (See the chapter "Writing About a Poem" for advice on both writing process and format guidelines.) Here is an essay written in response to this assignment by Becki Woods, a student of Mark Bernier, at Blinn College in Brenham, Texas.

Becki Woods

Professor Bernier

English 220

23 February 20xx

Elizabeth Bishop's Use of Imagery in "The Fish"

Upon first reading, Elizabeth Bishop's "The Fish" appears to be a simple fishing tale. A close investigation of the imagery in Bishop's highly detailed description, however, reveals a different sort of poem. The real theme of Bishop's poem is a compassion and respect for the fish's lifelong struggle to survive. By carefully and effectively describing the captured fish, his reaction to being caught, and the symbols of his past struggles to stay alive, Bishop creates, through her images of beauty, victory, and survival, something more than a simple tale.

The first four lines of the poem are quite ordinary and factual:

> I caught a tremendous fish
> and held him beside the boat
> half out of water, with my hook
> fast in a corner of his mouth. (1-4)

Except for _tremendous_, Bishop's persona uses no exaggerations--unlike most fishing stories--to set up the situation of catching the fish. The detailed description begins as the speaker recounts the event further, noticing something signally important about the captive fish: "He didn't fight" (5). At this point the poem begins to seem unusual: most fish stories are about how ferociously the prey resists being captured. The speaker also notes that the "battered and venerable / and homely" fish offered no resistance to being caught (8-9). The image of the submissive attitude of the fish is essential to the theme of the poem. It is his "utter passivity [that] makes [the persona's] detailed scrutiny possible" (McNally 192).

Once the image of the passive fish has been established, the speaker begins an examination of the fish itself, noting that "Here and there / his brown skin hung in strips / like ancient wall-paper" (9-11). By comparing the fish's skin to wallpaper, the persona creates, as Sybil Estess argues, "implicit suggestions of both artistry and decay" (713). Images of peeling wallpaper are instantly brought to mind. The comparison of the fish's skin and wallpaper, though "helpful in conveying an accurate notion of the fish's color to anyone with memories of Victorian parlors and their yellowed wallpaper . . . is," according to Nancy McNally, "even more useful in evoking the associations of deterioration which usually surround such memories" (192). The fish's faded beauty has been hinted at in the comparison, thereby setting up the detailed imagery that soon follows:

> He was speckled with barnacles,
> fine rosettes of lime,
> and infested
> with tiny white sea-lice,
> and underneath two or three
> rags of green weed hung down. (16-20)

The persona sees the fish as he is; the infestations and faults are not left out of the description. Yet, at the same time, the fisher "express[es] what [he/she] has sensed of the character of the fish" (Estess 714).

Bishop's persona notices "shapes like full-blown roses / stained and lost through age" on the fish's skin (14-15). The persona's perception of the fish's beauty is revealed along with a recognition of its faded beauty, which is best revealed in the description of the fish's being speckled with barnacles and spotted with lime. However, the fisher observes these spots and sees them as rosettes--as objects of beauty, not just ugly brown spots. These images contribute to the persona's recognition of beauty's having become faded beauty.

The poem next turns to a description of the fish's gills. The imagery in "While his gills were breathing in / the terrible oxygen" (22-23) leads "to the very structure of the creature" that is now dying (Hopkins 201). The descriptions of the fish's interior beauty--"the coarse white flesh / packed in like feathers," the colors "of his shiny entrails," and his "pink swim-bladder / like a big peony"--are reminders of the life that seems about to end (27-28, 31-33).

The composite image of the fish's essential beauty--his being alive--is developed further in the description of the five fish hooks that the captive, living fish carries in his lip:

> grim, wet, and weapon-like
>
> hung five old pieces of fish-line
>
> ....
>
> with all their five big hooks
>
> grown firmly in his mouth. (50-51, 54-55)

As if fascinated by them, the persona, observing how the lines must have been broken during struggles to escape, sees the hooks as "medals with their ribbons / frayed and

wavering, / a five-haired beard of wisdom / trailing from
his aching jaw" (61-64), and the fisher becomes enthralled
by re-created images of the fish's fighting desperately for
his life on at least five separate occasions--and winning.
Crale Hopkins suggests that "[i]n its capability not only
for mere existence, but for action, escaping from previous
anglers, the fish shares the speaker's humanity" (202), thus
revealing the fisher's deepening understanding of how he
must now act. The persona has "all along," notes Estess,
"describe[d] the fish not just with great detail but with an
imaginative empathy for the aquatic creature. In her more-
than-objective description, [the fisher] relates what
[he/she] has seen to be both the pride and poverty of the
fish" (715). It is at this point that the narrator of this
fishing tale has a moment of clarity. Realizing the fish's
history and the glory the fish has achieved in escaping
previous hookings, the speaker sees everything become,
"rainbow, rainbow, rainbow!" (75)--and then unexpectedly
lets the fish go.

Bishop's "The Fish" begins by describing an event that
might easily be a conventional story's climax: "I caught a
tremendous fish" (1). The poem, however, develops into a
highly detailed account of a fisher noticing both the age
and the faded beauty of the captive and his present beauty
and past glory as well. The fishing tale is not simply a
recounting of a capture; it is a gradually unfolding
epiphany in which the speaker sees the fish in an entirely
new light. The intensity of this encounter between an
apparently experienced fisher in a rented boat and battle-
hardened fish is delivered through the poet's skillful use
of imagery. It is through the description of the capture of
an aged fish that Bishop offers her audience her theme of
compassion derived from a respect for the struggle for
survival.

Works Cited

Bishop, Elizabeth. "The Fish." <u>An Introduction to Poetry</u>.
    Ed. X. J. Kennedy and Dana Gioia. 11th ed. New York:
    Longman, 2005. 97-98.

Estess, Sybil P. "Elizabeth Bishop: The Delicate Art of Map
    Making." <u>Southern Review</u> 13 (1977): 713-17.

Hopkins, Crale D. "Inspiration as Theme: Art and Nature in
    the Poetry of Elizabeth Bishop." <u>Arizona Quarterly</u> 32
    (1976): 200-02.

McNally, Nancy L. "Elizabeth Bishop: The Discipline of
    Description." <u>Twentieth-Century Literature</u> 11 (1966):
    192-94.

FURTHER SUGGESTIONS FOR WRITING

1. Choose, from "Poems for Further Reading," a poem that appeals to you. Then write a brief account of your experience in reading it, paying special attention to its imagery. What images strike you, and why? What do they contribute to the poem as a whole? Poems rich in imagery include Samuel Taylor Coleridge's "Kubla Khan," Robert Frost's "Birches," Charlotte Mew's "The Farmer's Bride," William Carlos Williams's "Spring and All (By the road to the contagious hospital)," and many more.

2. After you have read the haiku and the discussion of haiku-writing in this chapter, write three or four haiku of your own. Then write a brief prose account of your experience in writing them. What, if anything, did you find out?

6 Figures of Speech

WHY SPEAK FIGURATIVELY?

"I will speak daggers to her, but use none," says Hamlet, preparing to confront his mother. His statement makes sense only because we realize that *daggers* is to be taken two ways: literally (denoting sharp, pointed weapons) and nonliterally (referring to something that can be used *like* weapons—namely, words). Reading poetry, we often meet comparisons between two things whose similarity we have never noticed before. When Marianne Moore observes that a fir tree has "an emerald turkey-foot at the top," the result is a pleasure that poetry richly affords: the sudden recognition of likenesses.

A treetop like a turkey-foot, words like daggers—such comparisons are called **figures of speech.** In its broadest definition, a figure of speech may be said to occur whenever a speaker or writer, for the sake of freshness or emphasis, departs from the usual denotations of words. Certainly, when Hamlet says he will speak daggers, no one expects him to release pointed weapons from his lips, for *daggers* is not to be read solely for its denotation. Its connotations—sharp, stabbing, piercing, wounding—also come to mind, and we see ways in which words and daggers work alike. (Words too can hurt: by striking through pretenses, possibly, or by wounding their hearer's self-esteem.) In the statement "A razor is sharper than an ax," there is no departure from the usual denotations of *razor* and *ax*, and no figure of speech results. Both objects are of the same class; the comparison is not offensive to logic. But in "How sharper than a serpent's tooth it is to have a thankless child," the objects—snake's tooth (fang) and ungrateful offspring—are so unlike that no reasonable comparison may be made between them. To find similarity, we attend to the connotations of *serpent's tooth*—biting, piercing, venom, pain—rather than to its denotations. If we are aware of the connotations of *red rose* (beauty, softness, freshness, and so forth), then the line "My love is like a red, red rose" need not call to mind a woman with a scarlet face and a thorny neck.

Figures of speech are not devices to state what is demonstrably untrue. Indeed they often state truths that more literal language cannot communicate; they call attention to such truths; they lend them emphasis.

Alfred, Lord Tennyson   (1809–1892)*

THE EAGLE   1851

He clasps the crag with crooked hands;
Close to the sun in lonely lands,
Ringed with the azure world, he stands.

The wrinkled sea beneath him crawls;
He watches from his mountain walls,   5
And like a thunderbolt he falls.

This brief poem is rich in figurative language. In the first line, the phrase *crooked hands* may surprise us. An eagle does not have hands, we might protest; but the objection would be a quibble, for evidently Tennyson is indicating exactly how an eagle clasps a crag, in the way that human fingers clasp a thing. By implication, too, the eagle is a person. *Close to the sun,* if taken literally, is an absurd exaggeration, the sun being a mean distance of 93,000,000 miles from the earth. For the eagle to be closer to it by the altitude of a mountain is an approach so small as to be insignificant. But figuratively, Tennyson conveys that the eagle stands above the clouds, perhaps silhouetted against the sun, and for the moment belongs to the heavens rather than to the land and sea. The word *ringed* makes a circle of the whole world's horizons and suggests that we see the world from the eagle's height; the *wrinkled sea* becomes an aged, sluggish animal; *mountain walls,* possibly literal, also suggests a fort or castle; and finally the eagle itself is likened to a thunderbolt in speed and in power, perhaps also in that its beak is—like our abstract conception of a lightning bolt—pointed. How much of the poem can be taken literally? Only *he clasps the crag, he stands, he watches, he falls.* The rest is made of figures of speech. The result is that, reading Tennyson's poem, we gain a bird's-eye view of sun, sea, and land—and even of bird. Like imagery, figurative language refers us to the physical world.

William Shakespeare   (1564–1616)*

SHALL I COMPARE THEE TO   1609
A SUMMER'S DAY?

Shall I compare thee to a summer's day?
Thou art more lovely and more temperate.
Rough winds do shake the darling buds of May,
And summer's lease hath all too short a date.

Sometime too hot the eye of heaven shines,   5
And often is his gold complexion dimmed;
And every fair° from fair sometimes declines,   *fair one*
By chance, or nature's changing course, untrimmed.
But thy eternal summer shall not fade,
Nor lose possession of that fair thou ow'st°   *ownest, have*   10
Nor shall death brag thou wand'rest in his shade,
When in eternal lines to time thou grow'st.
    So long as men can breathe or eyes can see,
    So long lives this, and this gives life to thee.

Howard Moss   (1922–1987)

SHALL I COMPARE THEE TO A   1976
SUMMER'S DAY?

Who says you're like one of the dog days?
You're nicer. And better.
Even in May, the weather can be gray,
And a summer sub-let doesn't last forever.
Sometimes the sun's too hot;   5
Sometimes it is not.
Who can stay young forever?
People break their necks or just drop dead!
But you? Never!
If there's just one condensed reader left   10
Who can figure out the abridged alphabet,
    After you're dead and gone,
    In this poem you'll live on!

SHALL I COMPARE THEE TO A SUMMER'S DAY? (MOSS). *Dog days:* the hottest days of summer. The
ancient Romans believed that the Dog-star, Sirius, added heat to summer months.

QUESTIONS

1. In Howard Moss's streamlined version of Shakespeare, from a series called "Modified
   Sonnets (Dedicated to adapters, abridgers, digesters, and condensers everywhere),"
   to what extent does the poet use figurative language? In Shakespeare's original
   sonnet, how high a proportion of Shakespeare's language is figurative?
2. Compare some of Moss's lines to the corresponding lines in Shakespeare's sonnet.
   Why is *Even in May, the weather can be gray* less interesting than the original? In the
   lines on the sun (5–6 in both versions), what has Moss's modification deliberately
   left out? Why is Shakespeare's seeing death as a braggart memorable? Why aren't you
   greatly impressed by Moss's last two lines?

3. Can you explain Shakespeare's play on the word *untrimmed* (line 8)? Evidently the word can mean "divested of trimmings," but what other suggestions do you find in it?
4. How would you answer someone who argued, "Maybe Moss's language isn't as good as Shakespeare's, but the meaning is still there. What's wrong with putting Shakespeare into up-to-date words that can be understood by everybody?"

METAPHOR AND SIMILE

Life, like a dome of many-colored glass,
Stains the white radiance of Eternity.

The first of these lines (from Shelley's "Adonais") is a **simile:** a comparison of two things, indicated by some connective, usually *like, as, than,* or a verb such as *resembles.* A simile expresses a similarity. Still, for a simile to exist, the things compared have to be dissimilar in kind. It is no simile to say, "Your fingers are like mine"; it is a literal observation. But to say, "Your fingers are like sausages" is to use a simile. Omit the connective—say, "Your fingers are sausages"—and the result is a **metaphor,** a statement that one thing *is* something else, which, in a literal sense, it is not. In the second of Shelley's lines, it is *assumed* that Eternity is light or radiance, and we have an **implied metaphor,** one that uses neither a connective nor the verb *to be.* Here are examples:

Oh, my love is like a red, red rose.	*Simile*
Oh, my love resembles a red, red rose.	*Simile*
Oh, my love is redder than a rose.	*Simile*
Oh, my love is a red, red rose.	*Metaphor*
Oh, my love has red petals and sharp thorns.	*Implied metaphor*
Oh, I placed my love into a long-stem vase and I bandaged my bleeding thumb.	*Implied metaphor*

Often you can tell a metaphor from a simile by much more than just the presence or absence of a connective. In general, a simile refers to only one characteristic that two things have in common, while a metaphor is not plainly limited in the number of resemblances it may indicate. To use the simile "He eats like a pig" is to compare man and animal in one respect: eating habits. But to say "He's a pig" is to use a metaphor that might involve comparisons of appearance and morality as well.

For scientists as well as poets, the making of metaphors is customary. In 1933 George Lemaitre, the Belgian priest and physicist credited with the Big Bang theory of the origin of the universe, conceived of a primal atom that existed before anything else, which expanded and produced everything. And so, he remarked, making a wonderful metaphor, the evolution of the cosmos as it is today "can be compared to a display of fireworks that has just ended." As astrophysicist and poet Alan Lightman has noted, we can't help envisioning scientific discoveries in terms of things we know from daily life—spinning balls, waves in water, pendulums, weights on springs. "We have no other choice," Lightman reasons. "We cannot avoid forming mental pictures when we try to grasp the meaning of our equations, and how can we picture what we have not seen?"[1] In science as well as in poetry, it would seem, metaphors are necessary instruments of understanding.

In everyday speech, simile and metaphor occur frequently. We use metaphors ("She's a doll") and similes ("The tickets are selling like hotcakes") without being fully conscious of them. If, however, we are aware that words possess literal meanings as well as figurative ones, we do not write *died in the wool* for *dyed in the wool* or *tow the line* for *toe the line*, nor do we use **mixed metaphors** as did the writer who advised, "Water the spark of knowledge and it will bear fruit," or the speaker who urged, "To get ahead, keep your nose to the grindstone, your shoulder to the wheel, your ear to the ground, and your eye on the ball." Perhaps the unintended humor of these statements comes from our seeing that the writer, busy stringing together stale metaphors, was not aware that they had any physical reference.

Unlike a writer who thoughtlessly mixes metaphors, a good poet can join together incongruous things and still keep the reader's respect. In his ballad "Thirty Bob a Week," John Davidson has a British workingman tell how it feels to try to support a large family on small wages:

> It's a naked child against a hungry wolf;
> It's playing bowls upon a splitting wreck;
> It's walking on a string across a gulf
> With millstones fore-and-aft about your neck;
> But the thing is daily done by many and many a one;
> And we fall, face forward, fighting, on the deck.

Like the man with his nose to the grindstone, Davidson's wage earner is in an absurd fix; but his balancing act seems far from merely nonsensical. For every one of the poet's comparisons—of workingman to child, to bowler, to tight rope walker, and to seaman—offers suggestions of a similar kind. All help us see (and imagine) the workingman's hard life: a brave and unyielding struggle against impossible odds.

A poem may make a series of comparisons, like Davidson's, or the whole poem may be one extended comparison:

Emily Dickinson (1830–1886)*

MY LIFE HAD STOOD –   (ABOUT 1863)
A LOADED GUN

My Life had stood – a Loaded Gun –
In Corners – till a Day
The Owner passed – identified –
And carried Me away –

---

[1]"Physicists' Use of Metaphor," *The American Scholar* (Winter 1989): 99.

And now We roam in Sovreign Woods –
And now We hunt the Doe –
And every time I speak for Him –
The Mountains straight reply –

And do I smile, such cordial light
Upon the Valley glow –
It is as a Vesuvian face
Had let its pleasure through –

And when at Night – Our good Day done –
I guard My Master's Head –
'Tis better than the Eider-Duck's
Deep Pillow – to have shared –

To foe of His – I'm deadly foe –
None stir the second time –
On whom I lay a Yellow Eye –
Or an emphatic Thumb –

Though I than He – may longer live
He longer must – than I –
For I have but the power to kill,
Without – the power to die –

How much life metaphors bring to poetry may be seen by comparing two poems by Tennyson and Blake.

Alfred, Lord Tennyson (1809–1892)*

FLOWER IN THE CRANNIED WALL   1869

Flower in the crannied wall,
I pluck you out of the crannies,
I hold you here, root and all, in my hand,
Little flower—but *if* I could understand
What you are, root and all, and all in all,
I should know what God and man is.

How many metaphors does this poem contain? None. Compare it with a briefer poem on a similar theme: the quatrain that begins Blake's "Auguries of Innocence." (We follow here the opinion of W. B. Yeats, who, in editing Blake's poems, thought the lines ought to be printed separately.)

William Blake (1757–1827)*

To see a world in a grain of sand

(ABOUT 1803)

To see a world in a grain of sand
And a heaven in a wild flower,
Hold infinity in the palm of your hand
And eternity in an hour.

Set beside Blake's poem, Tennyson's—short though it is—seems lengthy. What contributes to the richness of "To see a world in a grain of sand" is Blake's use of a metaphor in every line. And every metaphor is loaded with suggestion. Our world does indeed resemble a grain of sand: in being round, in being stony, in being one of a myriad (the suggestions go on and on). Like Blake's grain of sand, a metaphor holds much, within a small circumference.

Sylvia Plath (1932–1963)*

Metaphors

1960

I'm a riddle in nine syllables,
An elephant, a ponderous house,
A melon strolling on two tendrils.
O red fruit, ivory, fine timbers!
This loaf's big with its yeasty rising.   5
Money's new-minted in this fat purse.
I'm a means, a stage, a cow in calf.
I've eaten a bag of green apples,
Boarded the train there's no getting off.

Questions

1. To what central fact do all the metaphors in this poem refer?
2. In the first line, what has the speaker in common with a riddle? Why does she say she has *nine* syllables?

N. Scott Momaday (b. 1934)

Simile

1974

What did we say to each other
that now we are as the deer
who walk in single file

with heads high
with ears forward   5
with eyes watchful
with hooves always placed on firm ground
in whose limbs there is latent flight

QUESTIONS

1. Momaday never tells us what was said. Does this omission keep us from understanding the comparison?
2. The comparison is extended with each detail adding some new twist. Explain the implications of the last line.

EXPERIMENT: *Likening*

Write a poem that follows the method of N. Scott Momaday's "Simile," consisting of one
long comparison between two objects. Possible subjects might include: Talking to a loved
one long-distance. What you feel like going to a weekend job. Being on a diet. Not being
noticed by someone you love. Winning a lottery.

Emily Dickinson (1830–1886)*

IT DROPPED SO LOW –   (ABOUT 1863)
IN MY REGARD

It dropped so low – in my Regard –
I heard it hit the Ground –
And go to pieces on the Stones
At bottom of my Mind –

Yet blamed the Fate that flung it – *less*   5
Than I denounced Myself,
For entertaining Plated Wares
Upon My Silver Shelf –

QUESTIONS

1. What is *it*? What two things are compared?
2. How much of the poem develops and amplifies this comparison?

Craig Raine (b. 1944)

A MARTIAN SENDS A POSTCARD HOME   1979

Caxtons are mechanical birds with many wings
and some are treasured for their markings—

they cause the eyes to melt
or the body to shriek without pain.

I have never seen one fly, but   5
sometimes they perch on the hand.

Mist is when the sky is tired of flight
and rests its soft machine on ground:

then the world is dim and bookish
like engravings under tissue paper.   10

Rain is when the earth is television.
It has the property of making colours darker.

Model T is a room with the lock inside—
a key is turned to free the world

for movement, so quick there is a film   15
to watch for anything missed.

But time is tied to the wrist
or kept in a box, ticking with impatience.

In homes, a haunted apparatus sleeps,
that snores when you pick it up.   20

If the ghost cries, they carry it
to their lips and soothe it to sleep

with sounds. And yet, they wake it up
deliberately, by tickling with a finger.

Only the young are allowed to suffer   25
openly. Adults go to a punishment room

with water but nothing to eat.
They lock the door and suffer the noises

alone. No one is exempt
and everyone's pain has a different smell.   30

At night, when all the colours die,
they hide in pairs

and read about themselves—
in colour, with their eyelids shut.

A MARTIAN SENDS A POSTCARD HOME. The title of this poem literally describes its contents. A Martian briefly describes everyday objects and activities on earth, but the visitor sees them all from an
alien perspective. The Martian/author lacks a complete vocabulary and sometimes describes general
categories of things with a proper noun (as in Model T in line 13). 1 *Caxtons:* Books, since William
Caxton (c. 1422–1491) was the first person to print books in England.

QUESTION

Can you recognize *everything* the Martian describes and translate it back into Earth-based English?

EXERCISE: *What Is Similar?*

Each of these quotations contains a simile or a metaphor. In each of these figures of speech, what two things is the poet comparing? Try to state exactly what you understand the two things to have in common: the most striking similarity or similarities that the poet sees.

1.   All the world's a stage,
   And all the men and women merely players:
   They have their exits and their entrances,
   And one man in his time plays many parts,
   His acts being seven ages.
                    —William Shakespeare, *As You Like It*

2. When the hounds of spring are on winter's traces . . .
                    —Algernon Charles Swinburne, "Atalanta in Calydon"

3. . . . the sun gnaws the night's bone
   down through the meat and gristle.
                    —John Ridland, "Elegy for My Aunt"

4. Art is long, and Time is fleeting,
   And our hearts, though strong and brave,
   Still, like muffled drums are beating
   Funeral marches to the grave.
                    —Henry Wadsworth Longfellow, "A Psalm of Life"

5. "Hope" is the thing with feathers –
   That perches in the soul –
   And sings the tune without the words –
   And never stops – at all –
                    —Emily Dickinson, an untitled poem

6. Why should I let the toad *work*
      Squat on my life?
   Can't I use my wit as a pitchfork
      And drive the brute off?
                    —Philip Larkin, "Toads"

7. I wear my patience like a light-green dress
   and wear it thin.
                    —Emily Grosholz, "Remembering the Ardèche"

8. a laugh maybe, like glasses on a shelf
   suddenly found by the sun . . .
                    —Beth Gylys, "Briefly"

9. Anew electric fence,
   Its five barbed wires tight
   As a steel-stringed banjo.
                    —Van K. Brock, "Driving at Dawn"

10. Spring stirs Gossamer Beynon Schoolmistress like a spoon.
                    —Dylan Thomas, *Under Milk Wood*

11. Our headlight caught, as in a flashbulb's flare,
    A pair of hitchhikers.
                    —Paul Lake, "Two Hitchhikers"

12. My life seems like those country western songs:
    Some man in black keeps walkin' out the door . . .
                    —Dessa Crawford, "With Our Boots On"

Other Figures

When Shakespeare asks, in a sonnet,

> O! how shall summer's honey breath hold out
> Against the wrackful siege of batt'ring days,

it might seem at first that he mixes metaphors. How can a *breath* confront the battering ram of an invading army? But it is summer's breath and, by giving it to summer, Shakespeare makes the season a man or woman. It is as if the fragrance of summer were the breath within a person's body, and winter were the onslaught of old age.

Such is one instance of **personification:** a figure of speech in which a thing, an animal, or an abstract term (*truth, nature*) is made human. A personification extends throughout this whole short poem.

James Stephens (1882–1950)*

The Wind   1915

The wind stood up and gave a shout.
He whistled on his fingers and

Kicked the withered leaves about
And thumped the branches with his hand

And said he'd kill and kill and kill,   5
And so he will and so he will.

The wind is a wild man, and evidently it is not just any autumn breeze but a hurricane or at least a stiff gale. In poems that do not work as well as this one, personification may be employed mechanically. Hollow-eyed personifications walk the works of lesser English poets of the eighteenth century: Coleridge has quoted the beginning of one such neoclassical ode, "Inoculation! heavenly Maid, descend!" It is hard for the contemporary reader to be excited by William Collins's "The Passions, An Ode for Music" (1747), which personifies, stanza by stanza, Fear, Anger, Despair, Hope, Revenge, Pity, Jealousy, Love, Hate, Melancholy, and Cheerfulness, and has them listen to Music, until even "Brown Exercise rejoiced to hear, / And Sport leapt up, and seized his beechen spear." Still, in "Two Sonnets on Fame" John Keats makes an abstraction come alive in seeing Fame as "a wayward girl."

Hand in hand with personification often goes **apostrophe**: a way of addressing someone or something invisible or not ordinarily spoken to. In an apostrophe, a poet (in these examples Wordsworth) may address an inanimate object ("Spade! with which Wilkinson hath tilled his lands"), some dead or absent person ("Milton! thou shouldst be living at this hour"), an abstract thing ("Return, Delights!"), or a spirit ("Thou Soul that art the eternity of thought"). More often than not, the poet uses apostrophe to announce a lofty and serious tone. An "O" may even be put in front of it ("O moon!") since, according to W. D. Snodgrass, every poet has a right to do so at least once in a lifetime. But apostrophe doesn't have to be highfalutin. It is a means of giving life to the inanimate. It is a way of giving body to the intangible, a way of speaking to it person to person, as in the words of a moving American spiritual: "Death, ain't you got no shame?"

Most of us, from time to time, emphasize a point with a statement containing exaggeration: "Faster than greased lightning," "I've told him a thousand times." We speak, then, not literal truth but use a figure of speech called **overstatement** (or **hyperbole**). Poets too, being fond of emphasis, often exaggerate for effect. Instances are Marvell's profession of a love that should grow "Vaster than empires, and more slow" and John Burgon's description of Petra: "A rose-red city, half as old as Time." Overstatement can be used also for humorous purposes, as in a fat woman's boast (from a blues song): "Every time I shake, some skinny gal loses her home."[2] The opposite is **understatement,** implying more than is said. Mark Twain in *Life on the Mississippi* recalls how, as an apprentice steamboat-pilot asleep when supposed to be on watch, he was roused by the pilot and sent clambering to the pilot house: "Mr. Bixby was close behind, commenting." Another example is Robert Frost's line "One could do worse than be a swinger of birches"—the conclusion of a poem that has suggested that to swing on a birch tree is one of the most deeply satisfying activities in the world.

In **metonymy,** the name of a thing is substituted for that of another closely associated with it. For instance, we say "The White House decided," and mean the president did. When John Dyer writes in "Grongar Hill,"

> A little rule, a little sway,
> A sun beam on a winter's day,
> Is all the proud and mighty have
> Between the cradle and the grave,

we recognize that *cradle* and *grave* signify birth and death. A kind of metonymy, **synecdoche** is the use of a part of a thing to stand for the whole of it or vice versa. We say "She lent a hand," and mean that she lent her entire presence. Similarly, Milton in "Lycidas" refers to greedy clergymen as "blind mouths." Another kind of metonymy is the **transferred epithet:** a device of emphasis in which the poet attributes some characteristic of a thing to another thing closely associated with it. When Thomas Gray observes that, in the evening pastures, "drowsy tinklings lull the distant folds," he well knows that sheep's bells do not drowse, but sheep do. When Hart Crane, describing the earth as seen from an airplane, speaks of "nimble blue plateaus," he attributes the airplane's motion to the earth.

Paradox occurs in a statement that at first strikes us as self-contradictory but that on reflection makes some sense. "The peasant," said G. K. Chesterton, "lives in a larger world than the globe-trotter." Here, two different meanings of *larger* are contrasted: "greater in spiritual values" versus "greater in miles." Some paradoxical statements, however, are much more than plays on words. In a moving sonnet, the blind John Milton tells how one night he dreamed he could see his dead wife. The poem ends in a paradox:

> But oh, as to embrace me she inclined,
> I waked, she fled, and day brought back my night.

EXERCISE: *Paradox*

What paradoxes do you find in the following poem? For each, explain the sense that underlies the statement.

---

[2]Quoted by Amiri Baraka [LeRoi Jones] in *Blues People* (New York: Morrow, 1963).

Chidiock Tichborne (1568?–1586)

ELEGY, WRITTEN WITH HIS OWN HAND   1586
IN THE TOWER BEFORE HIS EXECUTION

My prime of youth is but a frost of cares,
   My feast of joy is but a dish of pain,
My crop of corn is but a field of tares,°   *weeds*
   And all my good is but vain hope of gain:
The day is past, and yet I saw no sun,   5
And now I live, and now my life is done.

My tale was heard, and yet it was not told,
   My fruit is fall'n, and yet my leaves are green,
My youth is spent, and yet I am not old,
   I saw the world, and yet I was not seen: 10
My thread is cut, and yet it is not spun,
And now I live, and now my life is done.

I sought my death, and found it in my womb,
   I looked for life, and saw it was a shade,
I trod the earth, and knew it was my tomb,   15
   And now I die, and now I was but made:
My glass is full, and now my glass is run,
And now I live, and now my life is done.

ELEGY, WRITTEN WITH HIS OWN HAND. Accused of taking part in the Babington Conspiracy, a plot by Roman Catholics against the life of Queen Elizabeth I, eighteen-year-old Chidiock Tichborne was hanged, drawn, and quartered at the Tower of London. That is virtually all we know about him.

Asked to tell the difference between men and women, Samuel Johnson replied, "I can't conceive, madam, can you?" The great dictionary-maker was using a figure of speech known to classical rhetoricians as *paronomasia,* better known to us as a **pun** or play on words. How does a pun operate? It reminds us of another word (or other words) of similar or identical sound but of very different denotation. Although puns at their worst can be mere piddling quibbles, at best they can sharply point to surprising but genuine resemblances. The name of a dentist's country estate, Tooth Acres, is accurate: aching teeth paid for the property. In his novel *Moby-Dick,* Herman Melville takes up questions about whales that had puzzled scientists: for instance, are the whale's spoutings water or gaseous vapor? And when Melville speaks pointedly of the great whale "sprinkling and mistifying the gardens of the deep," we catch his pun, and conclude that the creature both mistifies and mystifies at once.

    In poetry, a pun may be facetious, as in Thomas Hood's ballad of "Faithless Nelly Gray":

    Ben Battle was a soldier bold,
       And used to war's alarms;

But a cannon-ball took off his legs,
    So he laid down his arms!

Or it may be serious, as in these lines on war by E. E. Cummings:

the bigness of cannon
is skillful,

(*is skillful* becoming *is kill-ful* when read aloud), or perhaps, as in Shakespeare's song in *Cymbeline*, "Fear no more the heat o' th' sun," both facetious and serious at once:

Golden lads and girls all must,
As chimney-sweepers, come to dust.

Poets often make puns on images, thereby combining the sensory force of imagery with the verbal pleasure of wordplay. Find and explain the punning images in these three poems.

Margaret Atwood (b. 1939)*

You fit into me   1971

you fit into me
like a hook into an eye

a fish hook
an open eye

John Ashbery (b. 1927)*

The Cathedral Is   1979

Slated for demolition

George Herbert (1593–1633)*

The Pulley   1633

   When God at first made man,
Having a glass of blessings standing by—
Let us (said he) pour on him all we can;
Let the world's riches, which dispersèd lie,
    Contract into a span.   5

So strength first made a way,
Then beauty flowed, then wisdom, honor, pleasure:
When almost all was out, God made a stay,
Perceiving that, alone of all His treasure,
    Rest in the bottom lay.   10

For if I should (said he)
Bestow this jewel also on My creature,
He would adore My gifts instead of Me,
And rest in Nature, not the God of Nature:
    So both should losers be.   15

Yet let him keep the rest,
But keep them with repining restlessness;
Let him be rich and weary, that at least,
If goodness lead him not, yet weariness
    May toss him to My breast.   20

QUESTIONS

1. What different senses of the word *rest* does Herbert bring into this poem?
2. How do God's words in line 16, *Yet let him keep the rest,* seem paradoxical?
3. What do you feel to be the tone of Herbert's poem? Does the punning make the poem seem comic?
4. Why is the poem called "The Pulley"? What is its implied metaphor?

To sum up: even though figures of speech are not to be taken *only* literally, they refer us to a tangible world. By *personifying* an eagle, Tennyson reminds us that the bird and humankind have certain characteristics in common. Through *metonymy,* a poet can focus our attention on a particular detail in a larger object; through *hyperbole* and *understatement,* make us see the physical actuality in back of words. *Pun* and *paradox* cause us to realize this actuality, too, and probably surprise us enjoyably at the same time. Through *apostrophe,* the poet animates the inanimate and asks it to listen—speaks directly to an immediate god or to the revivified dead. Put to such uses, figures of speech have power. They are more than just ways of playing with words.

Louis MacNeice (1907–1963)

PLAIN SPEAKING   1941

In the beginning and in the end the only decent
Definition is tautology: man is man,
Woman woman, and tree tree, and world world,
Slippery, self-contained; catch as catch can.

Which when caught between the beginning and end   5
Turn other than themselves, their entities unfurled,
Flapping and overlapping—a tree becomes
A talking tower, and a woman becomes world.

Catch them in nets, but either the thread is thin
Or the mesh too big or, thirdly, the fish die   10
And man from false communion dwindles back
Into a mere man under a mere sky.

But dream was dream and love was love and what
Happened happened—even if the judge said
It should have been otherwise—and glitter glitters   15
And I am I although the dead are dead.

QUESTIONS

1. What figure of speech is used predominantly in this poem? (Look up the definition of *tautology*; does MacNeice use the word in its literal sense, or could its use in the poem also be considered a figure of speech?)
2. Does the poem use any other figures of speech? Give examples.
3. What stages in a person's life does the poet seem to mean by *the beginning*, *the end*, and the time *between the beginning and end*? According to the text, how does the way we use words at each stage reveal our assumptions and/or expectations at that time of life?
4. Is the mood at the end of the poem one of defeat or affirmation? How does the use of tautologies in the last stanza help provide the answer?

FOR REVIEW AND FURTHER STUDY

Robert Frost   (1874–1963)*

THE SILKEN TENT   1942

She is as in a field a silken tent
At midday when a sunny summer breeze
Has dried the dew and all its ropes relent,
So that in guys° it gently sways at ease,   *attachments that steady it*
And its supporting central cedar pole,   5
That is its pinnacle to heavenward
And signifies the sureness of the soul,
Seems to owe naught to any single cord,
But strictly held by none, is loosely bound
By countless silken ties of love and thought   10
To everything on earth the compass round,
And only by one's going slightly taut
In the capriciousness of summer air
Is of the slightest bondage made aware.

QUESTIONS

1. Is Frost's comparison of a woman and tent a simile or a metaphor?
2. What are the ropes or cords?
3. Does the poet convey any sense of this woman's character? What sort of person do you believe her to be?
4. Paraphrase the poem, trying to state its implied meaning. (If you need to be refreshed about paraphrase, turn back to page 6.) Be sure to include the implications of the last three lines.

Denise Levertov (1923–1997)*

LEAVING FOREVER   1964

He says the waves in the ship's wake
are like stones rolling away.
I don't see it that way.
But I see the mountain turning,
turning away its face as the ship   5
takes us away.

QUESTIONS

1. What do you understand to be the man's feelings about leaving forever? How does the speaker feel? With what two figures of speech does the poet express these conflicting views?
2. Suppose that this poem had ended in another simile (instead of its three last lines):

    I see the mountain as a suitcase
    left behind on the shore
    as the ship takes us away.

    How is Denise Levertov's choice of a figure of speech a much stronger one?

Jane Kenyon (1947–1995)

THE SUITOR   1978

We lie back to back. Curtains
lift and fall,
like the chest of someone sleeping.
Wind moves the leaves of the box elder;
they show their light undersides,   5
turning all at once
like a school of fish.
Suddenly I understand that I am happy.
For months this feeling
has been coming closer, stopping   10
for short visits, like a timid suitor.

In each simile you find in "The Suitor," exactly what is the similarity?

EXERCISE: *Figures of Speech*

Identify the central figure of speech in the following three short poems.

Robert Frost   (1874–1963)*

THE SECRET SITS   1936

We dance round in a ring and suppose,
But the Secret sits in the middle and knows.

H. D. [Hilda Doolittle]   (1886–1961)*

LOVE THAT I BEAR   1921

Love that I bear
within my heart, O speak;
tell how beneath the serpent-spotted shell,
the cygnets wait,
how the soft owl   5
opens and flicks with pride,
eye-lids of great bird-eyes,
when underneath its breast
the owlets shrink and turn.

A. R. Ammons   (1926–2001)

COWARD   1975

Bravery runs in my family.

Kay Ryan   (b. 1945)*

TURTLE   1994

Who would be a turtle who could help it?
A barely mobile hard roll, a four-oared helmet,
she can ill afford the chances she must take
in rowing toward the grasses that she eats.
Her track is graceless, like dragging   5
a packing-case places, and almost any slope

defeats her modest hopes. Even being practical,
she's often stuck up to the axle on her way
to something edible. With everything optimal,
she skirts the ditch which would convert   10
her shell into a serving dish. She lives
below luck-level, never imagining some lottery
will change her load of pottery to wings.
Her only levity is patience,
the sport of truly chastened things.   15

QUESTION

How many metaphors, similes, or implied metaphors can you spot in this poem?

Robinson Jeffers   (1887–1962)*

HANDS   1929

Inside a cave in a narrow canyon near Tassajara
The vault of rock is painted with hands,
A multitude of hands in the twilight, a cloud of men's palms,
     no more,
No other picture. There's no one to say
Whether the brown shy quiet people who are dead intended   5
Religion or magic, or made their tracings
In the idleness of art; but over the division of years these
     careful
Signs-manual are now like a sealed message
Saying: "Look: we also were human; we had hands, not paws.
     All hail
You people with the cleverer hands, our supplanters   10
In the beautiful country; enjoy her a season, her beauty, and
     come down
And be supplanted; for you also are human."

QUESTION

Identify examples of personification and apostrophe in "Hands."

Robert Burns   (1759–1796)*

OH, MY LOVE IS LIKE A RED, RED ROSE   (ABOUT 1788)

Oh, my love is like a red, red rose
     That's newly sprung in June;
My love is like the melody
     That's sweetly played in tune.

So fair art thou, my bonny lass,
   So deep in love am I;
And I will love thee still, my dear,
   Till a' the seas gang° dry.   5

                                                 go

Till a' the seas gang dry, my dear,
   And the rocks melt wi' the sun;   10
And I will love thee still, my dear,
   While the sands o' life shall run.

And fare thee weel, my only love!
   And fare thee weel awhile!
And I will come again, my love   15
   Though it were ten thousand mile.

WRITER'S PERSPECTIVE

Robert Frost

Robert Frost on Writing

THE IMPORTANCE OF POETIC METAPHOR   1930

I do not think anybody ever knows the discreet use of metaphors, his own and other peoples, the discreet handling of metaphor, unless he has been properly educated in poetry.

    Poetry begins in trivial metaphors, pretty metaphors, "grace" metaphors, and goes on to the profoundest thinking that we have. Poetry provides the one permissible way of saying one thing and meaning another. People say, "Why don't you say what you mean?" We never do that, do we, being all of us too much poets. We like to talk in parables and in hints and in indirections—whether from diffidence or some other instinct.

    I have wanted in late years to go further and further in making metaphor the whole of thinking. I find someone now and then to agree with me that all thinking, except mathematical thinking, is metaphorical, or all thinking except scientific thinking. The mathematical might be difficult for me to bring in, but the scientific is easy enough.

What I am pointing out is that unless you are at home in the metaphor, unless you have had your proper poetical education in the metaphor, you are not safe anywhere. Because you are not at ease with figurative values: you don't know the metaphor in its strength and its weakness. You don't know how far you may expect to ride it and when it may break down with you. You are not safe in science; you are not safe in history.

From "Education by Poetry"

━━▣ WRITING CRITICALLY ▣━━

How Metaphors Enlarge a Poem's Meaning

Poems have the particular power of helping us see one thing by pointing out another. One of the most distinctive ways poems manage this feat is by calling a thing by a different name, in other words, by creating a metaphor. Paradoxically, by connecting an object to something else, a metaphor can reveal interesting aspects of the original thing we might either never have noticed or have considered unimportant.

Usually we can see the main point of a good metaphor immediately, but in interpreting a poem, the practical issue sometimes arises on how far to extend a comparison. All readers recognize that metaphors enlarge meaning, but they also know that there is always some limit to the comparison and that in most poems the limit remains unstated. If at the dinner table a big brother calls his kid brother "a pig," he probably does not mean to imply that the child has a snout and a kinky tail. Most metaphors have a finite set of associations—even insults from a big brother.

If you plan an essay on a highly metaphorical poem, it is often useful to examine the key comparison or comparisons in the poem. Jot down the major metaphors (or similes). Under each comparison make a two-column list—one marked "true," the other "false." Now start exploring the connections between the object the poem presents and the thing to which it is being compared. What aspects of the comparison are true? Make this list as long as possible. In the second list write the aspects that the two objects do not truly share; this list soon sets the limits of the metaphorical connections. In poems in which the metaphor is rich and resonant, the "true" list will be much longer than the "false" list. In other poems, those in which the metaphor is narrowly focused on only limited connections between the two objects, the "false" list will quickly outpace the "true" list. Finally, once you have listed the key comparisons in the poem, see if there is any obvious connection between all the metaphors or similes themselves. Do they have something in common? Are all of them threatening? Inviting? Nocturnal? Exaggerated? Their similarities, if any, will almost certainly be significant.

Don't spend more than a few minutes on each list. The object is not to list every possible connection, but only to determine the general scope of the metaphor and its implications. If the poem has a central metaphor, its scope and function should now be clear.

WRITING ASSIGNMENT

In a short essay (approximately 500 words) create your own extended simile or metaphor. Choose something from your life—perhaps a physical possession such as a car or coat, a part of your body such as your face or hair, or even a personal memory or emotion—and compare it to something else. You may begin by comparing what you choose to something it resembles physically, but you are free to use any comparison you find meaningful. Extend the metaphor as far as you can. Use hyperbole or understatement, as appropriate, but keep the metaphorical connection true enough for the reader to see and enjoy some connection. Feel free to be humorous. If you borrow a metaphor from some poem in this chapter, make sure you add an original twist of your own.

FURTHER SUGGESTIONS FOR WRITING

1. Freely using your imagination, write a paragraph in which you make as many hyperbolic statements as possible. Then write another version, changing all your exaggeration to understatement. Then, in a concluding paragraph, sum up what this experiment shows you about figurative language. Some possible topics are "The Most Gratifying (or Terrifying) Moment of My Life," "The Job I Almost Landed," "The Person I Most Admire."
2. Choose a short poem rich in figurative language: Sylvia Plath's "Metaphors," say, or Burns's "Oh, my love is like a red, red rose." Rewrite the poem, taking for your model Howard Moss's deliberately bepiddling version of "Shall I compare thee to a summer's day?" Eliminate every figure of speech. Turn the poem into language as flat and unsuggestive as possible. (Just ignore any rime or rhythm in the original.) Then, in a paragraph, indicate lines in your revised version that seem glaringly worsened. In conclusion, sum up what your barbaric rewrite tells you about the nature of poetry.

7 Song

SINGING AND SAYING

Most poems are more memorable than most ordinary speech, and when music is combined with poetry, the result can be more memorable still. The differences between speech, poetry, and song may appear if we consider, first of all, this fragment of an imaginary conversation between two lovers:

> Let's not drink; let's just sit here and look at each other. Or put a kiss
>   inside my goblet and I won't want anything to drink.

Forgettable language, we might think; but let's try to make it a little more interesting:

> Drink to me only with your eyes, and I'll pledge my love to you
>   with my eyes;
> Or leave a kiss within the goblet, that's all I'll want to drink.

The passage is closer to poetry, but still has a distance to go. At least we now have a figure of speech—the metaphor that love is wine, implied in the statement that one lover may salute another by lifting an eye as well as by lifting a goblet. But the sound of the words is not yet especially interesting. Here is another try, by Ben Jonson:

> Drink to me only with thine eyes,
>   And I will pledge with mine;
> Or leave a kiss but in the cup,
>   And I'll not ask for wine.

In these opening lines from Jonson's poem "To Celia," the improvement is noticeable. These lines are poetry; their language has become special. For one thing, the lines rime (with an additional rime sound on *thine*). There is interest, too, in the proximity of the words *kiss* and *cup:* the repetition (or alliteration) of the *k* sound. The rhythm of the lines has become regular; generally every other word (or syllable) is stressed:

> DRINK to me ON-ly WITH thine EYES,
>   And I will PLEDGE with MINE;
> Or LEAVE a KISS but IN the CUP,
>   And I'LL not ASK for WINE.

All these devices of sound and rhythm, together with metaphor, produce a pleasing effect—more pleasing than the effect of "Let's not drink; let's look at each other." But the words became more pleasing still when later set to music:

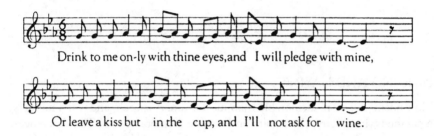

Drink to me on-ly with thine eyes, and I will pledge with mine,

Or leave a kiss but in the cup, and I'll not ask for wine.

In this memorable form, the poem is still alive today.

Ben Jonson   (1573?–1637)*

To Celia   1616

Drink to me only with thine eyes,
    And I will pledge with mine;
Or leave a kiss but in the cup,
    And I'll not ask for wine.
The thirst that from the soul doth rise   5
    Doth ask a drink divine;
But might I of Jove's nectar sup,
    I would not change for thine.

I sent thee late a rosy wreath,
    Not so much honoring thee   10
As giving it a hope that there
    It could not withered be.
But thou thereon didst only breathe,
    And sent'st it back to me;
Since when it grows, and smells, I swear,   15
    Not of itself but thee.

A compliment to a lady has rarely been put in language more graceful, more wealthy with interesting sounds. Other figures of speech besides metaphor make them unforgettable: for example, the hyperbolic tributes to the power of the lady's sweet breath, which can start picked roses growing again, and her kisses, which even surpass the nectar of the gods.

This song falls into stanzas—as many poems that resemble songs also do. A **stanza** (Italian for "stopping-place" or "room") is a group of lines whose pattern is repeated throughout the poem. Most songs have more than one stanza. When printed, the stanzas of songs and poems usually are set off from one another by space. When sung, stanzas of songs are indicated by a pause or by the introduction of a refrain, or chorus (a line or lines repeated). The word **verse,** which strictly refers to one line of a poem, is sometimes loosely used to mean a whole stanza: "All join in and sing the second verse!" In speaking of a stanza, whether sung or read, it is customary to indicate by a convenient algebra its **rime scheme,** the order in which rimed words recur. For instance, the rime scheme of this stanza by Herrick is *a b a b;* the first and third lines rime and so do the second and fourth:

> For shame or pity now incline
> To play a loving part,
> Either to send me kindly thine
> Or give me back my heart.

Refrains are words, phrases, or lines repeated at intervals in a song or song-like poem. A refrain usually follows immediately after a stanza, and when it does, it is called **terminal refrain.** A refrain whose words change slightly with each recurrence is called an **incremental refrain.** Sometimes we also hear an **internal refrain:** one that appears within a stanza, generally in a position that stays fixed throughout a poem. Both internal refrains and terminal refrains are used to great effect in the traditional song "The Cruel Mother."

Anonymous (traditional Scottish ballad)

The Cruel Mother

She sat down below a thorn,
> *Fine flowers in the valley,*
And there she has her sweet babe born
> *And the green leaves they grow rarely.*

"Smile na sae° sweet, my bonny babe,"   *so* 5
> *Fine flowers in the valley,*
"And° ye smile sae sweet, ye'll smile me dead."   *if*
> *And the green leaves they grow rarely.*

She's taen out her little pen-knife,
  Fine flowers in the valley,   10
And twinned° the sweet babe o' its life,   *severed*
  And the green leaves they grow rarely.

She's howket° a grave by the light of the moon,   *dug*
  Fine flowers in the valley,
And there she's buried her sweet babe in   15
  And the green leaves they grow rarely.

As she was going to the church,
  Fine flowers in the valley,
She saw a sweet babe in the porch
  And the green leaves they grow rarely.   20

"O sweet babe, and thou were mine,"
  Fine flowers in the valley,
"I wad cleed° thee in the silk so fine."   *dress*
  And the green leaves they grow rarely.

                                        25
"O mother dear, when I was thine,"
  Fine flowers in the valley,
"You did na prove to me sae kind."
  And the green leaves they grow rarely.

Taken by themselves, the refrain lines might seem mere pretty nonsense. But interwoven with the story of the murdered child, they form a terrible counterpoint. What do they come to mean? Possibly that Nature keeps going about her chores, unmindful of sin and suffering. The effect is an ironic contrast. Besides, by hearing the refrain over and over and over, we find it hard to forget.

    We usually meet poems as words on a page, but songs we generally first encounter as sounds in the air. Consequently, songs tend to be written in language simple enough to be understood on first hearing. But some contemporary songwriters have created songs that require listeners to pay close and repeated attention to their words. Beginning in the 1960s with performers like Bob Dylan, Leonard Cohen, Joni Mitchell, and Frank Zappa, some pop songwriters crafted deliberately challenging songs. More recently, Sting, Aimee Mann, Beck, and Suzanne Vega have written complex lyrics, often full of strange, dreamlike imagery. To unravel them, a listener may have to play the recording many times, with the treble turned up all the way. Anyone who feels that literary criticism is solely an academic enterprise should listen to high school and college students discuss the lyrics of their favorite songs.

    Many familiar poems began life as songs, but today, their tunes forgotten, they survive only in poetry anthologies. Shakespeare studded his plays with songs, and many of his contemporaries wrote verses to fit existing tunes. Some poets were themselves musicians (like Thomas Campion), and composed both words and music. In Shakespeare's day, **madrigals,** short secular songs for three or more voices arranged in counterpoint, enjoyed great popularity. A madrigal is always short, usually just one stanza, and rarely exceeds twelve or thirteen lines. Elizabethans loved to sing, and a person was considered a dolt if he or she could not join in a three-part song. Here is a madrigal from one of Shakespeare's comedies.

William Shakespeare   (1564–1616)*

TAKE, O, TAKE THOSE LIPS AWAY   (1604)

Take, O, take those lips away
   That so sweetly were forsworn,
And those eyes, the break of day,
   Lights that do mislead the morn;
But my kisses bring again, bring again,   5
Seals of love, but seal'd in vain, seal'd in vain.

TAKE, O, TAKE THOSE LIPS AWAY. This short song appears in *Measure for Measure*. It is sung by a boy in Act IV, just as we see Mariana, a deserted lover, for the first time.

Some poets who were not composers printed their work in madrigal books for others to set to music. In the seventeenth century, however, poetry and song seem to have fallen away from each other. By the end of the century, much new poetry, other than songs for plays, was written to be printed and to be silently read. Poets who wrote popular songs—like Thomas D'Urfey, compiler of the collection *Pills to Purge Melancholy*—were considered somewhat disreputable. With the notable exceptions of John Gay, who took existing popular tunes for *The Beggar's Opera,* and Robert Burns, who rewrote folk songs or made completely new words for them, few important English poets since Campion have been first-rate songwriters.

Occasionally, a poet has learned a thing or two from music. "But for the opera I could never have written *Leaves of Grass,*" said Walt Whitman, who loved the Italian art form for its expansiveness. Coleridge, Hardy, Auden, and many others have learned from folk ballads, and T. S. Eliot patterned his thematically repetitive *Four Quartets* after the structure of a quartet in classical music. "Poetry," said Ezra Pound, "begins to atrophy when it gets too far from music." Still, even in the twentieth century, the poet was more often a corrector of printer's proofs than a tunesmith or performer.

Some people think that to write poems and to travel about singing them, as many rock singer-composers now do, is a return to the venerable tradition of the **troubadours,** minstrels of the late Middle Ages. But there are differences. No doubt the troubadours had to please their patrons, but for better or worse their songs were not affected by a producer's video promotion budget or by the technical resources of a sound studio. Bob Dylan has denied that he is a poet, and Paul Simon once told an interviewer, "If you want poetry read Wallace Stevens."

Nevertheless, many rock lyrics have the verbal intensity of poetry. No rock lyric, however, can be judged independently of its musical accompaniment. A song joins words and music; a great song joins them inseparably. Although the words of a great song cannot stand on their own without their music, they are not invalidated as lyrics. Songwriters rarely create their lyrics to be read on the page. If the words seem rich and interesting in themselves, our enjoyment is only increased. Like most poems and songs of the past, most current songs may end up in the trash can of time. And yet, certain memorable rimed and rhythmic lines may live on, especially if they are expressed in stirring music and have been given wide exposure.

EXERCISE: *Comparing Poem and Song*

Compare the following poem by Edwin Arlington Robinson and a popular song lyric based on it. Notice what Paul Simon had to do to Robinson's original poem in order to make it into a song, and how Simon altered Robinson's conception.

Edwin Arlington Robinson   (1869–1935)*

RICHARD CORY   1897

Whenever Richard Cory went down town,
We people on the pavement looked at him:
He was a gentleman from sole to crown,
Clean favored, and imperially slim.

And he was always quietly arrayed,   5
And he was always human when he talked;
But still he fluttered pulses when he said,
"Good-morning," and he glittered when he walked.

And he was rich—yes, richer than a king—
And admirably schooled in every grace: 10
In fine,° we thought that he was everything   *in short*
To make us wish that we were in his place.

So on we worked, and waited for the light,
And went without the meat, and cursed the bread;
And Richard Cory, one calm summer night,   15
Went home and put a bullet through his head.

Paul Simon   (b. 1942)

RICHARD CORY   1966

With Apologies to E. A. Robinson

They say that Richard Cory owns
One half of this old town,
With elliptical connections
To spread his wealth around.
Born into Society,   5
A banker's only child,
He had everything a man could want:
Power, grace and style.

Refrain:

But I, I work in his factory
And I curse the life I'm livin'   10
And I curse my poverty
And I wish that I could be
Oh I wish that I could be
Oh I wish that I could be
Richard Cory.   15

The papers print his picture
Almost everywhere he goes:
Richard Cory at the opera,
Richard Cory at a show
And the rumor of his party   20
And the orgies on his yacht—
Oh he surely must be happy
With everything he's got.   *(Refrain.)*

He freely gave to charity,
He had the common touch,   25
And they were grateful for his patronage
And they thanked him very much,
So my mind was filled with wonder
When the evening headlines read:
"Richard Cory went home last night   30
And put a bullet through his head."   *(Refrain.)*

RICHARD CORY by Paul Simon. If possible, listen to the ballad sung by Simon and Garfunkel on
Sounds of Silence (Sony, 2001), © 1966 by Paul Simon. Used by permission.

Ballads

Any narrative song, like Paul Simon's "Richard Cory," may be called a **ballad.** In English, some of the most famous ballads are **folk ballads,** loosely defined as anonymous story-songs transmitted orally before they were ever written down. Sir Walter Scott, a pioneer collector of Scottish folk ballads, drew the ire of an old woman whose songs he had transcribed: "They were made for singing and no' for reading, but ye ha'e broken the charm now and they'll never be sung mair." The old singer had a point. Print freezes songs and tends to hold them fast to a single version. If Scott and others had not written them down, however, many would have been lost.

In his monumental work *The English and Scottish Popular Ballads* (1882–1898), the American scholar Francis J. Child winnowed out 305 folk ballads he considered authentic—that is, creations of illiterate or semiliterate people who had preserved them orally. Child, who worked by insight as well as by learning, did such a good job of telling the difference between folk ballads and other kinds that later scholars have added only about a dozen ballads to his count. Often called **Child ballads,** his texts include "The Three Ravens," "Sir Patrick Spence," "The Twa Corbies," "Edward," "The Cruel Mother," and many others still on the lips of singers. Here is one of the best-known Child ballads.

Anonymous   (traditional Scottish ballad)

Bonny Barbara Allan

It was in and about the Martinmas time,
  When the green leaves were afalling,
That Sir John Graeme, in the West Country,
  Fell in love with Barbara Allan.

He sent his men down through the town,   5
  To the place where she was dwelling;
"O haste and come to my master dear,
  Gin° ye be Barbara Allan."   *if*

O hooly,° hooly rose she up,   *slowly*
  To the place where he was lying,   10
And when she drew the curtain by:
  "Young man, I think you're dying."

"O it's I'm sick, and very, very sick,
  And 'tis a' for Barbara Allan."—
"O the better for me ye's never be,   15
  Tho your heart's blood were aspilling.

"O dinna ye mind,° young man," said she,   *don't you remember*
  "When ye was in the tavern adrinking,

That ye made the health° gae round and round,   *toasts*
   And slighted Barbara Allan?"   20

He turned his face unto the wall,
   And death was with him dealing:
"Adieu, adieu, my dear friends all,
   And be kind to Barbara Allan."

                                                                                               25
And slowly, slowly raise she up,
   And slowly, slowly left him,
And sighing said she could not stay,
   Since death of life had reft him.

She had not gane a mile but twa,
   When she heard the dead-bell ringing,   30
And every jow° that the dead-bell geid,   *stroke*
   It cried, "Woe to Barbara Allan!"

"O mother, mother, make my bed!
   O make it saft and narrow!
Since my love died for me today,   35
   I'll die for him tomorrow."

BONNY BARBARA ALLAN. 1 *Martinmas:* Saint Martin's day, November 11.

QUESTIONS

1. In any line does the Scottish dialect cause difficulty? If so, try reading the line aloud.
2. Without ever coming out and explicitly calling Barbara hard-hearted, this ballad reveals that she is. In which stanza and by what means is her cruelty demonstrated?
3. At what point does Barbara evidently have a change of heart? Again, how does the poem dramatize this change without explicitly talking about it?
4. In many American versions of this ballad, noble knight John Graeme becomes an ordinary citizen. The gist of the story is the same, but at the end are these further stanzas, incorporated from a different ballad:

> They buried Willie in the old churchyard
>   And Barbara in the choir;
> And out of his grave grew a red, red rose,
>   And out of hers a briar.
>
> They grew and grew to the steeple top
>   Till they could grow no higher;
> And there they locked in a true love's knot,
>   The red rose round the briar.

   Do you think this appendage heightens or weakens the final impact of the story? Can the American ending be defended as an integral part of a new song? Explain.
5. Paraphrase lines 9, 15–16, 22, 25–28. By putting these lines into prose, what has been lost?

As you can see from "Bonny Barbara Allan," in a traditional English or Scottish folk ballad the storyteller speaks of the lives and feelings of others. Even if the pronoun "I" occurs, it rarely has much personality. Characters often exchange dialogue, but no one character speaks all the way through. Events move rapidly, perhaps because some of the dull transitional stanzas have been forgotten. The events themselves, as ballad scholar Albert B. Friedman has said, are frequently "the stuff of tabloid journalism—sensational tales of lust, revenge and domestic crime. Unwed mothers slay their newborn babes; lovers unwilling to marry their pregnant mistresses brutally murder the poor women, for which, without fail, they are justly punished."[1] There are also many ballads of the supernatural ("The Twa Corbies") and of gallant knights ("Sir Patrick Spence"), and there are a few humorous ballads, usually about unhappy marriages.

A favorite pattern of ballad-makers is the so-called **ballad stanza,** four lines rimed *a b c b,* tending to fall into 8, 6, 8, and 6 syllables:

> Clerk Saunders and Maid Margaret
>   Walked owre yon garden green,
> And deep and heavy was the love
>   That fell thir twa between.°   *between those two*

Though not the only possible stanza for a ballad, this easily singable quatrain has continued to attract poets since the Middle Ages. Close kin to the ballad stanza is **common meter,** a stanza found in hymns such as "Amazing Grace," by the eighteenth-century English hymnist John Newton:

> Amazing grace! how sweet the sound
>   That saved a wretch like me!
> I once was lost, but now am found,
>   Was blind, but now I see.

Notice that its pattern is that of the ballad stanza except for its *two* pairs of rimes. That all its lines rime is probably a sign of more literate artistry than we usually hear in folk ballads. Another sign of schoolteachers' influence is that Newton's rimes are exact. (Rimes in folk ballads are often rough-and-ready, as if made by ear, rather than polished and exact, as if the riming words had been matched for their similar spellings. In "Barbara Allan," for instance, the hard-hearted lover's name rimes with *afalling, dwelling, aspilling, dealing,* and even with *ringing* and *adrinking.*) That so many hymns were written in common meter may have been due to convenience. If a congregation didn't know the tune to a hymn in common meter, they readily could sing its words to the tune of another such hymn they knew. Besides hymnists, many poets have favored common meter, among them A. E. Housman and Emily Dickinson.

---

[1]Introduction to *The Viking Book of Folk Ballads of the English-Speaking World,* ed. Albert B. Friedman (New York: Viking, 1956).

Related to traditional folk ballads but displaying characteristics of their own, **broadside ballads** (so called because they were printed on one sheet of paper) often were set to traditional tunes. Most broadside ballads were an early form of journalism made possible by the development of cheap printing and by the growth of audiences who could read, just barely. Sometimes merely humorous or tear-jerking, often they were rimed accounts of sensational news events. That they were widespread and often scorned in Shakespeare's day is attested by the character of Autolycus in *A Winter's Tale*, an itinerant hawker of ballads about sea monsters and strange pregnancies ("a usurer's wife was brought to bed of twenty money-bags"). Although many broadsides tend to be **doggerel** (verse full of irregularities due not to skill but to incompetence), many excellent poets had their work taken up and peddled in the streets—among them Marvell, Swift, and Byron.

Literary ballads, not meant for singing, are written by sophisticated poets for book-educated readers who enjoy being reminded of folk ballads. Literary ballads imitate certain features of folk ballads: they may tell of dramatic conflicts or of mortals who encounter the supernatural; they may use conventional figures of speech or ballad stanzas. Well-known poems of this kind include Keats's "La Belle Dame Sans Merci," Coleridge's "Rime of the Ancient Mariner," and (in our time) Dudley Randall's "Ballad of Birmingham."

Dudley Randall (1914–2000)*

BALLAD OF BIRMINGHAM   1966

*(On the Bombing of a Church in
Birmingham, Alabama, 1963)*

"Mother dear, may I go downtown
Instead of out to play,
And march the streets of Birmingham
In a Freedom March today?"

"No, baby, no, you may not go,   5
For the dogs are fierce and wild,
And clubs and hoses, guns and jail
Aren't good for a little child."

"But, mother, I won't be alone.
Other children will go with me,   10
And march the streets of Birmingham
To make our country free."

"No, baby, no, you may not go,
For I fear those guns will fire.
But you may go to church instead   15
And sing in the children's choir."

She has combed and brushed her night-dark hair,
And bathed rose petal sweet,
And drawn white gloves on her small brown hands,
And white shoes on her feet.   20

The mother smiled to know her child
Was in the sacred place,
But that smile was the last smile
To come upon her face.

                                                               25
For when she heard the explosion,
Her eyes grew wet and wild.
She raced through the streets of Birmingham
Calling for her child.

She clawed through bits of glass and brick,
Then lifted out a shoe.   30
"O here's the shoe my baby wore,
But, baby, where are you?"

QUESTIONS

1. This poem, about a dynamite blast set off in an African American church by a racial terrorist (later convicted), delivers a message without preaching. How would you sum up this message, its implied theme?
2. What is ironic in the mother's denying her child permission to take part in a protest march?
3. How does this modern poem resemble a traditional ballad?

EXPERIMENT: *Seeing the Traits of Ballads*

In "Poems for Further Reading" read the Child ballads "The Three Ravens" and "The Twa Corbies" (pages 442–44). With these ballads in mind, consider one or more of these modern poems:

W. H. Auden, "As I Walked Out One Evening" (page 448)
William Jay Smith, "American Primitive" (page 546)
William Butler Yeats, "Crazy Jane Talks with the Bishop" (page 571)

What characteristics of folk ballads do you find in them? In what ways do these modern poets depart from the traditions of folk ballads of the Middle Ages?

BLUES

Among the many song forms to have shaped the way poetry is written in English, no recent form has been more influential than the blues. Originally a type of folk music developed by black slaves in the South, **blues** songs have both a distinctive form and tone. They traditionally consist of three-line stanzas in which the first two identical lines are followed by a concluding riming third line:

To dream of muddy water—trouble is knocking at your door.
To dream of muddy water—trouble is knocking at your door.
Your man is sure to leave you and never return no more.

Early blues lyrics almost always spoke of some sadness, pain, or depriva-
tion—often the loss of a loved one. The melancholy tone of the lyrics, however, is not only world-weary but also world-wise. The blues expound the hard-
won wisdom of bitter life experience. They frequently create their special mood
through down-to-earth, even gritty, imagery drawn from everyday life. Although blues reach back into the nineteenth century, they were not widely
known outside African American communities before 1920, when the first
commercial recordings appeared. Their influence on both music and song from
that time was rapid and extensive. By 1930 James Weldon Johnson could declare, "It is from the blues that all that may be called American music derives
its most distinctive characteristic." Blues have not only become an enduring
category of popular music, they have also helped shape virtually all the major
styles of contemporary pop—jazz, rap, rock, gospel, country, and of course,
rhythm-and-blues.

The style and structure of blues have also influenced modern poets. Not only
have African American writers like Langston Hughes, Sterling A. Brown,
Etheridge Knight, and Sonia Sanchez written blues poems, but white poets as
dissimilar as W. H. Auden, Elizabeth Bishop, Donald Justice, and Sandra
McPherson have employed the form. The classic touchstones of the blues, however, remain the early singers such as Robert Johnson, Ma Rainey, Blind Lemon
Jefferson, Charley Patton, and—perhaps preeminently—Bessie Smith, "the
Empress of the Blues." Any form that has fascinated Bishop and Auden as well as
B. B. King, Mick Jagger, Tracy Chapman, and Eric Clapton surely deserves special notice. The blues remind us of how closely related song and poetry will al-
ways be. Here are the lyrics of one of Bessie Smith's earliest songs, based on a traditional folk blues, followed by a blues-influenced cabaret song written by W. H.
Auden (with the composer Benjamin Britten) for a night-club singer.

Bessie Smith (1898?–1937)
with Clarence Williams (1898–1965)

JAILHOUSE BLUES   1923

Thirty days in jail with my back turned to the wall.
Thirty days in jail with my back turned to the wall.
Look here, Mister Jailkeeper, put another gal in my stall.

I don't mind bein' in jail but I got to stay there so long.
I don't mind bein' in jail but I got to stay there so long.   5
Well, ev'ry friend I had has done shook hands and gone.

You better stop your man from ticklin' me under my chin.
You better stop your man from ticklin' me under my chin.
'Cause if he keep on ticklin' I'm sure gonna take him in.

10

Good mornin' blues, blues how do you do?
Good mornin' blues, blues how do you do?
Well, I just come here to have a few words with you.

W. H. Auden   (1907–1973)*

FUNERAL BLUES   1940

Stop all the clocks, cut off the telephone,
Prevent the dog from barking with a juicy bone,
Silence the pianos and muffled drum
Bring out the coffin, let the mourners come.

5

Let aeroplanes circle moaning overhead
Scribbling on the sky the message He Is Dead,
Tie crepe bows round the white necks of the public doves,
Let the traffic policemen wear black cotton gloves.

He was my North, my South, my East and West,
My working week and my Sunday rest,
10
My noon, my midnight, my talk, my song;
I thought that love would last for ever: I was wrong.

The stars are not wanted now: put out every one,
Pack up the moon and dismantle the sun,
Pour away the ocean and sweep up the woods;
15
For nothing now can ever come to any good.

QUESTIONS

What features of the traditional blues does Auden keep in his song? What features does he discard?

RAP

One of the most interesting musical and literary developments of the 1980s was the emergence of **rap,** a form of popular music in which words are recited to a driving rhythmic beat. It differs from mainstream popular music in several ways, but, most interesting in literary terms, rap lyrics are *spoken* rather than sung. In that sense, rap is a form of popular poetry as well as popular music. In most rap songs, the lead performer or "M.C." talks or recites, usually at top speed, long, rhythmic, four-stress lines that end in rimes. Although today most rap singers and groups use electronic or sampled backgrounds, rap began on city streets in the game of "signifying," in which two poets aim rimed insults at each other, sometimes accompanying their tirades with a beat made by clapping or finger-snapping. This game also includes boasts made by the players on both sides about their own abilities. Rap has developed so rapidly that it now uses a variety of metrical forms, but it is interesting to look more closely at some of the early work that established the genre. Most rap still follows the initial formula of rimed couplets that casually mix full rime with assonance. Here are a few lines from one of the first popular raps:

> I said, "By the way, baby, what's your name?"
> She said, "I go by the name Lois Lane.
> And you can be my boyfriend, you surely can
> Just let me quit my boyfriend, he's called Superman."

> —"Rapper's Delight," Sugarhill Gang, 1979

Rap is not written in the standard meters of English literary verse, but its basic measure does come out of the English tradition. Rap's characteristic four-stress, accentual line has been the most common meter for spoken popular poetry in English from Anglo-Saxon verse and the folk ballads to the work of Robert W. Service and Rudyard Kipling.

> What is a woman that you forsake her,
> And the hearth-fire and the home-acre,
> To go with the old grey Widow-maker?

> —"Harp Song of the Dane Women," Rudyard Kipling, 1906

The four-stress line is also a meter found throughout *Mother Goose*:

> Tom, Tom, the piper's son.
> Stole a pig and away did run
> The pig was eat, and Tom was beat
> Till he run crying down the street.

Rap deliberately makes use of stress-meter's ability to stretch and contract in syllable count. In fact, playing the syllable count against the beat is the basic metrical technique of rap. Like jazz, rap plays off a flexible rhythm against a fixed metrical beat, turning a traditional English folk meter into something distinctively African American. By hitting the beat hard while exploiting other elements of word music, rappers play interesting and elaborate games with the total rhythm of their lines. Here are the lyrics of an early rap recorded by Run D.M.C. that shows a sophisticated understanding of the traditions of English popular poetry (and makes direct references to a number of earlier literary works).

Run D.M.C. [J. Simmons/D. McDaniels]

from PETER PIPER   1986

Now Dr. Seuss and Mother Goose both did their thing
But Jam Master's getting loose and D.M.C.'s the king
'Cuz he's the adult entertainer, child educator
Jam Master Jay king of the cross-fader
He's the better of the best, best believe he's the baddest   5
Perfect timing when I'm climbing I'm the rhyming acrobatist
Lotta guts, when he cuts girls move their butts
His name is Jay, here to play, he must be nuts
And on the mix real quick, and I'd like to say
He's not Flash but he's fast and his name is Jay.   10

It goes a one, two, three and . . .
Jay's like King Midas, as I was told,
Everything that he touched turned to gold
He's the greatest of the great get it straight he's great
Claim fame 'cuz his name is known in every state   15
His name is Jay to see him play will make you say
God damn that D.J. made my day
Like the butcher, the baker, the candlestick maker
He's a maker, a breaker, and a title taker
Like the little old lady who lived in a shoe   20
If cuts were kids he would be through
Not lying y'all he's the best I know
And if I lie my nose will grow
Like a little wooden boy named Pinocchio
And you all know how the story go   25
Trix are for kids he plays much gigs
He's the big bad wolf and you're the 3 pigs
He's the big bad wolf in your neighborhood
Not bad meaning bad but bad meaning good . . . There it is!
We're Run D.M.C. got a beef to settle   30
Dee's not Hansel, he's not Gretel
Jay's a winner, not a beginner
His pocket gets fat, others' get thinner
Jump on Jay like cow jumped moon
People chase Jay like dish and spoon   35
And like all fairy tales end
You'll see Jay again my friend, hough!

PETER PIPER. (These lyrics were transcribed from the Run D.M.C. hit.) 2 *Jam Master Jay:* the DJ who
provides beats and scratching in the rap group. 4 *Cross-fader:* scratching device. 10 *Flash:* allusion either to Grandmaster Flash, another DJ, or the comic book superhero Flash; rap critics debate this
point.

For Review and Further Study

John Lennon   (1940–1980)
Paul McCartney   (b. 1942)

Eleanor Rigby   1966

Ah, look at all the lonely people!
Ah, look at all the lonely people!

Eleanor Rigby
Picks up the rice in the church where a wedding has been,
Lives in a dream,   5
Waits at the window
Wearing the face that she keeps in a jar by the door.
Who is it for?

All the lonely people,
Where do they all come from?   10
All the lonely people,
Where do they all belong?

Father McKenzie,
Writing the words of a sermon that no one will hear,
No one comes near   15
Look at him working,
Darning his socks in the night when there's nobody there.
What does he care?

All the lonely people
Where do they all come from?   20
All the lonely people
Where do they all belong?

Eleanor Rigby
Died in the church and was buried along with her name.
Nobody came.   25
Father McKenzie,
Wiping the dirt from his hands as he walks from the grave,
No one was saved.

All the lonely people,
Where do they all come from?   30
All the lonely people,
Where do they all belong?

Ah, look at all the lonely people!
Ah, look at all the lonely people!

Is there any reason to call this famous song lyric a ballad? Compare it with a traditional ballad, such as "Bonny Barbara Allan." Do you notice any similarity? What are the differences?

Bob Dylan (b. 1941)

THE TIMES THEY ARE a-CHANGIN' 1963

Come gather 'round people
Wherever you roam
And admit that the waters
Around you have grown
And accept it that soon   5
You'll be drenched to the bone.
If your time to you
Is worth savin'
Then you better start swimmin'
Or you'll sink like a stone   10
For the times they are a-changin'.

Come writers and critics
Who prophesize with your pen
And keep your eyes wide
The chance won't come again   15
And don't speak too soon
For the wheel's still in spin
And there's no tellin' who
That it's namin'.
For the loser now   20
Will be later to win
For the times they are a-changin'.

Come senators, congressmen
Please heed the call
Don't stand in the doorway   25
Don't block up the hall
For he that gets hurt
Will be he who has stalled
There's a battle outside
And it is ragin'.   30
It'll soon shake your windows
And rattle your walls
For the times they are a-changin'.

Come mothers and fathers
Throughout the land   35
And don't criticize
What you can't understand
Your sons and your daughters
Are beyond your command
Your old road is   40
Rapidly agin'.
Please get out of the new one
If you can't lend your hand
For the times they are a-changin'.

The line it is drawn   45
The curse it is cast
The slow one now
Will later be fast
As the present now
Will later be past   50
The order is
Rapidly fadin'.
And the first one now
Will later be last
For the times they are a-changin'.   55

QUESTIONS

1. What features does Dylan keep constant from stanza to stanza? What changes?
2. Who is addressed at the start of each stanza? How do those people affect what is said later in the same stanza?
3. Could the stanzas be sung in a different order without greatly changing the impact of the song? Or would any change undercut the structure of the song?
4. Do the words of this song work well on the page? Or is something essential lost when the music is taken away? Choose and defend one point of view.

Gwendolyn Brooks   (1917–2000)*

QUEEN OF THE BLUES   1945

Mame was singing
At the Midnight Club.
And the place was red
With blues.
She could shake her body   5
Across the floor.
For what did she have
To lose?

She put her mama
Under the ground   10
Two years ago.
(Was it three?)
She covered that grave
With roses and tears.
(A handsome thing   15
To see.)

She didn't have any
Legal pa
To glare at her,
To shame   20
Her off the floor
Of the Midnight Club.
Poor Mame.

She didn't have any
Big brother   25
To shout
"No sister of mine! . . ."
She didn't have any
Small brother
To think she was everything   30
Fine.

She didn't have any
Baby girl
With velvet
Pop-open eyes.   35
She didn't have any
Sonny boy
To tell sweet
Sonny boy lies.

"Show me a man   40
What will love me
Till I die.
Now show me a man
What will love me
Till I die.   45
Can't find no such man
No matter how hard
You try.
Go 'long, baby.
Ain't a true man left   50
In Chi.

"I loved my daddy.
But what did my daddy
Do?
I loved my daddy.   55
But what did my daddy
Do?
Found him a brown-skin chicken
What's gonna be
Black and blue.   60

"I was good to my daddy.
Gave him all my dough.
I say, I was good to my daddy.
I gave him all of my dough.
Scrubbed hard in them white folks'   65
Kitchens
Till my knees was rusty
And so'."

The M.C. hollered,
"Queen of the blues!
Folks, this is strictly   70
The queen of the blues!"
She snapped her fingers.
She rolled her hips.
What did she have
To lose?   75

But a thought ran through her
Like a fire.
"Men don't tip their
Hats to me.
They pinch my arms   80
And they slap my thighs.

But when has a man
Tipped his hat to me?"

Queen of the blues!
Queen of the blues!   85
Strictly, strictly,
The queen of the blues!

Men are low down
Dirty and mean.   90
Why don't they tip
Their hats to a queen?

QUESTIONS

1. How would you characterize the form of this poem? For what thematic reasons might the poet have chosen this form?
2. Do you think the poem would be more effective, or less so, if it were written in a more conventional "literary" style?

WRITER'S PERSPECTIVE

Paul McCartney

Paul McCartney on Writing

CREATING "ELEANOR RIGBY"   1978

Well, that ["Eleanor Rigby"] started off with sitting down at the piano and getting the first line of the melody, and playing around with the words. I think it was "Miss Daisy Hawkins" originally; then it was her picking up the rice in a church after a wedding. That's how nearly all our songs start, with the first line just suggesting itself from books or newspapers.

At first I thought it was a young Miss Daisy Hawkins, a bit like "Annabel Lee," but not so sexy; but then I saw I'd said she was picking up the rice in church, so she had to be a cleaner; she had missed the wedding, and she was suddenly lonely. In fact she had missed it all—she was the spinster type.

Jane° was in a play in Bristol then, and I was walking round the streets waiting for her to finish. I didn't really like "Daisy Hawkins"—I wanted a name that was more real. The thought just came: "Eleanor Rigby picks up the rice and lives in a dream"—so there she was. The next thing was Father McKenzie. It was going to be Father McCartney, but then I thought that was a bit of a hang-up for my Dad, being in this lonely song. So we looked through the phone book. That's the beauty of working at random—it does come up perfectly, much better than if you try to think it with your intellect.

Anyway there was Father McKenzie, and he was just as I had imagined him, lonely, darning his socks. We weren't sure if the song was going to go on. In the next verse we thought of a bin man, an old feller going through dustbins; but it got too involved—embarrassing. John and I wondered whether to have Eleanor Rigby and him have a thing going, but we couldn't really see how. When I played it to John we decided to finish it.

That was the point anyway. She didn't make it, she never made it with anyone, she didn't even look as if she was going to.

From *The Beatles in Their Own Words*

WRITING CRITICALLY

Is There a Difference Between Poetry and Song?

Poetry and song were originally one art, and even today the two forms remain closely related. We celebrate the beauty of a poem by praising its "music" just as we compliment a great song lyric by calling it "poetic." And yet a very simple distinction separates the two arts: in a song, the lyrics combine with music to create a collaborative total work, whereas in a poem the author must create all the effects by words alone.

In analyzing song lyrics as poetry, it is important to separate the words temporarily from their music. Before you transcribe the lyrics onto the page, listen to the song and jot down the three or four moments that affect you most powerfully. After you have transcribed the words, consult your notes and look at the lyrics. Are the effects that moved you in the recorded song still evident in the words alone? Or did they reside mostly in the music? Or did they perhaps originate in some special combination of words and music that is not adequately re-created by the text alone?

A song is no less powerful as a song just because the words don't stand on their own as poetry. A song is meant to be sung—transposing song lyrics onto the page changes their function. This exercise helps you understand lyrics as poetry, but do not scrutinize them unfairly relative to their original purpose.

Jane: refers to Jane Asher, a British actress McCartney was dating at the time.

Writing Assignment

Write a short paper (750–1000 words) in which you analyze the lyrics of a favorite song. Discuss what the words alone provide and what they lack in recreating the total power of the original song. The purpose of the paper is not to justify the song you have chosen as great poetry (though it may perhaps qualify); rather, it is to examine which parts of the song's power come solely from the words and which come from the music or performance. (Don't forget to provide your instructor with an accurate transcription of the song lyrics.)

Further Suggestions for Writing

1. Write a short study of a lyric (or lyrics) by a recent popular songwriter. Show why you believe the songwriter's work deserves the name of poetry.
2. Compare and contrast the English folk ballad "The Three Ravens" with the Scottish folk ballad "The Twa Corbies" (both in "Poems for Further Reading").
3. Compare the versions of "Richard Cory" by Edwin Arlington Robinson and by Paul Simon. Point out changes Simon apparently made in the poem to render it singable. What other changes did he make? How did he alter Robinson's story and its characters?
4. After listening to some recent examples of rap, compose a short rap lyric of your own, one that tells a story.

8 Sound

SOUND AS MEANING

Isak Dinesen, in a memoir of her life on a plantation in East Africa, tells how some Kikuyu tribesmen reacted to their first hearing of rimed verse:

> The Natives, who have a strong sense of rhythm, know nothing of verse, or at least did not know anything before the times of the schools, where they were taught hymns. One evening out in the maize-field, where we had been harvesting maize, breaking off the cobs and throwing them on to the ox-carts, to amuse myself, I spoke to the field laborers, who were mostly quite young, in Swahili verse. There was no sense in the verses, they were made for the sake of rime—"Ngumbe na-penda chumbe, Malaya mbaya. Wakamba na-kula mamba." The oxen like salt—whores are bad—The Wakamba eat snakes. It caught the interest of the boys, they formed a ring round me. They were quick to understand that meaning in poetry is of no consequence, and they did not question the thesis of the verse, but waited eagerly for the rime, and laughed at it when it came. I tried to make them themselves find the rime and finish the poem when I had begun it, but they could not, or would not, do that, and turned away their heads. As they had become used to the idea of poetry, they begged: "Speak again. Speak like rain." Why they should feel verse to be like rain I do not know. It must have been, however, an expression of applause, since in Africa rain is always longed for and welcomed.[1]

What the tribesmen had discovered is that poetry, like music, appeals to the ear. However limited it may be in comparison with the sound of an orchestra—or a

[1] Isak Dinesen, *Out of Africa* (New York: Random, 1972).

tribal drummer—the sound of words in itself gives pleasure. However, we might doubt Isak Dinesen's assumption that "meaning in poetry is of no consequence." "Hey nonny-nonny" and such nonsense has a place in song lyrics and other poems, and we might take pleasure in hearing rimes in Swahili; but most good poetry has meaningful sound as well as musical sound. Certainly the words of a song have an effect different from that of wordless music: they go along with their music and, by making statements, add more meaning. The French poet Isidore Isou, founder of a literary movement called *lettrisme,* maintained that poems can be written not only in words but also in letters (sample lines: *xyl, xyl, / prprali dryl / znglo trpylo pwi*). But the sound of letters alone, without denotation and connotation, has not been enough to make Letterist poems memorable. In the response of the Kikuyu tribesmen, there may have been not only the pleasure of hearing sounds but also the agreeable surprise of finding that things not usually associated had been brought together.

More powerful when in the company of meaning, not apart from it, the sounds of consonants and vowels can contribute greatly to a poem's effect. The sound of *s,* which can suggest the swishing of water, has rarely been used more accurately than in Surrey's line "Calm is the sea, the waves work less and less." When, in a poem, the sound of words working together with meaning pleases mind and ear, the effect is **euphony,** as in the following lines from Tennyson's "Come down, O maid":

> Myriads of rivulets hurrying through the lawn,
> The moan of doves in immemorial elms,
> And murmuring of innumerable bees.

Its opposite is **cacophony:** a harsh, discordant effect. It too is chosen for the sake of meaning. We hear it in Milton's scornful reference in "Lycidas" to corrupt clergymen whose songs "Grate on their scrannel pipes of wretched straw." (Read that line and one of Tennyson's aloud and see which requires lips, teeth, and tongue to do more work.) But note that although Milton's line is harsh in sound, the line (when we meet it in his poem) is pleasing because it is artful. In a famous passage from his *Essay on Criticism,* Pope has illustrated both euphony and cacophony. (Given here as Pope printed it, the passage relies heavily on italics and capital letters, for particular emphasis. If you will read these lines aloud, dwelling a little longer or harder on the words italicized, you will find that Pope has given you very good directions for a meaningful reading.)

Alexander Pope   (1688–1744)*

TRUE EASE IN WRITING COMES FROM ART,   1711
NOT CHANCE

True Ease in Writing comes from Art, not Chance,
As those move easiest who have learned to dance.
'Tis not enough no Harshness gives Offence,

The *Sound* must seem an *Echo* to the *Sense*.
Soft is the strain when *Zephyr*° gently blows,   *the west wind*   5
And the *smooth Stream* in *smoother Numbers*° flows;   *metrical rhythm*
But when loud Surges lash the sounding Shore,
The *hoarse, rough Verse* should like the *Torrent* roar.
When *Ajax* strives, some Rock's vast Weight to throw,
The Line too *labors*, and the Words move *slow*;   10
Not so, when swift *Camilla* scours the Plain,
Flies o'er th' unbending Corn, and skims along the Main.°   *expanse (of sea)*
Hear how *Timotheus'* varied Lays surprise,
And bid Alternate Passions fall and rise!
While, at each Change, the Son of *Lybian Jove*   15
Now *burns* with Glory, and then *melts* with Love;
Now his *fierce Eyes* with *sparkling Fury* glow;
Now *Sighs* steal out, and *Tears begin to flow*:
Persians and Greeks like *Turns of Nature* found,
And the *World's Victor* stood subdued by *Sound!*   20
The Pow'rs of Music all our Hearts allow;
And what *Timotheus* was, is *Dryden* now.

TRUE EASE IN WRITING COMES FROM ART, NOT CHANCE (*An Essay on Criticism*, lines 362–383).
9 *Ajax*: Greek hero, almost a superman, who in Homer's account of the siege of Troy hurls an enormous rock that momentarily flattens Hector, the Trojan prince (*Iliad* VII, 268–272). 11 *Camilla*: a kind of Amazon or warrior woman of the Volcians, whose speed and lightness of step are praised by the Roman poet Virgil: "She could have skimmed across an unmown grainfield / Without so much as bruising one tender blade; / She could have sped across an ocean's surge / Without so much as wetting her quicksilver soles" (*Aeneid* VII, 808–811). 13 *Timotheus*: favorite musician of Alexander the Great. In "Alexander's Feast, or The Power of Music," John Dryden imagines him: "Timotheus, placed on high / Amid the tuneful choir, / With flying fingers touched the lyre; / The trembling notes ascend the sky, / And heavenly joys inspire." 15 *Lybian Jove*: name for Alexander. A Libyan oracle had declared the king to be the son of the god Zeus Ammon.

Notice the pleasing effect of all the *s* sounds in the lines about the west wind and the stream, and in another meaningful place, the effect of the consonants in *Ajax strives*, a phrase that makes our lips work almost as hard as Ajax throwing the rock.

Is sound identical with meaning in lines such as these? Not quite. In the passage from Tennyson, for instance, the cooing of doves is not *exactly* a moan. As John Crowe Ransom pointed out, the sound would be almost the same but the meaning entirely different in "The murdering of innumerable beeves." While it is true that the consonant sound *sl-* will often begin a word that conveys ideas of wetness and smoothness—*slick, slimy, slippery, slush*—we are so used to hearing it in words that convey nothing of the kind—*slave, slow, sledgehammer*—that it is doubtful whether, all by itself, the sound communicates anything definite. The most beautiful phrase in the English language, according to Dorothy Parker, is *cellar door*. Another wit once nominated, as our most euphonious word, not *sunrise* or *silvery* but *syphilis*.

Relating sound more closely to meaning, the device called **onomatopoeia** is an attempt to represent a thing or action by a word that imitates the sound associated with it: *zoom, whiz, crash, bang, ding-dong, pitter-patter, yakety-yak*. Onomatopoeia is often effective in poetry, as in Emily Dickinson's line about the fly with its "uncertain stumbling Buzz," in which the nasal sounds *n, m, ng* and the sibilants *c, s* help make a droning buzz.

Like the Kikuyu tribesmen, others who care for poetry have discovered in the sound of words something of the refreshment of cool rain. Dylan Thomas, telling how he began to write poetry, said that from early childhood words were to him "as the notes of bells, the sounds of musical instruments, the noises of wind, sea, and rain, the rattle of milkcarts, the clopping of hooves on cobbles, the fingering of branches on the window pane, might be to someone, deaf from birth, who has miraculously found his hearing."[2] For readers, too, the sound of words can have a magical spell, most powerful when it points to meaning. James Weldon Johnson in *God's Trombones* has told of an old-time preacher who began his sermon, "Brothers and sisters, this morning I intend to explain the unexplainable—find out the indefinable—ponder over the imponderable—and unscrew the inscrutable!" The repetition of sound in *unscrew* and *inscrutable* has appeal, but the magic of the words is all the greater if they lead us to imagine the mystery of all Creation as an enormous screw that the preacher's mind, like a screwdriver, will loosen. Though the sound of a word or the meaning of a word may have value all by itself, both become more memorable when taken together.

William Butler Yeats (1865–1939)*

WHO GOES WITH FERGUS?   1892

Who will go drive with Fergus now,
And pierce the deep wood's woven shade,
And dance upon the level shore?
Young man, lift up your russet brow,
And lift your tender eyelids, maid,   5
And brood on hopes and fear no more.

And no more turn aside and brood
Upon love's bitter mystery;
For Fergus rules the brazen cars,°   *chariots*
And rules the shadows of the wood,   10
And the white breast of the dim sea
And all dishevelled wandering stars.

WHO GOES WITH FERGUS? *Fergus:* Irish king who gave up his throne to be a wandering poet.

[2]"Notes on the Art of Poetry," *Modern Poetics*, ed. James Scully (New York: McGraw-Hill, 1965).

QUESTIONS

1. In what lines do you find euphony?
2. In what line do you find cacophony?
3. How do the sounds of these lines stress what is said in them?

EXERCISE: *Listening to Meaning*

Read aloud the following brief poems. In the sounds of which particular words are meanings well captured? In which of the poems below do you find onomatopoeia?

John Updike   (b. 1932)*
RECITAL   1963

> ROGER BOBO GIVES
> RECITAL ON TUBA
> —*Headline in the Times*

Eskimos in Manitoba,
   Barracuda off Aruba,
Cock an ear when Roger Bobo
   Starts to solo on the tuba.

Men of every station—Pooh-Bah,   5
   Nabob, bozo, toff, and hobo—
Cry in unison, "Indubi-
   Tably, there is simply nobo-

Dy who oompahs on the tubo,
Solo, quite like Roger Bubo!"   10

William Wordsworth   (1770–1850)*
A SLUMBER DID MY SPIRIT SEAL   1800

A slumber did my spirit seal;
   I had no human fears—
She seemed a thing that could not feel
   The touch of earthly years

No motion has she now, no force;   5
   She neither hears nor sees;
Rolled round in earth's diurnal course,
   With rocks, and stones, and trees.

Emanuel di Pasquale   (b. 1943)

RAIN   1971

Like a drummer's brush,
the rain hushes the surface of tin porches.

Aphra Behn   (1640?–1689)

WHEN MAIDENS ARE YOUNG   1687

When maidens are young, and in their spring,
Of pleasure, of pleasure let 'em take their full swing,
  Full swing, full swing,
And love, and dance, and play, and sing,
For Silvia, believe it, when youth is done,   5
There's nought but hum-drum, hum-drum, hum-drum,
There's nought but hum-drum, hum-drum, hum-drum.

ALLITERATION AND ASSONANCE

Listening to a symphony in which themes are repeated throughout each movement, we enjoy both their recurrence and their variation. We take similar pleasure in the repetition of a phrase or a single chord. Something like this pleasure is
afforded us frequently in poetry.

    Analogies between poetry and wordless music, it is true, tend to break down
when carried far, since poetry—to mention a single difference—has denotation.
But like musical compositions, poems have patterns of sounds. Among such patterns long popular in English poetry is **alliteration,** which has been defined as a
succession of similar sounds. Alliteration occurs in the repetition of the same
consonant sound at the beginning of successive words—"round and round the
rugged rocks the ragged rascal ran," or in this delightful stanza by Witter Bynner,
written nearly a century ago as part of an elaborate literary hoax:

> If I were only dafter
>   I might be making hymns
> To the liquor of your laughter
>   Or the lacquer of your limbs.

Or it may occur inside the words, as in Milton's description of the gates of Hell:

>   On a sudden open fly
> With impetuous recoil and jarring sound
> The infernal doors, and on their hinges grate
> Harsh thunder, that the lowest bottom shook
> Of Erebus.

The former kind is called **initial alliteration,** the latter **internal alliteration** or **hidden alliteration.** We recognize alliteration by sound, not by spelling: *know* and *nail* alliterate, *know* and *key* do not. In a line by E. E. Cummings, "colossal hoax of clocks and calendars," the sound of *x* within *hoax* alliterates with the *cks* in *clocks.* Incidentally, the letter *r* does not *always* lend itself to cacophony: elsewhere in *Paradise Lost* Milton said that

> Heaven opened wide
> Her ever-during gates, harmonious sound
> On golden hinges moving . . .

By itself, a letter-sound has no particular meaning. This is a truth forgotten by people who would attribute the effectiveness of Milton's lines on the Heavenly Gates to, say, "the mellow *o*'s and liquid *l* of *harmonious* and *golden.*" Mellow *o*'s and liquid *l*'s occur also in the phrase *moldy cold oatmeal,* which may have a quite different effect. Meaning depends on larger units of language than letters of the alphabet.

Poetry formerly contained more alliteration than it usually contains today. In Old English verse, each line was held together by alliteration, a basic pattern still evident in the fourteenth century, as in the following description of the world as a "fair field" in *Piers Plowman:*

> A *f*eir *f*eld *f*ul of *f*olk *f*ond I ther bi-twene,
> Of alle *m*aner of *m*en, the *m*ene and the riche . . .

Most poets nowadays save alliteration for special occasions. They may use it to give emphasis, as Edward Lear does: "*F*ar and *f*ew, *f*ar and *f*ew, / Are the *l*ands where the Jumb*l*ies *l*ive." With its aid they can point out the relationship between two things placed side by side, as in Pope's line on things of little worth: "The courtier's *p*romises, and sick man's *p*rayers." Alliteration, too, can be a powerful aid to memory. It is hard to forget such tongue twisters as "Peter Piper picked a peck of pickled peppers," or common expressions like "green as grass," "tried and true," and "from stem to stern." In fact, because alliteration directs our attention to something, it had best be used neither thoughtlessly nor merely for decoration, lest it call attention to emptiness. A case in point may be a line by Philip James Bailey, a reaction to a lady's weeping: "I saw, but *sp*ared to *sp*eak." If the poet chose the word *spared* for any meaningful reason other than that it alliterates with *speak,* the reason is not clear.

As we have seen, to repeat the sound of a consonant is to produce alliteration, but to repeat the sound of a *vowel* is to produce **assonance.** Like alliteration, assonance may occur either initially—"all the *aw*ful *au*guries"[3]—or internally— Edmund Spenser's "Her goodly *ey*es like sapphires shining bright, / Her forehead

---

[3]Some prefer to call the repetition of an initial vowel-sound by the name of alliteration: "apt alliteration's artful aid."

ivory white . . . " and it can help make common phrases unforgettable: "eager beaver," "holy smoke." Like alliteration, it slows the reader down and focuses attention.

A. E. Housman   (1859–1936)*

EIGHT O'CLOCK   1922

He stood, and heard the steeple
   Sprinkle the quarters on the morning town.
One, two, three, four, to market-place and people
   It tossed them down.

Strapped, noosed, nighing his hour,   5
   He stood and counted them and cursed his luck;
And then the clock collected in the tower
   Its strength, and struck.

QUESTIONS

1. Why does the protagonist in this brief drama curse his luck? What is his situation?
2. For so short a poem, "Eight O'Clock" carries a great weight of alliteration. What patterns of initial alliteration do you find? What patterns of internal alliteration? What effect is created by all this heavy emphasis?

Robert Herrick   (1591–1674)*

UPON JULIA'S VOICE   1648

So smooth, so sweet, so silv'ry is thy voice,
As, could they hear, the damned would make no noise,
But listen to thee (walking in thy chamber)
Melting melodious words, to lutes of amber.

UPON JULIA'S VOICE. 4 *amber:* either the fossilized resin from which pipestems are sometimes made today, and which might have inlaid the body of a lute; or an alloy of four parts silver and one part gold.

QUESTIONS

1. Is Julia speaking or singing? How do we know for sure?
2. In what moments in this brief poem does the sound of words especially help convey meaning?
3. Does Herrick's reference to the *damned* (presumably howling from Hell's torments) seem out of place?

EXPERIMENT: *Reading for Assonance*

Try reading aloud as rapidly as possible the following poem by Tennyson. From the difficulties you encounter, you may be able to sense the slowing effect of assonance. Then read the poem aloud a second time, with consideration.

Alfred, Lord Tennyson   (1809–1892)*

THE SPLENDOR FALLS ON CASTLE WALLS   1850

<blockquote>

The splendor falls on castle walls
    And snowy summits old in story;
The long light shakes across the lakes,
    And the wild cataract leaps in glory.
Blow, bugle, blow, set the wild echoes flying,   5
Blow, bugle; answer, echoes, dying, dying, dying.

O hark, O hear! how thin and clear,
    And thinner, clearer, farther going!
O sweet and far from cliff and scar°   *jutting rock*
    The horns of Elfland faintly blowing!   10
Blow, let us hear the purple glens replying:
Blow, bugle; answer, echoes, dying, dying, dying.

O love, they die in yon rich sky,
    They faint on hill or field or river;
Our echoes roll from soul to soul,   15
    And grow for ever and for ever.
Blow, bugle, blow, set the wild echoes flying,
And answer, echoes, answer, dying, dying, dying.

</blockquote>

RIME

Isak Dinesen's tribesmen, to whom rime was a new phenomenon, recognized at once that rimed language is special language. So do we, for, although much English poetry is unrimed, rime is one means to set poetry apart from ordinary conversation and bring it closer to music. A **rime** (or rhyme), defined most narrowly, occurs when two or more words or phrases contain an identical or similar vowel-sound, usually accented, and the consonant-sounds (if any) that follow the vowel-sound are identical: *hay* and *sleigh*, *prairie schooner* and *piano tuner*.[4] From these examples it will be seen that rime depends not on spelling but on sound.

Excellent rimes surprise. It is all very well that a reader may anticipate which vowel-sound is coming next, for patterns of rime give pleasure by satisfying expectations; but riming becomes dull clunking if, at the end of each line,

---

[4]Some definitions of *rime* would apply the term to the repetition of any identical or similar sound, not only a vowel-sound. In this sense, assonance is a kind of rime; so is alliteration (called **initial rime**).

the reader can predict the word that will end the next. Hearing many a jukebox song for the first time, a listener can do so: *charms* lead to *arms*, *skies above* to *love*. As Alexander Pope observes of the habits of dull rimesters,

Where'er you find "the cooling western breeze,"
In the next line it "whispers through the trees";
If crystal streams "with pleasing murmurs creep,"
The reader's threatened (not in vain) with "sleep" . . .

But who—given the opening line of this comic poem—could predict the lines that follow?

William Cole   (1919–2000)

ON MY BOAT ON LAKE CAYUGA   1985

On my boat on Lake Cayuga
I have a horn that goes "Ay-oogah!"
I'm not the modern kind of creep
Who has a horn that goes "beep beep."

Robert Herrick, in a more subtle poem, made good use of rime to indicate a startling contrast:

Then while time serves, and we are but decaying,
Come, my Corinna, come, let's go a-Maying.

Though good rimes seem fresh, not all will startle, and probably few will call to mind things so unlike as *May* and *decay*, *Cayuga* and *Ay-oogah*. Some masters of rime often link words that, taken out of text, might seem common and unevocative. Here are the opening lines of Rachel Hadas's poem, "Three Silences," which describe an infant feeding at a mother's breast:

Of all the times when not to speak is best,
mother's and infant's is the easiest,
the milky mouth still warm against her breast.

Hadas's rime words are not especially memorable in themselves, and yet these lines are—at least in part because they rime so well. The quiet echo of sound at the end of each line reinforces the intimate tone of the mother's moment with her child. Poetic invention may be driven home without rime, but it is rime sometimes that rings the doorbell. Admittedly, some rimes wear thin from too much use. More difficult to use freshly than before the establishment of Tin Pan Alley, rimes such as *moon*, *June*, *croon* seem leaden and to ring true would need an extremely powerful context. *Death* and *breath* are a rime that poets have used with wearisome frequency; another is *birth*, *earth*, *mirth*. And yet we cannot exclude these from the diction of poetry, for they might be the very words a poet would need in order to say something new and original.

Good poets, said John Dryden, learn to make their rime "so properly a part of the verse, that it should never mislead the sense, but itself be led and governed by it." The comment may remind us that skillful rime—unlike poor rime—is never a distracting ornament. Like other patterns of sound, rime can help a poet to group ideas, emphasize particular words, and weave a poem together. It can start reverberations between words and can point to connections of meaning.

To have an **exact rime,** sounds following the vowel sound have to be the same: *red* and *bread, wealthily* and *stealthily, walk to her* and *talk to her.* If final consonant sounds are the same but the vowel sounds are different, the result is **slant rime,** also called **near rime, off rime,** or **imperfect rime:** *sun* riming with *bone, moon, rain, green, gone, thin.* By not satisfying the reader's expectation of an exact chime, but instead giving a clunk, a slant rime can help a poet say some things in a particular way. It works especially well for disappointed letdowns, negations, and denials, as in Blake's couplet:

He who the ox to wrath has moved
Shall never be by woman loved.

Many poets have admired the unexpected and arresting effects of slant rime. One of the first poets to explore the possibilities of rhyming consonants in a consistent way was Wilfred Owen, an English soldier in World War I, who wrote his best poems in the thirteen months before he was killed in action. Seeking a poetic language strong enough to describe the harsh reality of modern war, Owen experimented with matching consonant sounds in striking ways:

Now men will go content with what we spoiled
Or, discontent, boil bloody, and be spilled,
They will be swift with the swiftness of the tigress.
None will break ranks, though nations trek from progress.
Courage was mine, and I had mystery,
Wisdom was mine, and I had mastery:
To miss the march of this retreating world
Into vain citadels that are not walled.

Consonance, a kind of slant rime, occurs when the rimed words or phrases have the same beginning and ending consonant sounds but a different vowel, as in *chitter* and *chatter.* Owen rimes *spoiled* and *spilled* in this way. Consonance is used in a traditional nonsense poem, "The Cutty Wren": "'O where are you going?' says *Milder* to *Malder.*" (W. H. Auden wrote a variation on it that begins, "'O where are you going?' said *reader* to *rider*," thus keeping the consonance.)

End rime, as its name indicates, comes at the ends of lines, **internal rime** within them. Most rime tends to be end rime. Few recent poets have used internal rime so heavily as Wallace Stevens in the beginning of "Bantams in Pine-Woods": "Chieftain Iffucan of Azcan in caftan / Of tan with henna hackles, halt!" (lines also heavy on alliteration). A poet may employ both end rime and internal rime in the same poem, as in Robert Burns's satiric ballad "The Kirk's Alarm":

> Orthodox, Orthodox, wha believe in John Knox,
>   Let me sound an alarm to your conscience:
> There's a heretic blast has been blawn i' the wast,°   west
>   "That what is not sense must be nonsense."

Masculine rime is a rime of one-syllable words (*jail, bail*) or (in words of more than one syllable) stressed final syllables: *di-VORCE, re-MORSE*, or *horse, re-MORSE*. **Feminine rime** is a rime of two or more syllables, with stress on a syllable other than the last: *TUR-tle, FER-tile*, or (to take an example from Byron) *in-tel-LECT-u-al, hen-PECKED you all*. Often it lends itself to comic verse, but can occasionally be valuable to serious poems, as in Wordsworth's "Resolution and Independence":

> We poets in our youth begin in gladness,
> But thereof come in the end despondency and madness.

or as in Anne Sexton's seriously witty "Eighteen Days Without You":

> and of course we're not married, we are a pair of scissors
> who come together to cut, without towels saying His. Hers.

Artfully used, feminine rhyme can give a poem a heightened musical effect for the simple reason that it offers the listener twice as many rhyming syllables in each line. In the wrong hands, however, that sonic abundance has the unfortunate ability of making a bad poem twice as painful to endure. Poets can also mix masculine and feminine rhymes, as in the following sonnet by James Reeves.

James Reeves (1909–1978)

Rough Weather   1972

To share with you this rough, divisive weather
And not to grieve because we have to share it,
Desire to wear the dark of night together
And feel no colder that we do not wear it,
Because sometimes my sight of you is clearer,   5
The memory not clouded by the sense,
To know that nothing now can make you dearer
Than does the close touch of intelligence,
To be the prisoner of your kindnesses
And tell myself I want you to be free,   10
To wish you here with me despite all this,

To wish you here, knowing you cannot be—
This is a way of love in our rough season,
This side of madness, the other side of reason.

QUESTIONS

Which rhymes in the poem are feminine? Which are masculine?

Serious poems containing feminine rimes of three syllables have been attempted, notably by Thomas Hood in "The Bridge of Sighs":

> Take her up tenderly,
> Lift her with care;
> Fashioned so slenderly,
> Young, and so fair!

But the pattern is hard to sustain without lapsing into unintended comedy, as in the same poem:

> Still, for all slips of hers,
> One of Eve's family—
> Wipe those poor lips of hers,
> Oozing so clammily.

It works better when comedy is wanted.

Hilaire Belloc   (1870–1953)

THE HIPPOPOTAMUS   1896

I shoot the Hippopotamus
   with bullets made of platinum,
Because if I use leaden ones
   his hide is sure to flatten 'em.

In **eye rime,** spellings look alike but pronunciations differ—*rough* and *dough, idea* and *flea, Venus* and *menus.* Strictly speaking, eye rime is not rime at all.

Rime in American poetry suffered a significant fall from favor in the early 1960s. A new generation of poets took for models the open forms of Whitman, Pound, and William Carlos Williams. In the last few decades, however, some poets have been skillfully using rime again in their work. Often called the **New Formalists,** these poets include Julia Alvarez, Annie Finch, R. S. Gwynn, Rachel Hadas, Mark Jarman, Paul Lake, Charles Martin, Marilyn Nelson, Gjertrud Schnackenberg, and Timothy Steele. Their poems often use rime and meter to present unusual contemporary subjects, but they also sometimes write poems that recollect, converse, and argue with the poetry of the past.

Still, most American poets don't write in rime; some even consider its possibilities exhausted. Such a view may be a reaction against the wearing thin of rimes by overuse or the mechanical and meaningless application of a rime scheme. Yet anyone who listens to children skipping rope in the street, making up rimes to delight themselves as they go along, may doubt that the pleasures of rime are ended; and certainly the practice of Yeats and Emily Dickinson, to name only two, suggests that the possibilities of slant rime may be nearly infinite. If successfully employed, as it has been at times by a majority of English-speaking poets whose work we care to save, rime runs through its poem like a spine: the creature moves by means of it.

William Butler Yeats (1865–1939)*

LEDA AND THE SWAN   1924

A sudden blow: the great wings beating still
Above the staggering girl, her thighs caressed
By the dark webs, her nape caught in his bill,
He holds her helpless breast upon his breast.

How can those terrified vague fingers push   5
The feathered glory from her loosening thighs?
And how can body, laid in that white rush,
But feel the strange heart beating where it lies?

A shudder in the loins engenders there
The broken wall, the burning roof and tower   10
And Agamemnon dead.
             Being so caught up,
So mastered by the brute blood of the air,
Did she put on his knowledge with his power
Before the indifferent beak could let her drop?

QUESTIONS

1. According to Greek mythology, the god Zeus in the form of a swan descended on Leda, a Spartan queen. Among Leda's children were Clytemnestra, Agamemnon's unfaithful wife, who conspired in his murder, and Helen, on whose account the Trojan war was fought. What does a knowledge of these allusions contribute to our understanding of the poem's last two lines?
2. The slant rime *up* / *drop* (lines 11, 14) may seem accidental or inept. Is it? Would this poem have ended nearly so well if Yeats had made an exact rime like *up* / *cup* or like *stop* / *drop*?

Gerard Manley Hopkins   (1844–1889)*

GOD'S GRANDEUR   (1877)

The world is charged with the grandeur of God.
  It will flame out, like shining from shook foil;
  It gathers to a greatness, like the ooze of oil
Crushed. Why do men then now not reck his rod?
Generations have trod, have trod, have trod;   5
  And all is seared with trade; bleared, smeared with toil;
  And wears man's smudge and shares man's smell: the soil
Is bare now, nor can foot feel, being shod.

And for all this, nature is never spent;
  There lives the dearest freshness deep down things;   10
And though the last lights off the black West went
  Oh, morning, at the brown brink eastward, springs—
Because the Holy Ghost over the bent
  World broods with warm breast and with ah! bright wings.

GOD'S GRANDEUR. 1 *charged:* as though with electricity. 3–4 *It gathers . . . Crushed:* The grandeur of God will rise and be manifest, as oil rises and collects from crushed olives or grain. 4 *reck his rod:* heed His law. 10 *deep down things:* Tightly packing the poem, Hopkins omits the preposition *in* or *within* before *things.* 11 *last lights . . . went:* When in 1534 Henry VIII broke ties with the Roman Catholic Church and created the Church of England.

QUESTIONS

1. In a letter Hopkins explained *shook foil* (line 2): "I mean foil in its sense of leaf or tinsel. . . . Shaken goldfoil gives off broad glares like sheet lightning and also, and this is true of nothing else, owing to its zigzag dints and creasings and network of small many cornered facets, a sort of fork lightning too." What do you think he meant by the phrase *ooze of oil* (line 3)? Would you call this phrase an example of alliteration?
2. What instances of internal rime does the poem contain? How would you describe their effects?
3. Point out some of the poet's uses of alliteration and assonance. Do you believe that Hopkins perhaps goes too far in his heavy use of devices of sound, or would you defend his practice?
4. Why do you suppose Hopkins, in the last two lines, says *over the bent / World* instead of (as we might expect) *bent over the world?* How can the world be bent? Can you make any sense out of this wording, or is Hopkins just trying to get his rime scheme to work out?

Fred Chappell   (b. 1936)

NARCISSUS AND ECHO   1985

Shall the water not remember   *Ember*
my hand's slow gesture, tracing above   *of*
its mirror my half-imaginary   *airy*

portrait? My only belonging   *longing;*
is my beauty, which I take   *ache*   5
away and then return, as love   *of*
teasing playfully the one being   *unbeing.*
whose gratitude I treasure   *Is your*
moves me. I live apart   *heart*
from myself, yet cannot   *not*   10
live apart. In the water's tone,   *stone?*
that brilliant silence, a flower   *Hour,*
whispers my name with such slight   *light:*
moment, it seems filament of air,   *fare*
the world become cloudswell.   *well.*   15

NARCISSUS AND ECHO. This poem is an example of **Echo Verse**, a form (which dates back to late classical Greek poetry) in which the final syllables of the lines are repeated back as a reply or commentary, often a punning one. *Narcissus:* a beautiful young man, in Greek mythology, who fell in love with his own reflection in the water of a well. He gradually pined away because he could not reach his love; upon dying, he changed into the flower that bears his name. *Echo:* a nymph who, according to Roman tradition, loved Narcissus. When her love was not returned, she pined away until only her voice was left.

QUESTIONS

1. This poem is a dialogue. What is the relation between the two voices? Does the first voice hear the second?
2. How does the meaning of the poem change if we read the speech of each voice separately?
3. Is the echo technique used in this poem a gimmick? Or does it allow the poet to express something he might not be able to in any other way?

Robert Frost   (1874–1963)*

DESERT PLACES   1936

Snow falling and night falling fast, oh, fast
In a field I looked into going past,
And the ground almost covered smooth in snow,
But a few weeds and stubble showing last.

The woods around it have it—it is theirs.   5
All animals are smothered in their lairs,
I am too absent-spirited to count;
The loneliness includes me unawares.

And lonely as it is, that loneliness
Will be more lonely ere it will be less—   10
A blanker whiteness of benighted snow
With no expression, nothing to express.

They cannot scare me with their empty spaces
Between stars—on stars where no human race is.
I have it in me so much nearer home   15
To scare myself with my own desert places.

QUESTIONS

1. What are these desert places that the speaker finds in himself? (More than one theory is possible. What is yours?)
2. Notice how many times, within the short space of lines 8–10, Frost says *lonely* (or *loneliness*). What other words in the poem contain similar sounds that reinforce these words?
3. In the closing stanza, the feminine rimes *spaces*, *race is*, and *places* might well occur in light or comic verse. Does "Desert Places" leave you laughing? If not, what does it make you feel?

READING AND HEARING POEMS ALOUD

Thomas Moore's "The light that lies in women's eyes"—a line rich in internal rime, alliteration, and assonance—is harder to forget than "The light burning in the gaze of a woman." Effective on the page, Moore's line becomes even more striking when heard aloud. Practice reading poetry aloud—there is no better way to understand a poem than to effectively read it aloud. Developing skill at reading poems aloud will not only deepen your understanding of literature, it will also improve your ability to speak in public.

Before trying to read a poem aloud to other people, understand its meaning as thoroughly as possible. If you know what the poet is saying and the poet's attitude toward it, you will be able to find an appropriate tone of voice and to give each part of the poem a proper emphasis.

Except in the most informal situations and in some class exercises, read a poem to yourself before trying it on an audience. No actor goes before the footlights without first having studied the script, and the language of poems usually demands even more consideration than the language of most contemporary plays. Prepare your reading in advance. Check pronunciations you are not sure of. Underline things to be emphasized.

Read more slowly than you would read aloud from a newspaper. Keep in mind that you are saying something to somebody. Don't race through the poem as if you are eager to get it over with.

Don't lapse into singsong. A poem may have a definite swing, but swing should never be exaggerated at the cost of sense. If you understand what the poem is saying and utter the poem as if you do, the temptation to fall into such a mechanical intonation should not occur. Observe the punctuation, making slight pauses for commas, longer pauses for full stops (periods, question marks, exclamation points).

If the poem is rimed, don't raise your voice and make the rimes stand out unnaturally. They should receive no more volume than other words in the poem, though a faint pause at the end of each line will call the listener's attention to them. This advice is contrary to a school that holds that, if a line does not end in any punctuation, one should not pause but run it together with the line following. The trouble is that, from such a reading, a listener may not be able to identify the rimes; besides, the line, that valuable unit of rhythm, is destroyed.

In some older poems rimes that look like slant rimes may have been exact rimes in their day:

Still so perverse and opposite,
As if they worshiped God for spite.
       —Samuel Butler, *Hudibras* (1663)

Soft yielding minds to water glide away,
And sip, with nymphs, their elemental tea.
       —Alexander Pope, "The Rape of the Lock" (1714)

Tyger! Tyger! burning bright
In the forests of the night,
What immortal hand or eye
Could frame thy fearful symmetry?
       —William Blake, "The Tyger" (1794)

You may wish to establish a consistent policy toward such shifting usage: is it worthwhile to distort current pronunciation for the sake of the rime?

Listening to a poem, especially if it is unfamiliar, calls for concentration. Merciful people seldom read poetry uninterruptedly to anyone for more than a few minutes at a time. Robert Frost, always kind to his audiences, used to intersperse poems with many silences and seemingly casual remarks—shrewdly giving his hearers a chance to rest from their labors and giving his poems a chance to settle in.

If, in first listening to a poem, you don't take in all its meaning, don't be discouraged. With more practice in listening, your attention span and your ability to understand poems read aloud will increase. Incidentally, following the text of poems in a book while hearing them read aloud may increase your comprehension, but it may not necessarily help you to *listen*. At least some of the time, close your book and let your ears make the poems welcome. That way, their sounds may better work for you.

Hearing recordings of poets reading their work can help both your ability to read aloud and your ability to listen. Not all poets read their poems well, but there is much to be relished in both the highly dramatic reading style of a Dylan Thomas and the quiet underplay of a Robert Frost. You need feel no obligation, of course, to imitate the poet's reading of a poem. You have to feel about the poem in your own way, in order to read it with conviction and naturalness.

Even if you don't have an audience, the act of speaking poetry can have its own rewards. Perhaps that is what Yvor Winters meant when he said that, even though poetry was written for "the mind's ear" as well as the physical ear, "yet the mind's ear can be trained only by way of the other, and the matter, practically considered, comes inescapably back to the reading of poetry aloud."[5]

EXERCISE: *Reading for Sound and Meaning*

Read these brief poems aloud. What devices of sound do you find in each of them? Try to explain what sound contributes to the total effect of the poem and how it reinforces what the poet is saying.

Michael Stillman   (b. 1940)

IN MEMORIAM JOHN COLTRANE   1972

Listen to the coal
rolling, rolling through the cold
   steady rain, wheel on

wheel, listen to the
turning of the wheels this night   5
   black as coal dust, steel

on steel, listen to
these cars carry coal, listen
   to the coal train roll.

IN MEMORIAM JOHN COLTRANE. John Coltrane (1926–1967) was a saxophonist whose originality, passion, and technical wizardry have had a deep influence on the history of modern jazz.

William Shakespeare   (1564–1616)*

FULL FATHOM FIVE   ABOUT 1611
THY FATHER LIES

Full fathom five thy father lies;
   Of his bones are coral made;
Those are pearls that were his eyes:
   Nothing of him that doth fade,
But doth suffer a sea change   5
Into something rich and strange.
Sea nymphs hourly ring his knell:
   Ding-dong.
Hark! now I hear them—*Ding-dong, bell.*

FULL FATHOM FIVE THY FATHER LIES. The spirit Ariel sings this song in *The Tempest* to Ferdinand, prince of Naples, who mistakenly thinks his father is drowned.

[5]"The Audible Reading of Poetry" (1951), reprinted in *The Function of Criticism* (Denver: Swallow, 1957) 81.

Chryss Yost (b. 1966)

LAI WITH SOUNDS OF SKIN   2000

Shall we dress in skin,
our living linen?
bone weft,
pull of masculine
into feminine,   5
the heft,
the warp, weave and spin
of carded days in

tightly-twisted thin
yarns that we begin—   10
like wool
like *will*, like *has been*,
spoken to silken—
to spool:
thick bolts of linen,   15
skin to skein to skin.

LAI WITH SOUNDS OF SKIN. The *lai* is a French poetic form. Yost uses a version that consists of two, rhymed, eight-line stanzas in an intricate syllabic pattern. Yost's title not only announces the form of the poem but also makes a sexual pun suggesting the poem's subject.

T. S. Eliot (1888–1965)*

VIRGINIA   1934

Red river, red river,
Slow flow heat is silence
No will is still as a river
Still. Will heat move
Only through the mocking-bird   5
Heard once? Still hills
Wait. Gates wait. Purple trees,
White trees, wait, wait,
Delay, decay. Living, living,
Never moving. Ever moving   10
Iron thoughts came with me
And go with me:
Red river, river, river.

VIRGINIA. This poem is one of a series entitled "Landscapes."

T. S. Eliot

T. S. Eliot on Writing

THE MUSIC OF POETRY   1942

I would remind you, first, that the music of poetry is not something which exists apart from the meaning. Otherwise, we could have poetry of great musical beauty which made no sense, and I have never come across such poetry. The apparent exceptions only show a difference of degree: there are poems in which we are moved by the music and take the sense for granted, just as there are poems in which we attend to the sense and are moved by the music without noticing it. Take an apparently extreme example—the non-sense verse of Edward Lear. His non-sense is not vacuity of sense: it is a parody of sense, and that is the sense of it. *The Fumblies* is a poem of adventure, and of nostalgia for the romance of foreign voyage and exploration; *The Yongy-Bongy Bo* and *The Dong with a Luminous Nose* are poems of unrequited passion—"blues" in fact. We enjoy the music, which is of a high order, and we enjoy the feeling of irresponsibility towards the sense. Or take a poem of another type, the *Blue Closet* of William Morris. It is a delightful poem, though I cannot explain what it means and I doubt whether the author could have explained it. It has an effect somewhat like that of a rune or charm, but runes and charms are very practical formulae designed to produce definite results, such as getting a cow out of a bog. But its obvious intention (and I think the author succeeds) is to produce the effect of a dream. It is not necessary, in order to enjoy the poem, to know what the dream means; but human beings have an unshakeable belief that dreams mean something: they used to believe—and many still believe—that dreams disclose the secrets of the future; the orthodox modern faith is that they reveal the secrets—or at least the more horrid secrets—of the past.

.   .   .

So, while poetry attempts to convey something beyond what can be conveyed in prose rhythms, it remains, all the same, one person talking to another; and this is just as true if you sing it, for singing is another way of talking. The immediacy of poetry to conversation is not a matter on which we can lay down exact laws. Every revolution in poetry is apt to be, and sometimes to announce itself to be a return to common speech. . . .

It would be a mistake, however, to assume that all poetry ought to be melodious, or that melody is more than one of the components of the music of words. Some poetry is meant to be sung; most poetry, in modern times, is meant to be spoken—and there are many other things to be spoken of besides the murmur of innumerable bees or the moan of doves in immemorial elms. Dissonance, even cacophony, has its place: just as, in a poem of any length, there must be transitions between passages of greater and less intensity, to give a rhythm of fluctuating emotion essential to the musical structure of the whole; and the passages of less intensity will be, in relation to the level on which the total poem operates, prosaic—so that, in the sense implied by that context, it may be said that no poet can write a poem of amplitude unless he is a master of the prosaic.

From "The Music of Poetry"

WRITING CRITICALLY

Is It Possible to Write About Sound?

Sound represents an essential aspect of most poems, but it can be an elusive element to isolate for analysis. Even professional critics often disagree about the sonic effects of particular poems.

The easiest way to write about the sound of a poem is usually to focus your discussion. Rather than trying to explain every possible auditory element a poem possesses, concentrate on a single, clearly defined aspect that strikes you as especially noteworthy. For example, you might demonstrate how elements of sound in a poem emphasize its literal meaning. Don't look for hidden meanings. Simply try to understand how sound helps communicate the poem's main theme. Here you might examine how certain features (for example, rime, rhythm, meter, alliteration, and so forth) add force to the literal meaning of each line. Or, for ironic poems, you might look at how those same elements undercut and change the surface meaning of the poem.

A good way to begin this sort of writing assignment is to make a list of the main auditory elements you find in the poem. Does it contain rime, meter, alliteration, assonance, euphony, cacophony, repetition, or onomatopoeia? Note each striking instance of the relevant elements. (Remember that in such detailed analysis, it often helps to choose a short poem. If you want to discuss a longer work, focus on a short passage from it.) See if you can find a stylistic pattern in the items you list. Does this poet favor alliteration or repetition? Let your data build up before you force any conclusions on the poem. As your list grows, ideas will probably occur to you that were not apparent earlier.

Writing Assignment

In a short essay, examine how one or two elements of sound strengthen the literal meaning of a short poem. Review the conventional terms for elements of sound found in this chapter (alliteration, assonance, slant rime, euphony, and so on) to make sure you are describing correctly the elements you discuss. Support your argument with specific examples from the poem. Possible topics include "Rime and Repetition in Fred Chappell's 'Narcissus and Echo,'" "Alliteration in Shakespeare's 'Full Fathom Five,'" and "Assonance and Repetition in Tennyson's 'The Splendor Falls on Castle Walls.'"

Further Suggestions for Writing

1. Write about a personal experience with reading poems aloud.
2. Explain why contemporary poets are right (or wrong) to abandon rime.
3. Consider the verbal music in W. H. Auden's "As I Walked Out One Evening" (or another selection from "Poems for Further Reading"). Analyze the poem for language with ear appeal and show how the poem's sound is of a piece with its meaning.

9 Rhythm

STRESSES AND PAUSES

Rhythms affect us powerfully. We are lulled by a hammock's sway, awakened by an alarm clock's repeated yammer. Long after we come home from a beach, the rising and falling of waves and tides continue in memory. How powerfully the rhythms of poetry also move us may be felt in folk songs of railroad workers and chain gangs whose words were chanted in time to the lifting and dropping of a sledgehammer, and in verse that marching soldiers shout, putting a stress on every word that coincides with a footfall:

> Your LEFT! TWO! THREE! FOUR!
> Your LEFT! TWO! THREE! FOUR!
> You LEFT your WIFE and TWEN-ty-one KIDS
> And you LEFT! TWO! THREE! FOUR!
> You'll NEV-er get HOME to-NIGHT!

A rhythm is produced by a series of recurrences: the returns and departures of the seasons, the repetitions of an engine's stroke, the beats of the heart. A rhythm may be produced by the recurrence of a sound (the throb of a drum, a telephone's busy signal), but rhythm and sound are not identical. A totally deaf person at a parade can sense rhythm from the motions of the marchers' arms and feet, from the shaking of the pavement as they tramp. Rhythms inhere in the motions of the moon and stars, even though when they move, we hear no sound.

In poetry, several kinds of recurrent *sound* are possible, including (as we saw in the last chapter) rime, alliteration, and assonance. But most often when we speak of the **rhythm** of a poem, we mean the recurrence of stresses and pauses in it. When we hear a poem read aloud, stresses and pauses are, of course, part of its sound. It is possible to be aware of rhythms in poems read silently, too.

A **stress** (or **accent**) is a greater amount of force given to one syllable in speaking than is given to another. We favor a stressed syllable with a little more breath and emphasis, with the result that it comes out slightly louder, higher in pitch, or longer in duration than other syllables. In this manner we place a stress on the first syllable of words such as *eagle, impact, open,* and *statue,* and on the second syllable in *cigar, mystique, precise,* and *until.* Each word in English carries at least one stress, except (usually) for the articles *a, an,* and *the,* the conjunction *and,* and one-syllable prepositions: *at, by, for, from, of, to, with.* Even these, however, take a stress once in a while: "Get WITH it!" "You're not THE Dolly Parton?" One word by it-self is seldom long enough for us to notice a rhythm in it. Usually a sequence of at least a few words is needed for stresses to establish their pattern: a line, a passage, a whole poem. Strong rhythms may be seen in most Mother Goose rimes, to which children have been responding for hundreds of years. This rime is for an adult to chant while jogging a child up and down on a knee:

> Here goes my lord
> A trot, a trot, a trot, a trot!
> Here goes my lady
> A canter, a canter, a canter, a canter!
> Here goes my young master
> Jockey-hitch, jockey-hitch, jockey-hitch, jockey-hitch!
> Here goes my young miss
> An amble, an amble, an amble, an amble!
> The footman lags behind to tipple ale and wine
> And goes gallop, a gallop, a gallop, to make up his time.

More than one rhythm occurs in these lines, as the make-believe horse changes pace. How do these rhythms differ? From one line to the next, the interval be-tween stresses lengthens or grows shorter. In "a TROT a TROT a TROT a TROT," the stress falls on every other syllable. But in the middle of the line "A CAN-ter a CAN-ter a CAN-ter a CAN-ter," the stress falls on every third syl-lable. When stresses recur at fixed intervals as in these lines, the result is called a **meter.** The line "A trot a trot a trot a trot" is in **iambic meter,** a succession of al-ternate unstressed and stressed syllables.[1] Of all rhythms in the English language, this one is most familiar; most of our traditional poetry is written in it and ordi-nary speech tends to resemble it.

Stresses embody meanings. Whenever two or more fall side by side, words gain in emphasis. Consider these hard-hitting lines from John Donne, in which accent marks have been placed, dictionary-fashion, to indicate the stressed syllables:

> Bat·ter my heart, three-per·soned God, for You
> As yet but knock, breathe, shine, and seek to mend.
> That I may rise and stand, o'er throw me, and bend
> Your force to break, blow, burn, and make me new.

---

[1] Another kind of meter is possible, in which the intervals between stresses vary. This is **accentual meter,** not often found in contemporary poetry. It is discussed in the second part of this chapter.

Unstressed (or **slack**) **syllables** also can direct our attention to what the poet means. In a line containing few stresses and a great many unstressed syllables, there can be an effect not of power and force but of hesitation and uncertainty. Yeats asks in "Among School Children" what young mother, if she could see her baby grown to be an old man, would think him:

> A com·pen·sa·tion for the pang of his birth
> Or the un·cer·tain·ty of his set·ting forth?

When unstressed syllables recur in pairs, the result is a rhythm that trips and bounces, as in Robert Service's rollicking line:

> A bunch of the boys were whoop·ing it up in the Ma·la·mute
> sa·loon . . .

or in Poe's lines—also light but meant to be serious:

> For the moon nev·er beams with·out bring·ing me dreams
> Of the beau·ti·ful An·na·bel Lee.

Apart from the words that convey it, the rhythm of a poem has no meaning. There are no essentially sad rhythms, nor any essentially happy ones. But some rhythms enforce certain meanings better than others do. The bouncing rhythm of Service's line seems fitting for an account of a merry night in a Klondike saloon; but it may be distracting when encountered in Poe's wistful elegy.

The special power of poetry comes from allowing us to hear simultaneously every level of meaning in language—denotation and connotation, image and idea, abstract content and physical sound. Since sound stress is one of the ways that the English language most clearly communicates meaning, any regular rhythmic pattern will affect the poem's effect. Poets learn to use rhythms that reinforce the meaning and the tone of a poem. As film directors know, any movie scene's effect can change dramatically if different background music accompanies the images. Master of the suspense film Alfred Hitchcock, for instance, could fill an ordinary scene with tension or terror just by playing nervous, grating music underneath it. We also often notice the powerful effect rhythm has on meaning when an author goes awry and tries to create a particular mood in a manner that seems to pull us in an opposing direction. In Eliza Cook's "Song of the Sea-Weed," for instance, the poet depicts her grim and ghoulish scene in a bouncy ballad meter that makes the tone unintentionally comic:

> Many a lip is gaping for drink,
>   And madly calling for rain;
> And some hot brains are beginning to think
>   Of a messmate's opened vein.

EXERCISE: *Get with the Beat*

In each of the following passages the author has established a strong rhythm. Describe how the rhythm helps establish the tone and meaning of the poem. How does each poem's beat seem appropriate to the tone and subject?

1. I sprang to the stirrup, and Joris and he;
   I galloped, Dirck galloped, we galloped all three;
   "Good speed," cried the watch as the gatebolts undrew;
   "Speed!" echoed the wall to us galloping through.
   Behind shut the postern, the lights sank to rest,
   And into the midnight we galloped abreast.
   > —Robert Browning, from "How They Brought the Good News
   > from Ghent to Aix"

2. I couldn't be cooler, I come from Missoula,
   And I rope and I chew and I ride.
   But I'm a heroin dealer, and I drive a four-wheeler
   With stereo speakers inside.
   My ol' lady Phoebe's out rippin' off C.B.'s
   From the rigs at the Wagon Wheel Bar,
   Near a Montana truck stop and a shit-outta-luck stop
   For a trucker who's driven too far.
   > —Greg Keeler, from "There Ain't No Such Thing as a Montana
   > Cowboy" (a song lyric)

3. Of all the lives I cannot live,
   I have elected one

   to haunt me till the margins give
   and I am left alone

   One life has sounded in my voice
   and made me like a stone—

   one that the falling leaves can sink
   not over, but upon.
   > —Annie Finch, "Dickinson"

4. Oh newsprint moonprint Marilyn!
   Rub ink from a finger
   to make your beauty mark.
   > —Rachel Eisler, from "Marilyn's Nocturne" (a poem about a
   > newspaper photograph of Marilyn Monroe)

5. The master, the swabber, the boatswain, and I,
   The gunner and his mate
   Loved Moll, Meg, and Marian, and Margery,
   But none of us cared for Kate;
   For she had a tongue with a tang
   Would cry to a sailor "go hang!"—
   She loved not the savor of tar nor of pitch
   Yet a tailor might scratch her where'er she did itch;
   Then to sea, boys, and let her go hang!
   > —William Shakespeare, a song from *The Tempest*

Rhythms in poetry are due not only to stresses but also to pauses. "Every nice ear," observed Alexander Pope (*nice* meaning "finely tuned"), "must, I believe, have observed that in any smooth English verse of ten syllables, there is naturally a pause either at the fourth, fifth, or sixth syllable." Such a light but definite pause within a line is called a **cesura** (or **caesura**), "a cutting." More liberally than Pope, we apply the name to any pause in a line of any length, after any word in the line. In studying a poem, we often indicate a cesura by double lines (‖). Usually, a cesura will occur at a mark of punctuation, but there can be a cesura even if no punctuation is present. Sometimes you will find it at the end of a phrase or clause or, as in these lines by William Blake, after an internal rime:

> And priests in black gowns ‖ were walking their rounds
> And binding with briars ‖ my joys and desires.

Lines of ten or twelve syllables (as Pope knew) tend to have just one cesura, though sometimes there are more:

> Cover her face: ‖ mine eyes dazzle: ‖ she died young.

Pauses also tend to recur at more prominent places—namely, after each line. At the end of a verse (from *versus*, "a turning"), the reader's eye, before turning to go on to the next line, makes a pause, however brief. If a line ends in a full pause—usually indicated by some mark of punctuation—we call it **end-stopped.** All the lines in this passage from Christopher Marlowe's *Doctor Faustus* (in which Faustus addresses the apparition of Helen of Troy) are end-stopped:

> Was this the face that launch'd a thousand ships,
> And burnt the topless towers of Ilium?
> Sweet Helen, make me immortal with a kiss.
> Her lips suck forth my soul: see, where it flies!
> Come, Helen, come, give me my soul again.
> Here will I dwell, for heaven is in these lips,
> And all is dross that is not Helena.

A line that does not end in punctuation and that therefore is read with only a slight pause after it is called a **run-on line.** Because a run-on line gives us only part of a phrase, clause, or sentence, we have to read on to the line or lines following, in order to complete a thought. All these lines from Robert Browning's "My Last Duchess" are run-on lines:

> Sir, 'twas not
> Her husband's presence only, called that spot
> Of joy into the Duchess' cheek: perhaps
> Frà Pandolf chanced to say "Her mantle laps
> Over my lady's wrist too much," or "Paint
> Must never hope to reproduce the faint
> Half-flush that dies along her throat." Such stuff
> Was courtesy, she thought . . .[2]

---

[2]The complete poem, "My Last Duchess," appears on page 16.

A passage in run-on lines has a rhythm different from that of a passage like Marlowe's in end-stopped lines. When emphatic pauses occur in the quotation from Browning, they fall within a line rather than at the end of one. The passage by Marlowe and that by Browning are in lines of the same meter (iambic) and the same length (ten syllables). What makes the big difference in their rhythms is the running on, or lack of it.

To sum up: rhythm is recurrence. In poems, it is made of stresses and pauses. The poet can produce it by doing any of several things: making the intervals between stresses fixed or varied, long or short; indicating pauses (cesuras) within lines; end-stopping lines or running them over; writing in short or long lines. Rhythm in itself cannot convey meaning. And yet if a poet's words have meaning, their rhythm must be one with it.

Gwendolyn Brooks   (1917–2000)*
We Real Cool   1960

> The Pool Players.
> Seven at the Golden Shovel.

We real cool. We
Left school. We

Lurk late. We
Strike straight. We

Sing sin. We   5
Thin gin. We

Jazz June. We
Die soon.

Question
Describe the rhythms of this poem. By what techniques are they produced?

Alfred, Lord Tennyson   (1809–1892)*
Break, Break, Break   (1834)

Break, break, break,
   On thy cold gray stones, O Sea!
And I would that my tongue could utter
   The thoughts that arise in me.

O well for the fisherman's boy,   5
   That he shouts with his sister at play!
O well for the sailor lad,
   That he sings in his boat on the bay!

And the stately ships go on
   To their haven under the hill;   10
But O for the touch of a vanish'd hand,
   And the sound of a voice that is still!

Break, break, break,
   At the foot of thy crags, O Sea!
But the tender grace of a day that is dead   15
   Will never come back to me.

QUESTIONS

1. Read the first line aloud. What effect does it create at the beginning of the poem?
2. Is there a regular rhythmic pattern in this poem? If so, how would you describe it?
3. The speaker claims that his or her thoughts are impossible to utter. Using evidence from the poem, can you describe the speaker's thoughts and feelings?

Ben Jonson   (1573–1637)*

SLOW, SLOW, FRESH FOUNT, KEEP TIME   1600
WITH MY SALT TEARS

Slow, slow, fresh fount, keep time with my salt tears;
   Yet slower yet, oh faintly, gentle springs;
List to the heavy part the music bears,
   Woe weeps out her division° when she sings.   *a part in a song*
      Droop herbs and flowers,   5
      Fall grief in showers;
      Our beauties are not ours;
         Oh, I could still,
Like melting snow upon some craggy hill,
   Drop, drop, drop, drop,   10
Since nature's pride is now a withered daffodil.

SLOW, SLOW, FRESH FOUNT. The nymph Echo sings this lament over the youth Narcissus in Jonson's play *Cynthia's Revels*. In mythology, Nemesis, goddess of vengeance, to punish Narcissus for loving his own beauty, caused him to pine away and then transformed him into a narcissus (another name for a *daffodil*, line 11).

QUESTIONS

1. Read the first line aloud rapidly. Why is it difficult to do so?
2. Which lines rely most heavily on stressed syllables?
3. In general, how would you describe the rhythm of this poem? How is it appropriate to what is said?

Alexander Pope   (1688–1744)*

ATTICUS   1735

How did they fume, and stamp, and roar, and chafe?
And swear, not Addison himself was safe.

Peace to all such! but were there one whose fires
True genius kindles, and fair fame inspires;
Blest with each talent, and each art to please,   5
And born to write, converse, and live with ease,
Should such a man, too fond to rule alone,
Bear, like the Turk, no brother near the throne,
View him with scornful, yet with jealous eyes,
And hate for arts that caused himself to rise;   10
Damn with faint praise, assent with civil leer,
And, without sneering, teach the rest to sneer;
Willing to wound, and yet afraid to strike,
Just hint a fault, and hesitate dislike;
Alike reserved to blame, or to commend,   15
A timorous foe, and a suspicious friend;
Dreading e'en fools, by flatterers besieged,
And so obliging, that he ne'er obliged;
Like Cato, give his little Senate laws,
And sit attentive to his own applause: 20
While wits and Templars every sentence raise,
And wonder with a foolish face of praise—
Who but must laugh, if such a man there be?
Who would not weep, if Atticus were he?

ATTICUS. In this selection from "An Epistle to Dr. Arbuthnot," Pope has been referring to dull versifiers and their angry reception of his satiric thrusts at them. With *Peace to all such!* (line 3) he turns to
his celebrated portrait of a rival man of letters, Joseph Addison. 19 *Cato:* Roman senator about whom
Addison had written a tragedy. 21 *Templars:* London lawyers who dabbled in literature.

QUESTIONS

1. In these lines—one of the most famous damnations in English poetry—what positive
   virtues, in Pope's view, does Addison lack?
2. Which lines are end-stopped? What is the effect of these lines on the rhythm of this
   passage? (Suggestion: read "Atticus" aloud.)

EXERCISE: *Two Kinds of Rhythm*

The following compositions in verse have lines of similar length, yet they differ greatly in rhythm. Explain how they differ and why.

Sir Thomas Wyatt (1503?–1542)*

WITH SERVING STILL (1528–1536)

With serving still°   *continually*
   This have I won,
For my goodwill
   To be undone;

And for redress   5
   Of all my pain,
Disdainfulness
   I have again°;   *in return*
And for reward
   Of all my smart   10
Lo, thus unheard,
   I must depart!

Wherefore all ye
   That after shall
By fortune be,   15
   As I am, thrall,

Example take
   What I have won,
Thus for her sake
   To be undone!   20

Dorothy Parker (1893–1967)

RÉSUMÉ 1926

Razors pain you;
Rivers are damp;
Acids stain you;
And drugs cause cramp.
Guns aren't lawful;   5
Nooses give;
Gas smells awful;
You might as well live.

METER

To enjoy the rhythms of a poem, no special knowledge of meter is necessary. All you need do is pay attention to stresses and where they fall, and you will perceive the basic pattern, if there is any. However, there is nothing occult about the study of meter. Most people find they can master its essentials in no more time than it takes to learn a complicated game such as chess. If you take the time, you will then have the pleasure of knowing what is happening in the rhythms of many a fine poem, and pleasurable knowledge may even deepen your insight into poetry. The following discussion, then, will be of interest only to those who care to go deeper into **prosody,** the study of metrical structures in poetry.

Far from being artificial constructions found only in the minds of poets, meters occur in everyday speech and prose. As the following example will show, they may need only a poet to recognize them. The English satirist Max Beerbohm, after contemplating the title page of his first book, took his pen and added two more lines.

Max Beerbohm   (1872–1956)

ON THE IMPRINT OF THE FIRST   (1896)
ENGLISH EDITION OF
THE WORKS OF MAX BEERBOHM

"London: JOHN LANE, *The Bodley Head*
   New York: Charles Scribner's Sons."
This plain announcement, nicely read,
   Iambically runs.

In everyday life, nobody speaks or writes in perfect iambic rhythm, except at moments: "a HAM on RYE and HIT the MUStard HARD!" (As we have seen, iambic rhythm consists of a series of syllables alternately unstressed and stressed.) Poets rarely speak in it for long, either—at least, not with absolute consistency. If you read aloud Max Beerbohm's lines, you'll hear an iambic rhythm, but not an unvarying one. And yet all of us speak with a rising and falling of stress *somewhat like* iambic meter. Perhaps, as the poet and scholar John Thompson has maintained, "The iambic metrical pattern has dominated English verse because it provides the best symbolic model of our language."[3]

To make ourselves aware of a meter, we need only listen to a poem, or sound its words to ourselves. If we care to work out exactly what a poet is doing, we *scan* a line or a poem by indicating the stresses in it. **Scansion,** the art of so doing, is not just a matter of pointing to syllables; it is also a matter of listening to a poem and making sense of it. To scan a poem is one way to indicate how to read it aloud; in order to see where stresses fall, you have to see the places where the poet wishes to put emphasis. That is why, when scanning a poem, you may find yourself suddenly understanding it.

An objection might be raised against scanning: isn't it too simple to pretend that all language (and poetry) can be divided neatly into stressed syllables and

---

[3]*The Founding of English Metre* (New York: Columbia UP, 1966) 12.

unstressed syllables? Indeed it is. As the linguist Otto Jespersen has said, "In reality there are infinite gradations of stress, from the most penetrating scream to the faintest whisper."[4] However, the idea in scanning a poem is not to reproduce the sound of a human voice. For that we would do better to buy a tape recorder. To scan a poem, rather, is to make a diagram of the stresses (and absences of stress) we find in it. Various marks are used in scansion; in this book we use ´ for a stressed syllable and ˘ for an unstressed syllable.

There are four common accentual-syllabic meters in English—iambic, anapestic, trochaic, and dactylic. Each is named for its basic **foot** (usually a unit of two or three syllables that contains one strong stress) or building block. Here are some examples of each meter.

1. **Iambic**—a line made up primarily of **iambs,** an unstressed syllable followed by a stressed syllable, ˘´. The iambic measure is the most common meter in English poetry. Many writers, such as Robert Frost, feel iambs most easily capture the natural rhythms of our speech.

   ˘ ´ ˘ ´ ˘ ´ ˘ ´ ˘ ´
   But soft, | what light | through yon | der win | dow breaks?
   —*William Shakespeare*

   ˘ ´ ˘ ´ ˘ ´ ˘ ´ ˘ ´
   When I | have fears | that I | may cease | to be
   —*John Keats*

   ˘ ´ ˘ ´ ˘ ´ ˘ ´
   If we | had world | e·nough | and time
   ˘ ´ ˘ ´ ˘ ´ ˘ ´
   This coy | ness, la | dy, were | no crime
   —*Andrew Marvell*

   ˘ ´ ˘ ´ ˘ ´ ˘ ´
   My life | had stood – | a load | ed Gun
   —*Emily Dickinson*

2. **Anapestic**—a line made up primarily of **anapests,** two unstressed syllables followed by a stressed syllable, ˘˘´. Anapestic meter resembles iambic but contains an extra unstressed syllable. Totally anapestic lines often start to gallop, so poets sometimes slow them down by substituting an iambic foot (as Poe does in "Annabel Lee").

   ˘ ˘ ´ ˘ ˘ ´ ˘ ˘ ´ ˘ ˘ ´
   The As·syr | ian came down | like a wolf | on the fold

   ˘ ˘ ´ ˘ ˘ ´ ˘ ˘ ´ ˘ ˘ ´
   And his co | horts were gleam | ing in pur | ple and gold.

   ˘ ˘ ´ ˘ ˘ ´ ˘ ˘ ´ ˘ ˘ ´
   And the sheen | of their spears | was like stars | on the sea

   ˘ ˘ ´ ˘ ˘ ´ ˘˘ ´ ˘ ˘ ´
   When the blue | wave rolls night | ly on deep | Gal·i·lee.
   —*Lord Byron*

---

[4] "Notes on Metre," (1933), reprinted in *The Structure of Verse: Modern Essays on Prosody,* ed. Harvey Gross, 2nd ed. (New York: Ecco P, 1979).

Now this | is the Law | of the Jun | gle—as old | and as true
| as the sky

And the Wolf | that shall keep | it may pros | per, | but the wolf
| that shall break | it must die.

—Rudyard Kipling

It was ma | ny and ma | ny a year | a·go

In a king | dom by | the sea

That a maid | en there lived | whom you | may know

By the name | of An | na·bel Lee.

—Edgar Allan Poe

3. **Trochaic**—a line made up primarily of **trochees,** a stressed syllable followed by an unstressed syllable, ′⌣. The trochaic meter is often associated with songs, chants, and magic spells in English. Trochees make a strong, emphatic meter that is often very mnemonic. Shakespeare and Blake used trochaic meter to exploit its magical associations. Notice how Blake drops the unstressed syllable at the end of his lines from "The Tyger." (The location of a missing syllable in a metrical foot is usually marked with a caret sign, ⌄.)

Dou·ble, | dou·ble, | toil and | trou·ble

Fi·re | burn and | caul·dron | bub·ble.

—Shakespeare

Ty·ger, | ty·ger, | burn·ing | bright

In the | for·est | of the | night ⌄

—William Blake

Go and | catch a | fall·ing | star

—John Donne

4. **Dactylic**—a line made up primarily of **dactyls,** one stressed syllable followed by two unstressed syllables, ′⌣⌣. The dactylic meter is less common in English than in classical languages like Greek or Latin. Used carefully, dactylic meter can sound stately, as in Longfellow's *Evangeline,* but it also easily becomes a prancing, propulsive measure and is often used in comic verse. Poets often drop the unstressed syllables at the end of a dactylic line, the omission usually being noted with a caret sign, ⌄.

This is the | for·est pri | me·val. The | mur·mur·ing | pines and the
| hem·lock

—Henry Wadsworth Longfellow

Take her up | ten·der·ly

Lift her with | care

Fash·ioned so | slen·der·ly

Young and so | fair.

—Thomas Hood

Puss·y·cat, | puss·y·cat, | where have you | been?
—Mother Goose

Iambic and anapestic meters are called **rising** meters because their movement rises from an unstressed syllable (or syllables) to stress; trochaic and dactylic meters are called **falling.** In the twentieth century, the bouncing meters—anapestic and dactylic—were used more often for comic verse than for serious poetry. Called feet, though they contain no unaccented syllables, are the **monosyllabic foot** (´) and the **spondee** (´´). Meters are not ordinarily made up of them; if one were, it would be like the steady impact of nails being hammered into a board—no pleasure to hear or to dance to. But inserted now and then, they can lend emphasis and variety to a meter, as Yeats well knew when he broke up the predominantly iambic rhythm of "Who Goes with Fergus?" (page 168) with the line

And the white breast of the dim sea,

in which two spondees occur. Meters are classified also by line lengths: *trochaic monometer*, for instance, is a line one trochee long, as in this anonymous brief comment on microbes:

Adam
Had 'em.

A frequently heard metrical description is **iambic pentameter:** a line of five iambs, a meter especially familiar because it occurs in all blank verse (such as Shakespeare's plays and Milton's *Paradise Lost*), heroic couplets, and sonnets. The commonly used names for line lengths follow:

monometer	one foot
dimeter	two feet
trimeter	three feet
tetrameter	four feet

pentameter	five feet
hexameter	six feet
heptameter	seven feet
octameter	eight feet

Lines of more than eight feet are possible but are rare. They tend to break up into shorter lengths in the listening ear.

When Yeats chose the spondees *white breast* and *dim sea*, he was doing what poets who write in meter do frequently for variety—using a foot other than the expected one. Often such a substitution will be made at the very beginning of a line, as in the third line of this passage from Christopher Marlowe's *Tragical History of Doctor Faustus*:

> ˘ ′ | ˘ ′ | ˘ ′ | ˘ ˘ ′ | ˘ ˘ ′
> Was this | the face | that launched | a thou | sand ships
> ˘ ′ | ˘ ′ | ˘ ′ | ˘ ′ | ˘ ′
> And burnt | the top | less tow'rs | of Il | i·um?
> ′ ′ | ˘ ′ | ˘ ˘ ′ | ˘ ′ | ˘ ′
> Sweet Hel | en, make | me im·mor | tal with | a kiss.

How, we might wonder, can that last line be called iambic at all? But it is, just as a waltz that includes an extra step or two, or leaves a few steps out, remains a waltz. In the preceding lines the basic iambic pentameter is established, and though in the third line the regularity is varied from, it does not altogether disappear. It continues for a while to run on in the reader's mind, where (if the poet does not stay away from it for too long) the meter will be when the poem comes back to it.

Like a basic dance step, a meter is not to be slavishly adhered to. The fun in reading a metrical poem often comes from watching the poet continually departing from perfect regularity, giving a few heel-kicks to display a bit of joy or ingenuity, then easing back into the basic step again. Because meter is orderly and the rhythms of living speech are unruly, poets can play one against the other, in a sort of counterpoint. Robert Frost, a master at pitting a line of iambs against a very natural-sounding and irregular sentence, declared, "I am never more pleased than when I can get these into strained relation. I like to drag and break the intonation across the meter as waves first comb and then break stumbling on a shingle."[5]

Evidently Frost's skilled effects would be lost to a reader who, scanning a Frost poem or reading it aloud, distorted its rhythms to fit the words exactly to the meter. With rare exceptions, a good poem can be read and scanned the way we would speak its sentences if they were ours. This, for example, is an unreal scansion:

> ˘ ′ | ˘ ′ | ˘ ′ | ˘ ′ | ˘ ′
> That's my last Duch·ess paint·ed on the wall.

—because no speaker of English would say that sentence in that way. We are likely to stress *That's* and *last*.

---

[5]Letter to John Cournos in 1914, in *Selected Letters of Robert Frost*, ed. Lawrance Thompson (New York: Holt, 1964) 128.

Although in good poetry we seldom meet a very long passage of absolute metrical regularity, we sometimes find (in a line or so) a monotonous rhythm that is effective. Words fall meaningfully in Macbeth's famous statement of world-weariness: "Tomorrow and tomorrow and tomorrow . . ." and in the opening lines of Thomas Gray's "Elegy":

> ⌣ ′ ⌣ ′　⌣ ′ ⌣ ′　⌣ ′
> The cur·few tolls the knell of part·ing day,
> ⌣ ′ ⌣　′　′　′　⌣ ′　⌣ ′
> The low·ing herd wind slow·ly o'er the lea,
> ⌣ ′　⌣ ′　⌣ ′ ⌣　⌣ ′
> The plow·man home·ward plods his wear·y way,
> ⌣　′　⌣ ′　⌣ ′　⌣ ⌣　⌣ ′
> And leaves the world to dark·ness and to me.

Although certain unstressed syllables in these lines seem to call for more emphasis than others—you might, for instance, care to throw a little more weight on the second syllable of *curfew* in the opening line—we can still say that the lines are notably iambic. Their almost unvarying rhythm seems just right to convey the tolling of a bell and the weary setting down of one foot after the other.

Besides the two rising meters (iambic, anapestic) and the two falling meters (trochaic, dactylic), English poets have another valuable meter. It is **accentual meter,** in which the poet does not write in feet (as in the other meters) but instead counts accents (stresses). The idea is to have the same number of stresses in every line. The poet may place them anywhere in the line and may include practically any number of unstressed syllables, which do not count. In "Christabel," for instance, Coleridge keeps four stresses to a line, though the first line has only eight syllables and the last line has eleven:

> ′　′　′　′
> There is not wind e·nough to twirl
> ′　′　′　′
> The one red leaf, the last of its clan,
> ′　′　′　′
> That dan·ces as of·ten as dance it can,
> ′　′　′　′
> Hang·ing so light, and hang·ing so high,
> ′　′　′　′
> On the top-most twig that looks up at the sky.

The history of accentual meter is long and honorable. Old English poetry was written in a kind of accentual meter, but its line was more rule-bound than Coleridge's: four stresses arranged two on either side of a cesura, plus alliteration of three of the stressed syllables. In "Junk," Richard Wilbur revives the pattern:

> ′　′　′　′
> An axe an·gles ‖ from my neigh·bor's ash·can . . .

Many poets, from the authors of Mother Goose rimes to Gerard Manley Hopkins, have sometimes found accentual meters congenial. Recently, accentual meter has enjoyed huge popularity through rap poetry, which usually employs a four-stress line (see page 154 for further discussion of rap).

It has been charged that the importation of Greek names for meters and of the classical notion of feet was an unsuccessful attempt to make a Parthenon out of English wattles. The charge is open to debate, but at least it is certain that Greek names for feet cannot mean to us what they meant to Aristotle. Greek and Latin poetry is measured not by stressed and unstressed syllables, but by long and short vowel sounds. An iamb in classical verse is one short syllable followed by a long syllable. Such a meter constructed on the principle of vowel length is called a **quantitative meter.** Campion's "Rose-cheeked Laura" was an attempt to demonstrate it in English, but probably we enjoy the rhythm of the poem's well-placed stresses whether or not we notice its vowel sounds.

Thomas Campion   (1567–1620)

ROSE-CHEEKED LAURA, COME   1602

Rose-cheeked Laura, come,
Sing thou smoothly with thy beauty's
Silent music, either other
    Sweetly gracing.

Lovely forms do flow   5
From concent° divinely framèd;   *harmony*
Heav'n is music, and thy beauty's
    Birth is heavenly.

These dull notes we sing
Discords need for helps to grace them;   10
Only beauty purely loving
    Knows no discord,

But still moves delight,
Like clear springs renewed by flowing,
Ever perfect, ever in them-   15
    Selves eternal.

Although less popular among poets today than formerly, meter endures. Major poets from Shakespeare through Yeats have fashioned their work by it, and if we are to read their poems with full enjoyment, we need to be aware of it. To enjoy metrical poetry—even to write it—you do not have to slice lines into feet; you do need to recognize when a meter is present in a line, and when the line departs from it. An argument in favor of meter is that it reminds us of body rhythms such as breathing, walking, the beating of the heart. In an effective metrical poem, these rhythms cannot be separated from what the poet is saying—or, in the words of an old jazz song of Duke Ellington, "It don't mean a thing if you ain't got that swing." As critic Paul Fussell has put it: "No element of a poem is more basic—and I mean physical—in its effect upon the reader than the metrical element, and perhaps no technical triumphs reveal more readily than the metrical the poet's sympathy with that universal human nature . . . which exists outside his own."[6]

Vachel Lindsay (1879–1931)

FACTORY WINDOWS ARE ALWAYS BROKEN 1914

Factory windows are always broken.
Somebody's always throwing bricks,
Somebody's always heaving cinders,
Playing ugly Yahoo tricks.

Factory windows are always broken.   5
Other windows are let alone.
No one throws through the chapel-window
The bitter, snarling derisive stone.

Factory windows are always broken.
Something or other is going wrong.   10
Something is rotten—I think, in Denmark.
End of the factory-window song.

FACTORY WINDOWS ARE ALWAYS BROKEN. 4 *Yahoo:* a brutish uncivilized person (adopted from Jonathan Swift's *Gulliver's Travels.* 11 *Something is rotten . . . :* an allusion to a line from William Shakespeare's *Hamlet,* "Something is rotten in the state of Denmark."

QUESTIONS

1. Is the rhythm regular or irregular in this poem? If it is regular, how many strong beats are in each line?
2. What other devices of sound are in the poem?
3. What is the effect of the unusual last line? Does it change the tone of the poem, or is it in keeping with the earlier lines?

EXERCISE: *Meaningful Variation*

At what place or places in each of these passages does the poet depart from basic iambic meter? How does each departure help underscore the meaning?

1. Shadwell alone of all my sons is he
   Who stands confirmed in full stupidity.
   The rest to some faint meaning make pretense,
   But Shadwell never deviates into sense.
           —John Dryden, "Mac Flecknoe" (speech of Flecknoe, prince of
           Nonsense, referring to Thomas Shadwell, poet and playwright)

[6]*Poetic Meter and Poetic Form* (New York: Random, 1965) 110.

2. A needless Alexandrine ends the song
   That, like a wounded snake, drags its slow length along.
   —Alexander Pope, from *An Essay on Criticism*

3. Roll on, thou deep and dark blue Ocean—roll!
   Ten thousand fleets sweep over thee in vain;
   Man marks the earth with ruin—his control
   Stops with the shore; upon the watery plain
   The wrecks are all thy deed, nor doth remain
   A shadow of man's ravage, save his own,
   When, for a moment, like a drop of rain,
   He sinks into thy depths with bubbling groan,
   Without a grave, unknell'd, uncoffin'd, and unknown.
   —George Gordon, Lord Byron, *Childe Harold's Pilgrimage*

4. Deer walk upon our mountains, and the quail
   Whistle about us their spontaneous cries;
   Sweet berries ripen in the wilderness;
   And, in the isolation of the sky,
   At evening, casual flocks of pigeons make
   Ambiguous undulations as they sink,
   Downward to darkness, on extended wings.
   —Wallace Stevens, "Sunday Morning"

EXERCISE: *Recognizing Rhythms*

Which of the following poems contain predominant meters? Which poems are not wholly metrical, but are metrical in certain lines? Point out any such lines. What reasons do you see, in such places, for the poet's seeking a metrical effect?

Edna St. Vincent Millay   (1892–1950)*

COUNTING-OUT RHYME   1928

Silver bark of beech, and sallow
Bark of yellow birch and yellow
  Twig of willow.

Stripe of green in moosewood maple,
Color seen in leaf of apple,   5
  Bark of popple.

Wood of popple pale as moonbeam,
Wood of oak for yoke and barn-beam,
  Wood of hornbeam.

Silver bark of beech, and hollow   10
Stem of elder, tall and yellow
  Twig of willow.

A. E. Housman (1859–1936)*

WHEN I WAS ONE-AND-TWENTY   1896

When I was one-and-twenty
   I heard a wise man say,
"Give crowns and pounds and guineas
   But not your heart away;
Give pearls away and rubies   5
   But keep your fancy free."
But I was one-and-twenty,
   No use to talk to me.

When I was one-and-twenty
   I heard him say again,   10
"The heart out of the bosom
   Was never given in vain;
'Tis paid with sighs a plenty
   And sold for endless rue."
And I am two-and-twenty,   15
   And oh, 'tis true, 'tis true.

William Carlos Williams (1883–1963)*

HEEL & TOE TO THE END   1962

Gagarin says, in ecstasy,
he could have
gone on forever

he floated
ate and sang   5
and when he emerged from that

one hundred eight minutes off
the surface of
the earth he was smiling

Then he returned   10
to take his place
among the rest of us

from all that division and
subtraction a measure
toe and heel   15

heel and toe he felt
as if he had
been dancing

Heel & Toe to the End. 1 *Gagarin:* On April 12, 1961, Soviet cosmonaut Yuri Gagarin (1934–1968) became the first person ever to orbit the earth.

Walt Whitman   (1819–1892)*

Beat! Beat! Drums!   (1861)

Beat! beat! drums!—blow! bugles! blow!
Through the windows—through doors—burst like a ruthless force,
Into the solemn church, and scatter the congregation,
Into the school where the scholar is studying;
Leave not the bridegroom quiet—no happiness must he have now with   5
    his bride,
Nor the peaceful farmer any peace, ploughing his field or gathering his
    grain,
So fierce you whirr and pound you drums—so shrill you bugles blow.

Beat! beat! drums!—blow! bugles! blow!
Over the traffic of cities—over the rumble of wheels in the streets;
Are beds prepared for sleepers at night in the houses? no sleepers must   10
    sleep in those beds,
No bargainer's bargains by day—no brokers or speculators—would they
    continue?
Would the talkers be talking? would the singer attempt to sing?
Would the lawyer rise in the court to state his case before the judge?
Then rattle quicker, heavier drums—you bugles wilder blow.

Beat! beat! drums!—blow! bugles! blow!   15
Make no parley—stop for no expostulation,
Mind not the timid—mind not the weeper or prayer,
Mind not the old man beseeching the young man,
Let not the child's voice be heard, nor the mother's entreaties,
Make even the trestles to shake the dead where they lie awaiting the   20
    hearses.
So strong you thump O terrible drums—so loud you bugles blow.

David Mason (b. 1954)

SONG OF THE POWERS   1996

Mine, said the stone,
mine is the hour.
I crush the scissors,
such is my power.
Stronger than wishes,   5
my power, alone.

Mine, said the paper,
mine are the words
that smother the stone
with imagined birds,   10
reams of them, flown
from the mind of the shaper.

Mine, said the scissors,
mine all the knives
gashing through paper's   15
ethereal lives;
nothing's so proper
as tattering wishes.

As stone crushes scissors,
as paper snuffs stone   20
and scissors cut paper,
all end alone.
So heap up your paper
and scissor your wishes
and uproot the stone   25
from the top of the hill.
They all end alone
as you will, you will.

SONG OF THE POWERS. The three key images of this poem are drawn from the children's game of Scissors, Paper, Stone. In this game each object has a specific power: Scissors cuts paper, paper covers stone, and stone crushes scissors.

Langston Hughes (1902–1967)*

DREAM BOOGIE   1951

Good morning, daddy!
Ain't you heard
The boogie-woogie rumble
Of a dream deferred?

Listen closely:
You'll hear their feet
Beating out and beating out a—

> You think
> It's a happy beat?

Listen to it closely:
Ain't you heard
something underneath
like a—

> What did I say?

Sure,
I'm happy!
Take it away!

> Hey, pop!
> Re-bop!
> Mop!

> Y-e-a-h!

WRITER'S PERSPECTIVE

Gwendolyn Brooks

Gwendolyn Brooks on Writing

HEARING "WE REAL COOL"   1969

STAVROS: How about the seven pool players in the poem "We Real Cool"?

BROOKS: They have no pretensions to any glamor. They are supposedly dropouts, or at least they're in the poolroom when they should be possibly in school, since they're probably young enough or at least those I saw were when I looked in a poolroom, and they. . . . First of all, let me tell you how that's supposed to be said, because there's a reason why I set it out as I did. These are people who are essentially saying, "Kilroy is here. We *are*." But they're a little uncertain of the strength of their identity. The "We"—you're supposed to stop after the "We" and think about *validity*; of course, there's no way for you to tell whether it should be said softly or not, I suppose, but I say it rather softly because I want to represent their basic uncertainty, which they don't bother to question every day, of course.

STAVROS: Are you saying that the form of this poem, then, was determined by the colloquial rhythm you were trying to catch?

BROOKS: No, determined by my feelings about these boys, these young men.

From "On 'We Real Cool'"

◄▬▭ WRITING CRITICALLY ▭▬►

Freeze-Framing the Sound

If you plan to write about the rhythm of a poem, the best way to begin is nearly always by scanning. Although scansion may seem a bit intimidating at first, it is really not difficult; it is just a way of notating how to read the poem aloud. A scansion gives us a freeze-frame of the poem's most important sound patterns. And since stress reinforces meaning, it also helps us understand a poem better. Here is a simple way to get started:

1. Copy down the passage you want to analyze.
2. Mark the syllables on which the main speech stresses fall. (When in doubt, just read the line aloud several different ways and try to detect which way seems most natural.)
3. You might also want to make a few notes in the margin about other things that you notice. Are there rimes? How many syllables in each line? Are there any other recurring patterns of sound worth noting?

A simple scansion of the opening of Tennyson's poem "Break, Break, Break" (on page 193) might look like this in your notes:

Break, break, break	(3 syllables)
On thy cold gray stones, o sea	(7 syllables)/rime
And I would that my tongue could utter	(9 syllables)
The thoughts that arise in me.	(7 syllables)/rime

By now some basic organizing principles of the poem have become clear. The lines are rimed *a b c b,* but they contain an irregular number of syllables. The number of strong stresses, however, seems to be constant, at least in the opening stanza. Now that you have a visual diagram of the poem's sound, the rhythm will be much easier to write about.

WRITING ASSIGNMENT

Analyze the rhythm of a key passage from any poem in this chapter. Discuss how the poem uses rhythm to create certain effects. Incorporate into your analysis a scansion of the passage in question. (Your scansion need not identify every element of the poem's sound, but have it show all the elements you discuss.)

FURTHER SUGGESTIONS FOR WRITING

1. When has a rhythm of any kind (whether in poetry or not) stirred you, picked you up, and carried you along with it? Write an account of your experience.
2. The fact that most contemporary poets have given up meter, in the view of Stanley Kunitz, has made poetry "easier to write, but harder to remember." Why so? Comment on Kunitz's remark, or quarrel with it, in two or three paragraphs.
3. Robert Frost once claimed he tried to make poetry out of the "sound of sense." Writing to a friend, Frost discussed his notion that "the simple declarative sentence" in English often contained an abstract sound that helped communicate its meaning. "The best place to get the abstract sound of sense," wrote Frost, "is from voices behind a door that cuts off the words." Ask yourself how these sentences of dialogue would sound without the words in which they are embodied:

   > You mean to tell me you can't read?
   > I said no such thing.
   > Well read then.
   > You're not my teacher.

   Frost went on to say that "The reader must be at no loss to give his voice the posture proper to the sentence." Thinking about Frost's theory, can you see how it throws any light on one of his poems? In two or three paragraphs, discuss how Frost uses the "simple declarative sentence" as a distinctive rhythmic feature in his poetry.

10 *Closed Form*

Form, as a general idea, is the design of a thing as a whole, the configuration of all its parts. No poem can escape having some kind of form, whether its lines are as various in length as broomstraws or all in hexameter. To put this point in another way: if you were to listen to a poem read aloud in a language unknown to you, or if you saw the poem printed in that foreign language, whatever in the poem you could see or hear would be the form of it.[1]

Writing in **closed form,** a poet follows (or finds) some sort of pattern, such as that of a sonnet with its rime scheme and its fourteen lines of iambic pentameter. On a page, poems in closed form tend to look regular and symmetrical, often falling into stanzas that indicate groups of rimes. Along with William Butler Yeats, who held that a successful poem will "come shut with a click, like a closing box," the poet who writes in closed form apparently strives for a kind of perfection—seeking, perhaps, to lodge words so securely in place that no word can be budged without a worsening. For the sake of meaning, though, a competent poet often will depart from a symmetrical pattern. As Robert Frost observed, there is satisfaction to be found in things not mechanically regular: "We enjoy the straight crookedness of a good walking stick."

The poet who writes in **open form** usually seeks no final click. Often, such a poet views the writing of a poem as a process, rather than a quest for an absolute. Free to use white space for emphasis, able to shorten or lengthen lines as the sense seems to require, the poet lets the poem discover its shape as it goes along, moving as water flows downhill, adjusting to its terrain, engulfing obstacles. (Open form will provide the focus of the next chapter.)

---

[1] For a good summary of the uses of the term *form* in criticism of poetry, see the article "Form" by G. N. G. Orsini in *Princeton Encyclopedia of Poetry and Poetics,* 2nd ed., ed. Preminger, Warnke, and Hardison (Princeton: Princeton UP, 1975).

Most poetry of the past is in closed form, exhibiting at least a pattern of rime or meter, but since the early 1960s the majority of American poets have preferred forms that stay open. Lately, the situation has been changing yet again, with closed form reappearing in much recent poetry. Whatever the fashion of the moment, the reader who seeks a wide understanding of poetry of both the present and the past will need to know both the closed and open varieties.

Closed form gives some poems a valuable advantage: it makes them more easily memorable. The **epic** poems of nations—long narratives tracing the adventures of popular heroes: the Greek *Iliad* and *Odyssey*, the French *Song of Roland*, the Spanish *Cid*—tend to occur in patterns of fairly consistent line length or number of stresses because these works were sometimes transmitted orally. Sung to the music of a lyre or chanted to a drumbeat, they may have been easier to memorize because of their patterns. If a singer forgot something, the song would have a noticeable hole in it, so rime or fixed meter probably helped prevent an epic from deteriorating when passed along from one singer to another. It is no coincidence that so many English playwrights of Shakespeare's day favored iambic pentameter. Companies of actors, often called on to perform a different play each day, could count on a fixed line length to aid their burdened memories.

Some poets complain that closed form is a straitjacket, a limit to free expression. Other poets, however, feel that, like fires held fast in a narrow space, thoughts stated in a tightly binding form may take on a heightened intensity. "Limitation makes for power," according to one contemporary practitioner of closed form, Richard Wilbur; "the strength of the genie comes of his being confined in a bottle." Compelled by some strict pattern to arrange and rearrange words, delete, and exchange them, poets must focus on them the keenest attention. Often they stand a chance of discovering words more meaningful than the ones they started out with. And at times, in obedience to a rime scheme, the poet may be surprised by saying something quite unexpected. With the conscious portion of the mind, the poet may wish to express what seems to be a good idea. But a line ending in *year* must be followed by another ending in *atmosphere, beer, bier, bombardier, cashier, deer, friction-gear, frontier,* or some other rime word that otherwise might not have entered the poem. That is why rime schemes and stanza patterns can be mighty allies and valuable disturbers of the unconscious. As Rolfe Humphries has said about strict form: "It makes you think of better things than you would all by yourself."

FORMAL PATTERNS

The best-known one-line pattern for a poem in English is **blank verse:** unrimed iambic pentameter. (This pattern is not a stanza: stanzas have more than one line.) Most portions of Shakespeare's plays are in blank verse, and so are Milton's *Paradise Lost,* Tennyson's "Ulysses," certain dramatic monologues of Browning and Frost, and thousands of other poems. Here is a poem in blank verse that startles us by dropping out of its pattern in the final line. Keats appears to have written it late in his life to his fiancée Fanny Brawne.

John Keats (1795–1821)*

THIS LIVING HAND, NOW WARM AND CAPABLE   (1819?)

This living hand, now warm and capable
Of earnest grasping, would, if it were cold
And in the icy silence of the tomb,
So haunt thy days and chill thy dreaming nights
That thou wouldst wish thine own heart dry of blood   5
So in my veins red life might stream again,
And thou be conscience-calmed—see here it is—
I hold it towards you.

The **couplet** is a two-line stanza, usually rimed. Its lines often tend to be equal in length, whether short or long. Here are two examples:

Blow,
Snow!

As I in hoary winter's night stood shivering in the snow,
Surprised I was with sudden heat which made my heart to glow.

Actually, any pair of rimed lines that contains a complete thought is called a couplet, even if it is not a stanza, such as the couplet that ends a sonnet by Shakespeare. Unlike other stanzas, couplets are often printed solid, one couplet not separated from the next by white space. This practice is usual in printing the **heroic couplet**—or **closed couplet**—two rimed lines of iambic pentameter, the first ending in a light pause, the second more heavily end-stopped. George Crabbe, in *The Parish Register*, described a shotgun wedding:

Next at our altar stood a luckless pair,
Brought by strong passions and a warrant there:
By long rent cloak, hung loosely, strove the bride,
From every eye, what all perceived, to hide;
While the boy bridegroom, shuffling in his place,
Now hid awhile and then exposed his face.
As shame alternately with anger strove
The brain confused with muddy ale to move,
In haste and stammering he performed his part,
And looked the rage that rankled in his heart.

Though employed by Chaucer, the heroic couplet was named from its later use by Dryden and others in poems, translations of classical epics, and verse plays of epic heroes. It continued in favor through most of the eighteenth century. Much of our pleasure in reading good heroic couplets comes from the seemingly easy precision with which a skilled poet unites statements and strict pattern. In doing so, the poet may place a pair of words, phrases, clauses, or sentences side by side in agreement or similarity, forming a **parallel,** or in contrast and opposition, forming an **antithesis.** The effect is neat. For such skill in manipulating parallels and antitheses, John Denham's lines on the river Thames were much admired:

> O could I flow like thee, and make thy stream
> My great example, as it is my theme!
> Though deep, yet clear; though gentle, yet not dull;
> Strong without rage, without o'erflowing full.

These lines were echoed by Pope, ridiculing a poetaster, in two heroic couplets in *The Dunciad*:

> Flow, Welsted, flow! like thine inspirer, Beer:
> Though stale, not ripe; though thin, yet never clear;
> So sweetly mawkish, and so smoothly dull;
> Heady, not strong; o'erflowing, though not full.

Reading long poems in so exact a form, one may feel like a spectator at a Ping-Pong match, unless the poet skillfully keeps varying rhythms. One way of escaping such metronome-like monotony is to keep the cesura (see page 192) shifting about from place to place—now happening early in a line, now happening late—and at times unexpectedly to hurl in a second or third cesura. This skill, among other things, distinguishes the work of Dryden and Pope. If you care to see it in action, try working through Dryden's elegy for Oldham (page 470) or Pope's acid portrait of Atticus (page 195), noticing where the cesuras fall. You'll find that the pauses skip around with lively variety.

A **tercet** is a group of three lines. If rimed, they usually keep to one rime sound, as in this anonymous English children's jingle:

> Julius Caesar,
> The Roman geezer,
> Squashed his wife with a lemon-squeezer.

(That, by the way, is a great demonstration of surprising and unpredictable rimes.) *Terza rima,* the form Dante employs in *The Divine Comedy*, is made of tercets linked together by the rime scheme *a b a, b c b, c d c, d e d, e f e*, and so on. Harder to do in English than in Italian—with its greater resources of riming words—the form nevertheless has been managed by Shelley in "Ode to the West Wind" (with the aid of some slant rimes):

> Make me thy lyre, even as the forest is:
> What if my leaves are falling like its own!
> The tumult of thy mighty harmonies
>
> Will take from both a deep, autumnal tone,
> Sweet though in sadness. Be thou, spirit fierce,
> My spirit! Be thou me, impetuous one!

The workhorse of English poetry is the **quatrain,** a stanza consisting of four lines. Quatrains are used in more rimed poems than any other form.

Robert Graves   (1895–1985)*

COUNTING THE BEATS   1959

You, love, and I,
(He whispers) you and I,
And if no more than only you and I
What care you or I?

Counting the beats,   5
Counting the slow heart beats,
The bleeding to death of time in slow heart beats,
Wakeful they lie.

Cloudless day,
Night, and a cloudless day,   10
Yet the huge storm will burst upon their heads one day
From a bitter sky.

Where shall we be,
(She whispers) where shall we be,
When death strikes home, O where then shall we be   15
Who were you and I?

Not there but here,
(He whispers) only here,
As we are, here, together, now and here,
Always you and I.   20

Counting the beats,
Counting the slow heart beats,
The bleeding to death of time in slow heart beats,
Wakeful they lie.

QUESTION

What elements of sound and rhythm are consistent from stanza to stanza? Do any features change unpredictably from stanza to stanza?

Quatrains come in many line lengths, and sometimes contain lines of varying length, as in the ballad stanza (see page 150). Most often, poets rime the second and fourth lines of quatrains, as in the ballad, but the rimes can occur in any combination the poet chooses. Here are two quatrains from Tennyson's long, elegiac poem, *In Memoriam*. The poem's form—quatrains of iambic tetrameter with the unusual rime scheme *a b b a*—became so celebrated that this pattern is now called the "*In Memoriam* stanza":

Be near me when my light is low,
    When the blood creeps, and the nerves prick
    And tingle; and the heart is sick,
And all the wheels of being slow.

Be near me when the sensuous frame
    Is rack'd with pangs that conquer trust;
    And Time, a maniac scattering dust,
And Life, a Fury slinging flame.

Longer and more complicated stanzas are, of course, possible, but couplet, tercet, and quatrain have been called the building blocks of our poetry because most longer stanzas are made up of them. What short stanzas does John Donne mortar together to make the longer stanza of his "Song"?

John Donne   (1572–1631)*

SONG   1633

Go and catch a falling star,
    Get with child a mandrake root,
Tell me where all past years are,
    Or who cleft the Devil's foot,
Teach me to hear mermaids singing,   5
    Or to keep off envy's stinging,
        And find
        What wind
Serves to advance an honest mind.

If thou be'st borne to strange sights,   10
    Things invisible to see,
Ride ten thousand days and nights,
    Till age snow white hairs on thee,
Thou, when thou return'st, wilt tell me
    All strange wonders that befell thee,   15
        And swear
        Nowhere
Lives a woman true, and fair.

If thou findst one, let me know,
    Such a pilgrimage were sweet—   20
Yet do not, I would not go,
    Though at next door we might meet;
Though she were true, when you met her,
    And last, till you write your letter,
        Yet she   25
        Will be
False, ere I come, to two, or three.

Recently in vogue is a form known as **syllabic verse,** in which the poet establishes a pattern of a certain number of syllables to a line. Either rimed or rimeless but usually stanzaic, syllabic verse has been hailed as a way for poets to escape "the tyranny of the iamb" and discover less conventional rhythms, since, if they take as their line length an *odd* number of syllables, then iambs, being feet of *two* syllables, cannot fit perfectly into it. Offbeat victories have been scored in syllabics by such poets as W. H. Auden, W. D. Snodgrass, Donald Hall, Thom Gunn, and Marianne Moore. A well-known syllabic poem is Dylan Thomas's "Fern Hill" (page 556). Notice its shape on the page, count the syllables in its lines, and you'll perceive its perfect symmetry. Although it is like playing a game, the writing of such a poem is apparently more than finger exercise: the discipline can help a poet to sing well, though (with Thomas) singing "in . . . chains like the sea."

Poets who write in demanding forms seem to enjoy taking on an arbitrary task for the fun of it, as ballet dancers do, or weightlifters. Much of our pleasure in reading such poems comes from watching words fall into a shape. It is the pleasure of seeing any hard thing done skillfully—a leap executed in a dance, a basketball swished through a basket. Still, to be excellent, a poem needs more than skill; and to enjoy a poem it isn't always necessary for the reader to be aware of the skill that went into it. Unknowingly, the editors of the *New Yorker* once printed an **acrostic**—a poem in which the initial letter of each line, read downward, spells out a word or words—that named (and insulted) a well-known anthologist. Evidently, besides being ingenious, the acrostic was a printable poem. In the Old Testament book of Lamentations, profoundly moving songs tell of the sufferings of the Jews after the destruction of Jerusalem. Four of the songs are written as an alphabetical acrostic, every stanza beginning with a letter of the Hebrew alphabet. However ingenious, such sublime poetry cannot be dismissed as merely witty; nor can it be charged that a poet who writes in such a form does not express deep feeling.

Phillis Levin   (b. 1954)

Brief Bio   1995

Bearer of no news
Under the sun, except
The spring, I quicken
Time, drawing you to see
Earth's lightest pamphlet,   5
Reeling mosaic of rainbow dust,
Filament hinging a new set of wings,
Lord of no land, subject to flowers and wind,
Yesterday born in a palace that hangs by a thread.

Questions

1. What does the poem describe? (How can we know for sure if we have guessed the correct answer to the poem's riddle?)

2. What is the form of the poem?
3. How does the title relate to the rest of the poem?
4. Does the visual shape of the poem on the page suggest any image from the poem itself?

Patterns of sound and rhythm can, however, be striven after in a dull mechanical way, for which reason many poets today think them dangerous. Swinburne, who loved alliterations and tripping meters, had enough detachment to poke fun at his own excessive patterning:

> From the depth of the dreamy decline of the dawn through a
>   notable nimbus of nebulous noonshine,
>   Pallid and pink as the palm of the flag-flower that flickers with
>   fear of the flies as they float,
> Are the looks of our lovers that lustrously lean from a marvel of
>   mystic miraculous moonshine,
>   These that we feel in the blood of our blushes that thicken and
>   threaten with throbs through the throat?

This is bad, but bad deliberately. Viewed mechanically, as so many empty boxes somehow to be filled up, stanzas can impose the most hollow sort of discipline. If any good at all, a poem in a fixed pattern, such as a sonnet, is created not only by the craftsman's chipping away at it, but by the explosion of a sonnet-shaped *idea*.

Ronald Gross   (b. 1935)

YIELD   1967

Yield.
No Parking.
Unlawful to Pass.
Wait for Green Light.
Yield.   5

Stop.
Narrow Bridge.
Merging Traffic Ahead.
Yield.

Yield.   10

QUESTIONS

1. This poem by Ronald Gross is a "found poem." After reading it, how would you define **found poetry?**
2. Does "Yield" have a theme? If so, how would you state it?
3. What makes "Yield" mean more than traffic signs ordinarily mean to us?

Ronald Gross, who produces his "found poetry" by arranging prose from such unlikely places as traffic signs and news stories into poem-like lines, has told of making a discovery:

> As I worked with labels, tax forms, commercials, contracts, pin-up captions, obituaries, and the like, I soon found myself rediscovering all the traditional verse forms in found materials: ode, sonnet, epigram, haiku, free verse. Such finds made me realize that these forms are not mere artifices, but shapes that language naturally takes when carrying powerful thoughts or feelings.[2]

It is fun to see words tumble gracefully into such a shape. Consider, for instance, one famous "found poem," a sentence discovered in a physics textbook: "And so no force, however great, can stretch a cord, however fine, into a horizontal line which shall be absolutely straight."[3] What a good clear sentence containing effective parallels ("however great . . . however fine"), you might say, taking pleasure in it. Yet this plain statement gives extra pleasure if arranged like this:

> And so no force, however great,
>   Can stretch a cord, however fine,
>   Into a horizontal line
> Which shall be absolutely straight.

So spaced, in lines that reveal its built-in rimes and rhythms, the sentence would seem one of those "shapes that language naturally takes" that Ronald Gross finds everywhere. (It is possible, of course, that the textbook writer was gleefully planting a quatrain for someone to find; but perhaps it is more likely that he knew much rimed, metrical poetry by heart and couldn't help writing it unconsciously.) Inspired by pop artists who reveal fresh vistas in Brillo boxes and comic strips, found poetry has had a recent flurry of activity. Earlier practitioners include William Carlos Williams, whose long poem *Paterson* quotes historical documents and statistics. Prose, wrote Williams, can be a "laboratory" for poetry: "It throws up jewels which may be cleaned and grouped."

EXPERIMENT: *Finding a Poem*

In a newspaper, magazine, catalogue, textbook, or advertising throwaway, find a sentence or passage that (with a little artistic manipulation on your part) shows promise of becoming a poem. Copy it into lines like poetry, being careful to place what seem to be the most interesting words at the ends of lines to give them greatest emphasis. According to the rules of found poetry, you may excerpt, delete, repeat, and rearrange elements but not add anything. What does this experiment tell you about poetic form? About ordinary prose?

---

[2]"Speaking of Books: Found Poetry," *New York Times Book Review*, 11 June 1967. See also Gross's *Pop Poems* (New York: Simon, 1967).
[3]William Whewell, *Elementary Treatise on Mechanics* (Cambridge, England, 1819).

THE SONNET

When we speak, with Ronald Gross, of "traditional verse forms," we usually mean **fixed forms.** If written in a fixed form, a poem inherits from other poems certain familiar elements of structure: an unvarying number of lines, say, or a stanza pattern. In addition, it may display certain **conventions:** expected features such as themes, subjects, attitudes, or figures of speech. In medieval folk ballads a "milk-white steed" is a conventional figure of speech; and if its rider be a cruel and beautiful witch who kidnaps mortals, she is a conventional character. (*Conventional* doesn't necessarily mean uninteresting.)

In the poetry of western Europe and America, the **sonnet** is the fixed form that has attracted for the longest time the largest number of noteworthy practitioners. Originally an Italian form (*sonnetto:* "little song"), the sonnet owes much of its prestige to Petrarch (1304–1374), who wrote in it of his love for the unattainable Laura. So great was the vogue for sonnets in England at the end of the sixteenth century that a gentleman might have been thought a boor if he couldn't turn out a decent one. Not content to adopt merely the sonnet's fourteen-line pattern, English poets also tried on its conventional mask of the tormented lover. They borrowed some of Petrarch's similes (a lover's heart, for instance, is like a storm-tossed boat) and invented others. (If you would like more illustrations of Petrarchan conventions, see Shakespeare's sonnet on page 542.)

Soon after English poets imported the sonnet in the middle of the sixteenth century, they worked out their own rime scheme—one easier for them to follow than Petrarch's, which calls for a greater number of riming words than English can readily provide. (In Italian, according to an exaggerated report, practically everything rimes.) In the following **English sonnet,** sometimes called a **Shakespearean sonnet,** the rimes cohere in four clusters: *a b a b, c d c d, e f e f, g g.* Because a rime scheme tends to shape the poet's statements to it, the English sonnet has three places where the procession of thought is likely to turn in another direction. Within its form, a poet may pursue one idea throughout the three quatrains and then in the couplet end with a surprise.

William Shakespeare   (1564–1616)*

LET ME NOT TO THE MARRIAGE   1609
OF TRUE MINDS

Let me not to the marriage of true minds
Admit impediments; love is not love
Which alters when it alteration finds,
Or bends with the remover to remove.
O, no, it is an ever-fixèd mark   5
That looks on tempests and is never shaken;

It is the star to every wand'ring bark,
Whose worth's unknown, although his height be taken.
Love's not Time's fool, though rosy lips and cheeks
Within his bending sickle's compass° come;   *range*   10
Love alters not with his° brief hours and weeks   *Time's*
But bears° it out even to the edge of doom.   *endures*
    If this be error and upon me proved,
      I never writ, nor no man ever loved.

LET ME NOT TO THE MARRIAGE OF TRUE MINDS. 5 *ever-fixèd mark:* a sea-mark like a beacon or a light-
house that provides mariners with safe bearings. 7 *the star:* presumably the North Star, which gave
sailors the most dependable bearing at sea. 12 *edge of doom:* either the brink of death or—taken more
generally—Judgment Day.

Michael Drayton (1563–1631)

SINCE THERE'S NO HELP,   1619
COME LET US KISS AND PART

Since there's no help, come let us kiss and part;
Nay, I have done, you get no more of me,
And I am glad, yea, glad with all my heart
That thus so cleanly I myself can free;
Shake hands for ever, cancel all our vows,   5
And when we meet at any time again,
Be it not seen in either of our brows
That we one jot of former love retain.
Now at the last gasp of Love's latest breath,
When, his pulse failing, Passion speechless lies,   10
When Faith is kneeling by his bed of death,
And Innocence is closing up his eyes,
    Now if thou wouldst, when all have given him over,
    From death to life thou mightst him yet recover.

    Less frequently met in English poetry, the **Italian sonnet,** or **Petrarchan
sonnet,** follows the rime scheme *a b b a, a b b a* in its first eight lines, the **octave,**
and then adds new rime sounds in the last six lines, the **sestet.** The sestet may
rime *c d c d c d, c d e c d e, c d c c d c,* or in almost any other variation that doesn't
end in a couplet. This organization into two parts sometimes helps arrange the
poet's thoughts. In the octave, the poet may state a problem, and then, in the
sestet, may offer a resolution. A lover, for example, may lament all octave long
that a loved one is neglectful, then in line 9 begin to foresee some outcome: the
speaker will die, or accept unhappiness, or trust that the beloved will have a
change of heart.

Edna St. Vincent Millay   (1892–1950)*

What lips my lips have kissed,   1923
and where, and why

What lips my lips have kissed, and where, and why,
I have forgotten, and what arms have lain
Under my head till morning; but the rain
Is full of ghosts tonight, that tap and sigh
Upon the glass and listen for reply,   5
And in my heart there sits a quiet pain
For unremembered lads that not again
Will turn to me at midnight with a cry.
Thus in the winter stands the lonely tree,
Nor knows what birds have vanished one by one,   10
Yet knows its boughs more silent than before:
I cannot say what loves have come and gone,
I only know that summer sang in me
A little while, that in me sings no more.

In this Italian sonnet, the turn of thought comes at the traditional point—
the beginning of the ninth line. Many English-speaking poets, however, feel free
to vary its placement. In John Milton's commanding sonnet on his blindness
("When I consider how my light is spent" on page 516), the turn comes
midway through line 8, and no one has ever thought the worse of it for bending
the rules.

When we hear the terms *closed form* or *fixed form,* we imagine traditional poetic forms as a series of immutable rules. But, in the hands of the best poets, metrical forms are fluid concepts that change to suit the occasion. Here, for example,
is a haunting poem by Robert Frost that simultaneously fulfills the rules of two
traditional forms. Is it an innovative sonnet or a poem in *terza rima?* (See page
215 for a discussion of *terza rima.*) Frost combined the features of both forms to
create a compressed and powerfully lyric poem.

Robert Frost   (1874–1963)*

Acquainted with the Night   1928

I have been one acquainted with the night.
I have walked out in rain—and back in rain.
I have outwalked the furthest city light.

I have looked down the saddest city lane.
I have passed by the watchman on his beat   5
And dropped my eyes, unwilling to explain.

I have stood still and stopped the sound of feet
When far away an interrupted cry
Came over houses from another street,

But not to call me back or say good-bye;   10
And further still at an unearthly height,
One luminary clock against the sky

Proclaimed the time was neither wrong nor right
I have been one acquainted with the night.

"The sonnet," quipped Robert Bly, a contemporary poet-critic, "is where old professors go to die." And certainly in the hands of an unskilled practitioner, the form can seem moribund. Considering the impressive number of powerful sonnets by modern poets such as Yeats, Frost, Auden, Millay, Cummings, Kees, and Heaney, however, the form hardly appears to be exhausted. Like the hero of the popular ballad "Finnegan's Wake," literary forms (though not professors) declared dead have a startling habit of springing up again. No law compels sonnets to adopt an exalted tone, or confines them to an Elizabethan vocabulary. To see some of the surprising shapes contemporary sonnets take, read this selection of five recent examples.

Kim Addonizio   (b. 1954)

First Poem for You   1994

I like to touch your tattoos in complete
darkness, when I can't see them. I'm sure of
where they are, know by heart the neat
lines of lightning pulsing just above
your nipple, can find, as if by instinct, the blue   5
swirls of water on your shoulder where a serpent
twists, facing a dragon. When I pull you
to me, taking you until we're spent
and quiet on the sheets, I love to kiss
the pictures in your skin. They'll last until   10
you're seared to ashes; whatever persists
or turns to pain between us, they will still
be there. Such permanence is terrifying.
So I touch them in the dark; but touch them, trying.

Mark Jarman   (b. 1952)

Unholy Sonnet: After the Praying   1997

After the praying, after the hymn-singing,
After the sermon's trenchant commentary

On the world's ills, which make ours secondary,
After communion, after the hand-wringing,
And after peace descends upon us, bringing   5
Our eyes up to regard the sanctuary
And how the light swords through it, and how, scary
In their sheer numbers, motes of dust ride, clinging—
There is, as doctors say about some pain,
Discomfort knowing that despite your prayers,   10
Your listening and rejoicing, your small part
In this communal stab at coming clean,
There is one stubborn remnant of your cares
Intact. There is still murder in your heart.

QUESTIONS

1. What kind of sonnet is "Unholy Sonnet," English or Italian?
2. Does the poem have a turn of thought? If so, point out where it occurs and describe it.

R. S. Gwynn   (b. 1948)

SCENES FROM THE PLAYROOM   1986

Now Lucy with her family of dolls
Disfigures Mother with an emery board,
While Charles, with match and rubbing alcohol,
Readies the struggling cat, for Chuck is bored.

The young ones pour more ink into the water   5
Through which the latest goldfish gamely swims,
Laughing, pointing at naked, neutered Father.
The toy chest is a Buchenwald of limbs.

Mother is so lovely; Father, so late.
The cook is off, yet dinner must go on   10
With onions as her only cause for tears
She hacks the red meat from the slippery bone,
Setting the table, where the children wait,
Her grinning babies, clean behind the ears.

QUESTIONS

1. Explain the allusion to Buchenwald in line 8.
2. What do we know about this family and their lifestyle? What is revealed by the word *latest* (line 6)?
3. What do you think of these children and their parents? What does the poet think of them? By what details is his attitude made clear?

Timothy Steele   (b. 1948)*

SUMMER   1986

Voluptuous in plenty, summer is
Neglectful of the earnest ones who've sought her.
She best resides with what she images:
Lakes windless with profound sun-shafted water;
Dense orchards in which high-grassed heat grows thick;   5
The one-lane country road where, on his knees,
A boy initials soft tar with a stick;
Slow creeks which bear flecked light through depths of trees.

And he alone is summer's who relents
In his poor enterprisings; who can sense,   10
In alleys petal-blown, the wealth of chance;
Or can, supine in a deep meadow, pass
Warm hours beneath a moving sky's expanse,
Chewing the sweetness from long stalks of grass.

QUESTIONS

1. Define *voluptuous*. How does this word prepare us for the images to follow?
2. How many of the senses does this poem evoke?
3. What would be lost in the impact of line 5 if *dense* were omitted?
4. What images does the poem use to evoke the slow, heavy feeling of summer?

A. E. Stallings   (b. 1968)

SINE QUA NON   2002

Your absence, father, is nothing. It is nought—
The factor by which nothing will multiply,
The gap of a dropped stitch, the needle's eye
Weeping its black thread. It is the spot
Blindly spreading behind the looking glass.   5
It is the startled silences that come
When the refrigerator stops its hum,
And crickets pause to let the winter pass.

Your absence, father, is nothing—for it is
Omega's long last O, memory's elision,   10
The fraction of impossible division,
The element I move through, emptiness,
The void stars hang in, the interstice of lace,
The zero that still holds the sum in place.

SINE QUA NON. *Sine qua non* is from Latin, meaning literally, "without which not." Used to describe
something that is indispensable, an essential part, a prerequisite.

The Epigram

Oscar Wilde said that a cynic is "a man who knows the price of everything and the value of nothing." Such a terse, pointed statement is called an epigram. In poetry, however, an **epigram** is a form: "A short poem ending in a witty or ingenious turn of thought, to which the rest of the composition is intended to lead up" (according to the *Oxford English Dictionary*). Often it is a malicious gibe with an unexpected stinger in the final line—perhaps in the very last word.

Alexander Pope   (1688–1744)*

Epigram Engraved on the Collar of a Dog Which I Gave to His Royal Highness

1738

I am his Highness' dog at Kew;
Pray tell me, sir, whose dog are you?

Sir John Harrington   (1561?–1612)

Of Treason

1618

Treason doth never prosper; what's the reason?
For if it prosper, none dare call it treason.

Robert Herrick   (1591–1674)*

Moderation

1648

In things a moderation keep,
Kings ought to shear, not skin their sheep.

William Blake   (1757–1827)*

Her whole life is an epigram

(1793)

Her whole life is an epigram: smack smooth,° and neatly penned,   *perfectly smooth*
Platted° quite neat to catch applause, with a sliding noose at the end.   *plaited, woven*

E. E. Cummings   (1894–1962)*

a politician

1944

a politician is an arse upon
which everyone has sat except a man

Langston Hughes   (1902–1967)*

PRAYER   1955

Oh, God of dust and rainbows, help us see
That without dust the rainbow would not be.

J. V. Cunningham   (1911–1985)*

THIS Humanist WHOM NO BELIEFS   1947
CONSTRAINED

This Humanist whom no beliefs constrained
Grew so broad-minded he was scatter-brained.

John Frederick Nims   (1913–1999)

CONTEMPLATION   1967

"I'm Mark's alone!" you swore. Given cause to doubt you,
I think less of you, dear. But more about you.

Stevie Smith   (1902–1971)

THIS ENGLISHWOMAN   1937

This Englishwoman is so refined
She has no bosom and no behind.

Brad Leithauser   (b. 1953)

A VENUS FLYTRAP   1982

The humming fly is turned to carrion.
This vegetable's no vegetarian.

Dick Davis   (b. 1945)

FATHERHOOD   1991

O my children, whom I love,
Whom I snap at and reprove—
Bide your time and we shall see
Love and rage snap back at me.

Anonymous

EPITAPH ON A DENTIST

Stranger, approach this spot with gravity;
John Brown is filling his last cavity.

Hilaire Belloc   (1870–1956)

FATIGUE   1923

I'm tired of Love: I'm still more tired of Rhyme.
But Money gives me pleasure all the time.

Wendy Cope   (b. 1945)*

VARIATION ON BELLOC'S "FATIGUE"   1992

I hardly ever tire of love or rhyme—
That's why I'm poor and have a rotten time.

EXPERIMENT: *Expanding an Epigram*

Rewrite any of the preceding epigrams, taking them out of rime and adding a few more words to them. See if your revisions have nearly the same effect as the originals.

In English the only other fixed form to rival the sonnet and the epigram in favor is the **limerick:** five anapestic lines usually riming *a a b b a.* The limerick was made popular by Edward Lear (1812–1888), English painter and author of such nonsense poems as "The Owl and the Pussycat." Here is a sample, attributed to President Woodrow Wilson (1856–1924):

> I sat next to the Duchess at tea;
> It was just as I feared it would be:
>   Her rumblings abdominal
>   Were truly phenomenal
> And everyone thought it was me!

EXPERIMENT: *Contriving a Clerihew*

The **clerihew,** a fixed form named for its inventor, Edmund Clerihew Bentley (1875–1956), has straggled behind the limerick in popularity. Here are three examples: How would you define the form and what are its rules? Who or what is its conventional subject matter? Try writing your own example.

> James Watt
> Was the hard-boiled kind of Scot:
> He thought any dream
> Sheer waste of steam.
>   —W. H. Auden

Sir Christopher Wren
Said, "I am going to dine with some men.
If anybody calls
Say I am designing St. Paul's."
                    —Edmund Clerihew Bentley

Etienne de Silhouette
(It's a good bet)
Has the shadiest claim
To fame.
                    —Cornelius J. Ter Maat

OTHER FORMS

There are many other verse forms used in English. Some forms, like the villanelle and sestina (discussed below), come from other European literatures. But English has borrowed fixed forms from an astonishing variety of sources. The rubaiyat stanza (see pages 334–35), for instance, comes from Persian poetry; the haiku (see page 102) and tanka originated in Japan. Other borrowed forms include the ghazal (Arabic), pantoum (Malay), and sapphics (Greek). Even blank verse (see page 213), which seems as English as the royal family, began as an attempt by Elizabethan poets to copy an Italian eleven-syllable line. To conclude this chapter, here are poems in three widely used closed forms—the villanelle, triolet, and sestina. Their patterns, which are sometimes called "French forms," have been particularly fascinating to English-language poets because they do not merely require the repetition of rime sounds; instead, they demand more elaborate echoing, involving the repetition of either full words or whole lines of verse. Sometimes difficult to master, these forms can create a powerful musical effect unlike ordinary riming.

But first let's look at a recent poem in an unusual pattern to see how an unexpected form can suggest surprising images and ideas.

Robert Pinsky   (b. 1940)

ABC   2000

Any body can die, evidently. Few
Go happily, irradiating joy,

Knowledge, love. Many
Need oblivion, painkillers,
Quickest respite.   5

Sweet time unafflicted,
Various world:

X = your zenith.

1. What is the form of this poem?
2. If you rewrote the poem keeping all the ideas and images the same but changing the form, how much would that shift affect the poem's impact?

Dylan Thomas   (1914–1953)*

DO NOT GO GENTLE INTO THAT GOOD NIGHT   1952

Do not go gentle into that good night,
Old age should burn and rave at close of day;
Rage, rage against the dying of the light.

Though wise men at their end know dark is right,
Because their words had forked no lightning they   5
Do not go gentle into that good night.

Good men, the last wave by, crying how bright
Their frail deeds might have danced in a green bay,
Rage, rage against the dying of the light.

Wild men who caught and sang the sun in flight,   10
And learn, too late, they grieved it on its way,
Do not go gentle into that good night.

Grave men, near death, who see with blinding sight
Blind eyes could blaze like meteors and be gay,
Rage, rage against the dying of the light.   15

And you, my father, there on the sad height,
Curse, bless, me now with your fierce tears, I pray,
Do not go gentle into that good night.
Rage, rage against the dying of the light.

QUESTIONS

1. "Do not go gentle into that good night" is a **villanelle:** a fixed form originated by French courtly poets of the Middle Ages. What are its rules?
2. Whom does the poem address? What is the speaker saying?
3. Villanelles are sometimes criticized as elaborate exercises in trivial wordplay. How would you defend Thomas's poem against this charge?

Robert Bridges (1844–1930)

TRIOLET   1879

When first we met we did not guess
That Love would prove so hard a master;
Of more than common friendliness
When first we met we did not guess.
Who could foretell this sore distress,   5
This irretrievable disaster
When first we met—We did not guess
That Love would prove so hard a master.

TRIOLET. The **triolet** is a short lyric form borrowed from the French; its two opening lines are
repeated according to a set pattern, as Bridges's poem illustrates. The triolet is often used for light
verse, but Bridges's poem demonstrates how it can carry heavier emotional loads, if used with sufficient skill.

QUESTION

How do the first two lines change in meaning when they reappear at the end of the
poem?

Elizabeth Bishop (1911–1979)*

SESTINA   1965

September rain falls on the house.
In the failing light, the old grandmother
sits in the kitchen with the child
beside the Little Marvel Stove,
reading the jokes from the almanac,   5
laughing and talking to hide her tears.

She thinks that her equinoctial tears
and the rain that beats on the roof of the house
were both foretold by the almanac,
but only known to a grandmother.   10
The iron kettle sings on the stove.
She cuts some bread and says to the child,

It's time for tea now; but the child
is watching the teakettle's small hard tears
dance like mad on the hot black stove,   15
the way the rain must dance on the house.
Tidying up, the old grandmother
hangs up the clever almanac

on its string. Birdlike, the almanac
hovers half open above the child,   20
hovers above the old grandmother
and her teacup full of dark brown tears.
She shivers and says she thinks the house
feels chilly, and puts more wood in the stove.

It was to be, says the Marvel Stove.   25
I know what I know, says the almanac.
With crayons the child draws a rigid house
and a winding pathway. Then the child
puts in a man with buttons like tears
and shows it proudly to the grandmother.   30

But secretly, while the grandmother
busies herself about the stove,
the little moons fall down like tears
from between the pages of the almanac
into the flower bed the child   35
has carefully placed in the front of the house.

Time to plant tears, says the almanac.
The grandmother sings to the marvellous stove
and the child draws another inscrutable house.

SESTINA. As its title indicates, this poem is written in the trickiest of medieval fixed forms, that of the **sestina** (or "song of sixes"), said to have been invented in Provence in the thirteenth century by the troubadour poet Arnaut Daniel. In six six-line stanzas, the poet repeats six end-words (in a prescribed order), then reintroduces the six repeated words (in any order) in a closing **envoy** of three lines. Elizabeth Bishop strictly follows the troubadour rules for the order in which the end-words recur. (If you care, you can figure out the formula: in the first stanza, the six words are arranged A B C D E F; in the second, F A E B D C; and so on.) Notable sestinas in English have been written also by Sir Philip Sidney, Algernon Charles Swinburne, and Rudyard Kipling, more recently by Ezra Pound ("Sestina: Altaforte"), W. H. Auden ("Hearing of Harvests Rotting in the Valleys" and others), and by contemporary poets, among them John Ashbery, Tom Disch, Marilyn Hacker, Michael Heffernan, Donald Justice, Peter Klappert, and Mona Van Duyn.

QUESTIONS

1. A perceptive comment from a student: "Something seems to be going on here that the child doesn't understand. Maybe some terrible loss has happened." Test this guess by reading the poem closely.
2. Then consider this possibility. We don't know that "Sestina" is autobiographical; still, does any information about the poet's early life contribute to your reading of the poem? (See the chapter "Lives of the Poets.")
3. In the "little moons" that fall from the almanac (line 33), does the poem introduce dream or fantasy, or do you take these to be small round pieces of paper?
4. What is the tone of this poem—the speaker's apparent attitude toward the scene described?
5. In an essay, "The Sestina," in *A Local Habitation* (U of Michigan P, 1985), John Frederick Nims defends the form against an obvious complaint against it:

A shallow view of the sestina might suggest that the poet writes a stanza, and then is stuck with six words which he has to juggle into the required positions through five more stanzas and an envoy—to the great detriment of what passion and sincerity would have him say. But in a good sestina the poet has six words, six images, six ideas so urgently in his mind that he cannot get away from them; he wants to test them in all possible combinations and come to a conclusion about their relationship.

How well does this description of a good sestina fit "Sestina"?

EXPERIMENT: *Urgent Repetition*

Write a sestina and see what you find out by doing so. (Even if you fail in the attempt, you just might learn something interesting.) To start, pick six words you think are worth repeating six times. This elaborate pattern gives you much help: as John Ashbery has pointed out, writing a sestina is "like riding downhill on a bicycle and having the pedals push your feet." Here is some encouragement from a poet and critic, John Heath-Stubbs: "I have never read a sestina that seemed to me a total failure."

WRITER'S PERSPECTIVE

Robert Graves

Robert Graves on Writing

POETIC INSPIRATION AND POETIC FORM   1956

It is an axiom among poets that if one trusts whole-heartedly to poetic magic, one will be sure to solve any merely verbal problem or else discover that the verbal problem is hiding an imprecision in poetic thought.

I say magic, since the act of composition occurs in a sort of trance, distinguishable from dream only because the critical faculties are not dormant, but on the contrary, more acute than normally. Often a rugger° player is congratulated

rugger: rugby.

on having played the smartest game of his life, but regrets that he cannot re-member a single incident after the first five minutes, when he got kicked on the head. It is much the same with a poet when he completes a true poem. But often he wakes from the trance too soon and is tempted to solve the remaining prob-lems intellectually. Few self-styled poets have experienced the trance; but all who have, know that to work out a line by an exercise of reason, rather than by a deep-seated belief in miracle, is highly unprofessional conduct. If a trance has been interrupted, it is just too bad. The poem should be left unfinished, in the hope that suddenly, out of the blue, days or months later, it may start stirring again at the back of the mind, when the remaining problems will solve them-selves without difficulty.

. . .

It is unprofessional conduct to say: "When next I write a poem I shall use the sonnet form"—because the theme is by definition unforeseeable, and theme chooses metre. A poet should not be conscious of the metrical pattern of a poem he is writing until the first three or four lines have appeared; he may even find himself in the eleventh line of fourteen before realizing that a sonnet is on the way. Besides, metre is only a frame; the atmospheres of two sonnets can be so different that they will not be recognized as having the same form except by a careful count of lines and feet. Theme chooses metre; what is more, theme de-cides what rhythmic variations should be made on metre. The theory that all poems must be equally rich in sound is an un-English one, borrowed from Virgil. Rainbow-like passages are delightful every now and then, but they match a rare mood of opulence and exaltation which soon fatigues. The riches of *Paradise Lost* fatigue, and even oppress, all but musicians. Rainbows should make their appearances only when the moment has come to disclose the riches of the heart, or soul, or imagination; they testify to passing storms and are short-lived.

From "Harp, Anvil, Oar"

⊸▧ WRITING CRITICALLY ▧⊸

Turning Points

One possible definition of the sonnet might be a fourteen-line poem divided into two unequal parts. Italian sonnets divide their parts into the octave and the sestet, while the English sonnet is more lopsided, with a final couplet balanced against the first twelve lines. Some sonnets use less traditional arrangements, but generally poets build sonnets in which the unequal sections strongly contrast in tone, mood, theme, or point of view.

The moment when a sonnet changes its direction is commonly called "the turn." In a Shakespearean sonnet, the turn usually—but not always—comes in the final couplet. In modern sonnets, the turn is often less overt, but identifying the moment when the poem shifts will usually help you better understand both its theme and structure.

But how do you find the moment when a sonnet turns? Study the poem, latch on to the mood and manner of its opening lines. Is the feeling joyful or sad, loving or angry? Read the poem from this opening perspective until you feel it tug strongly in another direction. Sometimes the second part of a sonnet will directly contradict the opening. More often it explains, augments, or qualifies the opening.

WRITING ASSIGNMENT

Using any sonnet in the book, analyze and explain how the two parts of the poem combine to create a total effect neither part could achieve independently. In discussing the sonnet, identify the turning point and paraphrase what each of the poem's two sections say. In addition to the sonnets in this chapter, you might consider any of the following from "Poems for Further Reading": Elizabeth Barrett Browning's "How Do I Love Thee?"; Gerard Manley Hopkins's "The Windhover"; John Keats's "When I have fears that I may cease to be"; John Milton's "When I consider how my light is spent"; Wilfred Owen's "Anthem for Doomed Youth"; William Shakespeare's "When, in disgrace with Fortune and men's eyes"; or William Wordsworth's "Composed upon Westminster Bridge."

FURTHER SUGGESTIONS FOR WRITING

1. William Carlos Williams, in an interview, delivered this blast:

   > Forcing twentieth-century America into a sonnet—gosh, how I hate sonnets—
   > is like putting a crab into a square box. You've got to cut his legs off to make
   > him fit. When you get through, you don't have a crab any more.

   In a two-page essay, defend the modern American sonnet against Williams's charge. Or instead, open fire on it, using Williams's view for ammunition. Some sonnets to consider: R. S. Gwynn's "Scenes from the Playroom," Julia Alvarez's "The women on my mother's side were known" (page 310), and Kim Addonizio's "First Poem for You."

2. Write an unserious argument for or against the abolition of limericks. Give illustrations of limericks you think worthy of abolition (or preservation).

3. Compare Dylan Thomas's "Do not go gentle into that good night" with Wendy Cope's "Lonely Hearts" (page 70). Discuss how it is possible for the same form to be used to create such different kinds of poems.

11 *Open Form*

Writing in **open form,** a poet seeks to discover a fresh and individual arrangement for words in every poem. Such a poem, generally speaking, has neither a rime scheme nor a basic meter informing the whole of it. Doing without those powerful (some would say hypnotic) elements, the poet who writes in open form relies on other means to engage and to sustain the reader's attention. Novice poets often think that open form looks easy, not nearly so hard as riming everything; but in truth, formally open poems are easy to write only if written carelessly. To compose lines with keen awareness of open form's demands, and of its infinite possibilities, calls for skill: at least as much as that needed to write in meter and rime, if not more. Should the poet succeed, then the discovered arrangement will seem exactly right for what the poem is saying.

Denise Levertov   (1923–1997)*

ANCIENT STAIRWAY   1999

Footsteps like water hollow
the broad curves of stone
ascending, descending
century by century.
Who can say if the last   5
to climb these stairs
will be journeying
downward or upward?

Open form, in this brief poem, affords Denise Levertov certain advantages. Able to break off a line at whatever point she likes (a privilege not available to the poet writing, say, a conventional sonnet, who has to break off each line after its tenth syllable), she selects her pauses artfully. Line breaks lend emphasis: a word or phrase at the end of a line takes a little more stress (and receives a little more attention), because the ending of the line compels the reader to make a slight pause, if only for the brief moment it takes to sling back one's eyes and fix them on the line following. Slight pauses, then, follow the words and phrases *hollow / stone / descending / century / last / stairs / journeying / upward*— all these being elements that apparently the poet wishes to call our attention to. (The pause after a line break also casts a little more weight on the *first* word or phrase of each succeeding line.) Levertov makes the most of white space—another means of calling attention to things, as any good picture-framer knows. She has greater control over the shape of the poem, its look on the page, than would be allowed by the demands of meter; she uses that control to stack on top of one another lines that are (roughly) equivalent in width, like the steps of a staircase. The opening line with its quick stresses might suggest to us the many feet passing over the steps. From there, Levertov slows the rhythm to the heavy beats of lines 3–4, which could communicate a sense of repeated trudging up and down the stairs (in a particularly effective touch, all four of the stressed syllables in these two lines make the same sound), a sense that is reinforced by the poem's last line, which echoes the rhythm of line 3. Note too how, without being restricted by the need of a rime, she can order the terms in that last line according to her intended thematic emphasis. In all likelihood, we perceive these effects instinctively, not consciously (which may also be the way the author created them), but no matter how we apprehend them, they serve to deepen our understanding of and pleasure in the text.

Poetry in open form used to be called **free verse** (from the French *vers libre*), suggesting a kind of verse liberated from the shackles of rime and meter. "Writing free verse," said Robert Frost, who wasn't interested in it, "is like playing tennis with the net down." And yet, as Denise Levertov and many other poets demonstrate, high scores can be made in such an unconventional game, provided it doesn't straggle all over the court. For a successful poem in open form, the term *free verse* seems inaccurate. "Being an art form," said William Carlos Williams, "verse cannot be 'free' in the sense of having *no* limitations or guiding principles."[1] Various substitute names have been suggested: organic poetry, composition by field, raw (as against cooked) poetry, open form poetry. "But what does it matter what you call it?" remark the editors of a 1969 anthology called *Naked Poetry*. "The best poems of the last thirty years don't rhyme (usually) and don't move on feet of more or less equal duration (usually). That nondescription moves toward the only technical principle they all have in common."[2]

And yet many poems in open form have much more in common than absences and lacks. One positive principle has been Ezra Pound's famous suggestion

---

[1]"Free Verse," *Princeton Encyclopedia of Poetry and Poetics*, 2nd ed., 1975.
[2]Stephen Berg and Robert Mezey, eds., foreword, *Naked Poetry: Recent American Poetry in Open Forms* (Indianapolis: Bobbs, 1969).

that poets "compose in the sequence of the musical phrase, not in the sequence of the metronome"—good advice, perhaps, even for poets who write inside fixed forms. In Charles Olson's influential theory of **projective verse,** poets compose by listening to their own breathing. On paper, they indicate the rhythms of a poem by using a little white space or a lot, a slight indentation or a deep one, depending on whether a short pause or a long one is intended. Words can be grouped in clusters on the page (usually no more words than a lungful of air can accommodate). Heavy cesuras are sometimes shown by breaking a line in two and lowering the second part of it.[3]

To the poet working in open form, no less than to the poet writing a sonnet, line length can be valuable. Walt Whitman, who loved to expand vast sentences for line after line, knew well that an impressive rhythm can accumulate if the poet will keep long lines approximately the same length, causing a pause to recur at about the same interval after every line. Sometimes, too, Whitman repeats the same words at each line's opening. An instance is the masterly sixth section of "When Lilacs Last in the Dooryard Bloom'd," an elegy for Abraham Lincoln:

> Coffin that passes through lanes and streets,
> Through day and night with the great cloud darkening the land,
> With the pomp of the inloop'd flags with the cities draped in
>   black,
> With the show of the States themselves as of crape-veil'd women
>   standing,
> With processions long and winding and the flambeaus of the night,
> With the countless torches lit, with the silent sea of faces and the
>   unbared heads,
> With the waiting depot, the arriving coffin, and the somber faces,
> With dirges through the night, with the thousand voices rising
>   strong and solemn,
> With all the mournful voices of the dirges pour'd around the
>   coffin,
> The dim-lit churches and the shuddering organs—where amid
>   these you journey,
> With the tolling tolling bells' perpetual clang,
> Here, coffin that slowly passes,
> I give you my sprig of lilac.

There is music in such solemn, operatic arias. Whitman's lines echo another model: the Hebrew **psalms,** or sacred songs, as translated in the King James Version of the Bible. In Psalm 150, repetition also occurs inside of lines:

> Praise ye the Lord. Praise God in his sanctuary: praise him in the
>   firmament of his power.

[3]See Olson's essays "Projective Verse" and "Letter to Elaine Feinstein" in *Selected Writings,* edited by Robert Creeley (New York: New Directions, 1966). Olson's letters to Cid Corman are fascinating: *Letters for Origin, 1950–1955,* edited by Albert Glover (New York: Grossman, 1970).

Praise him for his mighty acts: praise him according to his excel-
lent greatness.
Praise him with the sound of the trumpet: praise him with the
psaltery and harp.
Praise him with the timbrel and dance: praise him with stringed
instruments and organs.
Praise him upon the loud cymbals: praise him upon the high
sounding cymbals.
Let every thing that hath breath praise the Lord. Praise ye the
Lord.

In Biblical Psalms, we are in the presence of (as Robert Lowell has said)
"supreme poems, written when their translators merely intended prose and were
forced by the structure of their originals to write poetry."[4]

Whitman was a more deliberate craftsman than he let his readers think, and
to anyone interested in writing in open form, his work will repay close study. He
knew that repetitions of any kind often make memorable rhythms, as in this passage from "Song of Myself," with every line ending on an -ing word (a stressed
syllable followed by an unstressed syllable):

Here and there with dimes on the eyes walking,
To feed the greed of the belly the brains liberally spooning,
Tickets buying, taking, selling, but in to the feast never once
going,
Many sweating, ploughing, thrashing, and then the chaff for
payment receiving,
A few idly owning, and they the wheat continually claiming.

Much more than simply repetition, of course, went into the music of those
lines—the internal rime *feed, greed,* the use of assonance, the trochees that begin
the third and fourth lines, whether or not they were calculated.

In such classics of open form poetry, sound and rhythm are positive forces.
When speaking a poem in open form, you often may find that it makes a difference for the better if you pause at the end of each line. Try pausing there, however briefly; but don't allow your voice to drop. Read just as you would normally
read a sentence in prose (except for the pauses, of course). Why do the pauses
matter? Open form poetry usually has no meter to lend it rhythm. *Some* lines in
an open form poem, as we have seen in Whitman's "dimes on the eyes" passage,
do fall into metrical feet; sometimes the whole poem does. Usually lacking
meter's aid, however, open form, in order to have more and more noticeable
rhythms, has need of all the recurring pauses it can get. When reading their own
work aloud, open form poets such as Robert Creeley and Allen Ginsberg often
pause very definitely at each line break.

[4]"On Freedom in Poetry," in Berg and Mezey, *Naked Poetry.*

Some poems, to be sure, seem more widely open in form than others. A poet, for instance, may employ rime, but have the rimes recur at various intervals; or perhaps rime lines of various lengths. (See T. S. Eliot's famous "The Love Song of J. Alfred Prufrock" on page 473. Is it a closed poem left ajar or an open poem trying to slam itself?) No law requires a poet to split thoughts into verse lines at all. Charles Baudelaire, Rainer Maria Rilke, Jorge Luis Borges, Alexander Solzhenitsyn, T. S. Eliot, and many others have written **prose poems,** in which, without caring that eye appeal and some of the rhythm of a line structure may be lost, the poet prints words in a block like a prose paragraph. For an example of a contemporary prose poem, see Carolyn Forché's "The Colonel" on page 248.

"Farewell, stale pale skunky pentameters (the only honest English meter, gloop! gloop!)," Kenneth Koch exulted, suggesting that it was high time to junk such stale conventions. Many poets who agree with him believe that it is wrong to fit words into any pattern that already exists, and instead believe in letting a poem seek its own shape as it goes along. (Traditionalists might say that that is what all good poems do anyway: sonnets rarely know they are going to be sonnets until the third line has been written. However, there is no doubt that the sonnet form already exists, at least in the back of the head of any poet who has ever read sonnets.) Some open form poets offer a historical motive: they want to reflect the nervous, staccato, disconnected pace of our bumper-to-bumper society. Others see open form as an attempt to suit thoughts and words to a more spontaneous order than the traditional verse forms allow. "Better," says Gary Snyder, quoting from Zen, "the perfect, easy discipline of the swallow's dip and swoop, 'without east or west.'"[5]

At the moment, much exciting new poetry is being written in both open form and closed. Today, a number of poets (labeled New Formalists) have taken up rime and meter and are writing sonnets, epigrams, and poems in rimed stanzas, giving "pale skunky pentameters" a fresh lease on life.[6] Meanwhile most younger poets continue to explore a wide range of open forms from conventional and conversational free verse to wildly challenging experimental styles. One West Coast poet, Jack Foley, often writes long free verse poems that involve two voices speaking simultaneously, which makes for exciting if also dizzying poetry readings. The contemporary American determination to play every possible trick that both written and spoken language allows is at least partially inspired by the early Modernist master E. E. Cummings, the smiling godfather of poetic experimentalists everywhere.

[5]"Some Yips & Barks in the Dark," in Berg and Mezey, *Naked Poetry.*
[6]For more samples of recent formal poetry than this book provides, see *Rebel Angels,* ed. Mark Jarman and David Mason (Brownsville: Story Line, 1996); *The Direction of Poetry,* ed. Robert Richman (Boston: Houghton, 1988); and *Ecstatic Occasions, Expedient Forms,* ed. David Lehman (Ann Arbor: U of Michigan P, 1996).

E. E. Cummings   (1894–1962)*

Buffalo Bill 's   1923

Buffalo Bill 's
defunct
    who used to
    ride a watersmooth-silver
                stallion   5
and break onetwothreefourfive pigeonsjustlikethat
                        Jesus
he was a handsome man
              and what i want to know is
how do you like your blueeyed boy   10
Mister Death

QUESTION

Cummings's poem would look like this if given conventional punctuation and set in a solid block like prose:

> Buffalo Bill's defunct, who used to ride a water-smooth silver stallion and break one, two, three, four, five pigeons just like that. Jesus, he was a handsome man. And what I want to know is: "How do you like your blue-eyed boy, Mister Death?"

If this were done, by what characteristics would it still be recognizable as poetry? But what would be lost?

W. S. Merwin   (b. 1927)

For the Anniversary of My Death   1967

Every year without knowing it I have passed the day
When the last fires will wave to me
And the silence will set out
Tireless traveler
Like the beam of a lightless star   5

Then I will no longer
Find myself in life as in a strange garment
Surprised at the earth
And the love of one woman
And the shamelessness of men   10
As today writing after three days of rain
Hearing the wren sing and the falling cease
And bowing not knowing to what

1. Read the poem aloud. Try pausing for a fraction of a second at the end of every line. Is there a justification for each line break?
2. The poem is divided into two asymmetrical sections. Does this formal division reflect some change or difference of meaning between the two sections?

William Carlos Williams (1883–1963)*

THE DANCE   1944

In Breughel's great picture, The Kermess,
the dancers go round, they go round and
around, the squeal and the blare and the
tweedle of bagpipes, a bugle and fiddles
tipping their bellies (round as the thick-   5
sided glasses whose wash they impound)
their hips and their bellies off balance
to turn them. Kicking and rolling about
the Fair Grounds, swinging their butts, those
shanks must be sound to bear up under such   10
rollicking measures, prance as they dance
in Breughel's great picture, The Kermess.

DETAIL. The Kermess *or* Peasant Dance *by Pieter Breughel the Elder* (1520?–1569).

THE DANCE. Breughel, a Flemish painter known for his scenes of peasant activities, represented in *The Kermess* a celebration on the feast day of a local patron saint.

QUESTIONS

1. Scan this poem and try to describe the effect of its rhythms.
2. Williams, widely admired for his free verse, insisted for many years that what he sought was a form not in the least bit free. What effect does he achieve by ending lines on such weak words as the articles *and* and *the?* By splitting *thick- | sided?* By splitting a prepositional phrase with the break at the end of line 8? By using line breaks to split *those* and *such* from what they modify? What do you think he is trying to convey?
3. Is there any point in his making line 12 a repetition of the opening line?
4. Look at the reproduction of Breughel's painting *The Kermess* (also called *Peasant Dance*). Aware that the rhythms of dancers, the rhythms of a painting, and the rhythms of a poem are not all the same, can you put in your own words what Breughel's dancing figures have in common with Williams's descriptions of them?
5. Compare with "The Dance" another poem that refers to a Breughel painting: W. H. Auden's "Museé des Beaux Arts" on page 450. What seems to be each poet's main concern: to convey in words a sense of the painting, or to visualize the painting in order to state some theme?

Stephen Crane (1871–1900)

THE HEART   1895

In the desert
I saw a creature, naked, bestial,
Who, squatting upon the ground,
Held his heart in his hands,
And ate of it.   5

I said, "Is it good, friend?"
"It is bitter—bitter," he answered;
"But I like it
Because it is bitter,
And because it is my heart."   10

Walt Whitman (1819–1892)*

CAVALRY CROSSING A FORD   1865

A line in long array where they wind betwixt green islands,
They take a serpentine course, their arms flash in the sun—hark to the
    musical clank,
Behold the silvery river, in it the splashing horses loitering stop to drink,
Behold the brown-faced men, each group, each person a picture, the
    negligent rest on the saddles,
Some emerge on the opposite bank, others are just entering the   5
    ford—while,
Scarlet and blue and snowy white,
The guidon flags flutter gayly in the wind.

QUESTIONS

The following nit-picking questions are intended to help you see exactly what makes these two open form poems by Crane and Whitman so different in their music.

1. What devices of sound occur in Whitman's phrase *silvery river* (line 3)? Where else in his poem do you find these devices?
2. Does Crane use any such devices?
3. In number of syllables, Whitman's poem is almost twice as long as Crane's. Which poem has more pauses in it? (Count pauses at the ends of lines, at marks of punctuation.)
4. Read the two poems aloud. In general, how would you describe the effect of their sounds and rhythms? Is Crane's poem necessarily an inferior poem for having less music?

Ezra Pound (1885–1972)*

THE GARRET   1915

Come, let us pity those who are better off than we are.
Come, my friend, and remember
    that the rich have butlers and no friends,
And we have friends and no butlers.
Come, let us pity the married and the unmarried.   5

Dawn enters with little feet
    like a gilded Pavlova,
And I am near my desire.
Nor has life in it aught better
Than this hour of clear coolness,   10
    the hour of waking together.

THE GARRET. 7 *Pavlova:* Anna Pavlova (1885–1931) was a celebrated Russian ballerina.

Wallace Stevens (1879–1955)*

THIRTEEN WAYS OF LOOKING   1923
AT A BLACKBIRD

I

Among twenty snowy mountains,
The only moving thing
Was the eye of the blackbird.

II

I was of three minds,
Like a tree   5
In which there are three blackbirds.

III

The blackbird whirled in the autumn winds.
It was a small part of the pantomime.

IV

A man and a woman
Are one.
A man and a woman and a blackbird
Are one.

V

I do not know which to prefer,
The beauty of inflections
Or the beauty of innuendoes,
The blackbird whistling
Or just after.

VI

Icicles filled the long window
With barbaric glass.
The shadow of the blackbird
Crossed it, to and fro.
The mood
Traced in the shadow
An indecipherable cause.

VII

O thin men of Haddam,
Why do you imagine golden birds?
Do you not see how the blackbird
Walks around the feet
Of the women about you?

VIII

I know noble accents
And lucid, inescapable rhythms;
But I know, too,
That the blackbird is involved
In what I know.

IX

When the blackbird flew out of sight,
It marked the edge
Of one of many circles.

X

At the sight of blackbirds
Flying in a green light,
Even the bawds of euphony   40
Would cry out sharply.

XI

He rode over Connecticut
In a glass coach.
Once, a fear pierced him,
In that he mistook   45
The shadow of his equipage
For blackbirds.

XII

The river is moving.
The blackbird must be flying.

XIII

It was evening all afternoon.   50
It was snowing
And it was going to snow.
The blackbird sat
In the cedar-limbs.

THIRTEEN WAYS OF LOOKING AT A BLACKBIRD.   25 *Haddam:* This biblical-sounding name is that of a
town in Connecticut.

QUESTIONS

1. What is the speaker's attitude toward the men of Haddam? What attitude toward
   this world does he suggest they lack? What is implied by calling them *thin* (line 25)?
2. What do the landscapes of winter contribute to the poem's effectiveness? If Stevens
   had chosen images of summer lawns, what would have been lost?
3. In which sections of the poem does Stevens suggest that a unity exists between
   human being and blackbird, between blackbird and the entire natural world? Can we
   say that Stevens "philosophizes"? What role does imagery play in Stevens's statement
   of his ideas?
4. What sense can you make of Part X? Make an enlightened guess.
5. Consider any one of the thirteen parts. What patterns of sound and rhythm do you
   find in it? What kind of structure does it have?
6. If the thirteen parts were arranged in some different order, would the poem be just as
   good? Or can we find a justification for its beginning with Part I and ending with Part
   XIII?
7. Does the poem seem an arbitrary combination of thirteen separate poems? Or is
   there any reason to call it a whole?

Carolyn Forché   (b. 1950)

THE COLONEL   1982

What you have heard is true. I was in his house. His wife carried a tray of coffee and sugar. His daughter filed her nails, his son went out for the night. There were daily papers, pet dogs, a pistol on the cushion beside him. The moon swung bare on its black cord over the house. On the television was a cop show. It was in English. Broken bottles were embedded in the walls around the house to scoop the kneecaps from a man's legs or cut his hands to lace. On the windows there were gratings like those in liquor stores. We had dinner, rack of lamb, good wine, a gold bell was on the table for calling the maid. The maid brought green mangoes, salt, a type of bread. I was asked how I enjoyed the country. There was a brief commercial in Spanish. His wife took everything away. There was some talk then of how difficult it had become to govern. The parrot said hello on the terrace. The colonel told it to shut up, and pushed himself from the table. My friend said to me with his eyes: say nothing. The colonel returned with a sack used to bring groceries home. He spilled many human ears on the table. They were like dried peach halves. There is no other way to say this. He took one of them in his hands, shook it in our faces, dropped it into a water glass. It came alive there. I am tired of fooling around he said. As for the rights of anyone, tell your people they can go fuck themselves. He swept the ears to the floor with his arm and held the last of his wine in the air. Something for your poetry, no? he said. Some of the ears on the floor caught this scrap of his voice. Some of the ears on the floor were pressed to the ground.

May 1978

QUESTIONS

1. Should we consider "The Colonel" a prose poem or a very short piece of prose? If it is poetry, what features distinguish it from prose? If it should be considered prose, what essential features of poetry does it lack?
2. Forché begins "The Colonel" by saying "What you have heard is true." Who is the *you?* Does she assume a specific person?
3. Should we believe that this story is true? If so, what leads us to believe its veracity?
4. Why does the author end "The Colonel" by giving a date?

VISUAL POETRY

Let's look at a famous poem with a distinctive visible shape. In the seventeenth century, ingenious poets trimmed their lines into the silhouettes of altars and crosses, pillars and pyramids. Here is one. Is it anything more than a demonstration of ingenuity?

George Herbert (1593–1633)*

Easter Wings   1633

Lord, who createdst man in wealth and store,
Though foolishly he lost the same,
Decaying more and more
Till he became
Most poor;
With thee
Oh, let me rise
As larks, harmoniously,
And sing this day thy victories;
Then shall the fall further the flight in me.

My tender age in sorrow did begin;
And still with sicknesses and shame
Thou didst so punish sin,
That I became
Most thin.
With thee
Let me combine,
And feel this day thy victory;
For if I imp my wing on thine,
Affliction shall advance the flight in me.

In the next-to-last line, *imp* is a term from falconry meaning to repair the wing of an injured bird by grafting feathers into it.

If we see it merely as a picture, we will have to admit that Herbert's word design does not go far. It renders with difficulty shapes that a sketcher's pencil could set down in a flash, in more detail, more accurately. Was Herbert's effort wasted? It might have been, were there not more to his poem than meets the eye. The mind, too, is engaged by the visual pattern, by the realization that the words *most thin* are given emphasis by their narrow form. Here, visual pattern points out meaning. Heard aloud, too, "Easter Wings" gives further pleasure. Its rimes, its rhythm are perceptible.

Ever since George Herbert's day, poets have continued to experiment with the looks of printed poetry. Notable efforts to entertain the eye are Lewis Carroll's rimed mouse's tail in *Alice in Wonderland*; and the *Calligrammes* of Guillaume Apollinaire, who arranged words in the shapes of a necktie, of the Eiffel Tower, of spears of falling rain. Here is a bird-shaped poem of more recent inspiration than Herbert's. What does its visual form have to do with what the poet is saying?

John Hollander   (b. 1929)

SWAN AND SHADOW   1969

                    Dusk
                Above the
            water hang the
                    loud
                    flies
                    Here
                    O so
                    gray
                    then
            What   A pale signal will appear
            When   Soon before its shadow fades
            Where   Here in this pool of opened eye
        In us   No Upon us As at the very edges
            of where we take shape in the dark air
                this object bares its image awakening
                    ripples of recognition that will
                        brush darkness up into light
even after this bird this hour both drift by atop the perfect sad instant now
                        already passing out of sight
                    toward yet-untroubled reflection
                this image bears its object darkening
            into memorial shades Scattered bits of
            light   No of water Or something across
            water   Breaking up No Being regathered
            soon   Yet by then a swan will have
            gone   Yet out of mind into what
                    vast
                    pale
                    hush
                    of a
                    place
                    past
            sudden dark as
                if a swan
                    sang

A whole poem doesn't need to be such a verbal silhouette, of course, for its appearance on the page to seem meaningful. In some lines of a longer poem, William Carlos Williams has conveyed the way an energetic bellhop (or hotel porter) runs downstairs:

ta tuck a
ta tuck a
ta tuck a
ta tuck a
ta tuck a

This is not only good onomatopoeia and an accurate description of a rhythm; the steplike appearance of the lines goes together with their meaning.

At least some of our pleasure in silently reading a poem derives from the way it looks upon its page. A poem in an open form can engage the eye with snowfields of white space and thickets of close-set words. A poem in stanzas can please us by its visual symmetry. And, far from being merely decorative, the visual devices of a poem can be meaningful, too. White space—as poets who work in open forms demonstrate—can indicate pauses. If white space entirely surrounds a word or phrase or line, then that portion of the poem obviously takes special emphasis. Typographical devices such as capital letters and italics also can lay stress upon words. In most traditional poems, a capital letter at the beginning of each new line helps indicate the importance the poet places on line-divisions, whose regular intervals make a rhythm out of pauses. And the poet may be trying to show us that certain lines rime by indenting them.

Some contemporary poets have taken advantage of the computer's ability to mix words and images. They use visual images as integral parts of their poems to explore possibilities beyond traditional prosody. Ezra Pound did similar things in his modernist epic, *The Cantos*, by incorporating Chinese ideograms, musical notations, and marginal notes into the text of the poem. More recently Terry Ehret created a sequence of poems that used ancient Egyptian hieroglyphics to prompt lyric meditations that are half translation and half free association. Here is one section from her poem sequence "Papyrus." (Note how Ehret uses a hieroglyph, a pictorial character used in ancient Egyptian writing, as the title of her short prose poem.)

Terry Ehret (b. 1955)

from PAPYRUS 1992

A lake. A night without moon. Distant memory of what the sun looks like rising. The darkness blows across the water like a wind. Passions that cool with age.

In recent decades, a movement called **concrete poetry** has traveled far and wide. Though practitioners of the art disagree over its definition, what most concretists seem to do is make designs out of letters and words. Other concrete poets wield typography like a brush dipped in paint, using such techniques as blow-up, montage, and superimposed elements (the same words printed many times on top of the same impression, so that the result is blurriness). They may even keep words in a usual order, perhaps employing white space as freely as any writer of open form verse. (More freely sometimes—Aram Saroyan has a concrete poem that consists of a page blank except for the word *oxygen*.) Poet Richard Kostelanetz has suggested that a more accurate name for concrete poetry might be "word-imagery." He sees it occupying an area somewhere between conventional poetry and visual art.

Admittedly, some concrete poems mean less than meets the eye. That many pretentious doodlers have taken up concretism may have caused a *Time* writer to sneer: did Joyce Kilmer miss all that much by never having seen a poem lovely as a

t

ttt

rrrrr

rrrrrrr

eeeeeeeee

???

Like other structures of language, however, concrete poems evidently can have the effect of poetry, if written by poets. Whether or not it ought to be dubbed "poetry," this art can do what poems traditionally have done: use language in delightful ways that reveal meanings to us.

Dorthi Charles   (b. 1963)

CONCRETE CAT   1971

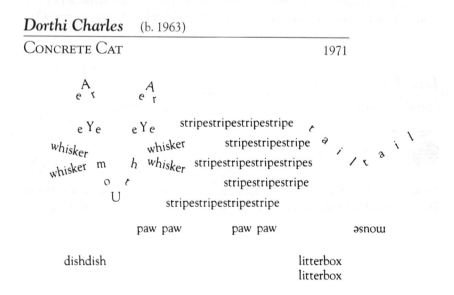

QUESTIONS

1. What does this writer indicate by capitalizing the *a* in *ear?* The *y* in *eye?* The *u* in *mouth?* By using spaces between the letters in the word *tail?*
2. Why is the word *mouse* upside down?
3. What possible pun might be seen in the cat's middle stripe?
4. What is the tone of "Concrete Cat"? How is it made evident?
5. Do these words seem chosen for their connotations or only for their denotations? Would you call this work of art a poem?

EXPERIMENT: *Do It Yourself*

Make a concrete poem of your own. If you need inspiration, pick some familiar object or animal and try to find words that look like it. For more ideas, study the typography of a magazine or newspaper; cut out interesting letters and numerals and try pasting them into arrangements. What (if anything) do your experiments tell you about familiar letters and words?

FURTHER SUGGESTIONS FOR WRITING

1. Consider whether concrete poetry is a vital art form or merely visual trivia.
2. Should a poem be illustrated, or is it better left to the mind's eye? Discuss this question in a brief essay. You might care to consider the illustrations in a collection of poems for children.

SEEING THE LOGIC OF OPEN FORM VERSE

Read the following poems in open form silently to yourself, noticing what each poet does with white space, repetitions, line breaks, and indentations. Then read the poems aloud, trying to indicate by slight pauses where lines end and also pausing slightly at any space inside a line. Can you see any reasons for the poet's placing his or her words in this arrangement rather than in a prose paragraph? Do any of these poets seem to care also about visual effect? (As with other kinds of poetry, there may not be any obvious logical reason for everything that happens in these poems.)

E. E. Cummings   (1894–1962)*

IN JUST-   1923

in Just-
spring   when the world is mud-
luscious the little
lame balloonman

whistles   far   and wee   5

and eddieandbill come
running from marbles and
piracies and it's
spring

when the world is puddle-wonderful   10

the queer
old balloonman whistles
far   and   wee
and bettyandisbel come dancing

from hop-scotch and jump-rope and   15

it's
spring
and
   the
      goat-footed   20

balloonMan   whistles
far
and
wee

Lucille Clifton   (b. 1936)

HOMAGE TO MY HIPS   1991

these hips are big hips.
they need space to
move around in.
they don't fit into little
petty places, these hips   5
are free hips.
they don't like to be held back.
these hips have never been enslaved,
they go where they want to go
they do what they want to do.   10
these hips are mighty hips.
these hips are magic hips.
i have known them
to put a spell on a man and
spin him like a top!   15

Carole Satyamurti (b. 1939)

I Shall Paint My Nails Red 1990

Because a bit of colour is a public service.

Because I am proud of my hands.

Because it will remind me I'm a woman.

Because I will look like a survivor.

Because I can admire them in traffic jams. 5

Because my daughter will say ugh.

Because my lover will be surprised.

Because it is quicker than dyeing my hair.

Because it is a ten-minute moratorium.

Because it is reversible. 10

QUESTION

"I Shall Paint My Nails Red" is written in free verse, but the poem has several organizing principles. How many can you discover?

Alice Fulton (b. 1952)

WHAT I LIKE 1983

Friend—the face I wallow toward
through a scrimmage of shut faces.
Arms like towropes to haul me home, aide-
memoire, my lost childhood docks, a bottled ark
in harbor. *Friend*—I can't forget 5
how even the word contains an *end*.
We circle each other in a scared bolero,
imagining stratagems: postures and imposters.
Cold convictions keep us solo. I ahem
and hedge my affections. Who'll blow the first kiss, 10
land it like the lifeforces we feel
tickling at each wrist? It should be easy
easy to take your hand, whisper down this distance
labeled hers or his: what I like about you is

QUESTION

Does this poem have an ending? Does it need to have an ending to be a successful poem?

Walt Whitman

Walt Whitman on Writing

THE POETRY OF THE FUTURE   1876

The poetry of the future, (a phrase open to sharp criticism, and not satisfactory to me, but significant, and I will use it)—the poetry of the future aims at the free expression of emotion, (which means far, far more than appears at first,) and to arouse and initiate, more than to define or finish. Like all modern tendencies, it has direct or indirect reference continually to the reader, to you or me, to the central identity of everything, the mighty Ego. (Byron's was a vehement dash, with plenty of impatient democracy, but lurid and introverted amid all its magnetism; not at all the fitting, lasting song of a grand, secure, free, sunny race.) It is more akin, likewise, to outside life and landscape, (returning mainly to the antique feeling,) real sun and gale, and woods and shores—to the elements themselves—not sitting at ease in parlor or library listening to a good tale of them, told in good rhyme. Character, a feature far above style or polish—a feature not absent at any time, but now first brought to the fore—gives predominant stamp to advancing poetry. . . .

Is there not even now, indeed, an evolution, a departure from the masters? Venerable and unsurpassable after their kind as are the old works, and always unspeakably precious as studies, (for Americans more than any other people,) is it too much to say that by the shifted combinations of the modern mind the whole underlying theory of first-class verse has changed?

From preface to the centennial edition of *Leaves of Grass*

Lining Up for Free Verse

"That's not poetry! It's just chopped-up prose." So runs one old-fashioned complaint about free verse. Such criticism may be true of inept poems, but in the best free verse the line endings transform language in ways beyond the possibilities of prose.

To understand the special effect of free verse, start by paying special attention to the line breaks. Look especially at the word at the end of each line, which receives special emphasis by its position. (In prose, we might easily pass over the word since in prose we read sentence by sentence.) Free verse almost always invites us to read more slowly and carefully than we would the same passage printed as prose. Look at how Wallace Stevens's lineation in "Thirteen Ways of Looking at a Blackbird" allows us not only to see but also to savor the implications of the ideas and images.

> I was of three minds,
> Like a tree
> In which there are three blackbirds.

On a purely semantic level, these lines may mean the same as the prose statement, "I was of three minds like a tree in which there are three blackbirds," but Stevens's arrangement into verse adds decisive emphasis at several points. Each of his three lines isolates and presents a separate image (the speaker, the tree, and the blackbirds). The placement of *three* at the same position at the end of the opening and closing line helps us feel the similar nature of the two statements. The short middle line allows us to see the image of the tree before we fully understand why it is parallel to the divided mind—thus adding a touch of suspense not in the prose. Ending each line with a key noun and image also gives the poem a concrete feel not altogether evident in the prose.

Even a short passage like Stevens's three lines suggests how powerfully the visual arrangement and rhythmic emphasis of free verse can amplify and transform the prose meaning of words.

WRITING ASSIGNMENT

Take any free verse poem and retype it as prose (adding conventional prose punctuation and capitalization, if necessary). Then compare the prose version to the original poem and discuss how the two passages differ in tone, rhythm, emphasis, or effect. Also acknowledge in what ways the two texts remain similar. Use any poem from this chapter or consider any of the following from "Poems for Further Reading": T. S. Eliot's "Journey of the Magi"; Ezra Pound's "The River Merchant's Wife: a Letter"; Theodore Roethke's "Elegy for Jane"; William Carlos Williams's "To Waken an Old Lady"; or James Wright's "A Blessing."

FURTHER SUGGESTIONS FOR WRITING

1. Compare any poem in this chapter or in "Poems for Further Reading" with a poem in rime and meter. Discuss several key features that they have in common despite their apparent differences in style. Features it might be useful to compare include imagery, tone, figures of speech, and word choice.
2. Is "free verse" totally free? Discuss this question in a short essay, drawing evidence from specific open form poems that you found interesting.

12 *Symbol*

The national flag is supposed to stir our patriotic feelings. When a black cat crosses his path, a superstitious man shivers, foreseeing bad luck. To each of these, by custom, our society expects a standard response. A flag, a black cat crossing one's path—each is a **symbol:** a visible object or action that suggests some further meaning in addition to itself. In literature, a symbol might be the word *flag* or the words *a black cat crossed his path* or every description of flag or cat in an entire novel, story, play, or poem.

A flag and the crossing of a black cat may be called **conventional symbols,** since they can have a conventional or customary effect on us. Conventional symbols are also part of the language of poetry, as we know when we meet the red rose, emblem of love, in a lyric, or the Christian cross in the devotional poems of George Herbert. More often, however, symbols in literature have no conventional, long-established meaning, but particular meanings of their own. In Melville's novel *Moby-Dick,* to take a rich example, whatever we associate with the great white whale is *not* attached unmistakably to white whales by custom. Though Melville tells us that men have long regarded whales with awe and relates Moby Dick to the celebrated fish that swallowed Jonah, the reader's response is to one particular whale, the creature of Herman Melville. Only the experience of reading the novel in its entirety can give Moby Dick his particular meaning.

We should say *meanings*, for as Eudora Welty has observed, it is a good thing Melville made Moby Dick a whale, a creature large enough to contain all that critics have found in him. A symbol in literature, if not conventional, has more than just one meaning. In "The Raven," by Edgar Allan Poe, the appearance of a strange black bird in the narrator's study is sinister; and indeed, if we take the poem seriously, we may even respond with a sympathetic shiver of dread. Does the bird mean death, fate, melancholy, the loss of a loved one, knowledge in the service of evil? All these, perhaps. Like any well-chosen symbol, Poe's raven sets going within the reader an unending train of feelings and associations.

We miss the value of a symbol, however, if we think it can mean absolutely anything we wish. If a poet has any control over our reactions, the poem will guide our responses in a certain direction.

T. S. Eliot (1888–1965)*

THE BOSTON EVENING TRANSCRIPT   1917

The readers of the *Boston Evening Transcript*
Sway in the wind like a field of ripe corn.

When evening quickens faintly in the street,
Wakening the appetites of life in some
And to others bringing the *Boston Evening Transcript*,   5
I mount the steps and ring the bell, turning
Wearily, as one would turn to nod good-bye to La Rochefoucauld,
If the street were time and he at the end of the street,
And I say, "Cousin Harriet, here is the *Boston Evening Transcript*."

The newspaper, whose name Eliot purposely repeats so monotonously, indicates what this poem is about. Now defunct, the *Transcript* covered in detail the slightest activity of Boston's leading families and was noted for the great length of its obituaries. Eliot, then, uses the newspaper as a symbol for an existence of boredom, fatigue (*Wearily*), petty and unvarying routine (since an evening newspaper, like night, arrives on schedule). The *Transcript* evokes a way of life without zest or passion, for, opposed to people who read it, Eliot sets people who do not: those whose desires revive, not expire, when the working day is through. Suggestions abound in the ironic comparison of the *Transcript*'s readers to a cornfield late in summer. To mention only a few: the readers sway because they are sleepy; they vegetate; they are drying up; each makes a rattling sound when turning a page. It is not necessary that we know the remote and similarly disillusioned friend to whom the speaker might nod: La Rochefoucauld, whose cynical *Maxims* entertained Parisian society under Louis XIV (sample: "All of us have enough strength to endure the misfortunes of others"). We understand that the nod is symbolic of an immense weariness of spirit. We know nothing about Cousin Harriet, whom the speaker addresses, but imagine from the greeting she inspires that she is probably a bore.

If Eliot wishes to say that certain Bostonians lead lives of sterile boredom, why does he couch his meaning in symbols? Why doesn't he tell us directly what he means? These questions imply two assumptions not necessarily true: first, that Eliot has a message to impart; second, that he is concealing it. We have reason to think that Eliot did not usually have a message in mind when beginning a poem, for as he once told a critic: "The conscious problems with which one is concerned in the actual writing are more those of a quasi-musical nature . . . than of a conscious exposition of ideas." Poets sometimes discover what they have to say while in the act of saying it. And it may be that in his *Transcript* poem, Eliot is saying exactly what he means. By communicating his meaning through symbols instead of statements, he may be choosing the only kind of language appropriate to an idea of great subtlety and complexity. (The paraphrase "Certain Bostonians are bored" hardly begins to describe the poem in all its possible meaning.) And by his use of symbolism, Eliot affords us the pleasure of finding our own entrances to his poem.

This power of suggestion that a symbol contains is, perhaps, its greatest advantage. Sometimes, as in the following poem by Emily Dickinson, a symbol will lead us from a visible object to something too vast to be perceived.

Emily Dickinson   (1830–1886)*

THE LIGHTNING IS A YELLOW FORK   (ABOUT 1870)

The Lightning is a yellow Fork
From Tables in the sky
By inadvertent fingers dropt
The awful Cutlery

Of mansions never quite disclosed   5
And never quite concealed
The Apparatus of the Dark
To ignorance revealed.

If the lightning is a fork, then whose are the fingers that drop it, the table from which it slips, the household to which it belongs? The poem implies this question without giving an answer. An obvious answer is "God," but can we be sure? We wonder, too, about these partially lighted mansions: if our vision were clearer, what would we behold?[1]

"But how am I supposed to know a symbol when I see one?" The best approach is to read poems closely, taking comfort in the likelihood that it is better not to notice symbols at all than to find significance in every literal stone and huge meanings in every thing. In looking for the symbols in a poem, pick out all

---

[1]In its suggestion of an infinite realm that mortal eyes cannot quite see, but whose nature can be perceived fleetingly through things visible, Emily Dickinson's poem, by coincidence, resembles the work of late-nineteenth-century French poets called **Symbolists.** To a symbolist the shirt-tail of Truth is continually seen disappearing around a corner. With their Neoplatonic view of ideal realities existing in a great beyond, whose corresponding symbols are the perceptible cats that bite us and tangible stones we stumble over, French poets such as Charles Baudelaire, Jules Laforgue, and Stéphane Mallarmé profoundly affected poets writing in English, notably Yeats (who said a poem "entangles . . . a part of the Divine essence") and Eliot. But in this chapter we consider symbolism as an element in certain poems, not Symbolism, the literary movement.

the references to concrete objects—newspapers, black cats, twisted pins. Consider these with special care. Notice any that the poet emphasizes by detailed description, by repetition, or by placing it at the very beginning or end of the poem. Ask: What is the poem about, what does it add up to? If, when the poem is paraphrased, the paraphrase depends primarily on the meaning of certain concrete objects, these richly suggestive objects may be the symbols.

There are some things a literary symbol usually is *not*. A symbol is not an abstraction. Such terms as *truth*, *death*, *love*, and *justice* cannot work as symbols (unless personified, as in the traditional figure of Justice holding a scale). Most often, a symbol is something we can see in the mind's eye: a newspaper, a lightning bolt, a gesture of nodding good-bye.

In narratives, a well-developed character who speaks much dialogue and is not the least bit mysterious is usually not a symbol. But watch out for an executioner in a black hood; a character, named for a Biblical prophet, who does little but utter a prophecy; a trio of old women who resemble the Three Fates. (It has been argued, with good reason, that Milton's fully rounded character of Satan in *Paradise Lost* is a symbol embodying evil and human pride, but a narrower definition of symbol is more frequently useful.) A symbol *may* be a part of a person's body (the baleful eye of the murder victim in Poe's story "The Tell-Tale Heart") or a look, a voice, or a mannerism.

A symbol usually is not the second term of a metaphor. In the line "The Lightning is a yellow Fork," the symbol is the lightning, not the fork.

Sometimes a symbol addresses a sense other than sight: the sound of a mysterious snapping string at the end of Chekhov's play *The Cherry Orchard;* or, in William Faulkner's tale "A Rose for Emily," the odor of decay that surrounds the house of the last survivor of a town's leading family—suggesting not only physical dissolution but also the decay of a social order. A symbol is a special kind of image, for it exceeds the usual image in the richness of its connotations. The dead wife's cold comb in the haiku of Buson (discussed on page 95) works symbolically, suggesting among other things the chill of the grave, the contrast between the living and the dead.

Holding a narrower definition than that used in this book, some readers of poetry prefer to say that a symbol is always a concrete object, never an act. They would deny the label "symbol" to Ahab's breaking his tobacco pipe before setting out to pursue Moby Dick (suggesting, perhaps, his determination to allow no pleasure to distract him from the chase) or to any large motion (as Ahab's whole quest). This distinction, while confining, does have the merit of sparing one from seeing all motion to be possibly symbolic. Some would call Ahab's gesture not a symbol but a **symbolic act.**

To sum up: a symbol radiates hints or casts long shadows (to use Henry James's metaphor). We are unable to say it "stands for" or "represents" a meaning. It evokes, it suggests, it manifests. It demands no single necessary interpretation, such as the interpretation a driver gives to a red traffic light. Rather, like Emily Dickinson's lightning bolt, it points toward an indefinite meaning, which may lie in part beyond the reach of words. In a symbol, as Thomas Carlyle said in *Sartor Resartus*, "the Infinite is made to blend with the Finite, to stand visible, and as it were, attainable there."

Thomas Hardy   (1840–1928)*

NEUTRAL TONES   1898

We stood by a pond that winter day,
And the sun was white, as though chidden of° God,   *rebuked by*
And a few leaves lay on the starving sod;
    —They had fallen from an ash, and were gray.

Your eyes on me were as eyes that rove   5
Over tedious riddles of years ago;
And some words played between us to and fro
    On which lost the more by our love.

The smile on your mouth was the deadest thing
Alive enough to have strength to die;   10
And a grin of bitterness swept thereby
    Like an ominous bird a-wing. . . .

Since then, keen lessons that love deceives,
And wrings with wrong, have shaped to me
Your face, and the God-curst sun, and a tree,   15
    And a pond edged with grayish leaves.

QUESTIONS

1. Sum up the story told in this poem. In lines 1–12, what is the dramatic situation? What has happened in the interval between the experience related in these lines and the reflection in the last stanza?
2. What meanings do you find in the title?
3. Explain in your own words the metaphor in line 2.
4. What connotations appropriate to this poem does the *ash* (line 4) have that *oak* or *maple* would lack?
5. What visible objects in the poem function symbolically? What actions or gestures?

If we read of a ship, its captain, its sailors, and the rough seas, and we realize we are reading about a commonwealth and how its rulers and workers keep it going even in difficult times, then we are reading an **allegory.** Closely akin to symbolism, allegory is a description—usually narrative—in which persons, places, and things are employed in a continuous and consistent system of equivalents.

Although more strictly limited in its suggestions than symbolism, allegory need not be thought inferior. Few poems continue to interest readers more than Dante's allegorical *Divine Comedy.* Sublime evidence of the appeal of allegory may be found in Christ's use of the **parable:** a brief narrative—usually allegorical but sometimes not—that teaches a moral.

Matthew 13:24–30 (King James Version, 1611)

THE PARABLE OF THE GOOD SEED

The kingdom of heaven is likened unto a man which sowed good seed
    in his field:
But while men slept, his enemy came and sowed tares among the
    wheat, and went his way.
But when the blade was sprung up, and brought forth fruit, then
    appeared the tares also.
So the servants of the householder came and said unto him, Sir, didst
    not thou sow good seed in thy field? From whence then hath it tares?
He said unto them, An enemy hath done this. The servants said unto   5
    him, Wilt thou then that we go and gather them up?
But he said, Nay; lest while ye gather up the tares, ye root up also the
    wheat with them.
Let both grow together until the harvest: and in the time of harvest I
    will say to the reapers, Gather ye together first the tares, and bind
    them in bundles to burn them: but gather the wheat into my barn.

The sower is the Son of man, the field is the world, the good seed are the children of the Kingdom, the tares are the children of the wicked one, the enemy is
the devil, the harvest is the end of the world, the reapers are angels. "As therefore the tares are gathered and burned in the fire; so shall it be in the end of this
world" (Matthew 13:36–42).

    Usually, as in this parable, the meanings of an allegory are plainly labeled or
thinly disguised. In John Bunyan's allegorical narrative *The Pilgrim's Progress*, it is
clear that the hero Christian, on his journey through places with such pointed
names as Vanity Fair, the Valley of the Shadow of Death, and Doubting Castle, is
the soul, traveling the road of life on the way toward Heaven. An allegory, when
carefully built, is systematic. It makes one principal comparison, the working out of
whose details may lead to further comparisons, then still further comparisons: Christian, thrown by Giant Despair into the dungeon of Doubting Castle, escapes by
means of a key called Promise. Such a complicated design may take great length to
unfold, as in Spenser's *Faerie Queene*; but the method may be seen in a short poem.

George Herbert   (1593–1633)*

THE WORLD   1633

Love built a stately house; where *Fortune* came,
And spinning phansies, she was heard to say,
That her fine cobwebs did support the frame,
Whereas they were supported by the same:
But *Wisdome* quickly swept them all away.   5

Then *Pleasure* came, who, liking not the fashion,
Began to make *Balcones*, *Terraces*,

Till she had weakened all by alteration:
But rev'rend *laws*, and many a *proclamation*
Reformed all at length with menaces.   10

The enter'd *Sinne* and with that Sycomore,
Whose leaves first sheltered man from drought & dew,
Working and winding slily evermore,
The inward walls and sommers cleft and tore:
But *Grace* shor'd these, and cut that as it grew.   15

Then *Sinne* combin'd with *Death* in a firm band
To raze the building to the very floore:
Which they effected, none could them withstand.
But *Love* and *Grace* took *Glorie* by the hand,
And built a braver Palace then before.   20

THE WORLD. 2 *phansies*: fancies. 10 *menaces*: threats. 14 *sommers*: summers: that is, beams or girders. 20 *then*: than.

QUESTIONS

1. What is the controlling image of this poem? What is that image an allegory of?
2. In each stanza of the poem, a similar pattern of action is repeated. What is that pattern, and how does it illuminate the poem's larger theme?
3. What is the "braver Palace" of the last line?

An object in allegory is like a bird whose cage is clearly lettered with its identity—"RAVEN, *Corvus corax*; habitat of specimen, Maine." A symbol, by contrast, is a bird with piercing eyes that mysteriously appears one evening in your library. It is there; you can touch it. But what does it mean? You look at it. It continues to look at you.

John Ciardi   (1916–1986)

MOST LIKE AN ARCH THIS MARRIAGE   1958

Most like an arch—an entrance which upholds
and shores the stone-crush up the air like lace.
Mass made idea, and idea held in place.
A lock in time. Inside half-heaven unfolds.

Most like an arch—two weaknesses that lean   5
into a strength. Two fallings become firm.
Two joined abeyances become a term
naming the fact that teaches fact to mean.

Not quite that? Not much less. World as it is,
what's strong and separate falters. All I do   10
at piling stone on stone apart from you
is roofless around nothing. Till we kiss

I am no more than upright and unset.
It is by falling in and in we make
the all-bearing point, for one another's sake,   15
in faultless failing, raised by our own weight.

QUESTION

Is this poem an allegory or merely a poem with a strong central symbol? (For the definition of allegory, see the Glossary of Literary Terms.)

Whether an object in literature is a symbol, part of an allegory, or no such thing at all, it has at least one sure meaning. Moby Dick is first a whale and the *Boston Evening Transcript* is a newspaper. Besides deriving a multitude of intangible suggestions from the title symbol in Eliot's long poem *The Waste Land*, its readers cannot fail to carry away a sense of the land's physical appearance: a river choked with sandwich papers and cigarette ends, London Bridge "under the brown fog of a winter dawn." A virtue of *The Pilgrim's Progress* is that its walking abstractions are no mere abstractions but are also human: Giant Despair is a henpecked husband. The most vital element of a literary work may pass us by, unless before seeking further depths in a thing, we look to the thing itself.

Robert Frost   (1874–1963)*

THE ROAD NOT TAKEN   1916

Two roads diverged in a yellow wood,
And sorry I could not travel both
And be one traveler, long I stood
And looked down one as far as I could
To where it bent in the undergrowth;   5

Then took the other, as just as fair,
And having perhaps the better claim,
Because it was grassy and wanted wear;
Though as for that the passing there
Had worn them really about the same,   10

And both that morning equally lay
In leaves no step had trodden black.
Oh, I kept the first for another day!
Yet knowing how way leads on to way,
I doubted if I should ever come back.   15

I shall be telling this with a sigh
Somewhere ages and ages hence:
Two roads diverged in a wood, and I—
I took the one less traveled by,
And that has made all the difference.   20

What symbolism do you find in this poem, if any? Back up your claim with evidence.

Christina Rossetti (1830–1894)

UPHILL   1862

Does the road wind uphill all the way?
   Yes, to the very end.
Will the day's journey take the whole long day?
   From morn to night, my friend.

But is there for the night a resting-place?   5
   A roof for when the slow dark hours begin.
May not the darkness hide it from my face?
   You cannot miss that inn.

Shall I meet other wayfarers at night?
   Those who have gone before.   10
Then must I knock, or call when just in sight?
   They will not keep you standing at that door.

Shall I find comfort, travel-sore and weak?
   Of labor you shall find the sum.
Will there be beds for me and all who seek?   15
   Yea, beds for all who come.

QUESTIONS

1. In reading this poem, at what line did you realize that the poet is building an allegory?
2. For what does each thing stand?
3. What does the title of the poem suggest to you?
4. Recast the meaning of line 14, a knotty line, in your own words.
5. Discuss the possible identities of the two speakers—the apprehensive traveler and the character with all the answers. Are they specific individuals? Allegorical figures?
6. Compare "Uphill" with Robert Creeley's "Oh No" (page 36). What striking similarities do you find in these two dissimilar poems?

Gjertrud Schnackenberg (b. 1953)

SUPERNATURAL LOVE   1985

My father at the dictionary-stand
Touches the page to fully understand
The lamplit answer, tilting in his hand

His slowly scanning magnifying lens,
A blurry, glistening circle he suspends   5
Above the word "Carnation." Then he bends

So near his eyes are magnified and blurred,
One finger on the miniature word,
As if he touched a single key and heard

A distant, plucked, infinitesimal string,   10
"The obligation due to every thing
That's smaller than the universe." I bring

My sewing needle close enough that I
Can watch my father through the needle's eye,
As through a lens ground for a butterfly   15

Who peers down flower-hallways toward a room
Shadowed and fathomed as this study's gloom
Where, as a scholar bends above a tomb

To read what's buried there, he bends to pore
Over the Latin blossom. I am four,   20
I spill my pins and needles on the floor

Trying to stitch "Beloved" X by X.
My dangerous, bright needle's point connects
Myself illiterate to this perfect text

I cannot read. My father puzzles why   25
It is my habit to identify
Carnations as "Christ's flowers," knowing I

Can give no explanation but "Because."
Word-roots blossom in speechless messages
The way the thread behind my sampler does   30

Where following each X I awkward move
My needle through the word whose root is love.
He reads, "A pink variety of Clove,

Carnatio, the Latin, meaning flesh."
As if the bud's essential oils brush   35
Christ's fragrance through the room, the iron-fresh

Odor carnations have floats up to me,
A drifted, secret, bitter ecstasy,
The stems squeak in my scissors, *Child, it's me,*

He turns the page to "Clove" and reads aloud: 40
"The clove, a spice, dried from a flower-bud."
Then twice, as if he hasn't understood,

He reads, "From French, for *clou,* meaning a nail."
He gazes, motionless. "Meaning a nail."
The incarnation blossoms, flesh and nail,   45

I twist my threads like stems into a knot
And smooth "Beloved," but my needle caught
Within the threads, *Thy blood so dearly bought,*

The needle strikes my finger to the bone.
I lift my hand, it is myself I've sewn,   50
The flesh laid bare, the threads of blood my own,

I lift my hand in startled agony
And call upon his name, "Daddy Daddy"—
My father's hand touches the injury

As lightly as he touched the page before,   55
Where incarnation bloomed from roots that bore
The flowers I called Christ's when I was four.

QUESTIONS

1. To understand this poem more fully, one would do well to emulate the speaker's father and consult the dictionary. Look up "incarnation": how do its various meanings help to illuminate the text?
2. Does the father's "magnifying lens" in line 4 seem to have any symbolic function? Explain.
3. What does X represent on the poem's literal level? What does it represent symbolically?
4. Why do you think the poet, instead of using three different riming words, ends all three lines of the fifteenth stanza with the word *nail*?
5. Words *as words* take on more than usual significance in this poem. Trace and discuss the occurrences of two of its key terms, *blossom* and *thread*.
6. What is the significance of the title?

FOR REVIEW AND FURTHER STUDY

Robinson Jeffers   (1887–1962)*

THE BEAKS OF EAGLES   1937

An eagle's nest on the head of an old redwood on one of the precipice-
    footed ridges
Above Ventana Creek, that jagged country which nothing but a falling
    meteor will ever plow; no horseman
Will ever ride there, no hunter cross this ridge but the winged ones, no
    one will steal the eggs from this fortress.
The she-eagle is old, her mate was shot long ago, she is now mated
    with a son of hers.
When lightning blasted her nest she built it again on the same tree, in   5
    the splinters of the thunderbolt.
The she-eagle is older than I; she was here when the fires of eighty-five
    raged on these ridges,

She was lately fledged and dared not hunt ahead of them but ate
    scorched meat. The world has changed in her time;
Humanity has multiplied, but not here; men's hopes and thoughts and
    customs have changed, their powers are enlarged,
Their powers and their follies have become fantastic,
The unstable animal never has been changed so rapidly. The motor   10
    and the plane and the great war have gone over him,
And Lenin has lived and Jehovah died: while the mother-eagle
Hunts her same hills, crying the same beautiful and lonely cry and is
    never tired; dreams the same dreams,
And hears at night the rock-slides rattle and thunder in the throats of
    these living mountains.
                    It is good for man
To try all changes, progress and corruption, powers, peace and anguish,   15
    not to go down the dinosaur's way
Until all his capacities have been explored: and it is good for him
To know that his needs and nature are no more changed in fact in ten
    thousand years than the beaks of eagles.

THE BEAKS OF EAGLES. 2 *Ventana Creek:* an isolated creek near Carmel, California. 10 *the great war:* World War I (1914–18). 11 *Lenin:* Vladimir Ilyich Lenin (1870–1924), the leader of the Russian Communist Revolution.

QUESTIONS

1. What does the speaker tell us about the eagle's habitat?
2. What do we know about the age of the eagle? What events have happened in her lifetime, both to her and to the outer world?
3. To what other creature is the eagle repeatedly compared?
4. What does the eagle come to symbolize by the end of the poem?
5. Would the meaning of the last line change significantly if the phrase *the beaks of eagles* became merely *eagles*? If so, how would it change?

Sara Teasdale (1884–1933)

THE FLIGHT   1926

We are two eagles
Flying together,
Under the heavens,
Over the mountains,
Stretched on the wind.   5
Sunlight heartens us,
Blind snow baffles us,
Clouds wheel after us,
Raveled and thinned.

We are like eagles;
But when Death harries us,
Human and humbled
When one of us goes,
Let the other follow—
Let the flight be ended,
Let the fire blacken,
Let the book close.

10

15

QUESTIONS

1. What do the two eagles experience together? What must they experience separately?
2. In the first stanza, the eagles are a metaphor. In the second stanza, the eagles become a simile. Does this change in the figure of speech have any significance?
3. What new metaphors are introduced in the second stanza?
4. What do the two eagles come to symbolize in this poem?

EXERCISE: *Symbol Hunting*

After you have read each of these poems, decide which description best suits it:

1. The poem has a central symbol.
2. The poem contains no symbolism, but is to be taken literally.

William Carlos Williams   (1883–1963)*

THE TERM   1937

A rumpled sheet
of brown paper
about the length

and apparent bulk
of a man was
rolling with the

wind slowly over
and over in
the street as

a car drove down
upon it and
crushed it to

the ground. Unlike
a man it rose
again rolling

with the wind over
and over to be as
it was before.

5

10

15

Ted Kooser (b. 1939)*

CARRIE   1979

"There's never an end to dust
and dusting," my aunt would say
as her rag, like a thunderhead,
scudded across the yellow oak
of her little house. There she lived   5
seventy years with a ball
of compulsion closed in her fist,
and an elbow that creaked and popped
like a branch in a storm. Now dust
is her hands and dust her heart.   10
There is never an end to it.

Rafael Campo (b. 1964)

WHAT THE BODY TOLD   1996

Not long ago, I studied medicine.
It was terrible, what the body told.
I'd look inside another person's mouth
And see the desolation of the world.
I'd see his genitals and think of sin.   5

Because my body speaks the stranger's language,
I've never understood those nods and stares.
My parents held me in their arms, and still
I think I've disappointed them; they care
And stare, they nod, they make their pilgrimage   10

To somewhere distant in my heart, they cry.
I look inside their other-person's mouths
And see the sleek interior of souls.
It's warm and red in there—like love, with teeth.
I've studied medicine until I cried   15

All night. Through certain books, a truth unfolds.
Anatomy and physiology,
The tiny sensing organs of the tongue—
Each nameless cell contributing its needs.
It was fabulous, what the body told.   20

Jon Stallworthy   (b. 1935)

AN EVENING WALK   1969

Taking my evening walk
where flats like liners ride
at anchor on a dark
phosphorus-rippled tide
of traffic, ebbing, flowing,   5
I heard from a kiosk
a telephone ringing;
from an empty kiosk.

Its dark voice welling up
out of the earth or air   10
for a moment made me stop,
listen, and consider
whether to break in
on its animal grief.
I could imagine   15
torrents of relief,

anger, explanation—
"*Oh for God's sake*"—but I'd
troubles of my own,
and passed on the other side.   20
All the same I wondered,
with every step I took,
what I would have heard
lifting it from the hook.

As I was returning   25
after the pubs were shut,
I found the bulb still burning
in the kiosk, but
the dark voice from the dark
had done with ringing: 30
the phone was off the hook
like a hanged man swinging.

Lorine Niedecker (1903–1970)*

POPCORN-CAN COVER (ABOUT 1959)

Popcorn-can cover
screwed to the wall
over a hole
    so the cold
can't mouse in   5

Wallace Stevens (1879–1955)*

ANECDOTE OF THE JAR 1923

I placed a jar in Tennessee,
And round it was, upon a hill.
It made the slovenly wilderness
Surround that hill.

The wilderness rose up to it,   5
And sprawled around, no longer wild.
The jar was round upon the ground
And tall and of a port in air.

It took dominion everywhere.
The jar was gray and bare.   10
It did not give of bird or bush,
Like nothing else in Tennessee.

William Butler Yeats

William Butler Yeats on Writing

POETIC SYMBOLS   1901

Any one who has any experience of any mystical state of the soul knows how there float up in the mind profound symbols, whose meaning, if indeed they do not delude one into the dream that they are meaningless, one does not perhaps understand for years. Nor I think has any one, who has known that experience with any constancy, failed to find some day, in some old book or on some old monument, a strange or intricate image that had floated up before him, and to grow perhaps dizzy with the sudden conviction that our little memories are but a part of some great Memory that renews the world and men's thoughts age after age, and that our thoughts are not, as we suppose, the deep, but a little foam upon the deep.

. . .

It is only by ancient symbols, by symbols that have numberless meanings besides the one or two the writer lays an emphasis upon, or the half-score he knows of, that any highly subjective art can escape from the barrenness and shallowness of a too conscious arrangement, into the abundance and depth of Nature. The poet of essences and pure ideas must seek in the half-lights that glimmer from symbol to symbol as if to the ends of the earth, all that the epic and dramatic poet finds of mystery and shadow in the accidental circumstances of life.

From "The Philosophy of Shelley's Poetry"

How to Read a Symbol

A symbol, to use poet John Drury's concise definition, is "an image that radiates meanings." Exactly what those meanings will be, however, often differs from poem to poem. In one poem snow may be a reassuring symbol of sleep and forgetfulness, while in another it becomes a chilling symbol of death. Both meanings easily connect to the natural image of snow, but in each poem, the author has nudged that image in a different direction.

The way a symbol has been used by earlier writers affects the way we grasp the image today. It would be difficult, for example, to put a great white whale in a contemporary poem without summoning up the symbolic association of Melville's Moby Dick. No matter how the poet chooses to handle it, the association will be there as a starting point.

Sometimes a poet gladly adopts the traditional symbolism of an image. In "Go, Lovely Rose" (page 562) Edmund Waller masterfully employs the image of the rose with all its conventional associations as a symbol of the transience of human beauty. William Butler Yeats believed that poetic symbols acquired their special power by thousands of years of use. Poets, therefore, had to employ symbols consistent with their ancient meanings. Contemporary poets, on the other hand, often enjoy turning traditional symbols upside down. In her poem, "The Victory" (page 99), Anne Stevenson presents the newborn child not as a conventional little angel or bundle of joy, but as a frightening, inhuman antagonist.

The same image, therefore, can often convey divergent meanings in different poems—even when the poems are written by contemporaries. Sara Teasdale and Robinson Jeffers, for example, were born only three years apart, and they often published poems in the same journals. Both employed the eagle as the central image of a poem (Teasdale's "The Flight" and Jeffers's "The Beaks of Eagles"), but the image came to symbolize different things in each poem.

When writing about the meaning (or meanings) of a symbol, follow the image through the poem and give it time to establish its own pattern of associations. Don't jump to quick conclusions. If the symbol is a traditional one (the cross, a rose, a reaper and so on), is it being used in the expected way? Or is the poet playing with its associations? And finally, if the image doesn't seem to radiate meanings above and beyond its literal sense, don't feel you have failed as a critic. Not everything is a symbol. As Sigmund Freud once commented about symbol-hunting, "Sometimes a cigar is just a cigar."

WRITING ASSIGNMENT

Compare the use of the eagle as a symbol in Sara Teasdale's "The Flight" and Robinson Jeffers's "The Beaks of Eagles." What does the central image of the eagle suggest in each poem? How does the symbolism differ in each? Are there any meaningful similarities between the two?

FURTHER SUGGESTIONS FOR WRITING

1. Discuss the symbolism in a poem in "Poems for Further Reading." Likely poems to study (among many) are T. S. Eliot's "The Love Song of J. Alfred Prufrock," Robert Lowell's "Skunk Hour," Gerard Manley Hopkins's "The Windhover," and Mary Jo Salter's "Welcome to Hiroshima."

2. Take a relatively simple, straightforward poem, such as William Carlos Williams's "This Is Just to Say" (page 54), and write a burlesque critical interpretation of it. Claim to discover symbols that the poem doesn't contain. While running wild with your "reading into" the poem, don't invent anything that you can't somehow support from the text of the poem itself. At the end of your burlesque, sum up in a paragraph what this exercise taught you about how to read poems, or how not to.

13 Myth and Narrative

Poets have long been fond of retelling **myths,** narrowly defined as traditional stories about the exploits of immortal beings. Such stories taken collectively may also be called **myth** or **mythology.** In one of the most celebrated collections of myth ever assembled, the *Metamorphoses*, the Roman poet Ovid told—to take one example from many—how Phaeton, child of the sun god, rashly tried to drive his father's fiery chariot on its daily round, lost control of the horses, and caused disaster both to himself and to the world. Our use of the term *myth* in discussing poetry, then, differs from its use in expressions such as "the myth of communism" and "the myth of democracy." In these examples, myth is used broadly to represent any idea people believe in, whether true or false. Nor do we mean—to take another familiar use of the word—a cock-and-bull story: "Judge Rapp doesn't roast speeders alive; that's just a *myth*." In the following discussion, *myth* will mean a kind of story—either from ancient or modern sources—whose actions implicitly symbolize some profound truth about human or natural existence.

Traditional myths tell us stories of gods or heroes—their battles, their lives, their loves, and often their suffering—all on a scale of magnificence larger than our life. These exciting stories usually reveal part of a culture's worldview. Myths often try to explain universal natural phenomena, like the phases of the moon or the turning of the seasons. But some myths tell the stories of purely local phenomena; one Greek legend, for example, recounts how grief-stricken King Aegeus threw himself into the sea when he mistakenly believed his son, Theseus, had been killed; consequently, the body of water between Greece and Turkey was called the Aegean Sea.

Modern psychologists, such as Sigmund Freud and Carl Jung, have been fascinated by myth and legend, since they believe these stories symbolically enact deep truths about human nature. Our myths, psychologists believe, express our wishes, dreams, and nightmares. Whether or not we believe myths, we recognize their psychological power. Even in the first century B.C., Roman poet Ovid did not believe in the literal truth of the legends he so suavely retold; he confessed, "I prate of ancient poets' monstrous lies."

And yet it is characteristic of a myth that it *can* be believed. Throughout history, myths have accompanied religious doctrines and rituals. They have helped sanction or recall the reasons for religious observances. A sublime instance is the New Testament account of the Last Supper. Because of its record of the words of Jesus, "Do this in remembrance of Me," Christians have continued to re-enact the offering and partaking of the body and blood of their Lord, under the appearances of bread and wine. It is essential to recall that, just because a myth narrates the acts of a god, we do not necessarily mean by the term a false or fictitious narrative. When we speak of the "myth of Islam" or "the Christian myth," we do so without implying either belief or disbelief.

Myths can also help sanction customs and institutions other than religious ones. At the same time that the baking of bread was introduced to ancient Greece—one theory goes—the myth of Demeter, goddess of grain, appeared. Demeter was a kindly deity who sent her emissary to teach humankind the valuable art of baking—thus helping to persuade the distrustful that bread was a good thing. Some myths seem designed to divert and regale, not to sanction anything. Such may be the story of the sculptor Pygmalion, who fell in love with the statue he had carved of a beautiful woman; so exquisite was his work, so deep was his feeling, that Aphrodite, the goddess of Love, brought the statue to life. And yet perhaps the story goes deeper than mere diversion: perhaps it is a way of saying that works of art achieve a reality of their own, that love can transform or animate its object.

How does a myth begin? Several theories have been proposed, none universally accepted. One is that a myth is a way to explain some natural phenomenon. Winter comes and the vegetation perishes because Persephone, child of Demeter, must return to the underworld for several months every year. This theory, as classical scholar Edith Hamilton has pointed out, may lead us to think incorrectly that Greek mythology was the creation of a primitive people. Tales of the gods of Mount Olympus may reflect an earlier inheritance, but the Greek myths known to us were transcribed in an era of high civilization. Anthropologists have questioned whether primitive people generally find beauty in the mysteries of nature. Many anthropologists emphasize the practical function of myth; in his influential work of comparative mythology, *The Golden Bough*, Sir James Frazer argued that most myths were originally expressions of human hope that nature would be fertile. Still another theory maintains that many myths began as real events; mythic heroes were real human beings whose deeds have been changed and exaggerated by posterity. Most present-day myth historians would say that different myths probably have different origins.

Poets have many coherent mythologies on which to draw; perhaps those most frequently consulted by British and American poets are the classical, the Christian, the Norse, the Native American, and the folk tales of the American frontier (embodying the deeds of superhuman characters such as Paul Bunyan). Some poets have taken inspiration from other myths as well: T. S. Eliot's *The Waste Land*, for example, is enriched by allusions to Buddhism and to pagan vegetation-cults. Robert Bly borrowed the terrifying Death Goddess of Aztec, Hindu, and Balinese mythology to make her the climactic figure of his long poem "The Teeth Mother Naked at Last."

A tour through any good art museum will demonstrate how thoroughly myth pervades the painting and sculpture of nearly every civilization. In literature, one evidence of its continuing value to recent poets and storytellers is how frequently ancient myths are retold. Even in modern society, writers often turn to myth when they try to tell stories of deep significance. Mythic structures still touch a powerful and primal part of the human imagination. William Faulkner's story "The Bear" recalls tales of Indian totem animals; John Updike's novel *The Centaur* presents the horse-man Chiron as a modern high-school teacher; James Joyce's *Ulysses* retells the *Odyssey* in modern Dublin; Rita Dove's play *The Darker Face of the Earth* recasts the story of Oedipus in the slave-era South; Bernard Shaw retells the story of Pygmalion in his popular Edwardian social comedy *Pygmalion*, later the basis of the hit musical *My Fair Lady*; Jean Cocteau's film *Orphée* shows us Eurydice riding to the underworld with an escort of motorcycles. Popular interest in such works may testify to the profound appeal myths continue to hold for us. Like other varieties of poetry, myth is a kind of knowledge, not at odds with scientific knowledge but existing in addition to it.

Robert Frost (1874–1963)*

NOTHING GOLD CAN STAY   1923

Nature's first green is gold,
Her hardest hue to hold.
Her early leaf's a flower;
But only so an hour.
Then leaf subsides to leaf.   5
So Eden sank to grief,
So dawn goes down to day.
Nothing gold can stay.

QUESTIONS

1. To what myth does this poem allude? Does Frost sound as though he believes in the myth or as though he rejects it?
2. When Frost says, "Nature's first green is gold," he is describing how many leaves first appear as tiny yellow buds and blossoms. But what else does this line imply?
3. What would happen to the poem's meaning if line 6 were omitted?

D. H. Lawrence   (1885–1930)*

BAVARIAN GENTIANS   1932

Not every man has gentians in his house
in soft September, at slow, sad Michaelmas.

Bavarian gentians, big and dark, only dark
darkening the daytime, torch-like with the smoking blueness of Pluto's
    gloom,
ribbed and torch-like, with their blaze of darkness spread blue   5
down flattening into points, flattened under the sweep of white day
torch-flower of the blue-smoking darkness, Pluto's dark-blue daze,
black lamps from the halls of Dis, burning dark blue,
giving off darkness, blue darkness, as Demeter's pale lamps give off
    light,
lead me then, lead the way.   10

Reach me a gentian, give me a torch!
let me guide myself with the blue, forked torch of this flower
down the darker and darker stairs, where blue is darkened on blueness
even where Persephone goes, just now, from the frosted September
to the sightless realm where darkness is awake upon the dark   15
and Persephone herself is but a voice
or a darkness invisible enfolded in the deeper dark
of the arms Plutonic, and pierced with the passion of dense gloom,
among the splendor of torches of darkness, shedding darkness on the
    lost bride and her groom.

BAVARIAN GENTIANS. 2 *Michaelmas:* The feast of St. Michael (September 29). 4 *Pluto:* Roman name
for Hades, in Greek mythology the ruler of the underworld, who abducted Persephone to be his bride.
Each spring Persephone returns to earth and is welcomed by her mother Demeter, goddess of fruitfulness; each winter she departs again, to dwell with her husband below. 8 *Dis:* Pluto's realm.

QUESTIONS

1. Read this poem aloud. What devices of sound do you hear in it?
2. What characteristics of gentians appear to remind Lawrence of the story of Persephone? What significance do you attach to the poem's being set in September? How
   does the fact of autumn matter to the gentians and to Persephone?

Thomas Hardy   (1840–1928)*

THE OXEN   1915

Christmas Eve, and twelve of the clock.
   "Now they are all on their knees,"

An elder said as we sat in a flock
    By the embers in hearthside ease.

We pictured the meek mild creatures where   5
    They dwelt in their strawy pen,
Nor did it occur to one of us there
    To doubt they were kneeling then.

So fair a fancy few would weave
    In these years! Yet, I feel,   10
If someone said on Christmas Eve,
    "Come; see the oxen kneel

"In the lonely barton° by yonder coomb°   *farmyard; a hollow*
    Our childhood used to know,"
I should go with him in the gloom,   15
    Hoping it might be so.

THE OXEN. This ancient belief has had wide currency among peasants and farmers of Western Europe. Some also say that on Christmas Eve the beasts can speak.

QUESTIONS

1. What body of myth is Hardy's subject and what are his speaker's attitudes toward it? Perhaps, in Hardy's view, the pious report about oxen is only part of it.
2. Read this poem aloud and notice its sound and imagery. What contrast do you find between the sounds of the first stanza and those of the last stanza? Which words make the difference? What images enforce a contrast in tone between the beginning of the poem and its ending?
3. G. K. Chesterton, writing as a defender of Christian faith, called Hardy's writings "the mutterings of the village atheist." See other poems by Hardy in "Poems for Further Reading." What do you think Chesterton might have meant? Can "The Oxen" be called a hostile mutter?

William Wordsworth   (1770–1850)*

THE WORLD IS TOO MUCH WITH US   1807

The world is too much with us; late and soon,
Getting and spending, we lay waste our powers;
Little we see in Nature that is ours;
We have given our hearts away, a sordid boon!
This Sea that bares her bosom to the moon;   5
The winds that will be howling at all hours,
And are up-gathered now like sleeping flowers;
For this, for everything, we are out of tune;
It moves us not. Great God! I'd rather be
A Pagan suckled in a creed outworn;   10

So might I, standing on this pleasant lea,
Have glimpses that would make me less forlorn;
Have sight of Proteus rising from the sea;
Or hear old Triton blow his wreathèd horn.

QUESTIONS

1. In this sonnet by Wordsworth what condition does the poet complain about? To what does he attribute this condition?
2. How does it affect him as an individual?

H. D. [Hilda Doolittle]   (1886–1961)*

HELEN   1924

All Greece hates
the still eyes in the white face,
the lustre as of olives
where she stands,
and the white hands.   5

All Greece reviles
the wan face when she smiles,
hating it deeper still
when it grows wan and white,
remembering past enchantments   10
and past ills.

Greece sees unmoved,
God's daughter, born of love,
the beauty of cool feet
and slenderest knees,   15
could love indeed the maid,
only if she were laid,
white ash amid funereal cypresses.

HELEN. In Greek mythology, Helen, most beautiful of all women, was the daughter of a mortal, Leda, by the god Zeus. Her abduction set off the long and devastating Trojan War. While married to Menelaus, king of the Greek city-state of Sparta, Helen was carried off by Paris, prince of Troy. Menelaus and his brother Agamemnon raised an army, besieged Troy for ten years, and eventually recaptured her. One episode of the Trojan War is related in the *Iliad*, Homer's epic poem, composed before 700 B.C.

ARCHETYPE

An important concept in understanding myth is the **archetype,** a basic image, character, situation, or symbol that appears so often in literature and legend that it evokes a deep universal response. (The Greek root of *archetype* means "original pattern.") The term was borrowed by literary critics from the writings of the Swiss psychologist Carl Jung, a serious scholar of myth and religion, who formulated a theory of the "collective unconscious," a set of primal memories common to the entire human race. Archetypal patterns emerged, he speculated, in prerational thought and often reflect key primordial experiences such as birth, growth, sexual awakening, family, generational struggle, and death, as well as primal elements such as fire, sun, moon, blood, and water. Jung also believed that these situations, images, and figures had actually been genetically coded into the human brain and are passed down to successive generations, but no one has ever been able to prove a biological base for the undeniable phenomenon of similar characters, stories, and symbols appearing across widely separated and diverse cultures.

Whatever their origin, archetypal images do seem verbally coded in most myths, legends, and traditional tales. One sees enough recurring patterns and figures from Greek myth to *Star Wars*, from Hindu epic to Marvel superhero comics, to strongly suggest that there is some common psychic force at work. Typical archetypal figures include the trickster, the cruel stepmother, the rebellious young man, the beautiful but destructive woman, and the stupid youngest son who succeeds through simple goodness. Any one of these figures can be traced from culture to culture. The trickster, for instance, appears in American Indian coyote tales, Norse myths about the fire god Loki, Marx Brothers films, and *Batman* comic books and cartoons featuring the Joker. Archetypal myths are the basic conventions of human storytelling, which we learn without necessarily being aware of the process. The patterns we absorb in our first nursery rhymes and fairy tales, as mythological critic Northrop Frye has demonstrated, underlie—though often very subtly—the most sophisticated poems and novels. One powerful archetype seen across many cultures is the demon-goddess who immobilizes men by locking them into a deathly trance or—in the most primitive forms of the myth—turning them to stone. Here is a modern version of this ancient myth in the following poem by Louise Bogan.

Louise Bogan   (1897–1970)*

MEDUSA   1923

I had come to the house, in a cave of trees,
Facing a sheer sky.
Everything moved,—a bell hung ready to strike,
Sun and reflection wheeled by.

When the bare eyes were before me   5
And the hissing hair,
Held up at a window, seen through a door.
The stiff bald eyes, the serpents on the forehead
Formed in the air.

This is a dead scene forever now.   10
Nothing will ever stir.
The end will never brighten it more than this,
Nor the rain blur.

The water will always fall, and will not fall,
And the tipped bell make no sound.   15
The grass will always be growing for hay
Deep on the ground.

And I shall stand here like a shadow
Under the great balanced day,
My eyes on the yellow dust, that was lifting in the wind,   20
And does not drift away.

MEDUSA. Medusa was one of the Gorgons of Greek mythology. Hideously ugly with snakes for hair,
Medusa turned those who looked upon her face into stone.

QUESTIONS

1. Who is the speaker of the poem?
2. Why are the first two stanzas spoken in the past tense while the final three are mainly in the future tense?
3. What is the speaker's attitude toward Medusa? Is there anything surprising about his or her reaction to being transformed into stone?
4. Does Bogan merely dramatize an incident from classical mythology, or does the poem suggest other interpretations as well?

PERSONAL MYTH

Sometimes poets have been inspired to make up myths of their own, to embody their own visions of life. "I must create a system or be enslaved by another man's," said William Blake, who in his "prophetic books" peopled the cosmos with supernatural beings having names such as Los, Urizen, and Vala (side by side with recognizable figures from the Old Testament and New Testament). This kind of system-making probably has advantages and drawbacks. T. S. Eliot, in his essay on Blake, wishes that the author of *The Four Zoas* had accepted traditional myths, and he compares Blake's thinking to a piece of home-made furniture whose construction diverted valuable energy from the writing of poems. Others have found Blake's untraditional cosmos an achievement—notably William Butler Yeats, himself the author of an elaborate personal mythology. Although we need not know all of Yeats's mythology to enjoy his poems, to know of its existence can make a few great poems deeper for us and less difficult.

William Butler Yeats (1865–1939)*

THE SECOND COMING   1921

Turning and turning in the widening gyre°   *spiral*
The falcon cannot hear the falconer;
Things fall apart; the center cannot hold;
Mere anarchy is loosed upon the world,
The blood-dimmed tide is loosed, and everywhere   5
The ceremony of innocence is drowned;
The best lack all conviction, while the worst
Are full of passionate intensity.

Surely some revelation is at hand;
Surely the Second Coming is at hand;   10
The Second Coming! Hardly are those words out
When a vast image out of *Spiritus Mundi*
Troubles my sight: somewhere in sands of the desert
A shape with lion body and the head of a man,
A gaze blank and pitiless as the sun,   15
Is moving its slow thighs, while all about it
Reel shadows of the indignant desert birds.
The darkness drops again; but now I know
That twenty centuries of stony sleep
Were vexed to nightmare by a rocking cradle,   20
And what rough beast, its hour come round at last,
Slouches towards Bethlehem to be born?

What kind of Second Coming does Yeats expect? Evidently it is not to be a Christian one. Yeats saw human history as governed by the turning of a Great Wheel, whose phases influence events and determine human personalities— rather like the signs of the Zodiac in astrology. Every two thousand years comes a horrendous moment: the Wheel completes a turn; one civilization ends and another begins. Strangely, a new age is always announced by birds and by acts of violence. Thus the Greek-Roman world arrives with the descent of Zeus in swan's form and the burning of Troy, the Christian era with the descent of the Holy Spirit—traditionally depicted as a dove—and the Crucifixion. In 1919 when Yeats wrote "The Second Coming," his Ireland was in the midst of turmoil and bloodshed; the Western Hemisphere had been severely shaken by World War I and the Russian Revolution. A new millennium seemed imminent. What sphinxlike, savage deity would next appear on earth, with birds proclaiming it angrily? Yeats imagines it emerging from *Spiritus Mundi*, Soul of the World, a collective unconscious from which a human being (since the individual soul touches it) receives dreams, nightmares, and racial memories.[1]

[1]Yeats fully explains his system in *A Vision* (1938; reprinted New York: Macmillan, 1956).

It is hard to say whether a poet who discovers a personal myth does so to have something to live by or to have something to write about. Robert Graves, who professed his belief in a White Goddess ("Mother of All Living, the ancient power of love and terror"), declared that he wrote his poetry in a trance, inspired by his Goddess-Muse.[2] Luckily, we do not have to know a poet's religious affiliation before we can read his or her poems. Perhaps most personal myths that enter poems are not acts of faith but works of art: stories that resemble traditional mythology.

Jonathan Holden   (b. 1941)

THE NAMES OF THE RAPIDS   1985

Snaggle-Tooth, Maytag, Taylor Falls—
long before we measured with our eyes
the true size of each monstrosity
its name, downriver, was famous to us.
It lay in wait, something to be slain   5
while our raft, errant, eddied
among glancing pinpricks of sun
and every bend giving way to bend
seemed a last reprieve.
But common terror has a raw taste.   10
It's all banality, as when
you stare straight into a bad cut—
this sense of being slightly more
awake than you might like.
When the raft pitches sideways off   15
a ledge, what you land on is less
than its name. It's a mechanism. None
of the demented expressions
that the fleshly water forms
over that stone profile   20
is more than another collision,
a fleeting logic lost and
forming, now lost in the melee.
When the world is most serious
we approach it with wholly open eyes   25
even as we start the plunge
and the stone explanation.

---

[2]See Graves's *The White Goddess*, rev. ed. (New York: Farrar, 1966), or for a terser statement of his position, see his lecture "The Personal Muse" in *On Poetry: Collected Talks and Essays* (New York: Doubleday, 1969).

1. From the names of the three rapids mentioned in line 1, describe what you think each one would probably be like.
2. How does personal myth function in this poem?

James Dickey (1923–1997)

THE HEAVEN OF ANIMALS   1962

Here they are. The soft eyes open.
If they have lived in a wood
It is a wood.
If they have lived on plains
It is grass rolling   5
Under their feet forever.

Having no souls, they have come,
Anyway, beyond their knowing.
Their instincts wholly bloom
And they rise.   10
The soft eyes open.

To match them, the landscape flowers,
Outdoing, desperately
Outdoing what is required:
The richest wood,   15
The deepest field.

For some of these,
It could not be the place
It is, without blood.
These hunt, as they have done,   20
But with claws and teeth grown perfect,

More deadly than they can believe.
They stalk more silently,
And crouch on the limbs of trees,
And their descent   25
Upon the bright backs of their prey

May take years
In a sovereign floating of joy.
And those that are hunted
Know this as their life,   30
Their reward: to walk

Under such trees in full knowledge
Of what is in glory above them,

And to feel no fear,
But acceptance, compliance.   35
Fulfilling themselves without pain

At the cycle's center,
They tremble, they walk
Under the tree,
They fall, they are torn,   40
They rise, they walk again.

QUESTIONS

1. In what ways does Dickey's animal heaven resemble the traditional Christian afterlife? In what ways does it differ?
2. How does the poem reconcile the carnivores' need to hunt with the well-being of the
   hunted animals?
3. Does the final stanza of the poem allude to any other part of the Christian mythos?

Diane Thiel (b. 1967)

MEMENTO MORI IN MIDDLE SCHOOL   2000

When I was twelve, I chose Dante's *Inferno*
in gifted class—an oral presentation
with visual aids. My brother, *il miglior fabbro*,

said he would draw the tortures. We used ten
red posterboards. That day, for school, I dressed   5
in pilgrim black, left earlier to hang them

around the class. The students were impressed.
The teacher, too. She acted quite amused
and peered too long at all the punishments.

We knew by reputation she was cruel.   10
The class could see a hint of twisted forms
and asked to be allowed to round the room

as I went through my final presentation.
We passed the first one, full of poets cut
out of a special issue of *Horizon*.   15

The class thought these were such a boring set,
they probably deserved their tedious fates.
They liked the next, though—bodies blown about,

the lovers kept outside the tinfoil gates.
We had a new boy in our class named Paolo   20
and when I noted Paolo's wind-blown state

and pointed out Francesca, people howled.
I knew that more than one of us not-so-
covertly liked him. It seemed like hours

before we moved on to the gluttons, though,   25
where they could hold the cool fistfuls of slime
I brought from home. An extra touch. It sold

in canisters at toy stores at the time.
The students recognized the River Styx,
the logo of a favorite band of mine.   30

We moved downriver to the town of Dis,
which someone loudly re-named Dis and Dat.
And for the looming harpies and the furies,

who shrieked and tore things up, I had clipped out
the shrillest, most deserving teacher's heads   35
from our school paper, then thought better of it.

At the wood of suicides, we quieted.
Though no one in the room would say a word,
I know we couldn't help but think of Fred.

His name was in the news, though we had heard   40
he might have just been playing with the gun.
We moved on quickly by that huge, dark bird

and rode the flying monster, Geryon,
to reach the counselors, each wicked face,
again, I had resisted pasting in.   45

To represent the ice in that last place,
where Satan chewed the traitors' frozen heads,
my mother had insisted that I take

an ice-chest full of popsicles—to end
my gruesome project on a lighter note.   50
"It *is* a comedy, isn't it," she said.

She hadn't read the poem, or seen our art,
but asked me what had happened to the sweet,
angelic poems I once read and wrote.

The class, though, was delighted by the treat,   55
and at the last round, they all pushed to choose
their colors quickly, so they wouldn't melt.

The bell rang. Everyone ran out of school,
as always, yelling at the top of their lungs,
The *Inferno* fast forgotten, but their howls   60

showed off their darkened red and purple tongues.

MEMENTO MORI IN MIDDLE SCHOOL. *Memento Mori*: Latin for "Remember you must die," the phrase now means any reminder of human mortality and the need to lead a virtuous life. 1 *Dante's* Inferno: The late medieval epic poem by the Italian poet Dante Alighieri decribes a Christian soul's journey through hell. (*Inferno* means "hell" in Italian.) 3 *il miglior fabbro*: the better craftsman—Dante's term for fellow poet Arnaut Daniel, which T. S. Eliot later famously quoted to praise Ezra Pound. 15 *Horizon*: a magazine of art and culture. 20–23: *Paolo . . . Francesca*: two lovers in Dante's *Inferno* who have been damned for their adultery. 29 *River Styx*: the sacred river that flows around hell to mark its boundary. 31 *Dis*: the main city of hell named after its ruler, Dis (Pluto). 43 *Geryon*: a mythical three-headed, three-bodied monster Dante places in his *Inferno*.

MYTH AND POPULAR CULTURE

If one can find myths in an art museum, one can also find them abundantly in popular culture. Movies and comic books, for example, are full of myths in modern guise. What is Superman, if not a mythic hero who has adapted himself to modern urban life? Marvel Comics even made the Norse thunder god, Thor, into a superhero, although they initially obliged him, like Clark Kent, to get a job. We also see myths retold on the technicolor screen. Sometimes Hollywood presents the traditional story directly, as in Walt Disney's *Cinderella;* more often the ancient tales acquire contemporary settings, as in another celluloid Cinderella story, *Pretty Woman.* (See how Anne Sexton has retold the Cinderella story from a feminist perspective, later in this chapter, or find a recording of Dana Dane's Brooklyn housing project version of the fairy tale done from a masculine perspective in his underground rap hit "Cinderfella.") George Lucas's *Star Wars* trilogy borrowed the structure of medieval quest legends. In quest stories, young knights pursued their destiny, often by seeking the Holy Grail, the cup Christ used at the Last Supper; in *Star Wars*, Luke Skywalker searched for his own parentage and identity, but his interstellar quest brought him to a surprisingly similar cast of knights, monsters, princesses, and wizards. Medieval Grail romances, which influenced Eliot's *The Waste Land*, also shaped films such as *The Fisher King* and *Brazil.* Science fiction also commonly uses myth to novel effect. Extraterrestrial visitors usually appear as either munificent mythic gods or nightmarish demons. Steven Spielberg's *E.T.*, for example, revealed a gentle, Christ-like alien recognized by innocent children, but persecuted by adults. E.T. even healed the sick, fell into a deathlike coma, and was resurrected.

It hardly matters whether the popular audience recognizes the literal source of a myth; the viewers intuitively understand the structure of the story and feel its deep imaginative resonance. That is why poets retell these myths; they are powerful sources of collective psychic energy, waiting to be tapped. Just as Hollywood screenwriters have learned that often the most potent way to use a myth is to disguise it, poets sometimes borrow the forms of popular culture to retell their myths. Here is a contemporary narrative poem that borrows imagery from motion pictures to reenact a story that not only predates cinema but, most probably, stretches back before the invention of writing itself.

Charles Martin (b. 1942)

TAKEN UP   1978

Tired of earth, they dwindled on their hill,
Watching and waiting in the moonlight until
The aspens' leaves quite suddenly grew still,

No longer quaking as the disc descended,
That glowing wheel of lights whose coming ended   5
All waiting and watching. When it landed

The ones within it one by one came forth,
Stalking out awkwardly upon the earth,
And those who watched them were confirmed in faith:

Mysterious voyagers from outer space,   10
Attenuated, golden—shreds of lace
Spun into seeds of the sunflower's spinning face—

Light was their speech, spanning mind to mind:
We come here not believing what we find—
Can it be your desire to leave behind   15

The earth, which those called angels bless,
Exchanging amplitude for emptiness?
And in a single voice they answered *Yes,*

Discord of human melodies all blent
To the unearthly strain of their assent.   20
Come then, the Strangers said, and those that were taken, went.

QUESTIONS

1. What myths does this poem recall?
2. This poem was written about the same time that Steven Spielberg's film *Close Encounters of the Third Kind* (1977) appeared. If you recall the movie, compare its ending with the ending of the poem. Martin had not seen the film before writing "Taken Up." How can we account for the similarity?

Why do poets retell myths? Why don't they just make up their own stories? First, using myth allows poets to be concise. By alluding to stories that their audiences know, they can draw on powerful associations with just a few words. If someone describes an acquaintance, "He thinks he's James Bond," that one allusion speaks volumes. Likewise, when Robert Frost inserts the single line, "So Eden sank to grief," in "Nothing Gold Can Stay," those five words summon up a wealth of associations. They tie the perishable quality of spring's beauty to the equally transient nature of human youth. They also suggest that everything in the human world is subject to time's ravages, that perfection is impossible for us to maintain, just as it was for Adam and Eve.

Second, poets know that many stories fall into familiar mythic patterns, and that the most powerful stories of human existence tend to be the same, generation after generation. Sometimes using an old story allows a writer to describe a new situation in a fresh and surprising way. Novels often try to capture the exact texture of a social situation; they need to present the everyday details to evoke the world in which their characters live. Myths tend to tell their stories more quickly and in more general terms. They give just the essential actions and leave out everything else. Narrative poems also work best when they focus on just the essential elements. Here are two modern narrative poems that retell traditional myths to make modern interpretations.

A. D. Hope (1907–2000)

IMPERIAL ADAM   1952

Imperial Adam, naked in the dew,
Felt his brown flanks and found the rib was gone.
Puzzled he turned and saw where, two and two,
The mighty spoor of Jahweh marked the lawn.

Then he remembered through mysterious sleep   5
The surgeon fingers probing at the bone,
The voice so far away, so rich and deep:
"It is not good for him to live alone."

Turning once more he found Man's counterpart
In tender parody breathing at his side.   10
He knew her at first sight, he knew by heart
Her allegory of sense unsatisfied.

The pawpaw drooped its golden breasts above
Less generous than the honey of her flesh;
The innocent sunlight showed the place of love;   15
The dew on its dark hairs winked crisp and fresh.

This plump gourd severed from his virile root,
She promised on the turf of Paradise
Delicious pulp of the forbidden fruit;
Sly as the snake she loosed her sinuous thighs,   20

And waking, smiled up at him from the grass;
Her breasts rose softly and he heard her sigh—
From all the beasts whose pleasant task it was
In Eden to increase and multiply

Adam had learned the jolly deed of kind: 25
He took her in his arms and there and then,
Like the clean beasts, embracing from behind,
Began in joy to found the breed of men.

Then from the spurt of seed within her broke
Her terrible and triumphant female cry,   30
Split upward by the sexual lightning stroke.
It was the beasts now who stood watching by:

The gravid elephant, the calving hind,
The breeding bitch, the she-ape big with young
Were the first gentle midwives of mankind;   35
The teeming lioness rasped her with her tongue;

The proud vicuña nuzzled her as she slept
Lax on the grass; and Adam watching too
Saw how her dumb breasts at their ripening wept,
The great pod of her belly swelled and grew,   40

And saw its water break, and saw, in fear,
Its quaking muscles in the act of birth,
Between her legs a pigmy face appear,
And the first murderer lay upon the earth.

IMPERIAL ADAM. Hope's poem retells the story of Adam and Eve. For the Biblical version, see Genesis 2:18–4:1. 4 *Jahweh:* the Lord of the Old Testament. The Hebrew name of God was written as JHVH, but it was considered too sacred to say aloud. Yahweh and Jehovah are the other most common versions of the vowel-less Hebrew name. 25 *deed of kind:* the act of procreation. This particular expression is usually used to describe the mating of animals. 44 *the first murderer:* Cain, Adam and Eve's first child, who murdered his brother, Abel. See Genesis 4:1–16.

QUESTIONS

1. Why is Adam called "imperial" What empire does he command?
2. What does Hope imply in lines 18–20, when he describes Eve's sexuality?
3. There is no serpent in Hope's version of the Adam and Eve story. And yet by the end of the poem, evil has entered Paradise. What has introduced it?
4. How does the last line of "Imperial Adam" affect the meaning of the poem?

Anne Sexton   (1928–1974)*

CINDERELLA   1971

You always read about it:
the plumber with twelve children
who wins the Irish Sweepstakes.
From toilets to riches.
That story.   5

Or the nursemaid,
some luscious sweet from Denmark
who captures the oldest son's heart.
From diapers to Dior.
That story.   10

Or a milkman who serves the wealthy,
eggs, cream, butter, yogurt, milk,
the white truck like an ambulance
who goes into real estate
and makes a pile.   15
From homogenized to martinis at lunch.

Or the charwoman
who is on the bus when it cracks up
and collects enough from the insurance.
From mops to Bonwit Teller.   20
That story.

Once
the wife of a rich man was on her deathbed
and she said to her daughter Cinderella:
Be devout. Be good. Then I will smile   25
down from heaven in the seam of a cloud.
The man took another wife who had
two daughters, pretty enough
but with hearts like blackjacks.
Cinderella was their maid.   30
She slept on the sooty hearth each night
and walked around looking like Al Jolson.
Her father brought presents home from town,
jewels and gowns for the other women
but the twig of a tree for Cinderella.   35
She planted that twig on her mother's grave
and it grew to a tree where a white dove sat.
Whenever she wished for anything the dove
would drop it like an egg upon the ground.
The bird is important, my dears, so heed him.   40

Next came the ball, as you all know.
It was a marriage market.
The prince was looking for a wife.
All but Cinderella were preparing
and gussying up for the big event.   45
Cinderella begged to go too.

Her stepmother threw a dish of lentils
into the cinders and said: Pick them
up in an hour and you shall go.
The white dove brought all his friends;   50
all the warm wings of the fatherland came,
and picked up the lentils in a jiffy.
No, Cinderella, said the stepmother,
you have no clothes and cannot dance.
That's the way with stepmothers.   55

Cinderella went to the tree at the grave
and cried forth like a gospel singer:
Mama! Mama! My turtledove,
send me to the prince's ball!
The bird dropped down a golden dress   60
and delicate little gold slippers.
Rather a large package for a simple bird.
So she went. Which is no surprise.
Her stepmother and sisters didn't
recognize her without her cinder face   65
and the prince took her hand on the spot
and danced with no other the whole day.

As nightfall came she thought she'd better
get home. The prince walked her home
and she disappeared into the pigeon house   70
and although the prince took an axe and broke
it open she was gone. Back to her cinders.

These events repeated themselves for three days.
However on the third day the prince
covered the palace steps with cobbler's wax   75
and Cinderella's gold shoe stuck upon it.
Now he would find whom the shoe fit
and find his strange dancing girl for keeps.
He went to their house and the two sisters
were delighted because they had lovely feet.   80
The eldest went into a room to try the slipper on
but her big toe got in the way so she simply
sliced it off and put on the slipper.
The prince rode away with her until the white dove
told him to look at the blood pouring forth.   85
That is the way with amputations.
They don't just heal up like a wish.
The other sister cut off her heel
but the blood told as blood will.
The prince was getting tired.   90

He began to feel like a shoe salesman.
But he gave it one last try.
This time Cinderella fit into the shoe
like a love letter into its envelope.

At the wedding ceremony   95
the two sisters came to curry favor
and the white dove pecked their eyes out.
Two hollow spots were left
like soup spoons.

Cinderella and the prince   100
lived, they say, happily ever after,
like two dolls in a museum case
never bothered by diapers or dust,
never arguing over the timing of an egg,
never telling the same story twice,   105
never getting a middle-aged spread,
their darling smiles pasted on for eternity.
Regular Bobbsey Twins.
That story.

CINDERELLA. 32 *Al Jolson:* Extremely popular American entertainer (1886–1950) who frequently
performed in blackface.

QUESTIONS

1. Most of Sexton's "Cinderella" straightforwardly retells a version of the famous fairy
   tale. But in the beginning and ending of the poem, how does Sexton change the
   story?
2. How does Sexton's refrain of "That story" alter the meaning of the episodes it describes? What is the tone of this poem (the poet's attitude toward her material)?
3. What does Sexton's final stanza suggest about the way fairy tales usually end?

Anne Sexton

Anne Sexton on Writing

TRANSFORMING FAIRY TALES   1970

[*To Paul Brooks°*]

October 14, 1970

Dear Paul,

I wanted to let some time elapse before I answered you so that I could think carefully about what you had to say. I've written seventeen "Transformations."° My goal was twenty, but I may have to make do with seventeen. Seventeen would be a nice book anyway, but I will wait a couple of months and see what comes. I am in the process of typing up the manuscript to submit to you.

But back to your comments. I realize that the "Transformations" are a departure from my usual style. I would say that they lack the intensity and perhaps some of the confessional force of my previous work. I wrote them because I had to . . . because I wanted to . . . because it made me happy. I would want to publish them for the same reason. I would like my readers to see this side of me, and it is not in every case the lighter side. Some of the poems are grim. In fact I don't know how to typify them except to agree that I have made them very contemporary. It would further be a lie to say that they weren't about me, because they are just as much about me as my other poetry.

I look at my work in stages, and each new book is a kind of growth and reaching outward and as always backward. Perhaps the critics will be unhappy with this book and some of my readers maybe will not like it either. I feel I will gain new readers and critics who have always disliked my work (and too true, the critics are not always kind to me) may come around. I have found the people I've shown them to apathetic in some cases and wildly excited in others. It often depends on their own feelings about Grimms' fairy tales.

[*To Kurt Vonnegut, Jr.*°]

November 17, 1970

Dear Kurt,

I meant to write you a postcard before your dentist appointment, but I was away at the time I should have sent it. Sorry. Your graph for "Cinderella" is right over my desk.

The enclosed manuscript is of my new book of poems. I've taken Grimms' Fairy Tales and "Transformed" them into something all of my own. The better books of fairy tales have introductions telling the value of these old fables. I feel my *Transformations* needs an introduction telling of the value of my (one could say) rape of them. Maybe that's an incorrect phrase. I do something very modern to them (have you ever tried to describe your own work? I find I am tongue-tied). They are small, funny and horrifying. Without quite meaning to I have joined the black humorists. I don't know if you know my other work, but humor was never a very prominent feature . . . terror, deformity, madness and torture were my bag. But this little universe of Grimm is not that far away. I think they end up being as wholly personal as my most intimate poems, in a different language, a different rhythm, but coming strangely, for all their story sound, from as deep a place.

From Anne Sexton: A Self-Portrait in Letters

Paul Brooks: Sexton's editor at Houghton Mifflin. He initially had reservations about Sexton's fairy tale poems. *"Transformations:"* title of Sexton's 1971 volume of poems that contained "Cinderella." *Kurt Vonnegut, Jr.:* popular author of *Cat's Cradle* (1963) and other novels.

━━◧═▷ WRITING CRITICALLY ◁═▩━━

Demystifying Myth

Myth often seems like an intimidating term. Asked to consider the mythic aspects of a poem, we often begin to worry about how well we remember the original story. Sometimes the version of the myth that we remember from a book or movie seems different from the story being referred to. Or one we have never before encountered feels oddly familiar. Myths often appear elusive because they are stories that lend themselves to adaptation. Two Greek versions of the same story will almost always differ widely in detail: new episodes appear, minor characters change names or vanish. What usually remains fixed, however, is the basic pattern. Orpheus always descends to the Underworld but is never able to rescue his beloved Eurydice. Superhuman Hercules inevitably goes mad and slaughters his wife and sons. Oedipus is always doomed to kill his father and unwittingly marry his widowed mother.

If the artistry of myth is in the details of the tale, the deeper psychological meaning is contained in its permanent underlying structure. In writing about myth, therefore, try to find the underlying pattern of the narrative in question. Does the basic shape of the poem's story seem familiar? Does that story have some recognizable source in myth or legend? If the poem has no obvious narrative line, does its movement call to mind other stories? In "Cinderella" Anne Sexton deliberately reminds us of the mythic patterns of her material ("the plumber with twelve children / who wins the Irish Sweepstakes. / From toilets to riches. / That story"). Although not all poems are conventional narratives, and few authors delight in leaving as many clues as Sexton, most authors do insert some luminous clues in their poems. Why? They want readers to hear the echoes of their sources, because writers understand the resonance of myth. "So Eden sank to grief," confides Frost in "Nothing Gold Can Stay," to let readers know that the poem is not only about spring. His reference to Eden encourages us to see the poem as a universal narrative rather than merely elegant natural description.

Once you have linked the poem to its mythic source, notice what new details the author has added. What do they tell us about his or her attitude toward the original source? Are important elements of the original discarded? What does their absence suggest about the author's primary focus? You can refresh your memory of the original myth by looking it up in a reference work such as *Brewer's Dictionary of Phrase and Fable*, but the essential thing is to recognize the basic narrative underlying the poem and to see how it shapes the new work's meaning. For a helpful overview of how critics analyze myth in literature, see the section "Mythological Criticism" in the chapter "Critical Approaches to Literature."

WRITING ASSIGNMENT

Provide a close reading of any poem from this book that uses a traditional myth or legend. In the course of your analysis, demonstrate how the author borrows or changes certain details of the myth to emphasize his or her meaning. In addition to the poems in this chapter, some selections to consider include: Fred Chappell's "Narcissus and Echo," T. S. Eliot's "Journey of the Magi," Anthony Hecht's "Adam," and William Butler Yeats's "The Magi" or "Leda and the Swan."

Here is an example of an essay on this assignment written by Heather Burke when she was a sophomore at Wesleyan University in Middletown, Connecticut.

Heather Burke

Professor Greene

English 150

18 January 20xx

The Bonds Between Love and Hatred in H.D.'s "Helen"

In her poem "Helen," H.D. examines the close connection between the emotions of love and hatred as embodied in the figure of Helen of Troy. Helen was the cause of the long and bloody Trojan War, and her homecoming is tainted by the memory of the suffering this war caused. As in many Imagist poems, the title is essential to the poem's meaning; it gives the reader both a specific mythic context and a particular subject. Without the title, it would be virtually impossible to understand the poem fully since Helen's name appears nowhere else in the text. The reader familiar with Greek myth knows that Helen, who was the wife of Menelaus, ran away with Paris. Their adultery provoked the Trojan War, which lasted for ten years and resulted in the destruction of Troy.

What is unusual about the poem is H.D.'s perspective on Helen of Troy. The poem refuses to romanticize Helen's story, but its stark new version is easy for a reader to accept. After suffering so much for the sake of one adulterous woman, how could the Greeks not resent her? Rather than idealizing the situation, H.D. describes the enmity which defiles Helen's homecoming and explores the irony of the hatred which "All Greece" feels for her.

The opening line of the poem sets its tone and introduces its central theme--hatred. Helen's beauty required thousands of men to face death in battle, but it cannot assuage the emotional aftermath of the war. Even though Helen is described as "God's daughter, born of love" (13), all she inspires now is resentment, and the poem explores the ways in which these two emotions are closely related.

In the first stanza, the poet uses the color white, as well as the radiance or luster connected with it, in her description of Helen, and this color will be associated with her throughout the poem:

> the still eyes in the white face,
>
> the lustre as of olives
>
> where she stands,
>
> and the white hands. (2-5)

As one of the foundations of agriculture and civilization, the olive was a crucial symbol in Greek culture. Helen's beauty is compared to the "lustre" of this olive. This word presumably refers to the radiance or light which the whiteness of her face reflects, but Helen's identification with this fruit also has an ironic connotation. The olive branch is a traditional symbol of peace, but the woman it is compared to was the cause of a bitter war.

The majority of the imagery in the poem is connected with the color white. H.D. uses white to describe Helen's skin; white would have been seen as the appropriate color for a rich and beautiful woman's skin in pre-twentieth century poetry. This color also has several connotations, all of which operate simultaneously in the poem. The color white has a connection to Helen's paternity; her immortal father Zeus took the form of a white swan when he made love to her mortal mother Leda. At the same time, whiteness suggests a certain chilliness, as with snow or frost. In the third stanza, H.D. makes this suggestion explicit with her use of the phrase "the beauty of cool feet" (14). This image also suggests the barrenness connected with such frigidity. In this sense, it is a very accurate representation of Helen, because in The Odyssey Homer tells us that ". . . the gods had never after granted Helen / a child to bring into the sunlit world / after the first, rose-lipped Hermoine"

(4.13-15). Helen is returned to her rightful husband, but after her adulterous actions, she is unable to bear him any more children. She is a woman who is renowned for exciting passion in legions of men, but that passion is now sterile.

Another traditional connotation of the color white is purity, but this comparison only accentuates Helen's sexual transgressions; she is hardly pure. H.D. emphasizes her lasciviousness through the use of irony. In the third stanza, she refers to Helen as a "maid." A maid is a virgin, but Helen is most definitely not virginal in any sense. In the following line, the poet rhymes "maid" with the word "laid," which refers to the placement of Helen's body on the funeral pyre. This particular word, however, deliberately emphasized by the rhyme, also carries slangy associations with the act of sexual intercourse. This connotation presents another ironic contrast with the word "maid."

The first line of the second stanza is almost identical to that of the first, and again we are reminded of the intense animosity that Helen's presence inspires. This hatred is now made more explicit. The word <u>revile</u> is defined by the <u>American Heritage College Dictionary</u> as "to denounce with abusive language" ("Revile"). Helen is a queen, but she is subjected to the insults of her subjects as well as the rest of Greece.

Helen's homecoming is not joyous, but a time of exile and penance. The war is over, but no one, especially Helen, can forget the past. Her memories seem to cause her wanness, which the dictionary defines as "indicating weariness, illness, or unhappiness" ("Wan"). Her face now ". . . grows wan and white, / remembering past enchantments / and past ills" (9-11). The enchantment she remembers is that of Aphrodite, the goddess who lured her from her husband and home to Paris's bed. The "ills" which Helen remembers can be seen as both her sexual offenses and the human losses sustained in the Trojan War. The use of the word <u>ills</u> works in conjunction with the word <u>wan</u> to demonstrate Helen's spiritual sickness; she is plagued by regret.

As the opening of the third stanza shows, the woman who was famous for her beauty and perfection now leaves Greece "unmoved." This opening may not echo the sharpness of those of the first two stanzas, but it picks up on the theme of Helen as a devalued prize. In the eyes of the Greeks, she is not the beauty who called two armies to battle but merely an unfaithful wife for whom many died needlessly.

The final lines of the poem reveal the one condition which could turn the people's hatred into love again. They "could love indeed the maid, / only if she were laid, / white ash amid funereal cypresses" (16-19). The Greeks can only forgive Helen once her body has been burned on the funeral pyre. These disturbing lines illustrate the destructive power of hatred; it can only be conquered by death. These lines also reveal the final significance of the color white. It suggests Helen's death. As Helen's face is pale and white in life, so her ashes will be in death. The flames of the funeral pyre are the only way to purify the flesh which was tainted by the figurative flames of passion. Death is the only way to restore Helen's beauty and make it immortal. While she is alive, her beauty is only a reminder of lost fathers, sons, and brothers. The people of Greece can only despise her while she is living, but they can love and revere the memory of her beauty once she is dead.

Works Cited

H. D. "Helen." <u>An Introduction to Poetry</u>. Ed. X. J. Kennedy
     and Dana Gioia. 11th ed. New York: Longman, 2005. 283.

Homer. <u>The Odyssey</u>. Trans. Robert Fitzgerald. New York:
     Noonday P, 1998.

"Revile." <u>American Heritage College Dictionary</u>. 4th ed. 2002.

"Wan." <u>American Heritage College Dictionary</u>. 4th ed. 2002.

FURTHER SUGGESTIONS FOR WRITING

1. Read the original version of either the story of Adam and Eve (the first four chapters of Genesis) or "Cinderella" (in Charles Perrault's *Mother Goose Tales*) and compare it to the corresponding poem in this chapter. Which elements in the myth does the poet change and which does he or she retain?
2. Write an explication of D. H. Lawrence's "Bavarian Gentians" or Thomas Hardy's "The Oxen." (For hints on writing about poetry by the method of explication, see the chapter "Writing About a Poem.")
3. Take any famous myth or fairy tale and retell it to reflect your personal philosophy.

14 *Poetry and Personal Identity*

Only a naive reader assumes that all poems directly reflect the personal experience of their authors. That would be like believing that a TV sitcom actually describes the real family life of its cast. As you will recall if you read "The Person in the Poem" (page 27), poets often speak in voices other than their own. These voices may be borrowed or imaginary. Stevie Smith appropriates the voice of a dead swimmer in her poem, "Not Waving but Drowning" (page 110), and Ted Hughes imagines a nonhuman voice in "Hawk Roosting" (page 30). Some poets also try to give their personal poems a universal feeling. Edna St. Vincent Millay's emotion-charged sonnet "Well, I Have Lost You; and I Lost You Fairly" describes the end of a difficult love affair with a younger man, but she dramatizes the situation in such a way that it seems deliberately independent of any particular time and place. Even her lover remains shadowy and nameless. No one has ever been able to identify the characters in Shakespeare's sonnets with actual people, but that fact does not diminish our pleasure in them as poems.

And yet there are times when poets try to speak openly in their own voices. What could be a more natural subject for a poet than examining his or her own life? The autobiographical elements in a poem may be indirect, as in Chidiock Tichborne's elegy, written before his execution for treason in 1586 (page 131), or it may form the central subject, as in Sylvia Plath's "Lady Lazarus," which discusses her suicide attempts. In either case, the poem's autobiographical stance affects a reader's response. Although we respond to a poem's formal elements, we cannot also help reacting to what we know about its human origins. To learn that the elegant elegy we have just read was written by an eighteen-year-old boy, who would soon be horribly executed, adds a special poignancy to the poem's content. Likewise, to read Plath's chilling exploration of her death wish, while knowing that within a few months the poet would kill herself, we receive an extra jolt of emotion. In a good autobiographical poem, that shock of veracity adds to the poem's power. In an unsuccessful poem, the autobiographical facts become a substitute for emotions not credibly conveyed by the words themselves.

One literary movement, **Confessional poetry,** has made such frank self-definition its main purpose. As the name implies, Confessional poetry renders personal experience as candidly as possible, even sharing confidences that may violate social conventions or propriety. Confessional poets sometimes shock their readers with admissions of experiences so intimate and painful—adultery, family violence, suicide attempts—that most people would try to suppress them, or at least not proclaim them to the world.

Some Confessional poets, such as Anne Sexton, W. D. Snodgrass, and Robert Lowell, underwent psychoanalysis, and at times their poems sound like patients telling their analysts every detail of their personal lives. For this reason, Confessional poems run the danger of being more interesting to their authors than to their readers. But when a poet successfully frames his or her personal experience so that the reader can feel an extreme emotion from the inside, the result can be powerful. Here is a chilling poem that takes us within the troubled psyche of a poet who contemplates suicide.

Sylvia Plath (1932–1963)*

Lady Lazarus (1962) 1965

I have done it again.
One year in every ten
I manage it—

A sort of walking miracle, my skin
Bright as a Nazi lampshade,   5
My right foot

A paperweight,
My face a featureless, fine
Jew linen.

Peel off the napkin   10
O my enemy.
Do I terrify?—

The nose, the eye pits, the full set of teeth?
The sour breath
Will vanish in a day.   15

Soon, soon the flesh
The grave cave ate will be
At home on me

And I a smiling woman.
I am only thirty.   20
And like the cat I have nine times to die.

This is Number Three.
What a trash
To annihilate each decade.

What a million filaments. 25
The peanut-crunching crowd
Shoves in to see

Them unwrap me hand and foot—
The big strip tease.
Gentleman, ladies, 30

These are my hands,
My knees.
I may be skin and bone,

Nevertheless, I am the same, identical woman.
The first time it happened I was ten. 35
It was an accident.

The second time I meant
To last it out and not come back at all.
I rocked shut

As a seashell. 40
They had to call and call
And pick the worms off me like sticky pearls.

Dying
Is an art, like everything else.
I do it exceptionally well. 45

I do it so it feels like hell.
I do it so it feels real.
I guess you could say I've a call.

It's easy enough to do it in a cell.
It's easy enough to do it and stay put. 50
It's the theatrical

Comeback in broad day
To the same place, the same face, the same brute
Amused shout:

"A miracle!" 55
That knocks me out.
There is a charge

For the eyeing of my scars, there is a charge
For the hearing of my heart—
It really goes. 60

And there is a charge, a very large charge,
For the word or a touch
Or a bit of blood

Or a piece of my hair or my clothes.
So, so, Herr Doktor.   65
So, Herr Enemy.

I am your opus,°   *work, work of art*
I am your valuable,
The pure gold baby

That melts to a shriek.   70
I turn and burn.
Do not think I underestimate your great concern.

Ash, ash—
You poke and stir.
Flesh, bone, there is nothing there—   75

A cake of soap,
A wedding ring,
A gold filling,

Herr God, Herr Lucifer,
Beware   80
Beware.

Out of the ash
I rise with my red hair.
And I eat men like air.

QUESTIONS

1. Although the poem is openly autobiographical, Plath uses certain symbols to represent herself (Lady Lazarus, a Jew murdered in a concentration camp, a cat with nine lives, and so on.). What do these symbols tell us about Plath's attitude toward herself and the world around her?
2. In her biography of Plath, *Bitter Fame*, the poet Anne Stevenson says that this poem penetrates "the furthest reaches of disdain and rage . . . bereft of all 'normal' human feelings." What do you think Stevenson means? Does anything in the poem strike you as particularly chilling?
3. The speaker in "Lady Lazarus" says, "Dying / Is an art, like everything else" (lines 43–44). What sense do you make of this metaphor?
4. Does the ending of "Lady Lazarus" imply that the speaker assumes that she will outlive her suicide attempts? Set forth your final understanding of the poem.

Not all autobiographical poetry needs to shock the reader, as Plath overtly does in "Lady Lazarus." Poets can also try to share the special moments that illuminate their day-to-day lives, as Elizabeth Bishop does in "Filling Station," when she describes a roadside gas station whose shabby bric-a-brac she saw as symbols of love. But when poets attempt to place their own lives under scrutiny, they face certain difficulties. Honest, thorough self-examination isn't as easy as it might seem. It is one thing to examine oneself in the mirror; it is quite another to sketch accurately what one sees there. Even if we have the skill to describe ourselves in words (or in paint) so that a stranger would recognize the self-portrait, there is the challenge of honesty. Drawing or writing our own self-portrait, most of us yield, often unconsciously, to the temptation of making ourselves a little nobler or better-looking than we really are. The best self-portraits, like Rembrandt's unflattering self-examinations, are usually critical. No one enjoys watching someone else preen in front of a dressing mirror, unless the intention is satiric.

Autobiographical poetry requires a hunger for honest self-examination. Many poets find that, in order to understand themselves and who they are, they must scrutinize more than the self in isolation. Other forces may shape their identities: their ethnic background, their families, their race, their gender, their religion, their economic status, and their age. Aware of these elements, many recent poets have written memorable personal poems. The Dominican American poet Julia Alvarez wrote an autobiographical sequence of thirty-three sonnets as she turned thirty-three. These poems frankly explore her conflicting identities as daughter, sister, divorcee, lover, writer, Dominican, and American. They earn the reader's trust by being open and self-critical. The subject of one sonnet is Alvarez's admission that she is not as beautiful as either her mother or her sister. Reading that admission, we instinctively sympathize with the author.

Julia Alvarez   (b. 1950)

THE WOMEN ON MY MOTHER'S SIDE   1984
WERE KNOWN (FROM "33")

The women on my mother's side were known
for beauty and were given lovely names
passed down for generations. I knew them
as my pretty aunts: Laura, who could turn
any head once, and Ada, whose husband   5
was so devoted he would lay his hand-
kerchief on seats for her and when she rose
thank her; there was Rosa, who got divorced
twice, her dark eyes and thick hair were to blame;
and my mother Julia, who was a catch   10
and looks it in her wedding photographs.
My sister got her looks, I got her name,
and it suits me that between resemblance
and words, I got the right inheritance.

CULTURE, RACE, AND ETHNICITY

One of the personal issues Julia Alvarez faces in "33" is her dual identity as Dominican and American. The daughter of immigrants, she was born in New York but spent her childhood in the Dominican Republic. Consequently, self-definition for her has meant resolving the claims of two potentially contradictory cultures. In this sonnet, Alvarez talks about inheriting two kinds of beauty from her mother's side of the family. First, there is the beauty of the flesh, which has been passed onto Alvarez's sister. Second, there is a poetic impulse to create beauty with words, fulfilled by the family names, which Alvarez herself has inherited. Here Alvarez touches on the central issue facing the autobiographical poet—using *words* to embody experience. For a writer, the gift of words is "the right inheritance," even if those words are, for an immigrant poet, sometimes in a different language from that of one's parents. American poetry is rich in immigrant cultures, as shown in the work of both first-generation writers such as Alvarez or John Ciardi and foreign-born authors such as Joseph Brodsky (Russia), Nina Cassian (Romania), Claude McKay (Jamaica), Eamon Grennan (Ireland), Thom Gunn (England), Shirley Geok-lin Lim (Malaysia), Emanuel di Pasquale (Italy), José Emilio Pacheco (Mexico), Herberto Padilla (Cuba), and Derek Walcott (St. Lucia). Some literary immigrants, such as the late Russian novelist and poet Vladimir Nabokov, make the difficult transition to writing in English. Others such as Cassian or Pacheco continue to write in their native languages. A few such as Brodsky write bilingually. Such texts often remind us of the multicultural nature of American poetry. Here is a poem by one literary immigrant that raises some important issues of personal identity.

Claude McKay   (1890–1948)

AMERICA   1922

Although she feeds me bread of bitterness,
And sinks into my throat her tiger's tooth,
Stealing my breath of life, I will confess
I love this cultured hell that tests my youth.
Her vigor flows like tides into my blood,   5
Giving me strength erect against her hate,
Her bigness sweeps my being like a flood.
Yet, as a rebel fronts a king in state,
I stand within her walls with not a shred
Of terror, malice, not a word of jeer.   10
Darkly I gaze into the days ahead,
And see her might and granite wonders there,
Beneath the touch of Time's unerring hand,
Like priceless treasures sinking in the sand.

1. Is "America" written in a personal or public voice? What specific elements seem personal? What elements seem public?
2. McKay was a black immigrant from Jamaica, but he does not mention either his race or national origin in the poem. Is his personal background important to understanding "America"?
3. "America" is written in a traditional form. How does the poem's form contribute to its impact?

Claude McKay's "America" raises the question of how an author's race and ethnic identity influence the poetry he or she writes. In the 1920s, for instance, there was an ongoing discussion among black poets as to whether their poetry should deal specifically with the African American experience. Did black poetry exist apart from the rest of American poetry or was it, as Robert Hayden would later suggest, "shaped over some three centuries by social, moral, and literary forces essentially American"? Should black authors primarily address a black audience or should they try to engage a broader literary public? Should black poetry focus on specifically black subjects, forms, and idioms or should it rely mainly on the traditions of English literature? Black poets divided into two camps. Claude McKay and Countee Cullen were among the writers who favored universal themes. (Cullen, for example, insisted he be called a "poet," not a "Negro poet.") Langston Hughes and Jean Toomer were among the "new" poets who felt that black poetry must reflect racial themes. They believed, as James Weldon Johnson had once said, that race was "perforce the thing that the American Negro Poet knows best." Writers on both sides of the debate produced excellent poems, but their work has a very different character. Compare McKay's "America" to a recent poem by Rhina Espaillat, which also examines the American experience from the viewpoint of individuals half inside and half outside mainstream society. Espaillat's poem also adds a new human dimension, the generation gap—familiar to anyone raised in an immigrant home—between those raised in "the old country" and those growing up (and feeling at home) in America.

Rhina Espaillat   (b. 1932)

BILINGUAL/BILINGÜE   1998

My father liked them separate, one there,
one here (allá y aquí), as if aware

that words might cut in two his daughter's heart
(el corazón) and lock the alien part

to what he was—his memory, his name   5
(su nombre)—with a key he could not claim.

"English outside this door, Spanish inside,"
he said, "y basta." But who can divide

the world, the word (mundo y palabra) from
any child? I knew how to be dumb   10

and stubborn (testaruda); late, in bed,
I hoarded secret syllables I read

until my tongue (mi lengua) learned to run
where his stumbled. And still the heart was one.

I like to think he knew that, even when,   15
proud (orgulloso) of his daughter's pen,

he stood outside mis versos, half in fear
of words he loved but wanted not to hear.

QUESTIONS

1. Espaillat's poem is full of Spanish words and phrases. (Even the title is given in both languages.) What does the Spanish add to the poem? Could we remove the phrases without changing the poem?
2. How does the father want to divide his daughter's world, at least in terms of language? Does his request suggest any other divisions he hopes to enforce in her life?
3. How does the daughter respond to her father's request to leave English outside their home?
4. "And still the heart was one," states the speaker of the poem. Should we take her statement at face value or do we sense a cost of her bilingual existence? Agree or disagree with the daughter's statement but state the reasons for your opinion.

The debate between ethnicity and universality has echoed among American writers of every racial and religious minority. Today, we find the same issues being discussed by Arab, Asian, Hispanic, Italian, Jewish, and Native American authors. There is, ultimately, no one correct answer to the questions of identity, for individual artists need the freedom to pursue their own imaginative vision. But considering the issues of race and ethnicity does help a poet think through the artist's sometimes conflicting responsibilities between group and personal identity. Even in poets who have pursued their individual vision, we often see how unmistakably they write from their racial, social, and cultural background. There may seem to be little overtly Hispanic content in Julia Alvarez's sonnet, but her poem implicitly reflects the close extended family structure of Latin cultures. Alvarez's poem also points out that we inherit our bodies as well as our cultures. Our body represents our genetic inheritance that goes back to the beginning of time. Sometimes a poet's ethnic background becomes part of his or her private mythology. In the following poem, Samuel Menashe talks about how his physical body is the center of his Jewish identity.

Samuel Menashe (b. 1925)

THE SHRINE WHOSE SHAPE I AM   1961

The shrine whose shape I am
Has a fringe of fire
Flames skirt my skin

There is no Jerusalem but this
Breathed in flesh by shameless love   5
Built high upon the tides of blood
I believe the Prophets and Blake
And like David I bless myself
With all my might

I know many hills were holy once   10
But now in the level lands to live
Zion ground down must become marrow
Thus in my bones I am the King's son
And through death's domain I go
Making my own procession   15

QUESTIONS

1. What does the poem tell you about the race and religion of the author? How is this information conveyed? Point to specific lines.
2. The ancient Jews located the center of Judaism at the Temple of Jerusalem, destroyed by the Romans in 70 A.D. When Menashe declares "There is no Jerusalem but this," what does he mean? What is he specifically referring to?
3. What does this poem imply about the nature of ethnic identity?

Francisco X. Alarcón (b. 1954)

THE X IN MY NAME   1993

the poor
signature
of my illiterate
and peasant
self   5
giving away
all rights
in a deceiving
contract for life

QUESTION

What does the speaker imply the X in his name signifies?

Wendy Rose (b. 1948)

FOR THE WHITE POETS 1977
WHO WOULD BE INDIAN

just once
just long enough
to snap up the words
fish-hooked
from our tongues.   5
You think of us now
when you kneel
on the earth,
turn holy
in a temporary tourism   10
of our souls.
With words
you paint your faces.
chew your doeskin,
touch breast to tree   15
as if sharing a mother
were all it takes,
could bring
instant and primal
knowledge.   20
You think of us only
when your voice
wants for roots,
when you have sat back
on your heels   25
and become primitive.
You finish your poem
and go back.

QUESTIONS

1. Who is the speaker of the poem? What is the speaker's attitude toward the persons
   addressed?
2. What does the speaker mean in line 16 by "sharing a mother"? Who or what is this
   "mother"?
3. Where do the "white poets" "go back" to in the last line?
4. Why does the speaker believe that "white poets" will always remain outside the
   American Indian's experience?

Sherman Alexie (b. 1966)

INDIAN BOY LOVE SONG (#1)   1992

Everyone I have lost
in the closing of a door
the click of the lock

is not forgotten, they
do not die but remain   5
within the soft edges
of the earth, the ash

of house fires and cancer
in sin and forgiveness
huddled under old blankets   10

dreaming their way into
my hands, my heart
closing tight like fists.

QUESTIONS

1. What is the significance of the simile that concludes the poem?
2. How does the poem's title affect your interpretation of the text? Explain.

Yusef Komunyakaa (b. 1947)

FACING IT   1988

My black face fades,
hiding inside the black granite.
I said I wouldn't,
dammit: No tears.
I'm stone. I'm flesh.   5
My clouded reflection eyes me
like a bird of prey, the profile of night
slanted against morning. I turn
this way—the stone lets me go.
I turn that way—I'm inside   10
the Vietnam Veterans Memorial
again, depending on the light
to make a difference.
I go down the 58,022 names,
half-expecting to find   15
my own in letters like smoke.
I touch the name Andrew Johnson;
I see the booby trap's white flash.
Names shimmer on a woman's blouse

but when she walks away $\qquad$ 20
the names stay on the wall.
Brushstrokes flash, a red bird's
wings cutting across my stare.
The sky. A plane in the sky.
A white vet's image floats $\qquad$ 25
closer to me, then his pale eyes
look through mine. I'm a window.
He's lost his right arm
inside the stone. In the black mirror
a woman's trying to erase names: $\qquad$ 30
No, she's brushing a boy's hair.

QUESTIONS

1. How does the title of "Facing It" relate to the poem? Does it have more than one meaning?
2. The narrator describes the people around him by their reflections on the polished granite rather than by looking at them directly. What does this indirect way of scrutinizing contribute to the poem?
3. This poem comes out of the life experience of a black Vietnam veteran. Is Komunyakaa's writing closer to McKay's "universal" method or closer to Toomer's "ethnic" style?

GENDER

In her celebrated study *You Just Don't Understand: Women and Men in Conversation* (1990), Georgetown University linguist Deborah Tannen explored how men and women use language differently. Tannen compared many everyday conversations between husbands and wives to "cross-cultural communications," as if people from separate worlds lived under the same roof. (Denise Levertov's "Leaving Forever," on page 135, describes the same situation quite vividly.) While analyzing the divergent ways in which women and men converse, Tannen carefully emphasizes that neither linguistic style is superior, only different.

While it would be simplistic to assume that all poems reveal the sex of their authors, many poems do become both richer and clearer when we examine their gender assumptions. Theodore Roethke's "My Papa's Waltz" (page 22) is hardly a macho poem, but it does reflect the complicated mix of love, authority, and violent horseplay that exists in many father-son relationships. By contrast, Sylvia Plath's "Metaphors" (page 124), which describes her own pregnancy through a series of images, deals with an experience that, by biological definition, only a woman can know first-hand. Feminist criticism has shown us how gender influences literary texts in subtler ways. (See "Critical Approaches to Literature" for a discussion of feminist theory.) The central insight of feminist criticism seems inarguable—our sex does often influence how we speak, write, and interpret language. But that insight need not be intimidating. It can also invite us to bring our whole life experience, as women or men, to reading a poem. It reminds us that poetry, the act of using language with the greatest clarity and specificity, is a means to see the world through the eyes of the opposite sex. Sometimes the messages we get from this exchange aren't pleasant, but at least they may shock us into better understanding.

Anne Stevenson   (b. 1933)*

SOUS-ENTENDU   1969

Don't think

that I don't know
that as you talk to me
the hand of your mind
is inconspicuously   5
taking off my stocking,
moving in resourceful blindness
up along my thigh.

Don't think
that I don't know   10
that you know
everything I say
is a garment.

SOUS-ENTENDU. The title is a French expression for "hidden meaning" or "implication." It describes something left unsaid but assumed to be understood.

QUESTIONS

1. What is left unsaid but assumed to be understood between the two people in this poem?
2. Could this poem have been written by a man? If so, under what circumstances? If not, why not?

Emily Grosholz   (b. 1950)

LISTENING   1992

Words in my ear, and someone still unseen
not yet quite viable, but quietly
astir inside my body;

not yet quite named, and yet
I weave a birthplace for him out of words.   5

Part of the world persists
distinct from what we say, but part will stay
only if we keep talking: only speech
can re-create the gardens of the world.

Not the rose itself,   10
but the School of Night assembled at its side
arguing, praising, whom we now recall.

A rose can sow its seed
alone, but poets need their auditors
and mothers need their language for a cradle.   15

My son still on his stalk
rides between the silence of the flowers
and conversation offered by his parents,
wise and foolish talk, to draw him out.

QUESTIONS

1. Who is the one listening in this poem? Who is the speaker?
2. What images does the speaker use to describe the person being addressed? What do these metaphors suggest about the relationship between speaker and listener?
3. How does the speaker compare the poet to the rose? How is this comparison relevant to the poem?

EXERCISE

Rewrite either of the following poems from the perspective of the opposite sex. Then evaluate in what ways the new poem has changed the original's meaning and in what ways the original poem comes through more or less unaltered.

Donald Justice   (b. 1925)*

MEN AT FORTY   1967

Men at forty
Learn to close softly
The doors to rooms they will not be
Coming back to.

At rest on a stair landing,   5
They feel it
Moving beneath them now like the deck of a ship,
Though the swell is gentle.

And deep in mirrors
They rediscover   10
The face of the boy as he practices tying
His father's tie there in secret

And the face of that father,
Still warm with the mystery of lather.
They are more fathers than sons themselves now.   15
Something is filling them, something

That is like the twilight sound
Of the crickets, immense,
Filling the woods at the foot of the slope
Behind their mortgaged houses.   20

Adrienne Rich   (b. 1929)*

WOMEN   1968

My three sisters are sitting
on rocks of black obsidian.
For the first time, in this light, I can see who they are.

My first sister is sewing her costume for the procession.
She is going as the Transparent Lady   5
and all her nerves will be visible.

My second sister is also sewing,
at the seam over her heart which has never healed entirely,
At last, she hopes, this tightness in her chest will ease.

My third sister is gazing
at a dark-red crust spreading westward far out on the sea.   10
Her stockings are torn but she is beautiful.

FOR REVIEW AND FURTHER STUDY

Shirley Geok-lin Lim   (b. 1944)

LEARNING TO LOVE AMERICA   1998

because it has no pure products

because the Pacific Ocean sweeps along the coastline
because the water of the ocean is cold
and because land is better than ocean

because I say we rather than they   5

because I live in California
I have eaten fresh artichokes
and jacarandas bloom in April and May

because my senses have caught up with my body
my breath with the air it swallows   10
my hunger with my mouth

because I walk barefoot in my house

because I have nursed my son at my breast
because he is a strong American boy
because I have seen his eyes redden when he is asked who he is   15
because he answers I don't know

because to have a son is to have a country
because my son will bury me here
because countries are in our blood and we bleed them

because it is late and too late to change my mind   20
because it is time.

LEARNING TO LOVE AMERICA. 1 *pure products*: an allusion to poem XVIII of *Spring and All* (1923) by
William Carlos Williams, which begins: "The pure products of America / go crazy—."

QUESTION

Do the reasons given in the poem suggest that the speaker really does love America?

Andrew Hudgins   (b. 1951)

ELEGY FOR MY FATHER, WHO IS NOT DEAD   1991

One day I'll lift the telephone
and be told my father's dead. He's ready.
In the sureness of his faith, he talks
about the world beyond this world
as though his reservations have   5
been made. I think he wants to go,
a little bit—a new desire
to travel building up, an itch
to see fresh worlds. Or older ones.
He thinks that when I follow him   10
he'll wrap me in his arms and laugh,
the way he did when I arrived
on earth. I do not think he's right.
He's ready. I am not. I can't
just say good-bye as cheerfully   15
as if he were embarking on a trip
to make my later trip go well.
I see myself on deck, convinced
his ship's gone down, while he's convinced
I'll see him standing on the dock   20
and waving, shouting, *Welcome back.*

QUESTIONS

1. The speaker describes his father's view of the afterlife in this poem. What image does he use to describe his father's vision of life after death?
2. What metaphor does the poet use to describe his own religious uncertainty?

Judith Ortiz Cofer   (b. 1952)

QUINCEAÑERA   1987

My dolls have been put away like dead
children in a chest I will carry
with me when I marry.
I reach under my skirt to feel
a satin slip bought for this day. It is soft   5
as the inside of my thighs. My hair
has been nailed back with my mother's
black hairpins to my skull. Her hands
stretched my eyes open as she twisted
braids into a tight circle at the nape   10
of my neck. I am to wash my own clothes
and sheets from this day on, as if
the fluids of my body were poison, as if
the little trickle of blood I believe
travels from my heart to the world were   15
shameful. Is not the blood of saints and
men in battle beautiful? Do Christ's hands
not bleed into your eyes from His cross?
At night I hear myself growing and wake
to find my hands drifting of their own will   20
to soothe skin stretched tight
over my bones.
I am wound like the guts of a clock,
waiting for each hour to release me.

QUINCEAÑERA. *Quinceañera:* a fifteen-year-old girl's coming-out party in Latin cultures.

QUESTIONS

1. What items and actions are associated with the speaker's new life? What items are put away?
2. What is the speaker waiting to release in the final two lines?
3. If the poem's title were changed to "Fifteen-Year-Old Girl," what would the poem lose in meaning?

Alastair Reid   (b. 1926)*

SPEAKING A FOREIGN LANGUAGE   1963

How clumsy on the tongue, these acquired idioms,
after the innuendos of our own. How far
we are from foreigners, what faith
we rest in one sentence, hoping a smile will follow
on the appropriate face, always wallowing   5
between what we long to say and what we can,
trusting the phrase is suitable to the occasion,
the accent passable, the smile real,
always asking the traveller's fearful question—
what is being lost in translation?   10
Something, to be sure. And yet, to hear
the stumbling of foreign friends, how little we care
for the wreckage of word or tense. How endearing they are,
and how our speech reaches out, like a helping hand,
or limps in sympathy. East to understand,   15
through the tangle of language, the heart behind
groping toward us, to make the translation of
syntax into love.

COMPARE

Compare Alastair Reid's poem to Rhina Espaillat's "Bilingual/Bilingüe." How does the
view of language differ in each poem? How is it similar?

Philip Larkin   (1922–1985)*

AUBADE   1977

I work all day, and get half-drunk at night.
Waking at four to soundless dark, I stare.
In time the curtain-edges will grow light.
Till then I see what's really always there:
Unresting death, a whole day nearer now,   5
Making all thought impossible but how
And where and when I shall myself die.
Arid interrogation: yet the dread
Of dying, and being dead,
Flashes afresh to hold and horrify.   10

The mind blanks at the glare. Not in remorse
—The good not done, the love not given, time
Torn off unused—nor wretchedly because
An only life can take so long to climb

Clear of its wrong beginnings, and may never; 15
But at the total emptiness for ever,
The sure extinction that we travel to
And shall be lost in always. Not to be here,
Not to be anywhere,
And soon; nothing more terrible, nothing more true. 20

This is a special way of being afraid.
No trick dispels. Religion used to try,
That vast moth-eaten musical brocade
Created to pretend we never die,
And specious stuff that says *No rational being* 25
Can fear a thing it will not feel, not seeing
That this is what we fear—no sight, no sound,
No touch or taste or smell, nothing to think with,
Nothing to love or link with,
The anaesthetic from which none come round. 30

And so it stays just on the edge of vision,
A small unfocused blur, a standing chill
That slows each impulse down to indecision.
Most things may never happen: this one will,
And realisation of it rages out 35
In furnace-fear when we are caught without
People or drink. Courage is no good:
It means not scaring others. Being brave
Lets no one off the grave.
Death is no different whined at than withstood. 40

Slowly light strengthens, and the room takes shape.
It stands plain as a wardrobe, what we know,
Have always known, known that we can't escape,
Yet can't accept. One side will have to go.
Meanwhile telephones crouch, getting ready to ring 45
In locked-up offices, and all the uncaring
Intricate rented world begins to rouse.
The sky is white as clay, with no sun.
Work has to be done.
Postmen like doctors go from house to house. 50

QUESTIONS

1. Is "Aubade" a Confessional poem? If so, what social taboo does it violate?
2. What embarrassing facts about the narrator does the poem reveal? Do these confessions lead us to trust or distrust him?
3. The narrator says that "Courage is no good" (stanza 4). How might he defend this statement?
4. Would a twenty-year-old reader respond differently to this poem than a seventy-year-old one? Would a devout Christian respond differently to the poem than an atheist?

Rhina Espaillat

Rhina Espaillat on Writing

BEING A BILINGUAL WRITER   1998

Recent interest in the phenomenon known as "Spanglish" has led me to reexamine my own experience as a writer who works chiefly in her second language, and especially to recall my father's inflexible rule against the mixing of languages. In fact, no English was allowed in that midtown Manhattan apartment that became home after my arrival in New York in 1939. My father read the daily paper in English, taught himself to follow disturbing events in Europe through the medium of English-language radio, and even taught me to read the daily comic strips, in an effort to speed my learning of the language he knew I would need. But that necessary language was banished from family conversation: it was the medium of the outer world, beyond the door; inside, among ourselves, only Spanish was permitted, and it had to be pure, grammatical, unadulterated Spanish.

At the age of seven, however, nothing seems more important than communicating with classmates and neighborhood children. For my mother, too, the new language was a way out of isolation, a means to deal with the larger world and with those American women for whom she sewed. But my father, a political exile waiting for changes in our native country, had different priorities; he lived in the hope of return, and believed that the new home, the new speech, were temporary. His theory was simple: if it could be said at all, it could be said best in the language of those authors whose words were the core of his education. But his insistence on pure Spanish made it difficult, sometimes impossible, to bring home and share the jokes of friends, puns, pop lyrics, and other staples of seven-year-old conversation. Table talk sometimes ended with tears or sullen silence.

And yet, despite the friction it caused from time to time, my native language was also a source of comfort—the reading that I loved, intimacy within the family, and a peculiar auditory delight best described as echoes in the mind. I learned early to relish words as counters in a game that could turn suddenly serious without losing the quality of play, and to value their sound as a meaning behind their meaning.

Nostalgia, a confusion of identity, the fear that if the native language is lost the self will somehow be altered forever; all are part of the subtle flavor of immigrant life, as well as the awareness that one owes gratitude to strangers for acts of communication that used to be simple and once imposed no such debt.

Memory, folklore, and food all become part of the receding landscape that language sets out to preserve. Guilt, too, adds to the mix, the suspicion that to love the second language too much is to betray those ancestors who spoke the first and could not communicate with us in the vocabulary of our education, our new thoughts. And finally, a sense of grievance and loss may spur hostility toward the new language and those who speak it, as if the common speech of the perceived majority could weld together a disparate population into a huge, monolithic, and threatening Other. That Other is then assigned traits and habits that preclude sympathy and mold "Us" into a unity whose cohesiveness gives comfort.

Luckily, there is another side to bilingualism: curiosity about the Other may be as natural and pervasive as group loyalty. If it weren't, travel, foreign residence, and intermarriage would be less common than they are. For some bilingual writers, the Other—and the language he speaks—are appealing. Some acknowledge and celebrate the tendency of languages to borrow from each other and produce something different in the process.

From afterword to *Where Horizons Go*

◄═══► WRITING CRITICALLY ◄═══►

Poetic Voice and Personal Identity

The poet Julia Alvarez has written about the fear, excitement, and surprise she felt coming home late one night to find copies of her first book of poems, *Homecoming* (1984), waiting by her front door. Reading her own poems in a printed book for the first time, she remarked, "What shocked me that midnight was that I heard my own voice loud and clear." Alvarez is not talking about hearing her physical voice, but about recognizing for the first time the specific personality that had emerged from her poems. She was surprised by the ways in which her verbal creation both resembled and differed from her actual self.

When critics discuss poetic voice, they often focus on matters of style—characteristic tone, word choice, figures of speech, and rhythms. An author's *personal* voice, however, encompasses more than style; it also includes characteristic themes and subjects. A recognizable poetic voice usually emerges only when a writer finds the right way of presenting the right subjects.

Finding an authentic voice has long been a central issue among women and minority poets. In exploring their subjects, which often lie outside existing traditions, these writers sometimes need to find innovative forms of expression. Edna

St. Vincent Millay, for instance, had to invent a new female voice to write the love poems that made her famous. Although her metrics were traditional, Millay's authoritative tone, self-assured manner, and sexual candor were revolutionary for her time. Sometimes a single word announces a new sort of voice; in Judith Ortiz Cofer's "Quinceañera," the title is a Spanish noun for which there is no one-word English equivalent. That one word suggests that we will be hearing a new voice.

When writing about voice in poetry, you will often find it illuminating to consider race, gender, age, ethnicity, and religious belief. Is the poem's perspective shaped by any of those elements of the author's identity? Don't limit the poem's meanings to those categories, but see if considering those concepts helps you understand the work better. Pay special attention to the way the poem's personal perspective is reflected in its formal aspects (imagery, tone, metaphor, and sound). Observing how formal aspects embody the author's special themes and subjects will be central to appreciating his or her voice. For further examination of these issues, you may want to read "Gender Criticism" in "Critical Approaches to Literature." Although that section discusses only one aspect of identity, the general principles it explores are relevant to the broader questions of how an author's life experience may influence the kinds of poetry he or she creates.

WRITING ASSIGNMENT

Analyze any poem in this chapter from the perspective of an author's race, gender, ethnicity, age, or religious beliefs. Describe how that perspective illuminates the meaning of the poem. Use whatever biographical research you can find, but make sure all of your arguments are specifically based on the poem itself and not merely on biographical data. For examples of similar analyses, see Darryl Pinckney's "Black Identity in Langston Hughes" (page 435) and Brett C. Millier's "On Elizabeth Bishop's 'One Art'" in the chapter "Critical Approaches to Literature." Short biographies of many of the poets in this book can be found in the chapter "Lives of the Poets."

FURTHER SUGGESTIONS FOR WRITING

1. Find another poem in "Poems for Further Reading" in which the poet, like Julia Alvarez, considers his or her own family. Tell in a paragraph or two what the poem reveals about the author.
2. Compare Larkin's "Aubade" with another poem about old age and death, such as William Butler Yeats's "Sailing to Byzantium" (page 379), Dylan Thomas's "Do not go gentle into that good night" (page 231), or William Shakespeare's "That time of year thou mayst in me behold" (page 542).

15 *Translation*

IS POETIC TRANSLATION POSSIBLE?

Poetry, said Robert Frost, is what gets lost in translation. If absolutely true, the comment is bad news for most of us, who have to depend on translations for our only knowledge of great poems in many other languages. However, some translators seem able to save a part of their originals and bring it across the language gap. At times they may even add more poetry of their own, as if to try to compensate for what is lost.

Unlike the writer of an original poem, the translator begins with a meaning that already exists. To convey it, the translator may decide to stick closely to the denotations of the original words or else to depart from them, more or less freely, to pursue something he or she values more. The latter aim is evident in the *Imitations* of Robert Lowell, who said he had been "reckless with literal meaning" and instead had "labored hard to get the tone." Particularly defiant of translation are poems in dialect, uneducated speech, and slang: what can be used for English equivalents? Ezra Pound, in a bold move, translates the song of a Chinese peasant in *The Classic Anthology Defined by Confucius:*

Yaller bird, let my corn alone,
Yaller bird, let my crawps alone,
These folks here won't let me eat,
I wanna go back whaar I can meet
the folks I used to know at home,
                  I got a home an' I wanna' git goin'.

Here, it is our purpose to judge a translation not by its fidelity to its original, but by the same standards we apply to any other poem written in English. To do so may be another way to see the difference between appropriate and inappropriate words.

Rainer Maria Rilke   (1875–1926)

EINGANG   1902

Wer du auch seist: Am Abend tritt hinaus
aus deiner Stube, drin du alles weißt;
als letztes vor der Ferne liegt dein Haus:
Wer du auch seist.
Mit deinen Augen, welche müde kaum   5
von der verbrauchten Schwelle sich befrein,
hebst du ganz langsam einen schwarzen Baum
und stellst ihn vor den Himmel: schlank, allein.
Und hast die Welt gemacht. Und sie ist groß
und win ein Wort, das noch im Schweigen reift.   10
Und wie dein Wille ihren Sinn begreift,
lassen sie deine Augen zärtlich los . . .

ENTRANCE   2001

Whoever you are: step out of doors tonight,
Out of the room that lets you feel secure.
Infinity is open to your sight.
Whoever you are.
With eyes that have forgotten how to see   5
From viewing things already too well-known,
Lift up into the dark a huge, black tree
And put it in the heavens: tall, alone.
And you have made the world and all you see.
It ripens like the words still in your mouth.   10
And when at last you comprehend its truth,
Then close your eyes and gently set it free.

—*Translated by Dana Gioia*

QUESTIONS

1. How well does the translation convey the poem's *poetry*? From what you can discern of
   the original (even if you do not understand German, you can note some of the poem's
   characteristics by studying its appearance on the page and, perhaps, hearing it read
   aloud), how does the translation convey the poem's formal characteristics and tone?
2. Note the title: what is it that the speaker is asking us to leave, and what does he
   desire us to enter into?

WORLD POETRY

English boasts one of the greatest poetic traditions in the world, with over six centuries of continuous literary culture from Geoffrey Chaucer to the present. It is the
language of Shakespeare, Milton, Pope, Keats, Tennyson, Dickinson, Whitman,
Frost, and Yeats. The primary language of over 400 million people, English is

spoken from London to San Francisco, Capetown to Sydney, Vancouver to Nassau. Yet English is the first language of only seven percent of the people of the globe. Mandarin Chinese has almost twice as many native speakers, and two other languages—Hindi and Spanish—have nearly as many speakers as English. Needless to say, all these tongues have rich and ancient literary traditions. To know only the poetry of English, therefore, is to experience a small fraction of world poetry.

Poetry is a universal human phenomenon. Every culture and every language group shape language into verse. To explore the poetry of other languages and cultures is a way of broadening one's vision of humanity. No one, of course, can ever master the whole field of human achievement in poetry, even in translation, but to know a few high spots from poets greatly esteemed by other nations can enlarge our notion of the art as well as enhance our sense of the world.

To gain some perspective on English poetry, one need only look at Chinese literature. China has the oldest uninterrupted literary tradition in the world, dating back at least 3400 years, and poetry has always been its central enterprise. Over a billion people speak one of the dialects of Chinese and all read the same written language. To give a taste of this unparalleled tradition, here is Li Po's "Drinking Alone Beneath the Moon," a classic of Chinese poetry, presented in four ways. First, the poem appears in its original Chinese characters; a phonetic transcription follows, along with a word-for-word literal translation into English. Finally, Li Po's poem is given in a poetic translation.

Li Po   (701–762)*

Drinking Alone Beneath the Moon (about 750)

月 下 獨 酌
花 間 一 壺 酒
獨 酌 無 相 親
舉 杯 邀 明 月
對 影 成 三 人
月 既 不 解 飲
影 徒 隨 我 身
暫 伴 月 將 影
行 樂 須 及 春
我 歌 月 徘 徊
我 舞 影 零 亂
醒 時 同 交 歡
醉 後 各 分 散
永 結 無 情 遊
相 期 邈 雲 漢

Yueh Hsia Tu Cho
MOON-BENEATH ALONE DRINK   (ABOUT 750)

Hua chien yi hu chiu
Flowers-among one pot wine
Tu cho wu hsiang ch'in (ts'ien)
Alone drink no mutual dear
Chü pei yueh ming yueh
Lift cup invite bright moon
Tuei ying ch'eng san jen (nzien)
Face shadow become three men
Yueh chi pu chieh yin
Moon not-only not understand drink   5
Ying t'u suei wo shen (sien)
Shadow in-vain follow my body
Chan pan yueh chiang ying
Temporarily accompany moon with shadow
Hsing lo hsü chi ch'un (ts'iuen)
Practice pleasure must catch spring
Wo ko yueh p' ai-huai
I sing moon linger-to-and-fro
Wo wu ying ling luan (luan)
I dance shadow scatter disorderly   10
Hsing shih t'ung chiao huan
Wake time together exchange joy
Tsui hou ko fen san (san)
Rapt-after each separate disperse
Yung chieh wu-ch'ing yu
Always tie no-passion friendship
Hsiang ch'i miao yun-han (xan)
Mutual expect distant Cloud-river

DRINKING ALONE BY MOONLIGHT   1919

A cup of wine, under the flowering trees;
I drink alone, for no friend is near.
Raising my cup I beckon the bright moon,
For he, with my shadow, will make three men.
The moon, alas, is no drinker of wine;   5
Listless, my shadow creeps about at my side.
Yet with the moon as friend and the shadow as slave
I must make merry before the Spring is spent.
To the songs I sing the moon flickers her beams;

In the dance I weave my shadow tangles and breaks.   10
While we were sober, three shared the fun;
Now we are drunk, each goes his way.
May we long share our odd, inanimate feast,
And meet at last on the Cloudy River of the sky.

—Translated by Arthur Waley

DRINKING ALONE BY MOONLIGHT. 14 *the Cloudy River of the sky:* the Milky Way.

QUESTIONS

1. Judging from the literal translation of Li Po's poem, discuss which aspects of the original seem to come across vividly in Arthur Waley's English version.
2. Which aspects change or disappear in Waley's version?
3. Take a line from Waley's version (perhaps one you don't especially like) and use the
   literal translation to offer a different translation.

EXERCISE: *Comparing Translations*

Which English translation of each of the following poems is the best poetry? The originals
may be of interest to some. For those who do not know the foreign language, the editor's
line-by-line prose paraphrases may help indicate what the translator had to work with and
how much of the translation is the translator's own idea. In which do you find the diction
most felicitous? In which do pattern and structure best move as one? What differences in
tone are apparent? It is doubtful that any one translation will surpass the others in every
detail.

Our verb *translate* is derived from the Latin word *translatus*, the past par-
ticiple of "to transfer" or "to carry across." The first set of translations tries to
carry across into English one of the most influential short poems ever written.
Horace's ode, which ends with the advice, *carpe diem* ("seize the day"), has left its
mark on countless poems. One even sees its imprint on contemporary novels
(such as Saul Bellow's *Seize the Day*) and films (such as *Dead Poets Society*) that
echo Horace's command to live in the present moment because no one knows
what the future will bring.

Horace   (65–8 B.C.)

ODES I (11)   (ABOUT 20 B.C.)

Tu ne quaesieris—scire nefas—quem mihi, quem tibi   1
finem di dederint, Leuconoe, nec Babylonios   2
temptaris numeros. Ut melius, quicquid erit, pati!   3
seu plures hiemes, seu tribuit Iuppiter ultimam,   4
quae nunc oppositis debilitat pumicibus mare   5

Tyrrhenum. Sapias, vina liques, et spatio brevi   6

spem longam reseces. Dum loquimur, fugerit invida   7

aetas: carpe diem, quam minimum credula postero.   8

ODES I (11). Prose translation: (1,2) Do not ask, Leuconoe—to know is not permitted—what end the gods have given to you and me, do not (3) consult Babylonian horoscopes. It will be better to endure whatever comes, (4) whether Jupiter grants us more winters or whether this is the last one, (5) which now against the opposite cliffs wears out (6) the Tuscan sea. Be wise, decant the wine, and since our space is brief, (7) cut back your far-reaching hope. Even while we talk, envious time has fled away: (8) seize the day, put little trust in what is to come.

HORACE TO LEUCONOE   1891

I pray you not, Leuconoe, to pore
With unpermitted eyes on what may be
Appointed by the gods for you and me,
Nor on Chaldean figures any more.
'T were infinitely better to implore   5
The present only:—whether Jove decree
More winters yet to come, or whether he
Make even this, whose hard, wave-eaten shore
Shatters the Tuscan seas to-day, the last—
Be wise withal, and rack your wine, nor fill   10
Your bosom with large hopes; for while I sing,
The envious close of time is narrowing;—
So seize the day, or ever it be past,
And let the morrow come for what it will.
                            —Translated by Edwin Arlington Robinson*

DON'T ASK   1963

Don't ask (we may not know), Leuconoe,
    What the gods plan for you or me.
        Leave the Chaldees to parse
        The sentence of the stars.

Better to bear the outcome, good or bad,   5
    Whether Jove purposes to add
        Fresh winters to the past
        Or to make this the last

Which now tires out the Tuscan sea and mocks
    Its strength with barricades of rocks.   10

Be wise, strain clear the wine
And prune the rambling vine

Of expectation. Life's short. Even while
  We talk Time, hateful, runs a mile.
    Don't trust tomorrow's bough   15
    For fruit. Pluck this, here, now.

—Translated by James Michie

A New Year's Toast   2000

Blanche—don't ask—it isn't right for us to know what ends
Fate may have in store for us. Don't dial up Psychic Friends.
Isn't it better just to take whatever the future sends,
Whether the new millennium goes off without a hitch
Or World War III is triggered by an old computer glitch?   5
Wise up. Have a drink. Keep plans to a modest pitch.
Even as we're talking here, we spend the time we borrow.
Seize Today—trust nothing to that sly old cheat, Tomorrow.

—Translated by A. E. Stallings

Questions

1. Which translation seems closest to the literal meaning of the Latin? Does that fidelity help or hinder its impact as a new poem in English?
2. In her translation, A. E. Stallings modernizes most of the images and allusions. What does this add to the translation's impact? Does it change the meaning of the original?
3. Which translation do you personally respond to most strongly? While recognizing the subjective nature of your preference, explain what aspects of the version appeal to you.

The next set of translations tries to recreate a short lyric by the classical Persian poet Omar Khayyam, the master of the *rubai*, a four-line stanza rimed *a a b a*. This Persian form was introduced into English by Edward FitzGerald (1809–1883) in his hugely popular translation, *The Rubaiyat of Omar Khayyam* (rubaiyat is the plural of rubai). In FitzGerald's Victorian version, Omar Khayyam became one of the most frequently quoted poets in English. Eugene O'Neill borrowed the title of his play *Ah, Wilderness!* from the *Rubaiyat* and expected his audience to catch the allusion. TV buffs may remember hearing Khayyam's poetry quoted habitually by the SWAT-team commander Howard Hunter on the classic series *Hill Street Blues*. Here are three poetic translations of a famous *rubai*. Which qualities of the original does each translation seem to capture?

Omar Khayyam   (1048–1131)

RUBAI   (ABOUT 1100)

Tongi-ye may-e la'l kh'aham o divani	1
Sadd-e ramaghi bayad o nesf-e nani	2
Vangah man o to neshasteh dar virani	3
Khoshtar bovad as mamlekat-e soltani.	4

RUBAI. Prose translation: (1) I want a jug of ruby wine and a book of poems. (2) There must be something to stop my breath from departing, and a half loaf of bread. (3) Then you and I sitting in some deserted ruin. (4)Would be sweeter than the realm of a sultan.

A BOOK OF VERSES UNDERNEATH THE BOUGH   1879

A Book of Verses underneath the Bough,
A Jug of Wine, a Loaf of Bread—and Thou
   Beside me singing in the Wilderness—
Oh, Wilderness were Paradise enow°!   *enough*

—*Translated by Edward FitzGerald**

OUR DAY'S PORTION   1968

Should our day's portion be one mancel loaf,
A haunch of mutton and a gourd of wine
Set for us two alone on the wide plain,
No Sultan's bounty could evoke such joy.

—*Translated by Robert Graves* and Omar Ali-Shah*

I NEED A BARE SUFFICIENCY   1992

I need a bare sufficiency—red wine,
   Some poems, half a loaf on which to dine
With you beside me in some ruined shrine:
   A king's state then is not as sweet as mine!

—*Translated by Dick Davis*

EXERCISE: *Persian Versions*

Write a *rubai* of your own on any topic. Some possible subjects include: what you plan to do next weekend to relax; advice to a friend to stop worrying; an invitation to a loved one; a four-line *carpe diem* ode. For your inspiration, here are a few more *rubaiyat* from Edward FitzGerald's celebrated translation.

Wake! For the Sun who scattered into flight
The Stars before him from the Field of Night,
    Drives Night along with them from Heaven, and strikes
The Sultan's Turret with a Shaft of Light.

* * * *

Come, fill the Cup, and in the Fire of Spring
Your Winter-garment of Repentence fling:
    The Bird of Time has but a little way
To flutter—and the Bird is on the Wing.

* * * *

Some for the Glories of this World; and some
Sigh for the Prophet's Paradise to come;
    Ah, take the Cash, and let the Credit go,
Nor heed the rumble of a Distant Drum!

* * * *

The Moving Finger writes; and, having writ,
Moves on: nor all your Piety nor Wit
    Shall lure it back to cancel half a Line
Nor all your Tears wash out a Word of it.

* * * *

Ah Love! could you and I with Him conspire
To grasp this sorry Scheme of Things entire,
    Would we not shatter it to bits—and then
Remould it nearer to the Heart's desire.

PARODY

There is another literary mode that is related to translation—namely, **parody**—in which one writer imitates another writer or work, usually for the purpose of poking fun. Parody can be considered an irreverent form of translation in which one poem is changed into another written in the same language but with a different effect (usually slipping from serious to silly). When one writer parodies another writer's work, it does not necessarily mean that the original poem is without merit. "Most parodies are written out of admiration rather than contempt," claimed critic Dwight Macdonald, who edited the anthology *Parodies* (1960), because there needs to be enough common sympathy between poet and parodist for the poem's essence not to be lost in the translation. It takes a fine poem to support an even passable parody. "Nobody is going to parody you if you haven't a style," remarked British critic Geoffrey Grigson.

What a parody mostly reveals is that any good poem becomes funny if you change one or more of the assumptions behind it. Gene Fehler, for example, takes Richard Lovelace's lover-soldier in "To Lucasta" (page 45) and turns him into a major league baseball player changing teams; what this new warrior loves, we soon discover, is neither honor nor his lady but a fat salary. Far from ridiculing Lovelace's original, Fehler's parody demonstrates that the poem is strong enough to support a comic translation into contemporary images.

Parodies remind us how much fun poetry can be—an aspect of the art sometimes forgotten during end-of-term exams and research papers. These comic transformations also teach us something essential about the original poems. Parodies are, as Dwight Macdonald said, "an intuitive kind of literary criticism, shorthand for what 'serious' critics must write out at length." If you try your hand at writing a parody, you will soon discover how deeply you need to understand the original work in order to reproduce its style and manner. You will also learn how much easier it is to parody a poem you really love.

Anonymous

WE FOUR LADS FROM   (ABOUT 1963)
LIVERPOOL ARE

We four lads from Liverpool are—
Paul in a taxi, John in a car,
George on a scooter, tootin' his hooter,
Following Ringo Starr.

Skillfully written, parody can be a devastating form of literary criticism. Rather than merely flinging abuse, the wise parodist imitates with understanding, even with sympathy. The many crude parodies of T. S. Eliot's difficult poem *The Waste Land* show parodists mocking what they cannot fathom, with the result that, instead of illuminating the original, they belittle it (and themselves). Good parodists have an ear for the sounds and rhythms of their originals, as does James Camp, who echoes Walt Whitman's stately "Out of the Cradle Endlessly Rocking" in his line "Out of the crock endlessly ladling" (what a weary teacher feels he is doing). Parody can be aimed at poems good or bad; yet there are poems of such splendor and dignity that no parodist seems able to touch them without looking like a small dog defiling a cathedral, and others so illiterate that good parody would be squandered on them. Sometimes parodies are even an odd form of flattery; poets poke fun at poems they simply can't get out of their heads any other way except by rewriting, as in the following parody, in which Wendy Cope delightfully imagines a rustic encounter like those in such classic Wordsworth poems as "We Are Seven" and "Resolution and Independence."

Wendy Cope   (b. 1945)*

A NURSERY RHYME (AS IT MIGHT HAVE   1986
BEEN WRITTEN BY WILLIAM WORDSWORTH)

The skylark and the jay sang loud and long,
The sun was calm and bright, the air was sweet,
When all at once I heard above the throng
Of jocund birds a single plaintive bleat.

And, turning, saw, as one sees in a dream,   5
It was a Sheep had broke the moorland peace
With his sad cry, a creature who did seem
The blackest thing that ever wore a fleece.

I walked towards him on the stony track
And, pausing for a while between two crags,   10
I asked him, "Have you wool upon your back?"
Thus he bespake, "Enough to fill three bags."

Most courteously, in measured tones, he told
Who would receive each bag and where they dwelt;
And oft, now years have passed and I am old,   15
I recollect with joy that inky pelt.

QUESTIONS

1. What characteristics of Wordsworth's poetry is Cope parodying here?
2. How would you describe the relationship between Cope's diction and the subject
   matter of the poem? Do they seem appropriate to one another or not?

Hugh Kingsmill
[Hugh Kingsmill Lunn]   (1889–1949)

WHAT, STILL ALIVE AT   (ABOUT 1920)
TWENTY-TWO?

What, still alive at twenty-two,
A clean, upstanding chap like you?
Sure, if your throat 'tis hard to slit,
Slit your girl's, and swing for it.

Like enough, you won't be glad   5
When they come to hang you, lad:
But bacon's not the only thing
That's cured by hanging from a string.

So, when the spilt ink of the night
Spreads o'er the blotting-pad of light   10
Lads whose job is still to do
Shall whet their knives, and think of you.

QUESTIONS

1. A. E. Housman considered this the best of many parodies of his poetry. Read his
   poems in this book, particularly "Eight O'Clock" (page 172), "When I was one-and-
   twenty" (page 206), and "To an Athlete Dying Young" (page 498). What characteristics of theme, form, and language does Hugh Kingsmill's parody convey?
2. What does Kingsmill exaggerate?

Bruce Bennett   (b. 1940)

THE LADY SPEAKS AGAIN   1992

"I lift my lamp beside the golden door."
More golden now than ever; don't ask why.
Just list your assets, where you can get more,
and who you know. No others need apply.

QUESTIONS

1. Who is the "lady" speaking? What poem is echoed in Bennett's parody?
2. Is Bennett making fun of the original poem (page 391)? Or is there another object
   for his satire?

Gene Fehler   (b. 1940)

IF RICHARD LOVELACE BECAME   1984
A FREE AGENT

Tell me not, fans, I am unkind
    For saying my good-bye
And leaving your kind cheers behind
    While I to new fans fly.

Now, I will leave without a trace   5
    And choose a rival's field;
For I have viewed the market place
    And seen what it can yield.

Though my disloyalty is such   10
    That all you fans abhor,
It's not that I don't love you much:
    I just love money more.

1. After comparing this parody to Richard Lovelace's "To Lucasta" (page 45), list the elements that Fehler keeps from the original and those he adds.
2. What ideals motivate the speaker of Lovelace's poem? What ideals motivate Fehler's free agent?

Aaron Abeyta   (b. 1971)

THIRTEEN WAYS OF LOOKING AT A TORTILLA   2001

i.
among twenty different tortillas
the only thing moving
was the mouth of the niño

ii.
i was of three cultures
like a tortilla   5
for which there are three bolios

iii.
the tortilla grew on the wooden table
it was a small part of the earth

iv.
a house and a tortilla
are one   10
a man a woman and a tortilla
are one

v.
i do not know which to prefer
the beauty of the red wall
or the beauty of the green wall   15
the tortilla fresh
or just after

vi.
tortillas filled the small kitchen
with ancient shadows
the shadow of Maclovia   20
cooking long ago
the tortilla
rolled from the shadow
the innate roundness

vii.
o thin viejos of chimayo
why do you imagine biscuits
do you not see how the tortilla
lives with the hands
of the women about you

viii.
i know soft corn
and beautiful inescapable sopapillas
but i know too
that the tortilla
has taught me what I know

ix.
when the tortilla is gone
it marks the end
of one of many tortillas

x.
at the sight of tortillas
browning on a black comal
even the pachucos of española
would cry out sharply

xi.
he rode over new mexico
in a pearl low rider
once he got a flat
in that he mistook
the shadow of his spare
for a tortilla

xii.
the abuelitas are moving
the tortilla must be baking

xiii.
it was cinco de mayo all year
it was warm
and it was going to get warmer
the tortilla sat
on the frijolito plate

25

30

35

40

45

50

WRITING EXERCISE

Try your hand at a parody of Wallace Stevens's "Thirteen Ways of Looking at a Blackbird" (page 245). Take any three or four stanzas from Stevens's poem and change the central image (as Aaron Abeyta did). If you are feeling ambitious, you might even try to parody all thirteen sections.

WRITER'S PERSPECTIVE

Arthur Waley

Arthur Waley on Writing

THE METHOD OF TRANSLATION   1919

It is commonly asserted that poetry, when literally translated, ceases to be poetry. This is often true, and I have for that reason not attempted to translate many poems which in the original have pleased me quite as much as those I have selected. But I present the ones I have chosen in the belief that they still retain the essential characteristics of poetry.

I have aimed at literal translation, not paraphrase. It may be perfectly legitimate for a poet to borrow foreign themes or material, but this should not be called translation.

Above all, considering imagery to be the soul of poetry, I have avoided either adding images of my own or suppressing those of the original.

Any literal translation of Chinese poetry is bound to be to some extent rhythmical, for the rhythm of the original obtrudes itself. Translating literally, without thinking about the meter of the version, one finds that about two lines out of three have a very definite swing similar to that of the Chinese lines. The remaining lines are just too short or too long, a circumstance very irritating to the reader, whose ear expects the rhythm to continue. I have therefore tried to produce regular rhythmic effects similar to those of the original. . . . In a few instances where the English insisted on being shorter than the Chinese, I have preferred to vary the meter of my version, rather than pad out the line with unnecessary verbiage.

I have not used rhyme because it is impossible to produce in English rhyme-effects at all similar to those of the original, where the same rhyme sometimes runs through a whole poem. Also, because the restrictions of rhyme necessarily injure either the vigor of one's language or the literalness of one's version. I do not, at any rate, know of any example to the contrary. What is generally known as "blank verse" is the worst medium for translating Chinese poetry, because the essence of blank verse is that it varies the position of its pauses, whereas in Chinese the stop always comes at the end of the couplet.

From A Hundred and Seventy Chinese Poems

═══▷ WRITING CRITICALLY ◁═══

Parody Is the Sincerest Form of Flattery

When Elizabeth Bishop taught at Harvard, a surprising question appeared on her take-home final exam. She asked students to write parodies of the three poets they had studied during the semester. This assignment was not for a creative writing class, but in her literature course on modern poetry. Bishop believed that in order to write a good parody one had to understand the original poem deeply. W. H. Auden went even further in declaring the value of parody. In designing his ideal college for aspiring poets, he declared that writing parodies would be the only authorized critical exercise in the curriculum.

Before writing a parody, select two or three poems by an author that seem characteristic of his or her style and concerns. Type out or photocopy the poems and then underline phrases or lines that represent the poet's particular sound. You might also make a short list of typical images, words, or even punctuation that the poet frequently uses. Now select one poem and start to imagine it in a different time or setting (as in Gene Fehler's "If Richard Lovelace Became a Free Agent"). Or conceive of the same ideas spoken by an altogether different person (as in Aaron Abeyta's "thirteen ways of looking at a tortilla"). Create a transposition that strikes you as potentially funny but still illuminates some aspect of the original. Try to keep your parody as close to the original poem as possible in terms of length, form, and syntax. You will be surprised by how much strength of expression you'll gain from the poet's line and sentence structure. Finally, have fun. If you don't enjoy your new poem, neither will a reader.

WRITING ASSIGNMENT

Write a parody of any poem in the book. (Remember, it will probably be funnier to your fellow students if it is one you have all studied.) Do your parody in either prose or verse, and make it follow the structure of the original as closely as possible. If you choose to write in verse, stick to the line structure of the original. It may be helpful to choose a model that isn't too difficult to copy (to parody a sonnet would require at least some command of rime and meter). Bring your parody to class and read it aloud.

FURTHER SUGGESTIONS FOR WRITING

1. Write your own version of Horace's "Carpe Diem" ode. Follow the original line by line but reset the poem in your home town (not ancient Tuscany) and address it to your best friend (not long-dead Leuconoe). Advise your friend in your new images to "seize the day."

2. Write a serious poem in the manner of Emily Dickinson, William Carlos Williams, E. E. Cummings, or any other modern poet whose work interests you and which you feel able to imitate. Try to make it good enough to slip into the poet's *Collected Poems* without anyone being the wiser. Read all the poet's poems in this book, or you can consult a larger selection or collection of the poet's work. Though it may be simplest to choose a particular poem as your model, you may echo any number of poems, if you like. It is probably a good idea to pick a subject or theme characteristic of the poet. This is a difficult project, but if you can do it even fairly well, you will know a great deal more about poetry and your poet.

16 *Critical Casebook: Latin American Poetry*

Most Americans experience poetry in only one language—English. Because English is a world language, with its native speakers spread across every continent, it is easy for us to underestimate the significance of poetry written in other tongues. Why is it important to experience poetry in a different language or translation? It matters because such poetry represents and illuminates a different cultural experience. Exposure to different cultures enriches our perspectives and challenges assumptions; it also helps us to understand our own culture better.

Latin American poetry is particularly relevant to the English speaker in the United States or Canada because of the long interconnected history of the Americas. Spanish is also an important world language—spoken by over 350 million people and the primary language in over twenty countries. The vast spread of Spanish has created an enormous and prominent body of literature, an international tradition in which Latin America has gradually replaced Spain as the center. Poetry occupies a very significant place in Latin American culture—a more public place than in the United States. Poetry even plays an important part of the popular culture in Latin America where the average person is able to name his or her favorite poets and can often recite some of their works from memory.

The tradition of Latin American poetry is long and rich. Many poets and scholars consider Sor Juana, a Catholic nun who lived in Mexico during the seventeenth century, to be the mother of Latin American poetry. Mexico's Nobel Laureate poet, Octavio Paz, acknowledges this lineage in his critical work on Sor Juana, *Traps of Faith* (1988), a quintessential book about her life and work. Sor Juana's writing was groundbreaking, not just in the context of Latin American poetry, but truly in the context of world literature, as she was the first writer in Latin America (and one of very few in her era) to address the rights of women to study and write. Her poems are also harbingers of important tendencies in Latin American poetry because of their heightened lyricism.

This lyrical quality finds new form and vitality in the works of the most widely known poets of Latin America—including César Vallejo, Pablo Neruda, Jorge Luis Borges, and Octavio Paz. Each of these poets addresses questions of cultural and personal identity in his work. Events of the twentieth century had great impact on both the subject matter and style of Latin American poets. The Spanish Civil War (1936–1939) sent many poets who had been living in Europe back to the Americas, conscious of the political and social values being tried and tested in Europe at the time.

Latin American women poets have carried on themes introduced by Sor Juana centuries earlier, often linking gender discrimination to other injustices. There is an acknowledged *"peso ancestral"* ("ancestral burden"), to quote Argentinian poet Alfonsina Storni, with which one must struggle. Storni's various struggles with such burdens throughout her life are a focus of her poetry. She filled her later poems with images of the sea and of release, and ended her life in 1938 by tragically walking into the sea. Storni's work is also characteristic of broader themes in Latin American poetry in that it takes on large social issues of the modern era, but does so through a unique and personal perspective.

Latin American poetry, particularly in the twentieth century, is marked by a recognition of the region as a unique blending of different cultures, European and indigenous, among others. It is also marked by a variety of artistic and political movements, of which surrealism is perhaps the most influential. The works of artists such as Mexican painter Frida Kahlo coincided with a body of new writing that emphasized a blurring of fantasy and reality. Some writers, such as Vallejo and Olga Orozco, became most well-known for their surrealist writing, while other poets, such as Neruda and Paz, incorporated some of the elements of the movement into their styles.

A number of Latin American poets were awarded the Nobel Prize in literature in the latter part of the twentieth century, including Paz, Neruda, and Gabriela Mistral. (Borges, to the astonishment of many critics, never won the award, though he captured nearly every other major international literary honor.) The importance of Spanish as a global language and in literature is reflected in the recognition of the stature of Latin American writers in the world. Even when decidedly political, Latin American poetry is known for its focus on the personal experience. One does not love one's country as a symbol, José Emilio Pacheco claims; rather one loves its people, its mountains, and three or four of its rivers.

Portrait of Sister Juana Inés de la Cruz *by unknown Mexican artist, eighteenth century*

Sor Juana Inés de la Cruz is said to have been born in Nepantla, Mexico, somewhere between 1648 and 1651. Very little is known about "Sister" Juana's life, since church records were destroyed during the Mexican Revolution. Passages from her famous Reply to Sor Philothea *allow a glimpse into her early life, such as her desire, at the age of six or seven, to wear boy's clothing and to study at the University in Mexico City. She also talks about cutting off her own hair in self-punishment for not having learned something she had set for herself as a task, saying "there was no cause for a head to be adorned with hair and naked of learning."*

In 1667 Sor Juana entered the convent of the "barefoot Carmelites," so-named because of the austere way of life they adopted, going either barefoot or wearing rope sandals. In 1669 she moved to the convent of San Jerónimo, where she studied and wrote until 1691. In her Reply, *she states that she chose the convent because it offered her more possibilities for engaging in her intellectual pursuits, which the restrictions of marriage at that time would not allow. The baroque period during which Sor Juana wrote required tight form and rime schemes. Though some of Sor Juana's poetry was commissioned, there are many poems in which we can see the poet's true spirit, especially in her love poems, which often transcend time in their intensity. In 1691 Sor Juana wrote the* Reply, *the first document in the Americas to argue for a woman's right to study and to write. The Church responded by demanding she give up her books and her instruments of writing. She renewed her vows to the Church, signing documents in her own blood. Sor Juana died during a devastating plague in 1695, after having given aid to a great number of the ill. Her famous* Reply *was first published, posthumously, in 1700.*

Asegura la Confianza de que Oculturá de todo un Secreto 1689

El paje os dirá, discreto,
como, luego que leí,
vuestro secreto rompí
por no romper el secreto.
Y aun hice más, os prometo:
los fragmentos, sin desdén,
del papel, tragué también;
que secretos que venero.
Aun en pedazos no quiero
que fuera del pecho estén.

She Promises to Hold a Secret in Confidence

2004

This page, discreetly, will convey
how, on the moment that I read it,
I tore apart your secret
not to let it be torn away
from me—and I will further say   5
what firm insurance followed:
those paper fragments, I also swallowed.
This secret, so dearly read—
I wouldn't want one shred
out of my chest, to be hollowed.   10

—*Translated by Diane Thiel*

Presente en que el Cariño Hace Regalo la Llaneza   1689

Lysi: a tus manos divinas
doy castañas espinosas,
porque donde sobran rosas
no pueden faltar espinas.
Si a su aspereza te inclinas
y con eso el gusto engañas,
perdona las malas mañas
de quien tal regalo te hizo;
perdona, pues que un erizo
sólo puede dar castañas.

A Simple Gift Made Rich by Affection

2004

Lysi, I give to your divine hand
these chestnuts in their thorny guise
because where velvet roses rise,
thorns also grow unchecked, unplanned.
If you're inclined toward their barbed brand   5
and with this choice, betray your taste,
forgive the ill-bred lack of taste
of one who sends you such a missive—
Forgive me, only this husk can give
the chestnut, in its thorns embraced.   10

—*Translated by Diane Thiel*

QUESTIONS

1. What literally is being described in "She Promises to Hold a Secret in Confidence"? Provide a paraphrase.
2. What interesting wordplay do you notice in each of these poems? Consider, for example, the use of "tore" and "be torn" in the first poem. Are there any other significant repetitions?
3. What stylistic and thematic similarities do you notice between these two poems?
4. How does the chestnut work as a metaphor in the second poem? What does the thorny husk seem to represent? What does the chestnut represent?
5. Read the excerpt from *Reply* and "Endgames" at the end of the chapter. How do these prose pieces change your reading of the poems?

PABLO NERUDA

Pablo Neruda

Pablo Neruda (1904–1973) was born Neftali Ricardo Reyes Basoalto in Parral, southern Chile. His mother died a month later, a fact which is said to have affected Neruda's choice of imagery throughout his life's work. He began writing poems as a child despite his family's disapproval; this disapproval led him, as a young man, to adopt the "working class" pen name Pablo Neruda. He published his first book, Crepusculario (Twilight), in 1923 and soon followed with his Veinte Poemas de Amor y una Canción Desperada (Twenty Love Poems and a Song of Despair). The book received vast attention, and Neruda decided to devote himself to writing poetry.

In 1927 Neruda served as a diplomat in Burma, his first in a long line of such diplomatic positions. He lived several years in Spain and chronicled the Spanish Civil War. Neruda journeyed home to Chile in 1938, then served as consul to Mexico, and returned again to Chile in 1943. When the Chilean government moved to the right, Neruda, who was a communist, went into hiding. During this time, he wrote his famous long sequence Canto General, which includes his "Alturas de Macchu Picchu" ("Heights of Macchu Picchu"), often considered the single most important modern Latin American poem.

In 1952, when the Chilean government ceased its persecution of leftist writers, Neruda returned to his native land and married his third wife, Matilde Urrutia. (His first two marriages had ended in divorce.) Neruda's later love poems were addressed to Matilde, including his Cien Sonetos de Amor (One Hundred Love Sonnets). These later poems bring his work full circle, returning to the themes and image-rich quality of his early Veinte Poemas de Amor. In 1970 Neruda was a candidate for the presidency of Chile, but withdrew to support the Socialist candidate, Salvador Allende. In 1973, just twelve days after the fall of Chile's democratic government, Neruda died of cancer in Santiago, Chile.

De tantos hombres que soy,
    que somos,
no puedo encontrar a ninguno:
se me pierden bajo la ropa,
se fueron a otra ciudad.

Cuando todo está preparado
para mostrarme inteligente
el tonto que llevo escondido
se toma la palabra en mi boca.

Otras veces me duermo en medio
de la sociedad distinguida
y cuando busco en mí al valiente,
un cobarde que no conozco
corre a tomar con mi esqueleto
mil deliciosas precauciones.

Cuando arde una casa estimada
en vez del bombero que llamo
se precipita el incendiario
y ése soy yo. No tengo arreglo.
Qué debo hacer para escogerme?
Cómo puedo rehabilitarme?

Todos los libros que leo
celebran héroes refulgentes
siempre seguros de sí mismos:
me muero de envidia por ellos,
y en los films de vientos y balas
me quedo envidiando al jinete,
me quedo admirando al caballo.

Pero cuando pido al intrépido
me sale el viejo perezoso,
y así yo no sé quién soy,
no sé cuántos soy o seremos.
Me gustaría tocar un timbre
y sacar el mí verdadero
porque si yo me necesito
no debo desaparecerme.

Of the many men who I am, who
    we are,
I can't find a single one;
they disappear among my clothes,
they've left for another city.

When everything seems to be set   5
to show me off as intelligent,
the fool I always keep hidden
takes over all that I say.

At other times, I'm asleep
among distinguished people,   10
and when I look for my brave self,
a coward unknown to me
rushes to cover my skeleton
with a thousand fine excuses.

                15
When a decent house catches fire,
instead of the fireman I summon,
an arsonist bursts on the scene,
and that's me. What can I do?
What can I do to distinguish myself?
How can I pull myself together?   20

All the books I read
are full of dazzling heroes,
always sure of themselves.
I die with envy of them;
and in films full of wind and bullets,   25
I goggle at the cowboys,
I even admire the horses.

But when I call for a hero,
out comes my lazy old self;
so I never know who I am,   30
nor how many I am or will be.
I'd love to be able to touch a bell
and summon the real me,
because if I really need myself,
I mustn't disappear.   35

Mientras escribo estoy ausente
y cuando vuelvo ya he partido:
voy a ver si a las otras gentes
les pasa lo que a mí me pasa,
si son tantos como soy yo,
si se parecen a sí mismos
y cuando lo haya averiguado
voy a aprender tan bien las cosas
que para explicar mis problemas
les hablaré de geografía.

While I am writing, I'm far away;
and when I come back, I've gone.
I would like to know if others
go through the same things that I do,
have as many selves as I have,   40
and see themselves similarly;
and when I've exhausted this problem,
I'm going to study so hard
that when I explain myself,
I'll be talking geography.   45

*—Translated by Alastair Reid**

QUESTIONS

1. In line 26, Reid translates Neruda's phrase "me quedo envidiando al jinete" as "I goggle at the cowboys." What does Reid gain or lose with that version? (In Spanish, *jinete* means *horseman* or *rider* but not specifically *cowboy*, which is *vaquero* or even— thanks to Hollywood— *cowboy*.) Neruda once told Reid, "Alastair, don't just translate my poems. I want you to improve them." Is this line an improvement?
2. How many men are in the speaker of the poem? What seems to be their relationship to one another?

CIEN SONETOS DE AMOR (V)   1959

No te toque la noche ni el aire ni la aurora,
sólo la tierra, la virtud de los racimos,
las manzanas que crecen oyendo el agua pura,
el barro y las resinas de tu país fragante.

Desde Quinchamalí donde hicieron tus ojos   5
hasta tus pies creados para mí en la Frontera
eres la greda oscura que conozco:
en tus caderas toco de nuevo todo el trigo.

Tal vez tú no sabías, aracuana,
que cuando antes de amarte me olvidé de tus besos   10
mi corazón quedó recordando tu boca

y fui como un herido por las calles
hasta que comprendí que había encontrado,
amor, mi territorio de besos y volcanes.

One Hundred Love Sonnets (V)　　　　1986

I did not touch your night, or your air, or dawn:
only the earth, the truth of the fruit in clusters,
the apples that swell as they drink the sweet water,
the clay and the resins of your sweet-smelling land.

From Quinchamalí where your eyes began,　　　　　　　　　　　5
to the Frontera where your feet were made for me,
you are my dark familiar clay: touching your hips,
I touch the wheat in its fields again.

Woman from Arauco, maybe you didn't know
how before I loved you I forgot your kisses.　　　　　　　　　10
But my heart went on, remembering your mouth—and I went on

and on through the streets like a man wounded,
until I understood, Love: I had found
my place, a land of kisses and volcanoes.

—Translated by Stephen Tapscott

One Hundred Love Sonnets.　5 *Quinchamalí*: small mountain town south of Santiago, Chile.
6 *Frontera*: frontier, border.　9 *Aruaco*: port city south of Santiago.

Questions

1. In Neruda's love sonnet, what extended metaphor does the speaker use to describe his love?
2. How does the direct address affect the immediacy of the poem? Does the "you" keep the reader out, or draw the reader in?

JORGE LUIS BORGES

Jorge Luis Borges

Jorge Luis Borges (1899–1986), a blind librarian who became one of the most influential writers ever to emerge from Latin America, was born in Buenos Aires. Borges's Protestant father and Catholic mother reflected Argentina's diverse background; their ancestry included Spanish, English, Italian, Portugese, and Indian blood. Borges's British grandmother lived with them, so "Georgie" and his younger sister were raised speaking both English and Spanish. Borges was taught at home by a British governess, until he went to school at the age of nine. The author later commented, "If I were asked to name the chief event in my life, I should say my father's library."

Caught in Europe by the outbreak of World War I, Borges lived in Switzerland and later Spain, where he joined the Ultraists, a group of experimental poets who renounced realism. Borges believed strongly in the power of the image and symbol, as opposed to the ornate, musical quality of fellow poets such as Ruben Darío. On returning to Argentina in 1921, he edited a poetry magazine printed in the form of a poster and affixed to city walls. In 1937, to help support his mother and dying father, the thirty-seven-year-old Borges (who still lived at home) got his first job as an assistant librarian. He had already published seven books of poetry and criticism, and had just begun writing short stories. Over the next fifteen years he published many of the stories that would earn him international acclaim.

During this decisive period, Borges encountered political trouble. For his opposition to the regime of Colonel Juan Perón, in 1946 Borges was forced to resign his post as a librarian and was mockingly offered a job as a chicken inspector. He refused the position and supported his mother and himself on his meager literary earnings. In 1955, after Perón was deposed, Borges became director of the National Library and a professor of English literature at the University of Buenos Aires. Suffering from poor eyesight since childhood, Borges eventually went blind. His eye problems may have encouraged him to work mainly in short, highly crafted forms in both prose and verse—brief stories, essays, and fables, as well as lyric poems full of elaborate music. In international terms, Borges is probably the most influential short story writer of the last half-century. Borges, however, considered himself first and foremost a poet.

Ni la intimidad de tu frente clara como una fiesta
ni la costumbre de tu cuerpo, aún misterioso y tácito y de niña,
ni la sucesión de tu vida asumiendo palabras o silencios
serán favor tan misterioso
como mirar tu sueño implicado   5
en la vigilia de mis brazos.
Virgen milagrosamente otra vez por la virtud absolutoria del sueño,
quieta y resplandeciente como una dicha que la memoria elige,
me darás esa orilla de tu vida que tú misma no tienes.
Arrojado a quietud,   10
divisaré esa playa última de tu ser
y te veré por vez primera, quizá,
como Dios ha de verte,
desbaratada la ficción del Tiempo,
sin el amor, sin mí.   15

Anticipation of Love   1972

Neither the intimacy of your look, your brow fair as a feast day,
not the favor of your body, still mysterious, reserved, and childlike,
nor what comes to me of your life, settling in words or silence,
will be so mysterious a gift
as the sight of your sleep, enfolded   5
in the vigil of my arms.
Virgin again, miraculously, by the absolving power of sleep,
quiet and luminous like some happy thing recovered by memory,
you will give me that shore of your life that you yourself do not own.
Cast up into silence   10
I shall discern that ultimate beach of your being
and see you for the first time, perhaps,
as God must see you—
the fiction of Time destroyed,
free from love, from me.   15

—*Translated by Robert Fitzgerald*

Questions

1. In "Anticipation of Love," note the translator's choice in line 4 to translate the
   Spanish "*favor*" (which translates more directly to "favor") to "gift." What do you
   think such a choice adds to the poem in English?
2. Why is the sleeping woman described as "virgin again"?
3. Does this poem describe a real event or only an imaginary one?

Los Enigmas   1964

Yo que soy el que ahora está cantando
Seré mañana el misterioso, el muerto,
El morador de un mágico y desierto
Orbe sin antes ni después ni cuando.
Así afirma la mística. Me creo   5
Indigno del Infierno o de la Gloria,
Pero nada predigo. Nuestra historia
Cambia como las formas de Proteo.
¿Qué errante laberinto, qué blancura
Ciega de resplandor será mi suerte,   10
Cuando me entregue el fin de esta aventura
La curiosa experiencia de la muerte?
Quiero beber su cristalino Olvido.
Ser para siempre; pero no haber sido.

The Enigmas   1972

I who am singing these lines today
Will be tomorrow the enigmatic corpse
Who dwells in a realm, magical and barren,
Without a before or an after or a when.
So say the mystics. I say I believe   5
Myself undeserving of Heaven or of Hell,
But make no predictions. Each man's tale
Shifts like the watery forms of Proteus.
What errant labyrinth, what blinding flash
Of splendor and glory shall become my fate   10
When the end of this adventure presents me with
The curious experience of death?
I want to drink its crystal-pure oblivion,
To be forever; but never to have been.

—*Translated by John Updike**

The Enigmas.   8 *Proteus:* Minor Greek god who had the ability to change form.

Questions

1. What is the speaker's most pressing question about his own future?
2. What is the main enigma or puzzle presented in "The Enigmas"?
3. What is the form of this poem?

OCTAVIO PAZ

Octavio Paz

Octavio Paz (1914–1998), the only Mexican author to win the Nobel Prize in literature, was born in Mexico City. Paz once commented that he came from "a typical Mexican family" because it combined European and Indian ancestors, but his background was quite distinguished. His father was a lawyer who had fought for the Mexican Revolution and served as secretary to guerilla leader, Emiliano Zapata. Paz's father retired and eventually went into exile in the United States after Zapata's 1919 assassination. "Impoverished by the revolution and civil war" his family lived in his grandfather's huge house in Mixoac, a suburb of Mexico City. "The house," he told an interviewer, "gradually crumbled around us," and the family abandoned rooms one by one as the roof collapsed. His grandfather had a library containing over six thousand books ("an enchanted cave," Paz later called it) where the young author immersed himself. Joining his father in exile, the young Paz lived for two years in Los Angeles. He then entered the National University of Mexico, but left in 1937 because he wanted to be a poet rather than a lawyer. Paz went to Spain to fight in the Spanish Civil War in 1937, but the Loyalist army refused to accept him because he didn't belong to the Communist Party (or any other political party). Paz refused to limit his political opinions to those of the two forces—military dictatorship or Marxist revolution—but worked toward democracy, "the mystery of freedom" as he called it in an early poem.

In 1945 Paz became a diplomat, spending years in San Francisco, New York, Geneva, and Delhi. In 1968 he resigned his post as ambassador to India in protest of the Mexican government's massacre of student demonstrators shortly before the Mexico City Olympic games. Paz then taught abroad at Cambridge University, the University of Texas, Harvard University, and other schools, but he always returned to Mexico City.

Paz's study of Mexican culture and national character, The Labyrinth of Solitude (1950), is a Latin American classic. Although deeply rooted in Mexican history and myth, the multilingual Paz was a true cosmopolitan. His study of the poetic process, The Bow and the Lyre (1956), ranged across world literature from Homer and Virgil to Whitman and Neruda. His Nobel Prize acceptance speech, published as "In Search of the Present" (1990), is a brilliant exploration of the cultural and imaginative relationship between the Old and New Worlds.

Con los Ojos Cerrados 1968	With Our Eyes Shut
Con los ojos cerrados Te iluminas por dentro Ertes la piedra ciega	With your eyes shut You light up from within You are blind stone
Noche a noche te labro Con los ojos cerrados Eres la piedra franca	Night by night I carve you With my eyes shut 5 You are clear stone
Nos volvemos inmensos Sólo por conocernos Con los ojos cerrados	We become immense Just knowing each other With our eyes shut

—*Translated by John Felstiner*

Questions

How do the refrains contribute to the musical quality of "With Our Eyes Shut"? What effects do the slight changes in phrasing this refrain create?

Certeza 1961	Certainty 1968
Si es real la luz blanca de esta lámpara, real la mano que escribe, ¿son reales los ojos que miran lo escrito?	If it is real the white light from this lamp, real the writing hand, are they real, the eyes looking at what I write?
De una palabra a la otra lo que digo se desvanece. Yo sé que estoy vivo entre dos paréntesis.	From one word to the other 5 what I say vanishes. I know that I am alive between two parentheses.

—*Translated by Charles Tomlinson*

Questions

In what ways is "Certainty" an *ars poetica* (poem about writing poetry)? What does the poem say about communication?

Surrealism in Latin American Poetry

Surrealism was one of the great artistic revolutions of the twentieth century. It first arose in the mockingly named "Dada" movement during World War I. (*Dada* is the French children's word for "hobbyhorse.") Dadaism was a radical rejection of the insanity perpetrated by the self-proclaimed "rational" world of the turbulent modern era. The approach was an attempt to shock the world out of its terrible self-destructive traditions. "The only way for Dada to continue," proclaimed poet André Breton, "is for it to cease to exist." Sure enough, the movement soon fell apart through its own excesses of energy and irreverence. In 1922 surrealism emerged as the successor to Dada, first as a literary movement, soon to spread to the visual arts, promoting the creation of fantastic, dreamlike works that reflected the unconscious mind. Fusing fact and myths, the movement sought to free art from the bounds of rationality. Not every modern writer embraced surrealism. Wallace Stevens referred mockingly to surrealism's dreamlike mixing of images as the act of making a "clam play an accordion."

Surrealism emphasized spontaneity rather than craft as the essential element in literary creation. Not all surrealist art, however, was spontaneous. Breton, for instance, spent six months on a poem of thirty words, in order to achieve what looked like spontaneity. And many surrealist visual artists would do several versions of the same "automatic drawing" in pursuit of the effect of immediacy. Breton's famous "Manifesto of Surrealism" (1924) launched a movement that continues to influence a great number of writers and artists around the world.

The early surrealists showed as much genius for absurd humor as for art, and their works often tried to shock and amuse. Marcel Duchamp once exhibited a huge printed reproduction of the *Mona Lisa* on which he had painted a large mustache. Louis Aragon's poem "Suicide" consisted only of the letters of the alphabet, and Breton once published a poem made up of names and numbers copied from the telephone directory. Is it any wonder that the surrealist motto was, "The approval of the public must be shunned at all cost"?

Surrealism's greatest international literary influence was on Latin American poetry. In the early twentieth century Latin America was much influenced by French culture, and literary innovations in Paris were quickly imported to Mexico City, Buenos Aires, and other New World capitals. In Latin America, however, surrealism lost much of the playfulness it exhibited in Europe, and the movement often took on a darker and more explicitly political quality. Surrealism also had a powerful effect on Latin American art. A tradition of surrealist painting emerged parallel to the movement in literature. One of the best known surrealist painters is the Mexican artist Frida Kahlo, whose work often created dreamlike visions of the human body, especially her own. In the *Two Fridas*, for example, she presents a frightening image of the body's interior exposed and mirrored. Kahlo's paintings are simultaneously personal and political—surrealistically portraying her own trauma, as well as the schism in her native country.

Many Latin American poets had periods that were strongly influenced by surrealism. César Vallejo, for instance, best known for the surrealist vanguardism of his second book, moved toward a more lyrical, inclusive style in his later work. Olga Orozco, as a translator of Breton, Paul Éluard, and other French surrealists, was strongly influenced by Parisian avant-garde poetry. Her work has a mysterious, dreamlike quality, as in the juxtapositions of "Reality and Desire." The repressiveness of Argentinian politics from the 1950s to the 1980s might have had an effect on her style as well, much in the way Dadaism emerged in Europe earlier in the century, as a response to violence. According to Octavio Paz, many poets, such as himself and Pablo Neruda, adopted surrealist processes, and their creative developments often coincided with the movement, although their work is not usually considered "surrealist."

Frida Kahlo   (1907–1957)

The Two Fridas   1939

The Two Fridas *by Frida Kahlo, c. 1939*

César Vallejo   (1892?–1938)

La Cólera que Quiebra   (1937) 1939
al Hombre en Niños

La cólera que quiebra al hombre en niños,
que quiebra al niño, en pájaros iguales,
y al pájaro, después, en huevecillos;
la cólera del pobre
tiene un aceite contra dos vinagres.   5

La cólera que el árbol quiebra en hojas,
a la hoja en botones desiguales
y al botón, en ranuras telescópicas;
la cólera del pobre
tiene dos ríos contra muchos mares.   10

La cólera que quiebra al bien en dudas,
a la duda, en tres arcos semejantes
y al arco, luego, en tumbas imprevistas;

la cólera del pobre
tiene un acero contra dos puñales.   15

    La cólera que quiebra el alma en cuerpos,
al cuerpo en órganos desemejantes
y al órgano, en octavos pensamientos;
la cólera del pobre
tiene un fuego central contra dos cráteres.   20

ANGER   1977

Anger which breaks a man into children,
Which breaks the child into two equal birds,
And after that the bird into a pair of little eggs:
The poor man's anger
Has one oil against two vinegars.   5

Anger which breaks a tree into leaves
And the leaf into unequal buds
And the bud into telescopic grooves;
The poor man's anger
Has two rivers against many seas.   10

Anger which breaks good into doubts
And doubt into three similar arcs
And then the arc into unexpected tombs;
The poor man's anger
Has one steel against two daggers.   15

Anger which breaks the soul into bodies
And the body into dissimilar organs
And the organ into octave thoughts;
The poor man's anger
Has one central fire against two craters.   20

—*Translated by Thomas Merton*

Olga Orozco   (b. 1920)

LA REALIDAD Y EL DESEO   1979

    A Luis Cernada

La realidad, sí, la realidad,
ese relámpago de lo invisible
que revela en nosotros la soledad de Dios.

Es este cielo que huye.
Es este territorio engalanado por las burbujas de la muerte.   5

Es esta larga mesa a la deriva
donde los comensales persisten ataviados por el prestigio de no estar.

A cada cual su copa
para medir el vino que se acaba donde empieza la sed.
Y cada cual su plato   10
para encerrar el hambre que se extingue sin saciarse jamás.
Y cada dos la división del pan:
el milagro al revés, la comunión tan sólo en lo imposible.
Y en medio del amor,
entre uno y otro cuerpo la caída,   15
algo que se asemeja al latido sombrío de unas alas que vuelven desde la
        eternidad,
al pulso del adiós debajo de la tierra.

La realidad, sí, la realidad:
un sello de clausura sobre todas las puertas del deseo.

REALITY AND DESIRE   1993

For Luis Cernada

Reality, yes, reality,
is the lightning-bolt of the invisible
that reveals in us the solitude of God.

This is the sky that escapes.
This is the territory adorned with the bubbles of death.   5
This is the big floating table
where the dinner-guests stay seated, wearing the prestige of
        not-being-there.

Each one has his goblet
to weigh the wine that ends where thirst begins.
Each one has his plate   10
that holds the hunger that ends but is never satisfied.
And for each pair their share of bread:
the miracle in reverse, solitary communion with the impossible.
And in the middle of love,
between one body and another, the fall,   15
something that seems like the shadowy throb of wings flying toward
        eternity,
to a pulse of farewell in the earth.

Reality, yes, reality:
the seal of cloister on all the gates of desire.

                                                            —*Translated by Stephen Tapscott*

POEMS FOR FURTHER READING

Alfonsina Storni   (1892–1938)

PESO ANCESTRAL   1919

Tú me dijiste: no lloró mi padre;
tú me dijiste: no lloró mi abuelo;
no han llorado los hombres de mi raza,
eran de acero.

Así diciendo te brotó una lágrima   5
y me cayó en la boca . . . más veneno
yo no he bebido nunca en otro vaso
así pequeño.

Débil mujer, pobre mujer que entiende,
dolor de siglos conocí al beberlo: 10
oh, el alma mía soportar no puede
todo su peso.

ANCESTRAL BURDEN   2004

You told me my father never cried
You told me my grandfather never cried.
The men of my lineage never cried
They were steel inside.

As you were saying this, you dropped a tear   5
that fell into my mouth—such poison
I have never drunk from any other cup
than this small one.

Weak woman, poor woman who understands
the ache of centuries I knew as I swallowed.   10
Oh, my spirit cannot carry all of its load.

—*Translated by Diane Thiel*

José Emilio Pacheco   (b. 1939)

ALTA TRAICIÓN   1969

No amo mi Patria. Su fulgor abstracto
es inasible.
Pero (aunque suene mal) daría la vida
por diez lugares suyos, cierta gente.
Puertos, bosques de piños, fortalezas,   5
una ciudad deshecha, gris, monstruosa,

varias figuras de su historia,
montañas
(y tres o cuatro ríos)

HIGH TREASON   1978

I do not love my country. Its abstract lustre
is beyond my grasp.
But (although it sounds bad) I would give my life
for ten places in it, for certain people,
seaports, pinewoods, fortresses,
a run-down city, gray, grotesque,
various figures from its history,
mountains
(And three or four rivers).

*—Translated by Alastair Reid**

QUESTIONS

1. What surreal effects do you find in Vallejo's and Orozco's poems? In other included poems? How is the Kahlo painting a quintessential example of surrealism?
2. How does the rhythm of Storni's poem (with its three longer lines and one shorter) contribute to the lyrical quality of the poem?

~ LATIN AMERICAN POETS ON POETRY ~

Sor Juana

REPLY TO SOR PHILOTHEA   (1691) 1700

TRANSLATED BY ALAN TRUEBLOOD

This was successful in one instance involving a very holy and very ingenuous prelate who thought studying was something for the Inquisition and ordered me to cease. I obeyed her (for the three months her right to so order me lasted) as regarded not taking a book in hand, but as to ceasing study altogether, it not being in my power, I could not carry it out. For, although I did not study from books, I did from everything God has created, all of it being my letters, and all this universal chain of being my book. I saw nothing without reflecting on it; I heard nothing without wondering at it—not even the tiniest, most material thing. For, as there is no created thing, no matter how lowly, in which one cannot recognize *me fecit Deus* [God made me], there is none that does not confound the mind once it stops to consider it. Thus, I repeat, I looked and marveled at all of them, so much so that simply from the person with whom I spoke, and from what that person said to me, countless reflections arose in my mind. What could be the origin of so great a variety of characters and minds, when all belonged to one species? Which humors and hidden qualities could bring this about? If I saw a figure, I at once fell to working out the relationship of its lines, measuring it with my mind and recasting it along different ones. Sometimes I would walk back and forth across the front of a sleeping-room of ours—a very large one—and observe how, though the lines of its two sides were parallel and its ceiling horizontal, one's vision made it appear as if the lines inclined toward each other and the ceiling were lower at the far end, from which I inferred that visual lines run straight but not parallel, tending rather toward a pyramidal figure. And I asked myself whether this could be the reason the ancients questioned whether the world was spherical or not. Because, although it appears to be, this could be an optical illusion, and show concavities where there might in fact be none.

This type of observation would occur to me about everything and still does, without my having any say in the matter; indeed, it continually irritates me because it tires my mind. I thought the same thing occurred in everyone's case, and with writing verse as well, until experience proved me wrong. This turn, or habit, of mind is so strong that I can look upon nothing without reflecting on it.

From *A Sor Juana Anthology*

Pablo Neruda

Towards the Splendid City   1971

I did not learn from books any recipe for writing a poem, and I, in my turn, will avoid giving any advice on mode or style which might give the new poets even a drop of supposed insight. When I am recounting in this speech something about past events, when reliving on this occasion a never-forgotten occurrence, in this place which is so different from what that was, it is because in the course of my life I have always found somewhere the necessary support, the formula which had been waiting for me not in order to be petrified in my words but in order to explain me to myself.

During this long journey I found the necessary components for the making of the poem. There I received contributions from the earth and from the soul. And I believe that poetry is an action, ephemeral or solemn, in which there enter as equal partners solitude and solidarity, emotion and action, the nearness to oneself, the nearness to mankind and to the secret manifestations of nature. And no less strongly I think that all this is sustained—man and his shadow, man and his conduct, man and his poetry—by an ever-wider sense of community, by an effort which will forever bring together the reality and the dreams in us because it is precisely in this way that poetry unites and mingles them. And therefore I say that I do not know, after so many years, whether the lessons I learned when I crossed a daunting river, when I danced around the skull of an ox, when I bathed my body in the cleansing water from the topmost heights—I do not know whether these lessons welled forth from me in order to be imparted to many others or whether it was all a message which was sent to me by others as a demand or an accusation. I do not know whether I experienced this or created it, I do not know whether it was truth or poetry, something passing or permanent, the poems I experienced in this hour, the experiences which I later put into verse.

From all this, my friends, there arises an insight which the poet must learn through other people. There is no insurmountable solitude. All paths lead to the same goal: to convey to others what we are. And we must pass through solitude and difficulty, isolation and silence in order to reach forth to the enchanted place where we can dance our clumsy dance and sing our sorrowful song—but in this dance or in this song there are fulfilled the most ancient rites of our conscience in the awareness of being human and of believing in a common destiny.

From Neruda's Nobel Prize lecture

Jorge Luis Borges

THE RIDDLE OF POETRY   1967

At the outset, I would like to give you fair warning of what to expect—or rather, of what not to expect—from me. I find that I have made a slip in the very title of my first lecture. The title is, if we are not mistaken, "The Riddle of Poetry," and the stress of course is on the first word, "riddle." So you may think the riddle is all-important. Or, what might be still worse, you may think I have deluded myself into believing that I have somehow discovered the true reading of the riddle. The truth is that I have no revelations to offer. I have spent my life reading, analyzing, writing (or trying my hand at writing), and enjoying. I found the last to be the most important thing of all. "Drinking in" poetry, I have come to a final conclusion about it. Indeed, every time I am faced with a blank page, I feel that I have to rediscover literature for myself. But the past is of no avail whatever to me. So, as I have said, I have only my perplexities to offer you. I am nearing seventy. I have given the major part of my life to literature, and I can offer you only doubts. . . .

For example, if I have to define poetry, and if I feel rather shaky about it, if I'm not too sure about it, I say something like: "Poetry is the expression of the beautiful through the medium of words artfully woven together." This definition may be good enough for a dictionary or a textbook, but we all feel that it is rather feeble. There is something far more important—something that may encourage us to go on not only trying our hand at writing poetry, but enjoying it and feeling that we know all about it.

This is that we *know* what poetry is. We know it so well that we cannot define it in other words, even as we cannot define the taste of coffee, the color red or yellow, or the meaning of anger, of love, of hatred, of the sunrise, of the sunset, or of our love for our country. These things are so deep in us that they can be expressed only by those common symbols that we share. So why should we need other words?

From *This Craft of Verse*

Octavio Paz

In Search of the Present   1990

Languages are vast realities that transcend those political and historical entities we call nations. The European languages we speak in the Americas illustrate this. The special position of our literatures when compared to those of England, Spain, Portugal and France depends precisely on this fundamental fact: they are literatures written in transplanted tongues. Languages are born and grow from the native soil, nourished by a common history. The European languages were rooted out from their native soil and their own tradition, and then planted in an unknown and unnamed world: they took root in the new lands and, as they grew within the societies of America, they were transformed. They are the same plant yet also a different plant. Our literatures did not passively accept the changing fortunes of the transplanted languages: they participated in the process and even accelerated it. They very soon ceased to be mere transatlantic reflections: at times they have been the negation of the literatures of Europe; more often, they have been a reply.

In spite of these oscillations the link has never been broken. My classics are those of my language and I consider myself to be a descendant of Lope and Quevedo,° as any Spanish writer would . . . yet I am not a Spaniard. I think that most writers of Spanish America, as well as those from the United States, Brazil and Canada, would say the same as regards the English, Portuguese and French traditions. To understand more clearly the special position of writers in the Americas, we should think of the dialogue maintained by Japanese, Chinese or Arabic writers with the different literatures of Europe. It is a dialogue that cuts across multiple languages and civilizations. Our dialogue, on the other hand, takes place within the same language. We are Europeans yet we are not Europeans. What are we then? It is difficult to define what we are, but our works speak for us.

                                                     From Paz's Nobel Prize lecture

⌇ Critics on Latin American Poetry ⌇

Stephanie Merrim   (b. 1951)

Endgames: Sor Juana Inés de la Cruz   1999

Why did Sor Juana write so much love poetry? Not only was it untoward for a nun, but love is a topic and emotion that seems to inspire true repugnance in Sor Juana. Consider the title of the following poems that revile love: "Which describes the catastrophe of the joys and desires of lovers," "Which resolves the question of which is more troublesome in conflicting emotions [*encontradas correspondencias*]:

Lope and Quevado: Lope de Vega (1562–1635) was a major Spanish dramatist and poet; Francisco Gomez de Quevedo (1580–1645) was a major Spanish novelist and poet. Their literary era is often referred to as the Golden Age.

to love or hate," "On a reasonable reflection which allays the pain of a passion," "Which offers a means to love without much grief." Sor Juana, as the titles suggest, is hardly a woman happy with love, an entranced woman in love. Happy or not, the sheer abundance of Sor Juana's love poetry—nearly fifty poems, about one-fifth of her poetry—has provoked scores of commentators to speculate about her motivation in writing it. Did Sor Juana write her amatory poetry in wake of a lost love? Conversely, was it a mere exercise, yet another of her experiments with a literary tradition, of her literary academy-inspired attempts to try her hand at them all? For to be a lyric poet was to be a love poet; love was poetry and poetry love (Frederick Luciani, *The Courtly Love Tradition in the Poetry of Sor Juana Inés de la Cruz*). Or, as Irving Leonard's influential interpretation would have it, did Sor Juana cipher into some of the love poetry an allegorical meaning, using the conventionalized forms of love poetry covertly to express the struggle between her love for church and for knowledge? Or was Sor Juana burdened less with abstract than with emotional struggles, with a melancholy for which the consecrated and depersonalized topics of courtly love provided an acceptable outlet?

From *Early Modern Women's Writing and Sor Juana Inés de la Cruz*

Alastair Reid (b. 1926)*

TRANSLATING NERUDA   1996

Translating someone's work, poetry in particular, has something about it akin to being possessed, haunted. Translating a poem means not only reading it deeply and deciphering it, but clambering about backstage among the props and the scaffolding. I found I could no longer read a poem of Neruda's simply as words on a page without hearing behind them that languid, caressing voice. Most important to me in translating these two writers [Neruda and Borges] was the sound of their voices in my memory, for it very much helped in finding the English appropriate to those voices. I found that if I learned poems of Neruda's by heart I could replay them at odd moments, on buses, at wakeful times in the night, until, at a certain point, the translation would somehow set. The voice was the clue: I felt that all Neruda's poems were fundamentally vocative—spoken poems, poems of direct address—and that Neruda's voice was in a sense the instrument for which he wrote. He once made a tape for me, reading pieces of different poems, in different tones and rhythms. I played it over so many times that I can hear it in my head at will. Two lines of his I used to repeat like a Zen koan, for they seemed to apply particularly to translating:

in this net it's not just the strings that count
but also the air that escapes through the meshes.

He often wrote of himself as having many selves, just as he had left behind him several very different poetic manners and voices.

From "Neruda and Borges"

Emir Rodríguez Monegal   (1921–1985)

BORGES AND PAZ   1973

There are few more tantalizing names in contemporary culture than Jorge Luis Borges and Octavio Paz. Both men have for a number of years transcended the somewhat parochial limits of their respective regions and have directed their work toward America (Latin or non-Latin) and Europe. To mention Paz or Borges in an international context today is to speak of writers who can demonstrate the intuition with which *El laberinto de la soledad* ends: today we Latin Americans are "for the first time in our history the contemporaries of all men." The frequency with which the works of Paz or Borges are quoted or alluded to in French or American, English or German criticism is sufficient proof of that contemporaneity, achieved with such difficulty by a culture which until very recently had been considered marginal, peripheral and merely colonial. . . .

In the context of present-day Spanish-American culture the names of Borges and Paz have even greater importance. In more than one sense they embody certain traits that should be taken into account before passing on to a more detailed analysis of them and their work. They share a certain intellectual attitude toward the esthetic phenomenon: an attitude which of course does not offer identical solutions to the same problems. Neither Paz nor Borges are disdainful of the day-to-day exercise of intelligence and erudition. They are highly educated poets, even in their impulsive or anguished moments. Lucid intelligence and intellectual enlightenment pervade their works and those works can sustain critical, profoundly personal meditation. Neither Paz nor Borges have renounced intellectuality: they realize that a poet cannot maintain an attitude of ignorance before the problems of language, esthetic phenomena and rhetorical speculation. As critics, they have both analyzed foreign works as well as their own; they have submitted the (ultimately unexplainable) phenomenon of poetic creation to tireless scrutiny.

To say this is not to assert, as some pretend to believe, that Paz and Borges are unaware of or hold in disdain the other faculties without which poetic creation or criticism is impossible. Paz's lyrical work begins with lucidity in order to reach the blinding glare of ecstasy; that of Borges makes use of the intellect in order to undermine and definitively destroy its own arrogance. Overwhelming intuition, the electric spark that leaps between two distant poles, the ability to seize by oblique methods the elusive core of reality are also characteristic of Paz's and Borges's works. But if their intelligence does not function in a vacuum, it is certainly the conducting medium of that poetic or critical charge both of their works contain.

They also share a deliberate, conscious and programmatic acceptance of a cultural tradition that comes to us from the West and transforms our literary task into the renewed construction and destruction of a dialogue begun many centuries ago on the shores of the Mediterranean. In both writers Americanism does not exclude but embodies that Mediterranean tradition. Too brilliant to ignore the fact that they are using a European verbal instrument, both look at reality from their respective Americas with the discipline they have acquired in vast multilingual libraries. Their Americanism is open.

From *The Perpetual Present*

QUESTIONS

1. Do the opening details included in Sor Juana's *Reply* surprise you? How does it change your reading of her poetry to know that the very act of writing was one of rebellion?
2. Consider the Nobel lectures of Paz and Neruda, and "The Riddle of Poetry" by Borges. What assertions do they make about "defining" poetry? Consider their included poems in terms of their prose comments.

SUGGESTIONS FOR WRITING

1. Consider Alfonsina Storni's "Ancestral Burden" and the two poems by Sor Juana. Discuss how each of the poems explores the experience and concerns of Latin American women. Use Sor Juana's prose piece *Reply* to inform your discussion of the poems.
2. Compare the love poems of Sor Juana, Pablo Neruda, and Jorge Luis Borges. In Stephanie Merrim's critical piece, she suggests some contradictory reasons for Sor Juana's many love poems. Use one of these reasons to support your assertions about love poetry.
3. Consider the surreal effects in Vallejo's and Orozco's poems, as well as in Frida Kahlo's painting, *The Two Fridas*. Examine other included poems for their surrealist techniques.
4. Consider the way personal and political themes merge in some of these poems. Compare Pacheco's "High Treason," Vallejo's "Anger," and Storni's "Ancestral Burden." Incorporate the prose pieces in your discussion. Paz speaks of language and identity in his Nobel acceptance speech. Use the prose comments by and about Paz and Borges to support your discussion of how the personal and political intersect in the poems.

17 *Recognizing Excellence*

Why do we call some poems "bad"? We are talking not about their moral implications. Rather, we mean that, for one or more of many possible reasons, the
poem has failed to move us or to engage our sympathies. Instead, it has made us
doubt that the poet is in control of language and vision; perhaps it has aroused
our antipathies or unwittingly appealed to our sense of the comic, though the
poet is serious. Some poems can be said to succeed despite burdensome faults.
But in general such faults are symptoms of deeper malady: some weakness in a
poem's basic conception or in the poet's competence.

Nearly always, a bad poem reveals only a dim and distorted awareness of its
probable effect on its audience. Perhaps the sound of words may clash with what
a poem is saying, as in the jarring last word of this opening line of a tender lyric
(author unknown, quoted by Richard Wilbur): "Come into the tent, my love,
and close the flap." A bad poem usually overshoots or falls short of its mark by
the poet's thinking too little or too much. Thinking too much, a poet contrives
an excess of ingenuity like that quoted by Alexander Pope in *Peri Bathous, or The
Art of Sinking in Poetry:* a hounded stag who "Hears his own feet, and thinks they
sound like more; / And fears the hind feet will o'ertake the fore." Thinking too
little, a poet writes redundantly, as Wordsworth in "The Thorn": "And they had
fixed the wedding-day, / The morning that must wed them both."

In a poem that has a rime scheme or a set line length, when all is well, pattern and structure move inseparably with the rest of the poem, the way a tiger's
skin and bones move with the tiger. But sometimes, in a poem that fails, the poet
evidently has had difficulty in fitting the statements into a formal pattern. English poets have long felt free to invert word order for a special effect (Milton: "ye
myrtles brown"), but the poet having trouble keeping to a rime scheme may invert words for no apparent reason but convenience. Needing a rime for *barge* may
lead to ending a line with *a police dog large* instead of *a large police dog*. Another
sign of trouble is a profusion of adjectives. If a line of iambic pentameter reads,

"Her lovely skin, like dear sweet white old silk," we suspect the poet of stuffing the line to make it long enough.

Even great poets write awful poems, and after their deaths, their worst efforts are collected with their masterpieces with no consumer warning labels to inform the reader. Some lines in the canon of celebrated bards make us wonder, "How could they have written this?" Wordsworth, Shelley, Whitman, and Browning are among the great whose failures can be painful, and sometimes an excellent poem will have a bad spot in it. To be unwilling to read them, though, would be as ill advised as to refuse to see Venice just because the Grand Canal is said to contain impurities. The seasoned reader of poetry thinks no less of Tennyson for having written, "Form, Form, Riflemen Form! . . . Look to your butts, and take good aims!" The collected works of a duller poet may contain no such lines of unconscious double meaning, but neither do they contain any poem as good as "Ulysses." If the duller poet never had a spectacular failure, it may be because of a failure to take risks. "In poetry," said Ronsard, "the greatest vice is mediocrity."

Often, inept poems fall into familiar categories. At one extreme is the poem written entirely in conventional diction, dimly echoing Shakespeare, Wordsworth, and the Bible, but garbling them. Couched in a rhythm that ticks along like a metronome, this kind of poem shows no sign that its author has ever taken a hard look at anything that can be tasted, handled, or felt. It employs loosely and thoughtlessly the most abstract of words: *love, beauty, life, death, time, eternity*. Littered with old-fashioned contractions (*'tis, o'er, where'er*), it may end in a simple preachment or platitude. George Orwell's complaint against much contemporary writing (not only poetry) is applicable: "As soon as certain topics are raised"—and one thinks of such standard topics for poetry as spring, a first kiss, and stars—"the concrete melts into the abstract and no one seems able to think of turns of speech that are not hackneyed." Writers, Orwell charged, too often make their sentences out of tacked-together phrases "like the sections of a prefabricated hen-house."[1] Versifiers often do likewise.

At the opposite extreme is the poem that displays no acquaintance with poetry of the past but manages, instead, to fabricate its own clichés. Slightly paraphrased, a manuscript once submitted to the *Paris Review* began:

Vile
    rottenflush
            o   —screaming—
            f CORPSEBLOOD!!   ooze
STRANGLE my
        eyes . . .
                        HELL's
            O, ghastly   stench**!!!

[1]George Orwell, "Politics and the English Language," *Shooting an Elephant and Other Essays* (New York: Harcourt, 1945).

At most, such a work has only a private value. The writer has vented personal frustrations upon words, instead of kicking stray dogs. In its way, "Vile Rotten-flush" is as self-indulgent as the oldfangled "first kiss in spring" kind of poem. "I dislike," said John Livingston Lowes, "poems that black your eyes, or put up their mouths to be kissed."

As jewelers tell which of two diamonds is fine by seeing which scratches the other, two poems may be tested by comparing them. This method works only on poems similar in length and kind: an epigram cannot be held up to test an epic. Most poems we meet are neither sheer trash nor obvious masterpieces. Because good diamonds to be proven need softer ones to scratch, in this chapter you will find a few clear-cut gems and a few clinkers.

Anonymous (English)

O MOON, WHEN I GAZE ON THY BEAUTIFUL FACE   (ABOUT 1900)

O Moon, when I gaze on thy beautiful face,
Careering along through the boundaries of space,
The thought has often come into my mind
If I ever shall see thy glorious behind.

O MOON. Sir Edmund Gosse, the English critic (1849–1928), offered this quatrain as the work of his servant, but there is reason to suspect him of having written it.

QUESTIONS

1. To what fact of astronomy does the last line refer?
2. Which words seem chosen with too little awareness of their denotations and connotations?
3. Even if you did not know that these lines probably were deliberately bad, how would you argue with someone who maintained that the opening O in the poem was admirable as a bit of concrete poetry?

Grace Treasone

LIFE   (ABOUT 1963)

Life is like a jagged tooth
that cuts into your heart;
fix the tooth and save the root,
and laughs, not tears, will start.

QUESTIONS

1. Try to paraphrase this poem. What is the poet saying?
2. How consistent is the working out of the comparison of life to a tooth?

Emily Dickinson (1830–1886)*

A DYING TIGER – MOANED FOR DRINK (ABOUT 1862)

A Dying Tiger – moaned for Drink –
I hunted all the Sand –
I caught the Dripping of a Rock
And bore it in my Hand –

His Mighty Balls – in death were thick – 5
But searching – I could see
A Vision on the Retina
Of Water – and of me –

'Twas not my blame – who sped too slow –
'Twas not his blame – who died 10
While I was reaching him –
But 'twas – the fact that He was dead –

QUESTIONS

How does this poem compare in success with other poems of Emily Dickinson that you
know? Justify your opinion by pointing to some of this poem's particulars.

EXERCISE: *Ten Terrible Moments in Poetry*

Here is a small anthology of bad moments in poetry.

For what reasons does each selection fail?

In which passages do you attribute the failure

  to inappropriate sound or diction?

  to awkward word order?

  to inaccurate metaphor?

  to excessive overstatement?

  to forced rime?

  to monotonous rhythm?

  to redundancy?

  to simple-mindedness or excessive ingenuity?

1. Last lines of *Enoch Arden* by Alfred, Lord Tennyson:

   So passed the strong heroic soul away.
   And when they buried him, the little port
   Had seldom seen a costlier funeral.

2. From *Purely Original Verse* (1891) by J. Gordon Coogler (1865–1901), of Columbia,
   South Carolina:

   Alas for the South, her books have grown fewer—
   She never was much given to literature.

3. From "Lines Written to a Friend on the Death of His Brother, Caused by a Railway Train Running Over Him Whilst He Was in a State of Inebriation" by James Henry Powell:

> Thy mangled corpse upon the rails in frightful shape was found.
> The ponderous train had killed thee as its heavy wheels went round,
> And thus in dreadful form thou met'st a drunkard's awful death
> And I, thy brother, mourn thy fate, and breathe a purer breath.

4. From *Dolce Far Niente* by the American poet Francis Saltus Saltus, who flourished in the 1890s:

> Her laugh is like sunshine, full of glee,
> And her sweet breath smells like fresh-made tea.

5. From another gem by Francis Saltus Saltus, "The Spider":

> Then all thy feculent majesty recalls
>   The nauseous mustiness of forsaken bowers,
> The leprous nudity of deserted halls—
>   The positive nastiness of sullied flowers.
>
> And I mark the colours yellow and black
>   That fresco thy lithe, dictatorial thighs,
> I dream and wonder on my drunken back
>   How God could possibly have created flies!

6. From "Song to the Suliotes" by George Gordon, Lord Byron:

> Up to battle! Sons of Suli
> Up, and do your duty duly!
> There the wall—and there the moat is:
> Bouwah! Bouwah! Suliotes,
> There is booty—there is beauty!
> Up my boys and do your duty!

7. From a juvenile poem of John Dryden, "Upon the Death of the Lord Hastings" (a victim of smallpox):

> Each little pimple had a tear in it,
> To wail the fault its rising did commit . . .

8. From "The Abbey Mason" by Thomas Hardy:

> When longer yet dank death had wormed
> The brain wherein the style had germed
>
> From Gloucester church it flew afar—
> The style called Perpendicular.—
>
> To Winton and to Westminster
> It ranged, and grew still beautifuller . . .

9. A metaphor from "The Crucible of Life" by the once-popular American newspaper poet Edgar A. Guest:

> Sacred and sweet is the joy that must come
> From the furnace of life when you've poured off the scum.

10. From an elegy for Queen Victoria by one of her subjects:

> Dust to dust, and ashes to ashes,
> Into the tomb the Great Queen dashes.

Sentimentality is a failure of writers who seem to feel a great emotion but who fail to give us sufficient grounds for sharing it. The emotion may be an anger greater than its object seems to call for, as in these lines to a girl who caused scandal (the exact nature of her act never being specified): "The gossip in each hall / Will curse your name . . . / Go! better cast yourself right down the falls!"[2] Or it may be an enthusiasm quite unwarranted by its subject: in *The Fleece* John Dyer temptingly describes the pleasures of life in a workhouse for the poor. The sentimental poet is especially prone to tenderness. Great tears fill his eyes at a glimpse of an aged grandmother sitting by a hearth. For all the poet knows, she may be the manager of a casino in Las Vegas who would be startled to find herself an object of pity, but the sentimentalist doesn't care to know about the woman herself. She is a general excuse for feeling maudlin. Any other conventional object will serve as well: a faded valentine, the strains of an old song, a baby's cast-off pacifier. An instance of such emotional self-indulgence is "The Old Oaken Bucket," by Samuel Woodworth, a stanza of which goes:

> How sweet from the green, mossy brim to receive it,
>   As, poised on the curb, it inclined to my lips!
> Not a full-flushing goblet could tempt me to leave it,
>   Tho' filled with the nectar that Jupiter sips.
> And now, far removed from the loved habitation,
>   The tear of regret will intrusively swell,
> As fancy reverts to my father's plantation,
>   And sighs for the bucket that hung in the well.

The staleness of the phrasing and imagery (Jove's nectar, *tear of regret*) suggests that the speaker is not even seeing the actual physical bucket, and the tripping meter of the lines is inappropriate to an expression of tearful regret. Perhaps the poet's nostalgia is genuine. Indeed, as Keith Waldrop has put it, "a bad poem is always sincere." However sincere in their feelings, sentimental poets fail as artists because they cannot separate their own emotional responses from those of the disinterested reader. Wet-eyed and sighing for a bucket, Woodworth achieves not pathos but **bathos:** a description that can move us to laughter instead of tears.[3] Tears, of course, can be shed for good reason. A piece of sentimentality is not to be confused with a well-wrought poem whose tone is tenderness.

---

[2]Ali. S. Hilmi, "The Preacher's Sermon," *Verse at Random* (Larnaca, Cyprus: Ohanian Press, 1953).
[3]*Bathos* in poetry can also mean an abrupt fall from the sublime to the trivial or incongruous. A sample, from Nicholas Rowe's play *The Fair Penitent:* "Is it the voice of thunder, or my father?" Another, from John Close, a minor Victorian: "Around their heads a dazzling halo shone, / No need of mortal robes, or any hat." When, however, such a letdown is used for a *desirable* effect of humor or contrast, it is usually called an **anticlimax:** as in Alexander Pope's lines on the queen's palace, "Here thou, great Anna! whom three realms obey, / Dost sometimes counsel take—and sometimes tea."

Rod McKuen   (b. 1933)

THOUGHTS ON CAPITAL PUNISHMENT   1954

There ought to be capital punishment for cars
that run over rabbits and drive into dogs
and commit the unspeakable, unpardonable crime
of killing a kitty cat still in his prime.

Purgatory, at the very least   5
                    should await the driver
   driving over a beast.

Those hurrying headlights coming out of the dark
that scatter the scampering squirrels in the park
should await the best jury that one might compose   10
of fatherless chipmunks and husbandless does.

And then found guilty, after too fair a trial
should be caged in a cage with a hyena's smile
or maybe an elephant with an elephant gun
should shoot out his eyes when the verdict is done.   15

There ought to be something, something that's fair
to avenge Mrs. Badger as she waits in her lair
for her husband who lies with his guts spilling out
cause he didn't know what automobiles are about.

Hell on the highway, at the very least   20
                    should await the driver
   driving over a beast.

Who kills a man kills a bit of himself
But a cat too is an extension of God.

William Stafford   (1914–1993)*

TRAVELING THROUGH THE DARK   1962

Traveling through the dark I found a deer
dead on the edge of the Wilson River road.
It is usually best to roll them into the canyon:
that road is narrow; to swerve might make more dead.

By glow of the tail-light I stumbled back of the car   5
and stood by the heap, a doe, a recent killing;
she had stiffened already, almost cold.
I dragged her off; she was large in the belly.

My fingers touching her side brought me the reason—
her side was warm; her fawn lay there waiting,   10
alive, still, never to be born.
Beside that mountain road I hesitated.

The car aimed ahead its lowered parking lights;
under the hood purred the steady engine.
I stood in the glare of the warm exhaust turning red;   15
around our group I could hear the wilderness listen.

I thought hard for us all—my only swerving—
then pushed her over the edge into the river.

QUESTIONS

1. Compare these poems by Rod McKuen and William Stafford. How are they similar?
2. Explain Stafford's title. Who are all those traveling through the dark?
3. Comment on McKuen's use of language. Consider especially: *unspeakable, unpardonable crime* (line 3), *kitty cat* (4), *scatter the scampering squirrels* (9), and *cause he didn't know* (19).
4. Compare the meaning of Stafford's last two lines and McKuen's last two. Does either poem have a moral? Can either poem be said to moralize?
5. Which poem might be open to the charge of sentimentality? Why?

In recent years, the belief that poetry cannot be popular has been shaken by practitioners of **cowboy poetry,** verse about life on the range, written by people who know that life firsthand. Usually realistic, riming and metrical, cowboy poetry is designed to be read aloud or recited to audiences such as the large throng that assembles each January at the Cowboy Poetry Gathering in Elko, Nevada. This kind of folk poetry "has its own criteria of good and bad," insists Gibbs Smith, publisher of two best-selling cowboy poetry anthologies; "it has its own rules; its own tradition, and we should respect that."[4] Devotees of cowboy poetry regard the following poem as a classic. Read it and see if you agree.

Wallace McRae   (b. 1936)

REINCARNATION   1980

"What does reincarnation mean?"
A cowpoke ast his friend.
His pal replied, "It happens when
Yer life has reached its end.
They comb yer hair, and warsh yer neck,   5

---

[4]Quoted by Sara Terry, "Poem on the Range," *Boston Globe Magazine,* Jan. 19, 1992. The anthologies, edited by Hal Cannon, are *Cowboy Poetry: A Gathering* and *New Cowboy Poetry* (Salt Lake City: Gibbs M. Smith, 1985 and 1990).

And clean yer fingernails,
And lay you in a padded box
Away from life's travails.

"The box and you goes in a hole,
That's been dug into the ground.   10
Reincarnation starts in when
Yore planted 'neath a mound.
Them clods melt down, just like yer box,
And you who is inside.
And then yore just beginnin's on   15
Yer transformation ride.

"In a while the grass'll grow
Upon yer rendered mound.
Till some day on yer moldered grave
A lonely flower is found.   20
And say a hoss should wander by
And graze upon this flower
That once wuz you, but now's become
Yer vegetative bower.

"The posey that the hoss done ate   25
Up, with his other feed,
Makes bone, and fat, and muscle
Essential to the steed.
But some is left that he can't use
And so it passes through,   30
And finally lays upon the ground.
This thing, that once wuz you.

"Then say, by chance, I wanders by
And sees this upon the ground,
And I ponders, and I wonders at,   35
This object that I found.
I thinks of reincarnation,
Of life, and death, and such,
And come away concludin': Slim,
You ain't changed, all that much."   40

QUESTIONS

1. If you were Slim, how would you react to that last line?
2. Discuss this harsh judgment: "This isn't much of a poem. The poet is only playing an elaborate joke on Slim and on the rest of us."
3. In general, do you believe that a poem is any the worse for a lack of total seriousness?
4. Take a close look at the poem's language. Which words or phrases seem unschooled cowboy speech? Which might be criticized as stilted or bookish? How do you account for this discrepancy?

5. Compare the poem's central idea with a similar notion advanced by Shakespeare's *Hamlet, Prince of Denmark:*

> *Hamlet:* A man may fish with the worm that hath eat of a king, and eat of the
> fish that hath fed of that worm.
> *King:* What dost thou mean by this?
> *Hamlet:* Nothing but to show you how a king may go to progress through the
> guts of a beggar. (4.3.27-32)

Notice that Hamlet, like Slim's friend, also puts his listener on the receiving end of an insult. But how might it be claimed that Shakespeare makes a simple idea rich and complicated?

6. Do you agree with Gibbs Smith that we should judge cowboy poetry only by its own rules (not oblige it to live up to standards we might apply to a passage of Shakespeare or a poem by Robert Frost)?

RECOGNIZING EXCELLENCE

How can we tell an excellent poem from any other? To give reasons for excellence in poetry is harder than to give reasons for failure in poetry (so often due to familiar kinds of imprecision and sentimentality). A bad poem tends to be stereotyped, an excellent poem unique. In judging either, we can have no absolute specifications. A poem is not like an electric toaster that an inspector can test using a check-off list. It has to be judged on the basis of what it is trying to be and how well it succeeds in the effort.

To judge a poem, we first have to understand it. At least, we need to understand it *almost* all the way; there are, to be sure, poems such as Hopkins's "The Windhover" (page 497), which most readers probably would call excellent even though its meaning is still being debated. Although it is a good idea to give a poem at least a couple of considerate readings before judging it, sometimes our first encounter starts turning into an act of evaluation. Moving along into the poem, becoming more deeply involved in it, we may begin forming an opinion. In general, the more a poem contains for us to understand, the more rewarding we are likely to find it. Of course, an obscure and highly demanding poem is not always to be preferred to a relatively simple one. Difficult poems can be pretentious and incoherent; still, there is something to be said for the poem complicated enough to leave us something to discover on our fifteenth reading (unlike most limericks, which yield their all at a look). Here is such a poem, one not readily fathomed and exhausted.

William Butler Yeats (1865–1939)*

SAILING TO BYZANTIUM   1927

That is no country for old men. The young
In one another's arms, birds in the trees
—Those dying generations—at their song,

The salmon-falls, the mackerel-crowded seas,
Fish, flesh, or fowl, commend all summer long   5
Whatever is begotten, born, and dies.
Caught in that sensual music all neglect
Monuments of unaging intellect.

An aged man is but a paltry thing,
A tattered coat upon a stick, unless   10
Soul clap its hands and sing, and louder sing
For every tatter in its mortal dress,
Nor is there singing school but studying
Monuments of its own magnificence;
And therefore I have sailed the seas and come   15
To the holy city of Byzantium.

O sages standing in God's holy fire
As in the gold mosaic of a wall,
Come from the holy fire, perne in a gyre,°   *spin down a spiral*
And be the singing-masters of my soul.   20
Consume my heart away; sick with desire
And fastened to a dying animal
It knows not what it is; and gather me
Into the artifice of eternity.

Once out of nature I shall never take   25
My bodily form from any natural thing,
But such a form as Grecian goldsmiths make
Of hammered gold and gold enameling
To keep a drowsy Emperor awake;
Or set upon a golden bough to sing   30
To lords and ladies of Byzantium
Of what is past, or passing, or to come.

SAILING TO BYZANTIUM. Byzantium was the capital of the Byzantine Empire, the city now called Istanbul. Yeats means, though, not merely the physical city. Byzantium is also a name for his conception of paradise.

Though *salmon-falls* (line 4) suggests Yeats's native Ireland, the poem, as we find out in line 25, is about escaping from the entire natural world. If the poet desires this escape, then probably the *country* mentioned in the opening line is no political nation but the cycle of birth and death in which human beings are trapped; and, indeed, the poet says his heart is "fastened to a dying animal." Imaginary landscapes, it would seem, are merging with the historical Byzantium. Lines 17–18 refer to mosaic images, adornments of the Byzantine cathedral of St. Sophia, in which the figures of saints are inlaid against backgrounds of gold. The clockwork bird of the last stanza is also a reference to something actual. Yeats noted: "I have read somewhere that in the Emperor's palace at Byzantium was a tree made of gold and silver, and artificial birds that sang." This description of the role the poet would seek—that of a changeless, immortal singer—directs us back to the earlier references to music and singing. Taken all together, they point toward the central metaphor of the poem: the craft of poetry can be a kind of singing. One kind of everlasting monument is a great poem. To study masterpieces of poetry is the only "singing school"—the only way to learn to write a poem.

We have no more than skimmed through a few of this poem's suggestions, enough to show that, out of allusion and imagery, Yeats has woven at least one elaborate metaphor. Surely one thing the poem achieves is that, far from merely puzzling us, it makes us aware of relationships between what a person can imagine and the physical world. There is the statement that a human heart is bound to the body that perishes, and yet it is possible to see consciousness for a moment independent of flesh, to sing with joy at the very fact that the body is crumbling away. Much of the power of Yeats's poem comes from the physical terms with which he states the ancient quarrel between body and spirit, body being a "tattered coat upon a stick." There is all the difference in the world between the work of the poet like Yeats whose eye is on the living thing and whose mind is awake and passionate, and that of the slovenly poet whose dull eye and sleepy mind focus on nothing more than some book read hastily long ago. The former writes a poem out of compelling need, the latter as if it seems a nice idea to write something.

Yeats's poem has the three qualities essential to beauty, according to the definition of Thomas Aquinas: wholeness, harmony, and radiance. The poem is all one; its parts move in peace with one another; it shines with emotional intensity. There is an orderly progression going on in it: from the speaker's statement of his discontent with the world of "sensual music," to his statement that he is quitting this world, to his prayer that the sages will take him in, and his vision of future immortality. And the images of the poem relate to one another—*dying generations* (line 3), *dying animal* (line 22), and the undying golden bird (lines 27–32)—to mention just one series of related things. "Sailing to Byzantium" is not the kind of poem that has, in Pope's words, "One simile, that solitary shines / In the dry desert of a thousand lines." Rich in figurative language, Yeats's whole poem develops a metaphor, with further metaphors as its tributaries.

"Sailing to Byzantium" has a theme that matters to us. What human being does not long, at times, to shed timid, imperfect flesh, to live in a state of absolute joy, unperishing? Being human, perhaps we too are stirred by Yeats's prayer: "Consume my heart away, sick with desire / And fastened to a dying animal. . . ." If it is true that in poetry, as Ezra Pound declared, "only emotion endures," then Yeats's poem ought to endure. (If you happen not to feel moved by this poem, try another—but come back to "Sailing to Byzantium" after a while.)

Most excellent poems, it might be argued, contain significant themes, as does "Sailing to Byzantium." But the presence of such a theme is not enough to render a poem excellent. Not theme alone makes an excellent poem, but how well a theme is stated.

Yeats's poem, some would say, is a match for any lyric in our language. Some might call it inferior to an epic (to Milton's *Paradise Lost*, say, or to the *Iliad*), but to make this claim is to lead us into a different argument: whether certain genres are innately better than others. Such an argument usually leads to a dead end. Evidently, *Paradise Lost* has greater range, variety, matter, length, and ambitiousness. But any poem—whether an epic or an epigram—may be judged by how well it fulfills the design it undertakes. God, who created both fleas and whales, pronounced all good. Fleas, like epigrams, have no reason to feel inferior.

EXERCISE: *Two Poems to Compare*

Here are two poems with a similar theme. Which contains more qualities of excellent poetry? Decide whether the other is bad or whether it may be praised for achieving something different.

Arthur Guiterman (1871–1943)

ON THE VANITY OF EARTHLY GREATNESS   1936

The tusks that clashed in mighty brawls
Of mastodons, are billiard balls.

The sword of Charlemagne the Just
Is ferric oxide, known as rust.

The grizzly bear whose potent hug   5
Was feared by all, is now a rug.

Great Caesar's bust is on the shelf,
And I don't feel so well myself.

Percy Bysshe Shelley (1792–1822)

OZYMANDIAS   1818

I met a traveler from an antique land
Who said: Two vast and trunkless legs of stone
Stand in the desert. Near them, on the sand,
Half sunk, a shattered visage lies, whose frown,
And wrinkled lip, and sneer of cold command,   5
Tell that its sculptor well those passions read
Which yet survive, stamped on these lifeless things,
The hand that mocked° them and the heart that fed;   *imitated*
And on the pedestal these words appear:
"My name is Ozymandias, king of kings: 10
Look on my works, ye Mighty, and despair!"
Nothing beside remains. Round the decay
Of that colossal wreck, boundless and bare
The lone and level sands stretch far away.

Some excellent poems of the past will remain sealed to us unless we are willing to sympathize with their conventions. Pastoral poetry, for instance— Marlowe's "Passionate Shepherd" and Milton's "Lycidas"—asks us to accept certain conventions and situations that may seem old-fashioned: idle swains, oaten flutes. We are under no grim duty, of course, to admire poems whose conventions do not appeal to us. But there is no point in blaming a poet for playing a particular game or for observing its rules.

Bad poems, of course, can be woven together out of conventions, like patchwork quilts made of old unwanted words. In Shakespeare's England, poets were busily imitating the sonnets of Petrarch, the Italian poet whose praise of his beloved Laura had become well known. The result of their industry was a surplus of Petrarchan **conceits,** or elaborate comparisons (from the Italian *concetto:* concept, bright idea). In a famous sonnet ("My mistress' eyes are nothing like the sun," page 542), Shakespeare, who at times helped himself generously from the Petrarchan stockpile, pokes fun at poets who thoughtlessly use such handed-down figures of speech.

There is no predictable pattern for poetic excellence. A reader needs to remain open to surprise and innovation. Remember, too, that a superb poem is not necessarily an uplifting one—full of noble sentiments and inspiring ideas. Some powerful poems deal with difficult and even unpleasant subjects. What matters is the compelling quality of the presentation, the evocative power of the language, and the depth of feeling and perception achieved by the total work. William Trevor once defined the short story as "an explosion of truth"; the same notion applies to poetry, with a special reminder that not all truths are pleasant. Robert Hayden's "The Whipping," for example, is a memorable but disturbing poem on a difficult subject, child abuse. Notice how Hayden refuses to sensationalize the topic into sociological clichés but instead reaches for its deeper human significance—not only for the victim, but also for the victimizer and even the observer.

Robert Hayden   (1913–1980)*

THE WHIPPING   1970

The old woman across the way
  is whipping the boy again
and shouting to the neighborhood
  her goodness and his wrongs.

Wildly he crashes through elephant ears,   5
  pleads in dusty zinnias,
while she in spite of crippling fat
  pursues and corners him.

She strikes and strikes the shrilly circling
    boy till the stick breaks 10
in her hand. His tears are rainy weather
    to woundlike memories:

My head gripped in bony vise
    of knees, the writhing struggle
to wrench free, the blows, the fear 15
    worse than blows that hateful

Words could bring, the face that I
    no longer knew or loved. . . .
Well, it is over now, it is over
    and the boy sobs in his room, 20

And the woman leans muttering against
    a tree, exhausted, purged—
avenged in part for lifelong hidings
    she has had to bear.

QUESTIONS

1. Who is the speaker of the poem? What is the speaker's relation to the people he observes in the opening stanza?
2. How does the scene being depicted change in the fourth stanza? Who are the people depicted here?
3. What reason does the speaker give for the old woman's violence? Does the speaker feel her reason is adequate to excuse her behavior?
4. How would you summarize the theme of this poem?

Sometimes poets use conventions in an innovative way, stretching the rules for new expressive ends. Here Elizabeth Bishop takes the form of the villanelle and bends the rules to give her poem a heartbreaking effect.

Elizabeth Bishop   (1911–1979)*

ONE ART   1976

The art of losing isn't hard to master;
so many things seem filled with the intent
to be lost that their loss is no disaster.

Lose something every day. Accept the fluster
of lost door keys, the hour badly spent. 5
The art of losing isn't hard to master.

Then practice losing farther, losing faster:
places, and names, and where it was you meant
to travel. None of these will bring disaster.

I lost my mother's watch. And look! my last, or   10
next-to-last, of three loved houses went.
The art of losing isn't hard to master.

I lost two cities, lovely ones. And, vaster,
some realms I owned, two rivers, a continent.
I miss them, but it wasn't a disaster.   15

—Even losing you (the joking voice, a gesture
I love) I shan't have lied. It's evident
the art of losing's not too hard to master
though it may look like (*Write* it!) like disaster.

QUESTIONS

1. What things has the speaker lost? Put together a complete list in the order she reveals them. What does the list suggest about her experience with loss?
2. Bishop varies the repeated lines that end with the word *disaster*. Look only at those lines: what do they suggest about the story being unfolded in the poem?
3. What effect does the parenthetical comment in the poem's last line create? Would the poem be different if it were omitted?
4. Compare this poem to other villanelles in this book, such as Dylan Thomas's "Do not go gentle into that good night" (page 231) and Wendy Cope's "Lonely Hearts" (page 70). In what ways does Bishop bend the rules of the form?

Like "One Art," many great poems engage our personal feelings and private concerns. Others explore larger historical issues and our relationship to them. The following poem, which is set in New York City on the day that Hitler invaded Poland and World War II started, was widely circulated in the weeks following the terrorist attacks of September 11, 2001.

W. H. Auden   (1907–1973)*
SEPTEMBER 1, 1939   1940

I sit in one of the dives
On Fifty-Second Street
Uncertain and afraid
As the clever hopes expire
Of a low dishonest decade: 5
Waves of anger and fear
Circulate over the bright
And darkened lands of the earth,
Obsessing our private lives;
The unmentionable odour of death   10
Offends the September night.

Accurate scholarship can
Unearth the whole offence
From Luther until now
That has driven a culture mad,   15
Find what occurred at Linz,
What huge imago made
A psychopathic god:
I and the public know
What all schoolchildren learn,   20
Those to whom evil is done
Do evil in return.

Exiled Thucydides knew
All that a speech can say
About Democracy,   25
And what dictators do,
The elderly rubbish they talk
To an apathetic grave;
Analysed all in his book,
The enlightenment driven away,   30
The habit-forming pain,
Mismanagement and grief:
We must suffer them all again.

Into this neutral air
Where blind skyscrapers use   35
Their full height to proclaim
The strength of Collective Man,
Each language pours its vain
Competitive excuse:
But who can live for long   40
In an euphoric dream;
Out of the mirror they stare,
Imperialism's face
And the international wrong.

Faces along the bar   45
Cling to their average day:
The lights must never go out,
The music must always play,
All the conventions conspire
To make this fort assume   50
The furniture of home;
Lest we should see where we are,
Lost in a haunted wood,

Children afraid of the night
Who have never been happy or good.   55

The windiest militant trash
Important Persons shout
Is not so crude as our wish:
What mad Nijinsky wrote
About Diaghilev   60
Is true of the normal heart;
For the error bred in the bone
Of each woman and each man
Craves what it cannot have,
Not universal love   65
But to be loved alone.

From the conservative dark
Into the ethical life
The dense commuters come,
Repeating their morning vow,   70
"I *will* be true to the wife,
I'll concentrate more on my work,"
And helpless governors wake
To resume their compulsory game:
Who can release them now,   75
Who can reach the deaf,
Who can speak for the dumb?

All I have is a voice
To undo the folded lie,
The romantic lie in the brain   80
Of the sensual man-in-the-street
And the lie of Authority
Whose buildings grope the sky:
There is no such thing as the State
And no one exists alone;   85
Hunger allows no choice
To the citizen or the police;
We must love one another or die.

Defenseless under the night
Our world in stupor lies;   90
Yet, dotted everywhere,
Ironic points of light
Flash out wherever the Just
Exchange their messages:

May I, composed like them   95
Of Eros and of dust,
Beleaguered by the same
Negation and despair,
Show an affirming flame.

SEPTEMBER 1, 1939. 2 *Fifty-Second Street;* in New York City. 14 *Luther:* German priest Martin Luther (1483–1546), whose 95 Theses (1517) ignited the Protestant Reformation. 16 *Linz:* town in Austria where Adolf Hitler was raised. 23 *Thucydides:* Greek historian of the fifth century B.C., whose *History of the Peloponnesian War* contains the famous oration by Pericles commemorating the Athenian war dead. 59–60 *What mad Nijinksy wrote / About Diaghilev:* Russian dancer Vaslav Nijinsky (1890–1960) wrote in his diary of the impresario Sergei Diaghilev (1872–1929): "Some politicians are hypocrites like Diaghilev, who does not want universal love, but to be loved alone. I want universal love."

QUESTIONS

1. How do the last two lines of the second stanza relate to the specific political and historical situation that the poem addresses? How valid do you find them as a description of human behavior in general?
2. What attitude does the poem take, especially in the third stanza, toward the use of patriotic appeals by heads of state to build support for war?
3. In the context of the poem's larger themes, why is it an "error" to desire "to be loved alone" (lines 62–66)?
4. What does Auden mean by "There is no such thing as the State" (line 84)?
5. Is this poem relevant to our times? Refer to particular situations and events to back up your response.

Excellent poetry might be easier to recognize if each poet had a fixed position on the slopes of Mount Parnassus, but, from one century to the next, the reputations of some poets have taken humiliating slides, or made impressive clambers. We decide for ourselves which poems to call excellent, but readers of the future may reverse our opinions. Most of us no longer would share this popular view of Walt Whitman held by one of his contemporaries:

> Walt Whitman (1819–1892), by some regarded as a great poet; by others, as no poet at all. Most of his so-called poems are mere catalogues of things, without meter or rime, but in a few more regular poems and in lines here and there he is grandly poetical, as in "O Captain! My Captain!"[5]

Walt Whitman (1819–1892)*

O CAPTAIN! MY CAPTAIN!   1865

O Captain! my Captain! our fearful trip is done,
The ship has weather'd every rack, the prize we sought is won,
The port is near, the bells I hear, the people all exulting,

[5] J. Willis Westlake, A. M., *Common-school Literature, English and American, with Several Hundred Extracts to be Memorized* (Philadelphia, 1898).

While follow eyes the steady keel, the vessel grim and daring;
　　But O heart! heart! heart!　　　　　　　　　　　　　　　　5
　　　　O the bleeding drops of red,
　　　　　　Where on the deck my Captain lies,
　　　　　　　　Fallen cold and dead.

O Captain! my Captain! rise up and hear the bells;
Rise up—for you the flag is flung—for you the bugle trills,　　10
For you bouquets and ribbon'd wreaths—for you the shores a-crowding,
For you they call, the swaying mass, their eager faces turning;
　　Here Captain! dear father!
　　　　This arm beneath your head!
　　　　　　It is some dream that on the deck,　　　　　　15
　　　　　　　　You've fallen cold and dead.

My Captain does not answer, his lips are pale and still,
My father does not feel my arm, he has no pulse nor will,
The ship is anchor'd safe and sound, its voyage closed and done,
From fearful trip the victor ship comes in with object won;　　20
　　Exult O shores, and ring O bells!
　　　　But I with mournful tread,
　　　　　　Walk the deck my Captain lies,
　　　　　　　　Fallen cold and dead.

O CAPTAIN! MY CAPTAIN! Written soon after the death of Abraham Lincoln, this was, in Whitman's lifetime, by far the most popular of his poems.

QUESTIONS

1. Compare this with other Whitman poems. In what ways is "O Captain! My Captain!" uncharacteristic of his works? Do you agree with J. Willis Westlake that this is one of the few occasions on which Whitman is "grandly poetical?"
2. Comment on the appropriateness of the poem's rhythms to its subject.
3. Do you find any evidence in this poem that an excellent poet wrote it?

　　In a sense, all readers of poetry are constantly reexamining the judgments of the past by choosing those poems they care to go on reading. In the end, we have to admit that the critical principles set forth in this chapter are all very well for admiring excellent poetry we already know, but they cannot be carried like a yardstick in the hand, to go out looking for it. As Ezra Pound said in his *ABC of Reading*, "A classic is classic not because it conforms to certain structural rules, or fits certain definitions (of which its author had quite probably never heard). It is classic because of a certain eternal and irrepressible freshness."

　　The best poems, like "Sailing to Byzantium," may offer a kind of religious experience. At the beginning of the twenty-first century, some of us rarely set foot outside an artificial environment. Whizzing down four-lane superhighways, we observe lakes and trees in the distance. In a way our cities are to us as anthills are to ants: no less than anthills, they are "natural" structures. But the "unnatural" world of school or business is, as Wordsworth says, too much with us. Locked in the shells of our ambitions, our self-esteem, we forget our kinship to earth and sea. We fabricate self-justifications. But a great poem shocks us into another order of perception. It points beyond language to something still more essential. It ushers us into an experience so moving and true that we feel (to quote King Lear) "cut to the brain." In bad or indifferent poetry, words are all there is.

Carl Sandburg (1878–1967)*

Fog   1916

The fog comes
on little cat feet.

It sits looking
over harbor and city
on silent haunches   5
and then moves on.

QUESTION

In lines 15–22 of "The Love Song of J. Alfred Prufrock" (page 473), T. S. Eliot also likens fog to a cat. Compare Sandburg's lines and Eliot's. Which passage tells us more about fogs and cats?

EXERCISE: *Reevaluating Popular Classics*

In this exercise you will read two of the most popular American poems of the nineteenth century. In their time, not only were these poems considered classics by serious critics, but thousands of ordinary readers knew them by heart. Recently, however, they have fallen out of critical favor.

   Your assignment is to read these poems carefully and make your own personal, tentative evaluation of each poem's merit. Here are some questions you might ask yourself, as you consider them.

- Do these poems engage your sympathies? Do they stir you and touch your feelings?
- What, if anything, might make them memorable? Do they have any vivid images? Any metaphors, understatement, overstatement, or other figures of speech? Do these poems appeal to the ear?
- Do the poems exhibit any wild incompetence? Do you find any forced rimes, inappropriate words, or other unintentionally comic features? Can the poems be accused of bathos or sentimentality, or do you trust the poet to report honest feelings?
- How well does the poet seem in control of language? Does the poet's language reflect in any detail the physical world we know?
- Do these poems seem entirely drawn from other poetry of the past, or do you have a sense that the poet is thinking and feeling on her (or his) own? Does the poet show any evidence of having read other poets' poetry?
- What is the poet trying to do in each poem? How successful, in your opinion, is the attempt?

Try setting these poems next to similar poems you know and admire. (You might try comparing Emma Lazarus's "The New Colossus" to Percy Bysshe Shelley's "Ozymandias," found in this chapter; both are sonnets, and their subjects have interesting similarities and contrasts. Or compare Edgar Allan Poe's "Annabel Lee" to A. E. Housman's "To an Athlete Dying Young," found in "Poems for Further Reading.")

Are these poems sufficiently rich and interesting to repay more than one reading?

Do you think that these poems still deserve to be considered classics? Or do they no longer speak powerfully to a contemporary audience?

Emma Lazarus (1849–1887)

THE NEW COLOSSUS   1883

Not like the brazen giant of Greek fame,
With conquering limbs astride from land to land;
Here at our sea-washed, sunset gates shall stand
A mighty woman with a torch, whose flame
Is the imprisoned lightning, and her name   5
Mother of Exiles. From her beacon-hand
Glows world-wide welcome; her mild eyes command
The air-bridged harbor that twin cities frame.
"Keep, ancient lands, your storied pomp!" cries she
With silent lips. "Give me your tired, your poor,   10
Your huddled masses yearning to breathe free,
The wretched refuse of your teeming shore.
Send these, the homeless, tempest-tost to me,
I lift my lamp beside the golden door!"

THE NEW COLOSSUS. In 1883, a committee formed to raise funds to build a pedestal for what would be the largest statue in the world, "Liberty Enlightening the World" by Fréderic-Auguste Bartholdi, which was a gift from the French people to celebrate America's centennial. American authors were asked to donate manuscripts for a fund-raising auction. The young poet Emma Lazarus, whose parents had come to America as immigrants, sent in this sonnet composed for the occasion. When President Grover Cleveland unveiled the Statue of Liberty in October 1886, Lazarus's sonnet was read at the ceremony. In 1903, the poem was carved on the statue's pedestal. The reference in the opening line to "the brazen giant of Greek fame" is to the famous Colossus of Rhodes, a huge bronze statue that once stood in the harbor on the Aegean island of Rhodes. Built to commemorate a military victory, it was one of the so-called Seven Wonders of the World.

Edgar Allan Poe   (1809–1849)*

ANNABEL LEE   1849

It was many and many a year ago,
   In a kingdom by the sea,
That a maiden there lived whom you may know
   By the name of Annabel Lee;
And this maiden she lived with no other thought   5
   Than to love and be loved by me.

I was a child and *she* was a child,
   In this kingdom by the sea,
But we loved with a love that was more than love—
   I and my Annabel Lee—   10
With a love that the wingéd seraphs of Heaven
   Coveted her and me.

And this was the reason that, long ago,
   In this kingdom by the sea,
A wind blew out of a cloud, chilling   15
   My beautiful Annabel Lee;
So that her highborn kinsmen came
   And bore her away from me,
To shut her up in a sepulchre
   In this kingdom by the sea.   20

The angels, not half so happy in Heaven,
   Went envying her and me:—
Yes!—that was the reason (as all men know,
   In this kingdom by the sea)
That the wind came out of the cloud by night,   25
   Chilling and killing my Annabel Lee.

But our love it was stronger by far than the love
   Of those who were older than we—
   Of many far wiser than we—
And neither the angels in Heaven above,   30
   Nor the demons down under the sea,
Can ever dissever my soul from the soul
   Of the beautiful Annabel Lee:—

For the moon never beams, without bringing me dreams
   Of the beautiful Annabel Lee;   35
And the stars never rise, but I feel the bright eyes
   Of the beautiful Annabel Lee:
And so, all the night-tide, I lie down by the side
Of my darling—my darling—my life and my bride,
   In the sepulchre there by the sea—   40
   In her tomb by the sounding sea.

Edgar Allan Poe

Edgar Allan Poe on Writing

A LONG POEM DOES NOT EXIST 1848

I hold that a long poem does not exist. I maintain that the phrase, "a long poem," is simply a flat contradiction in terms.

I need scarcely observe that a poem deserves its title only inasmuch as it excites, by elevating the soul. The value of the poem is in the ratio of its elevative excitement. But all excitements are, through a psychal necessity, transient. That degree of excitement which would entitle a poem to be so called at all cannot be sustained throughout a composition of any great length. After the lapse of half an hour, at the very utmost, it flags—fails—a revulsion ensues—and then the poem is in effect, and in fact, no longer such.

From "The Poetic Principle"

◄▬▭▭ WRITING CRITICALLY ▭▭▬►

How to Begin Evaluating a Poem

Evaluation is both the easiest and the hardest part of literary criticism. It is easy because we almost always have some immediate reaction to the poem or story we are reading. We like it or dislike it—sometimes passionately so. While that initial, unrehearsed response will often become part of our ultimate judgment, it will usually end up being no more than a departure point. Literary evaluation is also hard because we must balance this subjective response against the need to view the poem in an informed perspective. The question is not merely, does the work please or move us, but how well does it manage the literary tasks it sets out to perform? Not all good performances will necessarily be to our own taste. A good critic is willing both to admire a strong poem that he or she doesn't like and to admit that a personal favorite might not really be all that good.

Fair evaluation is so difficult that many contemporary theorists have declared it impossible. They maintain that some external factor—personal or ideological—will always get in the way of disinterested judgment. Some theorists even say that the very notion of disinterested evaluation is illusory: to judge one work of art better than another is always to impose a set of values on it. Although the issues raised by these critics are genuine, there are still both theoretical and practical reasons to evaluate literary works. First, some works of art set out very explicit generic expectations of how they wish to be judged. An epigram, for instance, usually seeks to be witty and concise. If it proves tiresome and verbose, it can fairly be said to fail. Second, there is a strong case to be made for the idea that it is also illusory to pretend we can refrain from judging works of art. Since quality is almost always implicitly evaluated, it may be more useful to make those judgments clear and explicit. Finally, there is the practical issue of time. No one can read (or reread) every work ever written. We need open and informed critical guidance on where best to focus our finite attention.

To begin evaluating a poem, first try to understand your own subjective response—don't pretend it doesn't exist. Admit, at least to yourself, whether the poem delights, moves, bores, or annoys you. Then try to determine what the poem seems designed to make you think and feel. Does it belong to some identifiable form or genre? (Is it, for instance, a love sonnet, narrative ballad, satire, or elegy?) How does its performance stack up against the expectations it creates? Considering those questions will give you some larger sense of perspective from which to evaluate the poem.

Next, move on to specific elements in the poem. How well do its language, imagery, symbols, and figures of speech work in communicating its meaning? Are the metaphors or similes effective? Is the imagery fresh and precise? Is the language ever unnecessarily vague or verbose? Does the poem ever fall into clichés or platitudes? (Although there are dozens of such questions to ask, focus on the specific questions that seem relevant to the particular poem. Finally, once you've examined the details of the poem critically, go back and reread it again—preferably aloud. Does the poem seem better or worse than it did initially? Try to base your final evaluation on your own honest reaction, but make sure you have nourished that personal response with careful critical examination so that your evaluation has grown into an informed judgment. (For further tips on the process of evaluation, read the checklist of critical questions found on page 390 under "Exercise: Reevaluating Popular Classics.")

WRITING ASSIGNMENT

Choose a short poem from this book that you particularly enjoy and write a defense of its excellence. In making your case, first set up the terms by which you will judge the poem and then demonstrate why such criteria are appropriate to this particular text. Finally, show specifically how the poem succeeds according to those standards.

Further Suggestions for Writing

1. Write a brief evaluation of either "The New Colossus" by Emma Lazarus or "Annabel Lee" by Edgar Allan Poe.
2. Concoct the worst poem you can possibly write and, in a brief accompanying essay, recount the difficulties you met and overcame in writing it. Quote, for example, any lines you wrote but had to discard for not being bad enough.
3. In "Poems for Further Reading," find a poem you particularly admire or dislike. In a brief essay (300–500 words), evaluate it. Refer to particulars in the poem to support your opinion of it.

18 *What Is Poetry?*

Archibald MacLeish   (1892–1982)

ARS POETICA   1926

A poem should be palpable and mute
As a globed fruit,

Dumb
As old medallions to the thumb,

Silent as the sleeve-worn stone   5
Of casement ledges where the moss has grown—

A poem should be wordless
As the flight of birds.

A poem should be motionless in time
As the moon climbs,   10

Leaving, as the moon releases
Twig by twig the night-entangled trees,

Leaving, as the moon behind the winter leaves,
Memory by memory the mind—

A poem should be motionless in time   15
As the moon climbs.

A poem should be equal to:
Not true.

For all the history of grief
An empty doorway and a maple leaf.   20

For love
The leaning grasses and two lights above the sea—

A poem should not mean
But be.

The title of Archibald MacLeish's provocative poem is Latin for "the poetic art" or "the art of poetry," and it is not unusual for poets to speculate in verse about their art. MacLeish, in fact, borrowed his title from the Roman poet Horace, who wrote a brilliant verse epistle on the subject during the reign of Caesar Augustus. In the two thousand years since then, there has been no shortage of opinions from fellow poets. There is something alluring and mysterious about poetry, even to its practitioners.

What, then, is poetry? By now, perhaps, you have formed your own idea, whether or not you can define it. Robert Frost made a try at a definition: "A poem is an idea caught in the act of dawning." Just in case further efforts at definition may be useful, here are a few memorable ones (including, for a second look, some given earlier):

> things that are true expressed in words that are beautiful.
> —*Dante*

> the art of uniting pleasure with truth by calling imagination to the help of reason.
> —*Samuel Johnson*

> the best words in the best order.
> —*Samuel Taylor Coleridge*

> the spontaneous overflow of powerful feelings.
> —*William Wordsworth*

> musical thought.
> —*Thomas Carlyle*

> emotion put into measure.
> —*Thomas Hardy*

> If I feel physically as if the top of my head were taken off, I know *that* is poetry.
> —*Emily Dickinson*

> speech framed . . . to be heard for its own sake and interest even over and above its interest of meaning.
> —*Gerard Manley Hopkins*

> a way of remembering what it would impoverish us to forget.
> —*Robert Frost*

> a revelation in words by means of the words.
> —*Wallace Stevens*

Poetry is prose bewitched.
　　　—Mina Loy

not the assertion that something is true, but the making of that truth
　　more fully real to us.
　　　—T. S. Eliot

the clear expression of mixed feelings.
　　　—W. H. Auden

the body of linguistic constructions that men usually refer to as poems.
　　　—J. V. Cunningham

hundreds of things coming together at the right moment.
　　　—Elizabeth Bishop

Verse should have two obligations: to communicate a precise instance
　　and to touch us physically, as the presence of the sea does.
　　　—Jorge Luis Borges

Reduced to its simplest and most essential form, the poem is a song.
　　Song is neither discourse nor explanation.
　　　—Octavio Paz

anything said in such a way, or put on the page in such a way, as to
　　invite from the hearer or the reader a certain kind of attention.
　　　—William Stafford

Poetry is life distilled.
　　　—Gwendolyn Brooks

A poem is something that penetrates for an instant into the unconscious.
　　　—Robert Bly

A poem differs from most prose in several ways. For one, both writer and
reader tend to regard it differently. The poet's attitude is something like this: I
offer this piece of writing to be read not as prose but as a poem—that is, more
perceptively, thoughtfully, and considerately, with more attention to sounds and
connotations. This is a great deal to expect, but in return, the reader, too, has a
right to certain expectations. Approaching the poem in the anticipation of out-
of-the-ordinary knowledge and pleasure, the reader assumes that the poem may
use certain enjoyable devices not available to prose: rime, alliteration, meter,
and rhythms—definite, various, or emphatic. (The poet may not *always* decide to
use these things.) The reader expects the poet to make greater use, perhaps, of resources of meaning such as figurative language, allusion, symbol, and imagery. As
readers of prose, we might seek no more than meaning: no more than what could
be paraphrased without serious loss. Meeting any figurative language or graceful
turns of word order, we think them pleasant extras. But in poetry all these "extras" matter as much as the paraphraseable content, if not more. For, when we
finish reading a good poem, we cannot explain precisely to ourselves what we

have experienced—without repeating, word for word, the language of the poem itself. Archibald MacLeish makes this point memorably in "*Ars Poetica*":

A poem should not mean
But be.

"Poetry is to prose as dancing is to walking," remarked Paul Valéry. It is doubtful, however, that anyone can draw an immovable boundary between poetry and prose. Certain prose needs only to be arranged in lines to be seen as poetry—especially prose that conveys strong emotion in vivid, physical imagery and in terse, figurative, rhythmical language. Even in translation the words of Chief Joseph of the Nez Percé tribe, at the moment of his surrender to the U.S. Army in 1877, still move us and are memorable:

Hear me, my warriors, my heart is sick and sad:
Our chiefs are killed,
The old men all are dead,
It is cold and we have no blankets.

The little children freeze to death.

Hear me, my warriors, my heart is sick and sad:
From where the sun now stands I will fight no more forever.

It may be that a poem can point beyond words to something still more essential. Language has its limits, and probably Edgar Allan Poe was the only poet ever to claim he could always find words for whatever he wished to express. For, of all a human being can experience and imagine, words say only part. "Human speech," said Flaubert, who strove after the best of it, "is like a cracked kettle on which we hammer out tunes to make bears dance, when what we long for is the compassion of the stars."

Like Yeats's chestnut-tree in "Among School Children" (which, when asked whether it is leaf, blossom, or bole, has no answer), a poem is to be seen not as a confederation of form, rime, image, metaphor, tone, and theme, but as a whole. We study a poem one element at a time because the intellect best comprehends what it can separate. But only our total attention, involving the participation of our blood and marrow, can see all elements in a poem fused, all dancing together. Yeats knew how to make poems and how to read them:

God guard me from those thoughts men think
In the mind alone;
He that sings a lasting song
Thinks in a marrow-bone.

Throughout this book, we have been working on the assumption that the patient and conscious explication of poems will sharpen unconscious perceptions. We can only hope that it will; the final test lies in whether you care to go on by yourself, reading other poems, finding in them pleasure and enlightenment. Pedagogy must have a stop; so too must the viewing of poems as if their elements fell into

chapters. For the total experience of reading a poem surpasses the mind's categories. The wind in the grass, says a proverb, cannot be taken into the house.

Ha Jin   (b. 1956)

MISSED TIME   2000

My notebook has remained blank for months
thanks to the light you shower
around me. I have no use
for my pen, which lies
languorously without grief.   5

Nothing is better than to live
a storyless life that needs
no writing for meaning—
when I am gone, let others say
they lost a happy man,   10
though no one can tell how happy I was.

19 *Two Critical Casebooks:*
Emily Dickinson and
Langston Hughes

EMILY DICKINSON

Amherst College Archives and Special
Collections.

Emily Dickinson (1830–1886) spent virtually all her life in her family home in
Amherst, Massachusetts. Her father Edward Dickinson was a prominent lawyer who
ranked as Amherst's leading citizen. (He even served a term in the U.S. Congress.)
Dickinson attended one year of college at Mount Holyoke Female Seminary in South
Hadley. She proved to be a good student, but, suffering from homesickness and poor
health, she did not return for the second year. This brief period of study and a few trips
to Boston, Philadelphia, and Washington, D.C., were the only occasions she left home
in her fifty-five-year life. As the years passed, Dickinson became more reclusive. She
stopped attending church (and refused to endorse the orthodox Congregationalist
creed). She also spent increasing time alone in her room—often writing poems. Dick-
inson never married, but she had a significant romantic relationship with at least one

unidentified man. Although scholars have suggested several likely candidates, the historical object of Dickinson's affections will likely never be known. What survives unmistakably, however, is the intensely passionate poetry written out of these private circumstances. By the end of her life, Dickinson had become a locally famous recluse; she rarely left home. She would greet visitors from her own upstairs room, clearly heard but never seen. In 1886 she was buried, according to her own instructions, within sight of the family home. Although Dickinson composed 1,775 known poems, she published only seven in her lifetime. She often, however, sent copies of poems to friends in letters, but only after her death would the full extent of her writings become known when a cache of manuscripts was discovered in a trunk in the homestead attic—handwritten little booklets of poems sewn together by the poet with needle and thread. From 1890 until the mid-twentieth century, nine posthumous collections of her poems were published by friends and relatives, some of whom rewrote her work and changed her idiosyncratic punctuation to make it more conventional. Thomas H. Johnson's three-volume edition of the Poems (1955) established a more accurate text. In relatively few and simple forms clearly indebted to the hymns she heard in church, Dickinson succeeded in being a true visionary and a poet of colossal originality.

⌒ POEMS ⌒

SUCCESS IS COUNTED
SWEETEST (1859) PUBLISHED 1878

Success is counted sweetest
By those who ne'er succeed.
To comprehend a nectar
Requires sorest need.

Not one of all the purple Host°   an army   5
Who took the Flag today
Can tell the definition
So clear of Victory

As he defeated – dying –
On whose forbidden ear   10
The distant strains of triumph
Burst agonized and clear!

WILD NIGHTS – WILD NIGHTS! (ABOUT 1861)

Wild Nights – Wild Nights!
Were I with thee
Wild Nights should be
Our luxury!

Futile – the Winds –
To a Heart in port –
Done with the Compass –
Done with the Chart!

Rowing in Eden –
Ah, the Sea!
Might I but moor – Tonight –
In Thee!

THERE'S A CERTAIN SLANT OF LIGHT   (ABOUT 1861)

There's a certain Slant of light,
Winter Afternoons –
That oppresses, like the Heft
Of Cathedral Tunes –

Heavenly Hurt, it gives us –
We can find no scar,
But internal difference,
Where the Meanings, are –

None may teach it – Any –
'Tis the Seal Despair –
An imperial affliction
Sent us of the Air –

When it comes, the landscape listens –
Shadows – hold their breath –
When it goes, 'tis like the Distance
On the look of Death –

I FELT A FUNERAL, IN MY BRAIN   (ABOUT 1861)

I felt a Funeral, in my Brain,
And Mourners to and fro
Kept treading – treading – till it seemed
That Sense was breaking through –

And when they all were seated,
A Service, like a Drum –
Kept beating – beating – till I thought
My Mind was going numb –

And then I heard them lift a Box
And creak across my Soul
With those same Boots of Lead, again,
Then Space – began to toll,

As all the Heavens were a Bell,
And Being, but an Ear,
And I, and Silence, some strange Race   15
Wrecked, solitary, here –

And then a Plank in Reason, broke,
And I dropped down, and down –
And hit a World, at every plunge,
And Finished knowing – then –   20

I'm Nobody! Who are you?   (ABOUT 1861)

I'm Nobody! Who are you?
Are you – Nobody – too?
Then there's a pair of us!
Don't tell! they'd banish us – you know!

How dreary – to be – Somebody!   5
How public – like a Frog –
To tell your name – the livelong June –
To an admiring Bog!

The Soul selects
her own Society   (ABOUT 1862)

The Soul selects her own Society –
Then – shuts the Door –
To her divine Majority –
Present no more –

Unmoved – she notes the Chariots – pausing –   5
At her low Gate –
Unmoved – an Emperor be kneeling
Upon her Mat –

I've known her – from an ample nation –
Choose One –   10
Then – close the Valves of her attention –
Like Stone –

Some keep the Sabbath going to Church   (1862) PUBLISHED 1864

Some keep the Sabbath going to Church –
I keep it, staying at Home –
With a Bobolink for a Chorister –
And an Orchard, for a Dome –

Some keep the Sabbath in Surplice –   5
I just wear my Wings –
And instead of tolling the Bell, for Church,
Our little Sexton – sings.

God preaches, a noted Clergyman –
And the sermon is never long,   10
So instead of getting to Heaven, at last –
I'm going, all along.

After great pain, a formal feeling comes   (1862)

After great pain, a formal feeling comes –
The Nerves sit ceremonious, like Tombs –
The stiff Heart questions was it He, that bore,
And Yesterday, or Centuries before?

The Feet, mechanical, go round –   5
Of Ground, or Air, or Ought –
A Wooden way
Regardless grown,
A Quartz contentment, like a stone –

This is the Hour of Lead –   10
Remembered, if outlived,
As Freezing persons, recollect the Snow –
First – Chill – then Stupor – then the letting go –

Much Madness is divinest Sense   (ABOUT 1862)

Much Madness is divinest Sense –
To a discerning Eye –
Much Sense – the starkest Madness –
'Tis the Majority
In this, as All, prevail –   5
Assent – and you are sane –
Demur – you're straightway dangerous –
And handled with a Chain

This is my letter to the World (1862)

This is my letter to the World
That never wrote to Me –
The simple News that Nature told –
With tender Majesty

Her Message is committed   5
To Hands I cannot see –
For love of Her – Sweet – countrymen –
Judge tenderly – of Me

I heard a Fly buzz – when I died (ABOUT 1862)

I heard a Fly buzz – when I died –
The Stillness in the Room
Was like the Stillness in the Air –
Between the Heaves of Storm –

The Eyes around – had wrung them dry –   5
And Breaths were gathering firm
For that last Onset – when the King
Be witnessed – in the Room –

I willed my Keepsakes – Signed away
What portion of me be   10
Assignable – and then it was
There interposed a Fly –

With Blue – uncertain stumbling Buzz –
Between the light – and me –
And then the Windows failed – and then   15
I could not see to see –

I started Early – Took my Dog (ABOUT 1862)

I started Early – Took my Dog –
And visited the Sea –
The Mermaids in the Basement
Came out to look at me –

And Frigates – in the Upper Floor   5
Extended Hempen Hands –
Presuming Me to be a Mouse –
Aground – upon the Sands –

But no Man moved Me – till the Tide
Went past my simple Shoe –   10
And past my Apron – and my Belt
And past my Bodice – too –

And made as He would eat me up –
As wholly as a Dew
Upon a Dandelion's Sleeve –   15
And then – I started – too –

And He – He followed – close behind –
I felt His Silver Heel
Upon my Ankle – Then my Shoes
Would overflow with Pearl –   20

Until We met the Solid Town –
No One He seemed to know –
And bowing – with a Mighty look –
At me – The Sea withdrew –

BECAUSE I COULD NOT STOP FOR DEATH   (ABOUT 1863)

Because I could not stop for Death –
He kindly stopped for me –
The Carriage held but just Ourselves –
And Immortality.

We slowly drove – He knew no haste   5
And I had put away
My labor and my leisure too,
For His Civility –

We passed the School, where Children strove
At Recess – in the Ring –   10
We passed the Fields of Gazing Grain –
We passed the Setting Sun –

Or rather – He passed Us –
The Dews drew quivering and chill –
For only Gossamer, my Gown –   15
My Tippet° – only Tulle –   cape

We passed before a House that seemed
A Swelling of the Ground –
The Roof was scarcely visible –
The Cornice – in the Ground –   20

Since then – 'tis Centuries – and yet
Feels shorter than the Day
I first surmised the Horses Heads
Were toward Eternity –

The Bustle in a House   (1866)

The Bustle in a House
The Morning after Death
Is solemnest of industries
Enacted upon Earth –

The Sweeping up the Heart   5
And putting Love away
We shall not want to use again
Until Eternity

Tell all the Truth but tell it slant   (About 1868)

Tell all the Truth but tell it slant –
Success in Circuit lies
Too bright for our infirm Delight
The Truth's superb surprise
As Lightning to the Children eased   5
With explanation kind
The Truth must dazzle gradually
Or every man be blind –

Compare

More poems by Emily Dickinson that are found in this book:

A Dying Tiger – moaned for Drink (page 373)
I like to see it lap the Miles (page 25)
It dropped so low – in my Regard (page 125)
The Lightning is a yellow Fork (page 261)
My Life had stood – a Loaded Gun (page 122)
A Route of Evanescence (page 100)

Emily Dickinson's room in Amherst, Massachusetts.

RECOGNIZING POETRY   (1870)

If I read a book [and] it makes my whole body so cold no fire ever can warm me I know *that* is poetry. If I feel physically as if the top of my head were taken off, I know *that* is poetry. These are the only ways I know it. Is there any other way.

How do most people live without any thoughts. There are many people in the world (you must have noticed them in the street) How do they live. How do they get strength to put on their clothes in the morning.

When I lost the use of my Eyes it was a comfort to think there were so few real *books* that I could easily find some one to read me all of them.

Truth is such a *rare* thing it is delightful to tell it.

I find ecstasy in living – the mere sense of living is joy enough.

From a conversation with Thomas Wentworth Higginson

COMPARE

Dickinson's famous comments on the nature of poetry, which are often quoted out of context, with their original source, a letter—not by the poet herself but by a visiting editor. (See the editor's letter that follows on page 412.)

25 April 1862

Mr. Higginson,

Your kindness claimed earlier gratitude – but I was ill – and write today, from my pillow.

Thank you for the surgery – it was not so painful as I supposed. I bring you others – as you ask – though they might not differ –

While my thought is undressed – I can make the distinction, but when I put them in the Gown – they look alike, and numb.

You asked how old I was? I made no verse – but one or two – until this winter
– Sir –

I had a terror – since September – I could tell to none – and so I sing, as the Boy does by the Burying Ground – because I am afraid – You inquire my Books – For Poets – I have Keats – and Mr and Mrs Browning. For Prose – Mr Ruskin – Sir Thomas Browne – and the Revelations.° I went to school – but in your manner of the phrase – had no education. When a little Girl, I had a friend, who taught me Immortality – but venturing too near, himself – he never returned – Soon after, my Tutor, died – and for several years, my Lexicon – was my only companion – Then I found one more – but he was not contented I be his scholar – so he left the Land.

You ask of my Companions Hills – Sir – and the Sundown – and a Dog – large as myself, that my Father bought me – They are better than Beings – because they know – but do not tell – and the noise in the Pool, at Noon – excels my Piano. I have a Brother and Sister – My Mother does not care for thought – and Father, too busy with his Briefs° – to notice what we do – He buys me many Books – but begs me not to read them – because he fears they joggle the Mind. They are religious – except me – and address an Eclipse, every morning – whom they call their "Father." But I fear my story fatigues you – I would like to learn – Could you tell me how to grow – or is it unconveyed – like Melody – or Witchcraft?

You speak of Mr Whitman – I never read his Book° – but was told that he was disgraceful –

I read Miss Prescott's "Circumstance,"° but it followed me, in the Dark – so I avoided her –

Two Editors of Journals came to my Father's House, this winter – and asked me for my Mind – and when I asked them "Why," they said I was penurious – and they, would use it for the World –

I could not weigh myself – Myself –

My size felt small – to me – I read your Chapters in the Atlantic – and experienced honor for you – I was sure you would not reject a confiding question –

Is this – Sir – what you asked me to tell you?

Your friend,
E – Dickinson
From a letter to Thomas Wentworth Higginson

SELF-DESCRIPTION. Emily Dickinson's letter was written to Thomas Wentworth Higginson, a noted writer. Dickinson had read his article of advice to young writers in the *Atlantic Monthly*. She sent him four poems and a letter asking if her verse was "alive." When he responded with comments and suggestions (the "surgery" Dickinson mentions in the second paragraph), she wrote him this letter about herself. *Mr Ruskin . . . Revelations:* in listing her favorite prose authors Dickinson chose John Ruskin (1819–1900), an English art critic and essayist, Sir Thomas Browne (1605–1682), a doctor and philosopher with a magnificent prose style, and the final book of the New Testament. *Briefs:* legal papers (her father was a lawyer). *Whitman . . . book: Leaves of Grass* (1855) by Walt Whitman was considered an improper book for women at this time because of the volume's sexual candor. *Miss Prescott's "Circumstance":* a story, also published in the *Atlantic Monthly*, that was full of violence.

Facsimile manuscript of "Some keep the Sabbath going to Church," printed on page 405.

CRITICS ON EMILY DICKINSON

Thomas Wentworth Higginson (1823–1911)

MEETING EMILY DICKINSON   1870

A large county lawyer's house, brown brick, with great trees & a garden—I sent up my card. A parlor dark & cool & stiffish, a few books & engravings & an open piano. . . .

A step like a pattering child's in entry & in glided a little plain woman with two smooth bands of reddish hair & a face a little like Belle Dove's; not plainer—with no good feature—in a very plain & exquisitely clean white pique & a blue net worsted shawl. She came to me with two day lilies which she put in a sort of childlike way into my hand & said "These are my introduction" in a soft frightened breathless childlike voice—& added under her breath Forgive me if I am frightened; I never see strangers & hardly know what I say—but she talked soon & thenceforward continuously—& deferentially—sometimes stopping to ask me to talk instead of her—but readily recommencing . . . thoroughly ingenuous & simple . . . & saying many things which you would have thought foolish & I wise—& some things you wd. hv. liked. I add a few over the page. . . .

"Women talk; men are silent; that is why I dread women."

"My father only reads on Sunday—he reads *lonely* & *rigorous* books."

"If I read a book [and] it makes my whole body so cold no fire ever can warm me I know *that* is poetry. If I feel physically as if the top of my head were taken off, I know *that* is poetry. These are the only ways I know it. Is there any other way."

"How do most people live without any thoughts. There are many people in the world (you must have noticed them in the street) How do they live. How do they get strength to put on their clothes in the morning"

"When I lost the use of my Eyes it was a comfort to think there were so few real *books* that I could easily find some one to read me all of them"

"Truth is such a *rare* thing it is delightful to tell it."

"I find ecstasy in living—the mere sense of living is joy enough"

I asked if she never felt want of employment, never going off the place & never seeing any visitor "I never thought of conceiving that I could ever have the slightest approach to such a want in all future time" (& added) "I feel that I have not expressed myself strongly enough."

She makes all the bread for her father only likes hers & says "& people must have puddings" this *very* dreamily, as if they were comets—so she makes them.

.   .   .

E D again

"Could you tell me what home is"

"I never had a mother. I suppose a mother is one to whom you hurry when you are troubled."

"I never knew how to tell time by the clock till I was 15. My father thought he had taught me but I did not understand & I was afraid to say I did not & afraid to ask any one else lest he should know."

Her father was not severe I should think but remote. He did not wish them to read anything but the Bible. One day her brother brought home Kavanagh° hid it under the piano cover & made signs to her & they read it: her father at last found it & was displeased. Perhaps it was before this that a student of his was amazed that they had never heard of Mrs. [Lydia Maria] Child° & used to bring them books & hide in a bush by the door. They were then little things in short dresses with their feet on the rungs of the chair. After the first book she thought in ecstasy "This then is a book! And there are more of them!"

"Is it oblivion or absorption when things pass from our minds?"

Major Hunt interested her more than any man she ever saw. She remembered two things he said—that her great dog "understood gravitation" & when he said he should come again "in a year. If I say a shorter time it will be longer."

When I said I would come again *some time* she said "Say in a long time, that will be nearer. Some time is nothing."

After long disuse of her eyes she read Shakespeare & thought why is any other book needed.

I never was with any one who drained my nerve power so much. Without touching her, she drew from me. I am glad not to live near her. She often thought me *tired* & seemed very thoughtful of others.

From a letter to his wife, August 16–17, 1870

Thomas H. Johnson   (1902–1985)

THE DISCOVERY OF EMILY DICKINSON'S MANUSCRIPTS   1955

Shortly after Emily Dickinson's death on May fifteenth, 1886, her sister Lavinia discovered a locked box in which Emily had placed her poems. Lavinia's amazement seems to have been genuine. Though the sisters had lived intimately together under the same roof all their lives, and though Lavinia had always been aware that her sister wrote poems, she had not the faintest concept of the great number of them. The story of Lavinia's willingness to spare them because she found no instructions specifying that they be destroyed, and her search for an editor and a publisher to give them to the world has already been told in some detail.

Lavinia first consulted the two people most interested in Emily's poetry, her sister-in-law Susan Dickinson, and Mrs. Todd. David Peck Todd, a graduate of Amherst College in 1875, returned to Amherst with his young bride in 1881 as director of the college observatory and soon became professor of Astronomy and Navigation. These were the months shortly before Mrs. Edward Dickinson's death, when neighbors were especially thoughtful. Mrs. Todd endeared herself to

---

Kavanagh: Kavanagh: A Tale (1849), an utterly innocuous work of fiction by the poet Henry Wadsworth Longfellow.   *Mrs. [Lydia Maria] Child:* anti-slavery writer and author (1802–1880) of didactic novels.

Emily and Lavinia by small but understanding attentions, in return for which Emily sent Mrs. Todd copies of her poems. At first approach neither Susan Dickinson nor Mrs. Todd felt qualified for the editorial task which they both were hesitant to undertake. Mrs. Todd says of Lavinia's discovery: "She showed me the manuscripts and there were over sixty little 'volumes,' each composed of four or five sheets of note paper tied together with twine. In this box she discovered eight or nine hundred poems tied up in this way."

. . .

As the story can be reconstructed, at some time during the year 1858 Emily Dickinson began assembling her poems into packets. Always in ink, they are gatherings of four, five, or six sheets of letter paper usually folded once but sometimes single. They are loosely held together by thread looped through them at the spine at two points equidistant from the top and bottom. When opened up they may be read like a small book, a fact that explains why Emily's sister Lavinia, when she discovered them after Emily's death, referred to them as "volumes." All of the packet poems are either fair copies or semifinal drafts, and they constitute two-thirds of the entire body of her poetry.

For the most part the poems in a given packet seem to have been written and assembled as a unit. Since rough drafts of packet poems are almost totally lacking, one concludes that they were systematically discarded. If the poems were in fact composed at the time the copies were made, as the evidence now seems to point, one concludes that nearly two-thirds of her poems were created in the brief span of eight years, centering on her early thirties. Her interest in the packet method of assembling the verses thus coincides with the years of fullest productivity. In 1858 she gathered some fifty poems into packets. There are nearly one hundred so transcribed in 1859, some sixty-five in 1860, and in 1861 more than eighty. By 1862 the creative drive must have been almost frightening; during that year she transcribed into packets no fewer than three hundred and sixty-six poems, the greater part of them complete and final texts.

Whether this incredible number was in fact composed in that year or represents a transcription of earlier worksheet drafts can never be established by direct evidence. But the pattern established during the preceding four years reveals a gathering momentum, and the quality of tenseness and prosodic skill uniformly present in the poems of 1861–1862 bears scant likeness to the conventionality of theme and treatment in the poems of 1858–1859. Excepting a half dozen occasional verses written in the early fifties, there is not a single scrap of poetry that can be dated earlier than 1858.

From The Poems of Emily Dickinson

Richard Wilbur   (b. 1921)*

THE THREE PRIVATIONS OF EMILY DICKINSON   1959

Emily Dickinson never lets us forget for very long that in some respects life gave her short measure; and indeed it is possible to see the greater part of her poetry as an effort to cope with her sense of privation. I think that for her there were three major privations: she was deprived of an orthodox and steady religious faith; she was deprived of love; she was deprived of literary recognition.

At the age of seventeen, after a series of revival meetings at Mount Holyoke Seminary, Emily Dickinson found that she must refuse to become a professing Christian. To some modern minds this may seem to have been a sensible and necessary step; and surely it was a step toward becoming such a poet as she became. But for her, no pleasure in her own integrity could then eradicate the feeling that she had betrayed a deficiency, a want of grace. In her letters to Abiah Root she tells of the enhancing effect of conversion on her fellow-students, and says of herself in a famous passage:

> I am one of the lingering bad ones, and so do I slink away, and pause and ponder, and ponder and pause, and do work without knowing why, not surely for this brief world, and more sure it is not for heaven, and I ask what this message *means* that they ask for so very eagerly: *you* know of this depth and fulness, will you try to tell me about it?

There is humor in that, and stubbornness, and a bit of characteristic lurking pride: but there is also an anguished sense of having separated herself, through some dry incapacity, from spiritual community, from purpose, and from magnitude of life. As a child of evangelical Amherst, she inevitably thought of purposive, heroic life as requiring a vigorous faith. Out of such a thought she later wrote:

> The abdication of Belief
> Makes the Behavior small –
> Better an ignis fatuus
> Than no illume at all –

That hers *was* a species of religious personality goes without saying; but by her refusal of such ideas as original sin, redemption, hell, and election, she made it impossible for herself—as Whicher observed—"to share the religious life of her generation." She became an unsteady congregation of one.

Her second privation, the privation of love, is one with which her poems and her biographies have made us exceedingly familiar, though some biographical facts remain conjectural. She had the good fortune, at least once, to bestow her heart on another; but she seems to have found her life, in great part, a history of loneliness, separation, and bereavement.

As for literary fame, some will deny that Emily Dickinson ever greatly desired it, and certainly there is evidence, mostly from her latter years, to support such a view. She *did* write that "Publication is the auction / Of the mind of man." And she *did* say to Helen Hunt Jackson, "How can you print a piece of your soul?" But earlier, in 1861, she had frankly expressed to Sue Dickinson the hope that "some-time" she might make her kinfolk proud of her. The truth is, I think, that Emily Dickinson knew she was good, and began her career with a normal appetite for recognition. I think that she later came, with some reason, to despair of being un-derstood or properly valued, and so directed against her hopes of fame what was by then a well-developed disposition to renounce. That she wrote a good number of poems about fame supports my view: the subjects to which a poet returns are those which vex him.

What did Emily Dickinson do, as a poet, with her sense of privation? One thing she quite often did was to pose as the laureate and attorney of the empty-handed, and question God about the economy of His creation. Why, she asked, is a fatherly God so sparing of His presence? Why is there never a sign that prayers are heard? Why does Nature tell us no comforting news of its Maker? Why do some receive a whole load, while others must starve on a crumb? Where is the benevolence in shipwreck and earthquake? By asking such questions as these, she turned complaint into critique, and used her own sufferings as experi-ential evidence about the nature of the deity. The God who emerges from these poems is a God who does not answer, an unrevealed God whom one cannot con-fidently approach through Nature or through doctrine.

From "Sumptuous Destitution"

Cynthia Griffin Wolff (b. 1935)

DICKINSON AND DEATH   1993

(A READING OF "BECAUSE I COULD NOT STOP FOR DEATH")

Modern readers are apt to comment upon the frequency with which Dickinson returns to this subject of death—"How morbid," people say. Perhaps. But if Dick-inson was morbid, so was everyone else in her culture. Poe's aestheticizing of death (along with the proliferation of Gothic fiction and poetry) reflects a perva-sive real-world concern: in mid-nineteenth-century America death rates were high. It was a truism that men had three wives (two of them having predeceased the spouse); infant mortality was so common that parents often gave several of their children the same name so that at least one "John" or "Lavinia" might sur-vive to adulthood; rapid urbanization had intensified the threat of certain dis-eases—cholera, typhoid, and tuberculosis.

Poe and the Gothic tradition were one response to society's anxiety about death. Another came from the pulpit: mid-nineteenth-century sermons took death as their almost constant subject. Somewhat later in the century, preachers would embrace a doctrine of consolation: God would be figured as a loving parent—almost motherly—who had prepared a home in heaven for us all, and ministers would tell the members of their congregation that they need not be apprehensive. However, stern traces of Puritanism still tinctured the religious discourse of Dickinson's young womanhood, and members of the Amherst congregation were regularly exhorted with blood-stirring urgency to reflect upon the imminence of their own demise. Repeatedly, then, in attempting to comprehend Dickinson's work, a reader must return to the fundamental tenets of Protestant Christianity, for her poetry echoes the Bible more often than any other single work or author.

In part this preoccupation with the doctrines of her day reflected a more general concern with the essential questions of human existence they addressed. In a letter to Higginson she once said, "To live is so startling, it leaves but little room for other occupations." And to her friend Mrs. Holland she wrote, "All this and more, though *is* there more? More than Love and Death? Then tell me its name." The religious thought and language of the culture was important to her poetry because it comprised the semiotic system that her society employed to discuss the mysteries of life and death. If she wished to contemplate these, what other language was there to employ?

In part, however, conventional Christianity—especially the latter-day Puritanism of Dickinson's New England—represented for Dickinson an ultimate expression of patriarchal power. Rebelling against its rule, upbraiding a "Father" in Heaven who required absolute "faith" from his followers, but gave no discernible response, became a way of attacking the very essence of unjust authority, especially male authority.

. . .

It is true that the stern doctrines of New England Protestantism offered hope for a life after death; yet in Dickinson's estimation, the trope that was used for this "salvation" revealed some of the most repellent features of God's power, for the invitation to accept "faith" had been issued in the context of a courtship with a macabre, sexual component. It was promised that those who had faith would be carried to Heaven by the "Bridegroom" Christ. "Blessed are they which are called unto the marriage supper of the Lamb" (Revelation 19:9). Nor did it escape Dickinson's notice that the perverse prurience of Poe's notions were essentially similar to this Christian idea of Christ's "love" for a "bride" which promised a reunion that must be "consummated" through death. Thus the poem that is, perhaps, the apotheosis of that distinctive Dickinson voice, "the speaking dead," offers an astonishing combination: this conventional promise of Christianity suffused with the tonalities of the Gothic tradition.

[Griffin quotes the entire text of "Because I could not stop for Death" found on page 407.]

The speaker is a beautiful woman (already dead!), and like some spectral Cinderella, she is dressed to go to a ball: "For only Gossamer, my Gown – / My Tippet – only Tulle –." Her escort recalls both the lover of Poe's configuration and the "Bridegroom" that had been promised in the Bible: "We slowly drove – He knew no haste / And I had put away / My labor and my leisure too, / For His Civility –". Their "Carriage" hovers in some surrealistic state that is exterior to both time and place: they are no longer earth-bound, not quite dead (or at least still possessed of consciousness), but they have not yet achieved the celebration that awaits them, the "marriage supper of the Lamb."

Yet the ultimate implication of this work turns precisely upon the *poet's* capacity to explode the finite temporal boundaries that generally define our existence, for there is a third member of the party—also exterior to time and location—and that is "Immortality." *True* immortality, the verse suggests, comes neither from the confabulations of a male lover nor from God's intangible Heaven. Irrefutable "Immortality" resides in the work of art itself, the creation of an empowered woman poet that continues to captivate readers more than one hundred years after her death. And this much-read, often-cited poem stands as patent proof upon the page of its own argument!

From "Emily Dickinson"

Judith Farr   (b. 1937)

A Reading of "My Life had stood – a Loaded Gun"[1]   1992

One of the notable qualities of this poem is its formidable directness of statement. Both the substance and the shape of the rhetoric seem straightforward. The ideas of guns and killing are not, superficially, invested by the speaker with negative properties. Far from it. The speaker recounts life with her master in tones of heady confidence and pleasure. If we did not know that this poem had been written by a woman—perhaps especially by "Miss Emily"—some of its presumed complexity and ominousness would be reduced. Let us say that Emily "when a Boy" is speaking; then it may be easier to credit the open delight of the speaker. Liberated from corners in the poem, he/she is freed into a grown-up gunman's life of authority and power, and she likes the idea exceedingly. All the piled-up, dynamic "And"s tell us so.

Or, if we cast her as a woman, she is what has been called "a man's woman"; everything he likes, *she* likes. She likes hunting, and her instincts are not pacifist or nurturing—no ducks and does for her. She smiles at her work of killing; Nature smiles with her (the firing of the gun makes a glow like Vesuvius); and at night she can pronounce the day good. (Hunting is, after all, not always a selfish sport; often it is a protective measure. "Sovereign Woods," of course, suggests a royal preserve, an unfair advantage for the hunter.) Because of her identification with the man, she is nearly human, but with a "Yellow Eye"—the color of explosion in an oval gunbarrel—and "emphatic Thumb." The American hunting pictures of Dickinson's day, like the landscapes of Bowles's favorite painter, Sanford Gifford, present hunting scenes like Dickinson's. Her buoyancy of tone accords with them, depicting easy days roaming in the open air, taking from an apparently complaisant nature all that the Master wants. If we imagine the speaker as a boy with his designated sponsor or master, then she is—up to the last qua-

---

[1]The full text of Dickinson's "My Life had stood – a Loaded Gun" appears on page 122.

train—learning how to be a man in the rustic world dreamed up by Fenimore Cooper.

"Owner," however, suggests sexual love, and to anyone versed in the language of Emily Dickinson, it inflects one of her central themes:

> 'Twas my one glory –
> Let it be
> Remembered
> I was owned of thee –

For that reason, and because there is such heroic intimacy between the gun and Master, one can see this as a poem of sexual love that emphasizes comradery, robust equality. It may be considered part of the Master cycle and related to "He touched me," where the speaker begins to "live" when Master touches her or carries her away. Although she is a woman, because the two are one in love she imagines herself like him; like him, empowered. . . . Here the speaker appropriates Master's masculinity; she is a loaded gun. Together they become one person, one royal We in a happy life of power. The speaker has always wanted to exercise her stored-up bullets or faculties; now she can. In a letter to her cousin Louise Norcross in 1880, Dickinson used these same images: "what is each instant but a gun, harmless because 'unloaded,' but that touched 'goes off'?" Although she omits one step, loading the gun, she is describing in her letter what she may be describing in her poem: love, "touching," as a means of being empowered.

There remains the final quatrain. It reads as a tightly wrought riddle, inviting explication. In one way, the stanza points up the incontrovertible difference between the mechanical gun and the human owner. He is the complete being, having both the power to die and the power to kill (even without her help). For all her fusion with him in their acts of love and death, she must still depend on him; she must be "carried." Thus this poem is often read—and read brilliantly—as a revelation of the limitations experienced by women under patriarchy, or even of the dependency of the female artist who needs male masters like Higginson to help her exercise her powers.

In reading this poem, however, I think that emphasis should always be placed on the pleasure the speaker experiences. The Master may be carrying her, but she is also speaking for him. He cannot do without her. That the gun's firing is compared to the pleasure of "a Vesuvian face" accents destruction, certainly; and it is hard to exempt this use of Vesuvius from all the others, always destructive, in the Dickinson canon. But the speaker seems to welcome her own destructiveness. She has been waiting a long time in many "corners" until the right lover lets her speak. For Dickinson, love is always the muse. Her variant for "the *power* to kill" in the penultimate line is *art*—which could make others die, from love or from aesthetic rapture. She herself—the gun, the artist—can never "die" like a real woman, however. She is but the arresting voice that speaks to and for the Master.

From *The Passion of Emily Dickinson*

LANGSTON HUGHES

Langston Hughes was born in Joplin, Missouri, in 1902. After his parents separated during his early years, he and his mother often lived a life of itinerant poverty, mostly in Kansas. Hughes attended high school in Cleveland, where as a senior he wrote "The Negro Speaks of Rivers." Reluctantly supported by his father, he attended Columbia University for a year before withdrawing. After a series of menial jobs, Hughes became a merchant seaman in 1923 and visited the ports of West Africa. For a time he lived in Paris, Genoa, and Rome, before returning to the United States. The publication of The Weary Blues (1926) earned him immediate fame, which he solidified a few months later with his pioneering essay "The Negro Artist and the Racial Mountain." In 1926 he also entered Lincoln University in Pennsylvania, from which he graduated in 1929. By then Hughes was already one of the central figures of the Harlem Renaissance, the flowering of African American arts and literature in the Harlem neighborhood of Upper Manhattan in New York City during the 1920s. A strikingly versatile author, Hughes worked in fiction, drama, translation, criticism, opera libretti, memoir, cinema, and songwriting, as well as poetry. He also became a tireless promoter of African American culture, crisscrossing the United States on speaking tours as well as compiling twenty-eight anthologies of African American folklore and poetry. His newspaper columns, which often reported conversations with an imaginary Harlem friend named Jesse B. Semple, nicknamed "Simple," attracted an especially large following. During the 1930s Hughes became involved in radical politics and traveled to the Soviet Union, but after World War II he gradually shifted to mainstream progressive politics. In his last years he became a spokesman for the moderate wing of the civil rights movement. He died in Harlem in 1967.

THE NEGRO SPEAKS OF RIVERS   (1921) 1926

I've known rivers:
I've known rivers ancient as the world and older than the flow of
    human blood in human veins.

My soul has grown deep like the rivers.

I bathed in the Euphrates when dawns were young.
I built my hut near the Congo and it lulled me to sleep.   5
I looked upon the Nile and raised the pyramids above it.
I heard the singing of the Mississippi when Abe Lincoln went down to
    New Orleans, and I've seen its muddy bosom turn all golden in the
    sunset.

I've known rivers:
Ancient, dusky rivers.

My soul has grown deep like the rivers.   10

MOTHER TO SON   (1922) 1932

Well, son, I'll tell you:
Life for me ain't been no crystal stair.
It's had tacks in it,
And splinters,
And boards torn up,   5
And places with no carpet on the floor—
Bare.
But all the time
I'se been a-climbin' on,
And reachin' landin's,   10
And turnin' corners,
And sometimes goin' in the dark
Where there ain't been no light.
So boy, don't you turn back.
Don't you set down on the steps   15
'Cause you finds it's kinder hard.
Don't you fall now—
For I'se still goin', honey,
I'se still climbin',
And life for me ain't been no crystal stair.   20

Dream Variations (1924) 1926

To fling my arms wide
In some place of the sun,
To whirl and to dance
Till the white day is done.
Then rest at cool evening   5
Beneath a tall tree
While night comes on gently,
 Dark like me—
That is my dream!

To fling my arms wide
In the face of the sun,   10
Dance! Whirl! Whirl!
Till the quick day is done.
Rest at pale evening . . .
A tall, slim tree . . .   15
Night coming tenderly
 Black like me.

I, Too 1926

I, too, sing America.

I am the darker brother.
They send me to eat in the kitchen
When company comes,
But I laugh,   5
And eat well,
And grow strong.

Tomorrow,
I'll be at the table
When company comes.   10
Nobody'll dare
Say to me,
"Eat in the kitchen,"
Then.

Besides,   15
They'll see how beautiful I am
And be ashamed—

I, too, am America.

Droning a drowsy syncopated tune,
Rocking back and forth to a mellow croon,
    I heard a Negro play.
Down on Lenox Avenue the other night
By the pale dull pallor of an old gas light   5
       He did a lazy sway. . . .
       He did a lazy sway. . . .
To the tune o' those Weary Blues.
With his ebony hands on each ivory key
He made that poor piano moan with melody.   10
       O Blues!
Swaying to and fro on his rickety stool
He played that sad raggy tune like a musical fool.
       Sweet Blues!
Coming from a black man's soul.   15
       O Blues!
In a deep song voice with a melancholy tone
I heard that Negro sing, that old piano moan—
       "Ain't got nobody in all this world,
        Ain't got nobody but ma self.   20
        I's gwine to quit ma frownin'
        And put ma troubles on the shelf."

Thump, thump, thump, went his foot on the floor.
He played a few chords then he sang some more—
       "I got the Weary Blues   25
        And I can't be satisfied.
        Got the Weary Blues
        And can't be satisfied—
        I ain't happy no mo'
        And I wish that I had died."   30
And far into the night he crooned that tune.
The stars went out and so did the moon.
The singer stopped playing and went to bed
While the Weary Blues echoed through his head.
He slept like a rock or a man that's dead.   35

THE WEARY BLUES. This poem quotes the first blues song Hughes had ever heard, "The Weary Blues," which begins, "I got de weary blues / And I can't be satisfied / . . . I ain't happy no mo' / And I wish that I had died."

Song for a Dark Girl   1927

Way Down South in Dixie
    (Break the heart of me)
They hung my black young lover
    To a cross roads tree.

Way Down South in Dixie   5
    (Bruised body high in air)
I asked the white Lord Jesus
    What was the use of prayer.

Way Down South in Dixie
    (Break the heart of me)   10
Love is a naked shadow
    On a gnarled and naked tree.

Desire   (1927) 1947

Desire to us
Was like a double death,
Swift dying
Of our mingled breath,
Evaporation   5
Of an unknown strange perfume
Between us quickly
In a naked
Room.

Prayer   (1931) 1947

Gather up
In the arms of your pity
The sick, the depraved.
The desperate, the tired,
All the scum   5
Of our weary city

Gather up
In the arms of your pity
Gather up
In the arms of your love—   10
Those who expect
No love from above.

Landlord, landlord,
My roof has sprung a leak.
Don't you 'member I told you about it
Way last week?

Landlord, landlord,   5
These steps is broken down.
When you come up yourself
It's a wonder you don't fall down.

Ten Bucks you say I owe you?
Ten Bucks you say is due?   10
Well, that's Ten Bucks more'n I'll pay you
Till you fix this house up new.

What? You gonna get eviction orders?
You gonna cut off my heat?
You gonna take my furniture and   15
Throw it in the street?

Um-huh! You talking high and mighty.
Talk on—till you get through.
You ain't gonna be able to say a word
If I land my fist on you.   20

Police! Police!
Come and get this man!
He's trying to ruin the government
And overturn the land!

Copper's whistle!   25
Patrol bell!
Arrest.

Precinct Station.
Iron cell.
Headlines in press: 30

MAN THREATENS LANDLORD

•

• •

TENANT HELD NO BAIL

•

• •

JUDGE GIVES NEGRO 90 DAYS IN COUNTY JAIL

END   1947

There are
No clocks on the wall,
And no time,
No shadows that move
From dawn to dusk   5
Across the floor.

There is neither light
Nor dark
Outside the door.

There is no door!   10

ISLAND   (1950) 1959

Wave of sorrow,
Do not drown me now:

I see the island
Still ahead somehow.

I see the island   5
And its sands are fair:

Wave of sorrow,
Take me there.

THEME FOR ENGLISH B   1951

The instructor said,

> *Go home and write*
> *a page tonight.*
> *And let that page come out of you—*
> *Then, it will be true.*   5

I wonder if it's that simple?
I am twenty-two, colored, born in Winston-Salem.
I went to school there, then Durham, then here
to this college on the hill above Harlem.
I am the only colored student in my class.   10
The steps from the hill lead down into Harlem,
through a park, then I cross St. Nicholas,
Eighth Avenue, Seventh, and I come to the Y,
the Harlem Branch Y, where I take the elevator
up to my room, sit down, and write this page: 15

It's not easy to know what is true for you and me
at twenty-two, my age. But I guess I'm what
I feel and see and hear, Harlem, I hear you:
hear you, hear me—we two—you, me, talk on this page.
(I hear New York, too.) Me—who?   20
Well, I like to eat, sleep, drink, and be in love.
I like to work, read, learn, and understand life.
I like a pipe for a Christmas present,
or records—Bessie, bop, or Bach.
I guess being colored doesn't make me not like   25
the same things other folks like who are other races.
So will my page be colored that I write?
Being me, it will not be white.

But it will be
a part of you, instructor.   30
You are white—
yet a part of me, as I am a part of you.
That's American.
Sometimes perhaps you don't want to be a part of me.
Nor do I often want to be a part of you.   35
But we are, that's true!
As I learn from you,
I guess you learn from me—
although you're older—and white—
and somewhat more free.   40

This is my page for English B.

THEME FOR ENGLISH B.   9 *College on the hill above Harlem:* Columbia University, where Hughes was
briefly a student. (Please note, however, that this poem is not autobiographical. The young speaker is
a character invented by the middle-aged author.)   24 *Bessie:* Bessie Smith (1898?–1937) was a popular blues singer often called the "Empress of the Blues." The lyrics to Smith's "Jailhouse Blues"
appear on page 153.

SUBWAY RUSH HOUR   1951

Mingled
breath and smell
so close
mingled
black and white   5
so near
no room for fear.

SLIVER   1951

Cheap little rhymes
A cheap little tune
Are sometimes as dangerous
As a sliver of the moon.
A cheap little tune   5
To cheap little rhymes
Can cut a man's
Throat sometimes.

HARLEM [DREAM DEFERRED]   1951

What happens to a dream deferred?

    Does it dry up
    like a raisin in the sun?
    Or fester like a sore—
    And then run?
    Does it stink like rotten meat?   5
    Or crust and sugar over—
    like a syrupy sweet?

    Maybe it just sags
    like a heavy load.   10

    Or does it explode?

HARLEM. This famous poem appeared under two titles in the author's lifetime. Both titles appear above.

COMPARE

More poems by Langston Hughes that are found in this book:
    Dream Boogie (page 208)
    Prayer (page 228)

Lenox Avenue, Harlem, in 1925.

THE NEGRO ARTIST AND THE RACIAL MOUNTAIN   1926

Most of my own poems are racial in theme and treatment, derived from the life I know. In many of them I try to grasp and hold some of the meanings and rhythms of jazz. I am as sincere as I know how to be in these poems and yet after every reading I answer questions like these from my own people: Do you think Negroes should always write about Negroes? I wish you wouldn't read some of your poems to white folks. How do you find anything interesting in a place like a cabaret? Why do you write about black people? You aren't black. What makes you do so many jazz poems?

But jazz to me is one of the inherent expressions of Negro life in America; the eternal tom-tom beating in the Negro soul—the tom-tom of revolt against weariness in a white world, a world of subway trains, and work, work, work; the tom-tom of joy and laughter, and pain swallowed in a smile. Yet the Philadelphia clubwoman is ashamed to say that her race created it and she does not like me to write about it. The old subconscious "white is best" runs through her mind. Years of study under white teachers, a lifetime of white books, pictures, and papers, and white manners, morals, and Puritan standards made her dislike the spirituals. And now she turns up her nose at jazz and all its manifestations—likewise almost everything else distinctly racial. She doesn't care for the Winold Reiss portraits of Negroes because they are "too Negro." She does not want a true picture of herself from anybody. She wants the artist to flatter her, to make the white world believe that all Negroes are as smug and as near white in soul as she wants to be. But, to my mind, it is the duty of the younger Negro artist, if he accepts any duties at all from outsiders, to change through the force of his art that old whispering "I want to be white," hidden in the aspirations of his people, to "Why should I want to be white? I am a Negro—and beautiful."

So I am ashamed for the black poet who says, "I want to be a poet, not a Negro poet," as though his own racial world were not as interesting as any other world. I am ashamed, too, for the colored artist who runs from the painting of Negro faces to the painting of sunsets after the manner of the academicians because he fears the strange un-whiteness of his own features. An artist must be free to choose what he does, certainly, but he must also never be afraid to do what he might choose.

From "The Negro Artist and the Racial Mountain"

COMPARE

Hughes's comments on the African American artist with Darryl Pinckney's critical observations on Langston Hughes's public identity as a black poet (page 435).

THE HARLEM RENAISSANCE   1940

White people began to come to Harlem in droves. For several years they packed the expensive Cotton Club on Lenox Avenue. But I was never there, because the Cotton Club was a Jim Crow club for gangsters and monied whites. They were not cordial to Negro patronage, unless you were a celebrity like Bojangles.° So Harlem Negroes did not like the Cotton Club and never appreciated its Jim Crow policy in the very heart of their dark community. Nor did ordinary Negroes like the growing influx of whites toward Harlem after sundown, flooding the little cabarets and bars where formerly only colored people laughed and sang, and where now the strangers were given the best ringside tables to sit and stare at the Negro customers—like amusing animals in a zoo.

The Negroes said: "We can't go downtown and sit and stare at you in your clubs. You won't even let us in your clubs." But they didn't say it out loud—for Negroes are practically never rude to white people. So thousands of whites came to Harlem night after night, thinking the Negroes loved to have them there, and firmly believing that all Harlemites left their houses at sundown to sing and dance in cabarets, because most of the whites saw nothing but the cabarets, not the houses.

Some of the owners of Harlem clubs, delighted at the flood of white patronage, made the grievous error of barring their own race, after the manner of the famous Cotton Club. But most of these quickly lost business and folded up, because they failed to realize that a large part of the Harlem attraction for

Bojangles: Bill "Bojangles" Robinson (1876–1949), dancer.

downtown New Yorkers lay in simply watching the colored customers amuse themselves. And the smaller clubs, of course, had no big floor shows or a name band like the Cotton Club, where Duke Ellington usually held forth, so, without black patronage, they were not amusing at all.

Some of the small clubs, however, had people like Gladys Bentley, who was something worth discovering in those days, before she got famous, acquired an accompanist, specially written material, and conscious vulgarity. But for two or three amazing years, Miss Bentley sat, and played a big piano all night long, literally all night, without stopping—singing songs like "The St. James Infirmary," from ten in the evening until dawn, with scarcely a break between the notes, sliding from one song to another, with a powerful and continuous underbeat of jungle rhythm. Miss Bentley was an amazing exhibition of musical energy—a large, dark, masculine lady, whose feet pounded the floor while her fingers pounded the keyboard—a perfect piece of African sculpture, animated by her own rhythm.

But when the place where she played became too well known, she began to sing with an accompanist, became a star, moved to a larger place, then downtown, and is now in Hollywood. The old magic of the woman and the piano and

The first and only issue of Fire!! *(1926), an influential journal of the Harlem Renaissance.*

the night and the rhythm being one is gone. But everything goes, one way or another. The '20's are gone and lots of fine things in Harlem night life have disappeared like snow in the sun—since it became utterly commercial, planned for the downtown tourist trade, and therefore dull.

The lindy-hoppers at the Savoy even began to practice acrobatic routines, and to do absurd things for the entertainment of the whites, that probably never would have entered their heads to attempt merely for their own effortless amusement. Some of the lindy-hoppers had cards printed with their names on them and became dance professors teaching the tourists. Then Harlem nights became show nights for the Nordics.

Some critics say that that is what happened to certain Negro writers, too—that they ceased to write to amuse themselves and began to write to amuse and entertain white people, and in so doing distorted and overcolored their material, and left out a great many things they thought would offend their American brothers of a lighter complexion. Maybe—since Negroes have writer-racketeers, as has any other race. But I have known almost all of them, and most of the good ones have tried to be honest, write honestly, and express their world as they saw it.

From *The Big Sea*

~ CRITICS ON LANGSTON HUGHES ~

Arnold Rampersad   (b. 1941)

HUGHES AS AN EXPERIMENTALIST   1991

From his first publication of verse in the *Crisis*, Hughes had reflected his admiration for Sandburg and Whitman by experimenting with free verse as opposed to committing himself conservatively to rhyme. Even when he employed rhyme in his verse, as he often did, Hughes composed with relative casualness—unlike other major black poets of the day, such as Countee Cullen and Claude McKay, with their highly wrought stanzas. He seemed to prefer, as Whitman and Sandburg had preferred, to write lines that captured the cadences of common American speech, with his ear always especially attuned to the variety of black American language. This last aspect was only a token of his emotional and aesthetic involvement in black American culture, which he increasingly saw as his prime source of inspiration, even as he regarded black Americans ("Loud laughers in the hands of Fate— / My People") as his only indispensable audience.

Early poems captured some of the sights and sounds of ecstatic black church worship ("Glory! Hallelujah!"), but Hughes's greatest technical accomplishment as a poet was in his fusing of the rhythms of blues and jazz with traditional poetry. This technique, which he employed his entire life, surfaced in his art around 1923 with the landmark poem "The Weary Blues," in which the persona recalls hearing a blues singer and piano player ("Sweet Blues! / Coming from a black man's soul") performing in what most likely is a speakeasy in Harlem. The persona recalls the plaintive verse intoned by the singer ("Ain't got nobody in all this world, / Ain't got nobody but ma self") but finally surrenders to the mystery and magic of the blues singer's art. In the process, Hughes had taken an indigenous African American art form, perhaps the most vivid and commanding of all, and preserved its authenticity even as he formally enshrined it in the midst of a poem in traditional European form.

"The Weary Blues," a work virtually unprecedented in American poetry in its blending of black and white rhythms and forms, won Hughes the first prize for poetry in May 1925 in the epochal literary contest sponsored by *Opportunity* magazine, which marked the first high point of the Harlem Renaissance. The work also confirmed his leadership, along with Countee Cullen, of all the younger poets of the burgeoning movement. For Hughes, it was only the first step in his poetical tribute to blues and jazz. By the time of his second volume of verse, *Fine Clothes to the Jew* (1927), he was writing blues poems without either apology or framing devices taken from the traditional world of poetry. He was also delving into the basic subject matters of the blues—love and raw sexuality, deep sorrow and sudden violence, poverty and heartbreak. These subjects, treated with sympathy for the poor and dispossessed, and without false piety, made him easily the most controversial black poet of his time.

From "Langston Hughes"

Rita Dove (b. 1952)* and Marilyn Nelson (b. 1946)*

LANGSTON HUGHES AND HARLEM   1998

Affectionately known for most of his life as "The Poet Laureate of Harlem," Langston Hughes was born in Missouri and raised in the Midwest, moving to Harlem only as a young man. There he discovered his spiritual home, in Harlem's heart of Blackness finding both his vocation—"to explain and illuminate the Negro condition in America"—and the proletarian voice of most of his best work. If Johnson was the Renaissance man of the Harlem Renaissance, Hughes was its greatest man of letters; he saw through publication more than a dozen collections of poems, ten plays, two novels, several collections of short fiction, one historical study, two autobiographical works, several anthologies, and many books for children. His essay, "The Negro Artist and the Racial Mountain," provided a personal credo and statement of direction for the poets of his generation, who, he says, "intend to express our individual dark-skinned selves without fear or shame . . . We know we are beautiful. And ugly too." His forthright commitment to the Negro people led him to explore with great authenticity the frustrated dreams of the Black masses and to experiment with diction, rhythm, and musical forms.

Hughes was ever quick to confess the influences of Whitman and Sandburg on his work, and his best poetry also reflects the influence of Sherwood Anderson's *Winesburg, Ohio*. Like these poets, Hughes collected individual voices; his work is a notebook of life-studies. In his best poems Hughes the man remains masked; his voices are the voices of the Negro race as a whole, or of individual Negro speakers. "The Negro Speaks of Rivers," a widely anthologized poem from his first book, *The Weary Blues* (1926), is a case in point. Here Hughes is visible only as spokesman for the race as he proclaims "I bathed in the Euphrates when dawns were young. / I built my hut near the Congo and it lulled me to sleep." Poems frequently present anonymous Black personae, each of whom shares a painful heritage and an ironic pride. As one humorous character announces:

> I do cooking,
> Day's work, too!
> Alberta K. Johnson
> *Madam* to you.

Hughes took poetry out of what Cullen called "the dark tower"—which was, and even during the Harlem Renaissance, ivy-covered and distant and took it directly to the people. His blues and jazz experiments described and addressed an audience for which music was a central experience; he became a spokesman for their troubles, as in "Po' Boy Blues":

> When I was home de
> Sunshine seemed like gold.
> When I was home de
> Sunshine seemed like gold.
> Since I come up North de
> Whole damn world's turned cold.

American democracy appears frequently in Hughes's work as the unfulfilled but potentially realizable dream of the Negro, who says in "Let America Be America Again":

> O, yes,
> I say it plain,
> America never was America *to* me
> And yet I swear this oath—America will be!

There are many fine poems in the Hughes canon, but the strongest single work is *Montage of a Dream Deferred* (1951), a collection of sketches, captured voices, and individual lives unified by the jazzlike improvisations on the central theme of "a dream deferred." Like many of his individual poems, this work is intended for performance: think of it as a Harlem *Under Milk Wood*. Hughes moves rapidly from one voice or scene to the next; from the person in "Blues in Dawn" who says "I don't dare start thinking in the morning," to, in "Dime," a snatch of conversation: "Chile, these steps is hard to climb. / Grandma, lend me a dime."

The moods of the poems are as varied as their voices, for Hughes includes the daylight hours as well as the night. There are the bitter jump-rope rhymes of disillusioned children, the naive exclamations of young lovers, the gossip of friends. A college freshman writes in his "Theme for English B": "I guess being colored doesn't make me not like / the same things other folks like who are other races." A jaded woman offers in "Advice" the observation that "birthing is hard / and dying is mean," and advises youth to "get yourself / a little loving / in between." "Hope" is a miniature vignette in which a dying man asks for fish, and "His wife looked it up in her dream book / and played it." The changing voices, moods, and rhythms of this collection are, as Hughes wrote in a preface, "Like be-bop . . . marked by conflicting change, sudden nuances. . . ." We are reminded throughout that we should be hearing the poem as music; as boogie-woogie, as blues, as bass, as saxophone. Against the eighty-odd dreams collected here, the refrain insists that these frustrated dreams are potentially dangerous:

> What happens to a dream deferred?

>> Does it dry up
>> like a raisin in the sun?
>> Or fester like a sore—
>> And then run?
>> Does it stink like rotten meat?
>> Or crust and sugar over—
>> like a syrupy sweet?

>> Maybe it just sags
>> like a heavy load.

>> *Or does it explode?*

More than any other Black poet, Langston Hughes spoke for the Negro people. Most of those after him have emulated his ascent of the Racial Mountain, his painfully joyous declaration of pride and commonality. His work offers white readers a glimpse into the social and the personal lives of Black America; Black readers recognize a proud affirmation of self.

From "A Black Rainbow: Modern Afro-American Poetry"

Darryl Pinckney (b. 1953)

BLACK IDENTITY IN LANGSTON HUGHES 1989

Fierce identification with the sorrows and pleasures of the poor black—"I myself belong to that class"—propelled Hughes toward the voice of the black Everyman. He made a distinction between his lyric and his social poetry, the private and the public. In the best of his social poetry he turned himself into a transmitter of messages and made the "I" a collective "I":

> I've known rivers:
> I've known rivers ancient as the world and older than the flow of
>> human blood in human veins.

> My soul has grown deep like the rivers.

> I bathed in the Euphrates when dawns were young.
> I built my hut near the Congo and it lulled me to sleep.

I looked upon the Nile and raised the pyramids above it.
I heard the singing of the Mississippi when Abe Lincoln went down to
    New Orleans, and I've seen its muddy bosom turn all golden in the
    sunset.

("The Negro Speaks of Rivers")

The medium conveys a singleness of intention: to make the black known. The straightforward, declarative style doesn't call attention to itself. Nothing distracts from forceful statement, as if the shadowy characters Sandburg wrote about in, say, "When Mammy Hums" had at last their chance to come forward and testify. Poems like "Aunt Sue's Stories" reflect the folk ideal of black women as repositories of racial lore. The story told in dramatic monologues like "The Negro Mother" or "Mother to Son" is one of survival—life "ain't been no crystal stair." The emphasis is on the capacity of black people to endure, which is why Hughes's social poetry, though not strictly protest writing, indicts white America, even taunts it with the steady belief that blacks will overcome simply by "keeping on":

I, too, sing America.

I am the darker brother.
They send me to the kitchen
When company comes,
But I laugh,
And eat well,
And grow strong.   ("I, Too")

Whites were not the only ones who could be made uneasy by Hughes's attempts to boldly connect past and future. The use of "black" and the invocation of Africa were defiant gestures back in the days when many blacks described themselves as brown. When Hughes answered Sandburg's "Nigger" ("I am the nigger, / Singer of Songs . . .") with "I am a Negro, / Black as the night is black, / Black like the depths of my Africa" ("Negro") he challenged the black middle class with his absorption in slave heritage.

From "Suitcase in Harlem"

Peter Townsend   (b. 1948)

Langston Hughes and Jazz   2000

Hughes's engagement with jazz was close and long-lived, from his "Weary Blues" of 1926 up to the time of his death in 1967. Jazz crops naturally out of the landscape of Hughes's poetry, which is largely that of the black communities of Harlem and Chicago, and it remains fluid in its significance. Hughes's earliest references to jazz, in poems like "Jazzonia" and "Jazz Band in a Parisian Cabaret," acknowledge the exoticism which was customary in the presentation of jazz in the 1920s, and the novelty which the music still possessed for Hughes himself:

> In a Harlem cabaret
> Six long-headed jazzers play
> A dancing girl whose eyes are bold
> Lifts high a dress of silken gold.   ("Jazzonia")

This novelty is compounded by a further level of exoticism for the white visitors to the black cabarets who figure frequently in Hughes's jazz world. "Jazz Band in a Parisian Cabaret," for instance, has the band

> Play it for the lords and ladies
> For the dukes and counts
> For the whores and gigolos
> For the American millionaires

and "Harlem Night Club" pictures "dark brown girls / In blond men's arms." In Hughes's more politically barbed poetry of the 1930s these comments on white voyeurism harden into his attitude in "Visitors to the Black Belt":

> You can say
> Jazz on the South Side—
> To me it's hell
> On the South Side.

At the same time, jazz is one of the threads that make up the fabric of urban life in the "Harlem Renaissance" period. In a poem entitled "Heart of Harlem" Hughes places jazz musicians such as Earl Hines and Billie Holiday alongside individuals of the stature of Adam Clayton Powell, Joe Louis and W. E. B. Dubois. Hughes's continuous awareness of the place of jazz in his community enables him to record its scenes and its changes across the decades. "Lincoln Theatre," a poem published in a collection in 1949, gives a memorably exact rendering of the sort of Swing Era performance, in a Harlem theater, that was discussed [earlier]:

> The movies end. The lights flash gaily on.
> The band down in the pit bursts into jazz.
> The crowd applauds a plump brown-skin bleached blonde
> Who sings the troubles every woman has.

Hughes responded with particular sympathy to jazz of the bebop period, which he saw as having great political significance. *Montage of a Dream Deferred*, published in 1951, is one of Hughes's most substantial sequences of poems, and it is shot through with references to jazz. His editorial note to the sequence explains the stylistic influence of bebop on its composition:

> This poem on contemporary Harlem, like bebop, is marked by conflicting changes, sudden nuances, sharp and impudent interjections, and passages sometimes in the manner of the jam session, sometimes the popular song, punctuated by the riffs, runs, breaks and distortions of the music of a community in transition.

As Hughes made clear in other places, he heard bebop as an expression of a dissi-
dent spirit within the younger black community:

> Little cullud boys with fears
> frantic, kick their draftee years
> into flatted fifths and flatter beers . . .

and "Dream Boogie" resounds with suggestions, threatening or impudent, that
well up in the music, the "boogie-woogie rumble":

> Listen to it closely
> Ain't you heard
> something underneath.

Bebop affected the forms of Hughes's poetry at the higher architectural
levels, dictating the structural rhythm of longer works like "Dream Deferred,"
but otherwise he employed a small range of simple verse forms that originate in
earlier styles of black music. A particular favourite was a two-stress line rhymed
in quatrains, derived from spirituals, and he also frequently used a looser form
drawn from the 12-bar blues. The first of these Hughes was able to use with remarkable flexibility, considering its brevity. The form is often used for aphoristic
effect, as in "Motto":

> I play it cool
> And dig all jive.
> That's the reason
> I stay alive.

or in "Sliver," a comment on the form itself:

> A cheap little tune
> To cheap little rhymes
> Can cut a man's
> Throat sometimes.

What is even more remarkable is the naturalness of its effect in these diverse
contexts. Hughes makes the form serve the purposes of narrative and description
just as flexibly as that of comment. It gives Hughes's verse its idiomatic flavor, so
that even where the subject is not jazz or even music, the verse is still permeated
with the qualities of black musical culture.

From Jazz in American Culture

Onwuchekwa Jemie   (b. 1940)

A READING OF "DREAM DEFERRED"   1976

The deferred dream is examined through a variety of human agencies, of inter-
locking and recurring voices and motifs fragmented and scattered throughout the

six sections of the poem. Much as in bebop, the pattern is one of constant reversals and contrasts. Frequently the poems are placed in thematic clusters, with poems within the cluster arranged in contrasting pairs. *Montage [of a Dream Deferred]* does not move in a straight line; its component poems move off in invisible directions, reappear and touch, creating a complex tapestry or mosaic.

The dream theme itself is carried in the musical motifs. It is especially characterized by the rumble ("The boogie-woogie ramble / Of a dream deferred")—that rapid thumping and tumbling of notes which so powerfully drives to the bottom of the emotions, stirring feelings too deep to be touched by the normal successions of notes and common rhythms. The rumble is an atomic explosion of musical energy, an articulate confusion, a moment of epiphany, a flash of blinding light in which all things are suddenly made clear. The theme is sounded at strategic times, culminating in the final section. . . .

The poet has taken us on a guided tour of microcosmic Harlem, day and night, past and present. And as a new day dawns and the poem moves into a summing up in the final section, he again poses the question and examines the possibilities:

What happens to a dream deferred?

Does it dry up
like a raisin in the sun?
Or fester like a sore—
And then run?
Does it stink like rotten meat?
Or crust and sugar over—
like a syrupy sweet?

Maybe it just sags
like a heavy load.

Or does it explode?

The images are sensory, domestic, earthy, like blues images. The stress is on deterioration—drying, rotting, festering, souring—on loss of essential natural quality. The raisin has fallen from a fresh, juicy grape to a dehydrated but still edible raisin to a sun-baked and inedible dead bone of itself. The Afro-American is not unlike the raisin, for he is in a sense a dessicated trunk of his original African self, used and abandoned in the American wilderness with the stipulation that he rot and disappear. Like the raisin lying neglected in the scorching sun, the black man is treated as a thing of no consequence. But the raisin refuses the fate assigned to it, metamorphoses instead into a malignant living sore that will not heal or disappear. Like the raisin, a sore is but a little thing, inconsequential on the surface but in fact symptomatic of a serious disorder. Its stink is like the stink of the rotten meat sold to black folks in so many ghetto groceries; meat no longer suitable for human use, deathly. And while a syrupy sweet is not central to the diet as meat might be, still it is a rounding-off final pleasure (dessert) at the end of a meal, or a delicious surprise that a child looks forward to at Halloween or

Christmas. But that final pleasure turns out to be a pain. Aged, spoiled candy leaves a sickly taste in the mouth; sweetness gone bad turns a treat into a trick.

The elements of the deferred dream are, like the raisin, sore, meat, and candy, little things of no great consequence in themselves. But their unrelieved accretion packs together considerable pressure. Their combined weight becomes too great to carry about indefinitely: not only does the weight increase from continued accumulation, but the longer it is carried the heavier it feels. The load sags from its own weight, and the carrier sags with it; and if he should drop it, it just might explode from all its strange, tortured, and compressed energies.

In short, a dream deferred can be a terrifying thing. Its greatest threat is its unpredictability, and for this reason the question format is especially fitting. Questions demand the reader's participation, corner and sweep him headlong to the final, inescapable conclusion.

From *Langston Hughes: An Introduction to the Poetry*

FOR FURTHER READING

You can study several other poets in depth in this book. The following writers are represented at length and also have short biographies in "Lives of the Poets."

Robert Frost—13 poems (plus Writer's Perspective)
William Shakespeare—9 poems
William Butler Yeats—8 poems (plus Writer's Perspective)
Thomas Hardy—7 poems
William Carlos Williams—7 poems
William Blake—6 poems

See the Index for specific details.

SUGGESTIONS FOR WRITING

1. Focusing on one or two poems, demonstrate how Dickinson's idiosyncratic capitalization and punctuation add special impact to her work.
2. How do the poems by Dickinson in this chapter and elsewhere in the book illustrate her statement (in "Recognizing Poetry" on page 409) that "I find ecstasy in living—the mere sense of living is joy enough"?
3. Compare and contrast the use of first-person voices in two poems by Langston Hughes (such as "I, Too" and "Theme for English B" or "Mother to Son" and "Island"). In what ways does the speaker's "I" differ in each poem and in what ways is it similar?
4. Discussing a single poem by Hughes, examine how musical forms (such as jazz, blues, or popular song) help shape the effect of the work.

20 Poems for Further Reading

The manuscript of John Donne's sonnet, "Death be not proud" (page 466).

Lord Randall

"O where ha you been, Lord Randal, my son?
And where ha you been, my handsome young man?"
"I ha been at the greenwood; mother, mak my bed soon,
For I'm wearied wi hunting, and fain wad lie down."

"An wha° met ye there, Lord Randal, my son?   *who*   5
An wha met you there, my handsome young man?"
"O I met wi my true-love; mother, mak my bed soon,
For I'm wearied wi hunting, and fain wad lie down."

"And what did she give you, Lord Randal, my son?
And what did she give you, my handsome young man?"   10
"Eels fried in a pan; mother, mak my bed soon,
For I'm wearied with hunting, and fain wad lie down."

"And wha gat° your leavins,° Lord Randal, my son?   *got; leftovers*
And wha gat your leavins, my handsome young man?"
"My hawks and my hounds; mother, mak my bed soon,   15
For I'm wearied wi hunting, and fain wad lie down."

"And what becam of them, Lord Randall, my son?
And what becam of them, my handsome young man?"
"They stretched their legs out an died; mother, mak my bed soon,
For I'm wearied wi hunting, and fain wad lie down."   20

"O I fear you are poisoned, Lord Randal, my son!
I fear you are poisoned, my handsome young man!"
"O yes, I am poisoned; mother, mak my bed soon,
For I'm sick at the heart, and I fain wad lie down."

"What d' ye leave to your mother, Lord Randal, my son?   25
What d' ye leave to your mother, my handsome young man?"
"Four and twenty milk kye°; mother, mak my bed soon,   *cow*
For I'm sick at the heart, and I fain wad lie down."

"What d' ye leave to your sister, Lord Randal, my son?
What d' ye leave to your sister, my handsome young man?"   30
"My gold and my silver; mother, mak my bed soon,
For I'm sick at the heart, and I fain wad lie down."

"What d' ye leave to your brother, Lord Randal, my son?
What d' ye leave to your brother, my handsome young man?"
"My house and my lands; mother, mak my bed soon,   35
For I'm sick at the heart, and I fain wad lie down."

"What d' ye leave to your true-love, Lord Randal, my son?
What d' ye leave to your true-love, my handsome young man?"
"I leave her hell and fire; mother, mak my bed soon,
For I'm sick at the heart, and I fain wad lie down."   40

COMPARE

"Lord Randall" with a modern ballad such as "Ballad of Birmingham" by Dudley Randall
(page 151).

Anonymous   (traditional English ballad)

THE THREE RAVENS

There were three ravens sat on a tree,
   Down a down, hay down, hay down,
There were three ravens sat on a tree,
   With a down,
There were three ravens sat on a tree,   5
They were as black as they might be.
   With a down derry, derry, derry, down, down.

The one of them said to his mate,
"Where shall we our breakfast take?"

"Down in yonder greene field,   10
There lies a knight slain under his shield.

"His hounds they lie down at his feet,
So well they can their master keep.

"His hawks they fly so eagerly,
There's no fowl dare him come nigh."   15

Down there comes a fallow doe,
As great with young as she might go.

She lift up his bloody head,
And kist his wounds that were so red.

She got him up upon her back,   20
And carried him to earthen lake.°   *the grave*

She buried him before the prime,°   *dawn*
She was dead herself ere evensong time.

God send every gentleman
Such hawks, such hounds, and such a leman.°   *lover*   25

THE THREE RAVENS. The lines of refrain are repeated in each stanza. "Perhaps in the folk mind the
doe is the form the soul of a human mistress, now dead, has taken," Albert B. Friedman has suggested
(in *The Viking Book of Folk Ballads*). "Most probably the knight's beloved was understood to be an enchanted woman who was metamorphosed at certain times into an animal." In lines 22 and 23, *prime*
and *evensong* are two of the canonical hours set aside for prayer and worship. Prime is at dawn, evensong at dusk.

Anonymous   (traditional Scottish ballad)

THE TWA CORBIES

As I was walking all alane,
I heard twa corbies° making a mane;°   *ravens; moan*
The tane° unto the t'other say,   *one*
"Where sall we gang° and dine today?"   *go*

"In behint yon auld fail dyke,°   *turf wall*   5
I wot° there lies a new slain knight;   *know*
And naebody kens° that he lies there,   *knows*
But his hawk, his hound, and lady fair.

"His hound is to the hunting gane,
His hawk to fetch the wild-fowl hame,   10
His lady's ta'en another mate,
So we may mak our dinner sweet.

"Ye'll sit on his white hause-bane,°   *neck bone*
And I'll pike out his bonny blue een;
Wi' ae° lock o' his gowden hair   *one*   15
We'll theek° our nest when it grows bare.   *thatch*

"Mony a one for him makes mane,
But nane sall ken where he is gane;
O'er his white banes, when they are bare,
The wind sall blaw for evermair."   20

THE TWA CORBIES. Sir Walter Scott, the first to print this ballad in his *Minstrelsy of the Scottish Border*
(1802–1803), calls it "rather a counterpart than a copy" of "The Three Ravens." M. J. C. Hodgart
and other scholars think he may have written most of it himself.

Anonymous (English lyric)

WESTERN WIND (ABOUT 1500)

Western wind, when wilt thou blow,
The° small rain down can rain?   *(so that) the*
Christ, if my love were in my arms,
And I in my bed again!

COMPARE

"Western Wind" with "The River-Merchant's Wife: a Letter" by Ezra Pound (page 530).

Anonymous (Navajo mountain chant)

LAST WORDS OF THE PROPHET

Farewell, my younger brother!
From the holy places the gods come for me.
You will never see me again; but when the showers pass and the
    thunders peal,
"There," you will say, "is the voice of my elder brother."
And when the harvest comes, of the beautiful birds and grasshoppers   5
    you will say,
"There is the ordering of my elder brother!"
          —Translated by Washington Matthews

COMPARE

"Last Words of the Prophet" with "A Slumber Did My Spirit Seal" by William Wordsworth (page 169).

Matthew Arnold (1822–1888)

DOVER BEACH 1867

The sea is calm tonight.
The tide is full, the moon lies fair
Upon the straits;—on the French coast the light
Gleams and is gone; the cliffs of England stand,
Glimmering and vast, out in the tranquil bay.   5
Come to the window, sweet is the night-air!
Only, from the long line of spray
Where the sea meets the moon-blanched land,
Listen! you hear the grating roar
Of pebbles which the waves draw back, and fling,   10
At their return, up the high strand,
Begin, and cease, and then again begin,

With tremulous cadence slow, and bring
The eternal note of sadness in.

Sophocles long ago   15
Heard it on the Aegean, and it brought
Into his mind the turbid ebb and flow
Of human misery; we
Find also in the sound a thought,
Hearing it by this distant northern sea.   20

The Sea of Faith
Was once, too, at the full, and round earth's shore
Lay like the folds of a bright girdle furled.
But now I only hear
Its melancholy, long, withdrawing roar,   25
Retreating, to the breath
Of the night-wind, down the vast edges drear
And naked shingles° of the world.   *gravel beaches*

Ah, love, let us be true
To one another! for the world, which seems   30
To lie before us like a land of dreams,
So various, so beautiful, so new,
Hath really neither joy, nor love, nor light,
Nor certitude, nor peace, nor help for pain;
And we are here as on a darkling° plain   *darkened or darkening* 35
Swept with confused alarms of struggle and flight,
Where ignorant armies clash by night.

COMPARE

"Dover Beach" with "Hap" by Thomas Hardy (page 488).

John Ashbery   (b. 1927)*

AT NORTH FARM   1984

Somewhere someone is traveling furiously toward you,
At incredible speed, traveling day and night,
Through blizzards and desert heat, across torrents, through narrow
        passes.
But will he know where to find you,
Recognize you when he sees you,   5
Give you the thing he has for you?

Hardly anything grows here,
Yet the granaries are bursting with meal,

The sacks of meal piled to the rafters.
The streams run with sweetness, fattening fish;   10
Birds darken the sky. Is it enough
That the dish of milk is set out at night,
That we think of him sometimes,
Sometimes and always, with mixed feelings?

COMPARE

"At North Farm" with "Uphill" by Christina Rossetti (page 267).

Margaret Atwood   (b. 1939)*

ROMANTIC   1995

Men and their mournful romanticisms
that can't get the dishes done—
that's freedom, that broken wineglass
in the cold fireplace.

When women wash underpants, it's a chore.   5
When men do it, an intriguing affliction.
How plangent, the damp socks flapping on the line,
how lost and single in the orphaning air . . .

She cherishes that sadness,
tells him to lie down on the grass,   10
closes each of his eyes with a finger,
applies her body like a poultice.

You poor thing, said the Australian woman
while he held our baby—
as if I had forced him to do it,   15
as if I had my high heel in his face.

Still, who's taken in?
Every time?
Us, and our empty hands, the hands
of starving nurses.   20

It's bullet holes we want to see in their skin,
scars, and the chance to touch them.

COMPARE

"Romantic" with "Power" by Adrienne Rich (page 535).

W. H. Auden

W. H. Auden   (1907–1973)*

As I Walked Out One Evening   1940

As I walked out one evening,
  Walking down Bristol Street,
The crowds upon the pavement
  Were fields of harvest wheat.

And down by the brimming river   5
  I heard a lover sing
Under an arch of the railway:
  "Love has no ending.

"I'll love you, dear, I'll love you
  Till China and Africa meet,   10
And the river jumps over the mountain
  And the salmon sing in the street,

"I'll love you till the ocean
  Is folded and hung up to dry
And the seven stars go squawking   15
  Like geese about the sky.

"The years shall run like rabbits,
  For in my arms I hold
The Flower of the Ages,
  And the first love of the world."   20

But all the clocks in the city
  Began to whirr and chime:

"O let not Time deceive you,
    You cannot conquer Time.

"In the burrows of the Nightmare   25
    Where Justice naked is,
Time watches from the shadow
    And coughs when you would kiss.

"In headaches and in worry
    Vaguely life leaks away,   30
And Time will have his fancy
    Tomorrow or today.

"Into many a green valley
    Drifts the appalling snow;
Time breaks the threaded dances   35
    And the diver's brilliant bow.

"O plunge your hands in water,
    Plunge them in up to the wrist;
Stare, stare in the basin
    And wonder what you've missed.   40

"The glacier knocks in the cupboard,
    The desert sighs in the bed,
And the crack in the teacup opens
    A lane to the land of the dead.

"Where the beggars raffle the banknotes   45
    And the Giant is enchanting to Jack,
And the Lily-white Boy is a Roarer,
    And Jill goes down on her back.

"O look, look in the mirror,
    O look in your distress;   50
Life remains a blessing
    Although you cannot bless.

"O stand, stand at the window
    As the tears scald and start;
You shall love your crooked neighbor   55
    With your crooked heart."

It was late, late in the evening,
    The lovers they were gone;
The clocks had ceased their chiming,
    And the deep river ran on.   60

COMPARE

"As I Walked Out One Evening" with "Dover Beach" by Matthew Arnold (page 445) and
"anyone lived in a pretty how town" by E. E. Cummings (page 71).

W. H. Auden   (1907–1973)*

MUSÉE DES BEAUX ARTS   1940

About suffering they were never wrong,
The Old Masters: how well they understood
Its human position; how it takes place
While someone else is eating or opening a window or just walking
    dully along;
How, when the aged are reverently, passionately waiting   5
For the miraculous birth, there always must be
Children who did not specially want it to happen, skating
On a pond at the edge of the wood:
They never forgot
That even the dreadful martyrdom must run its course   10
Anyhow in a corner, some untidy spot
Where the dogs go on with their doggy life and the torturer's horse
Scratches its innocent behind on a tree.

The Fall of Icarus *by Pieter Breughel the Elder (1520?–1569).*

In Brueghel's *Icarus*, for instance: how everything turns away
Quite leisurely from the disaster; the ploughman may   15
Have heard the splash, the forsaken cry,
But for him it was not an important failure; the sun shone
As it had to on the white legs disappearing into the green
Water; and the expensive delicate ship that must have seen
Something amazing, a boy falling out of the sky,   20
Had somewhere to get to and sailed calmly on.

COMPARE

"Musée des Beaux Arts" with "The Dance" by William Carlos Williams (page 243) and
the painting by Pieter Breughel to which each poem refers.

Elizabeth Bishop

Elizabeth Bishop   (1911–1979)*
FILLING STATION   1965

Oh, but it is dirty!
—this little filling station,
oil-soaked, oil-permeated
to a disturbing, over-all
black translucency.   5
Be careful with that match!

Father wears a dirty,
oil-soaked monkey suit
that cuts him under the arms,
and several quick and saucy   10
and greasy sons assist him

(it's a family filling station),
all quite thoroughly dirty.

Do they live in the station?
It has a cement porch   15
behind the pumps, and on it
a set of crushed and grease-
impregnated wickerwork;
on the wicker sofa
a dirty dog, quite comfy.   20

Some comic books provide
the only note of color—
of certain color. They lie
upon a big dim doily
draping a taboret°   stool   25
(part of the set), beside
a big hirsute begonia.

Why the extraneous plant?
Why the taboret?
Why, oh why, the doily?   30
(Embroidered in daisy stitch
with marguerites, I think,
and heavy with gray crochet.)

Somebody embroidered the doily.
Somebody waters the plant,   35
or oils it, maybe. Somebody
arranges the rows of cans
so that they softly say:
ESSO—SO—SO—SO
to high-strung automobiles.   40
Somebody loves us all.

COMPARE

"Filling Station" with "California Hills in August" by Dana Gioia (page 483) or "The splendor falls on castle walls" by Alfred, Lord Tennyson (page 173).

Detail of William Blake's The Tyger.

William Blake (1757–1827)*

The Tyger   1794

Tyger! Tyger! burning bright
In the forests of the night,
What immortal hand or eye
Could frame thy fearful symmetry?

In what distant deeps or skies   5
Burnt the fire of thine eyes?
On what wings dare he aspire?
What the hand dare seize the fire?

And what shoulder, and what art,
Could twist the sinews of thy heart?   10
And when thy heart began to beat,
What dread hand? and what dread feet?

What the hammer? what the chain?
In what furnace was thy brain?
What the anvil? what dread grasp   15
Dare its deadly terrors clasp?

When the stars threw down their spears,
And watered heaven with their tears,
Did he smile his work to see?
Did he who made the Lamb make thee?   20

Tyger! Tyger! burning bright
In the forests of the night,
What immortal hand or eye
Dare frame thy fearful symmetry?

COMPARE

"The Tyger" with "The Windhover" by Gerard Manley Hopkins (page 497).

William Blake

William Blake   (1757–1827)*

THE SICK ROSE   1794

O Rose, thou art sick!
The invisible worm
That flies in the night,
In the howling storm,

Has found out thy bed   5
Of crimson joy,
And his dark secret love
Does thy life destroy.

COMPARE

"The Sick Rose" with "The Man with Night Sweats" by Thom Gunn (page 484).

Eavan Boland   (b. 1944)

ANOREXIC   1980

Flesh is heretic.
My body is a witch.
I am burning it.

Yes I am torching
her curves and paps and wiles.   5
They scorch in my self denials.

How she meshed my head
in the half-truths
of her fevers

till I renounced   10
milk and honey
and the taste of lunch.

I vomited
her hungers.
Now the bitch is burning.   15

I am starved and curveless.
I am skin and bone.
She has learned her lesson.

Thin as a rib
I turn in sleep.   20
My dreams probe

a claustrophobia
a sensuous enclosure.
How warm it was and wide

once by a warm drum,   25
once by the song of his breath
and in his sleeping side.

Only a little more,
only a few more days
sinless, foodless,   30

I will slip
back into him again
as if I had never been away.

Caged so
I will grow   35
angular and holy

past pain,
keeping his heart
such company

as will make me forget
in a small space
the fall

into forked dark,
into python needs
heaving to hips and breasts   45
and lips and heat
and sweat and fat and greed.

COMPARE

"Anorexic" with "Her Kind" by Anne Sexton (page 34).

Gwendolyn Brooks   (1917–2000)*

THE MOTHER   1945

Abortions will not let you forget.
You remember the children you got that you did not get,
The damp small pulps with a little or with no hair,
The singers and workers that never handled the air.
You will never neglect or beat   5
Them, or silence or buy with a sweet.
You will never wind up the sucking-thumb
Or scuttle off ghosts that come.
You will never leave them, controlling your luscious sigh,
Return for a snack of them, with gobbling mother-eye.   10
I have heard in the voices of the wind the voices of my dim killed
     children.
I have contracted. I have eased
My dim dears at the breasts they could never suck.
I have said, Sweets, if I sinned, if I seized
Your luck   15
And your lives from your unfinished reach,
If I stole your births and your names,
Your straight baby tears and your games,
Your stilted or lovely loves, your tumults, your marriages, aches, and
     your deaths,

If I poisoned the beginnings of your breaths,   20
Believe that even in my deliberateness I was not deliberate.
Though why should I whine,
Whine that the crime was other than mine?—
Since anyhow you are dead.
Or rather, or instead,   25
You were never made.
But that too, I am afraid,
Is faulty: oh, what shall I say, how is the truth to be said?
You were born, you had body, you died.
It is just that you never giggled or planned or cried.   30

Believe me, I loved you all.
Believe me, I knew you, though faintly, and I loved, I loved you all.

COMPARE

"The Mother" with "Metaphors" by Sylvia Plath (page 124), and "The Victory" by Anne
Stevenson (page 99).

Gwendolyn Brooks   (1917–2000)*

THE PREACHER RUMINATES: 1945
BEHIND THE SERMON

I think it must be lonely to be God.
Nobody loves a master. No. Despite
The bright hosannas, bright dear-Lords, and bright
Determined reverence of Sunday eyes.

Picture Jehovah striding through the hall   5
Of His importance, creatures running out
From servant-corners to acclaim, to shout
Appreciation of His merit's glare.

But who walks with Him?—dares to take His arm,
To slap Him on the shoulder, tweak His ear,   10
Buy Him a Coca-Cola or a beer,
Pooh-pooh His politics, call Him a fool?

Perhaps—who knows?—He tires of looking down.
Those eyes are never lifted. Never straight.
Perhaps sometimes He tires of being great   15
In solitude. Without a hand to hold.

COMPARE

"the preacher ruminates: behind the sermon" with "Death be not proud" by John Donne
(page 466).

Elizabeth Barrett Browning   (1806–1861)*

How Do I Love Thee?   1850
Let Me Count the Ways

How do I love thee? Let me count the ways.
I love thee to the depth and breadth and height
My soul can reach, when feeling out of sight
For the ends of being and ideal grace.
I love thee to the level of every day's   5
Most quiet need, by sun and candle-light.
I love thee freely, as men strive for right.
I love thee purely, as they turn from praise.
I love thee with the passion put to use
In my old griefs, and with my childhood's faith.   10
I love thee with a love I seemed to lose
With my lost saints. I love thee with the breath,
Smiles, tears, of all my life; and, if God choose,
I shall but love thee better after death.

Compare

"How Do I Love Thee?" with "What lips my lips have kissed" by Edna St. Vincent Millay
(page 223).

Robert Browning   (1812–1889)*

Soliloquy of the Spanish Cloister   1842

Gr-r-r—there go, my heart's abhorrence!
    Water your damned flower-pots, do!
If hate killed men, Brother Lawrence,
    God's blood, would not mine kill you!
What? your myrtle-bush wants trimming?   5
    Oh, that rose has prior claims—
Needs its leaden vase filled brimming?
    Hell dry you up with its flames!

At the meal we sit together;
    Salve tibi! ° I must hear   *Hail to thee!*   10
Wise talk of the kind of weather,
    Sort of season, time of year:
*Not a plenteous cork-crop: scarcely
    Dare we hope oak-galls, I doubt;*
What's the Latin name for "parsley"?   15
    What's the Greek name for "swine's snout"?

Whew! We'll have our platter burnished,
    Laid with care on our own shelf!
With a fire-new spoon we're furnished,
    And a goblet for ourself,   20
Rinsed like something sacrificial
    Ere 'tis fit to touch our chaps—
Marked with L. for our initial!
    (He-he! There his lily snaps!)

Saint, forsooth! While Brown Dolores   25
    Squats outside the Convent bank
With Sanchicha, telling stories,
    Steeping tresses in the tank,
Blue-black, lustrous, thick like horsehairs,
    —Can't I see his dead eye glow,   30
Bright as 'twere a Barbary corsair's?
    (That is, if he'd let it show!)

When he finishes refection,
    Knife and fork he never lays
Cross-wise, to my recollection,   35
    As I do, in Jesu's praise.
I the Trinity illustrate,
    Drinking watered orange-pulp—
In three sips the Arian frustrate;
    While he drains his at one gulp!   40

Oh, those melons! if he's able
    We're to have a feast; so nice!
One goes to the Abbot's table,
    All of us get each a slice.
How go on your flowers? None double?   45
    Not one fruit-sort can you spy?
Strange!—And I, too, at such trouble,
    Keep them close-nipped on the sly!

There's a great text in Galatians,
    Once you trip on it, entails   50
Twenty-nine distinct damnations,
    One sure, if another fails;
If I trip him just a-dying,
    Sure of heaven as sure can be,
Spin him round and send him flying   55
    Off to hell, a Manichee?

Or, my scrofulous French novel
   On grey paper with blunt type!
Simply glance at it, you grovel
   Hand and foot in Belial's gripe;   60
If I double down its pages
   At the woeful sixteenth print,
When he gathers his greengages,
   Ope a sieve and slip it in't?

Or, there's Satan!—one might venture   65
   Pledge one's soul to him, yet leave
Such a flaw in the indenture
   As he'd miss till, past retrieve,
Blasted lay that rose-acacia
   We're so proud of! *Hy, Zy, Hine.* . . .   70
'St, there's Vespers! *Plena gratia*
   Ave, Virgo!° Gr-r-r—you swine!   *Hail, Virgin, full of grace!*

SOLILOQUY OF THE SPANISH CLOISTER. 3 *Brother Lawrence:* one of the speaker's fellow monks. 31 *Barbary corsair:* a pirate operating off the Barbary coast of Africa. 39 *Arian:* a follower of Arius, heretic who denied the doctrine of the Trinity. 49 *a great text in Galatians:* a difficult verse in this book of the Bible. Brother Lawrence will be damned as a heretic if he wrongly interprets it. 56 *Manichee:* another kind of heretic, one who (after the Persian philosopher Mani) sees in the world a constant struggle between good and evil, neither able to win. 60 *Belial:* here, not specifically Satan but (as used in the Old Testament) a name for wickedness. 70 *Hy, Zy, Hine:* possibly the sound of a bell to announce evening devotions.

COMPARE

"Soliloquy of the Spanish Cloister" with "In Westminster Abbey" by John Betjeman (page 39).

Geoffrey Chaucer (1340?–1400)

MERCILESS BEAUTY   (LATE 14TH CENTURY)

Your ÿen° two wol slee° me sodenly;   *eyes; slay*
I may the beautee of hem° not sustene,°   *them; resist*
So woundeth hit thourghout my herte kene.

And but° your word wo! helen° hastily   *unless; heal*
My hertes wounde, while that hit is grene,°   *new*   5
   Your ÿen two wol slee me sodenly;
   I may the beautee of hem not sustene.

Upon my trouthe° I sey you feithfully   *word*
That ye ben of my lyf and deeth the quene;
For with my deeth the trouthe° shal be sene.   truth   10
   Your ÿen two wol slee me sodenly;
   I may the beautee of hem not sustene,
   So woundeth it thourghout my herte kene.

MERCILESS BEAUTY. This poem is one of a group of three roundels, collectively titled "Merciles Beaute." A **roundel** (or **rondel**) is an English form consisting of 11 lines in 3 stanzas rimed with a refrain. 3 *So woundeth . . . kene:* "So deeply does it wound me through the heart."

COMPARE

"Merciless Beauty" with "My mistress' eyes are nothing like the sun" by William Shakespeare (page 542).

G. K. Chesterton   (1874–1936)

THE DONKEY   1900

When fishes flew and forests walked
   And figs grew upon thorn,
Some moment when the moon was blood
   Then surely I was born;

With monstrous head and sickening cry   5
   And ears like errant wings,
The devil's walking parody
   On all four-footed things.

The tattered outlaw of the earth,
   Of ancient crooked will;   10
Starve, scourge, deride me: I am dumb,
   I keep my secret still.

Fools! For I also had my hour;
   One far fierce hour and sweet:
There was a shout about my ears,   15
   And palms before my feet.

THE DONKEY. For more details of the donkey's hour of triumph see Matthew 21:1–8.

COMPARE

"The Donkey" with "The Tyger" by William Blake (page 453).

Samuel Taylor Coleridge   (1772–1834)

KUBLA KHAN   (1797–1798)

Or, a Vision in a Dream. A Fragment.

In Xanadu did Kubla Khan
A stately pleasure-dome decree:
Where Alph, the sacred river, ran
Through caverns measureless to man
    Down to a sunless sea.   5
So twice five miles of fertile ground
With walls and towers were girdled round;
And there were gardens bright with sinuous rills,
Where blossomed many an incense-bearing tree;
And here were forests ancient as the hills,   10
Enfolding sunny spots of greenery.

But oh! that deep romantic chasm which slanted
Down the green hill athwart a cedarn cover!
A savage place! as holy and enchanted
As e'er beneath a waning moon was haunted   15
By woman wailing for her demon-lover!
And from this chasm, with ceaseless turmoil seething,
As if this earth in fast thick pants were breathing,
A mighty fountain momently was forced:
Amid whose swift half-intermitted burst   20
Huge fragments vaulted like rebounding hail,
Or chaffy grain beneath the thresher's flail:
And 'mid these dancing rocks at once and ever
It flung up momently the sacred river.
Five miles meandering with a mazy motion   25
Through wood and dale the sacred river ran,
Then reached the caverns measureless to man,
And sank in tumult to a lifeless ocean:
And 'mid this tumult Kubla heard from far
Ancestral voices prophesying war!   30

    The shadow of the dome of pleasure
    Floated midway on the waves;
    Where was heard the mingled measure
    From the fountain and the caves.
It was a miracle of rare device,   35
A sunny pleasure-dome with caves of ice!

A damsel with a dulcimer
In a vision once I saw:
It was an Abyssinian maid,
And on her dulcimer she played,   40
Singing of Mount Abora.
Could I revive within me
Her symphony and song,
To such a deep delight 'twould win me,
That with music loud and long,   45
I would build that dome in air,
That sunny dome! those caves of ice!
And all who heard should see them there,
And all should cry, Beware! Beware!
His flashing eyes, his floating hair!   50
Weave a circle round him thrice,
And close your eyes with holy dread,
For he on honey-dew hath fed,
And drunk the milk of Paradise.

KUBLA KHAN. There was an actual Kublai Khan, a thirteenth-century Mongol emperor, and a Chinese city of Xanadu; but Coleridge's dream vision also borrows from travelers' descriptions of such other exotic places as Abyssinia and America. 51 *circle:* a magic circle drawn to keep away evil spirits.

COMPARE

"Kubla Khan" with "The Second Coming" by William Butler Yeats (page 286).

Billy Collins   (b. 1941)*

CARE AND FEEDING   2003

Because I will turn 420 tomorrow
in dog years
I will take myself for a long walk
along the green shore of the lake,

and when I walk in the door,   5
I will jump up on my chest
and lick my nose and ears and eyelids
while I tell myself again and again to get down.

I will fill my metal bowl at the sink
with cold fresh water,
and lift a biscuit from the jar   10
and hold it gingerly with my teeth.

Then I will make three circles
and lie down at my feet on the wood floor
and close my eyes   15
while I type all morning and into the afternoon,

checking every once in a while
to make sure I am still there,
reaching down
to stroke my furry, venerable head.   20

COMPARE

"Care and Feeding" with "For the Anniversary of My Death" by W. S. Merwin (page 242).

Hart Crane   (1899–1932)

MY GRANDMOTHER'S LOVE LETTERS   1926

There are no stars tonight
But those of memory.
Yet how much room for memory there is
In the loose girdle of soft rain.

There is even room enough
For the letters of my mother's mother,   5
Elizabeth,
That have been pressed so long
Into a corner of the roof
That they are brown and soft,   10
And liable to melt as snow.

Over the greatness of such space
Steps must be gentle.
It is all hung by an invisible white hair.
It trembles as birch limbs webbing the air.   15

And I ask myself:

"Are your fingers long enough to play
Old keys that are but echoes:
Is the silence strong enough
To carry back the music to its source   20

And back to you again
As though to her?"

Yet I would lead my grandmother by the hand
Through much of what she would not understand;
And so I stumble. And the rain continues on the roof   25
With such a sound of gently pitying laughter.

COMPARE

"My Grandmother's Love Letters" with "When You Are Old" by William Butler Yeats
(page 572).

E. E. Cummings   (1894–1962)*

SOMEWHERE I HAVE NEVER TRAVELLED,   1931
GLADLY BEYOND

somewhere i have never travelled,gladly beyond
any experience,your eyes have their silence:
in your most frail gesture are things which enclose me,
or which i cannot touch because they are too near

your slightest look easily will unclose me   5
though i have closed myself as fingers,
you open always petal by petal myself as Spring opens
(touching skilfully,mysteriously)her first rose

or if your wish be to close me,i and
my life will shut very beautifully,suddenly,   10
as when the heart of this flower imagines
the snow carefully everywhere descending;

nothing which we are to perceive in this world equals
the power of your intense fragility:whose texture
compels me with the colour of its countries,   15
rendering death and forever with each breathing

(i do not know what it is about you that closes
and opens;only something in me understands
the voice of your eyes is deeper than all roses)
nobody,not even the rain,has such small hands   20

COMPARE

"somewhere i have never travelled,gladly beyond" with "Merciless Beauty" by Geoffrey
Chaucer (page 461) or "Elegy for Jane" by Theodore Roethke (page 537).

John Donne

John Donne (1572–1631)*

DEATH BE NOT PROUD   (ABOUT 1610)

Death be not proud, though some have callèd thee
Mighty and dreadful, for thou art not so;
For those whom thou think'st thou dost overthrow
Die not, poor death, nor yet canst thou kill me.
From rest and sleep, which but thy pictures be,   5
Much pleasure, then from thee much more must flow,
And soonest our best men with thee do go,
Rest of their bones, and soul's delivery.
Thou art slave to fate, chance, kings, and desperate men,
And dost with poison, war, and sickness dwell,   10
And poppy, or charms can make us sleep as well,
And better than thy stroke; why swell'st thou then?
One short sleep past, we wake eternally,
And death shall be no more; death, thou shalt die.

COMPARE

Compare Donne's personification of Death in "Death be not proud" with Emily Dickinson's in "Because I could not stop for Death" (page 407).

John Donne (1572–1631)*

THE FLEA   1633

Mark but this flea, and mark in this
How little that which thou deny'st me is;
It sucked me first, and now sucks thee,
And in this flea our two bloods mingled be;
Thou know'st that this cannot be said   5
A sin, nor shame, nor loss of maidenhead,
   Yet this enjoys before it woo,
   And pampered swells with one blood made of two,
   And this, alas, is more than we would do.

Oh stay, three lives in one flea spare,   10
Where we almost, yea more than married are.
This flea is you and I, and this
Our marriage bed, and marriage temple is;
Though parents grudge, and you, we're met
And cloistered in these living walls of jet.   15
   Though use° make you apt to kill me,   *custom*
   Let not to that, self-murder added be,
   And sacrilege, three sins in killing three.

Cruel and sudden, hast thou since
Purpled thy nail in blood of innocence?   20
Wherein could this flea guilty be,
Except in that drop it sucked from thee?
Yet thou triumph'st, and say'st that thou
Find'st not thyself, nor me, the weaker now;
   'Tis true; then learn how false, fears be;   25
   Just so much honor, when thou yield'st to me,
   Will waste, as this flea's death took life from thee.

COMPARE

"The Flea" with "To His Coy Mistress" by Andrew Marvell (page 512).

John Donne (1572–1631)*

A Valediction: Forbidding Mourning (1611)

As virtuous men pass mildly away,
    And whisper to their souls to go,
Whilst some of their sad friends do say
    The breath goes now, and some say no:

So let us melt, and make no noise,   5
    No tear-floods, nor sigh-tempests move;
'Twere profanation of our joys
    To tell the laity° our love.   *common people*

Moving of th' earth° brings harms and fears;   *earthquake*
    Men reckon what it did and meant;   10
But trepidation of the spheres,
    Though greater far, is innocent.°   *harmless*

Dull sublunary lovers' love
    (Whose soul is sense) cannot admit
Absence, because it doth remove   15
    Those things which elemented° it.   *constituted*

But we, by a love so much refined
    That ourselves know not what it is,
Inter-assurèd of the mind,
    Care less, eyes, lips, and hands to miss.   20

Our two souls, therefore, which are one,
    Though I must go, endure not yet
A breach, but an expansiòn,
    Like gold to airy thinness beat.

If they be two, they are two so   25
    As stiff twin compasses are two:
Thy soul, the fixed foot, makes no show
    To move, but doth, if th' other do.

And though it in the center sit,
    Yet when the other far doth roam,   30
It leans and harkens after it,
    And grows erect as that comes home.

Such wilt thou be to me, who must,
  Like th' other foot, obliquely run;
Thy firmness makes my circle just,°   *perfect*   35
  And makes me end where I begun.

A VALEDICTION: FORBIDDING MOURNING. According to Donne's biographer Izaak Walton, Donne's wife received this poem as a gift before the poet departed on a journey to France. 11 *spheres:* in Ptolemaic astronomy, the concentric spheres surrounding the earth. The trepidation or motion of the ninth sphere was thought to change the date of the equinox. 19 *Inter-assurèd of the mind:* each sure in mind that the other is faithful. 24 *gold to airy thinness:* gold is so malleable that, if beaten to the thickness of gold leaf (1/250,000 of one inch), one ounce of gold would cover 250 square feet.

COMPARE

"A Valediction: Forbidding Mourning" with "To Lucasta" by Richard Lovelace (page 45).

Rita Dove

Rita Dove   (b. 1952)*

SUMMIT BEACH, 1921   1989

The Negro beach jumped to the twitch
of an oil drum tattoo and a mandolin,
sweaters flying off the finest brown shoulders
this side of the world.

She sat by the fire, shawl moored   5
by a single fake cameo. She was cold,
thank you, she did not care to dance—
the scar on her knee winking
with the evening chill.

Papa had said don't be so fast,   10
you're all you've got. So she refused

to cut the wing, though she let the boys
bring her sassafras tea and drank it down
neat as a dropped hankie.

Her knee had itched in the cast   15
till she grew mean from bravery.
She could wait, she was gold.
When the right man smiled it would be
music skittering up her calf

like a chuckle. She could feel   20
the breeze in her ears like water,
like the air as a child when
she climbed Papa's shed and stepped off
the tin roof into blue,

with her parasol and invisible wings.   25

COMPARE

"Summit Beach, 1921" with "Kite Poem" by James Merrill (page 513).

John Dryden   (1631–1700)

TO THE MEMORY OF MR. OLDHAM   1684

Farewell, too little and too lately known,
Whom I began to think and call my own;
For sure our souls were near allied, and thine
Cast in the same poetic mold with mine.
One common note on either lyre did strike,   5
And knaves and fools we both abhorred alike.
To the same goal did both our studies drive:
The last set out the soonest did arrive.
Thus Nissus fell upon the slippery place,
While his young friend performed and won the race.   10
O early ripe! to thy abundant store
What could advancing age have added more?
It might (what Nature never gives the young)
Have taught the numbers° of thy native tongue.   *meters*
But satire needs not those, and wit will shine   15
Through the harsh cadence of a rugged line.
A noble error, and but seldom made,
When poets are by too much force betrayed.
Thy gen'rous fruits, though gathered ere their prime,
Still showed a quickness; and maturing time   20
But mellows what we write to the dull sweets of rhyme.

Once more, hail, and farewell! farewell, thou young
But ah! too short, Marcellus of our tongue!
Thy brows with ivy and with laurels bound;
But fate and gloomy night encompass thee around.   25

To the Memory of Mr. Oldham. John Oldham, poet best remembered for his *Satires upon the Jesuits*, had died at thirty. 9–10 *Nissus; his young friend:* these two close friends, as Virgil tells us in the *Aeneid*, ran a race for the prize of an olive crown. 23 *Marcellus:* had he not died in his twentieth year, he would have succeeded the Roman emperor Augustus. 25 This line echoes the *Aeneid* (VI, 886), in which Marcellus is seen walking under the black cloud of his impending doom.

Compare

"To the Memory of Mr. Oldham" with "Elegy for Jane" by Theodore Roethke (page 537).

T. S. Eliot   (1888–1965)*

Journey of the Magi   1927

"A cold coming we had of it,
Just the worst time of the year
For a journey, and such a long journey:
The ways deep and the weather sharp,
The very dead of winter."   5
And the camels galled, sore-footed, refractory,
Lying down in the melting snow.
There were times we regretted
The summer palaces on slopes, the terraces,
And the silken girls bringing sherbet.   10
Then the camel men cursing and grumbling
And running away, and wanting their liquor and women,
And the night-fires going out, and the lack of shelters,
And the cities hostile and the towns unfriendly
And the villages dirty and charging high prices: 15
A hard time we had of it.
At the end we preferred to travel all night,
Sleeping in snatches,
With the voices singing in our ears, saying
That this was all folly.   20

Then at dawn we came down to a temperate valley,
Wet, below the snow line, smelling of vegetation;
With a running stream and a water-mill beating the darkness,
And three trees on the low sky,

And an old white horse galloped away in the meadow.   25
Then we came to a tavern with vine-leaves over the lintel,
Six hands at an open door dicing for pieces of silver,
And feet kicking the empty wine-skins.
But there was no information, and so we continued
And arrived at evening, not a moment too soon   30
Finding the place; it was (you may say) satisfactory.

All this was a long time ago, I remember,
And I would do it again, but set down
This set down
This: were we led all that way for   35
Birth or Death? There was a Birth, certainly,
We had evidence and no doubt. I had seen birth and death,
But had thought they were different; this Birth was
Hard and bitter agony for us, like Death, our death.
We returned to our places, these Kingdoms,   40
But no longer at ease here, in the old dispensation,
With an alien people clutching their gods.
I should be glad of another death.

JOURNEY OF THE MAGI. The story of the Magi, the three wise men who traveled to Bethlehem to be-hold the baby Jesus, is told in Matthew 2:1–12. That the three were kings is a later tradition. 1–5 *A cold coming . . . winter:* Eliot quotes with slight changes from a sermon preached on Christmas Day, 1622, by Bishop Lancelot Andrewes. 24 *three trees:* foreshadowing the three crosses on Calvary (see Luke 23:32–33). 25 *white horse:* perhaps the steed that carried the conquering Christ in the vision of St. John the Divine (Revelation 19:11–16). 41 *old dispensation:* older, pagan religion about to be dis-placed by Christianity.

COMPARE

"Journey of the Magi" with "The Magi" by William Butler Yeats (page 572).

T. S. Eliot

T. S. Eliot   (1888–1965)*

THE LOVE SONG OF J. ALFRED PRUFROCK   1917

> *S'io credessi che mia risposta fosse*
> *A persona che mai tornasse al mondo,*
> *Questa fiamma staria senza piu scosse.*
> *Ma perciocche giammai di questo fondo*
> *Non tornò vivo alcun, s'i'odo il vero,*
> *Senza tema d'infamia ti rispondo.*

Let us go then, you and I,
When the evening is spread out against the sky
Like a patient etherized upon a table;
Let us go, through certain half-deserted streets,
The muttering retreats   5
Of restless nights in one-night cheap hotels
And sawdust restaurants with oyster-shells:
Streets that follow like a tedious argument
Of insidious intent
To lead you to an overwhelming question . . .   10
Oh, do not ask, "What is it?"
Let us go and make our visit.

    In the room the women come and go
Talking of Michelangelo.

    The yellow fog that rubs its back upon the window-panes,   15
The yellow smoke that rubs its muzzle on the window-panes,
Licked its tongue into the corners of the evening,
Lingered upon the pools that stand in drains,
Let fall upon its back the soot that falls from chimneys,
Slipped by the terrace, made a sudden leap,   20

And seeing that it was a soft October night,
Curled once about the house, and fell asleep.

And indeed there will be time
For the yellow smoke that slides along the street
Rubbing its back upon the window-panes;   25
There will be time, there will be time
To prepare a face to meet the faces that you meet;
There will be time to murder and create,
And time for all the works and days of hands
That lift and drop a question on your plate;   30
Time for you and time for me,
And time yet for a hundred indecisions,
And for a hundred visions and revisions,
Before the taking of a toast and tea.

                                                                                35
In the room the women come and go
Talking of Michelangelo.

And indeed there will be time
To wonder, "Do I dare?" and, "Do I dare?"
Time to turn back and descend the stair,
With a bald spot in the middle of my hair—   40
(They will say: "How his hair is growing thin!")
My morning coat, my collar mounting firmly to the chin,
My necktie rich and modest, but asserted by a simple pin—
(They will say: "But how his arms and legs are thin!")
Do I dare   45
Disturb the universe?
In a minute there is time
For decisions and revisions which a minute will reverse.

For I have known them all already, known them all—
Have known the evenings, mornings, afternoons,   50
I have measured out my life with coffee spoons;
I know the voices dying with a dying fall
Beneath the music from a farther room.
So how should I presume?

                                                                                55
And I have known the eyes already, known them all—
The eyes that fix you in a formulated phrase,
And when I am formulated, sprawling on a pin,
When I am pinned and wriggling on the wall,
Then how should I begin
To spit out all the butt-ends of my days and ways?   60
And how should I presume?

And I have known the arms already, known them all—
Arms that are braceleted and white and bare

(But in the lamplight, downed with light brown hair!)
Is it perfume from a dress   65
That makes me so digress?
Arms that lie along a table, or wrap about a shawl.
    And should I then presume?
    And how should I begin?

                            . . . . .

Shall I say, I have gone at dusk through narrow streets   70
And watched the smoke that rises from the pipes
Of lonely men in shirt-sleeves, leaning out of windows? . . .

    I should have been a pair of ragged claws
Scuttling across the floors of silent seas.

                            . . . . .

And the afternoon, the evening, sleeps so peacefully!   75
Smoothed by long fingers,
Asleep . . . tired . . . or it malingers,
Stretched on the floor, here beside you and me.
Should I, after tea and cakes and ices,
Have the strength to force the moment to its crisis?   80
But though I have wept and fasted, wept and prayed,
Though I have seen my head (grown slightly bald) brought in upon a
        platter,
I am no prophet—and here's no great matter;
I have seen the moment of my greatness flicker,
And I have seen the eternal Footman hold my coat, and snicker,   85
And in short, I was afraid.

    And would it have been worth it, after all,
After the cups, the marmalade, the tea,
Among the porcelain, among some talk of you and me,
Would it have been worth while,   90
To have bitten off the matter with a smile,
To have squeezed the universe into a ball
To roll it towards some overwhelming question,
To say: "I am Lazarus, come from the dead,
Come back to tell you all, I shall tell you all"—   95
If one, settling a pillow by her head,
    Should say: "That is not what I meant at all.
    That is not it, at all."

    And would it have been worth it, after all,
Would it have been worth while,   100
After the sunsets and the dooryards and the sprinkled streets,
After the novels, after the teacups, after the skirts that trail along the
        floor—
And this, and so much more?—

It is impossible to say just what I mean!
But as if a magic lantern threw the nerves in patterns on a screen: 105
Would it have been worth while
If one, settling a pillow or throwing off a shawl,
And turning toward the window, should say:
  "That is not it at all,
  That is not what I meant, at all."   110

     . . . . .

No! I am not Prince Hamlet, nor was meant to be;
Am an attendant lord, one that will do
To swell a progress, start a scene or two,
Advise the prince; no doubt, an easy tool,
Deferential, glad to be of use,   115
Politic, cautious, and meticulous;
Full of high sentence, but a bit obtuse;
At times, indeed, almost ridiculous—
Almost, at times, the Fool.

  I grow old . . . I grow old . . .   120
I shall wear the bottoms of my trousers rolled.

  Shall I part my hair behind? Do I dare to eat a peach?
I shall wear white flannel trousers, and walk upon the beach.
I have heard the mermaids singing, each to each.

  I do not think that they will sing to me.   125

  I have seen them riding seaward on the waves
Combing the white hair of the waves blown back
When the wind blows the water white and black.

  We have lingered in the chambers of the sea
By sea-girls wreathed with seaweed red and brown   130
Till human voices wake us, and we drown.

The Love Song of J. Alfred Prufrock. The epigraph, from Dante's *Inferno*, is the speech of one dead and damned, who thinks that his hearer also is going to remain in Hell. Count Guido da Montefeltro, whose sin has been to give false counsel after a corrupt prelate had offered him prior absolution and whose punishment is to be wrapped in a constantly burning flame, offers to tell Dante his story: "If I thought my reply were to someone who could ever return to the world, this flame would waver no more. But since, I'm told, nobody ever escapes from this pit, I'll tell you without fear of ill fame." 29 *works and days*: title of a poem by Hesiod (eighth century B.C.), depicting his life as a hard-working Greek farmer and exhorting his brother to be like him. 82 *head . . . platter*: like that of John the Baptist, prophet and praiser of chastity, whom King Herod beheaded at the demand of Herodias, his unlawfully wedded wife (see Mark 6:17–28). 92–93 *squeezed . . . To roll it*: an echo from Marvell's "To His Coy Mistress," lines 41–42. 94 *Lazarus*: probably the Lazarus whom Jesus called forth from the tomb (John 11:1–44), but possibly the beggar seen in Heaven by the rich man in Hell (Luke 16:19–25).

Compare

"The Love Song of J. Alfred Prufrock" with "Acquainted with the Night" by Robert Frost (page 223).

Louise Erdrich

Louise Erdrich (b. 1954)

INDIAN BOARDING SCHOOL: THE RUNAWAYS   1984

Home's the place we head for in our sleep.
Boxcars stumbling north in dreams
don't wait for us. We catch them on the run.
The rails, old lacerations that we love,
shoot parallel across the face and break   5
just under Turtle Mountains. Riding scars
you can't get lost. Home is the place they cross.

The lame guard strikes a match and makes the dark
less tolerant. We watch through cracks in boards
as the land starts rolling, rolling till it hurts   10
to be here, cold in regulation clothes.
We know the sheriff's waiting at midrun
to take us back. His car is dumb and warm.
The highway doesn't rock, it only hums
like a wing of long insults. The worn-down welts   15
of ancient punishments lead back and forth.

All runaways wear dresses, long green ones,
the color you would think shame was. We scrub
the sidewalks down because it's shameful work.
Our brushes cut the stone in watered arcs   20
and in the soak frail outlines shiver clear
a moment, things us kids pressed on the dark
face before it hardened, pale, remembering
delicate old injuries, the spines of names and leaves.

INDIAN BOARDING SCHOOL: THE RUNAWAYS. 6. *Turtle Mountains:* in North Dakota and Manitoba.
The poet, of German and Native American descent, belongs to the Turtle Mountain Band of the
Chippewa.

COMPARE

"Indian Boarding School: The Runaways" with "For the White Poets Who Would Be Indian" by Wendy Rose (page 315).

B. H. Fairchild   (b. 1945)

A Starlit Night   2002

All over America at this hour men are standing
by an open closet door, slacks slung over one arm,
staring at wire hangers, thinking of taxes
or a broken faucet or their first sex: the smell
of back-seat Naugahyde, the hush of a maize field   5
like breathing, the stars rushing, rushing away.

And a woman lies in an unmade bed watching
the man she has known twenty-one, no,
could it be? twenty-two years, and she is listening
to the polonaise climbing up through radio static   10
from the kitchen where dishes are piled
and the linoleum floor is a great, gray sea.

It's the A-flat polonaise she practiced endlessly,
never quite getting it right, though her father,
calling from the darkened TV room, always said,   15
"Beautiful, kiddo!" and the moon would slide across
the lacquered piano top as if it were something
that lived underwater, something from far below.

They both came from houses with photographs,
the smell of camphor in closets, board games   20
with missing pieces, sunburst clocks in the kitchen
that made them, each morning, a little sad.
They didn't know what they wanted, every night,
every starlit night of their lives, and now they have it.

COMPARE

"A Starlit Night" with Wallace Stevens's "Disillusionment of Ten O'Clock" (page 84).

Robert Frost   (1874–1963)*

BIRCHES   1916

When I see birches bend to left and right
Across the lines of straighter darker trees,
I like to think some boy's been swinging them.
But swinging doesn't bend them down to stay
As ice storms do. Often you must have seen them   5
Loaded with ice a sunny winter morning
After a rain. They click upon themselves
As the breeze rises, and turn many-colored
As the stir cracks and crazes their enamel.
Soon the sun's warmth makes them shed crystal shells   10
Shattering and avalanching on the snow crust—
Such heaps of broken glass to sweep away
You'd think the inner dome of heaven had fallen.
They are dragged to the withered bracken by the load,
And they seem not to break; though once they are bowed   15
So low for long, they never right themselves:
You may see their trunks arching in the woods
Years afterwards, trailing their leaves on the ground
Like girls on hands and knees that throw their hair
Before them over their heads to dry in the sun.   20
But I was going to say when Truth broke in
With all her matter of fact about the ice storm
I should prefer to have some boy bend them
As he went out and in to fetch the cows—
Some boy too far from town to learn baseball,   25
Whose only play was what he found himself,
Summer or winter, and could play alone.
One by one he subdued his father's trees
By riding them down over and over again
Until he took the stiffness out of them,   30
And not one but hung limp, not one was left
For him to conquer. He learned all there was
To learn about not launching out too soon
And so not carrying the tree away
Clear to the ground. He always kept his poise   35
To the top branches, climbing carefully
With the same pains you use to fill a cup
Up to the brim, and even above the brim.
Then he flung outward, feet first, with a swish,
Kicking his way down through the air to the ground.   40
So was I once myself a swinger of birches.

And so I dream of going back to be.
It's when I'm weary of considerations,
And life is too much like a pathless wood
Where your face burns and tickles with the cobwebs   45
Broken across it, and one eye is weeping
From a twig's having lashed across it open.
I'd like to get away from earth awhile
And then come back to it and begin over.
May no fate willfully misunderstand me   50
And half grant what I wish and snatch me away
Not to return. Earth's the right place for love:
I don't know where it's likely to go better.
I'd like to go by climbing a birch tree,
And climb black branches up a snow-white trunk   55
Toward heaven, till the tree could bear no more,
But dipped its top and set me down again.
That would be good both going and coming back.
One could do worse than be a swinger of birches.

COMPARE

"Birches" with "Sailing to Byzantium" by William Butler Yeats (page 379).

Robert Frost   (1874–1963)*

MENDING WALL   1914

Something there is that doesn't love a wall,
That sends the frozen-ground-swell under it,
And spills the upper boulders in the sun;
And makes gaps even two can pass abreast.
The work of hunters is another thing: 5
I have come after them and made repair
Where they have left not one stone on a stone,
But they would have the rabbit out of hiding,
To please the yelping dogs. The gaps I mean,
No one has seen them made or heard them made,   10
But at spring mending-time we find them there.
I let my neighbor know beyond the hill;
And on a day we meet to walk the line
And set the wall between us once again.
We keep the wall between us as we go.   15
To each the boulders that have fallen to each.
And some are loaves and some so nearly balls
We have to use a spell to make them balance:

"Stay where you are until our backs are turned!"
We wear our fingers rough with handling them.   20
Oh, just another kind of outdoor game,
One on a side. It comes to little more:
There where it is we do not need the wall:
He is all pine and I am apple orchard.
My apple trees will never get across   25
And eat the cones under his pines, I tell him.
He only says, "Good fences make good neighbors."
Spring is the mischief in me, and I wonder
If I could put a notion in his head:
"*Why* do they make good neighbors? Isn't it   30
Where there are cows? But here there are no cows.
Before I built a wall I'd ask to know
What I was walling in or walling out,
And to whom I was like to give offence.
Something there is that doesn't love a wall,   35
That wants it down." I could say "Elves" to him,
But it's not elves exactly, and I'd rather
He said it for himself. I see him there
Bringing a stone grasped firmly by the top
In each hand, like an old-stone savage armed.   40
He moves in darkness as it seems to me,
Not of woods only and the shade of trees.
He will not go behind his father's saying,
And he likes having thought of it so well
He says again, "Good fences make good neighbors."   45

COMPARE

"Mending Wall" with "Digging" by Seamus Heaney (page 490).

Robert Frost   (1874–1963)*

STOPPING BY WOODS ON A   1923
SNOWY EVENING

Whose woods these are I think I know.
His house is in the village though;
He will not see me stopping here
To watch his woods fill up with snow.

My little horse must think it queer   5
To stop without a farmhouse near
Between the woods and frozen lake
The darkest evening of the year.

He gives his harness bells a shake
To ask if there is some mistake.   10
The only other sound's the sweep
Of easy wind and downy flake.

The woods are lovely, dark and deep,
But I have promises to keep,
And miles to go before I sleep,   15
And miles to go before I sleep.

COMPARE

"Stopping by Woods on a Snowy Evening" with "Desert Places" by Robert Frost (page 180).

Allen Ginsberg   (1926–1997)

A SUPERMARKET IN CALIFORNIA   1956

What thoughts I have of you tonight, Walt Whitman, for I walked
down the sidestreets under the trees with a headache self-conscious
looking at the full moon.

In my hungry fatigue, and shopping for images, I went into the neon
fruit supermarket, dreaming of your enumerations!

What peaches and what penumbras! Whole families shopping at
night! Aisles full of husbands! Wives in the avocados, babies in the
tomatoes!—and you, García Lorca, what were you doing down by the
watermelons?

I saw you, Walt Whitman, childless, lonely old grubber, poking
among the meats in the refrigerator and eyeing the grocery boys.

I heard you asking questions of each: Who killed the pork chops?   5
What price bananas? Are you my Angel?

I wandered in and out of the brilliant stacks of cans following you,
and followed in my imagination by the store detective.

We strode down the open corridors together in our solitary fancy
tasting artichokes, possessing every frozen delicacy, and never passing
the cashier.

Where are we going, Walt Whitman? The doors close in an hour.
Which way does your beard point tonight?

(I touch your book and dream of our odyssey in the supermarket and
feel absurd.)

Will we walk all night through solitary streets? The trees add shade   10
to shade, lights out in the houses, we'll both be lonely.

Will we stroll dreaming of the lost America of love past blue automobiles in driveways, home to our silent cottage?

Ah, dear father, graybeard, lonely old courage-teacher, what
America did you have when Charon quit poling his ferry and you got
out on a smoking bank and stood watching the boat disappear on the
black waters of Lethe?

A SUPERMARKET IN CALIFORNIA. *2 enumerations:* many of Whitman's poems contain lists of observed
details. *3 García Lorca:* modern Spanish poet who wrote an "Ode to Walt Whitman" in his book-
length sequence *Poet in New York. 12 Charon . . . Lethe:* Is the poet confusing two underworld rivers?
Charon, in Greek and Roman mythology, is the boatman who ferries the souls of the dead across the
River Styx. The River Lethe also flows through Hades, and a drink of its waters makes the dead lose
their painful memories of loved ones they have left behind.

COMPARE

"A Supermarket in California" with Walt Whitman's "To a Locomotive in Winter"
(page 24).

Dana Gioia   (b. 1950)

CALIFORNIA HILLS IN AUGUST   1982

I can imagine someone who found
these fields unbearable, who climbed
the hillside in the heat, cursing the dust,
cracking the brittle weeds underfoot,
wishing a few more trees for shade.   5

An Easterner especially, who would scorn
the meagerness of summer, the dry
twisted shapes of black elm,
scrub oak, and chaparral—a landscape
August has already drained of green.   10

One who would hurry over the clinging
thistle, foxtail, golden poppy,
knowing everything was just a weed,
unable to conceive that these trees
and sparse brown bushes were alive.   15

And hate the bright stillness of the noon,
without wind, without motion,
the only other living thing
a hawk, hungry for prey, suspended
in the blinding, sunlit blue.   20

And yet how gentle it seems to someone
raised in a landscape short of rain—

the skyline of a hill broken by no more
trees than one can count, the grass,
the empty sky, the wish for water.   25

COMPARE

"California Hills in August" with "To see a world in a grain of sand" by William Blake
(page 124).

Thom Gunn   (b. 1929)

THE MAN WITH NIGHT SWEATS   1992

I wake up cold, I who
Prospered through dreams of heat
Wake to their residue,
Sweat, and a clinging sheet.

My flesh was its own shield: 5
Where it was gashed, it healed.

I grew as I explored
The body I could trust
Even while I adored
The risk that made robust,   10

A world of wonders in
Each challenge to the skin.

I cannot but be sorry
The given shield was cracked,
My mind reduced to hurry,   15
My flesh reduced and wrecked.

I have to change the bed,
But catch myself instead

Stopped upright where I am
Hugging my body to me   20
As if to shield it from
The pains that will go through me,

As if hands were enough
To hold an avalanche off.

COMPARE

"The Man with Night Sweats" with "When I have fears that I may cease to be" by John
Keats (page 504).

Donald Hall   (b. 1928)

NAMES OF HORSES   1978

All winter your brute shoulders strained against collars, padding
and steerhide over the ash hames, to haul
sledges of cordwood for drying through spring and summer,
for the Glenwood stove next winter, and for the simmering range.

In April you pulled cartloads of manure to spread on the fields,   5
dark manure of Holsteins, and knobs of your own clustered with oats.
All summer you mowed the grass in meadow and hayfield, the mowing
    machine
clacketing beside you, while the sun walked high in the morning;

and after noon's heat, you pulled a clawed rake through the same acres,
gathering stacks, and dragged the wagon from stack to stack,   10
and the built hayrack back, uphill to the chaffy barn,
three loads of hay a day from standing grass in the morning.

Sundays you trotted the two miles to church with the light load
of a leather quartertop buggy, and grazed in the sound of hymns.
Generation on generation, your neck rubbed the windowsill   15
of the stall, smoothing the wood as the sea smooths glass.

When you were old and lame, when your shoulders hurt bending to
    graze,
one October the man, who fed you and kept you, and harnessed you
    every morning,
led you through corn stubble to sandy ground above Eagle Pond,
and dug a hole beside you where you stood shuddering in your skin,   20

and lay the shotgun's muzzle in the boneless hollow behind your ear,
and fired the slug into your brain, and felled you into your grave,
shoveling sand to cover you, setting goldenrod upright above you,
where by next summer a dent in the ground made your monument.

For a hundred and fifty years, in the pasture of dead horses,   25
roots of pine trees pushed through the pale curves of your ribs,
yellow blossoms flourished above you in autumn, and in winter
frost heaved your bones in the ground—old toilers, soil makers:

O Roger, Mackerel, Riley, Ned, Nellie, Chester, Lady Ghost.

COMPARE

"Names of Horses" with "The Bull Calf" by Irving Layton (page 508).

Thomas Hardy   (1840–1928)*

The Convergence of the Twain   1912

Lines on the Loss of the "Titanic"

I
In a solitude of the sea
Deep from human vanity,
And the Pride of Life that planned her, stilly couches she.

II
Steel chambers, late the pyres
Of her salamandrine fires,   5
Cold currents third,° and turn to rhythmic tidal lyres.   *thread*

III
Over the mirrors meant
To glass the opulent
The sea-worm crawls—grotesque, slimed, dumb, indifferent.

IV
Jewels in joy designed   10
To ravish the sensuous mind
Lie lightless, all their sparkles bleared and black and blind.

V
Dim moon-eyed fishes near
Gaze at the gilded gear
And query: "What does this vaingloriousness down here?" . . .   15

VI
Well: while was fashioning
This creature of cleaving wing,
The Immanent Will that stirs and urges everything

VII
Prepared a sinister mate
For her—so gaily great—   20
A Shape of Ice, for the time far and dissociate.

VIII
And as the smart ship grew
In stature, grace, and hue,
In shadowy silent distance grew the Iceberg too.

IX

Alien they seemed to be: 25
    No mortal eye could see
The intimate welding of their later history,

X

Or sign that they were bent
    By paths coincident
On being anon twin halves of one august event,   30

XI

Till the Spinner of the Years
    Said "Now!" And each one hears,
And consummation comes, and jars two hemispheres.

THE CONVERGENCE OF THE TWAIN. The luxury liner *Titanic*, supposedly unsinkable, went down in 1912 after striking an iceberg on its first Atlantic voyage. 5 *salamandrine:* like the salamander, a lizard that supposedly thrives in fires, or like a spirit of the same name that inhabits fire (according to alchemists).

COMPARE

"The Convergence of the Twain" with "Titanic" by David R. Slavitt (page 543).

Thomas Hardy

Thomas Hardy   (1840–1928)*

THE DARKLING THRUSH   1900

I leant upon a coppice gate
    When Frost was spectre-gray,
And Winter's dregs made desolate
    The weakening eye of day.

The tangled bine-stems scored the sky   5
    Like strings of broken lyres,
And all mankind that haunted nigh
    Had sought their household fires.

The land's sharp features seemed to be
    The Century's corpse outleant,   10
His crypt the cloudy canopy,
    The wind his death-lament.
The ancient pulse of germ and birth
    Was shrunken hard and dry,
And every spirit upon earth   15
    Seemed fervourless as I.

At once a voice arose among
    The bleak twigs overhead
In a full-hearted evensong
    Of joy illimited;   20
An aged thrush, frail, gaunt, and small,
    In blast-beruffled plume,
Had chosen thus to fling his soul
    Upon the growing gloom.

So little cause for carolings   25
    Of such ecstatic sound
Was written on terrestial things
    Afar or nigh around,
That I could think there trembled through
    His happy good-night air   30
Some blessed Hope, whereof he knew
    And I was unaware.

THE DARKLING THRUSH. Hardy set this poem on December 31, 1900, the last day of the nineteenth century.

COMPARE

"The Darkling Thrush" with "I Wandered Lonely as a Cloud" by William Wordsworth (page 31).

Thomas Hardy   (1840–1928)*

HAP   1866

If but some vengeful god would call to me
From up the sky, and laugh: "Thou suffering thing,
Know that thy sorrow is my ecstasy,
That thy love's loss is my hate's profiting!"

Then would I bear it, clench myself, and die,   5
Steeled by the sense of ire unmerited;
Half-eased in that a Powerfuller than I
Had willed and meted me the tears I shed.

But not so. How arrives it joy lies slain,
And why unblooms the best hope ever sown?   10
—Crass Casualty obstructs the sun and rain,
And dicing Time for gladness casts a moan . . .
These purblind Doomsters had as readily strown
Blisses about my pilgrimage as pain.

COMPARE

"Hap" with the Roman poet Horace's *carpe diem* ode on pages 333–34. Choose any of the three translations there of Horace's work or use the literal translation provided below the Latin original.

Robert Hayden

Robert Hayden   (1913–1980)*

THOSE WINTER SUNDAYS   1962

Sundays too my father got up early
and put his clothes on in the blueblack cold,
then with cracked hands that ached
from labor in the weekday weather made
banked fires blaze. No one ever thanked him.   5

I'd wake and hear the cold splintering, breaking.
When the rooms were warm, he'd call,
and slowly I would rise and dress,
fearing the chronic angers of that house,

Speaking indifferently to him,   10
who had driven out the cold
and polished my good shoes as well.
What did I know, what did I know
of love's austere and lonely offices?

COMPARE

"Those Winter Sundays" with "Daddy" by Sylvia Plath (page 526).

Seamus Heaney   (b. 1939)*

DIGGING   1966

Between my finger and my thumb
The squat pen rests; snug as a gun.

Under my window, a clean rasping sound
When the spade sinks into gravelly ground.
My father, digging. I look down   5

Till his straining rump among the flowerbeds
Bends low, comes up twenty years away
Stooping in rhythm through potato drills
Where he was digging.

The coarse boot nestled on the lug, the shaft   10
Against the inside knee was levered firmly.
He rooted out tall tops, buried the bright edge deep
To scatter new potatoes that we picked
Loving their cool hardness in our hands.

By God, the old man could handle a spade.   15
Just like his old man.

My grandfather cut more turf in a day
Than any other man on Toner's bog.
Once I carried him milk in a bottle
Corked sloppily with paper. He straightened up   20
To drink it, then fell to right away

Nicking and slicing neatly, heaving sods
Over his shoulder, going down and down
For the good turf. Digging.

The cold smell of potato mould, the squelch and slap   25
Of soggy peat, the curt cuts of an edge
Through living roots awaken in my head.
But I've no spade to follow men like them.

Between my finger and my thumb
The squat pen rests.   30
I'll dig with it.

COMPARE

"Digging" with "The Writer" by Richard Wilbur (page 564).

Seamus Heaney   (b. 1939)*

MOTHER OF THE GROOM   1972

What she remembers
Is his glistening back
In the bath, his small boots
In the ring of boots at her feet.

Hands in her voided lap,   5
She hears a daughter welcomed.
It's as if he kicked when lifted
And slipped her soapy hold.

Once soap would ease off
The wedding ring   10
That's bedded forever now
In her clapping hand.

COMPARE

"Mother of the Groom" with "Most Like an Arch This Marriage" by John Ciardi (page 265) and "The River Merchant's Wife: a Letter" by Ezra Pound (page 530).

Anthony Hecht

Anthony Hecht   (b. 1923)

ADAM   1967

Hath the rain a father? or who hath begotten the drops of dew?

"Adam, my child, my son,
These very words you hear
Compose the fish and starlight
Of your untroubled dream.
When you awake, my child,   5
It shall all come true.
Know that it was for you
That all things were begun."

Adam, my child, my son,
Thus spoke Our Father in heaven   10
To his first, fabled child,
The father of us all.
And I, your father, tell
The words over again
As innumerable men   15
From ancient times have done.

Tell them again in pain,
And to the empty air.
Where you are men speak
A different mother tongue.   20
Will you forget our games,
Our hide-and-seek and song?
Child, it will be long
Before I see you again.

Adam, there will be
Many hard hours,
As an old poem says,
Hours of loneliness.
I cannot ease them for you;
They are our common lot.
During them, like as not,
You will dream of me.

When you are crouched away
In a strange clothes closet
Hiding from one who's "It"
And the dark crowds in,
Do not be afraid—
O, if you can, believe
In a father's love
That you shall know some day.

Think of the summer rain
Or seedpearls of the mist;
Seeing the beaded leaf,
Try to remember me.
From far away
I send my blessing out
To circle the great globe.
It shall reach you yet.

25

30

35

40

45

ADAM. According to Genesis 2:6–7, God created Adam, the first man, from the dust of the earth; Adam is also the name of Anthony Hecht's first son. *Epigraph: "Hath the rain a father . . . ?":* These words are spoken to Job by the voice of God in Job 38:28.

COMPARE

"Adam" with "Imperial Adam" by A. D. Hope (page 293).

George Herbert

George Herbert   (1593–1633)*

LOVE   1633

Love bade me welcome; yet my soul drew back,
       Guilty of dust and sin.
But quick-eyed Love, observing me grow slack
       From my first entrance in,
Drew nearer to me, sweetly questioning   5
       If I lacked anything.

"A guest," I answered, "worthy to be here";
       Love said, "You shall be he."
"I, the unkind, ungrateful? Ah, my dear,
       I cannot look on Thee."   10
Love took my hand, and smiling did reply,
       "Who made the eyes but I?"

"Truth, Lord, but I have marred them; let my shame
       Go where it doth deserve."
"And know you not," says Love, "who bore the blame?"   15
       "My dear, then I will serve."
"You must sit down," says Love, "and taste My meat."
       So I did sit and eat.

COMPARE

"Love" with "Batter my heart, three-personed God" by John Donne (page 57).

Robert Herrick (1591–1674)*

TO THE VIRGINS, TO MAKE MUCH OF TIME   1648

Gather ye rose-buds while ye may,
    Old Time is still a-flying;
And this same flower that smiles today,
    Tomorrow will be dying.

The glorious lamp of heaven, the sun,   5
    The higher he's a-getting,
The sooner will his race be run,
    And nearer he's to setting.

That age is best which is the first,
    When youth and blood are warmer;   10
But being spent, the worse, and worst
    Times still succeed the former.

Then be not coy, but use your time,
    And while ye may, go marry;
For having lost but once your prime,   15
    You may for ever tarry.

COMPARE

"To the Virgins, to Make Much of Time" with "To His Coy Mistress" by Andrew Marvell
(page 512) and "Go, Lovely Rose" by Edmund Waller (page 562).

Gerard Manley Hopkins   (1844–1889)*

SPRING AND FALL   (1880)

To a young child

Márgarét, áre you gríeving
Over Goldengrove unleaving°   shedding its leaves
Leáves, líke the things of man, you
With your fresh thoughts care for, can you?
Áh! ás the heart grows older   5
It will come to such sights colder
By and by, nor spare a sigh
Though worlds of wanwood leafmeal lie;
And yet you *will* weep and know why.
Now no matter, child, the name: 10
Sórrow's spríngs áre the same.
Nor mouth had, no nor mind, expressed
What heart heard of, ghost° guessed: spirit

It ís the blight man was born for,
It is Margaret you mourn for.   15

COMPARE

"Spring and Fall" with "Aftermath" by Henry Wadsworth Longfellow (page 59).

Gerard Manley Hopkins

Gerard Manley Hopkins   (1844–1889)*

NO WORST, THERE IS NONE   (1884–1885)

No worst, there is none. Pitched past pitch of grief,
More pangs will, schooled at forepangs, wilder wring.
Comforter, where, where is your comforting?
Mary, mother of us, where is your relief?
My cries heave, herds-long; huddle in a main, a chief-   5
woe, world-sorrow; on an age-old anvil wince and sing—
Then lull, then leave off. Fury had shrieked "No ling-
ering! Let me be fell: force I must be brief."
O the mind, mind has mountains; cliffs of fall
Frightful, sheer, no-man-fathomed. Hold them cheap   10
May who ne'er hung there. Nor does long our small
Durance deal with that steep or deep. Here! creep,
Wretch, under a comfort serves in a whirlwind: all
Life death does end and each day dies with sleep.

COMPARE

"No worst, there is none" with "Hap" by Thomas Hardy (page 488).

Gerard Manley Hopkins   (1844–1889)*

THE WINDHOVER   (1877)

To Christ Our Lord

I caught this morning morning's minion, king-
   dom of daylight's dauphin, dapple-dawn-drawn Falcon, in his riding
   Of the rolling level underneath him steady air, and striding
High there, how he rung upon the rein of a wimpling wing
In his ecstasy! then off, off forth on swing,   5
   As a skate's heel sweeps smooth on a bow-bend: the hurl and gliding
   Rebuffed the big wind. My heart in hiding
Stirred for a bird, —the achieve of, the mastery of the thing!

Brute beauty and valor and act, oh, air, pride, plume, here
   Buckle! AND the fire that breaks from thee then, a billion   10
Times told lovelier, more dangerous, O my chevalier!

   No wonder of it: shéer plód makes plow down sillion°   *furrow*
Shine, and blue-bleak embers, ah my dear,
   Fall, gall themselves, and gash gold-vermilion.

THE WINDHOVER. A windhover is a kestrel, or small falcon, so called because it can hover upon the wind. 4 *rung . . . wing:* A horse is "rung upon the rein" when its trainer holds the end of a long rein and has the horse circle him. The possible meanings of *wimpling* include: (1) curving; (2) pleated, arranged in many little folds one on top of another; (3) rippling or undulating like the surface of a flowing stream.

COMPARE

"The Windhover" with "Batter my heart, three-personed God" by John Donne (page 57) and "Easter Wings" by George Herbert (page 249).

A. E. Housman   (1859–1936)*

LOVELIEST OF TREES, THE CHERRY NOW   1896

Loveliest of trees, the cherry now
Is hung with bloom along the bough,
And stands about the woodland ride°   *path*
Wearing white for Eastertide.

Now, of my threescore years and ten,   5
Twenty will not come again,
And take from seventy springs a score,
It only leaves me fifty more.

And since to look at things in bloom
Fifty springs are little room,
About the woodlands I will go
To see the cherry hung with snow.

10

COMPARE

"Loveliest of trees, the cherry now" with "To the Virgins, to Make Much of Time" by
Robert Herrick (page 495) and "Spring and Fall" by Gerard Manley Hopkins (page 495).

A. E. Housman (1859–1936)*

TO AN ATHLETE DYING YOUNG   1896

The time you won your town the race
We chaired you through the market-place;
Man and boy stood cheering by,
And home we brought you shoulder-high.

Today, the road all runners come,   5
Shoulder-high we bring you home,
And set you at your threshold down,
Townsman of a stiller town.

Smart lad, to slip betimes away
From fields where glory does not stay,   10
And early though the laurel grows
It withers quicker than the rose.

Eyes the shady night has shut
Cannot see the record cut,
And silence sounds no worse than cheers   15
After earth has stopped the ears.

Now you will not swell the rout
Of lads that wore their honors out,
Runners whom renown outran
And the name died before the man.   20

So set, before its echoes fade,
The fleet foot on the sill of shade,
And hold to the low lintel up
The still-defended challenge-cup.

And round that early-laureled head   25
Will flock to gaze the strengthless dead,
And find unwithered on its curls
The garland briefer than a girl's.

COMPARE

"To an Athlete Dying Young" with "Ex-Basketball Player" by John Updike (page 557).

Randall Jarrell

Randall Jarrell   (1914–1965)

THE DEATH OF THE BALL TURRET GUNNER   1945

From my mother's sleep I fell into the State
And I hunched in its belly till my wet fur froze.
Six miles from earth, loosed from its dream of life,
I woke to black flak and the nightmare fighters.
When I died they washed me out of the turret with a hose.

THE DEATH OF THE BALL TURRET GUNNER. Jarrell has written: "A ball turret was a plexiglass sphere set into the belly of a B-17 or B-24, and inhabited by two .50 caliber machine-guns and one man, a short small man. When this gunner tracked with his machine-guns a fighter attacking his bomber from below, he revolved with the turret; hunched in his little sphere, he looked like the fetus in the womb. The fighters which attacked him were armed with cannon firing explosive shells. The hose was a steam hose."

COMPARE

"The Death of the Ball Turret Gunner" with "Dulce et Decorum Est" by Wilfred Owen (page 46).

Robinson Jeffers   (1887–1962)*

To the Stone-cutters   1925

Stone-cutters fighting time with marble, you foredefeated
Challengers of oblivion
Eat cynical earnings, knowing rock splits, records fall down,
The square-limbed Roman letters
Scale in the thaws, wear in the rain. The poet as well   5
Builds his monument mockingly;
For man will be blotted out, the blithe earth die, the brave sun
Die blind, his heart blackening:
Yet stones have stood for a thousand years, and pained thoughts found
The honey peace in old poems.   10

Compare

"To the Stone-cutters" with "Not marble nor the gilded monuments" by William
Shakespeare (page 541).

Ben Jonson   (1573?–1637)*

On My First Son   (1603)

Farewell, thou child of my right hand, and joy.
My sin was too much hope of thee, loved boy;
Seven years thou wert lent to me, and I thee pay,
Exacted by thy fate, on the just day.
Oh, could I lose all father° now. For why   *fatherhood*   5
Will man lament the state he should envỳ—
To have so soon 'scaped world's and flesh's rage,
And, if no other misery, yet age.
Rest in soft peace, and asked, say, "Here doth lie
Ben Jonson his best piece of poetry,"   10
For whose sake henceforth all his vows be such
As what he loves may never like° too much.   *thrive*

On My First Son. 1 *child of my right hand:* Jonson's son was named Benjamin; this phrase translates
the Hebrew name. 4 *the just day:* the very day. The boy had died on his seventh birthday. 10 *poetry:*
Jonson uses the word *poetry* here reflecting its Greek root *poiesis,* which means *creation.*

Compare

"On My First Son" with " 'Out, Out—' " by Robert Frost (page 14).

Donald Justice   (b. 1925)*

COUNTING THE MAD   1960

This one was put in a jacket,
This one was sent home,
This one was given bread and meat
But would eat none,
And this one cried No No No No   5
All day long.

This one looked at the window
As though it were a wall,
This one saw things that were not there,
This one things that were,   10
And this one cried No No No No
All day long.

This one thought himself a bird,
This one a dog,
And this one thought himself a man,   15
An ordinary man,
And cried and cried No No No No
All day long.

COMPARE

"Counting the Mad" with "Embrace" by Billy Collins (page 109) and "Not Waving but Drowning" by Stevie Smith (page 110).

John Keats   (1795–1821)*

ODE ON A GRECIAN URN   1820

Thou still unravished bride of quietness,
    Thou foster-child of silence and slow time,
Sylvan historian, who canst thus express
    A flowery tale more sweetly than our rhyme:
What leaf-fringed legend haunts about thy shape   5
    Of deities or mortals, or of both,
        In Tempe or the dales of Arcady?
    What men or gods are these? What maidens loth?
What mad pursuit? What struggle to escape?
        What pipes and timbrels? What wild ecstasy?   10

Heard melodies are sweet, but those unheard
   Are sweeter; therefore, ye soft pipes, play on;
Not to the sensual° ear, but, more endeared,   *physical*
   Pipe to the spirit ditties of no tone:
Fair youth, beneath the trees, thou canst not leave   15
   Thy song, nor ever can those trees be bare;
      Bold Lover, never, never canst thou kiss,
Though winning near the goal—yet, do not grieve;
   She cannot fade, though thou hast not thy bliss,
   For ever wilt thou love, and she be fair!   20

Ah, happy, happy boughs! that cannot shed
   Your leaves, nor ever bid the Spring adieu;
And, happy melodist, unwearièd,
   For ever piping songs for ever new;
More happy love! more happy, happy love!   25
   For ever warm and still to be enjoyed,
      For ever panting, and for ever young;
All breathing human passion far above,
   That leaves a heart high-sorrowful and cloyed,
      A burning forehead, and a parching tongue.   30

Who are these coming to the sacrifice?
   To what green altar, O mysterious priest,
Lead'st thou that heifer lowing at the skies,
   And all her silken flanks with garlands drest?
What little town by river or sea shore,   35
   Or mountain-built with peaceful citadel,
      Is emptied of this folk, this pious morn?
And, little town, the streets for evermore
   Will silent be; and not a soul to tell
      Why thou art desolate, can e'er return.   40

O Attic shape! Fair attitude! with brede°   *design*
   Of marble men and maidens overwrought,
With forest branches and the trodden weed;
   Thou, silent form, dost tease us out of thought
As doth Eternity: Cold Pastoral!   45
   When old age shall this generation waste,
      Thou shalt remain, in midst of other woe
Than ours, a friend to man, to whom thou say'st,
Beauty is truth, truth beauty,—that is all
   Ye know on earth, and all ye need to know.   50

ODE ON A GRECIAN URN. *7 Tempe, dales of Arcady:* valleys in Greece. *41 Attic:* Athenian, possessing a classical simplicity and grace. *49–50:* if Keats had put the urn's words in quotation marks,
critics might have been spared much ink. Does the urn say just "beauty is truth, truth beauty," or does
its statement take in the whole of the last two lines?

COMPARE

"Ode on a Grecian Urn" with "Musée des Beaux Arts" by W. H. Auden (page 450).

John Keats (1795–1821)*

ON FIRST LOOKING INTO CHAPMAN'S HOMER

1816

Much have I traveled in the realms of gold,
    And many goodly states and kingdoms seen;
    Round many western islands have I been
Which bards in fealty to Apollo hold.
Oft of one wide expanse had I been told   5
    That deep-browed Homer ruled as his demesne,°   *domain*
    Yet did I never breathe its pure serene
Till I heard Chapman speak out loud and bold.
Then felt I like some watcher of the skies
    When a new planet swims into his ken;   10
Or like stout Cortez when with eagle eyes
    He stared at the Pacific—and all his men
Looked at each other with a wild surmise—
    Silent, upon a peak in Darien.

ON FIRST LOOKING INTO CHAPMAN'S HOMER. When one evening in October 1816 Keats's friend and former teacher Cowden Clarke introduced the young poet to George Chapman's vigorous Elizabethan translations of the *Iliad* and the *Odyssey*, Keats stayed up all night reading and discussing them in high excitement, then went home at dawn to compose this sonnet, which Clarke received at his breakfast table. 4 *fealty:* in feudalism, the loyalty of a vassal to his lord; *Apollo:* classical god of poetic inspiration. 11 *stout Cortez:* the best-known howler in English poetry. (What Spanish explorer *was* the first European to view the Pacific?) 14 *Darien:* old name for the Isthmus of Panama.

COMPARE

"On First Looking into Chapman's Homer" with "The Master" by Frederick Morgan (page 518) and "To the Stone-cutters" by Robinson Jeffers (page 500).

John Keats

John Keats   (1795–1821)*

WHEN I HAVE FEARS THAT I MAY CEASE TO BE   (1818)

When I have fears that I may cease to be
  Before my pen has gleaned my teeming brain,
Before high-pilèd books, in charact'ry,°   *written language*
  Hold like rich garners° the full-ripened grain;   *storehouses*
When I behold, upon the night's starred face,   5
  Huge cloudy symbols of a high romance,
And think that I may never live to trace
  Their shadows with the magic hand of chance;
And when I feel, fair creature of an hour,
  That I shall never look upon thee more,   10
Never have relish in the fairy° power   *supernatural*
  Of unreflecting love—then on the shore
Of the wide world I stand alone, and think
  Till love and fame to nothingness do sink.

WHEN I HAVE FEARS THAT I MAY CEASE TO BE.   12 *unreflecting:* thoughtless and spontaneous, rather
than deliberate.

COMPARE

"When I have fears that I may cease to be" with any of the three translations of Horace's
Carpe Diem ode (pages 334–35) or Philip Larkin's "Aubade" (page 323).

John Keats   (1795–1821)*

TO AUTUMN   1820

I

Season of mists and mellow fruitfulness,
  Close bosom-friend of the maturing sun;
Conspiring with him how to load and bless
  With fruit the vines that round the thatch-eaves run;
To bend with apples the mossed cottage-trees,   5
  And fill all fruit with ripeness to the core;
    To swell the gourd, and plump the hazel shells
  With a sweet kernel; to set budding more,
  And still more, later flowers for the bees,
  Until they think warm days will never cease,   10
    For Summer has o'er-brimmed their clammy cells.

II

Who hath not seen thee oft amid thy store?
  Sometimes whoever seeks abroad may find
Thee sitting careless on a granary floor,
  Thy hair soft-lifted by the winnowing wind;   15
Or on a half-reaped furrow sound asleep,
  Drowsed with the fume of poppies, while thy hook°   *sickle*
    Spares the next swath and all its twinèd flowers:
And sometimes like a gleaner thou dost keep
  Steady thy laden head across a brook;   20
  Or by a cider-press, with patient look,
    Thou watchest the last oozings hours by hours.

III

Where are the songs of Spring? Ay, where are they?
  Think not of them, thou hast thy music too,—
While barrèd clouds bloom the soft-dying day,   25
  And touch the stubble-plains with rosy hue;
Then in a wailful choir the small gnats mourn
  Among the river sallows,° borne aloft   *willows*
    Or sinking as the light wind lives or dies;
And full-grown lambs loud bleat from hilly bourn;   30
Hedge-crickets sing; and now with treble soft
The red-breast whistles from a garden-croft°   *garden plot*
  And gathering swallows twitter in the skies.

TO AUTUMN. 12 *thee:* Autumn personified. 15 *Thy hair . . . winnowing wind:* Autumn's hair is a billowing cloud of straw. In winnowing, whole blades of grain were laid on a granary floor and beaten with wooden flails, then the beaten mass was tossed in a blanket until the yellow straw (or *chaff*) drifted away on the air, leaving kernels of grain. 30 *bourn:* perhaps meaning a brook. In current English, the word is a cousin of burn, as in the first line of Gerard Manley Hopkins's "Inversnaid"; but in archaic English, which Keats sometimes liked to use, a *bourn* can also be a boundary, or a destination. What possible meaning makes most sense to you?

COMPARE

"To Autumn" with "Spring and Fall" by Gerard Manley Hopkins (page 495).

Philip Larkin

Philip Larkin   (1922–1985)*

HOME IS SO SAD   1964

Home is so sad. It stays as it was left,
Shaped to the comfort of the last to go
As if to win them back. Instead, bereft
Of anyone to please, it withers so,
Having no heart to put aside the theft   5

And turn again to what it started as,
A joyous shot at how things ought to be,
Long fallen wide. You can see how it was:
Look at the pictures and the cutlery.
The music in the piano stool. That vase.   10

COMPARE

"Home is so Sad" with "Dark house, by which once more I stand" by Alfred, Lord Tennyson (page 553) and "Piano" by D. H. Lawrence (page 10).

Philip Larkin (1922–1985)*

POETRY OF DEPARTURES 1955

Sometimes you hear, fifth-hand,
As epitaph:
He chucked up everything
And just cleared off,
And always the voice will sound   5
Certain you approve
This audacious, purifying,
Elemental move.

And they are right, I think.
We all hate home   10
And having to be there:
I detest my room,
Its specially-chosen junk,
The good books, the good bed,
And my life, in perfect order: 15
So to hear it said

He walked out on the whole crowd
Leaves me flushed and stirred,
Like *Then she undid her dress*
Or *Take that you bastard;*   20
Surely I can, if he did?
And that helps me stay
Sober and industrious.
But I'd go today,

Yes, swagger the nut-strewn roads,   25
Crouch in the fo'c'sle
Stubbly with goodness, if
It weren't so artificial,
Such a deliberate step backwards
To create an object: 30
Books; china; a life
Reprehensibly perfect.

COMPARE

"Poetry of Departures" with "I started Early – Took my Dog" by Emily Dickinson (page 406).

Irving Layton   (b. 1912)

THE BULL CALF   1959

The thing could barely stand. Yet taken
from his mother and the barn smells
he still impressed with his pride,
with the promise of sovereignty in the way
his head moved to take us in.   5
The fierce sunlight tugging the maize from the ground
licked at his shapely flanks.
He was too young for all that pride.
I thought of the deposed Richard II.

                                                                                10
"No money in bull calves," Freeman had said.
The visiting clergyman rubbed the nostrils
now snuffing pathetically at the windless day.
"A pity," he sighed.
My gaze slipped off his hat toward the empty sky
that circled over the black knot of men,   15
over us and the calf waiting for the first blow.

Struck,
the bull calf drew in his thin forelegs
as if gathering strength for a mad rush . . .
tottered . . . raised his darkening eyes to us,   20
and I saw we were at the far end
of his frightened look, growing smaller and smaller
till we were only the ponderous mallet
that flicked his bleeding ear
and pushed him over on his side, stiffly,   25
like a block of wood.

Below the hill's crest
the river snuffled on the improvised beach.
We dug a deep pit and threw the dead calf into it.
It made a wet sound, a sepulchral gurgle,   30
as the warm sides bulged and flattened.
Settled, the bull calf lay as if asleep,
one foreleg over the other,
bereft of pride and so beautiful now,
without movement, perfectly still in the cool pit,   35
I turned away and wept.

COMPARE

"The Bull Calf" with "Names of Horses" by Donald Hall (page 485).

Philip Levine   (b. 1928)

THEY FEED THEY LION   1972

Out of burlap sacks, out of bearing butter,
Out of black bean and wet slate bread,
Out of the acids of rage, the candor of tar,
Out of creosote, gasoline, drive shafts, wooden dollies,
They Lion grow.   5

　　　　　Out of the grey hills
Of industrial barns, out of rain, out of bus ride,
West Virginia to Kiss My Ass, out of buried aunties,
Mothers hardening like pounded stumps, out of stumps,
Out of the bones' need to sharpen and the muscles' to stretch,   10
They Lion grow.

　　　　　Earth is eating trees, fence posts,
Gutted cars, earth is calling her little ones,
"Come home, Come home!" From pig balls,
From the ferocity of pig driven to holiness,   15
From the furred ear and the full jowl come
The repose of the hung belly, from the purpose
They Lion grow.

　　　　　From the sweet glues of the trotters°   *cooked pigs feet*
Come the sweet kinks of the fist, from the full flower   20
Of the hams the thorax of caves,
From "Bow Down" come "Rise Up,"
Come they Lion from the reeds of shovels,
The grained arm that pulls the hands,
They Lion grow.   25

　　　　　From my five arms and all my hands,
From all my white sins forgiven, they feed,
From my car passing under the stars,
They Lion, from my children inherit,
From the oak turned to a wall, they Lion,   30
From they sack and they belly opened
And all that was hidden burning on the oil-stained earth
They feed they Lion and he comes.

COMPARE

"They Feed They Lion" with "Autumn Begins in Martins Ferry, Ohio" by James Wright
(page 569).

Adrian Louis (b. 1946)

LOOKING FOR JUDAS   1995

Weathered gray, the wooden walls
of the old barn soak in the bright
sparkling blood of the five-point mule
deer I hang there in the moonlight.
Gutted, skinned, and shimmering in eternal   5
nakedness, the glint in its eyes could
be stolen from the dry hills of Jerusalem.
They say before the white man
brought us Jesus, we had honor.
They say when we killed the Deer People,   10
we told them their spirits
would live in our flesh.
We used bows of ash, no spotlights, no rifles,
and their holy blood became ours.
Or something like that.   15

COMPARE

"Looking for Judas" with "The Negro Speaks of Rivers" (page 421) and "Song for a Dark Girl" (page 424) by Langston Hughes.

Robert Lowell (1917–1977)

SKUNK HOUR   1959

For Elizabeth Bishop

Nautilus Island's hermit
heiress still lives through winters in her Spartan cottage;
her sheep still graze above the sea.
Her son's a bishop. Her farmer
is first selectman in our village;   5
she's in her dotage.

Thirsting for
the hierarchic privacy
of Queen Victoria's century,
she buys up all   10
the eyesores facing her shore,
and lets them fall.

The season's ill—
we've lost our summer millionaire,
who seemed to leap from an L. L. Bean   15
catalogue. His nine-knot yawl
was auctioned off to lobstermen.
A red fox stain covers Blue Hill.

And now our fairy
decorator brightens his shop for fall;   20
his fishnet's filled with orange cork,
orange, his cobbler's bench and awl;
there is no money in his work,
he'd rather marry.

One dark night,   25
my Tudor Ford climbed the hill's skull;
I watched for love-cars. Lights turned down,
they lay together, hull to hull,
where the graveyard shelves on the town. . . .
My mind's not right.   30

A car radio bleats,
"Love, O careless Love. . . . " I hear
my ill-spirit sob in each blood cell,
as if my hand were at its throat. . . .
I myself am hell;   35
nobody's here—

only skunks, that search
in the moonlight for a bite to eat.
They march on their soles up Main Street:
white stripes, moonstruck eyes' red fire   40
under the chalk-dry and spar spire
of the Trinitarian Church.

I stand on top
of our back steps and breathe the rich air—
a mother skunk with her column of kittens swills the garbage pail.   45
She jabs her wedge-head in a cup
of sour cream, drops her ostrich tail,
and will not scare.

COMPARE

"Skunk Hour" with "Desert Places" by Robert Frost (page 180).

Andrew Marvell   (1621–1678)

To His Coy Mistress   1681

Had we but world enough and time,
This coyness,° lady, were no crime.   *modesty, reluctance*
We would sit down and think which way
To walk, and pass our long love's day.
Thou by the Indian Ganges' side   5
Should'st rubies find; I by the tide
Of Humber would complain.° I would   *sing sad songs*
Love you ten years before the Flood,
And you should, if you please, refuse
Till the conversion of the Jews.   10
My vegetable° love should grow   *vegetative, flourishing*
Vaster than empires, and more slow.
An hundred years should go to praise
Thine eyes, and on thy forehead gaze,
Two hundred to adore each breast,   15
But thirty thousand to the rest.
An age at least to every part,
And the last age should show your heart.
For, lady, you deserve this state,°   *pomp, ceremony*
Nor would I love at lower rate.   20
     But at my back I always hear
Time's wingèd chariot hurrying near,
And yonder all before us lie
Deserts of vast eternity.
Thy beauty shall no more be found,   25
Nor in thy marble vault shall sound
My echoing song; then worms shall try
That long preserved virginity,
And your quaint honor turn to dust,
And into ashes all my lust.   30
The grave's a fine and private place,
But none, I think, do there embrace.
     Now therefore, while the youthful hue
Sits on thy skin like morning glew°   *glow*
And while thy willing soul transpires   35
At every pore with instant° fires,   *eager*
Now let us sport us while we may;
And now, like amorous birds of prey,
Rather at once our time devour
Than languish in his slow-chapped° power.   *slow-jawed*   40
Let us roll all our strength and all

Our sweetness up into one ball
And tear our pleasures with rough strife
Thorough° the iron gates of life.   *through*
Thus, though we cannot make our sun   45
Stand still, yet we will make him run.

TO HIS COY MISTRESS. 7 *Humber:* a river that flows by Marvell's town of Hull (on the side of the world opposite from the Ganges). 10 *conversion of the Jews:* an event that, according to St. John the Divine, is to take place just before the end of the world. 35 *transpires:* exudes, as a membrane lets fluid or vapor pass through it.

COMPARE

"To His Coy Mistress" with "To the Virgins, to Make Much of Time" by Robert Herrick (page 495).

James Merrill   (1926–1995)

KITE POEM   1951

"One is reminded of a certain person,"
Continued the parson, settling back in his chair
With a glass of port, "who sought to emulate
The sport of birds (it was something of a chore)
By climbing up on a kite. They found his coat   5
Two counties away; the man himself was missing."

His daughters tittered: it was meant to be a lesson
To them—they had been caught kissing, or some such nonsense,
The night before, under the crescent moon.
So, finishing his pheasant, their father began   10
This thirty-minute discourse, ending with
A story improbable from the start. He paused for breath,

Having shown but a few of the dangers. However, the wind
Blew out the candles and the moon wrought changes
Which the daughters felt along their stockings. Then,   15
Thus persuaded, they fled to their young men
Waiting in the sweet night by the raspberry bed,
And kissed and kissed, as though to escape on a kite.

COMPARE

"Kite Poem" with "To the Virgins, to Make Much of Time" by Robert Herrick (page 495).

Charlotte Mew   (1869–1928)

THE FARMER'S BRIDE   1916

Three Summers since I chose a maid,
Too young maybe—but more's to do
At harvest-time than bide and woo.
   When us was wed she turned afraid
Of love and me and all things human;   5
Like the shut of a winter's day.
Her smile went out, and 'twasn't a woman—
     More like a little frightened fay.°   *elf*
       One night, in the Fall, she runned away.

"Out 'mong the sheep, her be," they said,   10
'Should properly have been abed;
But sure enough she wasn't there
Lying awake with her wide brown stare.
So over seven-acre field and up-along across the down
   We chased her, flying like a hare   15
Before our lanterns. To Church-Town
     All in a shiver and a scare
We caught her, fetched her home at last
     And turned the key upon her, fast.

She does the work about the house   20
As well as most, but like a mouse:
     Happy enough to chat and play
     With birds and rabbits and such as they,
     So long as men-folk keep away.
"Not near, not near!" her eyes beseech   25
When one of us comes within reach.
     The women say that beasts in stall
     Look round like children at her call.
     I've hardly heard her speak at all.

Shy as a leveret,° swift as he,   *hare*   30
Straight and slight as a young larch tree,
Sweet as the first wild violets, she,
To her wild self. But what to me?

The short days shorten and the oaks are brown,
   The blue smoke rises to the low gray sky,   35
One leaf in the still air falls slowly down,
   A magpie's spotted feathers lie
On the black earth spread white with rime,°   *frost*
The berries redden up to Christmas-time.
     What's Christmas-time without there be   40
     Some other in the house than we!

She sleeps up in the attic there
   Alone, poor maid. 'Tis but a stair
Betwixt us. Oh! my God! the down,
   The soft young down of her, the brown,   45
The brown of her—her eyes, her hair, her hair!

COMPARE

"The Farmer's Bride" with "Cinderella" by Anne Sexton (page 294).

Edna St. Vincent Millay

Edna St. Vincent Millay   (1892–1950)*

RECUERDO   1920

We were very tired, we were very merry—
We had gone back and forth all night on the ferry.
It was bare and bright, and smelled like a stable—
But we looked into a fire, we leaned across a table,
We lay on a hill-top underneath the moon;   5
And the whistles kept blowing, and the dawn came soon.

We were very tired, we were very merry—
We had gone back and forth all night on the ferry;
And you ate an apple, and I ate a pear,
From a dozen of each we had bought somewhere;   10
And the sky went wan, and the wind came cold,
And the sun rose dripping, a bucketful of gold.

We were very tired, we were very merry,
We had gone back and forth all night on the ferry.
We hailed, "Good morrow, mother!" to a shawl-covered head,   15
And bought a morning paper, which neither of us read;

And she wept, "God bless you!" for the apples and pears,
And we gave her all our money but our subway fares.

RECUERDO. The Spanish title means "a recollection" or "a memory."

COMPARE

"Recuerdo" with "A Blessing" by James Wright (page 568).

John Milton   (1608–1674)*

HOW SOON HATH TIME   1632

How soon hath time, the subtle thief of youth,
    Stol'n on his wing my three and twentieth year!
    My hasting days fly on with full career,
    But my late spring no bud or blossom show'th.
Perhaps my semblance might deceive the truth,   5
    That I to manhood am arriv'd so near,
    And inward ripeness doth much less appear,
    That some more timely-happy spirits endu'th.°   *endows*
Yet be it less or more, or soon or slow,
    It shall be still I strictest measure ev'n   10
    To that same lot, however mean or high,
Toward which Time leads me, and the will of Heav'n;
    All is, if I have grace to use it so,
    As ever in my great task-Master's eye.

COMPARE

"How soon hath time" with "When I have fears that I may cease to be" by John Keats
(page 504).

John Milton   (1608–1674)*

WHEN I CONSIDER HOW MY LIGHT IS SPENT   (1655?)

When I consider how my light is spent,
    Ere half my days in this dark world and wide,
    And that one talent which is death to hide
Lodged with me useless, though my soul more bent
To serve therewith my Maker, and present   5
    My true account, lest He returning chide;
    "Doth God exact day-labor, light denied?"
I fondly° ask. But Patience, to prevent   *foolishly*

That murmur, soon replies, "God doth not need
  Either man's work or His own gifts. Who best   10
  Bear His mild yoke, they serve Him best. His state
Is kingly: thousands at His bidding speed,
  And post o'er land and ocean without rest;
  They also serve who only stand and wait."

WHEN I CONSIDER HOW MY LIGHT IS SPENT. 1 *my light is spent:* Milton had become blind. 3 *that one talent:* For Jesus' parable of the talents (measures of money), see Matthew 25:14–30.

COMPARE

"When I consider how my light is spent" with "Batter my heart" by John Donne (page 57).

Marianne Moore

Marianne Moore   (1887–1972)*

POETRY   1921

I too, dislike it: there are things that are important beyond all this
               fiddle.
    Reading it, however, with a perfect contempt for it, one discovers
                  that there is in
    it after all, a place for the genuine.
        Hands that can grasp, eyes
           that can dilate, hair that can rise   5
               if it must, these things are important not because a
high sounding interpretation can be put upon them but because they
               are
    useful; when they become so derivative as to become
               unintelligible, the

same thing may be said for all of us—that we
    do not admire what
    we cannot understand. The bat,
        holding on upside down or in quest of something to   10

eat, elephants pushing, a wild horse taking a roll, a tireless wolf under
    a tree, the immovable critic twinkling his skin like a horse that
        feels a flea, the base-
ball fan, the statistician—case after case   15
    could be cited did
    one wish it; nor is it valid
        to discriminate against "business documents and

school-books"; all these phenomena are important. One must make a
        distinction
however: when dragged into prominence by half poets, the result
        is not poetry,   20
nor till the autocrats among us can be
    "literalists of
    the imagination"—above
        insolence and triviality and can present

for inspection, imaginary gardens with real toads in them, shall we
        have   25
    it. In the meantime, if you demand on one hand, in defiance of
        their opinion—
the raw material of poetry in
    all its rawness and
    that which is, on the other hand,
        genuine then you are interested in poetry.   30

COMPARE

Compare "Poetry" with *"Ars Poetica"* by Archibald MacLeish (page 396).

Frederick Morgan (b. 1922)

THE MASTER   1982

When Han Kan was summoned
to the imperial capital
it was suggested he sit at the feet of
the illustrious senior court painter
to learn from him the refinements of the art.   5

"No, thank you," he replied,
"I shall apprentice myself to the stables."

And he installed himself and his brushes amid the dung and the flies,
and studied the horses—their bodies' keen alertness—
eye-sparkle of one, another's sensitive stance,   10
the way a third moved graceful in his bulk—
and painted at last the emperor's favorite,
the charger named "Nightshining White,"

whose likeness after centuries still dazzles.

COMPARE

"The Master" with "Advice to a Friend Who Paints" by Kelly Cherry (page 62).

Marilyn Nelson

Marilyn Nelson   (b. 1946)*
A STRANGE BEAUTIFUL WOMAN   1985

A strange beautiful woman
met me in the mirror
the other night.
Hey,
I said,   5
what you doing here?
She asked me
the same thing.

COMPARE

Compare "A Strange Beautiful Woman" with "Embrace" by Billy Collins (page 109).

Howard Nemerov (1920–1991)

THE WAR IN THE AIR 1987

For a saving grace, we didn't see our dead,
Who rarely bothered coming home to die
But simply stayed away out there
In the clean war, the war in the air.

Seldom the ghosts came back bearing their tales   5
Of hitting the earth, the incompressible sea,
But stayed up there in the relative wind,
Shades fading in the mind,

Who had no graves but only epitaphs
Where never so many spoke for never so few: 10
Per ardua, said the partisans of Mars,
Per aspera, to the stars.

That was the good war, the war we won
As if there were no death, for goodness' sake,
With the help of the losers we left out there   15
In the air, in the empty air.

THE WAR IN THE AIR. 11–12 *Per ardua . . . Per aspera:* allusion to the English Royal Air Force's motto *"Per ardua ad astra,"* Latin for "through difficult things to the stars."

COMPARE

"The War in the Air" with "The Death of the Ball Turret Gunner" by Randall Jarrell (page 499) and "The Fury of Aerial Bombardment" by Richard Eberhart (page 69).

Lorine Niedecker

Lorine Niedecker (1903–1970)*

Sorrow Moves in Wide Waves   (ABOUT 1950)

Sorrow moves in wide waves,
    it passes, lets us be.
It uses us, we use it,
    it's blind while we see.

Consciousness is illimitable,   5
    too good to forsake
tho what we feel be misery
    and we know will break.

Old Mother turns blue and from us,
    "Don't let my head drop to the earth.   10
I'm blind and deaf." Death from the heart,
    a thimble in her purse.

"It's a long day since last night.
    Give me space. I need
floors. Wash the floors, Lorine!   15
    Wash clothes! Weed!"

Compare

"Sorrow Moves in Wide Waves" with "One Art" by Elizabeth Bishop (page 384).

Yone Noguchi (1875–1947)

A Selection of Hokku   1920

Leaves blown,
Birds flown away.

I wander in and out the Hall of Autumn.

     *   *

Are the fallen stars
Returning up the sky?—
The dews on the grass.

     *   *

Like a cobweb hung upon the tree,
A prey to wind and sunlight!
Who will say that we are safe and strong?

     *   *

Oh, How cool—
The sound of the bell
That leaves the bell itself.

HOKKU. *hokku* is an alternate form of the word *haiku*.

COMPARE

Compare Yone Noguchi's four hokku with any of the haiku by the "Three Masters,"
Basho, Buson, and Issa (page 103).

Sharon Olds

Sharon Olds   (b. 1942)*

The One Girl at the Boys' Party   1983

When I take my girl to the swimming party
I set her down among the boys. They tower and
bristle, she stands there smooth and sleek,
her math scores unfolding in the air around her.
They will strip to their suits, her body hard and   5
indivisible as a prime number,
they'll plunge in the deep end, she'll subtract
her height from ten feet, divide it into
hundreds of gallons of water, the numbers
bouncing in her mind like molecules of chlorine   10
in the bright blue pool. When they climb out,
her ponytail will hang its pencil lead
down her back, her narrow silk suit
with hamburgers and french fries printed on it
will glisten in the brilliant air, and they will   15
see her sweet face, solemn and
sealed, a factor of one, and she will
see their eyes, two each,
their legs, two each, and the curves of their sexes,
one each, and in her head she'll be doing her   20
wild multiplying, as the drops
sparkle and fall to the power of a thousand from her body.

Compare

"The One Girl at the Boys' Party" with "My Papa's Waltz" by Theodore Roethke (page 22).

Wilfred Owen (1893–1918)*

ANTHEM FOR DOOMED YOUTH   (1917?)

What passing-bells for these who die as cattle?
    Only the monstrous anger of the guns.
    Only the stuttering rifles' rapid rattle
Can patter out their hasty orisons.

No mockeries now for them; no prayers nor bells,   5
    Nor any voice of mourning save the choirs,—
The shrill, demented choirs of wailing shells;
    And bugles calling for them from sad shires.°   *counties*

What candles may be held to speed them all?
    Not in the hands of boys, but in their eyes   10
    Shall shine the holy glimmers of good-byes.
The pallor of girls' brows shall be their pall;
Their flowers the tenderness of patient minds,
And each slow dusk a drawing-down of blinds.

COMPARE

"Anthem for Doomed Youth" with "Facing It" by Yusef Komunyakaa (page 316).

Linda Pastan

Linda Pastan (b. 1932)

ETHICS   1981

In ethics class so many years ago
our teacher asked this question every fall:
if there were a fire in a museum
which would you save, a Rembrandt painting

or an old woman who hadn't many   5
years left anyhow? Restless on hard chairs
caring little for pictures or old age
we'd opt one year for life, the next for art
and always half-heartedly. Sometimes
the woman borrowed my grandmother's face   10
leaving her usual kitchen to wander
some drafty, half imagined museum.
One year, feeling clever, I replied
why not let the woman decide herself?
Linda, the teacher would report, eschews   15
the burdens of responsibility.
This fall in a real museum I stand
before a real Rembrandt, old woman,
or nearly so, myself. The colors
within this frame are darker than autumn,   20
darker even than winter—the browns of earth,
though earth's most radiant elements burn
through the canvas. I know now that woman
and painting and season are almost one
and all beyond saving by children.   25

COMPARE

"Ethics" with "Welcome to Hiroshima" by Mary Jo Salter (page 538).

Robert Phillips   (b. 1938)

RUNNING ON EMPTY   1981

As a teenager I would drive Father's
Chevrolet cross-county, given me

reluctantly: "Always keep the tank
half full, boy, half full, ya hear?"

The fuel gauge dipping, dipping   5
toward Empty, hitting Empty, then

—thrilling!—'way below Empty,
myself driving cross-county

mile after mile, faster and faster,
all night long, this crazy kid driving   10

the earth's rolling surface,
against all laws, defying chemistry,

rules, and time, riding on nothing
but fumes, pushing luck harder

than anyone pushed before, the wind   15
screaming past like the Furies . . .

I stranded myself only once, a white
night with no gas station open, ninety miles

from nowhere. Panicked for a while,
at standstill, myself stalled.   20

At dawn the car and I both refilled. But,
Father, I am running on empty still.

RUNNING ON EMPTY. 16 *Furies:* In Greek mythology, deities who pursue and torment evildoers.

COMPARE

"Running on Empty" with "Those Winter Sundays" by Robert Hayden (page 489) and
"My Papa's Waltz" by Theodore Roethke (page 22).

Sylvia Plath

Sylvia Plath (1932–1963)*

DADDY   (1962) 1965

You do not do, you do not do
Any more, black shoe
In which I have lived like a foot
For thirty years, poor and white,
Barely daring to breathe or Achoo.   5

Daddy, I have had to kill you.
You died before I had time—
Marble-heavy, a bag full of God,
Ghastly statue with one grey toe
Big as a Frisco seal   10

And a head in the freakish Atlantic
Where it pours bean green over blue
In the waters off beautiful Nauset.
I used to pray to recover you.
Ach, du.   15

In the German tongue, in the Polish town
Scraped flat by the roller
Of wars, wars, wars.
But the name of the town is common.
My Polack friend   20

Says there are a dozen or two.
So I never could tell where you
Put your foot, your root,
I never could talk to you.
The tongue stuck in my jaw.   25

It stuck in a barb wire snare.
Ich, ich, ich, ich,
I could hardly speak.
I thought every German was you.
And the language obscene   30

An engine, an engine
Chuffing me off like a Jew.
A Jew to Dachau, Auschwitz, Belsen.
I began to talk like a Jew.
I think I may well be a Jew.   35

The snows of the Tyrol, the clear beer of Vienna
Are not very pure or true.
With my gypsy ancestress and my weird luck
And my Taroc pack and my Taroc pack
I may be a bit of a Jew.   40

I have always been scared of *you*,
With your Luftwaffe, your gobbledygoo.
And your neat moustache
And your Aryan eye, bright blue.
Panzer-man, panzer-man, O You—   45

Not God but a swastika
So black no sky could squeak through.
Every woman adores a Fascist,
The boot in the face, the brute
Brute heart of a brute like you.   50

You stand at the blackboard, daddy,
In the picture I have of you,
A cleft in your chin instead of your foot
But no less a devil for that, no not
Any less the black man who   55

Bit my pretty red heart in two.
I was ten when they buried you.
At twenty I tried to die
And get back, back, back to you.
I thought even the bones would do.   60

But they pulled me out of the sack,
And they stuck me together with glue.
And then I knew what to do.
I made a model of you,
A man in black with a Meinkampf look   65

And a love of the rack and the screw.
And I said I do, I do.
So daddy, I'm finally through.
The black telephone's off at the root,
The voices just can't worm through.   70

If I've killed one man, I've killed two—
The vampire who said he was you
And drank my blood for a year,
Seven years, if you want to know.
Daddy, you can lie back now.   75

There's a stake in your fat black heart
And the villagers never liked you.
They are dancing and stamping on you.
They always *knew* it was you.
Daddy, daddy, you bastard, I'm through.   80

DADDY. Introducing this poem in a reading, Sylvia Plath remarked:

> The poem is spoken by a girl with an Electra complex. Her father died while she thought
> he was God. Her case is complicated by the fact that her father was also a Nazi and her
> mother very possibly part Jewish. In the daughter the two strains marry and paralyze each
> other—she has to act out the awful little allegory before she is free of it.

(Quoted by A. Alvarez, *Beyond All This Fiddle* [New York: Random, 1968].)

In some details "Daddy" is autobiography: the poet's father Otto Plath, a German, had come to the United States from Grabow, Poland. He had died following the amputation of a gangrened foot and leg when Sylvia was eight years old. Politically, Otto Plath was a Republican, not a Nazi, but was apparently a somewhat domineering head of the household. (See the recollections of the poet's mother Aurelia Schober Plath in her edition of *Letters Home* by Sylvia Plath [New York: Harper, 1975].

15 *Ach, du:* Oh, you. 27 *Ich, ich, ich, ich:* I, I, I, I. 51 *blackboard:* Otto Plath had been a professor of biology at Boston University. 65 *Meinkampf:* Adolf Hitler entitled his autobiography *Mein Kampf* ("My Struggle").

COMPARE

"Daddy" with "American Primitive" by William Jay Smith (page 546).

Edgar Allan Poe   (1809–1849)*

A DREAM WITHIN A DREAM   1849

Take this kiss upon the brow!
And, in parting from you now,
Thus much let me avow—
You are not wrong, who deem
That my days have been a dream;   5
Yet if Hope has flown away
In a night, or in a day,
In a vision, or in none,
Is it therefore the less *gone?*
All that we see or seem   10
Is but a dream within a dream.

I stand amid the roar
Of a surf-tormented shore,
And I hold within my hand
Grains of the golden sand—   15
How few! yet how they creep
Through my fingers to the deep,
While I weep—while I weep!
O God! can I not grasp
Them with a tighter clasp?   20
O God! can I not save
One from the pitiless wave?
Is *all* that we see or seem
But a dream within a dream?

COMPARE

"A Dream within a Dream" with "Dover Beach" by Matthew Arnold (page 445).

Alexander Pope   (1688–1744)*

A LITTLE LEARNING IS A DANG'ROUS THING (FROM AN ESSAY ON CRITICISM)   1711

A *little Learning* is a dang'rous Thing;
Drink deep, or taste not the *Pierian* Spring:
There *shallow Draughts* intoxicate the Brain,
And drinking *largely* sobers us again.
Fir'd at first Sight with what the *Muse* imparts,   5
In *fearless Youth* we tempt the Heights of Arts,
While from the bounded *Level* of our Mind,
Short Views we take, nor see the *Lengths behind,*
But *more advanc'd,* behold with strange Surprize
New, distant Scenes of *endless* Science rise!   10
So pleas'd at first, the towring *Alps* we try,
Mount o'er the Vales, and seem to tread the Sky;
Th' Eternal Snows appear already past,
And the first *Clouds* and *Mountains* seem the last:
But *those attain'd,* we tremble to survey   15
The growing Labours of the lengthen'd Way,
Th' *increasing* Prospect *tires* our wandring Eyes,
Hills peep o'er Hills, and *Alps* on *Alps* arise!

A LITTLE LEARNING IS A DANG'ROUS THING.   2 *Pierian Spring:* the spring of the Muses.

COMPARE

"A little Learning is a dang'rous Thing" with "The Writer" by Richard Wilbur (page 564).

Ezra Pound   (1885–1972)*

THE RIVER-MERCHANT'S WIFE: A LETTER   1915

While my hair was still cut straight across my forehead
I played about the front gate, pulling flowers.
You came by on bamboo stilts, playing horse,
You walked about my seat, playing with blue plums.
And we went on living in the village of Chokan: 5
Two small people, without dislike or suspicion.

At fourteen I married My Lord you.
I never laughed, being bashful.
Lowering my head, I looked at the wall.
Called to, a thousand times, I never looked back.   10

At fifteen I stopped scowling,
I desired my dust to be mingled with yours
Forever and forever and forever.
Why should I climb the lookout?

At sixteen you departed,   15
You went into far Ku-to-yen, by the river of swirling eddies,
And you have been gone five months.
The monkeys make sorrowful noise overhead.

You dragged your feet when you went out.
By the gate now, the moss is grown, the different mosses,   20
Too deep to clear them away!
The leaves fall early this autumn, in wind.
The paired butterflies are already yellow with August
Over the grass in the West garden;
They hurt me. I grow older.   25
If you are coming down through the narrows of the river Kiang,
Please let me know before hand,
And I will come out to meet you
    As far as Cho-fu-sa.

THE RIVER-MERCHANT'S WIFE: A LETTER. A free translation from the Chinese poet Li Po (eighth century).

COMPARE

"The River-Merchant's Wife: a Letter" with "A Valediction: Forbidding Mourning" by John Donne (page 468).

Dudley Randall

Dudley Randall   (1914–2000)*

A DIFFERENT IMAGE   1968

The age
requires this task:
create
a different image;
re-animate   5
the mask.

Shatter the icons of slavery and fear.
Replace
the leer
of the minstrel's burnt-cork face   10
with a proud, serene
and classic bronze of Benin.

COMPARE

"A Different Image" with "The Negro Speaks of Rivers" by Langston Hughes (page 421).

John Crowe Ransom (1888–1974)

PIAZZA PIECE   1927

—I am a gentleman in a dustcoat trying
To make you hear. Your ears are soft and small
And listen to an old man not at all,
They want the young men's whispering and sighing.
But see the roses on your trellis dying   5
And hear the spectral singing of the moon;
For I must have my lovely lady soon,
I am a gentleman in a dustcoat trying.

—I am a lady young in beauty waiting
Until my truelove comes, and then we kiss.   10
But what grey man among the vines is this
Whose words are dry and faint as in a dream?
Back from my trellis, Sir, before I scream!
I am a lady young in beauty waiting.

COMPARE

Compare "Piazza Piece" with "To His Coy Mistress" by Andrew Marvell (page 512).

Henry Reed (1914–1986)

NAMING OF PARTS   1946

Today we have naming of parts. Yesterday,
We had daily cleaning. And tomorrow morning,
We shall have what to do after firing. But today,
Today we have naming of parts. Japonica
Glistens like coral in all of the neighboring gardens,   5
        And today we have naming of parts.

This is the lower sling swivel. And this
Is the upper sling swivel, whose use you will see,
When you are given your slings. And this is the piling swivel,
Which in your case you have not got. The branches   10
Hold in the gardens their silent, eloquent gestures,
        Which in our case we have not got.

This is the safety-catch, which is always released
With an easy flick of the thumb. And please do not let me
See anyone using his finger. You can do it quite easy   15
If you have any strength in your thumb. The blossoms
Are fragile and motionless, never letting anyone see
        Any of them using their finger.

And this you can see is the bolt. The purpose of this
Is to open the breech, as you see. We can slide it   20
Rapidly backwards and forwards: we call this
Easing the spring. And rapidly backwards and forwards
The early bees are assaulting and fumbling the flowers:
       They call it easing the Spring.

They call it easing the Spring: it is perfectly easy   25
If you have any strength in your thumb: like the bolt,
And the breech, and the cocking-piece, and the point of balance,
Which in our case we have not got; and the almond-blossom
Silent in all of the gardens and the bees going backwards and forwards,
       For today we have naming of parts.   30

COMPARE

"Naming of Parts" with "The Fury of Aerial Bombardment" by Richard Eberhart (page 69).

Adrienne Rich   (b. 1929)*

LIVING IN SIN   1955

She had thought the studio would keep itself;
no dust upon the furniture of love.
Half heresy, to wish the taps less vocal,
the panes relieved of grime. A plate of pears,
a piano with a Persian shawl, a cat   5
stalking the picturesque amusing mouse
had risen at his urging.
Not that at five each separate stair would writhe
under the milkman's tramp; that morning light
so coldly would delineate the scraps   10
of last night's cheese and three sepulchral bottles;
that on the kitchen shelf among the saucers
a pair of beetle-eyes would fix her own—
envoy from some village in the moldings . . .
Meanwhile, he, with a yawn,   15
sounded a dozen notes upon the keyboard,
declared it out of tune, shrugged at the mirror,
rubbed at his beard, went out for cigarettes;
while she, jeered by the minor demons,
pulled back the sheets and made the bed and found   20
a towel to dust the table-top,
and let the coffee-pot boil over on the stove.
By evening she was back in love again,

though not so wholly but throughout the night
she woke sometimes to feel the daylight coming   25
like a relentless milkman up the stairs.

COMPARE

Compare and contrast "Living in Sin" with "Let me not to the marriage of true minds" by
William Shakespeare (page 221).

Adrienne Rich   (b. 1929)*

POWER   1978

Living   in the earth-deposits   of our history

Today a backhoe divulged   out of a crumbling flank of earth
one bottle   amber   perfect   a hundred-year-old
cure for fever   or melancholy   a tonic
for living on this earth   in the winters of this climate   5

Today I was reading about Marie Curie:
she must have known she suffered   from radiation sickness
her body bombarded for years   by the element
she had purified
It seems she denied to the end   10
the source of the cataracts on her eyes
the cracked and suppurating skin   of her finger-ends
till she could no longer hold   a test-tube or a pencil

She died   a famous woman   denying
her wounds   15
denying
her wounds   came   from the same source as her power

POWER. 6 *Marie Curie:* the Polish scientist (1867–1934) who helped discover polonium and
radium. She was the first person to win two Nobel Prizes.

COMPARE

"Power" with "Ethics" by Linda Pastan (page 524).

Edwin Arlington Robinson

Edwin Arlington Robinson   (1869–1935)*

MINIVER CHEEVY   1910

Miniver Cheevy, child of scorn,
    Grew lean while he assailed the seasons;
He wept that he was ever born,
    And he had reasons.

Miniver loved the days of old   5
    When swords were bright and steeds were prancing;
The vision of a warrior bold
    Would set him dancing.

Miniver sighed for what was not,
    And dreamed, and rested from his labors;   10
He dreamed of Thebes and Camelot,
    And Priam's neighbors.

Miniver mourned the ripe renown
    That made so many a name so fragrant;
He mourned Romance, now on the town,   15
    And Art, a vagrant.

Miniver loved the Medici,
    Albeit he had never seen one;
He would have sinned incessantly
    Could he have been one.   20

Miniver cursed the commonplace
    And eyed a khaki suit with loathing;
He missed the medieval grace
    Of iron clothing.

Miniver scorned the gold he sought,   25
    But sore annoyed was he without it;
Miniver thought, and thought, and thought,
    And thought about it.

Miniver Cheevy, born too late,
    Scratched his head and kept on thinking;   30
Miniver coughed, and called it fate,
    And kept on drinking.

MINIVER CHEEVY.   11 *Thebes:* a city in ancient Greece and the setting of many famous Greek myths;
Camelot: the legendary site of King Arthur's Court. 12 *Priam:* the last king of Troy; his "neighbors"
would have included Helen of Troy, Aeneas, and other famous figures. 17 *the Medici:* the ruling
family of Florence during the high Renaissance, the Medici were renowned patrons of the arts.

COMPARE

"Miniver Cheevy" with "Ulysses" by Alfred, Lord Tennyson (page 554).

Theodore Roethke

Theodore Roethke   (1908–1963)*

ELEGY FOR JANE   1953

> *My Student, Thrown by a Horse*

I remember the neckcurls, limp and damp as tendrils;
And her quick look, a sidelong pickerel smile;
And how, once startled into talk, the light syllables leaped for her,
And she balanced in the delight of her thought,
A wren, happy, tail into the wind,   5
Her song trembling the twigs and small branches.
The shade sang with her;

The leaves, their whispers turned to kissing;
And the mold sang in the bleached valleys under the rose.

Oh, when she was sad, she cast herself down into such a pure depth,   10
Even a father could not find her:
Scraping her cheek against straw;
Stirring the clearest water.

My sparrow, you are not here,
Waiting like a fern, making a spiny shadow.   15
The sides of wet stones cannot console me,
Nor the moss, wound with the last light.

If only I could nudge you from this sleep,
My maimed darling, my skittery pigeon.
Over this damp grave I speak the words of my love: 20
I, with no rights in this matter,
Neither father nor lover.

COMPARE

"Elegy for Jane" with "Annabel Lee" by Edgar Allan Poe (page 392).

Mary Jo Salter

Mary Jo Salter   (b. 1954)

WELCOME TO HIROSHIMA   1984

is what you first see, stepping off the train:
a billboard brought to you in living English
by Toshiba Electric. While a channel
silent in the TV of the brain

projects those flickering re-runs of a cloud   5
that brims its risen columnful like beer
and, spilling over, hangs its foamy head,
you feel a thirst for history: what year

it started to be safe to breathe the air,
and when to drink the blood and scum afloat   10
on the Ohta River. But no, the water's clear,
they pour it for your morning cup of tea

in one of the countless sunny coffee shops
whose plastic dioramas advertise
mutations of cuisine behind the glass: 15
a pancake sandwich; a pizza someone tops

with a maraschino cherry. Passing by
the Peace Park's floral hypocenter (where
how bravely, or with what mistaken cheer,
humanity erased its own erasure),   20

you enter the memorial museum
and through more glass are served, as on a dish
of blistered grass, three mannequins. Like gloves
a mother clips to coatsleeves, strings of flesh

hang from their fingertips; or as if tied   25
to recall a duty for us, *Reverence*
the dead whose mourners too shall soon be dead,
but all commemoration's swallowed up

in questions of bad taste, how re-created
horror mocks the grim original,   30
and thinking at last *They should have left it all*
you stop. This is the wristwatch of a child.

Jammed on the moment's impact, resolute
to communicate some message, although mute,
it gestures with its hands at eight-fifteen   35
and eight-fifteen and eight-fifteen again

while tables of statistics on the wall
update the news by calling on a roll
of tape, death gummed on death, and in the case
adjacent, an exhibit under glass   40

is glass itself: a shard the bomb slammed in
a woman's arm at eight-fifteen, but some
three decades on—as if to make it plain
hope's only as renewable as pain,

and as if all the unsung   45
debasements of the past may one day come
rising to the surface once again—
worked its filthy way out like a tongue.

COMPARE

"Welcome to Hiroshima" with "Ethics" by Linda Pastan (page 524) and "Ballad of Birmingham" by Dudley Randall (page 151).

William Shakespeare

William Shakespeare   (1564–1616)*

WHEN, IN DISGRACE WITH FORTUNE AND MEN'S EYES   1609

When, in disgrace with Fortune and men's eyes,
I all alone beweep my outcast state,
And trouble deaf heaven with my bootless° cries,   *futile*
And look upon myself and curse my fate,
Wishing me like to one more rich in hope,   5
Featured like him, like him with friends possessed,
Desiring this man's art, and that man's scope,
With what I most enjoy contented least,
Yet in these thoughts myself almost despising,
Haply° I think on thee, and then my state,   *luckily*   10
Like to the lark at break of day arising
From sullen earth, sings hymns at heaven's gate;
    For thy sweet love rememb'red such wealth brings
    That then I scorn to change my state with kings.

COMPARE

"When, in disgrace with Fortune and men's eyes" with "When I have fears that I may cease to be" by John Keats (page 504).

William Shakespeare (1564–1616)*

NOT MARBLE NOR THE GILDED MONUMENTS   1609

Not marble, nor the gilded monuments
Of princes, shall outlive this powerful rhyme;
But you shall shine more bright in these contents
Than unswept stone, besmeared with sluttish time.
When wasteful war shall statues overturn,   5
And broils root out the work of masonry,
Nor Mars his sword nor war's quick fire shall burn
The living record of your memory.
'Gainst death and all-oblivious enmity
Shall you pace forth; your praise shall still find room   10
Even in the eyes of all posterity
That wear this world out to the ending doom.
    So, till the judgment that yourself arise,
    You live in this, and dwell in lovers' eyes.

COMPARE

"Not marble nor the gilded monuments" with "To the Stone-cutters" by Robinson Jeffers (page 500).

William Shakespeare (1564–1616)*

WEARY WITH TOIL, I HASTE ME TO MY BED   1609

Weary with toil, I haste me to my bed,
The dear repose for limbs with travel tired;
But then begins a journey in my head,
To work my mind when body's work's expired:
For then my thoughts, from far where I abide,   5
Intend a zealous pilgrimage to thee,
And keep my drooping eyelids open wide,
Looking on darkness which the blind do see;
Save that my soul's imaginary sight
Presents thy shadow to my sightless view,   10
Which, like a jewel hung in ghastly night,
Makes black night beauteous, and her old face new.
    Lo, thus by day my limbs, by night my mind,
    For thee and for myself no quiet find.

COMPARE

"Weary with toil" with "What lips my lips have kissed, and where, and why" by Edna St. Vincent Millay (page 223) and "First Poem for You" by Kim Addonizio (page 224).

William Shakespeare (1564–1616)*

THAT TIME OF YEAR THOU MAYST IN ME BEHOLD   1609

That time of year thou mayst in me behold
When yellow leaves, or none, or few, do hang
Upon those boughs which shake against the cold,
Bare ruined choirs where late the sweet birds sang.
In me thou see'st the twilight of such day   5
As after sunset fadeth in the west,
Which by-and-by black night doth take away,
Death's second self that seals up all in rest.
In me thou see'st the glowing of such fire
That on the ashes of his youth doth lie,   10
As the deathbed whereon it must expire,
Consumed with that which it was nourished by.
   This thou perceiv'st, which makes thy love more strong,
   To love that well which thou must leave ere long.

COMPARE

"That time of year thou mayst in me behold" with "anyone lived in a pretty how town" by E. E. Cummings (page 71).

William Shakespeare (1564–1616)*

MY MISTRESS' EYES ARE NOTHING LIKE THE SUN   1609

My mistress' eyes are nothing like the sun;
Coral is far more red than her lips' red;
If snow be white, why then her breasts are dun;
If hairs be wires, black wires grow on her head.
I have seen roses damasked red and white,   5
But no such roses see I in her cheeks;
And in some perfumes is there more delight
Than in the breath that from my mistress reeks.
I love to hear her speak, yet well I know
That music hatch a far more pleasing sound;   10
I grant I never saw a goddess go:
My mistress, when she walks, treads on the ground.
   And yet, by heaven, I think my love as rare
   As any she,° belied with false compare.   *woman*

COMPARE

"My mistress' eyes are nothing like the sun" with "Homage to my hips" by Lucille Clifton (page 254) and "Crazy Jane Talks with the Bishop" by William Butler Yeats (page 571).

Louis Simpson   (b. 1923)

AMERICAN POETRY   1963

Whatever it is, it must have
A stomach that can digest
Rubber, coal, uranium, moons, poems.

Like the shark, it contains a shoe.
It must swim for miles through the desert   5
Uttering cries that are almost human.

COMPARE

"American Poetry" with *Ars Poetica* by Archibald MacLeish (page 396).

David R. Slavitt   (b. 1935)

TITANIC   1983

Who does not love the *Titanic*?
If they sold passage tomorrow for that same crossing,
who would not buy?

To go down . . . We all go down, mostly
alone. But with crowds of people, friends, servants,   5
well fed, with music, with lights! Ah!

And the world, shocked, mourns, as it ought to do
and almost never does. There will be the books and movies
to remind our grandchildren who we were
and how we died, and give them a good cry.   10

Not so bad, after all. The cold
water is anaesthetic and very quick.
The cries on all sides must be a comfort.

We all go: only a few, first-class.

COMPARE

"Titanic" with "The Convergence of the Twain" by Thomas Hardy (page 486).

Christopher Smart (1722–1771)

FOR I WILL CONSIDER MY CAT JEOFFRY (1759–1763)

For I will consider my Cat Jeoffry.
For he is the servant of the Living God, duly and daily serving him.
For at the first glance of the glory of God in the East he worships in his
    way.
For is this done by wreathing his body seven times round with elegant
    quickness.
For then he leaps up to catch the musk,° which is the   *catnip* 5
    blessing of God upon his prayer.
For he rolls upon prank to work it in.
For having done duty and received blessing he begins to consider
    himself.
For this he performs in ten degrees.
For first he looks upon his fore-paws to see if they are clean.
For secondly he kicks up behind to clear away there.   10
For thirdly he works it upon stretch° with   *he works his muscles, stretching*
    the fore-paws extended.
For fourthly he sharpens his paws by wood.
For fifthly he washes himself.
For sixthly he rolls upon wash.
For seventhly he fleas himself, that he may not be interrupted   15
    upon the beat.°   *his patrol*
For eighthly he rubs himself against a post.
For ninthly he looks up for his instructions.
For tenthly he goes in quest of food.
For having considered God and himself he will consider his neighbor.
For if he meets another cat he will kiss her in kindness.   20
For when he takes his prey he plays with it to give it a chance.
For one mouse in seven escapes by his dallying.
For when his day's work is done his business more properly begins.
For he keeps the Lord's watch in the night against the Adversary.
For he counteracts the powers of darkness by his electrical skin
    and glaring eyes.
       25
For he counteracts the Devil, who is death, by brisking about the life.
For in his morning orisons he loves the sun and the sun loves him.
For he is of the tribe of Tiger.
For the Cherub Cat is a term of the Angel Tiger.
For he has the subtlety and hissing of a serpent, which in goodness he   30
    suppresses.
For he will not do destruction if he is well-fed, neither will he spit
    without provocation.
For he purrs in thankfulness when God tells him he's a good Cat.
For he is an instrument for the children to learn benevolence upon.

For every house is incomplete without him, and a blessing is lacking in the spirit.

For the Lord commanded Moses concerning the cats at the departure of the Children of Israel from Egypt. 35

For every family had one cat at least in the bag.

For the English cats are the best in Europe.

For he is the cleanest in the use of his fore-paws of any quadruped.

For the dexterity of his defense is an instance of the love of God to him exceedingly.

For he is the quickest to his mark of any creature. 40

For he is tenacious of his point.

For he is a mixture of gravity and waggery.

For he knows that God is his Savior.

For there is nothing sweeter than his peace when at rest.

For there is nothing brisker than his life when in motion. 45

For he is of the Lord's poor, and so indeed is he called by benevolence perpetually—Poor Jeoffry! poor Jeoffry! the rat has bit thy throat.

For I bless the name of the Lord Jesus that Jeoffry is better.

For the divine spirit comes about his body to sustain it in complete cat.

For his tongue is exceeding pure so that it has in purity what it wants in music.

For he is docile and can learn certain things. 50

For he can sit up with gravity which is patience upon approbation.

For he can fetch and carry, which is patience in employment.

For he can jump over a stick which is patience upon proof positive.

For he can spraggle upon waggle at the word of command.

For he can jump from an eminence into his master's bosom. 55

For he can catch the cork and toss it again.

For he is hated by the hypocrite and miser.

For the former is afraid of detection.

For the latter refuses the charge.

For he camels his back to bear the first notion of business. 60

For he is good to think on, if a man would express himself neatly.

For he made a great figure in Egypt for his signal services.

For he killed the Icneumon-rat, very pernicious by land.

For his ears are so acute that they sting again.

For from this proceeds the passing quickness of his attention. 65

For by stroking of him I have found out electricity.

For I perceived God's light about him both wax and fire.

For the electrical fire is the spiritual substance which God sends from heaven to sustain the bodies both of man and beast.

For God has blessed him in the variety of his movements.

For, though he cannot fly, he is an excellent clamberer. 70

For his motions upon the face of the earth are more than any other quadruped.

For he can tread to all the measures upon the music.
For he can swim for life.
For he can creep.

FOR I WILL CONSIDER MY CAT JEOFFRY. This is a self-contained extract from Smart's long poem *Lord commanded Moses concerning the cats:* No such command is mentioned in Scripture. 54 *spraggle upon waggle:* W. F. Stead, in his edition of Smart's poem, suggests that this means Jeoffry will sprawl when his master waggles a finger or a stick. 59 *the charge:* perhaps the cost of feeding a cat.

COMPARE

"For I will consider my Cat Jeoffry" with "The Tyger" by William Blake (page 453).

William Jay Smith (b. 1918)

AMERICAN PRIMITIVE   1957

Look at him there in his stovepipe hat,
His high-top shoes, and his handsome collar;
Only my Daddy could look like that,
And I love my Daddy like he loves his Dollar.

The screen door bangs, and it sounds so funny—   5
There he is in a shower of gold;
His pockets are stuffed with folding money,
His lips are blue, and his hands feel cold.

He hangs in the hall by his black cravat,
The ladies faint, and the children holler: 10
Only my Daddy could look like that,
And I love my Daddy like he loves his Dollar.

COMPARE

"American Primitive" with "Daddy" by Sylvia Plath (page 526).

Cathy Song

Cathy Song   (b. 1955)

STAMP COLLECTING   1988

The poorest countries
have the prettiest stamps
as if impracticality were a major export
shipped with the bananas, t-shirts, and coconuts.
Take Tonga, where the tourists,   5
expecting a dramatic waterfall replete with birdcalls,
are taken to see the island's peculiar mystery:
hanging bats with collapsible wings
like black umbrellas swing upside down from fruit trees.
The Tongan stamp is a fruit.   10
The banana stamp is scalloped like a butter-varnished seashell.
The pineapple resembles a volcano, a spout of green on top,
and the papaya, a tarnished goat skull.

They look impressive,
these stamps of countries without a thing to sell   15
except for what is scraped, uprooted and hulled
from their mule-scratched hills.
They believe in postcards,
in portraits of progress: the new dam;
a team of young native doctors   20
wearing stethoscopes like exotic ornaments;
the recently constructed "Facultad de Medicina,"
a building as lack-lustre as an American motel.

The stamps of others are predictable.
Lucky is the country that possesses indigenous beauty.   25
Say a tiger or a queen.
The Japanese can display to the world
their blossoms: a spray of pink on green.
Like pollen, they drift, airborne.
But pity the country that is bleak and stark.   30

Beauty and whimsey are discouraged as indiscreet.
Unbreakable as their climate, a monument of ice,
they issue serious statements, commemorating
factories, tramways and aeroplanes;
athletes marbled into statues.   35
They turn their noses upon the world, these countries,
and offer this: an unrelenting procession
of a grim, historic profile.

COMPARE

"Stamp Collecting" with "The Virgins" by Derek Walcott (page 561).

William Stafford   (1914–1993)*

THE FARM ON THE GREAT PLAINS   1960

A telephone line goes cold;
birds tread it wherever it goes.
A farm back of a great plain
tugs an end of the line.

I call that farm every year,   5
ringing it, listening, still;
no one is home at the farm,
the line gives only a hum.

Some year I will ring the line
on a night at last the right one,   10
and with an eye tapered for braille
from the phone on the wall

I will see the tenant who waits—
the last one left at the place;
through the dark my braille eye   15
will lovingly touch his face.

"Hello, is Mother at home?"
No one is home today.
"But Father—he should be there."
No one—no one is here.   20

"But you—are you the one . . . ?"
Then the line will be gone
because both ends will be home:
no space, no birds, no farm.

My self will be the plain,   25
wise as winter is gray,
pure as cold posts go
pacing toward what I know.

COMPARE

"The Farm on the Great Plains" with "Piano" by D. H. Lawrence (page 10) and "Dark house, by which once more I stand" by Alfred, Lord Tennyson (page 553).

Wallace Stevens

Wallace Stevens   (1879–1955)*

PETER QUINCE AT THE CLAVIER   1923

I

Just as my fingers on these keys
Make music, so the selfsame sounds
On my spirit make a music, too.

Music is feeling, then, not sound;
And thus it is that what I feel,   5
Here in this room, desiring you,

Thinking of your blue-shadowed silk,
Is music. It is like the strain
Waked in the elders by Susanna.

Of a green evening, clear and warm,   10
She bathed in her still garden, while
The red-eyed elders watching, felt

The basses of their beings throb
In witching chords, and their thin blood
Pulse pizzicati of Hosanna.   15

                    II
In the green water, clear and warm,
Susanna lay.
She searched
The touch of springs,
And found   20
Concealed imaginings.
She sighed,
For so much melody.

Upon the bank, she stood
In the cool   25
Of spent emotions.
She felt, among the leaves,
The dew
Of old devotions.

She walked upon the grass,   30
Still quavering.
The winds were like her maids,
On timid feet,
Fetching her woven scarves,
Yet wavering.   35

A breath upon her hand
Muted the night.
She turned—
A cymbal crashed,
And roaring horns.   40

                    III
Soon, with a noise like tambourines,
Came her attendant Byzantines.
They wondered why Susanna cried
Against the elders by her side;

And as they whispered, the refrain   45
Was like a willow swept by rain.

Anon, their lamps' uplifted flame
Revealed Susanna and her shame.

And then, the simpering Byzantines
Fled, with a noise like tambourines.   50

                    IV
Beauty is momentary in the mind—
The fitful tracing of a portal;
But in the flesh it is immortal.

The body dies; the body's beauty lives.
So evenings die, in their green going,   55
A wave, interminably flowing.
So gardens die, their meek breath scenting
The cowl of winter, done repenting.
So maidens die, to the auroral
Celebration of a maiden's choral.   60

Susanna's music touched the bawdy strings
Of those white elders; but, escaping,
Left only Death's ironic scraping.
Now, in its immortality, it plays
On the clear viol of her memory,   65
And makes a constant sacrament of praise.

PETER QUINCE AT THE CLAVIER. In Shakespeare's *Midsummer Night's Dream*, Peter Quince is a
clownish carpenter who stages a mock-tragic play. 9 *Susanna:* In the Book of Susanna in the Apoc-
rypha, two lustful elders who covet Susanna, a virtuous married woman, hide in her garden, spy on
her as she bathes, then threaten to make false accusations against her unless she submits to them.
When she refuses, they cry out, and her servants come running. All ends well when the prophet
Daniel cross-examines the elders and proves them liars. 15 *pizzicati:* thin notes made by plucking a
stringed instrument. 42 *Byzantines:* Susanna's maidservants.

COMPARE

"Peter Quince at the Clavier" with "Ode on a Grecian Urn" by John Keats (page 501) or
"Sailing to Byzantium" by William Butler Yeats (page 379).

Wallace Stevens   (1879–1955)*

THE EMPEROR OF ICE-CREAM   1923

Call the roller of big cigars,
The muscular one, and bid him whip
In kitchen cups concupiscent curds.
Let the wenches dawdle in such dress
As they are used to wear, and let the boys   5
Bring flowers in last month's newspapers.
Let be be finale of seem.
The only emperor is the emperor of ice-cream.

Take from the dresser of deal,

Lacking the three glass knobs, that sheet   10
On which she embroidered fantails once
And spread it so as to cover her face.
If her horny feet protrude, they come
To show how cold she is, and dumb.
Let the lamp affix its beam.   15
The only emperor is the emperor of ice-cream.

The Emperor of Ice-Cream.   9 *deal:* fir or pine wood used to make cheap furniture.

COMPARE

"The Emperor of Ice-Cream" with "This living hand, now warm and capable" by John
Keats (page 214) and "A Slumber Did My Spirit Seal" by William Wordsworth (page
169).

Ruth Stone   (b. 1915)
SECOND HAND COAT   1982

I feel
in her pockets; she wore nice cotton gloves,
kept a handkerchief box, washed her undies,
ate at the Holiday Inn, had a basement freezer,
belonged to a bridge club.   5
I think when I wake in the morning
that I have turned into her.
She hangs in the hall downstairs,
a shadow with pulled threads.
I slip her over my arms, skin of a matron.   10
Where are you? I say to myself, to the orphaned body,
and her coat says,
Get your purse, have you got your keys?

COMPARE

"Second Hand Coat" with "Home is so Sad" by Philip Larkin (page 506).

Jonathan Swift   (1667–1745)
A DESCRIPTION OF THE MORNING   1711

Now hardly here and there an hackney-coach,°   horse-drawn cab
Appearing, showed the ruddy morn's approach.
Now Betty from her master's bed had flown
And softly stole to discompose her own.
The slipshod 'prentice from his master's door   5

Had pared the dirt, and sprinkled round the floor.
Now Moll had whirled her mop with dextrous airs,
Prepared to scrub the entry and the stairs.
The youth with broomy stumps began to trace
The kennel°-edge, where wheels had worn the place.   *gutter*   10
The small-coal man was heard with cadence deep
Till drowned in shriller notes of chimneysweep,
Duns° at his lordship's gate began to meet,   *bill-collectors*
And Brickdust Moll had screamed through half the street.
The turnkey° now his flock returning sees,   *jailkeeper* 15
Duly let out a-nights to steal for fees;
The watchful bailiffs° take their silent stands;   *constables*
And schoolboys lag with satchels in their hands.

A DESCRIPTION OF THE MORNING. 9 *youth with broomy stumps:* a young man sweeping the gutter's edge with worn-out brooms, looking for old nails fallen from wagonwheels, which were valuable. 14 *Brickdust Moll:* woman selling brickdust to be used for scouring.

COMPARE

"A Description of the Morning" with "London" by William Blake (page 82).

Alfred, Lord Tennyson   (1809–1892)*

DARK HOUSE, BY WHICH ONCE   1850
MORE I STAND

Dark house, by which once more I stand
    Here in the long unlovely street,
    Doors, where my heart was used to beat
So quickly, waiting for a hand,

A hand that can be clasped no more—   5
    Behold me, for I cannot sleep,
    And like a guilty thing I creep
At earliest morning to the door.

He is not here; but far away
    The noise of life begins again,   10
    And ghastly through the drizzling rain
On the bald street breaks the blank day.

DARK HOUSE. This poem is one part of the series *In Memoriam*, an elegy for Tennyson's friend Arthur Henry Hallam.

COMPARE

"Dark house, by which once more I stand" with "The piercing chill I feel" by Taniguchi Buson (page 94) and "Home is so Sad" by Philip Larkin (page 506).

Alfred, Lord Tennyson

Alfred, Lord Tennyson (1809–1892)*

ULYSSES   (1833)

It little profits that an idle king,
By this still hearth, among these barren crags,
Matched with an agèd wife, I mete and dole
Unequal laws unto a savage race
That hoard, and sleep, and feed, and know not me.   5
I cannot rest from travel; I will drink
Life to the lees. All times I have enjoyed
Greatly, have suffered greatly, both with those
That loved me, and alone; on shore, and when
Through scudding drifts the rainy Hyades   10
Vexed the dim sea. I am become a name;
For always roaming with a hungry heart
Much have I seen and known—cities of men
And manners, climates, councils, governments,
Myself not least, but honored of them all—   15
And drunk delight of battle with my peers,
Far on the ringing plains of windy Troy.
I am a part of all that I have met;
Yet all experience is an arch wherethrough
Gleams that untraveled world whose margin fades   20
Forever and forever when I move.
How dull it is to pause, to make an end,
To rust unburnished, not to shine in use!
As though to breathe were life! Life piled on life

Were all too little, and of one to me   25
Little remains; but every hour is saved
From that eternal silence, something more,
A bringer of new things; and vile it were
For some three suns to store and hoard myself,
And this grey spirit yearning in desire   30
To follow knowledge like a sinking star,
Beyond the utmost bound of human thought.
    This is my son, mine own Telemachus,
To whom I leave the scepter and the isle—
Well-loved of me, discerning to fulfill   35
This labor, by slow prudence to make mild
A rugged people, and through soft degrees
Subdue them to the useful and the good.
Most blameless is he, centered in the sphere
Of common duties, decent not to fail   40
In offices of tenderness, and pay
Meet adoration to my household gods,
When I am gone. He works his work, I mine.
    There lies the port; the vessel puffs her sail;
There gloom the dark, broad seas. My mariners,   45
Souls that have toiled, and wrought, and thought with me—
That ever with a frolic welcome took
The thunder and the sunshine, and opposed
Free hearts, free foreheads—you and I are old;
Old age hath yet his honor and his toil.   50
Death closes all; but something ere the end,
Some work of noble note, may yet be done,
Not unbecoming men that strove with Gods.
The lights begin to twinkle from the rocks;
The long day wanes; the low moon climbs; the deep   55
Moans round with many voices. Come, my friends,
'Tis not too late to seek a newer world.
Push off, and sitting well in order smite
The sounding furrows; for my purpose holds
To sail beyond the sunset, and the baths   60
Of all the western stars, until I die.
It may be that the gulfs will wash us down;
It may be we shall touch the Happy Isles,
And see the great Achilles, whom we knew.
Though much is taken, much abides; and though   65
We are not now that strength which in old days
Moved earth and heaven, that which we are, we are—

One equal temper of heroic hearts,
Made weak by time and fate, but strong in will
To strive, to seek, to find, and not to yield.   70

ULYSSES. 10 *Hyades:* daughters of Atlas, who were transformed into a group of stars. Their rising with the sun was thought to be a sign of rain. 63 *Happy Isles:* Elysium, a paradise believed to be attainable by sailing west.

COMPARE

"Ulysses" with "Sir Patrick Spence" (page 12).

Dylan Thomas   (1914–1953)*

FERN HILL   1946

Now as I was young and easy under the apple boughs
About the lilting house and happy as the grass was green,
      The night above the dingle° starry,   *wooded valley*
        Time let me hail and climb
      Golden in the heydays of his eyes,   5
And honored among wagons I was prince of the apple towns
And once below a time I lordly had the trees and leaves
        Trail with daisies and barley
      Down the rivers of the windfall light.

And as I was green and carefree, famous among the barns   10
About the happy yard and singing as the farm was home,
      In the sun that is young once only,
        Time let me play and be
      Golden in the mercy of his means,
And green and golden I was huntsman and herdsman, the calves   15
Sang to my horn, the foxes on the hills barked clear and cold,
        And the sabbath rang slowly
      In the pebbles of the holy streams.

All the sun long it was running, it was lovely, the hay
Fields high as the house, the tunes from the chimneys, it was air   20
      And playing, lovely and watery
        And fire green as grass.
      And nightly under the simple stars
As I rode to sleep the owls were bearing the farm away,
All the moon long I heard, blessed among stables, the nightjars   25
      Flying with the ricks, and the horses
        Flashing into the dark.

And then to awake, and the farm, like a wanderer white
With the dew, come back, the cock on his shoulder: it was all
      Shining, it was Adam and maiden, 30
            The sky gathered again
      And the sun grew round that very day.
So it must have been after the birth of the simple light
In the first, spinning place, the spellbound horses walking warm
      Out of the whinnying green stable 35
           On to the fields of praise.

And honored among foxes and pheasants by the gay house
Under the new made clouds and happy as the heart was long,
      In the sun born over and over,
           I ran my heedless ways, 40
      My wishes raced through the house high hay
And nothing I cared, at my sky blue trades, that time allows
In all his tuneful turning so few and such morning songs
      Before the children green and golden
           Follow him out of grace, 45

Nothing I cared, in the lamb white days, that time would take me
Up to the swallow thronged loft by the shadow of my hand,
      In the moon that is always rising,
           Nor that riding to sleep
      I should hear him fly with the high fields 50
And wake to the farm forever fled from the childless land.
Oh as I was young and easy in the mercy of his means,
           Time held me green and dying
      Though I sang in my chains like the sea.

COMPARE

"Fern Hill" with "in Just-" by E. E. Cummings (page 253) and "The World Is Too Much
with Us" by William Wordsworth (page 282).

John Updike   (b. 1932)*

EX-BASKETBALL PLAYER   1958

Pearl Avenue runs past the high-school lot,
Bends with the trolley tracks, and stops, cut off
Before it has a chance to go two blocks,
At Colonel McComsky Plaza. Berth's Garage
Is on the corner facing west, and there, 5
Most days, you'll find Flick Webb, who helps Berth out.

Flick stands tall among the idiot pumps—
Five on a side, the old bubble-head style,
Their rubber elbows hanging loose and low.
One's nostrils are two S's, and his eyes   10
An E and O. And one is squat, without
A head at all—more of a football type.

Once Flick played for the high-school team, the Wizards.
He was good: in fact, the best. In '46
He bucketed three hundred ninety points,   15
A county record still. The ball loved Flick.
I saw him rack up thirty-eight or forty
In one home game. His hands were like wild birds.

He never learned a trade, he just sells gas,
Checks oil, and changes flats. Once in a while,   20
As a gag, he dribbles an inner tube,
But most of us remember anyway.
His hands are fine and nervous on the lug wrench.
It makes no difference to the lug wrench, though.

Off work, he hangs around Mae's luncheonette.   25
Grease-gray and kind of coiled, he plays pinball,
Smokes those thin cigars, nurses lemon phosphates.
Flick seldom says a word to Mae, just nods
Beyond her face toward bright applauding tiers
Of Necco Wafers, Nibs, and Juju Beads.   30

COMPARE

"Ex-Basketball Player" with "To an Athlete Dying Young" by A. E. Housman (page 498).

Amy Uyematsu

Amy Uyematsu   (b. 1947)

THE TEN MILLION FLAMES OF LOS ANGELES   1998

A New Year's Poem, 1994

I've always been afraid of death by fire,
I am eight or nine when I see the remnants of a cross
burning on the Jacobs' front lawn,
seventeen when Watts explodes in '65,
forty-four when Watts blazes again in 1992.   5
For days the sky scatters soot and ash which cling to my skin,
the smell of burning metal everywhere. And I recall
James Baldwin's warning about the fire next time.

> *Fires keep burning in my city of the angels,*
> *from South Central to Hollywood,*   10
> *burn, baby, burn.*

In '93 LA's Santana winds incinerate Laguna and Malibu.
Once the firestorm begins, wind and heat regenerate
on their own, unleashing a fury so unforgiving
it must be a warning from the gods.   15

> *Fires keep burning in my city of the angels,*
> *how many does it take,*
> *burn, LA, burn.*

Everybody says we're all going to hell.
No home safe   20
from any tagger, gangster, carjacker, neighbor.
LA gets meaner by the minute
as we turn our backs

on another generation of young men,
become too used to this condition   25
of children killing children.
I wonder who to fear more.

>   *Fires keep burning in my city of angels,*
>   *but I hear someone whisper,*
>   *"Mi angelita, come closer."*   30

Though I ready myself for the next conflagration,
I feel myself giving in to something I can't name.
I smile more at strangers, leave big tips to waitresses,
laugh when I'm stuck on the freeway, content
just listening to B.B. King's "Why I Sing the Blues."   35

>   *"Mi angelita, mi angelita."*

I'm starting to believe in a flame
which tries to breathe in each of us.
I see young Chicanos fasting one more day
in a hunger strike for education,   40
read about gang members preaching peace in the 'hood,
hear Reginald Denny forgiving the men
who nearly beat him to death.
I look at people I know, as if for the first time,
sure that some are angels. I like the unlikeliness   45
of this unhandsome crew—the men losing their hair,
needing a shave, those with dark shining
eyes, and the grey-haired women, rage
and grace in each sturdy step.
What is this fire I feel, this fire which breathes freely   50
inside without burning them alive?

>   *Fires keep burning in my city of angels,*
>   *but someone calls to me.*
>   *"Angelita, do not run from the flame."*

THE TEN MILLION FLAMES OF LOS ANGELES: 4 *Watts:* African American neighborhood in Los Angeles, scene of race riots in 1965 and again in 1992 (following the acquittal of four white Los Angeles police officers who were caught on videotape beating Rodney King, a black motorist who had been stopped for speeding). 8 *James Baldwin:* writer and civil rights activist, author of two important books that were influential in the civil rights movement, *Go Tell It on the Mountain* (1953) and *Notes of a Native Son* (1955). 42 *Reginald Denny:* white truck-driver beaten by Watts rioters in 1992.

COMPARE

"The Ten Million Flames of Los Angeles" with "The Second Coming" by William Butler Yeats (page 286).

Derek Walcott

Derek Walcott (b. 1930)

THE VIRGINS   1976

Down the dead streets of sun-stoned Frederiksted,
the first free port to die for tourism,
strolling at funeral pace, I am reminded
of life not lost to the American dream;
but my small-islander's simplicities   5
can't better our new empire's civilized
exchange of cameras, watches, perfumes, brandies
for the good life, so cheaply underpriced
that only the crime rate is on the rise
in streets blighted with sun, stone arches   10
and plazas blown dry by the hysteria
of rumour. A condominium drowns
in vacancy; its bargains are dusted,
but only a jewelled housefly drones
over the bargains. The roulettes spin   15
rustily to the wind—the vigorous trade
that every morning would begin afresh
by revving up green water round the pierhead
heading for where the banks of silver thresh.

THE VIRGINS. The title of this poem refers to the Virgin Islands, a group of 100 small islands in the
Caribbean. 1 *Frederiksted:* the biggest seaport in St. Croix, the largest of the American Virgin Islands.
2 *free port:* a port city where goods can be bought and sold without paying customs taxes. 5 *small-
islander's:* Walcott was born on St. Lucia, another island in the West Indies. 16 *trade:* trade winds.

COMPARE

"The Virgins" with "London" by William Blake (page 82).

Edmund Waller (1606–1687)

Go, Lovely Rose   1645

Go, lovely rose,
Tell her that wastes her time and me
   That now she knows,
When I resemble° her to thee,   *compare*
How sweet and fair she seems to be.   5

   Tell her that's young
And shuns to have her graces spied,
   That hadst thou sprung
In deserts where no men abide,
Thou must have uncommended died.   10

   Small is the worth
Of beauty from the light retired:
   Bid her come forth,
Suffer herself to be desired,
And not blush so to be admired.   15

   Then die, that she
The common fate of all things rare
   May read in thee,
How small a part of time they share
That are so wondrous sweet and fair.   20

COMPARE

"Go, Lovely Rose" with "To the Virgins, to Make Much of Time" by Robert Herrick
(page 495) and "To His Coy Mistress" by Andrew Marvell (page 512).

Walt Whitman (1819–1892)*

A Noiseless Patient Spider   (1876)

A noiseless patient spider,
I mark'd where on a little promontory it stood isolated,
Mark'd how to explore the vacant vast surrounding,
It launch'd forth filament, filament, filament, out of itself,
Ever unreeling them, ever tirelessly speeding them.   5
And you O my soul where you stand,
Surrounded, detached, in measureless oceans of space,
Ceaselessly musing, venturing, throwing, seeking the spheres to
    connect them,
Till the bridge you will need be form'd, till the ductile anchor hold,
Till the gossamer thread you fling catch somewhere, O my soul.   10

COMPARE

"A Noiseless Patient Spider" with "Ulysses" by Alfred, Lord Tennyson (page 554) or "The Eagle" by Alfred, Lord Tennyson (page 119).

Walt Whitman

Walt Whitman   (1819–1892)*

I HEAR AMERICA SINGING   1860

I hear America singing, the varied carols I hear,
Those of mechanics, each one singing his as it should be blithe and
   strong,
The carpenter singing his as he measures his plank or beam,
The mason singing his as he makes ready for work, or leaves off work,
The boatman singing what belongs to him in his boat, the deckhand   5
   singing on the steamboat deck,
The shoemaker singing as he sits on his bench, the hatter singing as he
   stands,
The wood-cutter's song, the ploughboy's on his way in the morning, or
   at noon intermission or at sundown,
The delicious singing of the mother, or of the young wife at work, or of
   the girl sewing or washing,
Each singing what belongs to him or her and to none else,
The day what belongs to the day—at night the party of young fellows,   10
   robust, friendly,
Singing with open mouths their strong melodious songs.

COMPARE

"I Hear America Singing" with "I, Too" by Langston Hughes (page 422).

Richard Wilbur   (b. 1921)*

THE WRITER   1976

In her room at the prow of the house
Where light breaks, and the windows are tossed with linden,
My daughter is writing a story.

I pause in the stairwell, hearing
From her shut door a commotion of typewriter-keys   5
Like a chain hauled over a gunwale.

Young as she is, the stuff
Of her life is a great cargo, and some of it heavy:
I wish her a lucky passage.

But now it is she who pauses,   10
As if to reject my thought and its easy figure.
A stillness greatens, in which

The whole house seems to be thinking,
And then she is at it again with a bunched clamor
Of strokes, and again is silent.   15

I remember the dazed starling
Which was trapped in that very room, two years ago;
How we stole in, lifted a sash

And retreated, not to affright it;
And how for a helpless hour, through the crack of the door,   20
We watched the sleek, wild, dark

And iridescent creature
Batter against the brilliance, drop like a glove
To the hard floor, or the desk-top.

And wait then, humped and bloody,   25
For the wits to try it again; and how our spirits
Rose when, suddenly sure,

It lifted off from a chair-back,
Beating a smooth course for the right window
And clearing the sill of the world.   30

It is always a matter, my darling,
Of life or death, as I had forgotten. I wish
What I wished you before, but harder.

COMPARE

"The Writer" with "Digging" by Seamus Heaney (page 490).

C. K. Williams   (b. 1936)

ELMS   1987

All morning the tree men have been taking down the stricken elms
    skirting the broad sidewalks.
The pitiless electric chain saws whine tirelessly up and down their
    piercing, operatic scales
and the diesel choppers in the street shredding the debris chug
    feverishly, incessantly,
packing truckload after truckload with the feathery, homogenized, inert
    remains of heartwood,
twig and leaf and soon the block is stripped, it is as though illusions of   5
    reality were stripped:
the rows of naked facing buildings stare and think, their divagations
    more urgent than they were.
"The winds of time," they think, the mystery charged with fearful
    clarity: "The winds of time . . ."
All afternoon, on to the unhealing evening, minds racing, "Insolent,
    unconscionable, the winds of time . . ."

COMPARE

"Elms" With "Mutability" by William Wordsworth (page 74) and "Final Love Note" by
Clare Rossini (page 88).

William Carlos Williams   (1883–1963)*

SPRING AND ALL   1923

By the road to the contagious hospital
under the surge of the blue
mottled clouds driven from the
northeast—a cold wind. Beyond, the
waste of broad, muddy fields   5
brown with dried weeds, standing and fallen

patches of standing water
the scattering of tall trees

All along the road the reddish
purplish, forked, upstanding, twiggy   10
stuff of bushes and small trees
with dead, brown leaves under them
leafless vines—

Lifeless in appearance, sluggish
dazed spring approaches—   15

They enter the new world naked,
cold, uncertain of all
save that they enter. All about them
the cold, familiar wind—

Now the grass, tomorrow   20
the stiff curl of wildcarrot leaf
One by one objects are defined—
It quickens: clarity, outline of leaf

But now the stark dignity of
entrance—Still, the profound change   25
has come upon them: rooted, they
grip down and begin to awaken

COMPARE

"Spring and All" with "in Just-" by E. E. Cummings (page 253) and "Root Cellar" by
Theodore Roethke (page 96).

William Carlos Williams

William Carlos Williams (1883–1963)*

TO WAKEN AN OLD LADY   1921

Old age is
a flight of small
cheeping birds
skimming
bare trees
above a snow glaze.   5
Gaining and failing
they are buffeted

by a dark wind—
But what?   10
On harsh weedstalks
the flock has rested,
the snow
is covered with broken
seedhusks   15
and the wind tempered
by a shrill
piping of plenty.

COMPARE

"To Waken an Old Lady" with "Sorrow Moves in Wide Waves" by Lorine Niedecker
(page 521).

William Wordsworth

William Wordsworth (1770–1850)*

COMPOSED UPON WESTMINSTER BRIDGE   1807

Earth has not anything to show more fair:
Dull would he be of soul who could pass by
A sight so touching in its majesty:
This City now doth, like a garment, wear
The beauty of the morning; silent, bare,   5
Ships, towers, domes, theatres, and temples lie
Open unto the fields, and to the sky;
All bright and glittering in the smokeless air.
Never did sun more beautifully steep
In his first splendor, valley, rock, or hill;   10
Ne'er saw I, never felt, a calm so deep!

The river glideth at his own sweet will:
Dear God! the very houses seem asleep;
And all that mighty heart is lying still!

COMPARE

"Composed upon Westminster Bridge" with "London" by William Blake (page 82).

James Wright   (1927–1980)*

A BLESSING   1961

Just off the highway to Rochester, Minnesota,
Twilight bounds softly forth on the grass.
And the eyes of those two Indian ponies
Darken with kindness.
They have come gladly out of the willows   5
To welcome my friend and me.
We step over the barbed wire into the pasture
Where they have been grazing all day, alone.
They ripple tensely, they can hardly contain their happiness
That we have come.   10
They bow shyly as wet swans. They love each other.
There is no loneliness like theirs.
At home once more,
They begin munching the young tufts of spring in the darkness.
I would like to hold the slenderer one in my arms,   15
For she has walked over to me
And nuzzled my left hand.
She is black and white,
Her mane falls wild on her forehead,
And the light breeze moves me to caress her long ear   20
That is delicate as the skin over a girl's wrist.
Suddenly I realize
That if I stepped out of my body I would break
Into blossom.

COMPARE

"A Blessing" with "God's Grandeur" by Gerard Manley Hopkins (page 179).

James Wright (1927–1980)*

AUTUMN BEGINS IN MARTINS FERRY, OHIO   1963

In the Shreve High football stadium,
I think of Polacks nursing long beers in Tiltonsville,
And gray faces of Negroes in the blast furnace at Benwood,
And the ruptured night watchman of Wheeling Steel,
Dreaming of heroes.   5

All the proud fathers are ashamed to go home.
Their women cluck like starved pullets,
Dying for love.

Therefore,
Their sons grow suicidally beautiful   10
At the beginning of October,
And gallop terribly against each other's bodies.

COMPARE

"Autumn Begins in Martin's Ferry, Ohio" with "Ex-Basketball Player" by John Updike
(page 557).

Mary Sidney Wroth (1587?–1623?)

IN THIS STRANGE LABYRINTH   1621

In this strange labyrinth how shall I turn?
Ways are on all sides while the way I miss:
If to the right hand, there in love I burn;
Let me go forward, therein danger is;
If to the left, suspicion hinders bliss,   5
Let me turn back, shame cries I ought return
Nor faint though crosses with my fortunes kiss.
Stand still is harder, although sure to mourn;
Thus let me take the right, or left hand way;
Go forward, or stand still, or back retire;   10
I must these doubts endure without allay
Or help, but travail find for my best hire;
Yet that which most my troubled sense doth move
Is to leave all, and take the thread of love.

IN THIS STRANGE LABYRINTH. This sonnet comes from Wroth's *Urania* (1621), the first significant
sonnet sequence by a woman. Wroth was the niece of Sir Philip Sidney and of the countess of Pem-
broke as well as a distant relation of Sir Walter Raleigh. The *Labyrinth* of the title was the maze built
by Minos to trap the young men and women sacrificed to the Minotaur. King Minos's daughter Ari-
adne saved her beloved Theseus by giving him a skein of thread to guide his way through the
Labyrinth. (See the final line of the sonnet.)

COMPARE

"In this strange labyrinth" with "Let me not to the marriage of true minds" by William Shakespeare (page 221).

Sir Thomas Wyatt   (1503?–1542)*

THEY FLEE FROM ME THAT   (ABOUT 1535)
SOMETIME DID ME SEKË

They flee from me that sometime did me sekë
  With naked fotë° stalking in my chamber.   *foot*
I have seen them gentle, tame and mekë
  That now are wild, and do not remember
  That sometime they put themself in danger   5
To take bread at my hand; and now they range
Busily seeking with a continual change.

Thankèd be fortune, it hath been otherwise
  Twenty times better; but once in speciàll,
In thin array, after a pleasant guise,   10
  When her loose gown from her shoulders did fall,
  And she me caught in her armës long and small,
Therëwith all sweetly did me kiss,
And softly said, *Dear heart, how like you this?*

It was no dremë: I lay broadë waking.   15
  But all is turned thorough° my gentleness   *through*
Into a strangë fashion of forsaking;
  And I have leave to go of her goodness,
  And she also to use newfangleness.°   *to seek novelty*
But since that I so kindëly am served
                                 20
I would fain knowë what she hath deserved.

THEY FLEE FROM ME THAT SOMETIME DID ME SEKË. Some latter-day critics have called Sir Thomas Wyatt a careless poet because some of his lines appear faltering and metrically inconsistent; others have thought he knew what he was doing. It is uncertain whether the final *e*'s in English spelling were still pronounced in Wyatt's day as they were in Chaucer's, but if they were, perhaps Wyatt has been unjustly blamed. In this text, spellings have been modernized except in words where the final *e* would make a difference in rhythm. To sense how it matters, try reading the poem aloud leaving out the *e*'s and then putting them in wherever indicated. Sound them like the *a* in *sofa*. 20 *kindëly:* according to my kind (or hers); that is, as befits the nature of man (or woman). Perhaps there is also irony here, and the word means "unkindly."

COMPARE

"They flee from me that sometimes did me sekë" with "When, in disgrace with Fortune and men's eyes" by William Shakespeare (page 540).

William Butler Yeats

William Butler Yeats (1865–1939)*

Crazy Jane Talks with the Bishop   1933

I met the Bishop on the road
And much said he and I.
"Those breasts are flat and fallen now,
Those veins must soon be dry;
Live in a heavenly mansion,   5
Not in some foul sty."

"Fair and foul are near of kin,
And fair needs foul," I cried.
"My friends are gone, but that's a truth
Nor° grave nor bed denied,   *neither*   10
Learned in bodily lowliness
And in the heart's pride.

"A woman can be proud and stiff
When on love intent;
But Love has pitched his mansion in   15
The place of excrement;
For nothing can be sole or whole
That has not been rent."

Compare

"Crazy Jane Talks with the Bishop" with "The Flea" by John Donne (page 467) or "Down, Wanton, Down!" by Robert Graves (page 56).

William Butler Yeats (1865–1939)*
THE MAGI   1914

Now as at all times I can see in the mind's eye,
In their stiff, painted clothes, the pale unsatisfied ones
Appear and disappear in the blue depth of the sky
With all their ancient faces like rain-beaten stones,
And all their helms of silver hovering side by side,   5
And all their eyes still fixed, hoping to find once more,
Being by Calvary's turbulence unsatisfied,
The uncontrollable mystery on the bestial floor.

COMPARE

"The Magi" with "Journey of the Magi" by T. S. Eliot (page 471).

William Butler Yeats (1865–1939)*
WHEN YOU ARE OLD   1893

When you are old and grey and full of sleep,
And nodding by the fire, take down this book,
And slowly read, and dream of the soft look
Your eyes had once, and of their shadows deep;

How many loved your moments of glad grace,   5
And loved your beauty with love false or true,
But one man loved the pilgrim soul in you,
And loved the sorrows of your changing face;

And bending down beside the glowing bars,
Murmur, a little sadly, how Love fled   10
And paced upon the mountains overhead
And hid his face amid a crowd of stars.

COMPARE

"When You Are Old" with "Not marble nor the gilded monuments" by William
Shakespeare (page 541).

21 Lives of the Poets

Here you will find a brief biographical note for each poet represented in the book by more than one selection.

John Ashbery

John Ashbery, born in Rochester, New York, in 1927, was educated at Deerfield Academy, Harvard, and Columbia. In 1960 he became an art critic in Paris for the *New York Herald Tribune*, and from 1966 to 1972 served as executive editor of the magazine *Art News* in New York. His first full collection of poetry, *Some Trees* (1956), was chosen by W. H. Auden for publication in the Yale Series of Younger Poets; his *Self-Portrait in a Convex Mirror* (1976) garnered praise and three leading literary prizes, and sold well for a book of serious poetry. Ashbery has written plays and a novel (with James Schuyler), *A Nest of Ninnies* (1969). Some critics have speculated that Ashbery's experience as an art critic has tinged his poetry: that he performs in words what an abstract expressionist performs on canvas in oils.

His work can annoy readers who expect poems to make clear statements to be taken in only one way; others think him the foremost living American poet and major heir to the tradition of Wallace Stevens—that is, to the art of suggesting rather than depicting, of arranging words primarily for their own sake.

Margaret Atwood

Margaret Atwood, born in Ottawa in 1939, is a staunchly Canadian poet, short story writer, and novelist whose literary reputation has extended well beyond the borders of her native country. She published her first book of poems, *Double Persephone*, in 1962, the same year she graduated from the University of Toronto. She went on to earn a master's degree at Radcliffe and to study Victorian fantasy at Harvard. She has advanced her country's cultural identity by publishing *Survival* (1972), a book about Canadian literature, and by editing *The Oxford Book of Canadian Verse* (1982). Her fiction and poetry, at once comic and grim, often deal with alienation and the destructive nature of human relationships. Her novel *Cat's Eye* (1989) won attention on both sides of the Canadian border. The cream of her poetry has been skimmed in *Eating Fire: Selected Poems 1965–1995* (1998).

W. H. Auden

Wystan Hugh Auden (1907–1973), born in York, England, as a young man in the 1930s became the acknowledged spokesman for a generation of English poets that included Stephen Spender, C. Day Lewis, and Louis MacNeice. His early work was characterized by blithe wit, a Marxist outlook, and a knowledge of Freudian psychology; in later life, he professed Christianity and (in his views of poetry) increasing conservatism. In 1939 Auden emigrated to America, and in 1946 became a United States citizen. A prolific editor, anthologist, and translator of poetry, he collaborated on verse plays, travel memoirs, and (with his longtime companion Chester Kallman) librettos for operas, including Igor Stravinsky's *The Rake's Progress* (1951). He wrote influential criticism, notably that collected in *The Dyer's Hand* (1962). Auden divided his last years among England, Italy, Austria, and New York.

Matsuo Basho

Matsuo Basho (1644–1694) was born in Ueno, about thirty miles southwest of Kyoto, which was then the imperial capital of Japan. Basho's father was a samurai-class farmer with considerable land. Basho began writing poetry in adolescence, and he worked variously as a teacher, a waterworks official, and possibly even as a ninja spy. He eventually shaved his head and became a lay monk. In 1689 he and a friend took a five-month journey across Japan in which they covered 1233 miles by foot. *Narrow Road to the Far North*, his account of that trip (written in both verse and prose), is one of the classics of Japanese literature.

Elizabeth Bishop

Elizabeth Bishop (1911–1979) was born in Worcester, Massachusetts. After her father died (in her first year) and her mother was stricken with mental illness, she lived until age six with her grandmother in a coastal village in Nova Scotia. Because she suffered from asthma, Bishop received scant elementary schooling, but she read widely and deeply at home. At sixteen, she entered Walnut Hill, a boarding school, and later graduated from Vassar Collage. Her undergraduate poems won her the friendship of the poet Marianne Moore, who persuaded her not to go on to medical school, but instead to write. Fond of travel and flower-filled climates, Bishop lived for nine years in Key West, Florida, then for fifteen years in Brazil, dividing her time between the mountains and Rio de Janeiro. In 1966 she returned to the United States to teach: first at the University of Washington, then at Harvard from 1969 until 1977, when she retired. Most of her sparely disciplined work is contained in two volumes: *Complete Poems 1927–1979* (1983) and *Collected Prose* (1984). Her sharp-eyed poems, full of vivid images and apt metaphors, have influenced the work of other poets, among them her friends Randall Jarrell and Robert Lowell.

lifetime, Wordsworth and Coleridge were among the few admirers of his short lyrics; his "Prophetic Books" had to wait until the twentieth century for sympathetic readers.

William Blake

William Blake (1757–1827), poet, painter, and visionary, was born in the Soho district of London and early in life was apprenticed to an engraver. Becoming a skilled craftsman, he earned his living illustrating books, among them Dante's *Divine Comedy*, Milton's poems, and the Book of Job. A remarkable and original graphic artist whose only formal training came from a few months at the Royal Academy, Blake published his own poems, engraving them in a careful script embellished with hand-colored illustrations and decorations. His wife Catherine Boucher, whom he taught to read and write, shared his visions and helped him do the coloring. *Songs of Innocence* (1789) and *Songs of Experience* (1794), brief lyrics written from a child's point of view, are easy to enjoy; but anyone deeply interested in Blake copes also with the longer, more demanding "Prophetic Books," among them *The Book of Thel* (1789), *The Marriage of Heaven and Hell* (1790), and *Jerusalem* (1804–1820). In these later works, out of his readings in alchemy, the Bible, and the works of Plato and Swedenborg, Blake derived support for his lifelong hatred of scientific rationalism and created his own mythology, complete with devils and deities. A sympathizer with both the American and French revolutions, Blake was once accused of sedition, but the charges were dismissed. In his

Robert Bly

Robert Bly was born on a farm in Madison, Minnesota, in 1926, and continued to live there for most of his life. He graduated from Harvard, where he began studies in mathematics before deciding to devote his life to poetry. Rather than teaching, Bly has preferred to support himself and his family by giving poetry readings and by translating books and poems from Scandinavian and other languages. In 1958 he launched a poetry magazine, *The Fifties* (later renamed, as decades went by, *The Sixties* and *The Seventies*). In it he spoofed academic critics, urged American poets to open their work to dream and surrealism, and introduced in translation the work of important poets of Europe and Latin America. Bly has vitally influenced the work of James Wright, Donald Hall, and many younger poets. His readings, in which he sometimes chants and dons primitive masks, have drawn throngs. In the 1960s he organized (with David Ray) American Writers Against the Vietnam War, and over the years has championed many causes, usually pacifist and antinuclear. Lately he has been leading retreats for men, trying to help them understand their male natures. In 1990 Bly's *Iron John*, a book on contemporary male identity, became a national best-seller.

Louise Bogan

Louise Bogan (1897–1970) was born in Maine to parents of Irish descent. She spent her early years in several New England mill towns. Although she won a scholarship to Radcliffe, she left college to marry an army officer. Her husband's sudden death in 1920 left her alone with a small daughter. She boldly moved to Manhattan and began a literary career. Publishing her first book, *Body of This Death*, in 1923, Bogan developed an austere but emotional style of formal lyric that she continued to use until her final collection *The Blue Estuaries* in 1968. For nearly forty years Bogan reviewed poetry for the *New Yorker*. Underappreciated in their own time, Bogan's quiet poems have steadily risen in critical esteem since her death.

Jorge Luis Borges

See biographical note on page 353.

Gwendolyn Brooks

Gwendolyn Brooks (1917–2000), born in Topeka, Kansas, moved early in life to Chicago's South Side, whose people she has commemorated in her poetry and in a novel, *Maud Martha* (1953). Recipient of the Pulitzer Prize for poetry in 1950, for *Annie Allen*, Brooks has long been recognized as a leading voice in modern American letters. She combined several teaching positions with raising two children. From 1967, when she took part in a conference for black writers at Fisk University and

was impressed with young black poets' views, she was increasingly an activist, teaching teenage black writers in Chicago and addressing her work especially to black audiences. Instead of continuing to publish with a mainstream New York publishing house, she switched her work to Broadside, a small literary press in Detroit founded by black poet Dudley Randall. Her memoir *Report from Part One* (1972) discusses her altered outlook. In 1985 she was named consultant in poetry to the Library of Congress (the position now known as poet laureate of the United States). Her goals in life, she declared, were "to be clean of heart, clear of mind, and claiming of what is right and just."

Elizabeth Barrett Browning

Elizabeth Barrett (1806–1861) was born in a large country house outside Durham, England. The eldest of twelve children, she was raised in a close, affectionate family ruled by her possessive father. Ill health kept her at home as an adult, but she nonetheless achieved literary fame and corresponded with many famous writers. The day after she met one correspondent, Robert Browning, in 1845, he sent her a declaration of love, which she insisted he withdraw if he ever wanted to visit again. Gradually, however, she fell in love with her devoted visitor, but the courtship was conducted in secret, since her father had forbidden his children to marry. In 1846 she and Browning eloped to Italy, where the couple lived happily until her death in 1861. When

William Wordsworth died in 1850, Mrs. Browning was considered for the position of poet laureate (which eventually went to Tennyson). She was the most highly regarded woman poet of the nineteenth century, and her work was immensely popular with both critics and general readers.

Robert Browning

Robert Browning (1812–1889), born in a suburb of London, was educated mainly in his father's six-thousand-volume library. With *Pauline* (1833), he began to print his poetry. After the death of his wife Elizabeth Barrett Browning, with whom he had lived in Italy, he returned to England to become (Henry James wrote) an "accomplished, saturated, sane, sound man of the London world." There, as he neared sixty, he enjoyed late but loud applause and the adulation of the Browning Society: faithful readers whose local groups met over their teacups to explicate his work. Readers have most greatly favored Browning's story-poems in a form he perfected, the dramatic monologue—such as "My Last Duchess" and "Soliloquy of the Spanish Cloister"—in which he brings to life persons from the past (some of them famous), and has them speak their innermost thoughts and reveal their characters. His masterpiece, *The Ring and the Book* (1868–1869), is a long narrative poem in twelve monologues, based on a seventeenth-century Roman murder trial. Browning also wrote several plays, among them *A Blot in the 'Scutcheon* (1842). Through the praise and emulation of his later admirers Ezra Pound and T. S. Eliot, Browning has profoundly affected modern poetry. A formal experimenter, he speaks to us in energetic, punchy words—and like many later poets, he introduces learning into his poems without apology. More important, Browning is among the great yea-sayers in English poetry: an affirmer and celebrant of life.

Robert Burns

Robert Burns (1759–1796), the pre-eminent poet of Scotland, was born in a two-room farm cottage in Alloway, a hamlet on the River Doon, the son of a farmer who worked himself to death. For most of his days Burns too struggled to farm poor soil. Though his schooling lasted only three years, he eagerly read Shakespeare and Pope as a boy and let poetry pour from his own pen. Only in 1786, when he felt he needed money to emigrate to Jamaica, did he publish his *Poems, Chiefly in the Scottish Dialect*, depicting Scottish rural life with warm humor, tender compassion, and rugged exuberance. The book scored an immediate hit and Burns remained in Scotland for the rest of his days. After Edinburgh's stylish society, which had lionized him for a time, dropped him, he returned to his plough, married Jean Armour (who earlier had borne him two sets of twins), and continued to farm until 1791, when he retired to the easier life of a tax official. But, worn from toil, hardship, and poverty, Burns died at thirty-seven. Among his legacies are songs, such as "Flow Gently, Sweet Afton," "Comin' Through the Rye," and a song still heard in this country each New Year's Eve, "Auld Lang Syne." Like Hugh MacDiarmid, Burns wrote poetry in both standard English and Scots dialect—in the latter whenever, as in "The Jolly Beggars" and "Address to the Unco Guid," he expressed defiantly unconventional views.

Taniguchi Buson

Taniguchi Buson (1716–1783) was born on the outskirts of Osaka. Little is known about his childhood, but as a young man, he went to Edo (later called Tokyo) to study both painting and poetry. He soon became a celebrated painter as well as one of the "Three Masters" of classic haiku. Buson studied Buddhism for many years and may have considered becoming a priest. At forty-five, a prosperous artist, he married Tomo, who was also a poet. He lived a comfortable later life as an artist and teacher.

Billy Collins

Billy Collins was born in New York City in 1941. He graduated from Holy Cross College in 1963 and earned a Ph.D. in Romantic poetry from the University of California at Riverside in 1971. He has received fellowships from the New York Foundation for the Arts, the National Endowment for the Arts, and the Guggenheim Foundation, and was appointed Poet Laureate of the United States in 2001. Written in a witty and accessible style, his poems often begin with ordinary domestic situations and take them in some very surprising directions (although, as he demonstrates in "The Names," he is also capable of writing with great seriousness and power). His collections, including *Sailing Alone Around the Room: New and Selected*

Poems (2001) and *Nine Horses* (2002), have achieved phenomenal sales for books of poetry. Collins is a professor of English at Lehman College, City University of New York. He lives in Somers, New York.

Wendy Cope

Wendy Cope was born in Kent, England, in 1945. Her father, who was nearly sixty when she was born, was a poetry enthusiast of Victorian sensibilities, who often recited Tennyson and Fitzgerald's *Rubaiyat* to the family. After leaving school, she became a primary-school music teacher. Cope claims she "forgot about poetry for more than ten years." Her father's death in 1971, however, triggered a depression that eventually led her to seek psychological help. As she regained her self-esteem, Cope began reading poetry again and soon started writing. She first gained notice for her brilliant parodies of famous poems (which include a retelling of T. S. Eliot's *The Waste Land* in five limericks), but gradually her bittersweet and incisive love poems have become equally prized. Her three collections, *Making Cocoa for Kingsley Amis* (1986), *Serious Concerns*, (1992) and *If I Don't Know* (2001), have become bestsellers in England. In a 1998 BBC Radio 4 poll following the death of Ted Hughes, she was the respondents' first choice to succeed him as poet laureate.

E. E. Cummings

Edward Estlin Cummings (1894–1962) was born in Cambridge, Massachusetts, the son of a minister. As a young man at Harvard, he studied

Greek and Latin. In World War I, while serving as an ambulance driver, he was mistakenly arrested and confined to a French prison—an experience that gave rise to a novel filled with vivid portraits of his fellow prisoners, *The Enormous Room* (1922). Off and on throughout the 1920s, Cummings lived in Paris. In *Eimi* (1933) he scathingly and satirically reported on a trip to the Soviet Union. Although many of his lyric poems revel in typographical experiment, in theme and sentiment they are often more conventional than they appear. Besides poetry Cummings wrote essays, plays—including *Him* (1927) and *Santa Claus* (1946)—the ballet *Tom* (1935), and produced substantial work as a painter and a graphic artist. Throughout his career, he upheld simple themes: love is good, pomp is silly, one individual is worth a thousand faceless societies.

J. V. Cunningham

James Vincent Cunningham (1911–1985) was born in Maryland, but spent his early life in Montana. A Shakespeare scholar with a Stanford Ph.D., Cunningham taught English at Brandeis for many years (1953–1980) and for eight years served as chairman of the department. A reader of Latin and Greek, he became the modern master of the terse, pithy English verse epigram in the classical manner. All his poems have a similar brevity, firm control, and a cold, hardboiled manner. "Poetry is what looks like poetry, what sounds like poetry," he stated. "It is metrical composition." His relatively slim *Collected Poems and Epigrams* (1971) gathers most of his work in

verse; his *Collected Essays* (1976), most of his work in prose, including an earlier study, *Woe and Wonder: The Emotional Effect of Shakespearean Tragedy*. In a late critical work, *Dickinson: Lyric and Legend* (1980), Cunningham took a withering look at the bard of Amherst.

Emily Dickinson

See biographical note on page 401.

John Donne

John Donne (1572–1631), English poet and divine, wrote his subtle, worldly love lyrics as a young man in the court of Queen Elizabeth I. At the time, he came to be known in London as (wrote his contemporary, Richard Baker) "a great visitor of ladies, a great frequenter of plays, a great writer of conceited verses." The poems of his *Songs and Sonets* were first circulated in manuscript form, for in his lifetime Donne printed little. When in 1601 he married without the consent of his bride's father, he was dismissed from his secretarial post at court. For several years he endured poverty. His longer poems, *The First Anniversary* and *The Second Anniversary* (1611, 1612), suffused with gloom, see the order of the universe shaken by science and doubt. In 1615 Donne—apparently with some reluctance, for he had been raised a Catholic—became a priest of the Anglican church. From 1621 until his death, he was dean of St. Paul's Cathedral in London, where he preached sermons known for their eloquence. His "Holy Sonnets" date from later life. Almost forgotten for two centuries, Donne's work has had much influence in our time. H. J. C. Grierson published a great scholarly edition of it in 1912; shortly thereafter it was championed by T. S. Eliot.

Rita Dove

Rita Dove was born in Akron, Ohio, in 1952. She received her B.A. from Miami University of Ohio and her M.F.A. from the University of Iowa, and was a Fulbright scholar at the Universität Tübingen in Germany. From 1993 to 1995 she served as Poet Laureate of the United States. Her third book of poems, *Thomas and Beulah* (1986), was awarded the Pulitzer Prize. More recent collections include *Selected Poems* (1993), *Mother Love* (1995), and *On the Bus with Rosa Parks* (1999). She has also published a novel, a book of short stories, and a verse play, *The Darker Face of the Earth* (1994), which recasts the Oedipus myth in a drama set on a plantation in pre-Civil War Virginia. Dove's poetry often deals with themes of family, both present-day and historical, in a style that is concentrated and carefully wrought. She is Commonwealth Professor of English at the University of Virginia in Charlottesville, where she lives with her husband and daughter.

T. S. Eliot

Thomas Stearns Eliot (1888–1965) was born of a New England family that had moved to St. Louis. After study at Harvard, Eliot emigrated to London, and worked as a bank clerk and later an influential editor for the publishing house of Faber. In 1927 he became a British citizen and joined the Church of England. During the fire bombings of London in World War II, he served as an air-raid warden. Although Eliot strove to keep his private life private, biographer Peter Ackroyd in *T. S. Eliot* (1984) threw light upon his troubled early marriage. Early poems such as "The Love Song of J. Alfred Prufrock" (1917) and *The Waste Land* (1922), an allusive and seemingly disconnected complaint about the sterility of contemporary city life, enormously influenced young poets. Eliot was mainly responsible for bringing French symbolism into English poetry, and as a critic, he helped revive interest in John Donne and other Metaphysical poets. In an early essay, "Tradition and the Individual Talent" (1919), he finds a necessary continuity in Western civilization. *Four Quartets*, completed in 1943, was Eliot's last major work of poetry: an attempt to structure a long thematic poem like a work of music. In later years he devoted himself to writing verse plays for the London stage; the best received was *The Cocktail Party* (1950), in which Alec Guinness played a psychiatrist. In 1948 Eliot received the Nobel Prize in literature.

Robert Frost

Robert Frost (1874–1963), though born in San Francisco, came to be popularly known as a spokesman for rural New England. In periods of farming, teaching school, and raising chickens and writing for poultry journals, Frost struggled until his late thirties to support his family and to publish his poems, with little success. Moving to England to write and farm in 1912, he had his first two books published in London: *A Boy's Will*

(1913) and *North of Boston* (1914). Returning to America in 1915, he settled in New Hampshire, later teaching for many years (in a casual way) at Amherst College in Massachusetts. Audiences responded warmly to the poet's public readings; he was awarded four Pulitzer Prizes. In his later years the white-haired Frost became a sort of elder statesman and poet laureate of the John F. Kennedy administration, invited to read a poem at President Kennedy's inauguration and dispatched to Russia as a cultural emissary. Frost is sometimes admired for putting colloquial Yankee speech into poetry—and he did, but more essentially he mastered the art of laying conversational American speech along a metrical line. In a three-volume biography (1966–1976), Lawrance Thompson made Frost out to be an overweening egotist who tormented his family, and it has taken us decades to reestablish a more balanced—and properly admiring—view of him.

Robert Graves

Robert von Ranke Graves (1895–1985), one of the most prolifically talented writers of the twentieth century, was born in Wimbledon, England. His father Alfred Perceval Graves was a popular poet. During World War I, Graves enlisted in the Royal Welsh Fusiliers, a unit that saw ferocious combat. Wounded and mistakenly declared dead, Graves was demobilized with shell-shock. His youthful autobiography, *Goodbye to All That* (1929), ranks as the classic British memoir of World War I, and its stark accounts of the despair and brutality of trench warfare are still shocking today.

Moving to Majorca, Spain, in 1929, Graves wrote a series of best-selling historical novels, most famously *I, Claudius* and *Claudius the God* (both 1934). He later wrote an influential study of poetic mythology, *The White Goddess* (1948), which claims the matriarchal Moon Goddess as the true source of poetic inspiration. Graves's vast poetic output covers many subjects, but he is best remembered as a love poet, an area in which he has few modern equals.

Thomas Hardy

Thomas Hardy (1840–1928) was both a major Victorian novelist and a great poet of the twentieth century. After his novel *Jude the Obscure* (1896) was trounced by critics who objected to its dismal morbidity, Hardy, who by then had made a modest fortune from his fiction, switched exclusively to his first love, poetry. Hardy was born in the English county of Dorsetshire ("Wessex" in his fiction and poetry), and, as a young man, he worked as an architect. Determined to be a novelist, he first won success with *Far from the Madding Crowd* (1874), followed by *The Return of the Native* (1878), *The Mayor of Casterbridge* (1886), and his masterpiece, *Tess of the D'Urbervilles* (1891). After the death of his first wife Emma, with whom he appears to have had a rather cold and troubled relationship, Hardy was inspired to write a great spate of love poems in her memory. In old age he wrote a two-volume autobiography and charged his second wife, Florence, to publish it after his death under her own name. In both fiction and poetry, Hardy's view of the universe is somber: God appears to have forgotten us, and happiness usually arrives too late. *The Dynasts* (1903–1908), a long dramatic poem, makes amused gods sneer down on the Napoleonic wars. Many modern poets have credited Hardy with teaching them a good deal (probably about irony and the use of spoken language), among them W. H. Auden, Philip Larkin, Dylan Thomas, and W. D. Snodgrass.

Robert Hayden

Robert Hayden (1913–1980) was born in Detroit, Michigan. He attended Detroit City College (now called Wayne State University) and the University of Michigan, where he studied with W. H. Auden. In 1946 he began teaching at Fisk University in pre-civil-rights-era Nashville, where Hayden, an African American, experienced racial segregation for the first time. Although he lived in Nashville until 1968, he eventually sent his wife and daughter to New York, where schools were integrated. In 1941 he became a convert to the Baha'i faith, a universalist religion that emphasizes charity, tolerance, and equality; his poetry reflects the compassionate moral courage of that creed. Hayden edited the influential 1967 anthology *Kaleidoscope: Poems by American Negro Poets*. In 1976 he was appointed the Consultant in Poetry at the Library of Congress, the first African American to hold that influential office.

H. D. (*Hilda Doolittle*)

Hilda Doolittle (1886–1961), daughter of a Moravian mother and a professor of mathematics and astronomy, spent her first eight years in Bethlehem, Pennsylvania. At Bryn Mawr, she failed English and suffered a nervous collapse. By 1911 she had become a confirmed expatriate, living in London. At one time she was engaged to Ezra Pound, who submitted her early poems to Harriet Monroe's magazine *Poetry* and signed them "H. D. Imagiste." In 1913 she married poet and translator Richard Aldington, and in 1916 published *Sea Garden*, her first book of poems. During World War I, H. D. went through a marital breakup and a number of misfortunes, recalled in her novel *Palimpsest* (1926). Alone and in poor health, she was rescued by Winifred Ellerman, a writer signing herself Bryher, who adopted the poet's daughter by Cecil Gray and befriended H. D. for life. During 1933 and 1934, H. D. was a patient of Sigmund Freud, an experience she recalls in *Tribute to Freud* (1956). After World War II, the poet moved to Switzerland. Her last works of poetry were epic-long: *Trilogy* (1944–1946) and the dramatic monologue *Helen in Egypt* (1961). Her earlier poems are available in *Collected Poems 1912–1944* (1983), edited by Louis L. Martz. In 1960, back in the United States for the last time, H. D. received the American Academy of Arts and Letters Award of Merit for Poetry.

Seamus Heaney

Seamus Heaney, the best-known living Irish poet, was born on a farm in County Derry, Northern Ireland, in 1939. He taught at Queens University, Belfast, before leaving Northern Ireland in 1972 to make his home in Dublin. A guest lecturer at the University of California in Berkeley during the 1971–1972 academic year, he now divides his time between

Dublin and America, where he teaches at Harvard. Among his recent books of verse are *The Spirit Level* (1996), *Opened Ground* (1999), and a translation of the Anglo-Saxon epic *Beowulf* (2000). Rich with images of love and loss, Heaney's poetry draws inventively on the history of Ireland and the Irish from ancient times to the violent present. In 1995 he became the first Irish poet since W. B. Yeats to win the Nobel Prize in literature.

George Herbert

George Herbert (1593–1633), English devotional poet, the son of an aristocratic family, began writing poems as an undergraduate at Cambridge University. After dabbling for a time in worldly affairs, he entered the priesthood of the Church of England, to live out his days in a country parish. Herbert's poems have many references to music; according to his contemporary John Aubrey, he "had a very good hand on the lute, and set [to music] his own lyrics and sacred poems." Herbert did not publish his poems, but after his death friends collected them in *The Temple* (1633). The book is said to have stimulated Henry Vaughan to follow in Herbert's footsteps as a poet. Herbert makes the religious experience personal, definite, and familiar. For his use of startling "metaphysical" figures of speech, he has been compared with John Donne; but a rare sweetness and plain-spokenness make him unique among poets in English.

Robert Herrick

Robert Herrick (1591–1674), after serving as a goldsmith's apprentice, entered Cambridge University at twenty-two. For nine years he seems to have lived in London, consorting with a group of poets and wits whose chief was Ben Jonson. In 1629 he became parish priest in Dean Prior in rural Devonshire, where he lived out his days, sometimes chafing about the boorishness of his parishioners. When in 1647 the Puritans temporarily ousted him from his pulpit, Herrick returned to London. There at fifty-six, he published his first book, *Noble Numbers* (1647), all pious poems; he then reprinted them together with five times as many sportive, secular poems in *Hesperides* (1648). Unluckily, the books came too late to cause a stir, Herrick's early fame as a poet having withered and the vogue for chiseled classical lyrics having gone by. Like his master Jonson, Herrick writes song-like poems inspired by Greek and Latin pastoral (or shepherd-and-shepherdess) poetry. We go to him not for profound ideas, but for fresh, tough speech and resonant music. Herrick, who remained a bachelor, probably imagined the mistresses he praised. He declared in *Hesperides,* "To his book's end this last line he'd have placed: / Jocund his Muse was, but his life was chaste."

Gerard Manley Hopkins

Gerard Manley Hopkins (1844–1889), born in Essex, England, was, like Emily Dickinson, a major nineteenth-century poet not known until the following century. At twenty, a student at Oxford, he converted to Roman Catholicism and was received into that church by Cardinal Newman. Ordained a Jesuit, Hopkins at first served as a parish priest and teacher in working-class sections of large cities

(London, Glasgow, Liverpool, Manchester), where poverty and suffering distressed him. But his sermons were reportedly so strange (in one, he likened the church to a cow we milk and whose moo we follow) that his superiors removed him from public view, making him Professor of Greek at University College, Dublin. He died of typhoid fever at forty-four. Nearly thirty years after Hopkins's death, his friend Robert Bridges published his *Poems* (1918), having thought them too demanding for earlier readers. That much of Hopkins's work sounds odd to us may be due to the poet's admiration for Old English, with its gutsy monosyllables, and for Welsh poetry, rich in patterns of sound. Hopkins developed his own theory of versification, "sprung rhythm"—in brief, a kind of accentual verse. Though on entering the priesthood he had renounced poetry, he welcomed the suggestion of a superior that he contribute to a Jesuit magazine a poem on the drowning of five Franciscan nuns. The result, "The Wreck of the *Deutschland*," received a rejection slip. This challenging poem has been called "the dragon guarding the door to Hopkins's poetry," but most readers have gone in by the back door of his more quickly accessible nature poems. In these, the sensuous world bursts forth in irrepressible testimony to its Maker's glory.

A. E. Housman

A. E. Housman (1859–1936), English poet and professor of Latin, was born in a village in rural Shropshire, England. Although as a student at Oxford he distinguished himself as a promising scholar of the classics, he failed his exams, apparently because of some inner crisis precipitated by his love for a fellow male student. Determined to overcome this setback, Housman, while working as a clerk in the British patent office, at night wrote scholarly articles. Within ten years these academic writings, bristling with cold sarcasms and scathing putdowns of rival scholars, had won him such high repute that he was invited to be professor of Latin at the University of London. Later he moved on to the more prestigious Cambridge University, to spend the rest of his days living a retiring academic life befitting his shy temperament. Though Housman published only two slim collections of poems—the instantly and enormously popular *A Shropshire Lad* (1898) and the conclusively titled *Last Poems* (1922)—his place as a minor master of the English lyric seems unshakable. Like many Latin poets he admired, he insists in well-turned lines that life is short and comes to a bad end.

Langston Hughes

See biographical note on page 420.

Kobayashi Issa

Issa (1763–1827) was born Yataro Kobayashi in Kashiwabara, a mountain village in central Japan. His father was an educated farmer; his mother died when he was only two years old, and he was raised by his grandmother. At fifteen, he became an apprentice in Edo (now Tokyo). His father, who loved poetry, supported his writing. On his father's death, however, Issa's relatives disputed the will. The settlement required the poet to share the family house with his wrangling clan—by dividing it down the middle.

His final years were scarred by the deaths of his first wife and infant children. The poet's pen name, Issa, means "cup of tea."

Robinson Jeffers

John Robinson Jeffers (1887–1962) was born in Pittsburgh, but completed part of his early education in European boarding schools. In 1903 Jeffers's family moved to Southern California, where he entered Occidental College. Graduating at nineteen, he studied medicine, forestry, and literature on a graduate level before devoting his life to poetry. In 1906 he met Una Kuster, who was married to an attorney. Their tempestuous love affair eventually led, in 1913, to their marriage. In 1914 the couple visited Carmel, California, and Jeffers knew that it was his "inevitable place"—he would spend his remaining fifty-eight years there. With the help of a local stonemason, he built his own house on the edge of the Pacific, quarrying stone from the beach. Jeffers's poetry reflects the closeness to nature that made up his daily life. His philosophy of "inhumanism" refused to put mankind above the rest of nature; he demanded that humanity see itself as part of the vast interdependent reality of nature— a message that has made his poetry esteemed by environmentalists. Jeffers's Tor House in Carmel is now a national historic monument.

Ben Jonson

Ben Jonson (1573?–1637), posthumous son of a Scottish minister, was a native Londoner. As a boy, he received a firm grounding in Latin and Greek at Westminster School, but instead of enrolling in a university, took up bricklaying, then served as a soldier in Flanders. Home from the wars, he married and became an actor and playwright in London. Although a coolly rational classicist by persuasion, Jonson seems to have been an outspoken hothead, given to quarrels and brawls. In 1598 he killed a fellow actor in a duel and escaped the gallows only by claiming an ancient law that forbade hanging anyone who could read. From about 1606, Jonson frequented the Mermaid Tavern in London's Fleet Street, a favorite hangout of writers and actors. There, on the first Friday of each month, he presided over famed literary discussions; according to one report, his friend Shakespeare would take part at times and match wits with him. Later changing pubs (to the Devil and St. Dunstan), Jonson and his circle became known as the "Tribe of Ben"; Thomas Carew and Robert Herrick were younger members. Later Jonson became the leading writer of masques, elaborate plays with music and dancing produced at Court. As a poet, Jonson, in his precise Latinate lyrics, odes, and epigrams, helped get rid of worn-out Petrarchan conventions (those that Shakespeare mocks in "My mistress' eyes are nothing like the sun"). As a playwright, he excelled; his comedies, especially *Volpone, or The Fox* (1606) and *The Alchemist* (1610), are among the crown jewels of the English stage.

Donald Justice

Donald Justice was born in Miami, Florida, in 1925. He attended public schools, hoping at first to become a composer, but gradually his interests turned toward literature. After graduating from the University of Miami in

1945, he did graduate work at both the University of North Carolina and Stanford University before finishing a Ph.D. at the University of Iowa. Having spent four decades as a professor of creative writing, Justice is widely regarded as the most influential poetry teacher of his generation. His presence in the Iowa Writers' Workshops from 1957 to 1982 helped build it into national prominence. He later taught at the University of Florida in Gainesville. Justice's first book, *The Summer Anniversaries* (1960), won the Lamont Award, and over the course of his career, virtually every other prominent poetry prize has followed, most notably the Pulitzer and Bollingen Prizes. Retired from teaching, Justice lives in Iowa City. His *New and Selected Poems* was published in 1995.

John Keats

John Keats (1795–1821), son of a London stable-keeper, studied to become a physician and served as a surgeon's apprentice before deciding on poetry as a career. In 1817 he published his first book, *Poems,* which included "On First Looking into Chapman's Homer." Despite critics' hostility to his narrative poem *Endymion* (1818), Keats persisted. In 1818 he fell in love with sixteen-year-old Fanny Brawne, but, stricken with tuberculosis, he postponed plans for marriage. In 1820, shortly after the publication of his third and last book, Keats went to Italy in hopes of regaining his health, but his poetry soon slowed to a stop. In the following year, at twenty-five, he died in Rome and was buried there beneath the epitaph he wrote for himself: "Here lies one whose name was writ in water." His name, however, has continued to endure. No English poet wrote poems richer in sensuous imagery (as in his great odes, among them "Ode on Melancholy" and "To Autumn"), nor quite so beautifully reimagined the Middle Ages (in poems such as "La Belle Dame sans Merci" and "The Eve of St. Agnes"). He wrote several of the finest sonnets in the language; an unfinished epic of great interest, *Hyperion;* hilarious light verse; and scores of superb letters.

Ted Kooser

Ted Kooser, born in Ames, Iowa, in 1939, attended Iowa State University and then received a master's degree at the University of Nebraska in Lincoln. After teaching high school for one year, he took a job in the insurance industry in 1965 and has remained there ever since. Kooser's career, like his employment, has been unusual for an American poet. Although his early work gained little attention, his short, understated poems—many published by small presses—attracted a growing following. Kooser's poems are unmistakable. Brief, imagistic, and accessible, they usually describe a small everyday scene from American life in the Great Plains states, but midway there is almost always some unexpected but magical turn of imagination. Kooser lives on a small farm in Garland, Nebraska. His most recent book is *Braided Creek: A Conversation in Poetry* (2003), a collaboration with Jim Harrison.

Philip Larkin

Philip Larkin (1922–1985), born in Coventry, England, has been called the most influential British poet since

World War II. After studies at Oxford, he drifted into work as a librarian, and for many years was head librarian for the University of Hull. Early in his career Larkin wrote two novels, *Jill* (1946) and *A Girl in Winter* (1947). He also reviewed jazz recordings for a London newspaper. A self-declared foe of modernism in music, art, and literature, he published only four slim volumes of poems, traditional in form. The earliest collection was heavily indebted to Yeats: *The North Ship* (1945, which the author reissued in 1966 with a preface making fun of it). With *The Less Deceived* (1955), Larkin hit his characteristic stride, writing most of the poems in the voice of a tough-minded, disillusioned, self-deprecating man facing a dreary urban landscape of quiet frustration. This voice drew an immediate—and enduring—response from readers in postwar England.

instinctive natures, which we moderns (he argues) have neglected in favor of our overweening intellects. In *Lady Chatterley's Lover* (1928), he strove to restore explicit sexuality to English fiction. The book, which today seems tame and repetitious, was long banned in Britain and the United States. Deeper Lawrence novels include *Sons and Lovers* (1913), a veiled account of his breaking away from his fiercely possessive mother; *The Rainbow* (1915); *Women in Love* (1921); and *The Plumed Serpent* (1926), about a revival of pagan religion in Mexico. Besides fiction, Lawrence left a rich legacy of poetry, essays, criticism (*Studies in Classic American Literature*, 1923, is especially shrewd and funny), and travel writing. Lawrence exerted deep influence on others, both by the message in his work and by his personal magnetism.

D. H. Lawrence

David Herbert Lawrence (1885–1930) was born in Nottinghamshire, England, child of a coal-miner and a schoolteacher who hated her husband's toil and vowed that her son should escape it. He took up fiction writing, attaining early success. During World War I, Lawrence and his wife were unjustly suspected of treason (he because of his pacifism, she because of her aristocratic German birth). After the armistice they left England and, seeking a healthier climate for Lawrence, who suffered from tuberculosis, wandered in Italy, France, Australia, Mexico, and the American Southwest. Lawrence is an impassioned spokesman for our unconscious,

Denise Levertov

Denise Levertov (1923–1997) was born in Essex, England, daughter of a Welsh mother and a Russian Jewish-born priest of the Anglican church. She was educated at home, reading in her father's library. She served as a nurse in World War II. In 1947 she married an American novelist, Mitchell Goodman, and in the following year came to the United States. Her first book, published in England, had observed traditional poetic conventions (including rime and meter), but in America she discovered the work of William Carlos Williams and other open-form poets, and began to write in a different, freer mode. With Robert Creeley and others of the

Black Mountain group, she exerted much influence among younger poets. Her critical essays have been collected in *The Poet in the World* (1973) and *Light Up the Cave* (1981). Levertov was a tireless political activist, prominent in peace movements of the 1960s, 1970s, and 1980s.

Li Po

Very little is known with certainty about the life of Li Po (701–762), who is traditionally honored (with Tu Fu) as one of China's two greatest poets. He was probably born beyond the western borders of China in present-day Asiatic Russia. Having become famous in his youth for his poetry, he spent most of his later life wandering. His contemporaries considered his talent virtually supernatural, calling him the "Banished Immortal," a heavenly spirit who has been sent to earth as punishment for misbehavior, and Li Po was notorious for his heavy drinking. He was also careless about preserving his work, and the majority of his poems, which were sung or chanted, have been lost. Li Po died by drowning after falling into a river in a drunken attempt to embrace the moon's reflection.

Edna St. Vincent Millay

Edna St. Vincent Millay (1892–1950), born in Rockland, Maine, was the eldest of three daughters. When she was twelve, her father deserted the family. At twenty, she had already published "Renascence," one of her most celebrated poems. In 1917 she graduated from Vassar College and settled in Greenwich Village, where she became as famous for her vivacious personality, her bohemian life-style, her acting and playwriting, and her feminism, as for her verse. Even as she wrote *The Harp Weaver*, a serious volume of verse that won her a Pulitzer Prize in 1923, Millay did hack writing to pay her bills. Among other work for which she is known are verse dramas such as *Aria da Capo* (1920) and the sonnet cycle *Fatal Interview* (1931). In 1923 she married Eugen Jan Boissevain, Dutch businessman and widower of feminist Inez Milholland. In 1927 Millay's political activism expressed itself in poems about Sacco and Vanzetti, two anarchists convicted of murder, and involved her in an unsuccessful campaign to prevent their execution. Though she kept writing poetry well into the 1940s and received several honorary degrees, her reputation waned. Depressed after a nervous breakdown in 1944, she was troubled by a growing sense that the public had deserted her. Millay's life ended with a heart attack at the age of fifty-eight.

John Milton

John Milton (1608–1674), author of *Paradise Lost*, the greatest English epic, was born in London, the son of a scrivener who composed music. His mother early began schooling him to be a minister. He studied zealously. As he later recalled: "From my twelfth year I scarcely ever went to bed before midnight, which was the first cause of injury to my eyes." After he received his B.A. from Cambridge University in 1629, his father supported him through eight years of further study.

"Lycidas" (1638), a poem of this period, shows his deepening seriousness about religion and his growing resentment of corruption within the church, which were to lead him to the Puritan cause. Milton wrote much prose in the service of causes. In *Areopagitica* (1644), he argues for freedom of the press and opposes the strict censorship that had been imposed by Parliament. His unhappy marriage to Mary Powell led him to write tracts in favor of divorce. When Oliver Cromwell and the Puritans ousted King Charles and declared England a commonwealth, Milton's writings were remembered, and earned him a post as Cromwell's foreign secretary. His eyesight strained by years of hard study, Milton went blind and had to dictate his correspondence (in Latin) to clerks, one of whom was fellow poet Andrew Marvell. With the Restoration of Charles II in 1660, Milton's world came crashing down. In retirement, at last he turned to a project he had planned as a young man: his major heroic poem, *Paradise Lost* (1667), about Satan's rebellion and the Fall of Adam and Eve. This epic was followed by *Paradise Regained* (1671) and a verse drama modeled on a Greek tragedy, *Samson Agonistes* (1671).

Marianne Moore

Marianne Moore (1887–1972), whose poems earned praise from fellow poets as dissimilar as William Carlos Williams and T. S. Eliot, was born in Kirkwood, Missouri, a suburb of St. Louis. Her father abandoned the family in 1894, and Moore moved to Pennsylvania. In 1909 she graduated from Bryn Mawr, where a classmate was the poet H. D. For a time, Moore taught business courses at the U.S. Indian School in Carlisle, Pennsylvania, where the athlete Jim Thorpe was among her students. By 1915 her poems—witty, satirical, intellectual, disruptive, and innovative—had begun to appear in *Poetry* magazine. Until her mother died in 1947, Moore, a dutiful daughter, lived with her in Brooklyn, supporting herself by a series of conventional jobs. From 1925 to 1929 she edited the *Dial*, a literary magazine in whose pages she published many of the best poets of her day. Besides poems, Moore wrote essays, reviews, and translations, including *The Fables of La Fontaine* (1945). For her *Collected Poems* (1951), she won a Pulitzer Prize, the Bollingen Prize, and a National Book Award; her *Complete Poems* appeared in 1967. Late in life, Moore became a media figure for her fondness for the Brooklyn Dodgers and her penchant for three-cornered hats. She stayed in Brooklyn, writing and rewriting, through an active and vigorous old age.

Marilyn Nelson

Born in Cleveland, Ohio, in 1946, Marilyn Nelson was the daughter of a U.S. Air Force serviceman. Raised on one military base after another, she attended the University of California at Davis for her B.A. and completed a Ph.D. at the University of Minnesota. She is also a seminary-trained Lutheran lay minister. Two of her books, *The Homeplace* (1990) and *The*

Fields of Praise: New and Selected Poems (1997), have been finalists for the National Book Award. She currently teaches at the University of Delaware.

Pablo Neruda

See biographical note on page 349.

Lorine Niedecker

Lorine Niedecker (1903–1970) spent nearly all her life on Blackhawk Island near Fort Atkinson, Wisconsin, where her father worked as a carp fisherman. After two years at Beloit College, she returned home to care for her ailing mother. Following a brief marriage in 1928, Niedecker held jobs as a proofreader, librarian's assistant, and cleaning worker in a hospital. After her remarriage in 1963, she lived in Milwaukee, but on her husband's retirement the couple moved into a house they had built by the Rock River, and the poet returned to her native grounds. Although she lived an outwardly quiet life remote from publishing centers, Niedecker read widely and maintained a vigorous life of the mind. In the early 1930s she struck up a correspondence with poet and teacher Louis Zukofsky, who encouraged her poetry. In the 1950s poet Cid Corman printed her work in his avant-garde little magazine *Origin*. During her lifetime she published sparingly, but *From This Condensery: The Complete Writing of Lorine Niedecker* (1985) contains a large body of poems, as well as critical essays, experimental prose, and five radio plays. Her life and work are the subject of Kristine Thatcher's play *Niedecker*, given an off-Broadway production in 1989.

Sharon Olds

Sharon Olds was born in San Francisco in 1942 and attended Stanford University. After graduation in 1964, she moved East and eventually took a Ph.D. from Columbia University in 1972. Her first collection of poems, *Satan Says* (1980), was well received, but her second volume, *The Dead and the Living* (1984), scored a major critical success by winning both the Lamont Award and National Book Critics Circle Award. Olds's work often graphically depicts the passions, joys, and pain of family life. She currently teaches at New York University.

Wilfred Owen

Wilfred Owen (1893–1918) was, like A. E. Housman, a native of Shropshire, England. He attended London University and for a time served as lay assistant to a minister, helping the sick and poor. In 1916, during World War I, he enlisted in the British army, became a company commander, and in less than two years wrote all his famous antiwar poems of life in the trenches. The army seems suddenly to have changed Owen from a competent minor poet with little to say into a powerful voice of pacifism. At age twenty-five, while trying to get his men across a canal under enemy fire on the French front, he was killed in action only a week before the war ended. Though Owen published only four poems, after his death a collection of his work was edited by another front-line war poet, Siegfried Sassoon (1920). Owen is preeminent among English poets who wrote of that conflict, and the reputation of his work has continued to grow.

Octavio Paz

See biographical note on page 356.

Sylvia Plath

Sylvia Plath (1932–1963), one of the most remarkable poets in English of the past half-century, was born in Boston, the daughter of German immigrants who both taught at Boston University. The death of her father when the poet was eight was a trauma from which she seems never quite to have recovered. As a scholarship-winning student at Smith College, Plath revealed early promise, and her work soon received publication. Like Esther Greenwood, protagonist of her one novel *The Bell Jar* (1963), Plath won a student contest that sent her to work in New York for a national magazine, and struggled with a year-long siege of mental illness for which she underwent shock treatments. Returning to Smith, she graduated with top honors. Later she studied at Cambridge University in England, where she met and in 1956 married the poet Ted Hughes. Estranged from her husband, she committed suicide in London, leaving two children and, in manuscript form, the intense, powerful poems that went

into her posthumous, highly acclaimed collection, *Ariel* (1965).

Edgar Allan Poe

Edgar Allan Poe (1809–1849) was born in Boston, the son of itinerant actors. He lost his father in 1810 and his mother the next year. Taken in by a well-to-do Richmond merchant, Poe was given an excellent education, but he eventually dropped out of both the University of Virginia and West Point. He became a celebrated journalist, and he edited major journals such as *Southern Literary Messenger*, *Burton's Gentleman's Magazine*, and *Broadway Journal*, to which he contributed stories, poems, articles, and reviews. His romantic idealism, argumentative personality, heavy drinking, and difficult personal life, however, kept him from achieving financial security. After the death of his wife in 1847, Poe began drinking more heavily, and his mental and physical health deteriorated. He was only forty years old when he died in Baltimore on October 7, 1849. The exact circumstances of his death have never been adequately explained.

Alexander Pope

Alexander Pope (1688–1744), the leading English poet of the early eighteenth century, was born in London, son of a Roman Catholic linen merchant. A sickly, stunted, pockmarked child, he suffered from weak health and continual exhaustion throughout his life, and was said to have worn padded clothes to disguise his misshapen frame. Pope excelled early as a poet, composing his *Pastorals* (1709) at age sixteen. His rimed translations of the *Iliad* (1720) and the *Odyssey* (1725–1726) and his edition of Shakespeare (1725), best-sellers in their day, made him independently wealthy, and he was able to buy an estate at Twickenham and live in style. Pope did not write an epic, but instead translated epics and wrote great mock epics: *The Rape of the Lock* (1714), in which he voices compassion for women transformed into wives, and *The Dunciad* (1728–1743), in which he mocks his many literary enemies. He was a master satirist and splendid craftsman of the heroic couplet. Romantic critics generally think him no poet at all, but G. K. Chesterton remarked, "If Pope be not a poet, then who is?"

Ezra Pound

Ezra Pound (1885–1972), among the most influential (and still controversial) modern poets, was born in Hailey, Idaho. He readied himself for a teaching career, but when in 1907 he lost his job at Wabash College for sheltering a penniless prostitute, he left America. Settling in England and later in Paris, he wielded influence on the work of T. S. Eliot, whose long poem *The Waste Land* he edited; W. B. Yeats, whom he served as secretary and critic; and James Joyce. Pound was perpetually championing writers then unknown, such as Robert Frost. In 1924 Pound settled permanently in Italy, where he came to admire Mussolini's economic policies. During World War II he made broadcasts to America by Italian radio, deemed treasonous. When American armed forces

arrested him in 1945, Pound spent three weeks in a cage in an army camp in Pisa. Flown to the United States to stand trial, he was declared incompetent and for twelve years was confined in St. Elizabeths in Washington, a hospital for the criminally insane. In 1958, upon the intervention of Robert Frost, Archibald MacLeish, and other old friends, he was pronounced incurable and allowed to return to Italy to spend his last, increasingly silent years. In his prime, Pound was a swaggeringly confident critic, a berater of smugness and mediocrity, a delectable humorist. Among his lasting books are *Personae* (enlarged edition, 1949), short poems; *ABC of Reading* (1934), an introduction to poetry; and *Literary Essays* (1954). His *Cantos*, a vast poem woven of historical themes and published in installments over forty years, was never finished. Pound was a great translator of poetry from Italian, Provençal, Chinese, and other languages. Pare away his delusions, and a remarkable human being and splendid poet remains.

Dudley Randall

Dudley Randall (1914–2000) was born in Washington, D.C. He graduated from Wayne State University and the University of Michigan, and worked as librarian and poet-in-residence at the University of Detroit. A pioneer in the modern movement to publish the work of black writers, Randall founded what has been called the most influential small publishing house in America, Broadside Press. He also edited an important anthology, *The Black Poets* (1971). Randall's *A Litany* of Friends: New and Selected Poems was published in 1981.

Alastair Reid

Alastair Reid was born in Whithorn, Scotland, in 1926. His college work at St. Andrews was interrupted by service in the Royal Navy during World War II, but he eventually graduated with a degree in classics. After teaching for a few years in America, Reid began to spend part of each year in Majorca with Robert Graves, with whom he collaborated on translations and an opera libretto. Soon Reid became one of the most admired translators of Spanish-language poetry; his versions of the poetry of Pablo Neruda and Jorge Luis Borges are particularly noteworthy. His own poetry, collected in *Weatherings* (1978), is rich and arresting. For years Reid wrote for the *New Yorker*. Married twice, he has one son. He currently lives in the Dominican Republic.

Andrienne Rich

Adrienne Rich was born in Baltimore in 1929. Since the selection of her first volume by W. H. Auden for the Yale Series of Younger Poets in 1951, her work has continually broken new ground, moving from closed forms to feminist poetics and radical politics. A selection of her poems is collected in *The Fact of a Doorframe: Poems 1950–2001* (2002). Her prose works include *On Lies, Secrets, and Silence* (1979), *Blood, Bread, and Poetry* (1986), and *What Is Found There* (1993). Her work has received many awards—most notably the Lenore Marshall / Nation Award, the Lambda Literary Award, the Frost Medal from the Poetry Society of America, the Wallace Stevens Award of the Academy of American Poets, the Lannan Foundation Lifetime Achievement Award, and the Bollingen Prize.

Edwin Arlington Robinson

Edwin Arlington Robinson (1869–1935) was raised in Gardiner, Maine, the model for Tilbury Town, the setting for many of his poems. After a stint at Harvard, Robinson moved to New York City. Initially, he published three books, but slowly sank into poverty and alcoholism. In 1902 President Theodore Roosevelt discovered Robinson's work and obtained for him a government position with virtually no duties. Robinson used this fortunate intercession to embark on a series of literary projects, and he gradually became the most widely esteemed American poet of the early twentieth century. He won the Pulitzer Prize three times in seven years, and his long poem *Tristram* (1927) became a best-seller. Although Robinson's work has suffered from critical neglect in recent years, he remains an important American poet. His austere style, penetrating psychology, and bitter realism represent a turning point in American poetry from nineteenth-century romanticism to the threshold of modernism. His work decisively influenced the poetry of Robert Frost.

Theodore Roethke

Theodore Roethke (1908–1963) was born in Saginaw, Michigan, where his family ran a large greenhouse. (No poet seems wealthier in his knowledge of vegetation.) He went to the University of Michigan and (for a year) to Harvard. As a young poet teaching college at a time when creative writing teachers without Ph.D.s were suspect, Roethke held impermanent jobs before coming to rest at the University of Washington in Seattle. There, from 1947 until his death, he was an influential teacher of poetry and poetry writing; among his students were Carolyn Kizer, David Wagoner, and James Wright. Roethke was a large, heavyset man light on his feet (he once coached varsity tennis at Lafayette), and would sometimes prepare for a poetry reading by pacing the stage like an athlete warming up. His poetry developed from rather conventional and imitative lyrics through a phase of disconnected stream of consciousness into (at the end) a meditative poetry reminiscent in its open lines of Walt Whitman's.

Kay Ryan

Kay Ryan was born in San Jose, California, in 1945 and was raised in the dry landscapes of the San Joaquin Valley and Mojave Desert. She studied literature in college but never took a writing course. For the past twenty years she has taught remedial English at the College of Marin, a two-year public college, and has also taught writing at San Quentin Prison. Ryan's literary career was slow in building. Her first book was privately printed, but her short and evocatively compressed poetry has slowly gained her a significant reputation. Her recent books include *Elephant Rocks* (1996) and *Say Uncle* (2000). She lives in Fairfax, California.

Carl Sandburg

The first important American poet to be raised in a home where English was a second language, Carl Sandburg (1878–1967) was born in Galesburg, Illinois, the oldest of seven children of poor Swedish immigrants. Leaving school after the eighth grade, he had many jobs, including milkman, bricklayer, and farm laborer. After serving in the Spanish-American War, he paid his way through college by working as a fireman. Sandburg achieved fame with the publication of *Chicago Poems* (1916), which established him as the leading populist in Modernist American poetry. A handsome, charismatic man, he toured the nation reciting his poems and singing folksongs. He won the Pulitzer Prize not only in poetry but also in history, for his multivolume biography of Abraham Lincoln.

Anne Sexton

Anne Sexton (1928–1974) was born in Newton, Massachusetts, to an old and prominent New England family. She attended boarding school and finishing school, but never went on to college. In 1948 she eloped with Alfred Sexton (always known as "Kayo" to his wife and family). Beautiful, elegant, and commanding, Sexton dreamed of becoming a model, but shortly after the birth of her second daughter she suffered the first of many nervous breakdowns. Her fragile mental health would take her in and out of hospitals for the rest of her life. After watching a television program on "How to Write a Sonnet" in 1956, Sexton, encouraged by her psychiatrist, began composing poetry. Dedicating herself to writing, she made astonishing progress and soon published her work in leading journals and magazines such as the *Hudson Review* and the *New Yorker*. Her strongly emotional and confessional poems earned her wide acclaim, and her third volume, *Live or Die* (1967), won the Pulitzer Prize. Fame, however, could not assuage the pain of her troubled psyche or the increasing disorder of her personal life. In October 1974 Sexton committed suicide. She was only forty-five years old.

William Shakespeare

William Shakespeare (1564–1616), the supreme writer of English, was born, baptized, and buried in the market town of Stratford-on-Avon, eighty miles from London. Son of a glovemaker and merchant who was high bailiff (or mayor) of the town, he probably attended grammar school and learned to read Latin authors in the original. At eighteen, he married Anne Hathaway, twenty-six, by whom he had three children, including twins. By 1592 he had become well known and envied as an actor and playwright in London. From 1594 until he retired, he belonged to the same theatrical company, the Lord Chamberlain's Men (later renamed the King's Men in honor of their patron, James I), for whom he wrote thirty-six plays—some of them, such as *Hamlet* and *King Lear*, profound reworkings of old plays. As an actor, Shakespeare is believed to have played supporting roles, such as the ghost of Hamlet's father. The company prospered, moved into the Globe in 1599, and in 1608 bought the fashionable Blackfriars as well; Shakespeare owned an interest in both theaters. When plagues shut down the theaters from 1592 to 1594, Shakespeare turned to poetry; his great *Sonnets* (not published until 1609) probably date from the 1590s. Plays were regarded as entertainments of little literary merit, like comic books today, and Shakespeare did not bother to supervise their publication. He did, however, carefully see through press his sonnets and the narrative poems *Venus and Adonis* (1593) and *The Rape of Lucrece* (1594).

Stevie Smith

Stevie Smith (1902–1971) was born in Hull, Yorkshire, christened Florence Margaret Smith. Being wiry and short, she acquired her nickname from a popular jockey, Stevie Donahue. For more than sixty years, beginning at age three, Smith lived with her aunt in Palmers Green, a suburb of London, and worked for thirty years as a publisher's secretary. *Novel on Yellow Paper* (1936) is the best known of her three novels. Her poetry readings, in public and on BBC radio, widened her audience. *Collected Poems* (1976) is illustrated with her own witty, slapdash, and rakishly charming drawings. *Me Again: Uncollected Writings* (1982) contains poems, stories, essays, and a play for radio. In the film *Stevie* (1978), based on a stage play by Hugh Whitemore, Glenda Jackson plays the poet with keen insight and power.

Sor Juana

See biographical note on page 347.

William Stafford

William Stafford (1914–1993), born in Hutchinson, Kansas, graduated from the University of Kansas and later took a doctorate at the University of Iowa. During World War II he was interned as a conscientious objector, an experience he recalls in his prose memoir *Down in My Heart* (1947). For many years he taught at Lewis and Clark College in Portland, Oregon, and in 1970 and 1971 he served as Consultant in Poetry for the Library of Congress. *Traveling Through the Dark* (1962) won the National Book Award, and in 1977 Stafford published a large volume of his collected poems, *Stories That Could Be True*. In much of his work he traced the landscapes of the Midwest and of the Pacific Northwest, where he long lived. He described his poetry as "much like talk, with some enhancement." Shortly before his death in 1993, Stafford was chosen in a national poll of American writers as the poet most highly regarded by his peers.

Timothy Steele

Timothy Steele was born in Burlington, Vermont, in 1948. He did his undergraduate work at Stanford. After taking his doctorate in English at Brandeis, where he studied with J. V. Cunningham, Steele returned to California, where he has taught ever since. His first book of poems, *Uncertainties and Rest,* appeared in 1979 and has been followed by two other collections. His study *Missing Measures: Modern Poetry and the Revolt Against Meter* (1990) has been one of the most influential books of literary history of recent years. Steele writes exclusively in traditional forms. His work is characterized by a Yankee reticence and a precise but understated style that holds considerable power within these strict limits. He currently teaches at California State University, Los Angeles.

James Stephens

James Stephens (1882–1950), born in Dublin, Ireland, was a famous member of the Irish Literary Renaissance, a movement early in the century that included William Butler Yeats and the playwrights Lady Gregory, J. M. Synge, and Sean O'Casey. As a young man, Stephens took a job as a typist in a lawyer's office, where access to a typewriter started him writing fantastic fiction, some of it based on Irish folklore, such as his most popular novel, *The Crock of Gold* (1912). Other imaginative novels followed, including *The Demi-Gods* (1914) and *Deirdre* (1923). *Irish Fairy Tales* (1920) retells classic legends for young readers. Although best remembered for such books, Stephens was a considerable poet as well. His first collection appeared in 1909, and in 1926 he published his *Collected Poems*. Some of his poems are actually free translations from the Irish: "A Glass of Beer," for instance, is a version of a seven-teenth-century poem by Dáibhí Ó Bruadair.

Wallace Stevens

Wallace Stevens (1879–1955) was born in Reading, Pennsylvania; his father was a successful lawyer; his mother, a former schoolteacher. As a special student at Harvard, he became president of the student literary maga-zine, the *Harvard Advocate,* but he did not want a liberal arts degree. Instead, he became a lawyer in New York City, and in 1916 joined the legal staff of the Hartford Accident and Indemnity Company. In 1936 he was elected a vice president. Stevens, who would write poems in his head while walking to work and then dictate them to his secretary, was a leading expert on surety claims. Once asked how he was able to combine poetry and insurance, he replied that the two occupations had an element in common: "calcu-lated risk." As a young man in New York, Stevens made lasting friendships with the poets Marianne Moore and William Carlos Williams, but he did not seek literary society. Though his poems are full of references to Europe and remote places, his only travels were annual vacation trips to Key West. He printed his early poems in *Poetry* magazine, but did not publish a book until *Harmonium* appeared in 1923, when he was forty-four. Living quietly in Hartford, Connecticut, Stevens sought to discover order in a chaotic world with his subtle and ex-otic imagination. His critical essays, collected in *The Necessary Angel* (1951), and his *Letters* (1966), edited by his daughter Holly Stevens, reveal a penetrating, philosophic mind. His *Collected Poems* (1954), published on his seventy-fifth birthday, garnered important prizes and belated recogni-tion for Stevens as a major American poet.

Anne Stevenson

Anne Stevenson is the quintessential transatlantic poet. Born in England in 1933 of American parents, she was ed-ucated in the United States. After graduating from the University of Michigan, she returned to England. She has taught in both countries and now lives in Durham, England. Com-bining two cultures in her background, Stevenson has also combined the ca-reers of scholar and poet. In 1966 she published the first full-length study of Elizabeth Bishop, and in 1989 she re-leased *Bitter Fame: A Life of Sylvia Plath*, a controversial but authoritative biography. Stevenson's *Collected Poems* appeared in 1996. Gathering poems from her ten previous books of verse, this substantial volume confirmed her position as a major contemporary poet.

Alfred, Lord Tennyson

Alfred Tennyson (1809–1892) was born in Lincolnshire, England, the son of an alcoholic rural minister. When Queen Victoria made him a baron in 1883 (at seventy-five), he added the "Lord" to his byline. A precocious poet, Tennyson began writing verse at five, and while still in his teens collab-orated with his brother Charles on *Poems by Two Brothers* (1827). As a student at Cambridge, he was unusual: he kept a snake for a pet, won a medal for poetry, and left without earning a degree. But in college he made influential friendships, especially that of Arthur Hallam, whose death in 1833 inspired Tennyson's *In Memoriam* (1850), the elegiac sequence that contains "Dark house by which once more I stand." The year 1850 was a banner one for Tennyson in other ways: he at last felt prosperous enough to marry Emily Sellwood, who had remained engaged to him for fourteen years, and Queen Victoria named him poet laureate, in which capacity he served for four decades, writing poems for state occasions. Between 1859 and 1888 Tennyson completed *Idylls of the King*, a twelve-part narrative poem about Arthur and his Round Table. In his mid-sixties he wrote several plays. A spokesman for the Victorian age and its militant colonialism, Tennyson is still respected as a poet of varied assets, including an excellent ear.

Dylan Thomas

Dylan Thomas (1914–1953) was born in the coastal town of Swansea, Wales, the son of a teacher of English. Much of Thomas's life was a bitter struggle to support his wife and children, a struggle intensified by his fondness for spending freely. Lacking a university education, Thomas found most paying literary work barred to him in Britain, although late in life he received many assignments to write film and radio scripts. A resonant reader-aloud of poetry, he made broadcasts for BBC radio and undertook several immensely popular reading tours of America, preceded by a reputation for heavy drinking and gustatorial lovemaking. He died in a hospital in New York City after drinking a procession of straight whiskeys, apparently courting the end. Thomas wrote not only poems (in the early ones he brought surrealism into English poetry), but also remarkable stories and a "play for voices," *Under Milk Wood* (1954), based on memories of his home town in Wales.

John Updike

John Updike, born in Pennsylvania in 1932, is primarily regarded as a novelist. But his first book was verse, *The Carpentered Hen* (1954), from which we take "Ex-Basketball Player"; and ever since, he has continued to produce verse both light and serious. He received his B.A. from Harvard, then went to Oxford to study drawing and fine art. From 1955 to 1957 he worked on the staff of the *New Yorker*. Though he left the magazine to write full-time, he has continued to supply it with bright stories and searching book reviews. Updike has published nearly fifty books. His *Collected Poems* was published in 1993. His most recent volume of verse is *Americana* (2001).

Walt Whitman

Walt Whitman (1819–1892) was born on Long Island, son of an impoverished farmer. He spent his early years as a school teacher, a temperance propagandist, a carpenter, a printer, and a newspaper editor on the Brooklyn *Eagle*. He began writing poetry in his youth, sometimes declaiming his lines above the crash of waves on New York beaches. Apparently he was also inspired to write wide, spacious, confident lines by attending performances of Italian opera. His self-published *Leaves of Grass* (1855) won praise from Ralph Waldo Emerson and gained Whitman readers in England. For the rest of his life, he kept revising and enlarging it, ceasing only with a ninth or "deathbed edition" in 1891–1892. Americans at first were slow to accept Whitman's unconventionally open verse forms, his sexual frankness, and his gregarious egoism. The poet of boundless faith in American democracy, Whitman tempered his vision by his experiences as a volunteer hospital nurse during the Civil War (described in his poems *Drum-Taps* and his wartime letters). After the war, he held secretarial jobs to support himself, and lost one such job when his employer's scandalized eye fell upon the *Leaves*. In old age, a semi-invalid after a stroke, Whitman made his home in Camden, New Jersey. Before he died, he saw his work finally winning respect and worldwide acceptance. Whitman's influence on later American poetry has been profound, both by the example of his open forms and by his bold encompassing of subject matter that had formerly been considered unpoetic. (In "Song of the Exposition," read aloud at an industrial show in New York, the poet exclaims of his Muse: "She's here, install'd amid the kitchen ware!")

Richard Wilbur

Richard Wilbur, born in 1921 in New York City, graduated from Amherst College, then served in the army during World War II. He has taught English at Harvard, Wellesley, Wesleyan, and Smith. With his first two collections, *The Beautiful Changes* (1947) and *Ceremony* (1950), Wilbur acquired a high reputation for a poetry of sensitivity, wit, grace, and command of traditional forms. Besides writing poetry, for which he has received many prizes, including two Pulitzer Prizes and a National Book Award, he has edited the poetry of Shakespeare and Poe. He has written song lyrics for *Candide*, a Broadway musical by Lillian Hellman and Leonard Bernstein (1956); *Loudmouse*, a story for children (1963); *Responses*, literary criticism (1976); and he has translated plays of Molière and Racine into wonderfully skillful English verse. He divides his time between Cummington, Massachusetts, where he has a home adjacent to an apple orchard, and Key West, Florida. In 1987 he was named United States poet laureate by the Library of Congress. His *New and Collected Poems* (1988) gathers most of his original work in poetry.

William Carlos Williams

William Carlos Williams (1883–1963) was born in Rutherford, New Jersey, where he remained in later life as a practicing pediatrician. While studying for his M.D. degree at the University of Pennsylvania, he made friends with the poets Ezra Pound and H. D. (Hilda Doolittle). Surprisingly prolific for a busy doctor, Williams wrote (besides poetry) novels and short stories, plays, criticism, and essays in history (*In the American Grain*, 1939). He kept a fliptop desk in his office and between patients would haul out his typewriter and dash off poems. His encouragement of younger poets, among them Allen Ginsberg (whose doctor he was when Ginsberg was a baby), and the long-sustained example of his formally open poetry made him an appealing father figure to the generation of the Beat poets and the Black Mountain poets—Ginsberg, Gary Snyder, and Robert Creeley. But he also had great influence on Robert Lowell, and on an entire younger generation of American poets in our day. Williams believed in truth-telling about ordinary life, championed plain speech "out of the mouths of Polish mothers," and insisted that there can be "no ideas but in things." Combining poetry with prose (including documents and statistics), his long poem in five parts, *Paterson* (1946–1958), explores the past, present, and future of the New Jersey industrial city near which Williams lived for most of his days.

William Wordsworth

William Wordsworth (1770–1850) was born in England's Lake District, whose landscapes and people were to inform many of his poems. As a young man, he visited France, sympathized with the Revolution, and met a young Frenchwoman who bore him a child. The Reign of Terror prevented him from returning to France, and he and Annette Vallon never married. With his sister Dorothy (1771–1855), his lifelong intellectual companion and the author of remarkable journals, he settled in Dorsetshire. Later they moved to Grasmere, in the Lake District, where Wordsworth lived the rest of his life. In 1798 his friendship with Samuel Taylor Coleridge resulted in their joint publication of *Lyrical Ballads*, a book credited with introducing Romanticism to English poetry. (Wordsworth contributed "Tintern

Abbey" and other poems.) To the second edition of 1800, Wordsworth supplied a preface calling for a poetry written "in the real language of men." Time brought him a small official job, a marriage, a swing from left to right in his political sentiments, and appointment as poet laureate. Although he kept on writing, readers have generally preferred his earlier poems. *The Prelude*, a long poem-memoir completed in 1805, did not appear until after the poet's death. One of the most original of writers, Wordsworth—especially for his poems of nature and simple rustics—occupies a popular place in English poetry, much like that of Robert Frost in America.

James Wright

James Wright (1927–1980) was born in Martins Ferry, Ohio. After taking his doctorate at the University of Washington, where he studied with Theodore Roethke, he taught at the University of Minnesota, Macalester College, and Hunter College in New York. His first book *A Green Wall* (1957), in the Yale Series of Younger Poets, established him as a traditional formalist of great skill. With Robert Bly, by whom he was persuaded to branch out of traditional forms, he translated the poems of César Vallejo, Pablo Neruda, and Georg Trakl. In 1972 he received the Pulitzer Prize for his *Collected Poems*. Wright was a memorable teacher, a great quoter of poetry from memory, and a fine critic. "I try and say how I love my country and how I despise the way it is treated," he declared. "I try and speak of the beauty and again of the ugliness in the lives of the poor and neglected."

Sir Thomas Wyatt

Sir Thomas Wyatt (1503?–1542) was both poet and man of action: diplomat, soldier, and courtier. He was born in his father's castle in Kent, England, and, as a boy, he was sent to Court. In 1516 he entered St. John's College, Cambridge. Wyatt twice saw the inside of prison when he slipped from the favor of King Henry VIII. He is thought to have been a lover of Anne Boleyn, later the king's wife, a fact that perhaps affects some of his remarkable love lyrics. A prominent man in Tudor England, Wyatt carried out diplomatic missions, served as ambassador to Spain, was a member of Parliament and the king's privy council, and was Commander of the Fleet. His mission to Italy in 1527 had great consequence for English poetry, for he brought back knowledge of the works of Petrarch and other Italian love poets. In imitation of them, Wyatt wrote some of the first sonnets in our language—also lyrics, rondels, satires, and psalms.

William Butler Yeats

William Butler Yeats (1865–1939), poet and playwright, an Irishman of English ancestry, was born in Dublin, the son of painter John Butler Yeats. For a time he studied art himself and was irregularly schooled in Dublin and in London. Early in life Yeats sought to transform Irish folklore and legend into mellifluous poems. He overcame shyness to take an active part in cataclysmic events: he became involved in the movement for an Irish nation (partly drawn into it by his unrequited love for Maud Gonne, a crusading nationalist) and in founding the Irish Literary Theatre (1898) and the Irish National Theatre, which in 1904 moved to the renowned Abbey Theatre in Dublin. Dublin audiences were difficult: in 1899 they jeered Yeats's first play, The Countess Cathleen, for portraying a woman who, defying the church, sells her soul to the devil to buy bread for starving peasants. Eventually Yeats retired from the fray, to write plays presented in drawing rooms, such as Purgatory. After the establishment of the Irish Free State, Yeats served as a senator (1922–1928). His lifelong interest in the occult culminated in his writing of A Vision (1925), a view of history as governed by the phases of the moon; Yeats believed the book was inspired by spirit masters who dictated communications to his wife Georgie Hyde-Lees. Had Yeats stopped writing in 1900, he would be remembered as an outstanding minor Victorian. Instead, he went on to become one of the most influential poets of the twentieth century.

WRITING

22 *Writing About Literature*

In the study of literature, common sense (poet Gerard Manley Hopkins assures us) is never out of place. For most of a class hour, a professor once rhapsodized about the arrangement of the contents of W. H. Auden's *Collected Poems*. Auden, he claimed, was a master of thematic continuity, who had brilliantly placed the poems in an order that (to the ingenious mind) best complemented each other. Near the end of the hour, his theories were punctured—with a great inaudible pop—when a student, timidly raising a hand, pointed out that Auden had arranged the poems in the book not by theme but in alphabetical order according to the first word of each poem. The professor's jaw dropped: "Why didn't you say that sooner?" The student was apologetic: "I—I was afraid I'd sound too *ordinary*." Don't be afraid to state a conviction, though it seems obvious. Does it matter that you may be repeating something that, once upon a time or even just the other day, has been said before? There are excellent old ideas as well as new.

BEGINNING

Offered a choice of literary works to write about, you probably will do best if you choose what appeals to you. And how to find out what appeals? Whether you plan to write a short paper that requires no research beyond the story or poem or play itself, or a long paper that will take you to the library or the Internet, the first stage of your project is reading carefully—and taking notes. To focus your attention, one time-honored method is to read with a pencil, marking (if the book is yours) passages that stand out in importance, jotting brief notes in a margin ("*Key symbol—this foreshadows the ending*," "*Dramatic irony*," or other possibly useful remarks). In a long story or poem or play, some students asterisk passages that cry for comparison—for instance, all the places in which they find the same theme or symbol. Later, at a glance, they can review the highlights of a work and, when writing a paper about it, quickly refer to evidence. Students who dislike marking up a book may prefer to take notes on looseleaf notebook paper, holding one sheet beside a page in the book and giving it the book's page number. Later, in writing a paper, they can place book page and companion note page together again. This method has the advantage of affording a lot of room for note taking; it is a good one for short poems closely packed with complexities.

KEEPING A JOURNAL

After you have taken some notes, reflect on them. Before you go to the library to consult other people's published thoughts, try to work out your own. There is much to be said for the gut reaction of the first-time reader of a work of literature. That reaction is pure, forceful, and unadulterated by too much outside knowledge. It may contain insights that are unique to the reader, insights that will be lost if not written down immediately and explored by that reader.

To be sure that the power of that initial reaction is not lost, many instructors ask students to keep a journal: a day-to-day account of what they read and how they react to it. A great advantage in keeping a journal is that you can express your thoughts and feelings immediately, in your own words, before they grow cold. You can set down all your miscellaneous reactions to what you read, whether or not they fit into a paper topic. (If you have to write a paper later on, your journal just might suggest topics galore.) Depending on what your instructor thinks is essential, your journal may take in all your reading for the course, or you may concentrate on the work of some writer or writers, or on one kind of story. As you read, you can jot down anything that you wish to remember. Does a theme in a story or a line of dialogue strike you forcefully? Make a note of it. Does something in the story not make sense? Record your bewilderment.

Your journal is personal: a place for you to sound off, to express your feelings. Don't just copy your class notes into it; don't simply quote the stories. The mere length of your entries will not impress your instructor either: try for insights. A paragraph or two will probably suffice to set down your main reactions to most stories. In keeping a journal (a kind of writing primarily for yourself), you don't rewrite; so you need not feel obliged to polish your prose. Your aim is to store information without delay, to wrap words around your reactions and observations.

Keeping a journal will be satisfying only if you keep it up-to-date. Record your feelings and insights while you still have a story freshly in mind. Get weeks behind, and you will have to grind out a journal from scratch, the night before it is due, and the whole project will decay into meaningless drudgery. If you faithfully do a little reading and writing every day or so, you will find yourself keeping track of the life of your mind. When your journal is closed, you will have a lively record not only of the literature you have read but also of your personal involvement with it.

Using Critical Sources
and Maintaining Academic Integrity

Certain literary works, because they offer intriguing difficulties, have attracted professional critics by the score. On library shelves, great phalanxes of critical books now stand at the side of James Joyce's complex novels *Ulysses* and *Finnegans Wake* and T. S. Eliot's allusive poem *The Waste Land*. The student who undertakes to study such works seriously is well advised to profit from the critics' labors. Chances are, too, that even in discussing a relatively uncomplicated work, you will want to seek the aid of some critics. If you quote them, quote them exactly, in quotation marks, and give them credit. When employed in any but the most superlative student paper, a brilliant phrase (or even a not-so-brilliant sentence) from a renowned critic is likely to stand out like a golf ball in a garter snake's midriff, and most English instructors are likely to recognize it. If you rip off the critic's words, then go ahead and steal the whole essay, for good critics write in seamless unities. Then, when apprehended, you can exclaim—like the student whose term paper was found to be the work of a well-known scholar—"I've been robbed! That paper cost me fifty dollars!" This student not only cheated his teacher but himself, having got nothing for his college tuition but a little practice in typing. Giving proper acknowledgment to works and ideas not your own is both a moral and legal obligation. Take it seriously.

A later chapter, "Writing a Research Paper," will discuss the topic of plagiarism and academic integrity in greater depth; for now, students should simply remember that claiming another's work as one's own is the worst offense of the learning community. It negates the very purpose of education, which is to learn to think for oneself. Even if you summarize a critic's idea in your own words rather than quote his or her exact words, you have to give credit to your source. Nothing is cheaper to give than proper credit.

Discovering Essay Ideas

Writing is not likely to proceed in a straight line. Like thought, it often goes by fits and starts, by charges and retreats and mopping-up operations. All the while you read other critics' thoughts and take notes, you discover material to write about; all the while you turn over your topic in your mind, you plan your paper. It is the nature of ideas, those headstrong things, to happen in any order they desire. While you continue to plan, while you write a draft, and while you revise, expect to keep discovering new thoughts—perhaps the best thoughts of all. If you do, be sure to invite them in.

Choosing an Appropriate Topic

Choose a topic appropriate to the assigned length of your paper. How do you know the probable length of your discussion until you write it? When in doubt, you are better off to define your topic narrowly. Your paper will be stronger if you go more deeply into your subject than if you choose some gigantic subject and then find yourself able to touch on most aspects of it only superficially. A thorough explication of a short story is hardly possible in a paper of 250 words. There are, in truth, four-line poems whose surface 250 words might only begin to scratch. A profound topic ("The Character of Shakespeare's Hamlet") might overflow a book, but a more focused topic ("Hamlet's Views of Acting" or "Hamlet's Puns") might result in a manageable paper.

Many student writers find it helpful in defining a topic to state an emerging idea for a paper in a provisional **thesis sentence:** a summing-up of the one main idea or argument that the paper will embody. A good statement of a thesis is not just a disembodied subject; it comes with both subject and verb. ("The Downfall of Oedipus Rex" is not yet a complete idea for a paper; "What Caused the Downfall of Oedipus Rex?" is.) "The Isolation of Laura in *The Glass Menagerie*" might be a decent title for a paper, but it isn't a useful thesis because it doesn't indicate what one might say about that isolation (nor what Tennessee Williams is saying about it). It may be obvious that isolation isn't desirable, but a clearer and more workable thesis sentence might be, "In *The Glass Menagerie*, the playwright shows how Laura's isolation leads her to take refuge in a world of dreams."

Think of your thesis sentence as the announcement of the argument you intend to prove. Once you've said what it is, the rest of the paper will be the presentation of the evidence you've gathered from the text or your research to support your argument. If you find you can't support certain aspects of the statement, then refine it so that you can. Until you turn it in, your essay is a work-in-progress. Anything can be changed and should be if it doesn't further the development of the paper's main idea.

Topic in hand (which may get drastically changed as you continue), you begin to sort out your miscellaneous notes, and the thoughts and impressions you recorded in your journal. If you can see that you haven't had enough ideas, you may wish to brainstorm or freewrite—to set yourself, say, fifteen minutes in which to write down as fast as you can all the ideas on your topic that come into your head, without worrying whether they are going to be useful. (You can look over the results and decide that later.) Write rapidly and uncritically, letting your thoughts tumble onto paper as fast as your pen or computer can capture them. This method will often goad the unconscious into coming up with unexpectedly good ideas; at least you will generate more potentially useful raw material.

Outlining

To outline or not to outline? Unless your topic, by its nature, suggests some obvious way to organize your paper ("An Explication of a Wordsworth Sonnet" might mean simply working through the poem line by line), then some kind of outline will probably help. In high school or other prehistoric times, you perhaps learned how to construct a beautiful outline, laid out with Roman numerals, capital letters, Arabic numerals, and lowercase letters. It was a thing of beauty and symmetry, and it possibly even had something to do with paper writing. But if now you are skeptical of the value of outline, reflect: not every outline needs to be detailed and elaborate. Some students, of course, find it helpful to outline in detail—particularly if they are planning a long research paper involving several literary works, comparing and contrasting several aspects of them. For a 500-word analysis of a short story's figures of speech, though, all you might need is a simple list of points to make, scribbled down in the order in which you will make them. This order is probably not, of course, the order in which the points first occurred to you. Thoughts, when they first come to mind, can arrive as a confused rabble.

While granting the need for order in a piece of writing, the present authors confess that they are reluctant outliners. Their tendency (or curse) is to want to keep whatever random thoughts occur to them, to polish their prose right then and there, and finally to try to juggle their disconnected paragraphs into something like logical order. The usual result is that they have large blocks of illogical thought left over. This process is wasteful, and if you can learn to live with an outline, then you belong to the legion of the blessed and will never know the pain of scrapping pages that cost you hours. On the other hand, you will never know the joy of meandering—of bursting into words and surprising yourself. As novelist E. M. Forster remarked, "How do I know what I think until I see what I say?"

An outline, if you use one, is not meant to stand as an achievement in itself. It should—as Ezra Pound said literary criticism ought to do—consume itself and disappear. Here is a once-valuable outline not worth keeping—a very informal one that enabled a student to organize the paper comparing "Design" by Robert Frost (see page 618) with "Wing-Spread" by Abbie Huston Evans (page 626). Before he wrote, the student jotted down the points he had in mind. Looking over this "mess of garbage" (as he then regarded it), he could see that, among his scattered thoughts, two topics predominated. One was about figures of speech and about connotations, and these ideas he decided to join under the heading LANGUAGE. His other emerging idea had to do with the two poets' quite different themes. Having perceived that his thoughts weren't totally jumbled, he then proceeded through his list, numbering with the same numbers any ideas that seemed to go together, and so arranging them in the order he wanted to follow. His outline then looked like this:

```
        Wing-Spread good, Design better
    l.
        Frost is in the sonnet tradition

    3.  Themes--Evans: "Be small."

            Frost: "Is there any design in universe?"

        Evan's word cable--suggests suspension bridge   A

        Is Evans thinking of serpent in Eden?

        Figures of speech--Evans doesn't use many--

            gives the moth a gender    B

        Frost's words--more connotations in 'em    A

        Frost's puns    B also similes.
```

2. LANGUAGE

Labeling with "A" the two points about words full of connotations, and with "B" the two points about figures of speech, the student indicated to himself that these points were to be taken up together. He found, as you can see in the finished essay on page 627, two ideas that didn't seem to relate to his purpose. These were the points about Frost's being in the sonnet tradition and about Evans's possible interest in the Garden of Eden serpent. Reluctantly but wisely, he decided to leave them out. These ideas might have led him to make interesting comments on the individual poems, but they would not have got him to *compare* the poems, as the assignment asked. Having made this rough outline, he felt encouraged to return to the two poems; and, on rereading them, he noticed some further points, which now fell readily into his plan. One of these points was that Frost's poem also contains similes. He added it to his outline and so remembered it.

DRAFTING AND REVISING, OR CREATIVITY VS. ANALYSIS

Seated at last or striking some other businesslike stance,[1] you prepare to write, only to find yourself besieged with petty distractions. All of a sudden you remember a friend you had promised to call, some double-A batteries you were supposed to pick up, a neglected Coke (in another room) growing warmer and flatter by the minute. If your paper is to be written, you have only one course of action: collar these thoughts and for the moment banish them.

When first you draft your paper—that is, when you write it out in the rough— you will probably do best to write rapidly. At this early stage, you don't need to be fussy about spelling, grammar, and punctuation. To be sure, those picayune details matter, but you can worry about them later, when you are **editing** (combing through your draft repairing grammar, cutting excess words, making small verbal improvements) and **proofreading** (going over your finished paper line by line, checking it for typographical or other mistakes). At the moment, you want your creative mind to take charge of the writing process; this part of yourself has the good ideas and the insights; it has the confidence. Indulge your creative mind: get your thoughts down on paper and forget about checking spellings in the dictionary. Your analytical, critical mind can do all that later. Now is the time to forge ahead, to believe in yourself and the force of your ideas. Perhaps when you write your draft, you won't even want to look at all those notes on your reading that you collected so industriously. When you come to a place where a note will fit, you might just insert a reminder to yourself, such as SEE CARD 19 or SEE ARISTOTLE ON COMEDY.

Let us admit that writing about literature is a more formal kind of writing than turning out a narrative essay called, "My Most Exciting Experience." You may need to draft some of your paper slowly and painstakingly. You'll find yourself coping with all sorts of small problems, many of them simple and mechanical. What, for instance, will you call the author whose work you are dealing with? Decide at the outset. Most

---

[1]Vladimir Nabokov, author of *Lolita* and *Pale Fire,* wrote most of his novels on large index cards while standing up—eventually buying a lectern to work on.

critics favor the author's last name alone: "Dickinson implies . . ." ("Miss Dickinson" or "Ms. Dickinson" may sound too fussy, overly polite; "Emily," too chummy.) Will you include footnotes in your paper, and if so, do you know how they work? (Some pointers on handling the pesky things are given in the chapter "Writing a Research Paper.")

Using Literary Terminology

One more word of friendly advice. In this book you are offered a vocabulary with which to discuss literature: a flurry of terms such as *irony*, *symbol*, and *image*, printed in **boldface** when first introduced. (All these boldface words are defined again in the Glossary of Literary Terms found at the end of this book.) In your writing, you may decide to enlist a few of these terms. Literary terminology sometimes sounds so impressive that a beginning critic can be tempted to use it indiscriminately. Nothing is less sophisticated or more opaque, however, than too many technical terms thrown together for grandiose effect: "The mythic *symbolism* of this *archetype* is the *antithesis* of the *dramatic situation*." Far better to choose plain words you're already at ease with. Your instructor has met many a critical term before and is not likely to be impressed by the mere sight of another one. Knowingly selected and placed, a critical term can help sharpen a thought and make it easier to handle. It is less cumbersome, for example, to refer to the *tone* of a story than to say, "the way the author makes you feel that she feels about what she is talking about."

Just remember that even graduate students working toward their doctorates in literature have trouble with the incomprehensibility of some specimens of literary theory. Thus, rather than modeling your writing on the turgid and jargon-filled prose too frequently found in contemporary criticism, aim for intelligent clarity in your own essays. It is, in fact, possible to discuss a complex idea in clear prose. When you use specialized terms, do so to smooth the way for your reader—to make your meaning more precise. They should not serve as stumbling blocks to understanding, or semantic puzzles that your teacher must tease out.

Revising

When you write your first draft, by the way, leave plenty of space between lines and set enormous margins. Then, when later thoughts come to you, you can easily squeeze them in.

Does any writer write with perfection on the first try? Some writers have claimed to do so—among them the English novelist Anthony Trollope, who thought it "unmanly" not to write a thought precisely the first time. Jack Kerouac, leading novelist of the Beat Generation of the 1950s, believed in spontaneous prose. He wrote entire novels on uncut ribbons of teletype paper, thus saving himself the interruption of stopping at the bottom of each page. His specialty, though, was fiction of ecstasy and hallucination, not essays in explication, or comparison and contrast. For most of us, however, good writing is largely a matter of revising—of going back over our first thoughts word by word. Now you can turn on your analytical mind and be as critical of your creativity as the final product warrants. Of course, painstaking revision is more than a matter of tidying up grammar and spelling; in the process of reconsidering our words, we sometimes discover fresher and sharper ideas. "Writing and rewriting," says John Updike, "are a constant search for what one is saying."

To achieve effective writing, you must have the courage to be wild. Aware that no reader need see your rough drafts, you can treat them mercilessly—tear them apart, rearrange their pieces, reassemble them into a stronger order. The art of revising calls for a textbook in itself, but here are a few simple suggestions:

1. Insofar as your deadline allows, be willing to revise as many times as need be.

2. Don't think of revision as the simple chore of fixing up spelling mistakes. That's proofreading, and it comes last. When you revise, be willing to cut and slash, to discover new insights, to move blocks of words around so that they follow in a stronger order. Stand ready to question your whole approach to a work of literature, to entertain the notion of throwing everything you have written into the wastebasket and starting over again.

3. At this stage, you may find it helpful to enlist outside advice—from your instructor, from your roommate or your mate, from any friend who will read your rough draft and give you a reaction. If you can enlist such a willing reader, ask him or her: What isn't clear to you?

4. If you (or your willing reader) should find any places that aren't readily understandable, single them out for rewriting. After all, you don't need to revise a whole draft if only parts of it need work. Try rewriting any troublesome passage or paragraph.

5. Short, skimpy paragraphs of one or two sentences may indicate places that call for more thought or more material. Can you supply them with more evidence, more explanation, more example and illustration?

6. A time-tested method of revising is to lay aside your paper for a while, forget about it, and then after a long interval (the Roman poet Horace recommended nine years, but obviously that's a bit long for most students), go back to it for a fresh look. If you have time, take a nap or a walk, or at least a yawn and a stretch before you take yet another look. Remember that the literal meaning of "revision" is "to see again."

7. When your paper is in a *last* draft—then it's time to edit it. Once you have your ideas in firm shape, you can check those uncertain spellings, look up the agreement of subjects and verbs in a grammar book or handbook, make your pronouns and antecedents agree, cut needless words, pull out a weak word and send in a stronger one. Back when you were drafting, being prematurely fussy about such small things might have frozen you up. But once you feel satisfied that you have made yourself clear, you can be as fussy as you like.

The Form of Your Finished Paper

Now that you have smoothed your final draft as fleck-free as you can, your instructor may have specific advice for the form of your finished paper. If none is forthcoming, follow the guidelines in the MLA *Handbook for Writers of Research Papers*, which you will find more fully described in the chapter "Writing a Research paper." In brief:

1. Choose standard letter-size ($8\frac{1}{2} \times 11$) white paper.

2. Give your name, your instructor's name, the course number, and the date at the top left-hand corner of your first page.

3. Title your paper and make that title reflect your thesis. A title such as "Essay on *The Glass Menagerie*" is not a title at all, but a file folder heading; your final paper requires something far more original. Most writers don't give their work a title until after they've completed it. At that point, you will be able to provide a fresh, focused title.

4. Leave an inch or more of margin on all four sides of each page and a few inches of blank paper or an additional sheet after your conclusion, so that your instructor can offer comments. If you include a Works Cited section, it belongs on a separate page.

5. Double-space, including quotations and notes. Don't forget to double-space the Works Cited page too.

6. Give your last name and the page number in the top right-hand corner of each page, one-half inch from the top.

And what of titles of works discussed: when do you put them in quotation marks and when do you underline them? One rule of thumb is that titles of works shorter than book length rate quotation marks (poems, short stories, articles); but titles of books (including book-length poems such as *The Odyssey*), plays, and periodicals take underlining or italics. (In a manuscript to be typeset, an <u>underline</u> is a signal to the compositor to use *italics*.)

Using Spell-Check and Grammar-Check Programs

Most computers have a program to automatically check spelling. These devices make it much easier to proofread your papers, but they will not catch all errors. It is still crucial that you proofread and correct your papers in the old-fashioned way—read them yourself.

The most common type of error that occurs is when the spell checker approves of a perfectly acceptable word that is incorrect in context. *In* or *it* frequently is mistyped as *is*, for example, and the spell checker won't catch the misspelling. Likewise, *the* is often erroneously keyboarded as *he*. This produces memorable spell-check-approved sentences such as "It Edna St. Vincent Millay's sonnet, we hear he voice of feminist concerns not often found is Modernist poetry." No human reader would ever approve of this pseudosentence, but a computer might.

Another common problem is that the names of most authors, places, and special literary terms won't be in many standard spell-check memories. Unfamiliar words will be identified during the spell-check process, but you still must intervene to correct possible errors made during keyboarding. Check all proper nouns carefully, so that Robert Forst, Gwendolyn Broks, or Emily Dickenson don't make unauthorized appearances midway in your otherwise exemplary paper. As the well-known authors Dina Gioia, Dan Goia, Dana Glola, Dona Diora, and Dana Gioia advise, always check the spelling of all names.

As a final warning about letting your computer write your finished paper, here are some cautionary verses that have circulated over the last few years on the Internet. (Based on a charming piece of light verse by Jerrold H. Zar, "Candidate for a Pullet Surprise," this version reflects additions and revisions by numerous anonymous Internet collaborators.)

A LITTLE POEM REGARDING COMPUTER SPELL CHECKERS   2000?

Eye halve a spelling checker
  It came with my pea sea
It plainly marques four my revue
  Miss steaks eye kin knot sea.

Eye strike a key and type a word   5
  And weight four it two say
Weather eye am wrong oar write
  It shows me strait a weigh.

As soon as a mist ache is made
  It nose bee fore two long   10
And eye can put the error rite
  Its rare lea ever wrong.

Eye have run this poem threw it
  I am shore your pleased two no
Its letter perfect awl the weigh   15
  My checker tolled me sew.

In addition to spell-check programs, most computers also feature grammar checkers. These programs will highlight sentences that have obvious grammatical mistakes: subjects and verbs that don't agree, sentence fragments, dangling modifiers. Unfortunately, if you don't know what is wrong with your sentence in the first place, the grammar program won't tell you. You can try recasting the sentence until the highlighting disappears (indicating that it's now grammatically correct), or you can simply be sure that you have a good grasp of grammar already. Most colleges offer brief refresher courses in grammar, and, of course, writers' handbooks with grammar rules are readily available. Still, the best way to improve your grammar, your spelling, and your general command of language is to read widely and well. To that end, we urge you to read the works of literature collected in this book beyond those texts assigned to you by your teacher. A well-furnished mind is a great place to live, an address you'll want to have forever.

What to do now but hand in your paper? "And good riddance!" you may feel, after such an expenditure of thinking, time, and energy. But a good paper is not only worth submitting, it is also worth keeping. If you return to it after a while, you may find to your surprise that it will preserve and even renew what you have learned.

23 *Writing About a Poem*

Assignment: write a paper about a poem. You can approach your paper as a grim duty: any activity can look like a dull obligation. For Don Juan, in Spanish legend, even making love became a chore. But the act of writing, like the act of love, is easier if your feelings take part in it. Write about something you dislike and don't understand, and you not only set for yourself the labors of Hercules, but you also guarantee your reader discouragingly hard labor, too.

To write about a poem well, you need first to experience it. It helps to live with the poem for as long as possible; there is little point in trying to fully understand the poem in a ten-minute tour of inspection on the night before the paper falls due. However challenging, writing about poetry has immediate rewards. To mention just one, the poem you spend time writing about is going to mean much more to you than poems skimmed over ever do.

Most of the problems you will meet in writing about a poem are the same ones you encounter in writing about a play or a story: finding a topic, organizing your thoughts, writing, revising. For general advice on writing papers about any kind of literature, see the earlier chapter, "Writing About Literature," on page 605. In a few ways, however, a poem requires a different approach. In this chapter we will deal briefly with some of them and will offer a few papers that students have written. We think you will agree that these papers are interesting, and we assure you that most students can write equally good papers.

Briefer than most stories and plays, lyric poems look easier to write about. They call, however, for your keenest attention. You may find that, before you can discuss a short poem, you will have to read it slowly and painstakingly, with your mind (like your pencil) sharp and ready. Unlike a play or a short story, a lyric poem tends to have very little plot, and perhaps you will find little to say about what happens in it. In order to understand a poem, you'll need to notice elements other than narrative: the connotations or suggestions of its words, surely, and the rhythm of phrases and lines. The subtleties of language are so essential to a poem (and so elusive) that Robert Frost was moved to say, "Poetry is what gets lost in translation." Once in a while, of course, you'll read a story whose prose abounds in sounds, rhythms, figures of speech, imagery, and other elements you expect of poetry. Certain novels of Herman Melville and William Faulkner contain paragraphs that, if extracted, seem in themselves prose poems—so lively are they in their wordplay, so rich in metaphor. But such writing is exceptional, and the main business of most fiction is to get a story told. An extreme case of a fiction writer who didn't want his prose to sound poetic is Georges Simenon, best known for his mystery novels, who said that whenever he noticed in his manuscript any word or phrase that called attention to itself, he struck it out. This method of writing would never do for a poet, who revels in words and phrases that fix themselves in memory. It is safe to say that, in order to write well about a poem, you have to read it carefully enough to remember at least part of it word for word.

Let's consider three commonly useful approaches to writing about poetry.

EXPLICATING

In an **explication** (literally, "an unfolding") of a poem, a writer explains the entire poem in detail, unraveling any complexities to be found in it. This method is a valuable one in approaching a lyric poem, especially if the poem is rich in complexities (or in suggestions worth rendering explicit). Most poems that you'll ever be asked to explicate are short enough to discuss thoroughly within a limited time; fully to explicate a long and involved work, such as John Milton's epic *Paradise Lost*, might require a lifetime. (To explicate a short passage of Milton's long poem, however, would be a practical and interesting course assignment.)

The writer of an explication tries to examine and unfold all the details in a poem that a sensitive reader might consider. These might include allusions, the denotations or connotations of words, the possible meanings of symbols, the effects of certain sounds and rhythms and formal elements (rime schemes, for instance), the sense of any statements that contain irony, and other particulars. Not intent on ripping a poem to pieces, the author of a useful explication instead tries to show how each part contributes to the whole.

An explication is easy to organize. You can start with the first line of the poem and keep working straight on through. An explication should not be confused with a paraphrase. A paraphrase simply puts the literal meaning of a poem into plain prose sense: it is a sort of translation that might prove helpful in clarifying a poem's main theme. Perhaps in writing an explication, you will wish to do some paraphrasing, but an explication (unlike a paraphrase) does not simply restate. It explains a poem, in great detail.

Here, for example, is a famous poem by Robert Frost, followed by a student's concise explication. (The assignment was to explain whatever in "Design" seemed most essential, in not more than 750 words.)

Robert Frost   (1874–1963)

DESIGN   1936

I found a dimpled spider, fat and white,
On a white heal-all, holding up a moth
Like a white piece of rigid satin cloth—
Assorted characters of death and blight
Mixed ready to begin the morning right,   5
Like the ingredients of a witches' broth—
A snow-drop spider, a flower like a froth,
And dead wings carried like a paper kite.

What had that flower to do with being white,
The wayside blue and innocent heal-all?   10
What brought the kindred spider to that height,
Then steered the white moth thither in the night?
What but design of darkness to appall?—
If design govern in a thing so small.

Ted Jasper

Professor Hirsch

English 130

21 November 20xx

       An Unfolding of Robert Frost's "Design"

    "I always wanted to be very observing," Robert Frost
once told an audience, after reading his poem "Design." Then
he added, "But I have always been afraid of my own
observations" (qtd. in Cook 126-27). What could Frost have
observed that could scare him? Let's examine the poem in
question and see what we discover.

    Starting with the title, "Design," any reader of this
poem will find it full of meaning. As the Merriam-Webster
Dictionary defines design, the word can denote among other
things a plan, purpose, or intention ("Design"). Some

---

arguments for the existence of God (I remember from Sunday School) are based on the "argument from design": that because the world shows a systematic order, there must be a Designer who made it. But the word design can also mean "a deliberate undercover project or scheme" such as we attribute to a "designing person" ("Design"). As we shall see, Frost's poem incorporates all of these meanings. His poem raises the old philosophic question of whether there is a Designer, an evil Designer, or no Designer at all.

Like many other sonnets, "Design" is divided into two parts. The first eight lines draw a picture centering on the spider, who at first seems almost jolly. It is dimpled and fat like a baby, or Santa Claus. The spider stands on a wildflower whose name, heal-all, seems ironic: a heal-all is supposed to cure any disease, but this flower has no power to restore life to the dead moth. (Later, in line ten, we learn that the heal-all used to be blue. Presumably, it has died and become bleached-looking.) In the second line we discover, too, that the spider has hold of another creature, a dead moth. We then see the moth described with an odd simile in line three: "Like a white piece of rigid satin cloth." Suddenly, the moth becomes not a creature but a piece of fabric--lifeless and dead--and yet satin has connotations of beauty. Satin is a luxurious material used in rich formal clothing, such as coronation gowns and brides' dresses. Additionally, there is great accuracy in the word: the smooth and slightly plush surface of satin is like the powder-smooth surface of moths' wings. But this "cloth," rigid and white, could be the lining to Dracula's coffin.

In the fifth line an invisible hand enters. The characters are "mixed" like ingredients in an evil potion. Some force doing the mixing is behind the scene. The characters in themselves are innocent enough, but when brought together, their whiteness and look of <u>rigor mortis</u> are overwhelming. There is something diabolical in the spider's feast. The "morning right" echoes the word <u>rite</u>, a ritual--in this case apparently a Black Mass or a Witches' Sabbath. The simile in line seven ("a flower like a froth") is more ambiguous and harder to describe. A froth is white, foamy, and delicate--something found on a brook in the woods or on a beach after a wave recedes. However, in the natural world, froth also can be ugly: the foam on a polluted stream or a rabid dog's mouth. The dualism in nature--its beauty and its horror--is there in that one simile.

So far, the poem has portrayed a small, frozen scene, with the dimpled killer holding its victim as innocently as a boy holds a kite. Already, Frost has hinted that Nature may be, as Radcliffe Squires suggests, "Nothing but an ash-white plain without love or faith or hope, where ignorant appetites cross by chance" (87). Now, in the last six lines of the sonnet, Frost comes out and directly states his theme. What else could bring these deathly pale, stiff things together "but design of darkness to appall?" The question is clearly rhetorical; we are meant to answer, "Yes, there does seem an evil design at work here!" I take the next-to-last line to mean, "What except a design so dark and sinister that we're appalled by it?" "Appall," by the way, is the second pun in the poem: it sounds like <u>a pall</u> or shroud. (The derivation of <u>appall</u>, according to <u>Merriam-Webster</u>, is ultimately from a Latin word meaning "to be pale"--an interesting word choice for a poem full of white pale images ["Appall"].) <u>Steered</u> carries the suggestion of a steering-wheel or rudder that some pilot had to control. Like the word <u>brought</u>, it implies that some invisible force charted the paths of spider, heal-all, and moth, so that they arrived together.

Having suggested that the universe is in the hands of that sinister force (an indifferent God? Fate? the Devil?),

Frost adds a note of doubt. The Bible tells us that "His eye is on the sparrow," but at the moment the poet doesn't seem sure. Maybe, he hints, when things in the universe drop below a certain size, they pass completely out of the Designer's notice. When creatures are this little, maybe God doesn't bother to govern them but just lets them run wild. And possibly the same mindless chance is all that governs human lives. And because this is even more senseless than having an angry God intent on punishing us, it is, Frost suggests, the worst suspicion of all.

Works Cited

"Appall." <u>Merriam-Webster Online</u>. 2004. Merriam-Webster.
    14 Oct. 20xx <http://www.m-w.com/>.

Cook, Reginald. <u>Robert Frost: A Living Voice</u>. Amherst: U of
    Massachusetts P, 1974.

"Design." <u>Merriam-Webster Online</u>. 2004. Merriam-Webster.
    14 Oct. 20xx <http://www.m-w.com/>.

Frost, Robert. "Design." <u>Collected Poems, Prose and Plays</u>.
    New York: Library of America, 1995. 275.

Squires, Radcliffe. <u>The Major Themes of Robert Frost</u>. Ann
    Arbor: U of Michigan P, 1963.

This excellent paper, while finding something worth unfolding in every line in Frost's poem, does so without seeming mechanical. Notice that, although the student proceeds sequentially through the poem from the title to the last line, he takes up, when necessary, some points, out of order. In paragraph two, for example, the writer looks ahead to the end of the poem and briefly states the poem's main theme. (He does so in order to relate this theme to the poem's title.) In the third paragraph, he explicates the poem's *later* image of the heal-all, relating it to the first image. He also comments on the form of the poem ("Like many other sonnets"), on its similes and puns, and on its denotations and connotations.

This paper also demonstrates good use of manuscript form, following the *MLA Handbook,* 6th ed. Brief references (in parentheses) tell us where the writer found Frost's remarks and give page numbers for his quotation from a book by Radcliffe Squires. At the end of the paper, a list of Works Cited uses the abbreviations for *University* and *Press* that the *MLA Handbook* recommends.

It might seem that to work through a poem line by line is a mechanical task, and yet there can be genuine excitement in doing so. Randall Jarrell once wrote an explication of "Design" in which he managed to convey just such excitement. See if you can sense Jarrell's joy in writing about the poem.

> Frost's details are so diabolically good that it seems criminal to leave some unremarked; but notice how *dimpled, fat,* and *white* (all but one; all but one) come from our regular description of any baby; notice how the *heal-all,* because of its name, is the one flower in all the world picked to be the altar for this Devil's Mass; notice how *holding up* the moth brings something ritual and hieratic, a ghostly, ghastly formality, to this priest and its sacrificial victim; notice how terrible to the fingers, how full of the stilling rigor of death, that *white piece of rigid satin cloth* is. And *assorted characters of death and blight* is, like so many things in this poem, sharply ambiguous: *a mixed bunch of actors* or *diverse representative signs.* The tone of the phrase *assorted characters of death and blight* is beautifully developed in the ironic Breakfast-Club-calisthenics, Radio-Kitchen heartiness of *mixed ready to begin the morning right* (which assures us, so unreassuringly, that this isn't any sort of Strindberg *Spook Sonata,* but hard fact), and concludes in the *ingredients* of the witches' broth, giving the soup a sort of cuddly shimmer that the cauldron in *Macbeth* never had; the *broth,* even, is brought to life—we realize that witches' broth *is* broth, to be supped with a long spoon.[1]

Evidently, Jarrell's cultural interests are broad: ranging from August Strindberg's groundbreaking modern play down to *The Breakfast Club* (a once-popular radio program that cheerfully exhorted its listeners to march around their tables). And yet breadth of knowledge, however much it deepens and enriches Jarrell's writing, isn't all that he brings to the reading of poetry. For him an explication isn't a dull plod, but a voyage of discovery. His prose—full of figures of speech (*diabolically good, cuddly shimmer*)—conveys the apparent delight he takes in showing off his findings. Such a joy, of course, can't be acquired deliberately. But it can grow, the more you read and study poetry.

ANALYZING

An **analysis** of a poem, like a news commentator's analysis of a crisis in the Middle East or a chemist's analysis of an unknown fluid, separates its subject into elements, as a means to understanding that subject—to see what composes it. Usually, the writer of

---

[1] *Poetry and the Age* (New York: Knopf, 1953), 42–43.

such an essay singles out one of these elements for attention: "Imagery of Light and Darkness in Frost's 'Design' "; "The Character of Satan in Milton's *Paradise Lost*."

Like explication, analysis can be particularly useful in dealing with a short poem. Unlike explication (which inches through a poem line by line), analysis often suits a long poem, too, because it allows the writer to discuss just one manageable element in the poem. A good analysis casts intense light on a poem from one direction. If you care enough about a poem and about some perspective on it—its theme, say, or its symbolism or its singability—writing an analysis can enlighten and give pleasure.

In this book you probably have met a few brief analyses: the discussion of connotations in John Masefield's "Cargoes" (page 82), for instance, or the examination of symbols in T. S. Eliot's "The *Boston Evening Transcript*" (page 260). In fact, most of the discussions in this book are analytic. Temporarily, we have separated the whole art of poetry into elements such as tone, irony, literal meaning, suggestions, imagery, figures of speech, sound, rhythm, and so on. No element of a poem, of course, exists apart from all the other elements. Still, by taking a closer look at particular elements, one at a time, we see them more clearly and can more easily study them.

Long analyses of metrical feet, rime schemes, and indentations tend to make ponderous reading. Such formal and technical elements are perhaps the hardest to discuss engagingly. And yet formal analysis (at least a little of it) can be interesting and illuminating; it can measure the very pulse beat of lines. If you do care about the technical side of poetry, then write about it, by all means. You will probably find it helpful to learn the terms for the various meters, stanzas, fixed forms, and other devices, so that you can summon them to your aid with confidence. Here is a short formal analysis of "Design" by a student who evidently cares for technicalities and finds an interesting way to talk about them. Concentrating on Frost's use of the sonnet form in "Design," the student casts light on the entire poem.

Lopez 1

Guadalupe Lopez
Professor Faber
English 210
16 April 20xx

The Design of Robert Frost's "Design"

For "Design" the sonnet form has at least two
advantages. As in most Italian sonnets, the poem's argument
falls into two parts. In the octave Robert Frost's persona
draws a still-life of a spider, a flower, and a moth; then

---

in the sestet he contemplates the meaning of his still-life. The sestet focuses on a universal: the possible existence of a vindictive deity who causes the spider to catch the moth and, no doubt, also causes--when viewed anthropomorphically --other suffering.

Frost's persona weaves his own little web. The unwary audience is led through the poem's argument from its opening "story" to a point at which something must be made of the story's symbolic significance. Even the rhyme scheme contributes to the poem's successful leading of the audience toward the sestet's theological questioning. The word <u>white</u> ends the first line of the sestet, and the same vowel sound is echoed in the lines that follow. All in all, half of the sonnet's lines end in the "ite" sound, as if to render significant the wh<u>ite</u>ness--the symbolic innocence--of nature's representation of a greater truth.

A sonnet has a familiar design, and the poem's classical form points to the thematic concern that there seems to be an order to the universe that might be perceived by looking at even seemingly insignificant natural events. The sonnet must follow certain conventions, and nature, though not as readily apprehensible as a poetic form, is apparently governed by a set of laws. There is a ready-made irony in Frost's choosing such an order-driven form to meditate on whether or not there is any order in the universe. However, whether or not his questioning sestet is actually approaching an answer or, indeed, the answer, Frost has approached an order that seems to echo a larger order in his using the sonnet form. An approach through poetic form and substance is itself significant in Frost's own estimation, for Frost argues that what a poet achieves in writing poetry is "a momentary stay against confusion" (777).

Although design clearly governs in this poem--in this "thing so small"--the design is not entirely predictable.

The poem does start out in the form of an Italian sonnet, relying on only two rhyming sounds. However, unlike an Italian sonnet, one of the octave's rhyming sounds--the "ite"--continues into the sestet. And additionally, "Design" ends in a couplet, much in the manner of the Shakespearean sonnet, which frequently offers, in the final couplet, a summing up of the sonnet's argument. Perhaps not only nature's "story" of the spider, the flower, and the moth but also Frost's poem itself echoes the larger universe. It looks perfectly orderly until the details are given their due.

Work Cited

Frost, Robert. "The Figure a Poem Makes." Collected Poems, Prose and Plays. New York: Library of America, 1995. 776-78.

COMPARING AND CONTRASTING

To write a **comparison** of two poems, you place them side by side and point out their likenesses; to write a **contrast,** you point out their differences. If you wish, you can combine the two methods in the same paper. For example, even though you may emphasize similarities, you may also call attention to significant differences, or vice versa.

Such a paper makes the most sense if you pair two poems that have much in common. It would be possible to compare Wallace McRae's comic cowboy poem "Reincarnation" with Thomas Gray's profoundly elegiac "Elegy Written in a Country Churchyard" but comparison would be difficult, perhaps futile. Though both poems are in English and both deal with the themes of death and transfiguration, the two seem hopelessly remote from each other—in diction, tone, complexity, and scope. Your first task, therefore, is to choose two poems that shed light on one another when they are examined together.

Having found a pair of poems that illuminate each other, you then try to demonstrate in your paper further, unsuspected resemblances—not just those that are obvious ("'Design' and 'Wing-Spread' are both about bugs"). The interesting resemblances are ones that take thinking to discover. Similarly, you may want to show noteworthy differences—besides those your reader will see without any help.

In comparing two poems, you may be tempted to discuss one of them and be done with it, then spend the latter half of your paper discussing the other. This simple way of organizing an essay can be dangerous if it leads you to keep the two poems in total isolation from each other. The whole idea of such an assignment, of course, is to see what can be learned by comparing the two poems. There is nothing wrong in discussing all of poem A first, then discussing poem B—*if* in discussing B, you keep looking back at A. Another procedure is to keep comparing the two poems all the way through your paper—dealing first, let's say, with their themes; then with their central metaphors; and finally, with their respective merits.

More often than not, a comparison is a kind of analysis—a study of a theme common to two poems, for instance, or of two poets' similar fondness for the myth of Eden. You also can evaluate poems by comparing and contrasting them, placing them side by side in order to decide which poet deserves the brighter laurels. Here, for example, is a poem by Abbie Huston Evans, followed by a paper that considers Frost's "Design" and Evans's "Wing-Spread." By comparing and contrasting the two poems for both their language and their themes, this student shows us reasons for his evaluation.

Abbie Huston Evans   (1881–1979)

Wing-Spread   1938

The midge spins out to safety
Through the spider's rope;
But the moth, less lucky,
Has to grope.

Mired in glue-like cable   5
See him foundered swing
By the gap he opened
With his wing,

Dusty web enlacing
All that blue and beryl.   10
In a netted universe
Wing-spread is peril.

Tom Munjee

Professor Mickey

English 110

21 October 20xx

"Wing-Spread" Does a Dip

Abbie Huston Evans's "Wing-Spread" is an effective short poem, but it lacks the complexity and depth of Robert Frost's "Design." These two poems were published only two years apart, and both present a murderous spider and an unlucky moth, but Frost's treatment differs from Evans's approach in at least two important ways. First, Frost uses poetic language more evocatively than Evans. Second, "Design" digs more deeply into the situation to uncover a more memorable theme.

If we compare the language of the two poems, we find "Design" is full of words and phrases rich with suggestions. The language of "Wing-Spread," by comparison, seems thinner. Frost's "dimpled spider, fat and white," for example, is certainly a more suggestive description. Actually, Evans does not describe her spider; she just says, "the spider's rope." (Evans does vividly show the spider and moth in action. In Frost's poem, they are already dead and petrified.) In "Design," the spider's dimples show that it is like a chubby little baby. This seems an odd way to look at a spider, but it is more original than Evans's conventional view (although I like her word cable, suggesting that the spider's web is a kind of high-tech food trap). Frost's word-choice--his repetition of white--paints a more striking scene than Evans's slightly vague "All that blue and beryl." Except for her brief personification of the moth in the second stanza, Evans hardly uses any figures of speech, and even this one is not a clear personification--

she simply gives the moth a sex by referring to it as "him." Frost's striking metaphors, similes, and even puns (right, appall), show him, as usual, to be a master of figures of speech. He calls the moth's wings "satin cloth" and "a paper kite;" Evans just refers in line 8 to a moth's wing. As far as the language of the two poems goes, we might as well compare a vase brimming with flowers and a single flower stuck in a vase. In fairness to Evans, I would say that her poem, while lacking complexity, still makes its point effectively. Her poem has powerful sounds: short lines with the riming words coming at us again and again.

In theme, however, "Wing-Spread" seems much more narrow than "Design." The first time I read Evans's poem, all I felt was: Ho hum, the moth's wings were too wide and got stuck. The second time I read it, I realized that she was saying something with a universal application. This message comes out in line 11, in "a netted universe." That metaphorical phrase is the most interesting part of her poem. Netted makes me imagine the universe as being full of nets rigged by someone who is fishing for us. Maybe, like Frost, Evans sees an evil plan operating. She does not, though, investigate it. She says that the midge escapes because it is tiny. On the other hand, things with wide wing-spreads get stuck. Her theme as I read it is, "Be small and inconspicuous if you want to survive," or maybe, "Isn't it too bad that in this world the big beautiful types crack up and die, while the little puny punks keep sailing?" Now, this is a valuable idea. I have often thought that very same thing myself. But Frost's closing note ("If design govern in a thing so small") is really devastating because it raises a huge uncertainty. "Wing-Spread" leaves us with not much besides a moth stuck in a web and a moral. In both language and theme, "Design" climbs to a higher altitude.

Works Cited

Evans, Abbie Huston. "Wing-Spread." An Introduction to
    Poetry. Ed. X. J. Kennedy and Dana Gioia. 11th ed. New
    York: Longman, 2005. 626.

Frost, Robert. "Design." Collected Poems, Prose and Plays.
    New York: Library of America, 1995. 275.

HOW TO QUOTE A POEM

When you discuss a short poem, you should usually quote the whole text of the poem at the beginning of your paper, with its lines numbered. Then you can refer to it with ease, and your instructor can follow you without having to juggle a book. Ask your instructor, however, whether he or she prefers the full text to be quoted this way. Quoted to illustrate some point, memorable lines can add interest to your paper. Good commentators on poetry tend to be apt quoters, helping their readers to experience a word, a phrase, a line, or a passage that otherwise might be neglected. Quoting poetry accurately, however, raises certain difficulties you don't face in quoting prose.

If you are quoting fewer than four lines of poetry, you should transform the line arrangement into prose form, separating each line by a space, diagonal (/), and a space. The diagonal (/) indicates the writer's respect for where the poet's lines begin and end. Do not change the poet's capitalization or punctuation. Be sure to identify the line numbers you are quoting, as follows:

> The color white preoccupies Frost. The spider is "fat
> and white, / On a white heal-all" (1-2), and even the
> victim moth is pale, too.

There are also lines to think about—important and meaningful units whose shape you will need to preserve. If you are quoting four or more lines, it is good policy to arrange the lines that you are quoting just as they occur in the poem, white space and all, and to identify the line numbers you are quoting. In general, follow these rules:

1. Indent the quotation one inch, or ten spaces, from the left-hand margin.
2. Double-space between the quoted lines.
3. Type the poem exactly as it appears in the original; you do not need to use quotation marks.
4. Cite the line numbers you are quoting in parentheses.

At the outset, the poet tells us of his discovery of

        a dimpled spider, fat and white,

    On a white heal-all, holding up a moth

    Like a white piece of rigid satin cloth--

    Assorted characters of death and blight (1-4)

and implies that the small killer is both childlike

and sinister.

When you are beginning the quotation in the middle of a line of verse, position your starting word as closely as possible to where it occurs in the poem (as in the above example)—not at the left-hand margin.

    If a line you are quoting is too long to fit on one line, you should indent it one-quarter inch, or three spaces, as follows:

    What had that flower to do with being

       white,

    The wayside blue and innocent heal-all?

    What brought the kindred spider to that

       height,

    Then steered the white moth thither in the

       night? (9-12)

    If you omit words from the lines you quote, indicate the omission with an ellipsis (. . .), as in the following example:

The color white preoccupies Frost in his description

of the spider "fat and white, / On a white heal-all

... / Like a white piece of rigid satin cloth" (1-3).

There's no need for an ellipsis, if the lines you are quoting go right to the end of a sentence in the original, or if it is obvious that only a phrase is being quoted.

The speaker says that he "found a dimpled spider,"

and he goes on to portray it as a kite-flying boy.

If you leave out whole lines of verse, indicate the omission by a line of spaced periods about the length of a line of the poem you are quoting.

```
Maybe, she hints, when things in the universe drop

below a certain size, they pass completely out of the

Designer's notice:
```

> The midge spins out to safety
>
> Through the spider's rope;
>
> . . . .
>
> In a netted universe
>
> Wing-spread is peril. (1-2, 11-12)

Before You Begin

You will probably already have spent considerable time in reading, thinking, and feeling. Having selected your topic, you will have taken a further look at the poem or poems you have chosen, letting further thoughts and feelings come to you. The quality of your paper will depend, above all, on the quality of your preparation. Now you are ready at last to write.

Try to make the language with which you analyze a poem as fresh and accurate as possible. It is easy to fall into habitual expression—especially to overuse a few convenient words. Mechanical language may tempt you to think of the poem in mechanical terms. Here, for instance, is a plodding discussion of Robert Frost's poem:

```
The symbols Frost uses in "Design" are very

successful. Frost makes the spider stand for Nature.

He wants us to see nature as blind and cruel. He also

employs good sounds. He uses a lot of i's because he

is trying to make you think of falling rain.
```

What's wrong with this "analysis"? The underscored words are worth questioning here. While understandable, the words *employs* and *uses* seem to lead the writer to see Frost only as a conscious tool-manipulator. To be sure, Frost in a sense "uses" symbols, but did he grab hold of them and lay them into his poem? For all we know, perhaps the symbols arrived quite unbidden and used the poet. To write a good poem, Frost maintained, a poet himself has to be surprised. (How, by the way, can we hope to know what a poet *wants* to do? And there isn't much point in saying that the poet is *trying* to do something. He has already done it, if he has written a good poem.) At least it is likely that Frost didn't plan to fulfill a certain quota of i-sounds. Writing his poem, not by following a blueprint but probably by bringing it slowly to the surface of his mind, Frost no doubt had enough to do without trying to engineer the reactions of his possible audience. Like all true symbols, Frost's spider doesn't *stand for* anything. The writer would be closer to the truth to say that the spider *suggests* or *reminds us* of Nature or of certain forces in the natural world. (Symbols just hint; they don't indicate.)

After the student discussed the paper in a conference with his instructor, he rewrote the two sentences:

```
The symbols in Frost's "Design" are highly effective.

The spider, for instance, suggests the blindness and

cruelty of Nature. Frost's word-sounds, too, are part

of the meaning of his poem, for the i's remind the

reader of falling rain.
```

Not every reader of "Design" will hear rain falling, but the student's revision probably comes closer to describing the experience of the poem most of us know.

In writing about poetry, an occasional note of self-doubt can be useful—now and then a *perhaps* or *a possibly* or an *it seems*. Such qualifying expressions may seem timid shilly-shallying, but at least they keep the writer from thinking, "I know all there is to know about this poem."

Facing the showdown with your empty sheaf of paper or blank computer screen, however, you can't worry forever about your critical vocabulary. To do so is to risk the fate of the centipede in a bit of comic verse, who was running along efficiently until someone asked, "Pray, which leg comes after which?" whereupon "He lay distracted in a ditch / Considering how to run." It is a safe bet that your instructor is human. Your main task as a writer is to communicate to another human being your sensitive reading of a poem.

SUGGESTIONS FOR WRITING

Topics for Brief Papers (250–500 words)

1. Write a concise *explication* of a short poem of your choice or one suggested by your instructor. In a paper this brief, you probably won't have room to explain everything in the poem; explain what you think most needs explaining. (An illustration of an explication appears on page 618.)

2. Write an *analysis* of a short poem that focuses on how one of its key elements shapes its meaning. (An illustration of an analysis appears on page 623.) For examples, here are a few specific topics:

   > Kinds of Irony in Hardy's "The Workbox"
   >
   > The Attitude of the Speaker in Marvell's "To His Coy Mistress"
   >
   > The Theme of Pastan's "Ethics"
   >
   > The Rhythms of Plath's "Daddy"
   >
   > An Extended Metaphor in Yeats's "Long-legged Fly." (Explain the one main comparison that the poem makes and show how the

whole poem makes it. Other likely poems for a paper on extended metaphor: Dickinson's "Because I could not stop for Death," Frost's "The Silken Tent," Lowell's "Skunk Hour," Rich's "Aunt Jennifer's Tigers," Stevenson's "The Victory.")

(To locate any of these poems, see the Index of Authors and Titles.)

3. Select a poem in which the main speaker is a character who for any reason interests you. You might consider, for instance, Betjeman's "In Westminster Abbey," Browning's "Soliloquy of the Spanish Cloister," Eliot's "The Love Song of J. Alfred Prufrock," or Rhina Espaillat's "Bilingual/Bilingüe." Then write a brief profile of this character, drawing only on what the poem tells you (or reveals). What is the character's approximate age? Situation in life? Attitude toward self? Attitude toward others? General personality? Do you find this character admirable?

4. Although each of these poems tells a story, what happens in the poem isn't necessarily obvious: Cummings's "anyone lived in a pretty how town," Eliot's "The Love Song of J. Alfred Prufrock," Robinson's "Luke Havergal," Stevenson's "The Victory," Wright's "A Blessing." Choose one of these poems, and in a paragraph sum up what you think happens in it. Then in a second paragraph, ask yourself: what, *besides* the element of story, did you consider in order to understand the poem?

5. Think of someone you know (or someone you can imagine) whose attitude toward poetry in general is one of dislike. Suggest a poem for that person to read—a poem that you like—and, addressing your skeptical reader, point out whatever you find to enjoy in it, something that you think the skeptic just might enjoy too.

Topics for More Extensive Papers (600–1,000 words)

1. Write an explication of a poem short enough for you to work through line by line—for instance, Dickinson's "My Life had stood – a Loaded Gun" or Stevie Smith's "Not Waving But Drowning," or Frost's "Nothing Gold Can Stay." As if offering your reading experience to a friend who hasn't read the poem before, try to point out all the leading difficulties you encountered and set forth in detail your understanding of any lines that contain such difficulties.

2. Write an explication of a longer poem—for instance, Eliot's "The Love Song of J. Alfred Prufrock," Hardy's "The Convergence of the Twain," Plath's "Lady Lazarus," or Stevens's "Peter Quince at the Clavier." Although you will not be able to go through every line of the poem, explain what you think most needs explaining.

3. In this book you will find numerous poems by each of these poets: Auden, Blake, Dickinson, Donne, Eliot, Frost, Hardy, Hopkins, Hughes, Keats, Cummings, Shakespeare, Stevens, Tennyson, Whitman, William Carlos Williams, Wordsworth, and Yeats; and multiple selections for many more. After you read a few poems by a poet who interests you, write an analysis of *more than one* of the poet's poems. To do this, you need to select one characteristic theme (or

other element) to deal with—something typical of the poet's work not found only in a single poem. Here are a few specific topics for such an analysis:

> Love and Loss in Alfred, Lord Tennyson's Poetry
>
> The Cost of Achieving Individual Identity: The Work of Adrienne Rich
>
> How Emily Dickinson's Lyrics Resemble Hymns
>
> The Humor of Robert Frost
>
> Folk Elements in the Poetry of Langston Hughes
>
> John Keats's Sensuous Imagery
>
> The Vocabulary of Music in Poems of Wallace Stevens
>
> Non-free Verse: Patterns of Sound in Three Poems of William Carlos Williams

4. Compare and contrast two poems in order to evaluate them. Which is more satisfying and effective poetry? To make a meaningful comparison, be sure to choose two poems that genuinely have much in common, perhaps a similar theme or subject. (For an illustration of such a paper, see the one given in this chapter. For suggestions of poems to compare, see "Poems for Further Reading.")

5. Evaluate by the method of comparison two versions of a poem, one an early draft and one a late draft, or perhaps two translations from another language. For parallel versions to work on, see Chapter 15, "Translation."

6. If the previous topic appeals to you, consider this. In 1912, twenty-four years before he published "Design," Robert Frost sent a correspondent this early version:

In White

A dented spider like a snow drop white
On a white Heal-all, holding up a moth
Like a white piece of lifeless satin cloth—
Saw ever curious eye so strange a sight?—
Portent in little, assorted death and blight   5
Like ingredients of a witches' broth?—
The beady spider, the flower like a froth,
And the moth carried like a paper kite.

What had that flower to do with being white,
The blue prunella every child's delight.   10
What brought the kindred spider to that height?
(Make we no thesis of the miller's plight.)
What but design of darkness and of night?
Design, design! Do I use the word aright?

Compare "In White" with "Design." In what respects is the finished poem superior?

Topics for Long Papers (1,500 words or more)

1. Write a line-by-line explication of a poem rich in matters to explain or of a longer poem that offers ample difficulty. While relatively short, Donne's "A Valediction: Forbidding Mourning" or Hopkins's "The Windhover" are poems that will take a good bit of time to explicate. Even a short, apparently simple poem such as Frost's "Stopping by Woods on a Snowy Evening" can provide more than enough to explicate thoughtfully in a longer paper.

2. Write an analysis of the work of one poet (as suggested above, in the third topic for more extensive papers) in which you go beyond this book to read an entire collection of that poet's work.

3. Write an analysis of a certain theme (or other element) that you find in the work of two or more poets. It is probable that in your conclusion you will want to set the poets' work side by side, comparing or contrasting it, and perhaps making some evaluation. Sample topics include:

   > Langston Hughes, Gwendolyn Brooks, and Dudley Randall as Prophets of Social Change

   > What It Is to Be a Woman: The Special Knowledge of Sylvia Plath, Anne Sexton, and Adrienne Rich

   > Popular Culture as Reflected in the Poetry of Wendy Cope, Michael B. Stillman, Gene Fehler, and Charles Martin

   > The Complex Relations Between Fathers and Sons in the Poetry of Robert Hayden, Andrew Hudgins, and Robert Phillips

   > Making Up New Words for New Meanings: Neologisms in Lewis Carroll and Kay Ryan

4. Select one of the "Writer's Perspectives" that are found at the end of each chapter, and use the ideas it contains to cast light on a poem by the same author. Do Frost's ideas on metaphors seem consistent with his own poetic practice? How do Ezra Pound's comments on imagery help us read his poems?

24 *Writing a Research Paper*

DOING RESEARCH FOR AN ESSAY

For short essays, students are usually asked simply to explore their own responses to a work of literature. This task requires thought and reflection, but doesn't demand research. Many people do their best thinking while walking—in nature, in a park, or even just across campus. Imagine, then, that your initial reaction to a story or poem draws you into the quiet forest of your own deepest insights. That's a valuable place, where epiphanies can occur. Carefully note down those thoughts in your reading journal for they will form the creative core of your essay

Later, when a research paper is assigned, you will need to step from the forest of your own reflections into the clearing where other minds meet. That clearing is usually your school's library, though it may be a virtual space visited via your computer's Internet connection. Once in that place where thoughts are shared via published work, you will need to find, read, and assimilate published material that expands and corroborates some aspect of your gut reaction to a piece of literature.

How to Get Started

Unfortunately for novice researchers, sometimes the first material uncovered in the library or on the Internet isn't the desired evidence needed to support a main idea. Worse, you may find your idea has already been examined a dozen times over. Like Odysseus, tie yourself to the mast so that when you hear the siren voices of published professors, you can listen without abandoning your own point of view. Your idea may have been treated, but not yet by you—your particular take on a topic is bound to be different from someone else's. After all, thousands of books have been written on Shakespeare's plays, and there are still new things to say.

Don't forget that the ideal research paper is still based on your *own* observations and interpretations of a literary text. You come up with the point you want to support with research, and then you find the material that will help you demonstrate its

636

plausibility. Of course, sometimes you will find that certain ideas are unworkable. There may be a flaw in your initial observation based on something you didn't know about the context of the piece or its author. For example, perhaps you read William Butler Yeats's poem "Who Goes With Fergus?" and assumed that "brazen cars" were pink Cadillacs and "the white breast of the dim sea" was that huge, white, gelatinous sea creature recently found off the coast of Chile. Obviously, if you then try to write a paper about Yeats's poem in light of phat rides and freaky sea creatures, you won't get anything for your pains but a hysterically laughing instructor who might give your paper an "F" for "Funny."

In the beginning, your research will show you both where you might have misinterpreted and how others have treated your idea. Of course, it is annoying to find that you may be wrong about something, or that someone else has taken off with what you thought was your original argument, but don't let these discoveries put you off. Now you're getting to the vexed center of your subject, and soon you will be able to compare your own ideas against the others and use some of those seemingly similar arguments to refine your thoughts. It is always a good idea to concede the presence of other ideas as you sharpen your own. For example, you may have noticed something strange about the body of Arnold Friend in Joyce Carol Oates's story "Where Are You Going, Where Have You Been?" Perhaps you noticed he has trouble standing in his shoes and you want to explore that odd detail. If you do some research on this character, you may find Arnold Friend referred to as the devil (who has cloven hoofs and hence might have problems with standard-issue cowboy boots), or as the wolf in "Little Red Riding Hood" (also a character not accustomed to standing on his hind legs in human clothes). At that point you may think, "Okay, my idea is shot. Everyone has written about this aspect of the Oates character." Well, just sharpen your focus. Can you think of other stories that deal with potentially supernatural characters, possibly evil ones? What about "Young Goodman Brown"? Or Flannery O'Connor's "A Good Man Is Hard to Find"? How might you compare Arnold Friend with Hawthorne's devil or O'Connor's Misfit?

Or perhaps it is the general topic of physical abnormalities in literature that really intrigues you. You might explore what descriptions of unusual characteristics have to say about human perception, about outer and inner selves, appearance and reality. Several works in this book treat characters that, in one way or another, are unusual. Compare them to Arnold Friend, or find some articles on typical human responses to physical differences in a few popular psychology journals and see where that takes you. Your initial idea is always the most important one you will have because it is your purest response to the work you have read, but sometimes it is only the jumping-off point to other ideas, an indicator of a more general topic that you will focus on and refine in your paper.

Notecards

Once you have done a little initial research—enough to refine your topic to one that you can usefully pursue in a research paper, start taking notes on everything you are reading that relates to your topic. One method of taking notes is to write on index cards—the 3- × 5-inch kind for brief notes and titles, 5- × 8-inch cards for longer notes. Write on one side only; notes on the back of a card are often later overlooked. Cards are easy to shuffle and order, and will help you better organize your material. To save work, instead of copying on a card the title and author of a book you're taking a note on, just keep a numbered list of the books you're using. Then, when making a note, you need write only the book's identifying number and page references on the card in order to identify your source.

You can organize your notes based on the books you're taking them from, or by the theme you are exploring. However, whichever method you choose, be sure you keep track of the source of all quoted material. Certainly, it is easier to take notes while you read than to have to run back to the library during the final typing. Bear in mind the cautionary tale of historian Doris Kearns Goodwin. She was charged with plagiarizing sections of two of her famous books when her words were found to be jarringly similar to those published in other books. She was forced to admit that the plagiarism occurred because she had not clearly marked on her notecards what were her own ideas and words and what were comments from other sources. Goodwin's once enormous reputation is still suffering from these charges, but you can learn from her mistakes and save your own reputation—and your grades.

Photocopying

As photocopy machines are to be found in practically all libraries, you do not need to spend hours copying by hand whole poems and long prose passages. If accuracy is essential (and surely it is), then copying a long poem or prose passage is worth the small investment. Copyright law permits students and scholars to reproduce a single copy in this fashion; it does not, however, permit making a dozen or more copies for public sale. Of course, it is also helpful to make copies of the critical passages you are using from research articles or books—having material from those texts verbatim will help you to accurately quote and cite your sources.

EVALUATING AND USING INTERNET SOURCES

The Internet can be a valuable tool to student researchers. Not only can students access libraries and universities around the world; they can also access countless online publications and Web sites. But it is important to remember that a Web site can be created by anyone with access to a computer and the Internet—no matter how poorly qualified that person might be. Therefore, students must remain analytical or discerning when they enter the World Wide Web or they may find themselves tangled in the spidery threads of a dubious site.

A good place to begin your search is through your own college library. College libraries subscribe to specialized online or CD-ROM database services covering all academic subjects. When searching for articles and books on literary topics, you can also use the *MLA International Bibliography*. If you are not familiar with how to use your library's database system, ask the reference librarian for help—all too often students ignore this primary source of help and leave the library complaining, "I can't find anything on my topic."

Of course, if you are a bit adventurous and want to navigate the Web on your own, you need to make sure that you find reliable sources. Many Internet search engines (e.g., *Yahoo!*) arrange subject directories in a hierarchy, allowing you to go from very general topic areas into more specific ones (e.g., Path: Humanities; Literature; Literary Criticism); this structure *may* be helpful in trying to find a topic on which to write an essay. Remember that if you use general phrases or terms on one of these search engines (e.g., the author's name and the story title), you most likely will get thousands of hits, but only a few of them will be usable sources for a literary research paper. For example, if you enter the phrase CHARLOTTE PERKINS GILMAN'S THE YELLOW WALLPAPER on the search line, you will get Web sites on which you can buy the book, paper assignments that have been posted for classes that use the Internet as a communication tool, and even some listings for stores that sell yellow wallpaper.

A more efficient way to search is by using KEYWORDS to search a specified topic and use the available "advanced" search options (e.g., *Alta Vista*'s "More Precision" search option). When you search using keywords, the results will contain those keywords (LITERARY CRITICISM ON GILMAN'S THE YELLOW WALLPAPER or SYMBOLISM IN HAWTHORNE'S YOUNG GOODMAN BROWN). However, even a keyword search may not provide you with the reputable sources you need, as anyone with Internet access can post a document on the Web. So how do you unlock the Web and gain access to sites that will truly help you to accomplish your task, namely, to write a well-supported literary research paper?

Using Reliable Web Sites and Metapages

One way to increase the likelihood that you will find useful and reliable material on the Web is to begin searching at a reliable Web site. The Library of Congress is an excellent starting point and you don't have to travel to Washington to use it. There are eight alcoves in the Main Reading Room of the Library of Congress, and in recent years they have added a ninth—a virtual alcove that provides an annotated collection of Web sites in the Humanities and Social Sciences Division. For your purpose—writing a literary research paper—access the Subject Index (http://www.loc.gov/rr/main/alcove9/), select "Literature," and then select "Literary Criticism." You will be given a list of metapages and Web sites with collections of critical and biographical material on authors and their works. (A metapage is a page that provides links to other Web sites.)

There are Web-based libraries that are also useful starting points. The *Internet Public Library* (http://www.ipl.org) allows you to search for literary criticism by author, work, country of origin, or literary period. The University of Michigan School of Information and Library Studies started the Internet Public Library in 1995, and it maintains the site. *Library Spot* (http://www.libraryspot.com) is a portal to over 5,000 libraries around the world, periodicals, online texts, reference works, and links to metapages and Web sites on any topic including literary criticism. It is a carefully maintained library site published by Start Spot Mediaworks, Inc., in the North-western University/Evanston Research Park in Evanston, Illinois.

The *Voice of the Shuttle* (http://www.vos.ucsb.edu/) is another useful Web site for the literary researcher. Here you will find research links in over 25 categories in the Humanities and Social Sciences, including online texts, libraries, academic Web sites, and metapages. The site was developed and is maintained by Dr. Alan Liu of the English Department of the University of California, Santa Barbara.

All the Web sites mentioned here are reliable points from which to begin your research. (You should be aware that some journals and university Web sites might not be fully accessible to you from home and might require access through your college library's Internet database connection.) When you follow the links posted on reliable sites, you should access trustworthy material. Of course the ultimate determination of whether a source is reliable falls to you—and you need to know how to make that determination.

Putting Sources to the Test

When evaluating any Web site, the first thing to look for is AUTHORSHIP or SPONSORSHIP of the site. Is the author/sponsor known to you or reputable by associa-tion? Is contact information provided on the site? A government or university-sponsored site is considered to be reliable. We can contact them via e-mail, U.S. mail, or telephone. When you access a book excerpt or article in a periodical, you should also look closely at the information provided on the author. Is this someone known for expertise in the field? Are the author's academic or association credentials presented?

DATE OF PUBLICATION could be another important factor to consider when de-ciding on the suitability of an online document. In some cases you may want to base your essay on the most current literary theory, and so will want to use the most re-cently published material. Always check for a publication date. If the document lists an edition number, make sure that you are using the latest edition of the material.

When using periodicals, consider the TITLE OF THE MAGAZINE OR JOURNAL. Is it an academic journal or a popular magazine? What type of reputation does it have? Obviously, you do not want to use a magazine that periodically reports on Elvis sight-ings and alien births. And you most likely will want to limit your use of popular mag-azines in favor of scholarly journals published to enhance the study of literature.

If you need help in analyzing Internet sources, there are several good Web sites that offer support. Cornell University has two good documents posted: "Critically Ana-lyzing Information Sources" (<http://www.library.cornell.edu> Path: Research & Sub-ject Guides; Critically Analyzing Information Sources) and "Distinguishing Scholarly Journals from Other Periodicals" (<http://www.library.cornell.edu> Path: Research & Subject Guides; Distinguishing Scholarly Journals from Other Periodicals). The UCLA College Library also provides valuable information: "Thinking Critically about World Wide Web Resources" (<http://www.library.ucla.edu/libraries/college/help/critical/index.htm>) and "Thinking Critically about Discipline-Based World Wide Web Re-sources" (<http://www/library.ucla.edu/libraries/college/help/critical/discipline.htm>).

GUARDING ACADEMIC INTEGRITY

Papers for Sale Are Papers That "F"ail

Do not be seduced by the apparent ease of cheating by computer. Your Internet searches may turn up several sites that offer term papers to download. (Just as you can find pornography; political propaganda, and questionable get-rich-quick schemes!) These sites will often want money for what they offer, but some will not, happy just to strike a blow against the "oppressive" insistence of English teachers that students learn to think and write.

Plagiarized term papers are an old game: the fraternity file and the "research-assistance" service have been around far longer than the computer. It may seem easy enough to download a paper, put your name at the head of it, and turn it in for an easy grade. Such papers usually stick out like a sore thumb, however, as any writing teacher can tell you. The style will be wrong, the work will not be consistent with other work by the same student in any number of ways, and the teacher will sometimes have seen the same phony paper before. The ease with which electronic texts are reproduced makes it even more likely that the same paper will appear again and again. It is far better to take the "C" or "D" you have earned for your own work, no matter how mediocre, than to try and pass off someone else's work as your own. Even if, somehow, your instructor does not recognize your submission as a plagiarized paper, you have diminished your character through dishonesty and lost an opportunity to learn something on your own.

A Final Word of Warning on Internet Plagiarism

The battle against academic dishonesty, moreover, may now have been won by computer program designers. Professors now can use plagiarism detection services to identify plagiarism. Questionable research papers can even be sent to services (e.g., Turnitin.com, EVE2) that will perform complex searches of the Internet to locate sources of plagiarized material. The research paper will be returned with plagiarized sections annotated and the source URLs documented. The end result—a failing grade on the essay, perhaps a failing grade for the course, and, depending on the policies of your university, the very real possibility of expulsion.

ACKNOWLEDGING AND DOCUMENTING SOURCES

Acknowledging Your Sources

It is essential to give credit to any critics who supplied you with ideas, information, or specific phrases, and to do so properly means being painstaking. To paraphrase a critic, you do more than just rearrange the critic's words and phrases; you translate them into language of your own. Suppose you wish to refer to an insight of Randall Jarrell, who commented as follows on the images of spider, flower, and moth in Robert Frost's poem "Design":

> Notice how the *heal-all*, because of its name, is the one flower in all the world picked to be the altar for this Devil's Mass; notice how *holding up* the

moth brings something ritual and hieratic, a ghostly, ghastly formality, to this priest and its sacrificial victim.

It would be incorrect to say, without quotation marks:

```
Frost picks the heal-all as the one flower in all the
world to be the altar for this Devil's Mass. There is
a ghostly, ghastly formality to the spider holding up
the moth, like a priest holding a sacrificial victim.
```

This rewording, although not exactly in Jarrell's language, manages to steal his memorable phrases without giving him credit. Nor is it sufficient just to include Jarrell's essay in the Works Cited list at the end of your paper. If you do, you are still a crook; you merely point to the scene of your crime. What is needed, clearly, is to think through Jarrell's words to the point he is making; and if you want to keep any of his striking phrases (and why not?), put them exactly as he wrote them in quotation marks:

```
As Randall Jarrell points out, Frost portrays the
spider as a kind of priest in a Mass, or Black Mass,
elevating the moth like an object for sacrifice, with
"a ghostly, ghastly formality" (42).
```

To be scrupulous in your acknowledgment, tell where you found your quotation from Jarrell, citing the page reference, as detailed in the next section.

Documenting Your Sources

When you quote from other writers, when you borrow their information, or when you summarize or paraphrase their ideas, make sure you give them their due. Document everything you take. Identify the writer by name; cite not only the very book, magazine, newspaper, pamphlet, letter, or other source you are using, but also the page or pages from which you are quoting.

By so doing, you invite your readers to go to your original source and check up on you. Most readers won't bother, of course, but at least your invitation enlists their confidence. Besides, the duty to document keeps you carefully looking at your sources—and so helps keep your writing accurate and responsible. The latest and most efficient way for writers to document their sources is that recommended in the *MLA Handbook for Writers of Research Papers*, 6th ed. (New York: Mod. Lang. Assn., 2003). In the long run, whether you write a long term paper citing dozens of sources or a short paper citing only three or four, the MLA's advice will save you and your reader time and trouble.

These pointers cannot take the place of the *MLA Handbook* itself, but the gist of the method is this: begin by listing your sources—all the works from which you're going to quote, summarize, paraphrase, or take information. Later on, when you key your paper in finished form, you're going to *end* it with a neat copy of this list (once called a "bibliography," now entitled "Works Cited"). Then, in writing your paper, every time you refer to one of these works, you need give only enough information to help a reader locate it under "Works Cited." Usually, you can just give (in parentheses) an author's last name and a page citation. If you were writing, for example, a paper on Weldon Kees's sonnet "For My Daughter" and wanted to include an observation from Samuel Maio's book *Creating Another Self*, you would incorporate the information right in the text of your paper, most often at the end of a sentence:

```
One critic has observed that the distinctive tone of

"For My Daughter" depends on Kees's combination of

personal subject matter with an impersonal voice

(Maio 123).
```

If you wanted to cite *two* books or magazine articles by Maio in your paper, how would the reader tell them apart? In your text, condense the title of each book or article into a word or two. Remember that condensed book titles are also underlined or italicized, and condensed article titles are still placed within quotation marks:

```
One critic has observed that the distinctive tone of

"For My Daughter" depends on Kees's combination of

personal subject matter with an impersonal voice

(Maio, Creating 123).
```

If you have already mentioned the name of the author in your sentence, you need give only the page number when you refer to the source:

```
As Samuel Maio has observed, Kees creates a

distinctive tone in this sonnet by combining a

personal subject with an impersonal voice (123).
```

If you wanted to quote more than four lines, you should set it off from the body of your paper. Start a new line; indent one inch (or ten typewriter spaces); type the quote, double-spaced. After the period at the end of the quotation, put the page reference in parentheses. You do not need to use quotation marks.

Samuel Maio made an astute observation about the
nature of Kees's distinctive tone:

> Kees has therefore combined a personal
> subject matter with an impersonal voice--
> that is, one that is consistent in its tone
> evenly recording the speaker's thoughts
> without showing any emotional intensity
> which might lie behind those thoughts. (123)

The beauty of this documentation method is that you don't have to stop the flow of your thought with a detailed footnote identifying your source. At the end of your paper, in your list of works cited, your reader can find a fuller description of your source—in this case, a critical book:

Maio, Samuel. <u>Creating Another Self: Voice in Modern American Personal Poetry</u>. Kirksville, MO: Thomas Jefferson UP, 1995.

Documentation may seem tedious, but rest assured, your instructor simply wants to smooth the path between your paper and your interested readers. Documenting sources may look arcane, but it is really simple and logical: it's not for your benefit, it's for someone else reading your paper who wants to pursue a topic that you have researched. That interested reader resembles you when you were first in the library searching for material—he or she wants to find all the cited sources that relate to their own particular interest in the subject under scrutiny. Your paper is kindly providing the necessary information for that reader to track down those sources. In the community of researchers, this is not just required—it is common courtesy to one's fellow thinkers.

Works Cited List

At the end of your research paper, you should include a complete list of all the works you have cited. The MLA *Handbook* provides complete instructions for citing a myriad of different types of sources, from books to online databases. Here is a partial checklist of the *Handbook*'s recommendations for presenting such a list.

1. Start a new page for the Works Cited list, and continue the page numbering from the body of your paper.
2. Center the title, "Works Cited," one inch from the top of the page.
3. Double-space between all lines (including after the title and between entries).
4. Type each entry beginning at the left-hand margin. If an entry runs longer than a single line, indent the following lines one-half inch (or five full spaces) from the left-hand margin.

5. Alphabetize each entry according to the author's last name.
6. Include three sections in each entry: author, title, publication or access information. You will, however, give slightly different information for a book, journal article, online source, or other references.

Citing Print Sources

For a book cite:

  a. **Author's full name** as it appears on the title page, last name first, followed by a period.
  b. **Book's full title** (and subtitle, if it has one, separated by a colon) followed by a period. Remember to underline or italicize the title.
  c. **Publication information:** city of publication followed by a colon, the name of the publisher followed by a comma, and the year of publication followed by a period.

  (1) **Make your citation of the city of publication brief, but clear.** If the title page lists more than one city, cite only the first. For U.S. cities, you need not provide the state unless the name of the city alone may be confusing or is unfamiliar. For cities outside the United States, add a country abbreviation if the city is unfamiliar. For Canadian cities, use the province abbreviation. (Examples: Rome, GA; Leeds, Eng.; Victoria, BC)

  (2) **Shorten the publisher's name.** Eliminate articles (*A, An, The*), business abbreviations (*Co., Corp., Inc., Ltd.*), and descriptive words (*Books, House, Press, Publishers*). The exception is a university press, for which you should use the letters *U* (for University) and *P* (for Press). Use only the first listed *surname* of the publisher. Examples below:

Publisher's Name	**Proper Citation**
Harvard University Press	Harvard UP
University of Chicago Press	U of Chicago P
Farrar, Straus and Giroux, Inc.	Farrar
Alfred A. Knopf, Inc.	Knopf

The final citation for a book should read:

```
Author's last name, First name. Book Title. Publication city:
    Publisher, Year.
```

For a journal article cite:

  a. **Author's name,** last name first, followed by a period.
  b. **Title of the article,** followed by a period, all within quotation marks.
  c. **Publication information:** journal title (underlined or italicized); volume number; the year of publication in parentheses, followed by a colon; and,

finally, the inclusive page numbers of the entire article followed by a period.

The final citation for a journal article should read:

```
Author's last name, First name. "Article Title." Journal Volume
    (Year): Pages.
```

If the journal starts the pagination of *each* issue from page one (in contrast to continuous numbering from the previous issue), then you must give both the volume and issue number, with a period between the two. For example, if the article you cite appears in volume 5, issue 2 of such a journal, cite it as 5.2.

```
Author's last name, First name. "Article Title." Journal
    Volume.Issue (Year): Pages.
```

Citing Internet Sources

If you decide to gather source material from the Internet, you must make a careful record of the required bibliographic information for documentation, just as you do for print sources. However, documentation of Internet sources is a bit more complex than it is for print sources. Make a list of the documentation information that you will need *before* you begin your Internet search; recording the information as you go will ensure that you can document a source correctly and find that item on the Web again should you need to do so.

To document an Internet source, you will need the following: author's name when available; title of the document; full information about any previous or simultaneous publication in print form; title of the scholarly project, database, periodical, or professional or personal site; name of the editor of the scholarly project or database; date of electronic publication or last update; name of the institution or organization sponsoring or associated with the site; date when you accessed the source; the Web site address or URL. (Not all the listed information will be available or appropriate for each Internet source—this is a listing of all the possible data you will need for documentation). Many Web sites provide much of this information at the start or end of an article or at the bottom of a Web site home page.

The basic components of any Internet citation are:
    a. **Author's name,** last name first, followed by a period.
    b. **Title of document,** followed by a period, all within quotation marks.
    c. **Print publication information,** if available: title of periodical or book underlined or italicized, volume number and date of publication followed by a period (if page numbers are given, insert a colon followed by the page numbers).
    d. **Electronic publication information:** the title of the Web site, underlined or italicized, followed by a period; editor's name or version number if pro-

vided, followed by a period; the date of electronic publication or the latest update, followed by a period; the name of any organization or institution sponsoring the site, followed by a period.

e. **Access information:** the date that you viewed the document online, followed by the URL (uniform resource locator) enclosed in angle brackets.

(1) If the URL is very long and complicated, give the URL for the site's search page. If no specific URL was assigned to the document, give the URL for the site's home page.

(2) If you accessed a document that does not show a specific URL through a series of links from a Web site's home page, insert the word *Path* followed by a colon after the angle bracket enclosing the URL, and give the title of each link, separating each with a semicolon.

In many cases, not all this information is available for an Internet source. However, when available, the final citation for a document obtained on the Web should read:

```
Author's Last Name, First Name. "Document Title." Print
    Periodical Title Volume (Date of Print Publication): Page
    Numbers. Title of Internet Site. Site Editor. Date of
    Electronic Publication. Web Site Sponsor. Your Access Date
    <URL>.
```

Sample Works Cited List

For a paper on Weldon Kees's "For My Daughter," a student's Works Cited list might look as follows:

```
                          Works Cited
Grosholz, Emily. "The Poetry of Memory." Weldon Kees: A
    Critical Introduction. Ed. Jim Elledge. Metuchen, NJ:
    Scarecrow, 1985. 46-47.
Howard, Ben. "Four Voices." Weldon Kees: A Critical
    Introduction. Ed. Jim Elledge. Metuchen, NJ: Scarecrow,
    1985. 177-79.
Kees, Weldon. The Collected Poems of Weldon Kees. Ed. Donald
    Justice. Lincoln: U of Nebraska P, 1975.
Maio, Samuel. Creating Another Self: Voice in Modern American
    Personal Poetry. Kirksville, MO: Thomas Jefferson UP,
    1995.
Nelson, Raymond. "The Fitful Life of Weldon Kees." American
    Literary History 1 (1989): 816-52.
```

Reidel, James. <u>Vanished Act: The Life and Art of Weldon Kees</u>.

    Lincoln: U of Nebraska P, 2003.

Ross, William T. <u>Weldon Kees</u>. Twayne's US Authors Ser. 484.

    Boston: Twayne, 1985.

<u>Weldon Kees</u>. Ed. James Reidel. 2003. Nebraska Center for

    Writers, Creighton University. 26 Aug. 2004

        <http://mockingbird.creighton.edu/NCW/kees.htm>.

"Weldon Kees." <u>Online Poetry Classroom</u>. 2003. Academy of

    American Poets. 20 Sept. 2004

        <http://www.onlinepoetryclassroom.org/

    poets/poets.cfm?prmID=744>.

See the Reference Guide for Citations at the end of this chapter for additional examples of the types of citations that you are likely to need for your essays or check the 6th edition of the MLA *Handbook*.

Endnotes and Footnotes

It is imperative to keep the citations and quotations in your text brief and snappy, lest they hinder the flow of your prose. You may wish to append a note supplying a passage of less important (yet possibly valuable) information or making careful qualifying statements ("On the other hand, not every expert agrees. John Binks finds that poets are often a little magazine's only cash customers; while Molly MacGuire maintains that . . ."). If you want to insert such an aside and suspect that you can't put it in your text without awkwardly interrupting your paper, then cast it into an **endnote** (a note placed at the end of a paper), or a **footnote** (a note placed at the bottom of a page).

How do you drop in such notes? The number of each consecutive note comes (following any punctuation) after the last word of a sentence. So that the number will stand out, use the "Insert Footnote" option or create a superscript number from the Font menu in your word-processing program, thus lifting the number slightly above the level of your prose.

as other observers have claimed.[1]

When you use the "Insert Footnote" option in your word-processing program, the formatting and placement of the footnote at the bottom of the page will be done automatically.

    [1] John Binks, to name only one such observer, finds that poets are often . . .

Although now useful mainly for such asides, endnotes and footnotes are time-honored ways to document *all* sources in a research paper. Indeed, some instructors still prefer them to a Works Cited list and ask students to use notes to indicate every writer cited. In a brief paper containing only one or two citations, endnotes or footnotes may be simpler and less showy than a Works Cited list that has only two entries. Once again, always check with your instructor on the preferred style.

The *MLA Handbook* encourages writers to use endnotes rather than footnotes in research papers. Endnotes are listed on a new page at the end of your essay text (number this page in sequence with the previous page). Center the title "Notes" one inch from the top of the page, double-space, and follow this format: indent each entry one-half inch from the left-hand margin, subsequent lines in the entry should begin at the left margin, type the notes consecutively and double-spaced. In notes, the author's first name comes first. (In a list of Works Cited, you put the last name first, so that you can readily arrange your list of authors in alphabetical order.)

An endnote identifying a magazine article looks like this:

¹⁶ Louise Horton, "Who Reads Small Literary Magazines and What Good Do They Do?" <u>Texas Review</u> 9.1 (1984): 108-09.

An endnote referencing a book looks like this:

¹⁷ Elizabeth Frank, <u>Louise Bogan: A Portrait</u> (New York: Knopf, 1985) 59-60.

Should you return later to cite another place in Frank's book, you need not repeat all its information. Just write:

¹⁸ Frank 192.

If in your paper you refer to two sources by Elizabeth Frank, give the full title of each in the first note citing it. Then, if you cite it again, use a shortened form of its title:

¹⁹ Frank, <u>Bogan</u> 192.

If you do use footnotes to document all your sources, format them as you do endnotes. Begin to type footnotes four lines below the text on your page, *single-spaced*, with the first line indented one-half inch from the left margin and subsequent lines brought to the left margin. Double-space between entries, and indent the first line of each. Two footnotes at the bottom of the page look like this:

¹⁶ Louise Horton, "Who Reads Small Literary Magazines and What Good Do They Do?" <u>Texas Review</u> 9.1 (1984): 108-09.

¹⁷ John Binks, to name only one such observer, finds that poets are often . . .

CONCLUDING THOUGHTS

A well-crafted research essay is a wondrous thing—as delightful, in its own way, as a well-crafted poem or short story or play. Good essays prompt thought and add to knowledge. Writing a research paper sharpens your own mind and exposes you to the honed insights of other thinkers. Think of anything you write as a piece that could be published for the benefit of other people interested in your topic. After all, such a goal is not as far-fetched as it seems: this textbook, for example, features a number of papers written by students. Why shouldn't yours number among them? Aim high.

Reference Guide for Citations

Here is a comprehensive summary of the types of citations you are likely to need for most student papers. The format follows the current MLA standards for Works Cited lists.

Print Publications
Books

No Author Listed

A Keepsake Anthology of the Fiftieth Anniversary Celebration of the Consultantship In Poetry. Washington: Library of Congress, 1987.

One Author

Middlebrook, Diane Wood. Anne Sexton: A Biography. Boston: Houghton, 1991.

Two or Three Authors

Jarman, Mark, and Robert McDowell. The Reaper: Essays. Brownsville, OR: Story Line, 1996.

Four or More Authors

Phillips, Rodney, et al. The Hand of the Poet. New York: Rizzoli, 1997.

or

Phillips, Rodney, Susan Benesch, Kenneth Benson, and Barbara Bergeron. The Hand of the Poet. New York: Rizzoli, 1997.

Two Books by Same Author

Bawer, Bruce. The Aspect of Eternity. St. Paul: Graywolf, 1993.

---. Diminishing Fictions: Essays on the Modern American Novel and Its Critics. St. Paul: Graywolf, 1988.

Corporate Author

Poets and Writers. <u>A Writer's Guide to Copyright</u>. New York:
      Poets & Writers, 1979.

Author and Editor

Shakespeare, William. <u>The Sonnets</u>. Ed. G. Blakemore Evans.
      Cambridge, Eng.: Cambridge UP, 1996.

One Editor

Monteiro, George, ed. <u>Conversations with Elizabeth Bishop</u>.
      Jackson: UP of Mississippi, 1996.

Two Editors

Craig, David, and Janet McCann, eds. <u>Odd Angles of Heaven:
      Contemporary Poetry by People of Faith</u>. Wheaton, IL:
      Shaw, 1994.

Translation

Dante Alighieri. <u>Inferno: A New Verse Translation</u>. Trans.
      Michael Palma. New York: Norton, 2002.

Introduction, Preface, Foreword, or Afterword

Thwaite, Anthony, Preface. <u>Contemporary Poets</u>. Ed. Thomas
      Riggs. 6th ed. New York: St. James, 1996. vii-viii.
Lapham, Lewis. Introduction. <u>Understanding Media: The
      Extensions of Man</u>. By Marshall McLuhan. Cambridge: MIT P,
      1994. vi-x.

Work in an Anthology

Allen, Dick. "The Emperor's New Clothes." <u>Poetry After
      Modernism</u>. Ed. Robert McDowell. Brownsville, OR: Story
      Line, 1991. 71-99.

Translation in an Anthology

Neruda, Pablo. "We Are Many." Trans. Alastair Reid. An
    Introduction to Poetry. Ed. X. J. Kennedy and Dana Gioia.
    11th ed. New York: Longman, 2005. 350.

Multivolume Work

Wellek, René. A History of Modern Criticism, 1750-1950. 8 vols.
    New Haven: Yale UP, 1955-92.

One Volume of a Multivolume Work

Wellek René. A History of Modern Criticism, 1750-1950. Vol. 7.
    New Haven: Yale UP, 1991.

Book in a Series

Ross, William T. Weldon Kees. Twayne's US Authors Ser. 484.
    Boston: Twayne, 1985.

Republished Book

Ellison, Ralph. Invisible Man. 1952. New York: Vintage, 1995.

Revised or Subsequent Editions

Janouch, Gustav. Conversations with Kafka. Trans. Goronwy Rees.
    Rev. ed. New York: New Directions, 1971.

Reference Books

Signed Article in Reference Book

Cavoto, Janice E. "Harper Lee's To Kill a Mockingbird." The
    Oxford Encyclopedia of American Literature. Ed. Jay
    Parini. Vol. 2. New York: Oxford UP, 2004. 418-21.

Unsigned Encyclopedia Article—Standard Reference Book
"James Dickey." The New Encyclopaedia Britannica: Micropaedia.
15th ed. 1987.

Dictionary Entry
"Design." Merriam-Webster's Collegiate Dictionary. 11th ed.
2003.

Periodicals

Journal with Continuous Paging
Balée, Susan. "Flannery O'Connor Resurrected." Hudson Review
47 (1994): 377-93.

Journal That Pages Each Issue Separately
Salter, Mary Jo. "The Heart Is Slow to Learn." New Criterion
10.8 (1992): 23-29.

Signed Magazine Article
Gioia, Dana. "Studying with Miss Bishop." New Yorker 5 Sept.
1986: 90-101.

Unsigned Magazine Article
"The Real Test." New Republic 5 Feb. 2001: 7.

Newspaper Article
Lyall, Sarah. "In Poetry, Ted Hughes Breaks His Silence on
Sylvia Plath." New York Times 19 Jan. 1998, natl. ed.:
A1+.

Signed Book Review
Harper, John. "Well-Crafted Tales with Tabloid Titles." Rev. of
Tabloid Dreams, by Robert Olen Butler. Orlando Sentinel 15
Dec. 1996: D4.

Unsigned, Untitled Book Review
Rev. of Otherwise: New and Selected Poems, by Jane Kenyon.
Virginia Quarterly Review 72 (1996): 136.

ELECTRONIC PUBLICATIONS

Online Resources

Web Site

Voice of the Shuttle. Ed. Alan Liu. 2003. U of California,
    Santa Barbara. 17 Oct. 2003 <http://vos.ucsb.edu/>.

Document on a Web Site

"Wallace Stevens." Poetry Exhibits. 31 Jan. 2001. The Academy
    of American Poets. 20 Sept. 2003 <http://www.poets.org/
    poets/poets.cfm?45442B7C000C07070C>.

Document on a Web Site: Citing a Path

"Wallace Stevens." Poetry Exhibits. 31 Jan. 2001. The Academy
    of American Poets. 20 Sept. 2003 <http://www.poets.org>.
    Path: Find a Poet; S; Stevens, Wallace.

Document on a Web Site: Citing a Search Page

"A Hughes Timeline." PBS Online. 2001. Public Broadcasting
    Service. 20 Sept. 2003 <http://www.pbs.org/search>.

An Entire Online Book

Jewett, Sarah Orne. The Country of the Pointed Firs. Boston:
    Houghton, 1910. Bartleby.com:Great Books Online. Ed.
    Steven van Leeuwen. 1999. 10 Oct. 2003
    <http://www.bartleby.com/125/>.

Online Reference Database

Encyclopaedia Britannica Online. 2002. Encyclopaedia
    Britannica. 15 Feb. 2003 <http://www.britannica.com/>.

Article in Online Scholarly Journal

Hoffman, Tyler B. "Emily Dickinson and the Limit of War." Emily
    Dickinson Journal 3.2 (1994). 15 Mar. 2004
    <http://www.colorado.edu/EDIS/journal/articles/
    III.2.Hoffman.html>.

Article from a Scholarly Journal, Part of an Archival Database

Oates, Joyce Carol. "'Soul at the White Heat': The Romance of
    Emily Dickinson's Poetry." <u>Critical Inquiry</u> 13.4 (1987).
    <u>Literary Criticism on the Web</u>. Ed. Randy Souther. 7 July
    2003 <http://start.at/literarycriticism>. Path: D;
    Dickinson; Joyce Carol Oates on Emily Dickinson; "Soul at
    the White Heat."

Article in Online Newspaper

Atwood, Margaret. "The Writer: A New Canadian Life-Form."
    <u>New York Times on the Web</u> 18 May 1997. 20 Aug. 2003
    <http://www.nytimes.com/books/97/05/18/
    bookend/bookend.html>.

Article in Online Magazine

Garner, Dwight. "The Salon Interview: Jamaica Kincaid."
    <u>Salon</u> 13 Jan. 1996. 15 Feb. 2004
    <http://www.salonmagazine.com/05/features/kincaid.html>.

Article Accessed via a Library Subscription Service

Seitler, Dana. "Unnatural Selection: Mothers, Eugenic Feminism,
    and Charlotte Perkins Gilman's Regeneration Narratives."
    <u>American Quarterly</u> 55.1 (2003): 61-87. ProQuest. Arcadia U
    Landman Lib., Glenside, PA. 7 July 2003
    <http://www.il.proquest.com/proquest/>.

Online Posting

Grossenbacher, Laura. "Comments about the Ending Illustration."
    Online Posting. 4 Sept. 1996. <u>The Yellow Wallpaper Site</u>.
    14 Mar. 2001 <http://www.cwrl.utexas.edu/
    ~daniel/amlit/wallpaper/readcomments.html>.

CD-ROM Reference Works

CD-ROM Publication

"Appall." <u>The Oxford English Dictionary</u>. 2nd ed. CD-ROM.
    Oxford: Oxford UP, 1992.

Periodically Published Information, Collected on CD-ROM

Kakutani, Michiko. "Slogging Surreally in the Vietnamese
Jungle." Rev. of The Things They Carried, by Tim O'Brien.
New York Times Ondisc. CD-ROM. UMI-ProQuest. Oct. 1993.

MISCELLANEOUS SOURCES

Compact Disc (CD)

Shakespeare, William. The Complete Arkangel Shakespeare: 38
Fully-Dramatized Plays. Narr. Eileen Atkins and John
Gielgud. Read by Imogen Stubbs, Joseph Fiennes, et al.
Audio Partners, 2003.

Audiocassette

Roethke, Theodore. Theodore Roethke Reads His Poetry.
Audiocassette. Caedmon, 1972.

Videocassette

Henry V. By William Shakespeare. Dir. Laurence Olivier. Perf.
Laurence Olivier. Two Cities Films. 1944. Videocassette.
Paramount, 1988.

DVD

Hamlet. By William Shakespeare. Perf. Laurence Olivier, Eileen
Herlie, and Basil Sydney. Two Cities Films. 1948. DVD.
Criterion, 2000.

Film

Hamlet. By William Shakespeare. Dir. Franco Zeffirelli. Perf.
Mel Gibson, Glenn Close, Helena Bonham Carter, Alan Bates,
and Paul Scofield. Warner, 1991.

Television or Radio Program

Moby Dick. By Herman Melville. Dir. Franc Roddam. Perf. Patrick
Stewart and Gregory Peck. 2 episodes. USA Network. 16-17
Mar. 1998.

25 *Critical Approaches to Literature*

> Literary criticism should arise out of a debt of love.
> —George Steiner

Literary criticism is not an abstract, intellectual exercise; it is a natural human response to literature. If a friend informs you she is reading a book you have just finished, it would be odd indeed if you did not begin swapping opinions. Literary criticism is nothing more than discourse—spoken or written—about literature. A student who sits quietly in a morning English class, intimidated by the notion of literary criticism, will spend an hour that evening talking animatedly about the meaning of rock lyrics or comparing the relative merits of the *Star Wars* trilogies. It is inevitable that people will ponder, discuss, and analyze the works of art that interest them.

The informal criticism of friends talking about literature tends to be casual, unorganized, and subjective. Since Aristotle, however, philosophers, scholars, and writers have tried to create more precise and disciplined ways of discussing literature. Literary critics have borrowed concepts from other disciplines, such as philosophy, history, linguistics, psychology, and anthropology, to analyze imaginative literature more perceptively. Some critics have found it useful to work in the abstract area of **literary theory,** criticism that tries to formulate general principles rather than discuss specific texts. Mass media critics, such as newspaper reviewers, usually spend their time evaluating works—telling us which books are worth reading, which plays not to bother seeing. But most serious literary criticism is not primarily evaluative; it assumes we know that *Othello* or *The Metamorphosis* is worth reading. Instead, such criticism is analytic; it tries to help us better understand a literary work.

In the following pages you will find overviews of ten critical approaches to literature. While these ten methods do not exhaust the total possibilities of literary criticism, they represent the most widely used contemporary approaches. Although presented separately, the approaches are not necessarily mutually exclusive; many critics mix methods to suit their needs and interests. For example, a historical critic may use formalist techniques to analyze a poem; a biographical critic will frequently use psychological theories to analyze an author. The summaries neither try to provide a history of each approach, nor do they try to present the latest trends in each school. Their purpose is to give you a practical introduction to each critical method and then provide representative examples of it. If one of these critical methods interests you, why not try to write a class paper using the approach?

FORMALIST CRITICISM

Formalist criticism regards literature as a unique form of human knowledge that needs to be examined on its own terms. "The natural and sensible starting point for work in literary scholarship," René Wellek and Austin Warren wrote in their influential *Theory of Literature*, "is the interpretation and analysis of the works of literature themselves." To a formalist, a poem or story is not primarily a social, historical, or biographical document; it is a literary work that can be understood only by reference to its intrinsic literary features, that is, those elements found in the text itself. To analyze a poem or story, therefore, the formalist critic focuses on the words of the text rather than facts about the author's life or the historical milieu in which it was written. The critic would pay special attention to the formal features of the text—the style, structure, imagery, tone, and genre. These features, however, are usually not examined in isolation, because formalist critics believe that what gives a literary text its special status as art is how all its elements work together to create the reader's total experience. As Robert Penn Warren commented, "Poetry does not inhere in any particular element but depends upon the set of relationships, the structure, which we call the poem."

A key method that formalists use to explore the intense relationships within a poem is **close reading,** a careful step-by-step analysis and explication of a text. (For further discussion of explication, see page 617.) The purpose of close reading is to understand how various elements in a literary text work together to shape its effects on the reader. Since formalists believe that the various stylistic and thematic elements of literary work influence each other, these critics insist that form and content cannot be meaningfully separated. The complete interdependence of form and content is what makes a text literary. When we extract a work's theme or paraphrase its meaning, we destroy the aesthetic experience of the work.

When Robert Langbaum examines Robert Browning's "My Last Duchess," he uses several techniques of formalist criticism. First, he places the poem in relation to its literary form, the dramatic monologue. Second, he discusses the dramatic structure of the poem—why the duke tells his story, whom he addresses, and the physical circumstances in which he speaks. Third, Langbaum analyzes how the duke tells his story—his tone, manner, even the order in which he makes his disclosures. Langbaum neither introduces facts about Browning's life into his analysis, nor relates the poem to the historical period or social conditions that produced it. He focuses on the text itself to explain how it produces a complex effect on the reader.

Cleanth Brooks   (1906–1994)

THE FORMALIST CRITIC   1951

Here are some articles of faith I could subscribe to:

That literary criticism is a description and an evaluation of its object.

That the primary concern of criticism is with the problem of unity—the kind of whole which the literary work forms or fails to form, and the relation of the various parts to each other in building up this whole.

That the formal relations in a work of literature may include, but certainly exceed, those of logic.

That in a successful work, form and content cannot be separated.

That form is meaning.

That literature is ultimately metaphorical and symbolic.

That the general and the universal are not seized upon by abstraction, but got at through the concrete and the particular.

That literature is not a surrogate for religion.

That, as Allen Tate says, "specific moral problems" are the subject matter of literature, but that the purpose of literature is not to point a moral.

That the principles of criticism define the area relevant to literary criticism; they do not constitute a method for carrying out the criticism.

.   .   .

The formalist critic knows as well as anyone that poems and plays and novels are written by men—that they do not somehow happen—and that they are written as expressions of particular personalities and are written from all sorts of motives—for money, from a desire to express oneself, for the sake of a cause, etc. Moreover, the formalist critic knows as well as anyone that literary works are merely potential until they are read—that is, that they are recreated in the minds of actual readers, who vary enormously in their capabilities, their interests, their prejudices, their ideas. But the formalist critic is concerned primarily with the work itself. Speculation on the mental processes of the author takes the critic away from the work into biography and psychology. There is no reason, of course, why he should not turn away into biography and psychology. Such explorations are very much worth making. But they should not be confused with an account of the work. Such studies describe the process of composition, not the structure of the thing composed, and they may be performed quite as validly for the poor work as for the good one. They may be validly performed for any kind of expression—non-literary as well as literary.

From "The Formalist Critic"

Robert Langbaum   (b. 1924)

ON ROBERT BROWNING'S "MY LAST DUCHESS"   1957

When we have said all the objective things about Browning's "My Last Duchess,"
we will not have arrived at the meaning until we point out what can only be sub-
stantiated by an appeal to effect—that moral judgment does not figure importantly
in our response to the duke, that we even identify ourselves with him. But how is
such an effect produced in a poem about a cruel Italian duke of the Renaissance
who out of unreasonable jealousy has had his last duchess put to death, and is now
about to contract a second marriage for the sake of dowry? Certainly, no summary
or paraphrase would indicate that condemnation is not our principal response.
The difference must be laid to form, to that extra quantity which makes the difference in artistic discourse between content and meaning.

   The objective fact that the poem is made up entirely of the duke's utterance
has of course much to do with the final meaning, and it is important to say that
the poem is in form a monologue. But much more remains to be said about the
way in which the content is laid out, before we can come near accounting for the
whole meaning. It is important that the duke tells the story of his kind and generous last duchess to, of all people, the envoy from his prospective duchess. It is
important that he tells his story while showing off to the envoy the artistic
merits of a portrait of the last duchess. It is above all important that the duke
carries off his outrageous indiscretion, proceeding triumphantly in the end
downstairs to conclude arrangements for the dowry. All this is important not
only as content but also as form, because it establishes a relation between the
duke on the one hand, and the portrait and the envoy on the other, which determines the reader's relation to the duke and therefore to the poem—which determines, in other words, the poem's meaning.

   The utter outrageousness of the duke's behavior makes condemnation the
least interesting response, certainly not the response that can account for the
poem's success. What interests us more than the duke's wickedness is his immense attractiveness. His conviction of matchless superiority, his intelligence
and bland amorality, his poise, his taste for art, his manners—high-handed aristocratic manners that break the ordinary rules and assert the duke's superiority
when he is being most solicitous of the envoy, waiving their difference of rank
("Nay, we'll go / Together down, sir"); these qualities overwhelm the envoy,
causing him apparently to suspend judgment of the duke, for he raises no demur.
The reader is no less overwhelmed. We suspend moral judgment because we
prefer to participate in the duke's power and freedom, in his hard core of character fiercely loyal to itself. Moral judgment is in fact important as the thing to
be suspended, as a measure of the price we pay for the privilege of appreciating to
the full this extraordinary man.

   It is because the duke determines the arrangement and relative subordina-
tion of the parts that the poem means what it does. The duchess's goodness
shines through the duke's utterance; he makes no attempt to conceal it, so

preoccupied is he with his own standard of judgment and so oblivious of the world's. Thus the duchess's case is subordinated to the duke's, the novelty and complexity of which engages our attention. We are busy trying to understand the man who can combine the connoisseur's pride in the lady's beauty with a pride that caused him to murder the lady rather than tell her in what way she displeased him, for in that

> would be some stooping; and I choose
> Never to stoop.

> (lines 42–43)

The duke's paradoxical nature is fully revealed when, having boasted how at his command the duchess's life was extinguished, he turns back to the portrait to admire of all things its life-likeness:

> There she stands
> As if alive.

> (lines 46–47)

This occurs ten lines from the end, and we might suppose we have by now taken the duke's measure. But the next ten lines produce a series of shocks that outstrip each time our understanding of the duke, and keep us panting after revelation with no opportunity to consolidate our impression of him for moral judgment. For it is at this point that we learn to whom he has been talking; and he goes on to talk about dowry, even allowing himself to murmur the hypocritical assurance that the new bride's self and not the dowry is of course his object. It seems to me that one side of the duke's nature is here stretched as far as it will go; the dazzling figure threatens to decline into paltriness admitting moral judgment, when Browning retrieves it with two brilliant strokes. First, there is the lordly waiving of rank's privilege as the duke and the envoy are about to proceed downstairs, and then there is the perfect all-revealing gesture of the last two and a half lines when the duke stops to show off yet another object in his collection:

> Notice Neptune, though,
> Taming a sea-horse, thought a rarity,
> Which Claus of Innsbruck cast in bronze for me!

> (lines 54–56)

The lines bring all the parts of the poem into final combination, with just the relative values that constitute the poem's meaning. The nobleman does not hurry on his way to business, the connoisseur cannot resist showing off yet another precious object, the possessive egotist counts up his possessions even as he moves toward the acquirement of a new possession, a well-dowered bride; and most important, the last duchess is seen in final perspective. She takes her place as one of a line of objects in an art collection; her sad story becomes the *cicerone's* anecdote° lending piquancy to the portrait. The duke has taken from her what he wants, her beauty, and thrown the life away; and we watch with awe as he proceeds to take what he wants from the envoy and by implication from the new duchess. He carries all before him by sheer force of will so undeflected by ordinary compunctions as even, I think, to call into question—the question rushes into place behind the startling illumination of the last lines, and lingers as the poem's haunting afternote—the duke's sanity.

From *The Poetry of Experience*

BIOGRAPHICAL CRITICISM

Biographical criticism begins with the simple but central insight that literature is written by actual people and that understanding an author's life can help readers more thoroughly comprehend the work. Anyone who reads the biography of a writer quickly sees how much an author's experience shapes—both directly and indirectly—what he or she creates. Reading that biography will also change (and usually deepen) our response to the work. Sometimes even knowing a single important fact illuminates our reading of a poem or story. Learning, for example, that poet Josephine Miles was confined to a wheelchair or that Weldon Kees committed suicide at forty-one will certainly make us pay attention to certain aspects of their poems we might otherwise have missed or considered unimportant. A formalist critic might complain that we would also have noticed those things through careful textual analysis, but biographical information provides the practical assistance of underscoring subtle but important meanings in the poems. Though many literary theorists have assailed biographical criticism on philosophical grounds, the biographical approach to literature has never disappeared because of its obvious practical advantage in illuminating literary texts.

It may be helpful here to make a distinction between biography and biographical criticism. **Biography** is, strictly speaking, a branch of history; it provides a written account of a person's life. To establish and interpret the facts of a poet's life, for instance, a biographer would use all the available information—not just personal documents such as letters and diaries but also the poems for the possible light they might shed on the subject's life. A biographical *critic*, however, is not concerned with recreating the record of an author's life. Biographical criticism focuses on explicating the literary work by using the insight provided by knowledge of the author's life. Quite often, biographical critics, such as Brett C. Millier in her discussion of Elizabeth Bishop's "One Art," will examine the drafts of a poem or story to see both how the work came into being and how it might have been changed from its autobiographical origins.

A reader, however, must use biographical interpretations cautiously. Writers are notorious for revising the facts of their own lives; they often delete embarrassments

---

cicerone's anecdote: The Duke's tale. (In Italian, a *cicerone* is one who conducts guided tours for sightseers.)

and invent accomplishments while changing the details of real episodes to improve their literary impact. John Cheever, for example, frequently told reporters about his sunny, privileged youth; after the author's death, his biographer Scott Donaldson discovered a childhood scarred by a distant mother; a failed, alcoholic father; and nagging economic uncertainty. Likewise, Cheever's outwardly successful adulthood was plagued by alcoholism, sexual promiscuity, and family tension. The chilling facts of Cheever's life significantly changed the way critics read his stories. The danger in the case of a famous writer (Sylvia Plath and F. Scott Fitzgerald are two modern examples) is that the life story can overwhelm and eventually distort the work. A savvy biographical critic always remembers to base an interpretation on what is in the text itself; biographical data should amplify the meaning of the text, not drown it out with irrelevant material.

Leslie Fiedler (1917–2003)

THE RELATIONSHIP OF POET AND POEM   1960

A central dogma of much recent criticism asserts that biographical information is irrelevant to the understanding and evaluation of poems, and that conversely, poems cannot legitimately be used as material for biography. This double contention is part of a larger position which holds that history is history and art is art, and that to talk about one in terms of the other is to court disaster. Insofar as this position rests upon the immortal platitude that it is good to know what one is talking about, it is unexceptionable; insofar as it is a reaction based upon the procedures of pre-Freudian critics, it is hopelessly outdated; and insofar as it depends upon the extreme nominalist definition of a work of art, held by many "formalists" quite unawares, it is metaphysically reprehensible. It has the further inconvenience of being quite unusable in the practical sphere (all of its proponents, in proportion as they are sensitive critics, immediately betray it when speaking of specific works, and particularly of large bodies of work); and, as if that were not enough, it is in blatant contradiction with the assumptions of most serious practicing writers.

That the anti-biographical position was once "useful," whatever its truth, cannot be denied; it was even once, what is considerably rarer in the field of criticism, amusing; but for a long time now it has been threatening to turn into one of those annoying clichés of the intellectually middle-aged, profferred with all the air of a stimulating heresy. The position was born in dual protest against an excess of Romantic criticism and one of "scientific scholarship." Romantic aesthetics appeared bent on dissolving the formally realized "objective" elements in works of art into "expression of personality"; while the "scholars," in revolt against Romantic subjectivity, seemed set on casting out all the more shifty questions of value and *gestalt* as "subjective," and concentrating on the kind of "facts" amenable to scientific verification. Needless to say, it was not the newer psychological sciences that the "scholars" had in mind, but such purer disciplines as physics and biology. It was at this point that it became fashionable to talk about literary study as "research," and graphs and tables began to appear in analyses of works of art.

. . .

The poet's life is the focusing glass through which pass the determinants of the shape of his work: the tradition available to him, his understanding of "kinds," the impact of special experiences (travel, love, etc.). But the poet's life is more than a burning glass; with his work, it makes up his total meaning. I do not intend to say, of course, that some meanings of works of art, satisfactory and as far as they go sufficient, are not available in the single work itself (only a really *bad* work depends for all substantial meaning on a knowledge of the life-style of its author); but a whole body of work will contain larger meanings, and, where it is available, a sense of the life of the writer will raise that meaning to a still higher power. The latter two kinds of meaning fade into each other; for as soon as two works by a single author are considered side by side, one has begun to deal with biography—that is, with an interconnectedness fully explicable only in terms of a personality, inferred or discovered.

One of the essential functions of the poet is the assertion and creation of a personality, in a profounder sense than any nonartist can attain. We ask of the poet a definition of man, at once particular and abstract, stated and acted out. It is impossible to draw a line between the work the poet writes and the work he lives, between the life he lives and the life he writes. And the agile critic, therefore, must be prepared to move constantly back and forth between life and poem, not in a pointless circle, but in a meaningful spiraling toward the absolute point.

No! in Thunder

Brett C. Millier   (b. 1958)

ON ELIZABETH BISHOP'S "ONE ART"   1993

Elizabeth Bishop left seventeen drafts of the poem "One Art" among her papers. In the first draft, she lists all the things she's lost in her life—keys, pens, glasses, cities—and then she writes "One might think this would have prepared me / for losing one average-sized not exceptionally / beautiful or dazzlingly intelligent person . . . / But it doesn't seem to have at all. . . ." By the seventeenth draft, nearly every word has been transformed, but most importantly, Bishop discovered along the way that there might be a way to master this loss.

One way to read Bishop's modulation between the first and last drafts from "the loss of you is impossible to master" to something like "I am still the master of losing even though losing you looks like a disaster" is that in the writing of such a disciplined, demanding poem as this villanelle ("[*Write* it!]") lies the potential mastery of the loss. Working through each of her losses—from the bold, painful catalog of the first draft to the finely-honed and privately meaningful final version—is the way to overcome them or, if not to overcome them, then to see the way in which she might possibly master herself in the face of loss. It is all, perhaps "one art"—writing elegy, mastering loss, mastering grief, self-mastery. Bishop had a precocious familiarity with loss. Her father died before her first birthday, and four years later her mother disappeared into a sanitarium, never to be seen by her daughter again. The losses in the poem are real: time in the form of the "hour badly spent" and, more tellingly for the orphaned Bishop "my mother's watch": the lost houses, in Key West, Petrópolis, and Ouro Prêto, Brazil. The city of Rio de Janeiro and the whole South American continent (where she had lived for nearly two decades) were lost to her with the suicide of her Brazilian companion. And currently, in the fall of 1975, she seemed to have lost her dearest friend and lover, who was trying to end their relationship. But each version of the poem distanced the pain a little more, depersonalized it, moved it away from the tawdry self-pity and "confession" that Bishop disliked in so many of her contemporaries.

Bishop's friends remained for a long time protective of her personal reputation, and unwilling to have her grouped among lesbian poets or even among the other great poets of her generation—Robert Lowell, John Berryman, Theodore Roethke—as they seemed to self-destruct before their readers' eyes. Bishop herself taught them this reticence by keeping her private life to herself, and by investing what "confession" there was in her poems deeply in objects and places, thus deflecting biographical inquiry. In the development of this poem, discretion is both a poetic method, and a part of a process of self-understanding, the seeing of a pattern in her own life.

Adapted by the author from *Elizabeth Bishop: Life and the Memory of It*

HISTORICAL CRITICISM

Historical criticism seeks to understand a literary work by investigating the social, cultural, and intellectual context that produced it—a context that necessarily includes the artist's biography and milieu. Historical critics are less concerned with explaining a work's literary significance for today's readers than with helping us understand the work by recreating, as nearly as possible, the exact meaning and impact it had on its original audience. A historical reading of a literary work begins by exploring the possible ways in which the meaning of the text has changed over time. An analysis of William Blake's poem "London," for instance, carefully examines how certain words had different connotations for the poem's original readers than they do today. It also explores the probable associations an eighteenth-century English reader would have made with certain images and characters, like the poem's persona, the chimney sweep—a type of exploited child laborer who, fortunately, no longer exists in our society.

Reading ancient literature, no one doubts the value of historical criticism. There have been so many social, cultural, and linguistic changes that some older texts are incomprehensible without scholarly assistance. But historical criticism can even help one better understand modern texts. To return to Weldon Kees's "For My Daughter" for example, one learns a great deal by considering two rudimentary historical facts—the year in which the poem was first published (1940) and the nationality of its author (American)—and then asking how this information has shaped the meaning of the poem. In 1940 war had already broken out in Europe, and most Americans realized that their country, still recovering from the Depression, would soon be drawn into it. For a young man like Kees, the future seemed bleak, uncertain, and personally dangerous. Even this simple historical analysis helps explain at least part of the bitter pessimism of Kees's poem, though a psychological critic would rightly insist that Kees's dark personality also played a crucial role. In writing a paper on a poem, you might explore how the time and place of its creation affect its meaning. For a splendid example of how to recreate the historical context of a poem's genesis, read the following account by Hugh Kenner of Ezra Pound's imagistic "In a Station of the Metro."

Hugh Kenner (1923–2003)

IMAGISM   1971

For it was English post-Symbolist verse that Pound's Imagism set out to reform, by deleting its self-indulgences, intensifying its virtues, and elevating the glimpse into the vision. The most famous of all Imagist poems commenced, like any poem by Arthur Symons,° with an accidental glimpse. Ezra Pound, on a visit to Paris in 1911, got out of the Metro at La Concorde, and "saw suddenly a beautiful face, and then another and another, and then a beautiful child's face, and then another beautiful woman, and I tried all that day to find words for what they had meant to me, and I could not find any words that seemed to me worthy, or as lovely as that sudden emotion."

The oft-told story is worth one more retelling. This was just such an experience as Arthur Symons cultivated, bright unexpected glimpses in a dark setting, instantly to melt into the crowd's kaleidoscope. And a poem would not have given Symons any trouble. But Pound by 1911 was already unwilling to write a Symons poem.

He tells us that he first satisfied his mind when he hit on a wholly abstract vision of colors, splotches on darkness like some canvas of Kandinsky's (whose work he had not then seen). This is a most important fact. Satisfaction lay not in preserving the vision, but in devising with mental effort an abstract equivalent for it, reduced, intensified. He next wrote a 30-line poem and destroyed it; after six months he wrote a shorter poem, also destroyed; and after another year, with,

---

Arthur Symons: Symons (1865–1945) was a British poet who helped introduce French symbolist verse into English. His own verse was often florid and impressionistic.

as he tells us, the Japanese *hokku* in mind, he arrived at a poem which needs every one of its 20 words, including the six words of its title:

IN A STATION OF THE METRO

The apparition of these faces in the crowd;
Petals on a wet, black bough.

We need the title so that we can savor that vegetal contrast with the world of machines: this is not any crowd, moreover, but a crowd seen underground, as Odysseus and Orpheus and Koré saw crowds in Hades. And carrying forward the suggestion of wraiths, the word "apparition" detaches these faces from all the crowded faces, and presides over the image that conveys the quality of their separation:

Petals on a wet, black bough.

Flowers, underground; flowers, out of the sun; flowers seen as if against a natural gleam, the bough's wetness gleaming on its darkness, in this place where wheels turn and nothing grows. The mind is touched, it may be, with a memory of Persephone, as we read of her in the 106th Canto,

Dis' bride, Queen over Phlegethon,
girls faint as mist about her.

—the faces of those girls likewise "apparitions."
What is achieved, though it works by way of the visible, is no picture of the thing glimpsed, in the manner of

The light of our cigarettes
Went and came in the gloom.

It is a simile with "like" suppressed: Pound called it an equation, meaning not a redundancy, *a* equals *a*, but a generalization of unexpected exactness. The statements of analytic geometry, he said, "are 'lords' over fact. They are the thrones and dominations that rule over form and recurrence. And in like manner are great works of art lords over fact, over race-long recurrent moods, and over tomorrow." So this tiny poem, drawing on Gauguin and on Japan, on ghosts and on Persephone, on the Underworld and on the Underground, the Metro of Mallarmé's capital and a phrase that names a station of the Metro as it might a station of the Cross, concentrates far more than it need ever specify, and indicates the means of delivering post-Symbolist poetry from its pictorialist impasse. "An 'Image' is that which presents an intellectual and emotional complex in an instant of time": that is the elusive Doctrine of the Image. And, just 20 months later, "The image . . . is a radiant node or cluster; it is what I can, and must perforce, call a VORTEX, from which, and through which, and into which, ideas are constantly rushing." And: "An *image* . . . is real because we know it directly."

From *The Pound Era*

Joseph Moldenhauer   (b. 1934)

"To His Coy Mistress" and the Renaissance Tradition   1968

Obedient to the neoclassical aesthetic which ruled his age, Andrew Marvell strove for excellence within established forms rather than trying to devise unique forms of his own. Like Herrick, Ben Jonson, and Campion, like Milton and the Shakespeare of the sonnets, Marvell was derivative. He held imitation to be no vice; he chose a proven type and exploited it with a professionalism rarely surpassed even in a century and a land as amply provided with verse craftsmen as his. Under a discipline so willingly assumed, Marvell's imagination flourished, producing superb and enduring examples of the verse types he attempted.

. . .

When he undertook to write a *carpe diem* lyric in "To His Coy Mistress," Marvell was working once more within a stylized form, one of the favorite types in the Renaissance lyric catalogue. Again he endowed the familiar model with his own special sensibility, composing what for many readers is the most vital English instance of the *carpe diem* poem. We can return to it often, with undiminished enthusiasm—drawn not by symbolic intricacy, though it contains two or three extraordinary conceits, nor by philosophical depth, though it lends an unusual seriousness to its theme—but drawn rather by its immediacy and concreteness, its sheer dynamism of statement within a controlled structure.

The *carpe diem* poem, whose label comes from a line of Horace and whose archetype for Renaissance poets was a lyric by Catullus, addresses the conflict of beauty and sensual desire on the one hand and the destructive force of time on the other. Its theme is the fleeting nature of life's joys; its counsel, overt or implied, is Horace's "seize the present," or, in the language of Herrick's "To the Virgins,"

> Gather ye Rose-buds while ye may,
> Old Time is still a flying.

It takes rise from that most pervasive and aesthetically viable of all Renaissance preoccupations, man's thralldom to time, the limitations of mortality upon his senses, his pleasures, his aspirations, his intellectual and creative capacities. Over the exuberance of Elizabethan and seventeenth-century poetry the pall of death continually hovers, and the lyrics of the age would supply a handbook of strategies for the circumvention of decay. The birth of an heir, the preservative balm of memory, the refuge of Christian resignation or Platonic ecstasy—these are some solutions which the poets offer. Another is the artist's ability to immortalize this world's values by means of his verse. Shakespeare's nineteenth and fifty-fifth sonnets, for example, employ this stratagem for the frustration of "Devouring Time," as does Michael Drayton's "How Many Paltry, Foolish, Painted Things." In such poems the speaker's praise of the merits of the beloved is coupled with a celebration of his own poetic gift, through which he can eternize those merits as a "pattern" for future men and women.

The *carpe diem* lyric proposes a more direct and immediate, if also more temporary, solution to the overwhelming problem. Whether subdued or gamesome in tone, it appeals to the young and beautiful to make time their own for a while, to indulge in the "harmless folly" of sensual enjoyment. Ordinarily, as in "To His Coy Mistress" and Herrick's "Corrina's Going A-Maying," the poem imitates an express invitation to love, a suitor's immodest proposal to his lady. Such works are both sharply dramatic and vitally rhetorical; to analyze their style and structure is, in effect, to analyze a persuasive appeal.

From "The Voices of Seduction in 'To His Coy Mistress'"

Psychological Criticism

Modern psychology has had an immense effect on both literature and literary criticism. The psychoanalytic theories of the Austrian neurologist Sigmund Freud changed our notions of human behavior by exploring new or controversial areas such as wish fulfillment, sexuality, the unconscious, and repression. Perhaps Freud's greatest contribution to literary study was his elaborate demonstration of how much human mental process was unconscious. He analyzed language, often in the form of jokes and conversational slips of the tongue (now often called "Freudian slips"), to show how it reflected the speaker's unconscious fears and desires. He also examined symbols not only in art and literature but also in dreams to study how the unconscious mind expressed itself in coded form to avoid the censorship of the conscious mind. His theory of human cognition asserted that much of what we apparently forget is actually stored deep in the subconscious mind, including painful traumatic memories from childhood that have been repressed.

Freud admitted that he himself had learned a great deal about psychology from studying literature. Sophocles, Shakespeare, Goethe, and Dostoyevsky were as important to the development of his ideas as were his clinical studies. Some of Freud's most influential writing was, in a broad sense, literary criticism, such as his psychoanalytic examination of Sophocles' Oedipus in *The Interpretation of Dreams* (1900). In analyzing Sophocles' tragedy, *Oedipus the King*, Freud paid the classical Greek dramatist the considerable compliment that the playwright had such profound insight into human nature that his characters display the depth and complexity of real people. In focusing on literature, Freud and his disciples like Carl Jung, Ernest Jones, Marie Bonaparte, and Bruno Bettelheim endorsed the belief that great literature truthfully reflects life.

Psychological criticism is a diverse category, but it often employs three approaches. First, it investigates the creative process of the arts: what is the nature of literary genius, and how does it relate to normal mental functions? Such analysis may also focus on literature's effects on the reader. How does a particular work register its impact on the reader's mental and sensory faculties? The second approach involves the psychological study of a particular artist. Most modern literary biographers employ psychology to understand their subject's motivations and behavior. One book, Diane Middlebrook's controversial *Anne Sexton: A Biography* (1991), actually used tapes of the poet's sessions with her psychiatrist as material for the study. The third common approach is the analysis of fictional characters. Freud's study of Oedipus is the prototype for this approach, which tries to bring modern insights about human behavior into the study of how fictional people act. While psychological criticism carefully examines the surface of the literary work, it customarily speculates on what lies underneath the text—the unspoken or perhaps even unspeakable memories, motives, and fears that covertly shape the work, especially in fictional characterizations.

Sigmund Freud (1856–1939)

THE DESTINY OF OEDIPUS   1900

TRANSLATED BY JAMES STRACHEY

If *Oedipus the King* moves a modern audience no less than it did the contemporary Greek one, the explanation can only be that its effect does not lie in the contrast between destiny and human will, but is to be looked for in the particular nature of the material on which that contrast is exemplified. There must be something which makes a voice within us ready to recognize the compelling force of destiny in the *Oedipus*, while we can dismiss as merely arbitrary such dispositions as are laid down in *Die Ahnfrau*° or other modern tragedies of destiny. And a factor of this kind is in fact involved in the story of King Oedipus. His destiny moves us only because it might have been ours—because the oracle laid the same curse upon us before our birth as upon him. It is the fate of all of us, perhaps, to direct our first sexual impulse towards our mother and our first hatred and our first murderous wish against our father. Our dreams convince us that that is so. King Oedipus, who slew his father Laius and married his mother Jocasta, merely shows us the fulfillment of our own childhood wishes. But, more fortunate than he, we have meanwhile succeeded, insofar as we have not become psychoneurotics, in detaching our sexual impulses from our mothers and in forgetting our jealousy of our fathers. Here is one in whom these primeval wishes of our childhood have been fulfilled, and we shrink back from him with the whole force of the repression by which those wishes have since that time been held down within us. While the poet, as he unravels the past, brings to light the guilt of Oedipus, he is at the same time compelling us to recognize our own inner minds, in which those same impulses, though suppressed, are still to be found. The contrast with which the closing Chorus leaves us confronted—

> look upon Oedipus.
> This is the king who solved the famous riddle
> And towered up, most powerful of men.
> No mortal eyes but looked on him with envy,
> Yet in the end ruin swept over him.

Die Ahnfrau: "The Foremother," a verse play by Franz Grillparzer (1791–1872), Austrian dramatist and poet.

—strikes as a warning at ourselves and our pride, at us who since our childhood have grown so wise and so mighty in our own eyes. Like Oedipus, we live in ignorance of these wishes, repugnant to morality, which have been forced upon us by Nature, and after their revelation we may all of us well seek to close our eyes to the scenes of our childhood.

From The Interpretation of Dreams

Harold Bloom   (b. 1930)

POETIC INFLUENCE   1975

Let me reduce my argument to the hopelessly simplistic; poems, I am saying, are neither about "subjects" nor about "themselves." They are necessarily about *other poems*; a poem is a response to a poem, as a poet is a response to a poet, or a person to his parent. Trying to write a poem takes the poet back to the origins of what a poem *first was* for him, and so takes the poet back beyond the pleasure principle to the decisive initial encounter and response that began him. We do not think of W. C. Williams as a Keatsian poet, yet he *began and ended as one*, and his late celebration of his Greeny Flower is another response to Keats's odes. *Only a poet challenges a poet as poet*, and so only a poet makes a poet. To the poet-in-a-poet, a poem is always *the other man*, the precursor, and so a poem is always a person, always the father of one's Second Birth. To live, the poet must *misinterpret* the father, by the crucial act of misprision, which is the rewriting of the father.

But who, what is the poetic father? The voice of the other, of the *daimon*, is always speaking in one; the voice that cannot die because already it has survived death—*the dead poet lives in one*. In the last phase of strong poets, they attempt to join the undying *by living in the dead poets* who are already alive in them. This late Return of the Dead recalls us, as readers, to a recognition of the original motive for the catastrophe of poetic incarnation. Vico, who identified the origins of poetry with the impulse towards divination (to foretell, but also to become a god by foretelling), implicitly understood (as did Emerson, and Wordsworth) that a poem is written to escape dying. Literally, poems are refusals of mortality. Every poem therefore has two makers: the precursor, and the ephebe's rejected mortality.

A poet, I argue in consequence, is not so much a man speaking to men as a man rebelling against being spoken to by a dead man (the precursor) outrageously more alive than himself.

From A Map of Misreading

MYTHOLOGICAL CRITICISM

Mythological critics look for the recurrent universal patterns underlying most literary works. **Mythological criticism** is an interdisciplinary approach that combines the insights of anthropology, psychology, history, and comparative religion. If psychological criticism examines the artist as an individual, mythological criticism explores the artist's common humanity by tracing how the individual imagination uses symbols and situations—consciously or unconsciously—in ways that transcend its own historical milieu and resemble the mythology of other cultures or epochs.

A central concept in mythological criticism is the **archetype,** a symbol, character, situation, or image that evokes a deep universal response. The idea of the archetype came into literary criticism from the Swiss psychologist Carl Jung, a lifetime student of myth and religion. Jung believed that all individuals share a "collective unconscious," a set of primal memories common to the human race, existing below each person's conscious mind. Archetypal images (which often relate to experiencing primordial phenomena like the sun, moon, fire, night, and blood), Jung believed, trigger the collective unconscious. We do not need to accept the literal truth of the collective unconscious, however, to endorse the archetype as a helpful critical concept. Northrop Frye defined the archetype in considerably less occult terms as "a symbol, usually an image, which recurs often enough in literature to be recognizable as an element of one's literary experience as a whole."

Identifying archetypal symbols and situations in literary works, mythological critics almost inevitably link the individual text under discussion to a broader context of works that share an underlying pattern. In discussing Shakespeare's *Hamlet,* for instance, a mythological critic might relate Shakespeare's Danish prince to other mythic sons avenging the deaths of their fathers, like Orestes from Greek myth or Sigmund of Norse legend; or, in discussing *Othello,* relate the sinister figure of Iago to the devil in traditional Christian belief. Critic Joseph Campbell took such comparisons even further; his compendious study *The Hero with a Thousand Faces* demonstrates how similar mythic characters appear in virtually every culture on every continent.

Carl G. Jung   (1875–1961)
THE COLLECTIVE UNCONSCIOUS AND ARCHETYPES   1931
TRANSLATED BY R. F. C. HULL

A more or less superficial layer of the unconscious is undoubtedly personal. I call it the *personal unconscious.* But this personal unconscious rests upon a deeper layer, which does not derive from personal experience and is not a personal acquisition but is inborn. This deeper layer I call the *collective unconscious.* I have chosen the term "collective" because this part of the unconscious is not individual but universal; in contrast to the personal psyche, it has contents and modes of behavior that are more or less the same everywhere and in all individuals. It is, in other words, identical in all men and thus constitutes a common psyche substrate of a suprapersonal nature which is present in every one of us.

Psychic existence can be recognized only by the presence of contents that are *capable of consciousness.* We can therefore speak of an unconscious only in so far as we are able to demonstrate its contents. The contents of the personal unconscious are chiefly the *feeling-toned complexes,* as they are called; they constitute the personal and private side of psychic life. The contents of the collective unconscious, on the other hand, are known as *archetypes.* . . .

For our purposes this term is apposite and helpful, because it tells us that so far as the collective unconscious contents are concerned we are dealing with archaic or—I would say—primordial types, that is, with universal images that have existed since the remotest times. The term "representations collectives," used by Lévy-Bruhl to denote the symbolic figures in the primitive view of the world, could easily be applied to unconscious contents as well, since it means practically the same thing. Primitive tribal lore is concerned with archetypes that have been modified in a special way. They are no longer contents of the unconscious, but have already been changed into conscious formulae taught according to tradition, generally in the form of esoteric teaching. This last is a typical means of expression for the transmission of collective contents originally derived from the unconscious.

Another well-known expression of the archetypes is myth and fairy tale. But here too we are dealing with forms that have received a specific stamp and have been handed down through long periods of time. The term "archetype" thus applies only indirectly to the "representations collectives," since it designates only those psychic contents which have not yet been submitted to conscious elaboration and are therefore an immediate datum of psychic experience. In this sense there is a considerable difference between the archetype and the historical formula that has evolved. Especially on the higher levels of esoteric teaching the archetypes appear in a form that reveals quite unmistakably the critical and evaluating influence of conscious elaboration. Their immediate manifestation, as we encounter it in dreams and visions, is much more individual, less understandable, and more naïve than in myths, for example. The archetype is essentially an unconscious content that is altered by becoming conscious and by being perceived, and it takes its color from the individual consciousness in which it happens to appear.

From *The Collected Works of C. G. Jung*

Northrop Frye (1912–1991)

MYTHIC ARCHETYPES   1957

We begin our study of archetypes, then, with a world of myth, an abstract or purely literary world of fictional and thematic design, unaffected by canons of plausible adaptation to familiar experience. In terms of narrative, myth is the imitation of actions near or at the conceivable limits of desire. The gods enjoy beautiful women, fight one another with prodigious strength, comfort and assist man, or else watch his miseries from the height of their immortal freedom. The fact that myth operates at the top level of human desire does not mean that it necessarily presents its world as attained or attainable by human beings. . . .

Realism, or the art of verisimilitude, evokes the response "How like that is to what we know!" When what is written is *like* what is known, we have an art of extended or implied simile. And as realism is an art of implicit simile, myth is an art of implicit metaphorical identity. The word "sun-god," with a hyphen used instead of a predicate, is a pure ideogram, in Pound's terminology, or literal metaphor, in ours. In myth we see the structural principles of literature isolated; in realism we see the *same* structural principles (not similar ones) fitting into a context of plausibility. (Similarly in music, a piece by Purcell and a piece by Benjamin Britten may not be in the least *like* each other, but if they are both in D major their tonality will be the same.) The presence of a mythical structure in realistic fiction, however, poses certain technical problems for making it plausible, and the devices used in solving these problems may be given the general name of *displacement*.

Myth, then, is one extreme of literary design; naturalism is the other, and in between lies the whole area of romance, using that term to mean, not the historical mode of the first essay, but the tendency, noted later in the same essay, to displace myth in a human direction and yet, in contrast to "realism," to conventionalize content in an idealized direction. The central principle of displacement is that what can be metaphorically identified in a myth can only be linked in romance by some form of simile: analogy, significant association, incidental accompanying imagery, and the like. In a myth we can have a sun-god or a tree-god; in a romance we may have a person who is significantly associated with the sun or trees.

From *Anatomy of Criticism*

SOCIOLOGICAL CRITICISM

Sociological criticism examines literature in the cultural, economic, and political context in which it is written or received. "Art is not created in a vacuum," critic Wilbur Scott observed, "it is the work not simply of a person, but of an author fixed in time and space, answering a community of which he is an important, because articulate part." Sociological criticism explores the relationships between the artist and society. Sometimes it looks at the sociological status of the author to evaluate how the profession of the writer in a particular milieu affected what was written. Sociological criticism also analyzes the social content of literary works—what cultural, economic, or political values a particular text implicitly or explicitly promotes. Finally, sociological criticism examines the role the audience has in shaping literature. A sociological view of Shakespeare, for example, might look at the economic position of Elizabethan playwrights and actors; it might also study the political ideas expressed in the plays or discuss how the nature of an Elizabethan theatrical audience (which was usually all male unless the play was produced at court) helped determine the subject, tone, and language of the plays.

An influential type of sociological criticism has been Marxist criticism, which focuses on the economic and political elements of art. Marxist criticism, like the work of the Hungarian philosopher Georg Lukacs, often explores the ideological content of literature. Whereas a formalist critic would maintain that form and content are inextricably blended, Lukacs believed that content determines form and that, therefore, all art is political. Even if a work of art ignores political issues, it makes a political statement, Marxist critics believe, because it endorses the economic and political status quo. Consequently, Marxist criticism is frequently evaluative and judges some literary work better than others on an ideological basis; this tendency can lead to reductive judgment, as when Soviet critics rated Jack London a novelist superior to William Faulkner, Ernest Hemingway, Edith Wharton, and Henry James, because he illustrated the principles of class struggle more clearly. London was America's first major working-class writer. To examine the political ideas and observations found in his fiction can be illuminating, but to fault other authors for lacking his instincts and ideas is not necessarily helpful in understanding their particular qualities. There is always a danger in sociological criticism—Marxist or otherwise—of imposing the critic's personal politics on the work in question and then evaluating it according to how closely it endorses that ideology. As an analytical tool, however, Marxist criticism and sociological methods can illuminate political and economic dimensions of literature that other approaches overlook.

Georg Lukacs   (1885–1971)

CONTENT DETERMINES FORM   1962

What determines the style of a given work of art? How does the intention determine the form? (We are concerned here, of course, with the intention realized in the work; it need not coincide with the writer's conscious intention.) The distinctions that concern us are not those between stylistic "techniques" in the formalistic sense. It is the view of the world, the ideology or *Weltanschauung*° underlying a writer's work, that counts. And it is the writer's attempt to reproduce this view of the world which constitutes his "intention" and is the formative principle underlying the style of a given piece of writing. Looked at in this way, style ceases to be a formalistic category. Rather, it is rooted in content; it is the specific form of a specific content.

　　Content determines form. But there is no content of which Man himself is not the focal point. However various the *données*° of literature (a particular experience, a didactic purpose), the basic question is, and will remain: what is Man?

　　Here is a point of division: if we put the question in abstract, philosophical terms, leaving aside all formal considerations, we arrive—for the realist school— at the traditional Aristotelian dictum (which was also reached by other than purely aesthetic considerations): Man is *zoon politikon,*° a social animal. The Aristotelian dictum is applicable to all great realistic literature. Achilles and Werther, Oedipus and Tom Jones, Antigone and Anna Karenina: their individual existence—their *Sein an sich,*° in the Hegelian terminology; their "ontological being," as a more fashionable terminology has it—cannot be distinguished from their social and historical environment. Their human significance, their specific individuality cannot be separated from the context in which they were created.

From *Realism in Our Time*

Weltanschauung: German for "world view," an outlook on life.　*données* French for "given"; it means the materials a writer uses to create his or her work or the subject or purpose of a literary work.　*zoon politikon:* Greek for "political animal."　*Sein an sich:* the German philosopher G. W. F. Hegel's term for "pure existence."

Alfred Kazin   (1915–1998)

Walt Whitman and Abraham Lincoln   1984

In Lincoln's lifetime Whitman was the only major writer to describe him with love. Whitman identified Lincoln with himself in the worshipful fashion that became standard after Lincoln's death. That Lincoln was a class issue says a good deal about the prejudices of American society in the East. A leading New Yorker, George Templeton Strong, noted in his diary that while he never disavowed the "lank and hard featured man," Lincoln was "despised and rejected by a third of the community, and only tolerated by the other two-thirds." Whitman the professional man of the people had complicated reasons for loving Lincoln. The uneasiness about him among America's elite was based on the fear that this unknown, untried man, elected without administrative experience (and without a majority) might not be up to his "fearful task."

. . . .

Whitman related himself to the popular passion released by war and gave himself to this passion as a political cause. He understood popular opinion in a way that Emerson, Thoreau, and Hawthorne did not attempt to understand it. Emerson said, like any conventional New England clergyman, that the war was holy. He could not speak for the masses who bore the brunt of the war. Whitman was able to get so much out of the war, to create a lasting image of it, because he knew what people were feeling. He was not above the battle like Thoreau and Hawthorne, not suspicious of the majority like his fellow New Yorker Herman Melville, who in "The House-top," the most personal poem in *Battle-Pieces*, denounced the "ship-rats" who had taken over the city in the anti-draft riots of 1863.

Despite Whitman's elusiveness—he made a career out of longings it would have ended that career to fulfill—he genuinely felt at home with soldiers and other "ordinary" people who were inarticulate by the standards of men "from the schools." He was always present, if far from available, presenting the picture of a nobly accessible and social creature. He certainly got on better with omnibus drivers, workingmen, and now "simple" soldiers (especially when they were wounded and open to his ministrations) than he did with "scribblers." By the time Whitman went down after Fredericksburg to look for brother George, the war was becoming a revolution of sorts and Whitman's old radical politics were becoming "the nation." This made him adore Lincoln as the symbol of the nation's unity. An essential quality of Whitman's Civil War "memoranda" is Whitman's libidinous urge to associate himself with the great, growing, ever more powerful federal cause. Whitman's characteristic lifelong urge to join, to combine, to see life as movement, unity, totality, became during the Civil War an actively loving association with the broad masses of the people and *their* war. In his cult of the Civil War, Whitman allies himself with a heroic and creative energy which sees itself spreading out from the people and their representative men, Lincoln and Whitman.

Hawthorne's and Thoreau's horror of America as the Big State did not reflect Whitman's image of the Union. His passion for the "cause" reflected his intense faith in democracy at a juncture when the United States at war represented the revolutionary principle to Marx, the young Ibsen, Mill, Browning, Tolstoy. Whitman's deepest feeling was that his own rise from the city streets, his future as a poet of democracy, was tied up with the Northern armies.

From An American Procession

GENDER CRITICISM

Gender criticism examines how sexual identity influences the creation and reception of literary works. Gender studies began with the feminist movement and were influenced by such works as Simone de Beauvoir's *The Second Sex* (1949) and Kate Millett's *Sexual Politics* (1970) as well as sociology, psychology, and anthropology. Feminist critics believe that culture has been so completely dominated by men that literature is full of unexamined "male-produced" assumptions. They see their criticism correcting this imbalance by analyzing and combatting patriarchal attitudes. Feminist criticism has explored how an author's gender influences—consciously or unconsciously—his or her writing. While a formalist critic like Allen Tate emphasized the universality of Emily Dickinson's poetry by demonstrating how powerfully the language, imagery, and mythmaking of her poems combine to affect a generalized reader, Sandra M. Gilbert, a leading feminist critic, has identified attitudes and assumptions in Dickinson's poetry that she believes are essentially female. Another important theme in feminist criticism is analyzing how sexual identity influences the reader of a text. If Tate's hypothetical reader was deliberately sexless, Gilbert's reader sees a text through the eyes of his or her sex. Finally, feminist critics carefully examine how the images of men and women in imaginative literature reflect or reject the social forces that have historically kept the sexes from achieving total equality.

Recently, gender criticism has expanded beyond its original feminist perspective. Critics have explored the impact of different sexual orientations on literary creation and reception. A men's movement has also emerged in response to feminism, seeking not to reject feminism but to rediscover masculine identity in an authentic, contemporary way. Led by poet Robert Bly, the men's movement has paid special attention to interpreting poetry and fables as myths of psychic growth and sexual identity.

Elaine Showalter   (b. 1941)

TOWARD A FEMINIST POETICS   1979

Feminist criticism can be divided into two distinct varieties. The first type is concerned with *woman as reader*—with woman as the consumer of male-produced literature, and with the way in which the hypothesis of a female reader changes our apprehension of a given text, awakening us to the significance of its sexual codes. I shall call this kind of analysis the *feminist critique,* and like other kinds of critique it is a historically grounded inquiry which probes the ideological assumptions of literary phenomena. Its subjects include the images and stereotypes of women in literature, the omissions of and misconceptions about women in criticism, and the fissures in male-constructed literary history. It is also concerned with the exploitation and manipulation of the female audience, especially in popular culture and film; and with the analysis of woman-as-sign in semiotic systems. The second type of feminist criticism is concerned with *woman as writer*—with woman as the producer of textual meaning, with the history, themes, genres, and structures of literature by women. Its subjects include the psychodynamics of female creativity; linguistics and the problem of a female language; the trajectory of the individual or collective female literary career; literary history; and, of course, studies of particular writers and works. No term exists in English for such a specialized discourse, and so I have adapted the French term *la gynocritique:* "gynocritics" (although the significance of the male pseudonym in the history of women's writing also suggested the term "georgics").

The feminist critique is essentially political and polemical, with theoretical affiliations to Marxist sociology and aesthetics; gynocritics is more self-contained and experimental, with connections to other modes of new feminist research. In a dialogue between these two positions, Carolyn Heilbrun, the writer, and Catharine Stimpson, editor of the journal *Signs: Women in Culture and Society,* compare the feminist critique to the Old Testament, "looking for the sins and errors of the past," and gynocritics to the New Testament, seeking "the grace of imagination." Both kinds are necessary, they explain, for only the Jeremiahs of the feminist critique can lead us out of the "Egypt of female servitude" to the promised land of the feminist vision. That the discussion makes use of these Biblical metaphors points to the connections between feminist consciousness and conversion narratives which often appear in women's literature; Carolyn Heilbrun comments on her own text, "When I talk about feminist criticism, I am amazed at how high a moral tone I take."

From "Toward a Feminist Poetics"

Sandra M. Gilbert (b. 1936) and Susan Gubar (b. 1944)

THE FREEDOM OF EMILY DICKINSON   1985

[Emily Dickinson] defined herself as a *woman* writer, reading the works of female precursors with special care, attending to the implications of novels like Charlotte Brontë's *Jane Eyre*, Emily Brontë's *Wuthering Heights*, and George Eliot's *Middlemarch* with the same absorbed delight that characterized her devotion to Elizabeth Barrett Browning's *Aurora Leigh*. Finally, then, the key to her enigmatic identity as a "supposed person" who was called the "Myth of Amherst" may rest, not in investigations of her questionable romance, but in studies of her unquestionably serious reading as well as in analyses of her disquietingly powerful writing. Elliptically phrased, intensely compressed, her poems are more linguistically innovative than any other nineteenth-century verses, with the possible exception of some works by Walt Whitman and Gerard Manley Hopkins, her two most radical male contemporaries. Throughout her largely secret but always brilliant career, moreover, she confronted precisely the questions about the individual and society, time and death, flesh and spirit, that major precursors from Milton to Keats had faced. Dreaming of "Amplitude and Awe," she recorded sometimes vengeful, sometimes mystical visions of social and personal transformation in poems as inventively phrased and imaginatively constructed as any in the English language.

Clearly such accomplishments required not only extraordinary talent but also some measure of freedom. Yet because she was the unmarried daughter of conservative New Englanders, Dickinson was obliged to take on many household tasks; as a nineteenth-century New England wife, she would have had the same number of obligations, if not more. Some of these she performed with pleasure; in 1856, for instance, she was judge of a bread-baking contest, and in 1857 she won a prize in that contest. But as Higginson's "scholar," as a voracious reader and an ambitious writer, Dickinson had to win herself time for "Amplitude and Awe," and it is increasingly clear that she did so through a strategic withdrawal from her ordinary world. A story related by her niece Martha Dickinson Bianchi reveals that the poet herself knew from the first what both the price and the prize might be: on one occasion, said Mrs. Bianchi, Dickinson took her up to the room in which she regularly sequestered herself, and, mimicking locking herself in, "thumb and forefinger closed on an imaginary key," said "with a quick turn of her wrist, 'It's just a turn—and freedom, Matty!'"

In the freedom of her solitary, but not lonely, room, Dickinson may have become what her Amherst neighbors saw as a bewildering "myth." Yet there, too, she created myths of her own. Reading the Brontës and Barrett Browning, studying Transcendentalism and the Bible, she contrived a theology which is powerfully expressed in many of her poems. That it was at its most hopeful a female-centered theology is revealed in verses like those she wrote about the women artists she admired, as well as in more general works like her gravely pantheistic address to the "Sweet Mountains" who "tell me no lie," with its definition of the hills around Amherst as "strong Madonnas" and its description of the writer herself as "The Wayward Nun – beneath the Hill – / Whose service is to You – ." As Dickinson's admirer and descendant Adrienne Rich has accurately observed, this passionate poet consistently chose to confront her society—to "have it out"—"on her own premises."

From introduction to Emily Dickinson,
The Norton Anthology of Literature by Women

READER-RESPONSE CRITICISM

Reader-response criticism attempts to describe what happens in the reader's mind while interpreting a text. If traditional criticism assumes that imaginative writing is a creative act, reader-response theory recognizes that reading is also a creative process. Reader-response critics believe that no text provides self-contained meaning; literary texts do not exist independently of readers' interpretations. A text, according to this critical school, is not finished until it is read and interpreted. As Oscar Wilde remarked in the preface to his novel *The Picture of Dorian Gray* (1891), "It is the spectator, and not life that art really mirrors." The practical problem then arises, however, that no two individuals necessarily read a text in exactly the same way. Rather than declare one interpretation correct and the other mistaken, reader-response criticism recognizes the inevitable plurality of readings. Instead of trying to ignore or reconcile the contradictions inherent in this situation, it explores them.

The easiest way to explain reader-response criticism is to relate it to the common experience of rereading a favorite book after many years. Rereading a novel as an adult, for example, that "changed your life" as an adolescent, is often a shocking experience. The book may seem substantially different. The character you remembered liking most now seems less admirable, and another character you disliked now seems more sympathetic. Has the book changed? Very unlikely, but *you* certainly have in the intervening years. Reader-response criticism explores how the different individuals (or classes of individuals) see the same text differently. It emphasizes how religious, cultural, and social values affect readings; it also overlaps with gender criticism in exploring how men and women read the same text with different assumptions.

While reader-response criticism rejects the notion that there can be a single correct reading for a literary text, it doesn't consider all readings permissible. Each text creates limits to its possible interpretations. As Stanley Fish admits in the following critical selection, we cannot arbitrarily place an Eskimo in William Faulkner's story "A Rose for Emily" (though Professor Fish does ingeniously imagine a hypothetical situation where this bizarre interpretation might actually be possible).

Stanley Fish   (b. 1938)

An Eskimo "A Rose for Emily"   1980

The fact that it remains easy to think of a reading that most of us would dismiss out of hand does not mean that the text excludes it but that there is as yet no elaborated interpretive procedure for producing that text. . . . Norman Holland's analysis of Faulkner's "A Rose for Emily" is a case in point. Holland is arguing for a kind of psychoanalytic pluralism. The text, he declares, is "at most a matrix of psychological possibilities for its readers," but, he insists, "only some possibilities . . . truly fit the matrix": "One would not say, for example, that a reader of . . . 'A Rose for Emily' who thought the 'tableau' [of Emily and her father in the doorway] described an Eskimo was really responding to the story at all—only pursuing some mysterious inner exploration."

Holland is making two arguments: first, that anyone who proposes an Eskimo reading of "A Rose for Emily" will not find a hearing in the literary community. And that, I think, is right. ("We are right to rule out at least some readings.") His second argument is that the unacceptability of the Eskimo reading is a function of the text, of what he calls its "sharable promptuary," the public "store of structured language" that sets limits to the interpretations the words can accommodate. And that, I think, is wrong. The Eskimo reading is unacceptable because there is at present no interpretive strategy for producing it, no way of "looking" or reading (and remember, all acts of looking or reading are "ways") that would result in the emergence of obviously Eskimo meanings. This does not mean, however, that no such strategy could ever come into play, and it is not difficult to imagine the circumstances under which it would establish itself. One such circumstance would be the discovery of a letter in which Faulkner confides that he has always believed himself to be an Eskimo changeling. (The example is absurd only if one forgets Yeats's *Vision* or Blake's Swedenborgianism° or James Miller's recent elaboration of a homosexual reading of *The Waste Land*.) Immediately the workers in the Faulkner industry would begin to reinterpret the canon in the light of this newly revealed "belief" and the work of reinterpretation would involve the elaboration of a symbolic or allusive system (not unlike mythological or typological criticism) whose application would immediately transform the text into one informed everywhere by Eskimo meanings. It might seem that I am admitting that there is a text to be transformed, but the object of transformation would be the text (or texts) given by whatever interpretive strategies the Eskimo strategy was in the process of dislodging or expanding. The result would be that whereas we now have a Freudian "A Rose for Emily," a mythological "A Rose for Emily," a Christological "A Rose for Emily," a regional "A Rose for Emily," a sociological "A Rose for Emily," a linguistic "A Rose for Emily," we would in addition have an Eskimo "A Rose for Emily," existing in some relation of compatibility or incompatibility with the others.

Again the point is that while there are always mechanisms for ruling out readings, their source is not the text but the presently recognized interpretive strategies for producing the text. It follows, then, that no reading, however outlandish it might appear, is inherently an impossible one.

From *Is There a Text in This Class?*

Robert Scholes   (b. 1929)

"How Do We Make a Poem?"   1982

Let us begin with one of the shortest poetic texts in the English language, "Elegy" by W. S. Merwin:

Who would I show it to

One line, one sentence, unpunctuated, but proclaimed an interrogative by its grammar and syntax—what makes it a poem? Certainly without its title it would not be a poem; but neither would the title alone constitute a poetic text. Nor do the two together simply make a poem by themselves. Given the title and the

Yeats's Vision *or Blake's* Swedenborgianism: Irish poet William Butler Yeats and Swedish mystical writer Emanuel Swedenborg both claimed to have received revelations from the spirit world; some of Swedenborg's ideas are embodied in the long poems of William Blake.

text, the *reader* is encouraged to make a poem. He is not forced to do so, but there is not much else he can do with this material, and certainly nothing else so rewarding. (I will use the masculine pronoun here to refer to the reader, not because all readers are male but because I am, and my hypothetical reader is not a pure construct but an idealized version of myself.)

How do we make a poem out of this text? There are only two things to work on, the title and the question posed by the single, colloquial line. The line is not simply colloquial, it is prosaic; with no words of more than one syllable, concluded by a preposition, it is within the utterance range of every speaker of English. It is, in a sense, completely intelligible. But in another sense it is opaque, mysterious. Its three pronouns—who, I, it—pose problems of reference. Its conditional verb phrase—would . . . show to—poses a problem of situation. The context that would supply the information required to make that simple sentence meaningful as well as intelligible is not there. It must be supplied by the reader.

To make a poem of this text the reader must not only know English, he must know a poetic code as well: the code of the funeral elegy, as practiced in English from the Renaissance to the present time. The "words on the page" do not constitute a poetic "work," complete and self-sufficient, but a "text," a sketch or outline that must be completed by the active participation of a reader equipped with the right sort of information. In this case part of that information consists of an acquaintance with the elegiac tradition: its procedures, assumptions, devices, and values. One needs to know works like Milton's "Lycidas," Shelley's "Adonais," Tennyson's "In Memoriam," Whitman's "When Lilacs Last in the Dooryard Bloomed," Thomas's "Refusal to Mourn the Death by Fire of a Child in London," and so on, in order to "read" this simple poem properly. In fact, it could be argued that the more elegies one can bring to bear on a reading of this one, the better, richer poem this one becomes. I would go even further, suggesting that a knowledge of the critical tradition—of Dr. Johnson's objections to "Lycidas," for instance, or Wordsworth's critique of poetic diction—will also enhance one's reading of this poem. For the poem is, of course, an anti-elegy, a refusal not simply to mourn, but to write a sonorous, eloquent, mournful, but finally acquiescent, accepting—in a word, "elegiac"—poem at all.

Reading the poem involves, then, a special knowledge of its tradition. It also involves a special interpretive skill. The forms of the short, written poem as they have developed in English over the past few centuries can be usefully seen as compressed, truncated, or fragmented imitations of other verbal forms, especially the play, story, public oration, and personal essay. The reasons for this are too complicated for consideration here, but the fact will be apparent to all who reflect upon the matter. Our short poems are almost always elliptical versions of what can easily be conceived of as dramatic, narrative, oratorical, or meditative texts. Often, they are combinations of these and other modes of address. To take an obvious example, the dramatic monologue in the hands of Robert Browning is like a speech from a play (though usually more elongated than most such speeches). But to "read" such a monologue we must imagine the setting, the situation, the context, and so on. The dramatic monologue is "like" a play but gives us less information of certain sorts than a play would, requiring us to provide that information by decoding the clues in the monologue itself in the light of our understanding of the generic model. Most short poems work this way. They require both special knowledge and special skills to be "read."

To understand "Elegy" we must construct a situation out of the clues provided. The "it" in "Who would I show it to" is of course the elegy itself. The "I" is the potential writer of the elegy. The "Who" is the audience for the poem. But the verb phrase "would . . . show to" indicates a condition contrary to fact. Who would I show it to *if* I were to write it? This implies in turn that for the potential elegiac poet there is one person whose appreciation means more than that of all the rest of the potential audience for the poem he might write, and it further implies that the death of this particular person is the one imagined in the poem. If this person were dead, the poet suggests, so would his inspiration be dead. With no one to write for, no poem would be forthcoming. This poem is not only a "refusal to mourn," like that of Dylan Thomas, it is a refusal to elegize. The whole elegiac tradition, like its cousin the funeral oration, turns finally away from mourning toward acceptance, revival, renewal, a return to the concerns of life, symbolized by the very writing of the poem. Life goes on; there *is* an audience; and the mourned person will live through accomplishments, influence, descendants, and also (not least) in the elegiac poem itself. Merwin rejects all that. *If* I wrote an elegy for X, the person for whom I have always written, X would not be alive to read it; therefore, there is no reason to write an elegy for the one person in my life who most deserves one; therefore, there is no reason to write any elegy, anymore, ever. Finally, and of course, this poem called "Elegy" is not an elegy.

From Semiotics and Interpretation

DECONSTRUCTIONIST CRITICISM

Deconstructionist criticism rejects the traditional assumption that language can accurately represent reality. Language, according to deconstructionists, is a fundamentally unstable medium; consequently, literary texts, which are made up of words, have no fixed, single meaning. Deconstructionists insist, according to critic Paul de Man, on "the impossibility of making the actual expression coincide with what has to be expressed, of making the actual signs coincide with what is signified." Since they believe that literature cannot definitively express its subject matter, deconstructionists tend to shift their attention away from *what* is being said to *how* language is being used in a text.

Paradoxically, deconstructionist criticism often resembles formalist criticism; both methods usually involve close reading. But while a formalist usually tries to demonstrate how the diverse elements of a text cohere into meaning, the deconstructionist approach attempts to show how the text "deconstructs," that is, how it can be broken down—by a skeptical critic—into mutually irreconcilable positions. A biographical or historical critic might seek to establish the author's intention as a means to interpreting a literary work, but deconstructionists reject the notion that the critic should endorse the myth of authorial control over language. Deconstructionist critics like Roland Barthes and Michel Foucault have therefore called for "the death of the author," that is, the rejection of the assumption that the author, no matter how ingenious, can fully control the meaning of a text. They have also announced the death of literature as a special category of writing. In their view, poems and novels are merely words on a page that deserve no privileged status as art; all texts are created equal—equally untrustworthy, that is.

Deconstructionists focus on how language is used to achieve power. Since they believe, in the words of critic David Lehman, that "there are no truths, only rival interpretations," deconstructionists try to understand how some "interpretations" come to be regarded as truth. A major goal of deconstruction is to demonstrate how those supposed truths are at best provisional and at worst contradictory.

Deconstruction, as you may have inferred, calls for intellectual subtlety and skill. If you pursue your literary studies beyond the introductory stage, you will want to become more familiar with its assumptions. Deconstruction may strike you as a negative, even destructive, critical approach, and yet its best practitioners are adept at exposing the inadequacy of much conventional criticism. By patient analysis, they can sometimes open up the most familiar text and find unexpected significance.

Roland Barthes   (1915–1980)

THE DEATH OF THE AUTHOR   1968

TRANSLATED BY STEPHEN HEATH

Succeeding the Author, the scriptor no longer bears within him passions, humours, feelings, impressions, but rather this immense dictionary from which he draws a writing that can know no halt: life never does more than imitate the book, and the book itself is only a tissue of signs, an imitation that is lost, infinitely deferred.

Once the Author is removed, the claim to decipher a text becomes quite futile. To give a text an Author is to impose a limit on that text, to furnish it with a final signified, to close the writing. Such a conception suits criticism very well, the latter then allotting itself the important task of discovering the Author (or its hypostases: society, history, psyché, liberty) beneath the work: when the Author has been found, the text is "explained"—victory to the critic. Hence there is no surprise in the fact that, historically, the reign of the Author has also been that of the Critic, nor again in the fact that criticism (be it new) is today undermined along with the Author. In the multiplicity of writing, everything is to be *disentangled*, nothing *deciphered*; the structure can be followed, "run" (like the thread of a stocking) at every point and at every level, but there is nothing beneath: the space of writing is to be ranged over, not pierced; writing ceaselessly posits meaning ceaselessly to evaporate it, carrying out a systematic exemption of meaning. In precisely this way literature (it would be better from now on to say *writing*), by refusing to assign a "secret," an ultimate meaning, to the text (and to the world as text), liberates what may be called an anti-theological activity, an activity that is truly revolutionary since to refuse to fix meaning is, in the end, to refuse God and his hypostases—reason, science, law.

From "The Death of the Author"

Geoffrey Hartman   (b. 1929)

On Wordsworth's "A Slumber Did My Spirit Seal"   1987

Take Wordsworth's well-known lyric of eight lines, one of the "Lucy" poems, which has been explicated so many times without its meaning being fully determined:

> A slumber did my spirit seal;
>   I had no human fears:
> She seemed a thing that could not feel
>   The touch of earthly years.
>
> No motion has she now, no force;
>   She neither hears nor sees;
> Rolled round in earth's diurnal course,
>   With rocks, and stones, and trees.

It does not matter whether you interpret the second stanza (especially its last line) as tending toward affirmation, or resignation, or a grief verging on bitterness. The tonal assignment of one rather than another possible meaning, to repeat Susanne Langer° on musical form, is curiously open or beside the point. Yet the lyric does not quite support Langer's general position, that "Articulation is its life, but not assertion," because the poem is composed of a series of short and definitive statements, very like assertions. You could still claim that the poem's life is not in the assertions but somewhere else: but where then? What would articulation mean in that case? Articulation is not anti-assertive here; indeed the sense of closure is so strong that it thematizes itself in the very first line.

Nevertheless, is not the harmony or aesthetic effect of the poem greater than this local conciseness; is not the sense of closure broader and deeper than our admiration for a perfect technical construct? The poem is surely something else than a fine box, a well-wrought coffin.

That it is a kind of epitaph is relevant, of course. We recognize, even if genre is not insisted on, that Wordsworth's style is laconic, even lapidary. There may be a mimetic or formal motive related to the ideal of epitaphic poetry. But the motive may also be, in a precise way, meta-epitaphic. The poem, first of all, marks the closure of a life that has never opened up: Lucy is likened in other poems to a hidden flower or the evening star. Setting overshadows rising, and her mode of existence is inherently inward, westering. I will suppose then, that Wordsworth was at some level giving expression to the traditional epitaphic wish: Let the earth rest lightly on the deceased. If so, his conversion of this epitaphic formula is so complete that to trace the process of conversion might seem gratuitous. The formula, a trite if deeply grounded figure of speech, has been catalyzed out of existence. Here it is formula itself, or better, the adjusted words of the mourner that lie lightly on the girl and everyone who is a mourner.

I come back, then, to the "aesthetic" sense of a burden lifted, rather than denied. A heavy element is made lighter. One may still feel that the term "elation" is

---

Susanne Langer: Langer (1895–1985) was an American philosopher who discussed the relationship between aesthetics and artistic form.

inappropriate in this context; yet elation is, as a mood, the very subject of the first stanza. For the mood described is love or desire when it *eternizes* the loved person, when it makes her a star-like being that "could not feel / The touch of earthly years." This *naive* elation, this spontaneous movement of the spirit upward, is reversed in the downturn or catastrophe of the second stanza. Yet this stanza does not close out the illusion; it preserves it within the elegaic form. The illusion is elated, in our use of the word: *aufgehoben*° seems the proper term. For the girl is still, and all the more, what she seemed to be: beyond touch, like a star, if the earth in its daily motion is a planetary and erring rather than a fixed star, and if all on this star of earth must partake of its sublunar, mortal, temporal nature.

. . . .

To sum up: In Wordsworth's lyric the specific gravity of words is weighed in the balance of each stanza; and this balance is as much a judgment on speech in the context of our mortality as it is a meaningful response to the individual death. At the limit of the medium of words, and close to silence, what has been purged is not concreteness, or the empirical sphere of the emotions—shock, disillusion, trauma, recognition, grief, atonement—what has been purged is a series of flashy schematisms and false or partial mediations: artificial plot, inflated consolatory rhetoric, the coercive absolutes of logic or faith.

From "Elation in Hegel and Wordsworth"

Cultural Studies

Unlike the other critical approaches discussed in this chapter, cultural criticism (or **cultural studies**) does not offer a single way of analyzing literature. No central methodology is associated with cultural studies. Nor is cultural criticism solely, or even mainly, concerned with literary texts in the conventional sense. Instead, the term *cultural studies* refers to a relatively recent interdisciplinary field of academic inquiry. This field borrows methodologies from other approaches to analyze a wide range of cultural products and practice.

To understand cultural studies, it helps to know a bit about its origins. In the English-speaking world, the field was first defined at the Centre for Contemporary Cultural Studies of Birmingham University in Britain. Founded in 1964, this graduate program tried to expand the range of literary study beyond traditional approaches to canonic literature in order to explore a broader spectrum of historical, cultural, and political issues. The most influential teacher at the Birmingham Centre was Raymond Williams (1921–1983), a Welsh socialist with wide intellectual interests. Williams argued that scholars should not study culture as a canon of great works by individual artists but rather examine it as an evolutionary process that involves the entire society. "We cannot separate literature and art," Williams said, "from other kinds of social practice." The cultural critic, therefore, does not study fixed

---

aufgehoben: German for "taken up" or "lifted up," but this term can also mean "canceled" or "nullified." Hartman uses the term for its double meaning.

aesthetic objects as much as dynamic social processes. The critic's challenge is to identify and understand the complex forms and effects of the process of culture.

A Marxist intellectual, Williams called his approach cultural materialism (a reference to the Marxist doctrine of dialectical materialism), but later scholars soon discarded that name for two broader and more neutral terms, cultural criticism and cultural studies. From the start, this interdisciplinary field relied heavily on literary theory, especially Marxist and feminist criticism. It also employed the documentary techniques of historical criticism combined with political analysis focused on issues of social class, race, and gender. (This approach flourished in the United States, where it is called New Historicism.) Cultural studies is also deeply antiformalist, since the field concerns itself with investigating the complex relationship among history, politics, and literature. Cultural studies rejects the notion that literature exists in an aesthetic realm separate from ethical and political categories.

A chief goal of cultural studies is to understand the nature of social power as reflected in "texts." For example, if the object of analysis were a sonnet by Shakespeare, the cultural studies adherent might investigate the moral, psychological, and political assumptions reflected in the poem and then deconstruct them to see what individuals, social classes, or gender might benefit from having those assumptions perceived as true. The relevant mission of cultural studies is to identify both the overt and covert values reflected in a cultural practice. The cultural studies critic also tries to trace out and understand the structures of meaning that hold those assumptions in place and give them the appearance of objective representation. Any analytical technique that helps illuminate these issues is employed.

In theory, a cultural studies critic might employ any methodology. In practice, however, he or she will most often borrow concepts from deconstruction, Marxist analysis, gender criticism, race theory, and psychology. Each of these earlier methodologies provides particular analytical tools that cultural critics find useful. What cultural studies borrows from deconstructionism is its emphasis on uncovering conflict, dissent, and contradiction in the works under analysis. Whereas traditional critical approaches often sought to demonstrate the unity of a literary work, cultural studies often seeks to portray social, political, and psychological conflicts it masks. What cultural studies borrows from Marxist analysis is an attention to the ongoing struggle between social classes, each seeking economic (and therefore political) advantage. Cultural studies often asks questions about what social class created a work of art and what class (or classes) served as its audience. Among the many things that cultural studies borrowed from gender criticism and race theory is a concern with social inequality between the sexes and races. It seeks to investigate how these inequities have been reflected in the texts of a historical period or a society. Cultural studies is, above all, a political enterprise that views literary analysis as a means of furthering social justice.

Since cultural studies does not adhere to any single methodology (or even a consistent set of methodologies), it is impossible to characterize the field briefly, because there are exceptions to every generalization offered. What one sees most clearly are characteristic tendencies, especially the commitment to examining issues of class, race, and gender. There is also the insistence on expanding the focus of critical inquiry beyond traditional high literary culture. British cultural studies guru Anthony Easthope can, for example, analyze with equal aplomb Gerard Manley Hopkins's "The

Windhover," Edgar Rice Burrough's *Tarzan of the Apes*, a Benson and Hedges's ciga-rette advertisement, and Sean Connery's eyebrows. Cultural studies is infamous—even among its practitioners—for its habitual use of literary jargon. It is also notorious for its complex intellectual analysis of mundane materials such as Easthope's analysis of a cig-arette ad, which may be interesting in its own right but remote from most readers' lit-erary experience. Some scholars, such as Heather Glen, however, use the principles of cultural studies to provide new social, political, and historical insights on canonic texts such as William Blake's "London." Omnivorous, iconoclastic, and relentlessly ana-lytic, cultural criticism has become a major presence in contemporary literary studies.

Mark Bauerlein   (b. 1959)
WHAT IS CULTURAL STUDIES?   1997

Traditionally, disciplines naturally fell into acknowledged subdivisions, for ex-ample, as literary criticism broke up into formalist literary criticism, philological criticism, narratological analysis, and other methodologically distinguished pur-suits, all of which remained comfortably within the category "literary criticism." But cultural studies eschews such institutional disjunctions and will not let any straitening adjective precede the "cultural studies" heading. There is no distinct formalist cultural studies or historicist cultural studies, but only cultural studies. (Feminist cultural studies may be one exception.) Cultural studies is a field that will not be parceled out to the available disciplines. It spans culture at large, not this or that institutionally separated element of culture. To guarantee this tran-scendence of disciplinary institutions, cultural studies must select a name for it-self that has no specificity, that has too great an extension to mark off any expe-dient boundaries for itself. "Cultural studies" serves well because, apart from distinguishing between "physical science" and "cultural analysis," the term pro-vides no indication of where any other boundaries lie.

This is exactly the point. To blur disciplinary boundaries and frustrate the in-tellectual investments that go along with them is a fundamental motive for cultural studies practice, one that justifies the vagueness of the titular term. This explains why the related label "cultural criticism," so much in vogue in 1988, has declined. The term "criticism" has a narrower extension than does "studies," ruling out some empirical forms of inquiry (like field work) that "studies" admits. "Studies" pre-serves a methodological openness that "criticism" closes. Since such closures have suspect political intentions behind them, cultural studies maintains its institutional purity by disdaining disciplinary identity and methodological uniformity.

. . .

A single approach will miss too much, will overlook important aspects of cul-ture not perceptible to that particular angle of vision. A multitude of approaches will pick up an insight here and a piece of knowledge there and more of culture will enter into the inquiry. A diversity of methods will match the diversity of culture, thereby sheltering the true nature of culture from the reductive appropriations of formal disciplines.

But how do cultural critics bring all these methods together into a coherent inquiry? Are there any established rules of incorporating "important insights and knowledge" coming out of different methods into a coherent scholarly project of cultural studies? How might a scholar use both phonemic analysis and deconstruction in a single inquiry when deconstructionist arguments call into question the basic premises of phonetics? What scholar has the competence to handle materials from so many disciplines in a rigorous and knowing manner? Does cultural criticism as a "studies" practice offer any transdisciplinary evaluative standards to apply to individual pieces of cultural criticism? If not, if there is no clear methodological procedures or evaluative principles in cultural studies, it is hard to see how one might popularize it, teach it, make it into a recognized scholarly activity. In practical terms, one does not know how to communicate it to others or show students how to do it when it assumes so many different methodological forms. How does one create an academic department out of an outspokenly antidisciplinary practice? What criteria can faculty members jointly invoke when they are trying to make curricular and personnel decisions?

Once again, this is precisely the point. One reason for the generality of the term is to render such institutional questions unanswerable. Cultural studies practice mingles methods from a variety of fields, jumps from one cultural subject matter to another, simultaneously proclaims superiority to other institutionalized inquiries (on a correspondence to culture basis) and renounces its own institutionalization—gestures that strategically forestall disciplinary standards being applied to it. By studying culture in heterogenous ways, by clumping texts, events, persons, objects, and ideologies into a cultural whole (which, cultural critics say, is reality) and bringing a melange of logical argument, speculative propositions, empirical data, and political outlooks to bear upon it, cultural critics invent a new kind of investigation immune to methodological attack.

From *Literary Criticism: An Autopsy*

Heather Glen

THE STANCE OF OBSERVATION IN   1983
WILLIAM BLAKE'S "LONDON"

In choosing to present his vision of social disaster thus, Blake was engaging with a familiar literary mode. The assumption of a stance of "observation," freely passing judgment on that which is before it, is common to much eighteenth-century literature: "There mark what ills the scholar's life assail".[1] But nowhere is it more prominent than in that which attempts to describe London, a place of bewildering diversity, changing and growing rapidly, in which a new kind of anonymity and alienation was becoming a remarked-upon fact of life. Indeed, it

---

[1] Johnson, "The Vanity of Human Wishes," I. 159. The opening lines of this poem are perhaps the dramatization *par excellence* of this stance: "Let observation with extensive view, / Survey mankind, from China to Peru; / Remark each anxious toil, each eager strife, / And watch the busy scenes of crouded life."

seems that in the literature of London the implications of this state were beginning to become an explicit preoccupation. Thus, Ben Sedgly in 1751:

> No man can take survey of this opulent city, without meeting in his way, many melancholy instances resulting from this consumption of spirituous liquors: poverty, diseases, misery and wickedness, are the daily observations to be made in every part of this great metropolis: whoever passes along the streets, may find numbers of abandoned wretches stretched upon the cold pavement, motionless and insensible, removed only by the charity of passengers from the danger of being crushed by carriages, trampled by horses, or strangled with filth in the common sewers.

"Take survey of," "meeting in his way," "observations to be made," "whoever passes along the streets may find"—the sense throughout is of an anonymous and freely observing stranger, rather than of a member of a society who sees himself as shaped by it and interacting with others within it. Perhaps such a perspective is natural in a documentary work such as Sedgly's. But this sense of the self in the city is central, too, to much of the most powerful imaginative literature of the century, literature which is after all not merely a description of or meditation upon the world, but the recreation of a certain mode of being within it. It is a sense that informs the novels of Defoe: the figures of Roxana and Colonel Jack and Moll Flanders move through the streets from adventure to adventure with a freedom from social constraint which is only possible because of the nature of London life. It is to be found in Gay's *Trivia* and *The Beggar's Opera*; in Boswell's *Journal*; in Johnson's *London*, and even in those of his essays which seem to have nothing to do with London at all:

> He that considers how little he dwells upon the condition of others, will learn how little the attention of others is attracted by himself. While we see multitudes passing before us, of whom perhaps not one appears to deserve our notice, or excites our sympathy, we should remember, that we likewise are lost in the same throng, that eye which happens to glance upon us is turned in a moment on him that follows us, and that the utmost which we can reasonably hope or fear is to fill a vacant hour with prattle, and be forgotten.[2]

Here, the tone is one of judicious moralizing. But the imagery is that of the confusing eighteenth-century London street, in which relations with one's fellow beings involve attracting attention, deserving notice, glancing and turning, even *exciting* sympathy: in which the other is the object of observation rather than one with whom one interacts. And the supposedly free individual who sees those who pass before him as a mighty spectacle is himself "lost in the same throng."

The eighteenth-century London street was not, then, merely a place where suffering and distress could be seen on a hitherto unprecedented scale: it was also a place where that sense of the other as object—often as feeble and wretched object—which Blake exposes in "The Human Abstract" ("we . . . make somebody Poor") was the dominant mode of relationship. And it is a sense which is an

[2]Samuel Johnson, *The Rambler*, 159.

ironic point of reference in "London." For this poem begins with a speaker who seems to be a detached observer, who wanders "thro'" the streets of the city and "marks" the sights before him. Yet his is not the lively and distinctive London of Defoe or Gay or Johnson: what he records is not variety, but sameness. To him, both streets and river are simply "charter'd": the different faces which pass all bear the same message, "Marks of weakness, marks of woe." And the tight quatrain with its present indicative tense conveys not flexible responsiveness to constantly changing possibilities, but entrapment. What this speaker sees is fatally linked to the way in which he sees it. In the notebook draft, the second word of the third line was "see": Blake's alteration limits any incipient sense of freedom. The triple beat of "mark"—an active verb materializing into two plural nouns—registers a new consciousness of this "I"'s implication in the world "thro'" which he wanders. What he observes is the objectification of his own activity.

"Mark" is not the only change which Blake made in this stanza. In the notebook draft, the first two lines read:

I wander thro' each dirty street,
Near where the dirty Thames does flow.

The substitution, in the engraved version, of "charter'd," signals a complex process of poetic thought. For "charter'd" in 1793 was a word at the centre of political debate: a word whose accepted meaning of "granted privileges or rights" had been challenged by Paine a year earlier, in a book whose sales had by now reached 200,000:

> It is a perversion of terms to say, that a charter gives rights. It operates by a contrary effect, that of taking rights away. Rights are inherently in all the inhabitants; but charters, by annulling those rights in the majority, leave the right by exclusion in the hands of a few . . . all charters have no other than an indirect negative operation. They do not give rights to A, but they make a difference in favour of A by taking away the right of B, and consequently are instruments of injustice.[3]

No contemporary of Blake's could have read the two altered opening lines of his poem as an objective description of the trading organization of the city. Their repetition of "charter'd" forces into prominence the newly, ironically recognized sense that the very language of "objective" description may be riddled with ideological significance: that beneath the assurance of polite usage may lurk another, "cheating" meaning. And this sense informs the stanza in a peculiar way. It is as though beneath the polite surface—the observer in London wandering the streets of a city whose "charter'd" organization he notes, as the guidebooks noted its commercial organization, and whose manifestations of distress and depravity he, like hundreds of other eighteenth-century writers, remarks—there is another set of meanings, which are the *reverse* of those such description could customarily bear. They are not meanings private to Blake: and they are meanings which focus in those sound-linked and repeated words, "mark" and "charter'd."

From *Vision and Disenchantment*

[3]Paine, *Rights of Man*, ed. Henry Collins (Harmondsworth: Penguin, 1969), 242–43.

Glossary of Literary Terms

Abstract diction *See* **Diction.**

Accent An emphasis or stress placed on a syllable in speech. Clear pronunciation of polysyllabic words almost always depends on correct placement of their accents (e.g., *de*-sert and de-*sert* are two different words and parts of speech, depending on their accent). Accent or speech stress is the basis of most meters in English. (*See also* **Accentual meter, Meter.**)

Accentual meter A meter that uses a consistent number of strong speech stresses per line. The number of unstressed syllables may vary, as long as the accented syllables do not. Much popular poetry, such as rap and nursery rhymes, is written in accentual meter.

Acrostic A poem in which the initial letters of each line, when read downward, spell out a hidden word or words (often the name of a beloved person). Acrostics date back as far as the Hebrew Bible and classical Greek poetry.

Allegory A narrative in verse or prose in which the literal events (persons, places, and things) consistently point to a parallel sequence of symbolic ideas. This narrative strategy is often used to dramatize abstract ideas, historical events, religious systems, or political issues. An allegory has two levels of meaning: a literal level that tells a surface story and a symbolic level in which the abstract ideas unfold. The names of allegorical characters often hint at their symbolic roles. For example, in Nathaniel Hawthorne's "Young Goodman Brown," Faith is not only the name of the protagonist's wife but also a symbol of the protagonist's religious faith.

Alliteration The repetition of two or more consonant sounds in successive words in a line of verse or prose. Alliteration can be used at the beginning of words ("cool cats"—**initial alliteration**) or internally on stressed syllables ("In *k*itchen *c*ups concupiscent curds"—which combines initial and **internal alliteration**). Alliteration was a central feature of Anglo-Saxon poetry and is still used by contemporary writers.

All-knowing narrator *See* **Omniscient narrator.**

Allusion A brief (and sometimes indirect) reference in a text to a person, place, or thing—fictitious or actual. An allusion may appear in a literary work as an initial quotation, a passing mention of a name, or as a phrase borrowed from another writer—often carrying the meanings and implications of the original. Allusions imply a common set of knowledge between reader and writer and operate as a literary shorthand to enrich the meaning of a text.

Analysis The examination of a piece of literature as a means of understanding its subject or structure. An effective analysis often clarifies a work by focusing on a single element such as tone, irony, symbolism, imagery, or rhythm in a way that enhances the reader's understanding of the whole. *Analysis* comes from the Greek word meaning to "undo," to "loosen."

Anapest A metrical foot in verse in which two unstressed syllables are followed by a stressed syllable, as in "on a *boat*" or "in a *slump*." (*See also* **Meter.**)

Antithesis Words, phrases, clauses, or sentences set in deliberate contrast to one another. Antithesis balances opposing ideas, tones, or structures, usually to heighten the effect of a statement.

Apostrophe A direct address to someone or something. In poetry an apostrophe often addresses something not ordinarily spoken to (e.g., "O mountain!"). In an apostrophe, a speaker may address an inanimate object, a dead or absent person, an abstract thing, or a spirit. Apostrophe is often used to provide a speaker with means to articulate thoughts aloud.

Archetype A recurring symbol, character, landscape, or event found in myth and literature across different cultures and eras. The idea of the archetype came into literary criticism from the Swiss psychologist Carl Jung who believed that all individuals share a "collective unconscious," a set of primal memories common to the human race that exists in our subconscious. An example of an archetypal character is the devil who may appear in pure mythic form (as in John Milton's *Paradise Lost*) but occurs more often in a disguised form like Fagin in Charles Dickens's *Oliver Twist* or Abner Snopes in William Faulkner's "Barn Burning."

Assonance The repetition of two or more vowel sounds in successive words, which creates a kind of rhyme. Like alliteration, the assonance may occur initially ("*all* the *awful auguries*") or internally ("wh*i*te l*i*lacs"). Assonance may be used to focus attention on key words or concepts. Assonance also helps make a phrase or line more memorable.

Auditory imagery A word or sequence of words that refers to the sense of hearing. (*See also* **Imagery.**)

Augustan age This term has two related meanings. First, it originally referred to the greatest period of Roman literature under the Emperor Augustus (27 B.C.–14 A.D.) in which Virgil, Horace, and Ovid wrote. Second, it refers to the early eighteenth century in English literature, a neoclassical period dominated by Alexander Pope, Thomas Gray, and Jonathan Swift. English Augustan poetry was characteristically formal in both structure and diction.

Ballad Traditionally, a song that tells a story. The ballad was originally an oral verse form—sung or recited and transmitted from performer to performer without being written down. Ballads are characteristically compressed, dramatic, and objective in their narrative style. There are many variations to the ballad form, most consisting of quatrains (made up of lines of three or four metrical feet) in a simple rhyme scheme. (*See also* **Ballad stanza.**)

Ballad stanza The most common pattern of ballad makers consists of four lines rhymed *abcb*, in which the first and third lines have four metrical feet and the second and fourth lines have three feet (4, 3, 4, 3).

Bathos In poetry, an unintentional lapse from the sublime to the ridiculous or trivial. Bathos differs from anticlimax, in that the latter is a deliberate effect, often for the purpose of humor or contrast, whereas bathos occurs through failure.

Biographical criticism The practice of analyzing a literary work by using knowledge of the author's life to gain insight.

Biography A factual account of a person's life, examining all available information or texts relevant to the subject.

Blank verse The most common and well-known meter of unrhymed poetry in English. Blank verse contains five iambic feet per line and is never rhymed. (*Blank* means "unrhymed.") Many literary works have been written in blank verse, including Tennyson's "Ulysses" and Frost's "The Mending Wall." Shakespeare's plays are written primarily in blank verse. (*See also* **Iambic pentameter**.)

Blues A type of folk music originally developed by African Americans in the South, often about some pain or loss. Blues lyrics traditionally consist of three-line stanzas in which the first two identical lines are followed by a third concluding, rhyming line. The influence of the blues is fundamental in virtually all styles of contemporary pop—jazz, rap, rock, gospel, country, and rhythm and blues.

Broadside ballads Poems printed on a single sheet of paper, often set to traditional tunes. Most broadside ballads, which originated in the late sixteenth century, were an early form of verse journalism, cheap to print, and widely circulated. Often they were humorous or pathetic accounts of sensational news events.

Cacophony A harsh, discordant sound often mirroring the meaning of the context in which it is used. For example, "Grate on the scrannel pipes of wretched straw" (Milton's "Lycidas"). The opposite of cacophony is **euphony**.

Caesura, cesura A pause within a line of verse. Traditionally, caesuras appear near the middle of a line, but their placement may be varied to create expressive rhythmic effects. A caesura will usually occur at a mark of punctuation, but there can be a caesura even if no punctuation is present.

Carpe diem Latin for "seize the day." Originally said in Horace's famous "Odes I (11)," this phrase has been applied to characterize much lyric poetry concerned with human mortality and the passing of time.

Child ballads American scholar Francis J. Child compiled a collection of over three hundred authentic ballads in his book *The English and Scottish Popular Ballads* (1882–1898). He demonstrated that these ballads were the creations of oral folk culture. These works have come to be called Child ballads.

Clerihew A comic verse form named for its inventor, Edmund Clerihew Bentley. A clerihew begins with the name of a person and consists of two metrically awkward, rhymed couplets. Humorous and often insulting, clerihews serve as ridiculous biographies, usually of famous people.

Closed couplet Two rhymed lines that contain an independent and complete thought or statement. The closed couplet usually pauses lightly at the end of the first line; the second is more heavily end-stopped, or "closed." When such couplets are written in rhymed iambic pentameter, they are called **heroic couplets**. (*See also* **Couplet**.)

Closed form A generic term that describes poetry written in some preexisting pattern of meter, rhyme, line, or stanza. A closed form produces a prescribed structure as in the triolet, with a set rhyme scheme and line length. Closed forms include the sonnet, sestina, villanelle, ballade, and rondeau.

Close reading A method of analysis involving careful step-by-step explication of a poem in order to understand how various elements work together. Close reading is a common practice of formalist critics in the study of a text.

Colloquial English The casual or informal but correct language of ordinary native speakers, which may include contractions, slang, and shifts in grammar, vocabulary, and diction. Wordsworth helped introduce colloquialism into English poetry, challenging the past constraints of highly formal language in verse and calling for the poet to become "a man speaking to men." Conversational in tone, *colloquial* is derived from the Latin *colloquium*, "speaking together." (*See also* **Diction, Levels of diction.**)

Common meter A highly regular form of ballad meter with two sets of rhymes—*abab*. "Amazing Grace" and many other hymns are in common meter. (*See also* **Ballad stanza.**)

Comparison In the analysis or criticism of literature, one may place two works side-by-side to point out their similarities. The product of this, a comparison, may be more meaningful when paired with its counterpart, a **contrast**.

Conceit A poetic device using elaborate comparisons, such as equating a loved one with the graces and beauties of the world. Most notably used by the Italian poet Petrarch in praise of his beloved Laura, *conceit* comes from the Italian *concetto*, "concept" or "idea."

Concrete diction *See* **Diction.**

Concrete poetry A visual poetry composed exclusively for the page in which a picture or image is made of printed letters and words. Concrete poetry attempts to blur the line between language and visual art. Concrete poetry was especially popular as an experimental movement in the 1960s.

Confessional poetry A poetic genre emerging in the 1950s and 1960s primarily concerned with autobiography and the unexpurgated exposure of the poet's personal life. Notable practitioners included Robert Lowell, W. D. Snodgrass, and Anne Sexton.

Connotation An association or additional meaning that a word, image, or phrase may carry, apart from its literal denotation or dictionary definition. A word picks up connotations from all the uses to which it has been put in the past. For example, an owl in literature is not merely the literal bird. It also carries the many associations (connotations, that is) attached to it.

Consonance Also called **Slant rhyme**. A kind of rhyme in which the linked words share similar consonant sounds but different vowel sounds, as in *reason* and *raisin*, *mink* and *monk*. Sometimes only the final consonant sound is identical, as in *fame* and *room*, *crack* and *truck*. Used mostly by modern poets, consonance often registers more subtly than exact rhyme, lending itself to special poetic effects.

Contrast A contrast of two works of literature is developed by placing them side-by-side to point out their differences. This method of analysis works well with its opposite, a **comparison**, which focuses on likenesses.

Convention Any established feature or technique in literature that is commonly understood by both authors and readers. A convention is something generally agreed on to be appropriate for its customary uses, such as the sonnet form for a love poem or the opening "Once upon a time" for a fairy tale.

Conventional symbols Literary symbols that have a conventional or customary effect on most readers. We would respond similarly to a black cat crossing our path or a young bride in a white dress. These are conventional symbols because they carry recognizable connotations and suggestions.

Couplet A two-line stanza in poetry, usually rhymed, which tends to have lines of equal length. Shakespeare's sonnets were famous for ending with a summarizing, rhymed couplet: "Give my love fame faster than Time wastes life; / So thou preven-t'st his scythe and crookèd knife." (*See also* **Closed couplet.**)

Cowboy poetry A contemporary genre of folk poetry written by people with firsthand experience in the life of horse, trail, and ranch. Plainspoken and often humorous, cowboy poetry is usually composed in rhymed ballad stanzas and meant to be recited aloud.

Cultural studies A contemporary interdisciplinary field of academic study that focuses on understanding the social power encoded in "texts." Cultural studies defines "texts" more broadly than literary works; they include any analyzable phenomenon from a traditional poem to an advertising image or an actor's face. Cultural studies has no central critical methodology but uses whatever intellectual tools are appropriate to the analysis at hand.

Dactyl A metrical foot of verse in which one stressed syllable is followed by two unstressed syllables (*bat*-ter-y or *par*-a-mour). The dactylic meter is less common to English than it was to classical Greek and Latin verse. Longfellow's *Evangeline* is the most famous English-language long dactylic poem.

Deconstructionist criticism A school of criticism that rejects the traditional assumption that language can accurately represent reality. Deconstructionists believe that literary texts can have no single meaning; therefore, they concentrate their attentions on *how* language is being used in a text, rather than on *what* is being said.

Decorum Propriety or appropriateness. In poetry, decorum usually refers to a level of diction that is proper to use in a certain occasion. Decorum can also apply to characters, setting, and the harmony that exists between the elements in a poem. For example, aged nuns speaking inner-city jive might violate decorum.

Denotation The literal, dictionary meaning of a word. (*See also* **Connotation.**)

Dialect A particular variety of language spoken by an identifiable regional group or social class of persons. Dialects are often used in literature in an attempt to present a character more realistically and to express significant differences in class or background.

Diction Word choice or vocabulary. Diction refers to the class of words that an author decides is appropriate to use in a particular work. Literary history is the story of diction being challenged, upheld, and reinvented. **Concrete diction** involves a highly specific word choice in the naming of something or someone. **Abstract diction** contains words that express more general ideas or concepts. More concrete diction would offer *boxer puppy* rather than *young canine, Lake Ontario* rather than *body of fresh water*. Concrete words refer to what we can immediately perceive with our senses. (*See also* **Levels of diction**.)

Didactic poetry Kind of poetry intended to teach the reader a moral lesson or impart a body of knowledge. Poetry that aims for education over art.

Dimeter A verse meter consisting of two metrical feet, or two primary stresses, per line.

Doggerel Verse full of irregularities often due to the poet's incompetence. Doggerel is crude verse that brims with cliché, obvious rhyme, and inept rhythm.

Dramatic irony A special kind of suspenseful expectation, when the audience or reader understands the implication and meaning of a situation onstage and foresees the oncoming disaster (in tragedy) or triumph (in comedy) but the character does not. The irony forms between the contrasting levels of knowledge of the character and the reader.

Dramatic monologue A poem written as a speech made by a character at some decisive moment. The speaker is usually addressing a silent listener as in T. S. Eliot's "The Love Song of J. Alfred Prufrock" or Robert Browning's "My Last Duchess."

Dramatic poetry Any verse written for the stage, as in the plays of classical Greece, the Renaissance (Shakespeare), and neoclassical periods (Molière, Racine). Also a kind of poetry that presents the voice of an imaginary character (or characters) speaking directly, without any additional narration by the author. In poetry, the term usually refers to the dramatic monologue, a lyric poem written as a speech made by a character at some decisive moment, such as Lord, Alfred Tennyson's "Ulysses." (*See also* **Dramatic monologue**.)

Echo verse A poetic form in which the final syllables of the lines are repeated back as a reply or commentary, often using puns. Echo verse dates back to late classical Greek poetry. Fred Chappell's "Narcissus and Echo" is a contemporary example of this form.

Editing The act of rereading a draft in order to correct mistakes, cut excess words, and make improvements.

Elegy A lament or a sadly meditative poem, often written on the occasion of a death or other solemn theme. An elegy is usually a sustained poem in a formal style.

Endnote An additional piece of information that the author includes in a note at the end of a paper. Endnotes usually contain information that the author feels is important to convey but not appropriate to fit into the main body of text. (*See also* **Footnote**.)

End rhyme Rhyme that occurs at the ends of lines, rather than within them (as internal rhyme does). End rhyme is the most common kind of rhyme in English-language poetry.

End-stopped line A line of verse that ends in a full pause, usually indicated by a mark of punctuation.

English sonnet Also called **Shakespearean sonnet**. The English sonnet has a rhyme scheme organized into three quatrains with a final couplet: *abab cdcd efef gg*. The poem may turn, that is, shift in mood or tone, between any of the quatrains (although it usually occurs on the ninth line). (*See also* **Sonnet**.)

Envoy A short, often summarizing stanza that appears at the end of certain poetic forms (most notably the sestina, chant royal, and the French ballade). The envoy contains the poet's parting words. The word comes from the French *envoi*, meaning "sending forth."

Epic A long narrative poem usually composed in an elevated style tracing the adventures of a legendary or mythic hero. Epics are usually written in a consistent form and meter throughout. Famous epics include Homer's *Iliad* and *Odyssey*, Virgil's *Aeneid*, and Milton's *Paradise Lost*.

Epigram A very short poem, often comic, usually ending with some sharp turn of wit or meaning.

Epigraph A brief quotation preceding a story or other literary work. An epigraph usually suggests the subject, theme, or atmosphere the story will explore.

Euphony The harmonious effect when the sounds of the words connect with the meaning in a way pleasing to the ear and mind. An example is found in Tennyson's lines, "The moan of doves in immemorial elms, / And murmuring of innumerable bees." The opposite of euphony is **cacophony**.

Exact rhyme A full rhyme in which the sounds following the initial letters of the words are identical in sound, as in *follow* and *hollow*, *go* and *slow*, *disband* and *this hand*.

Explication Literally, an "unfolding." In an explication an entire poem is explained in detail, addressing every element and unraveling any complexities as a means of analysis.

Eye rhyme Rhyme in which the spelling of the words appears alike, but the pronunciations differ, as in *laughter* and *daughter*, *idea* and *flea*.

Falling meter Trochaic and dactylic meters are called falling meters because their first syllable is accented, followed by one or more unaccented syllables. A foot of falling meter falls in its level of stress, as in the words *co*-medy or *aw*-ful.

Feminine rhyme A rhyme of two or more syllables with a stress on a syllable other than the last, as in *tur*-tle and *fer*-tile. (*See also* **Masculine rhyme, Rhyme.**)

Feminist criticism *See* **Gender criticism.**

Figure of speech An expression or comparison that relies not on its literal meaning, but rather on its connotations and suggestions. For example, "He's dumber than dirt" is not literally true; it is a figure of speech. Major figures of speech include **metaphor, metonymy, simile,** and **synecdoche.**

Fixed form A traditional verse form requiring certain predetermined elements of structure, for example, a stanza pattern, set meter, or predetermined line length. A fixed form like the sonnet, for instance, must have no more or less than fourteen lines, rhymed according to certain conventional patterns. (*See also* **Closed form.**)

Folk ballads Anonymous narrative songs, usually in ballad meter, that were originally transmitted orally. Although most well-known ballads have been transcribed and published in order to protect them from being lost, they were originally created for oral performance, often resulting in many versions of a single ballad.

Folk epic Also called **Traditional epic.** A long narrative poem that traces the adventures of a tribe or nation's popular heroes. Some examples of epics are the *Iliad* and the *Odyssey* (Greek), *The Song of Roland* (French), and *The Cid* (Spanish). A folk epic originates in an oral tradition as opposed to a literary epic, which is written by an individual author consciously emulating earlier epic poetry.

Folklore The body of traditional wisdom and customs—including songs, stories, myths, and proverbs—of a people as collected and continued through oral tradition.

Foot The unit of measurement in metrical poetry. Different meters are identified by the pattern and order of stressed and unstressed syllables in their foot, usually containing two or three syllables, with one syllable accented.

Footnote An additional piece of information that the author includes at the bottom of a page, usually noted by a small reference number in the main text. A footnote might supply the reader with brief facts about a related historical figure or event, the definition of a foreign word or phrase, or any other relevant information that may help in understanding the text. (*See also* **Endnote.**)

Form The means by which a literary work conveys its meaning. Traditionally, form refers to the way in which an artist expresses meaning rather than the content of that meaning, but it is now commonplace to note that form and content are inextricably related. Form, therefore, is more than the external framework of a literary work. It includes the totality of ways in which it unfolds and coheres as a structure of meaning and expression.

Formal English The heightened, impersonal language of educated persons, usually only written, although possibly spoken on dignified occasions. (*See also* **Levels of diction.**)

Formalist criticism A school of criticism which argues that literature may only be discussed on its own terms; that is, without outside influences or information. A key method that formalists use is close reading, a step-by-step analysis of the elements in a text.

Found poetry Poetry constructed by arranging bits of "found" prose. A found poem is a literary work made up of nonliterary language arranged for expressive effect.

Free verse From the French *vers libre*. Free verse describes poetry that organizes its lines without meter. It may be rhymed (as in some poems by H. D.), but it usually is not. There is no one means of organizing free verse, and different authors have used irreconcilable systems. What unites the two approaches is a freedom from metrical regularity. (*See also* **Open form.**)

Gender criticism Gender criticism examines how sexual identity influences the creation, interpretation, and evaluation of literary works. This critical approach began with feminist criticism in the 1960s and 1970s which stated that literary study had been so dominated by men that it contained many unexamined "male-produced" assumptions. Feminist criticism sought to address this imbalance in two ways: first in insisting that sexless interpretation was impossible, and second by articulating responses to the texts that were explicitly male or female. More recently, gender criticism has focused on gay and lesbian literary identity as interpretive strategies.

General English The ordinary speech of educated native speakers. Most literate speech and writing is general English. Its diction is more educated than **colloquial English**, yet not as elevated as **formal English**. (*See also* **Levels of diction.**)

Haiku A Japanese verse form that has three unrhymed lines of five, seven, and five syllables. Traditional haiku is often serious and spiritual in tone, relying mostly on imagery, and usually set in one of the four seasons.

Heptameter A verse meter consisting of seven metrical feet, or seven primary stresses, per line.

Heroic couplet *See* **Closed couplet**.

Hexameter A verse meter consisting of six metrical feet, or six primary stresses, per line.

Historical criticism The practice of analyzing a literary work by investigating the social, cultural, and intellectual context that produced it—a context that necessarily includes the artist's biography and milieu. Historical critics strive to recreate the exact meaning and impact a work had on its original audience.

Hyperbole *See* **Overstatement**.

Iamb A metrical foot in verse in which an unaccented syllable is followed by an accented one, as in "ca-*ress*" or "a *cat*" (‿ ′). The iambic measure is the most common meter used in English poetry.

Iambic meter A verse meter consisting of a specific recurring number of iambic feet per line. (*See also* **Iamb, Iambic pentameter.**)

Iambic pentameter The most common meter in English verse—five iambic feet per line. Many fixed forms, such as the sonnet and heroic couplets, are written in iambic pentameter. Unrhymed iambic pentameter is called **blank verse**.

Image A word or series of words that refers to any sensory experience (usually sight, although also sound, smell, touch, or taste). An image is a direct or literal recreation of physical experience and adds immediacy to literary language.

Imagery The collective set of images in a poem or other literary work.

Implied metaphor A metaphor that uses neither connectives nor the verb *to be*. If we say, "John crowed over his victory," we imply metaphorically that John is a rooster but do not say so specifically. (*See also* **Metaphor**.)

Incremental refrain A refrain whose words change slightly with each recurrence. (*See also* **Refrain**.)

Initial alliteration *See* **Alliteration**.

Internal alliteration *See* **Alliteration**.

Internal refrain A refrain that appears within a stanza, generally in a position that stays fixed throughout a poem. (*See also* **Refrain**.)

Internal rhyme Rhyme that occurs within a line of poetry, as opposed to **end rhyme**. Read aloud, these Wallace Stevens lines are rich in internal rhyme: "Chieftain Iffucan of Azcan in caftan / Of tan with henna hackles, halt!" (from "Bantams in Pine-Woods").

Ironic point of view The perspective of a character or narrator whose voice or position is rich in ironic contradictions. (*See also* **Irony**.)

Irony A literary device in which a discrepancy of meaning is masked beneath the surface of the language. Irony is present when a writer says one thing but means something quite the opposite. There are many kinds of irony, but the two major varieties are **verbal irony** (in which the discrepancy is contained in words) and **situational irony** (in which the discrepancy exists when something is about to happen to a character or characters who expect the opposite outcome). (*See also* **Cosmic irony, Irony of fate, Sarcasm, Verbal irony.**)

Irony of fate A type of situational irony that can be used for either tragic or comic purposes. Irony of fate is the discrepancy between actions and their results, between what characters deserve and what they get, between appearance and reality.

Italian sonnet Also called **Petrarchan sonnet**, a sonnet with the following rhyme pattern for the first eight lines (the **octave**): *abba, abba*; the final six lines (the **sestet**) may follow any pattern of rhymes, as long as it does not end in a couplet. The poem traditionally turns, or shifts in mood or tone, after the octave. (*See also* **Sonnet.**)

Levels of diction In English, there are conventionally four basic levels of formality in word choice, or four levels of diction. From the least formal to the most elevated they are **vulgate, colloquial English, general English**, and **formal English**. (*See also* **Diction.**)

Limerick A short and usually comic verse form of five anapestic lines usually rhyming *aabba*. The first, second, and fifth lines traditionally have three stressed syllables each; the third and fourth have two stresses each (3, 3, 2, 2, 3).

Literary ballad Ballad not meant for singing, written for literate readers by sophisticated poets rather than arising from the anonymous oral tradition. (*See also* **Ballad.**)

Literary epic A crafted imitation of the oral folk epic written by an author living in a society where writing has been invented. Examples of the literary epic are *The Aeneid* by Virgil and *The Divine Comedy* by Dante Alighieri. (*See also* **Folk epic.**)

Literary theory Literary criticism that tries to formulate general principles rather than discuss specific texts. Theory operates at a high level of abstraction and often focuses on understanding basic issues of language, communication, art, interpretation, culture, and ideological content.

Lyric A short poem expressing the thoughts and feelings of a single speaker. Often written in the first person, lyric poetry traditionally has a songlike immediacy and emotional force.

Madrigal A short secular song for three or more voices arranged in counterpoint. The madrigal is often about love or pastoral themes. It originated in Italy in the fourteenth century and enjoyed great success during the Elizabethan Age.

Masculine rhyme Either a rhyme of one syllable words (as in *fox* and *socks*) or—in polysyllabic words—a rhyme on the stressed final syllables: con-*trive* and sur-*vive*. (*See also* **Feminine rhyme.**)

Metaphor A statement that one thing *is* something else, which, in a literal sense, it is not. By asserting that a thing is something else, a metaphor creates a close association between the two entities and usually underscores some important similarity between them. An example of metaphor is "Richard is a pig."

Meter A recurrent, regular, rhythmic pattern in verse. When stresses recur at fixed intervals, the result is meter. Traditionally, meter has been the basic organizational device of world poetry. There are many existing meters, each identified by the different patterns of recurring sounds. In English most common meters involve the arrangement of stressed and unstressed syllables.

Metonymy Figure of speech in which the name of a thing is substituted for that of another closely associated with it. For instance, in saying "The White House decided," one could mean that the president decided.

Mixed metaphor A metaphor that trips over another metaphor—usually unconsciously—already in the statement. Mixed metaphors are the result of combining two or more incompatible metaphors resulting in ridiculousness or nonsense. For example, "Mary was such a tower of strength that she breezed her way through all the work" ("towers" do not "breeze").

Monologue An extended speech by a single character. The term originated in drama, where it describes a solo speech that has listeners (as opposed to a **soliloquy**, where the character speaks only to himself or herself). A poem can be written in monologue form if it is an unbroken speech by one character to another silent character or characters.

Monometer A verse meter consisting of one metrical foot, or one primary stress, per line.

Monosyllabic Foot A foot, or unit of meter, that contains only one syllable.

Motif An element that recurs significantly throughout a narrative. A motif can be an image, idea, theme, situation, or action (and was first commonly used as a musical term for a recurring melody or melodic fragment). A motif can also refer to an element that recurs across many literary works like a beautiful lady in medieval romances who turns out to be an evil fairy or three questions that are asked a protagonist to test his or her wisdom.

Myth A traditional narrative of anonymous authorship that arises out of a culture's oral tradition. The characters in traditional myths are usually gods or heroic figures. Myths characteristically explain the origins of things—gods, people, places, plants, animals, and natural events—usually from a cosmic view. A culture's values and belief systems are traditionally passed from generation to generation in myth. In literature, myth may also refer to boldly imagined narratives that embody primal truths about life. Myth is usually differentiated from legend, which has a specific historical base.

Mythological criticism The practice of analyzing a literary work by looking for recurrent universal patterns. Mythological criticism explores the artist's common humanity by tracing how the individual imagination uses myths and symbols that are shared by different cultures and epochs.

Narrative poem A poem that tells a story. Narrative is one of the four traditional modes of poetry, along with lyric, dramatic, and didactic. **Ballads** and **epics** are two common forms of narrative poetry.

Neoclassical period *See* **Augustan age**.

New Formalism A term for a recent literary movement (begun around 1980) in which young poets began using rhyme, meter, and narrative again. New Formalists attempt to write poetry that appeals to an audience beyond academia. Timothy Steele, Gertrude Schnackenberg, R. S. Gwynn, David Mason, and Marilyn Nelson are poets commonly associated with the movement.

Octameter A verse meter consisting of eight metrical feet, or eight primary stresses, per line.

Octave A stanza of eight lines. *Octave* is a term usually used when speaking of sonnets to indicate the first eight-line section of the poem, as distinct from the *sestet* (the final six lines). Some poets also use octaves as separate stanzas as in W. B. Yeats's "Sailing to Byzantium," which employs the *ottava rima* ("eighth rhyme") stanza—*abababcc*.

Off rhyme *See* **Slant rhyme**.

Omniscient narrator Also called **all-knowing narrator**. A narrator who has the ability to move freely through the consciousness of any character. The omniscient narrator also has complete knowledge of all of the external events in a story. (*See also* **Nonparticipant narrator**.)

Onomatopoeia A literary device that attempts to represent a thing or action by the word that imitates the sound associated with it (e.g., *crash, bang, pitter-patter*).

Open form Verse that has no set formal scheme—no meter, rhyme, or even set stanzaic pattern. Open form is always in free verse. (*See also* **Free verse**.)

Oral tradition The tradition within a culture that transmits narratives by word of mouth from one generation to another. Fables, folktales, ballads, and songs are examples of some types of narratives found originally in an oral tradition.

Overstatement Also called **hyperbole**. Exaggeration used to emphasize a point.

Parable A brief, usually allegorical narrative that teaches a moral. The parables found in Christian literature, such as "The Parable of the Prodigal Son" (Luke 15:11–32), are classic examples of the form. In parables, unlike fables (where the moral is explicitly stated within the narrative), the moral themes are implicit and can often be interpreted in several ways.

Paradox A statement that at first strikes one as self-contradictory, but that on reflection reveals some deeper sense. Paradox is often achieved by a play on words.

Parallelism An arrangement of words, phrases, clauses, or sentences side-by-side in a similar grammatical or structural way. Parallelism organizes ideas in a way that demonstrates their coordination to the reader.

Paraphrase The restatement in one's own words of what we understand a literary work to say. A paraphrase is similar to a summary, although not as brief or simple.

Parody A mocking imitation of a literary work or individual author's style, usually for comic effect. A parody typically exaggerates distinctive features of the original for humorous purposes.

Pentameter A verse meter consisting of five metrical feet, or five primary stresses, per line. In English, the most common form of pentameter is iambic.

Persona Latin for "mask." A fictitious character created by an author to be the speaker of a poem, story, or novel. A persona is always the narrator of the work and not merely a character in it.

Personification A figure of speech in which a thing, an animal, or an abstract term is endowed with human characteristics. Personification allows an author to dramatize the nonhuman world in tangibly human terms.

Petrarchan sonnet *See* **Italian sonnet**.

Poetic diction Strictly speaking, *poetic diction* means any language deemed suitable for verse, but the term generally refers to elevated language intended for poetry rather than common use. Poetic diction often refers to the ornate language used in literary periods such as the Augustan age, when authors employed a highly specialized vocabulary for their verse. (*See also* **Diction.**)

Portmanteau word An artificial word that combines parts of other words to express some combination of their qualities. Sometimes portmanteau words prove so useful that they become part of the standard language. For example, *smog* from *smoke* and *fog*; or *brunch* from *breakfast* and *lunch*.

Print culture A culture that depends primarily on the printed word—in books, magazines, and newspapers—to distribute and preserve information. In recent decades the electronic media have taken over much of this role from print.

Projective verse Charles Olson's theory that poets compose by listening to their own breathing and using it as a rhythmic guide rather than poetic meter or form. (*See also* **Open form.**)

Prose poem Poetic language printed in prose paragraphs, but displaying the careful attention to sound, imagery, and figurative language characteristic of poetry.

Prosody The study of metrical structures in poetry. (*See also* **Scansion.**)

Psalms Sacred songs, usually referring to the 150 Hebrew poems collected in the Old Testament.

Psychological criticism The practice of analyzing a literary work through investigating three major areas: the nature of literary genius, the psychological study of a particular artist, and the analysis of fictional characters. This methodology uses the analytical tools of psychology and psychoanalysis to understand the underlying motivations and meanings of a literary work.

Pun A play on words in which one word is substituted for another similar or identical sound, but of very different meaning.

Quantitative meter A meter constructed on the principle of vowel length. Such quantities are difficult to hear in English, so this meter remains slightly foreign to our language. Classical Greek and Latin poetry were written in quantitative meters.

Quatrain A stanza consisting of four lines. Quatrains are the most common stanza used in English-language poetry.

Rap A popular style of music that emerged in the 1980s in which lyrics are spoken or chanted over a steady beat, usually sampled or prerecorded. Rap lyrics are almost always rhymed and very rhythmic—syncopating a heavy metrical beat in a manner similar to jazz. Originally an African American form, rap is now international. In that way, rap can be seen as a form of popular poetry.

Reader-response criticism The practice of analyzing a literary work by describing what happens in the reader's mind while interpreting the text. Reader-response critics believe that no literary text exists independently of readers' interpretations and that there is no single fixed interpretation of any literary work.

Refrain A word, phrase, line, or stanza repeated at intervals in a song or poem. The repeated chorus of a song is a refrain.

Rhyme, Rime Two or more words that contain an identical or similar vowel sound, usually accented, with following consonant sounds (if any) identical as well: *queue* and *stew, prairie schooner* and *piano tuner*. (*See also* **Consonance, Exact rhyme**.)

Rhyme scheme, Rime scheme Any recurrent pattern of rhyme within an individual poem or fixed form. A rhyme scheme is usually described by using small letters to represent each end rhyme—*a* for the first rhyme, *b* for the second, and so on. The rhyme scheme of a stanza of **common meter** or hymn meter, for example, would be notated as *abab*.

Rhythm The pattern of stresses and pauses in a poem. A fixed and recurring rhythm in a poem is called **meter**.

Rising meter A meter whose movement rises from an unstressed syllable (or syllables) to a stressed syllable (for-*get*, in De-*troit*). Iambic and anapestic are examples of rising meter.

Rondel A thirteen-line English verse form consisting of three stanzas rhymed with a refrain.

Run-on line A line of verse that does not end in punctuation, but carries on grammatically to the next line. Such lines are read aloud with only a slight pause at the end. A run-on line is also called *enjambment*.

Sarcasm A conspicuously bitter form of irony in which the ironic statement is designed to hurt or mock its target. (*See also* **Irony**.)

Satiric poetry Poetry that blends criticism with humor to convey a message. Satire characteristically uses irony to make its points. Usually, its tone is one of detached amusement, withering contempt, and implied superiority.

Scansion A practice used to describe rhythmic patterns in a poem by separating the metrical feet, counting the syllables, marking the accents, and indicating the pauses. Scansion can be very useful in analyzing the sound of a poem and how it should be read aloud.

Sentimentality A usually pejorative description of the quality of a literary work that tries to convey great emotion but fails to give the reader sufficient grounds for sharing it.

Sestet A poem or stanza of six lines. *Sestet* is a term usually used when speaking of sonnets, to indicate the final six-line section of the poem, as distinct from the octave (the first eight lines). (*See also* **Sonnet**.)

Sestina A complex verse form ("song of sixes") in which six end words are repeated in a prescribed order through six stanzas. A sestina ends with an **envoy** of three lines in which all six words appear—for a total of thirty-nine lines. Originally used by French and Italian poets, the sestina has become a popular modern form in English.

Shakespearean sonnet *See* **English sonnet**.

Simile A comparison of two things, indicated by some connective, usually *like, as, than*, or a verb such as *resembles*. A simile usually compares two things that initially seem unlike but are shown to have a significant resemblance. "Cool as a cucumber" and "My love is like a red, red rose" are examples of similes.

Slack syllable An unstressed syllable in a line of verse.

Slant rhyme A rhyme in which the final consonant sounds are the same but the vowel sounds are different, as in letter and litter, bone and bean. Slant rhyme may also be called *near rhyme*, *off rhyme*, or *imperfect rhyme*. (*See also* **Consonance**.)

Sociological criticism The practice of analyzing a literary work by examining the cultural, economic, and political context in which it was written or received. Sociological criticism primarily explores the relationship between the artist and society.

Soliloquy Originating in drama, a speech by a character alone onstage in which he or she utters his or her thoughts aloud. The soliloquy is important in drama because it gives the audience insight into a character's inner life, private motivations, and uncertainties.

Sonnet From the Italian *sonnetto*: "little song." A traditional and widely used verse form, especially popular for love poetry. The sonnet is a fixed form of fourteen lines, traditionally written in iambic pentameter, usually made up of an **octave** (the first eight lines) and a concluding **sestet** (six lines). There are, however, several variations, most conspicuously the Shakespearean, or English sonnet, which consists of three quatrains and a concluding couplet. Most sonnets turn, or shift in tone or focus, after the eight lines, although the placement may vary. (*See also* **English sonnet, Italian sonnet**.)

Spondee A metrical foot of verse containing two stressed syllables (′ ′) often substituted into a meter to create extra emphasis.

Stanza From the Italian, meaning "stopping-place" or "room." A recurring pattern of two or more lines of verse, poetry's equivalent to the paragraph in prose. The stanza is the basic organizational principle of most formal poetry.

Stress An emphasis or accent placed on a syllable in speech. Clear pronunciation of polysyllabic words almost always depends on correct placement of their stress. (For instance, *de*-sert and de-*sert* are two different words and parts of speech, depending on their stress.) Stress is the basic principle of most English-language meter.

Style All the distinctive ways in which an author, genre, movement, or historical period uses language to create a literary work. An author's style depends on his or her characteristic use of diction, imagery, tone, syntax, and figurative language.

Surrealism A modernist movement in art and literature that tries to organize art according to the irrational dictates of the unconscious mind. Founded by the French poet André Breton, Surrealism sought to reach a higher plane of reality by abandoning logic for the seemingly absurd connections made in dreams and other unconscious mental activities.

Syllabic verse A verse form in which the poet establishes a pattern of a certain number of syllables to a line. Syllabic verse is the most common meter in most Romance languages such as Italian, French, and Spanish; it is less common in English because it is difficult to hear syllable count. Syllabic verse was used by several Modernist poets, most conspicuously Marianne Moore.

Symbol A person, place, or thing in a narrative that suggests meanings beyond its literal sense. Symbol is related to allegory, but it works more complexly. In an allegory an object has a single additional significance. By contrast, a symbol usually contains multiple meanings and associations. In Herman Melville's *Moby-Dick*, for example, the great white whale does not have just a single significance but accrues powerful associations as the narrative progresses.

Symbolic act An action whose significance goes well beyond its literal meaning. In literature, symbolic acts usually involve some conscious or unconscious ritual element like rebirth, purification, forgiveness, vengeance, or initiation.

Symbolist movement An international literary movement that originated with nineteenth-century French poets such as Charles Baudelaire, Arthur Rimbaud, and Paul Verlaine. Symbolists aspired to make literature resemble music. They avoided direct statement and exposition for powerful evocation and suggestion. Symbolists also considered the poet as a seer who could look beyond the mundane aspects of the everyday world to capture visions of a higher reality.

Symbolists Members of the Symbolist movement.

Synecdoche The use of a significant part of a thing to stand for the whole of it or vice versa. To say *wheels* for *car* or *rhyme* for *poetry* are examples of synecdoche. (*See also* **Metonymy**.)

Tactile imagery A word or sequence of words that refers to the sense of touch. (*See also* **Imagery**.)

Tercet A group of three lines of verse, usually all ending in the same rhyme. (*See also* **Terza rima**.)

Terminal refrain A refrain that appears at the end of each stanza in a song or poem. (*See also* **Refrain**.)

Terza rima A verse form made up of three-line stanzas that are connected by an overlapping rhyme scheme (*aba, bcb, cdc, ded*, etc.). Dante employs *terza rima* in *The Divine Comedy*.

Tetrameter A verse meter consisting of four metrical feet, or four primary stresses, per line.

Theme The central thought of a poem. A short work may have a single obvious theme, but longer works can contain multiple themes.

Thesis sentence A summing-up of the one main idea or argument that an essay or critical paper will embody.

Tone The attitude toward a subject conveyed in a literary work. No single stylistic device creates tone; it is the net result of the various elements an author brings to creating the works, feeling, and manner. Tone may be playful, sarcastic, ironic, sad, solemn, or any other possible attitude. A writer's tone plays an important role in establishing the reader's relationship to the characters or ideas presented in a literary work.

Traditional epic *See* **Folk epic**.

Transferred epithet A figure of speech in which the poet attributes some characteristic of a thing to another thing closely associated with it. Transferred epithet is a kind of metonymy. It usually places an adjective next to a noun in which the connection is not strictly logical (Milton's phrase "blind mouths" or Hart Crane's "nimble blue plateaus") but has expressive power.

Trimeter A verse meter consisting of three metrical feet, or three primary stresses, per line.

Triolet A short lyric form of eight rhymed lines borrowed from the French. The two opening lines are repeated according to a set pattern. Triolets are often playful, but dark lyric poems like Robert Bridge's "Triolet" demonstrate the form's flexibility.

Trochaic, trochee A metrical foot in which a stressed syllable is followed by an unstressed syllable (′ ⌣) as in the words *sum*-mer and *chor*-us. The trochaic meter is often associated with songs, chants, and magic spells in English.

Troubadours The minstrels of the late Middle Ages. Originally, troubadours were lyric poets living in southern France and northern Italy who sang to aristocratic audiences mostly of chivalry and love.

Understatement An ironic figure of speech that deliberately describes something in a way that is less than the true case.

Verbal irony A statement in which the speaker or writer says the opposite of what is really meant. For example, a friend might comment, "How graceful you are!" after you trip clumsily on a stair.

Verse From the Latin *versum*, "to turn." Verse has two major meanings. First, it refers to any single line of poetry. Second, it refers to any composition in lines of more or less regular rhythm—in contrast to prose.

Vers libre *See* **Free verse**.

Villanelle A fixed form developed by French courtly poets of the Middle Ages in imitation of Italian folk song. A villanelle consists of six rhymed stanzas in which two lines are repeated in a prescribed pattern.

Visual imagery A word or sequence of words that refers to the sense of sight or presents something one may see.

Vulgate From the Latin word *vulgus*, "mob" or "common people." The lowest level of formality in language, vulgate is the diction of the common people with no pretensions at refinement or elevation. The vulgate is not necessarily vulgar in the sense of containing foul or inappropriate language; it refers simply to unschooled, everyday language.

Acknowledgments

LITERARY ACKNOWLEDGMENTS

Aaron Abeyta: "thirteen ways of looking at a tortilla" from *Colcha* by Aaron Abeyta. Copyright © 2000. Reprinted by permission of the University Press of Colorado.

Kim Addonizio: "First Poem for You," copyright © 1994 by Kim Addonizio. Reprinted from *The Philosopher's Club* by Kim Addonizio, with the permission of BOA Editions, Ltd., Rochester, NY.

Francisco X. Alarcón: "The X in My Name" from *No Golden Gate for Us* by Francisco X. Alarcón. Copyright © 1993 by Francisco X. Alarcón. Reprinted by permission of Pennywhistle Press, Tesuque, NM 87574.

Sherman Alexie: "Indian Boy Love Song (#1)" reprinted from *The Business of Fancy Dancing*, © 1992 by Sherman Alexie, by permission of Hanging Loose Press.

Julia Alvarez: "The Women On My Mother's Side Were Known" from *Homecoming*. Copyright © 1984, 1996 by Julia Alvarez. Published by Plume, an imprint of The Penguin Group; originally published by Grove Press. Reprinted by permission of Susan Bergholz Literary Services, New York. All rights reserved.

A. R. Ammons: "Coward" reprinted by permission of the author.

John Ashbery: "At North Farm" from *A Wave* by John Ashbery. Copyright © 1981, 1982, 1983, 1984 by John Ashbery. "The Cathedral Is" from *As We Know* by John Ashbery. Copyright © 1979 by John Ashbery. Reprinted by permission of Georges Borchardt, Inc. for the author.

Margaret Atwood: "Romantic" from *Morning in the Burned House* by Margaret Atwood. Copyright © 1995 by Margaret Atwood. Reprinted by permission of Houghton Mifflin Company. All rights reserved. "You fit into me" from *Power Politics* by Margaret Atwood. Copyright © 1971 by Margaret Atwood. (House of Anansi Press Ltd.) Reprinted by permission.

W. H. Auden: "James Watt" from *Academic Graffiti* by W. H. Auden and Sanjust Filippo (illustrator), copyright © 1972 by W. H. Auden. Illustration copyright © 1972 by Sanjust Filippo. "Funeral Blues," copyright 1940 and renewed 1968 by W. H. Auden, "Musée des Beaux Arts," copyright 1940 and renewed 1968 by W. H. Auden, "The Unknown Citizen," copyright 1940 and renewed 1968 by W. H. Auden, "As I Walked Out One Evening," copyright 1940 and renewed 1968 by W. H. Auden, "September 1, 1939," copyright 1940 and renewed 1968 by W. H. Auden. All from *Collected Poems* by W. H. Auden. Used by permission of Random House, Inc. and Faber and Faber Ltd.

Roland Barthes: "The Death of the Author" from *Image/Music/Text*, translated by Stephen Heath. Reprinted by permission of Farrar, Straus & Giroux, LLC.

Mark Bauerlein: From *Literary Criticism: An Autopsy* by Mark Bauerlein. Copyright © 1997 University of Pennsylvania Press. Reprinted by permission.

Max Beerbohm: "On the imprint of the first English edition of The Works of Max Beerbohm." Final two lines inscribed by Max Beerbohm in a presentation copy of his book. Used by permission of Sir. Geoffrey Keynes.

Hilaire Belloc: "The Hippopotamus" from *Cautionary Verses* by Hilaire Belloc. Reprinted by permission of Peters Fraser & Dunlop.

Bruce Bennett: "The Lady Speaks Again" from *Taking Off* by Bruce Bennett (Orchises Press). Copyright © 1992 by Bruce Bennett. Reprinted by permission of the author.

Connie Bensley: "Last Haiku" and "The Covetous Cat" from *Choosing to Be a Swan*, Bloodaxe Books, 1994. Reprinted by permission of the publisher.

John Betjeman: "In Westminster Abbey" from *Collected Poems* by John Betjeman. Reprinted by permission of John Murray, London.

Elizabeth Bishop: "The Fish," "Filling Station," "One Art" and "Sestina" from *The Complete Poems 1927–1979* by Elizabeth Bishop. Copyright © 1979, 1983 by Alice Helen Methfessel. Reprinted by permission of Farrar, Straus and Giroux, LLC.

Chana Bloch: "Tired Sex" from *Mrs. Dumpty*, © 1998. Reprinted by permission of The University of Wisconsin Press.

Harold Bloom: "Poetic Influence" from *A Map of Misreading* by Harold Bloom. Copyright © 1975 by Oxford University Press. Used by permission of Oxford University Press, Inc.

Robert Bly: "Driving to Town Late to Mail a Letter" from *Silence in the Snow Fields* by Robert Bly, Wesleyan University Press. Copyright © 1959, 1960, 1961, 1962, by Robert Bly. Reprinted by permission of the author.

Eavan Boland: "Anorexic" from *An Origin Like Water: Collected Poems 1967–1987* by Eavan Boland. Copyright © 1996 by Eavan Boland. Used by permission of W. W. Norton & Company, Inc.

Jorge Luis Borges: "The Enigmas" translated by John Updike, copyright © 1999 by Maria Kodama; translation copyright © 1999 by John Updike from *Selected Poems* by Jorge Borges, edited by Alexander Coleman. Used by permission of Viking Penguin, a division of Penguin Group (USA) Inc. "Los Enigmas" by Jorge Borges reprinted by permission of Emece Editores S. A. "Amarosa Anticipación (Anticipation of Love)" translated by Robert Fitzgerald from *Jorge Luis Borges: Selected Poems 1923–1967* by Jorge Luis Borges, copyright © 1968, 1969, 1970, 1971, 1972 by Jorge Luis Borges, Emece Editores, S. A. and Norman Thomas Di Giovanni. Used by permission of Dell Publishing, a division of Random House, Inc. Excerpt from *This Craft of Verse: The Charles Eliot Norton Lectures 1967–1968* by Jorge Luis Borges, edited by Calin-Andrei Mihailescu, pp. 1–2, 17–18, Cambridge, Mass: Harvard University Press, copyright © 2000 by the President and Fellows of Harvard College. Reprinted by permission of the publisher.

Cleanth Brooks: Excerpts from "The Formalist Critic," copyright 1951 by Cleanth Brooks. Originally appeared in *The Kenyon Review*. Reprinted by permission of Patricia Sue Brooks.

Gwendolyn Brooks: "Queen of the Blues," "The Independent Man" "The Preacher Ruminates: Behind the Sermon" from *Blacks*. Reprinted by consent of Brooks Permissions. "The Mother" and "We Real Cool" from *Blacks*. Reprinted by permission of the author. Excerpt entitled "On 'We Real Cool'" from *Part One* by Gwendolyn Brooks. Reprinted by permission of the author.

Jennifer Brutschy: "Born Again" from *The San Francisco Haiku Anthology*, edited by J. Ball. Reprinted by permission of the author.

Buson: "The piercing chill I feel" from *An Introduction to Haiku* by Harold G. Henderson, copyright © 1958 by Harold G. Henderson. Used by permission of Doubleday, a division of Random House. "I Go" from *The Essential Haiku: Versions of Basho, Buson & Issa*, edited and with an Introduction by Robert Hass. Introduction and selection copyright © 1994 by Robert Hass. Unless otherwise noted, all translations copyright © 1994 by Robert Hass. Reprinted by permission of Harper-Collins Publishers, Inc.

Rafael Campo: "What the Body Told" from *What the Body Told*, by Rafael Campo. Copyright © 1996 by Rafael Campo. Reprinted by permission of Georges Borchardt, Inc. for the author.

Fred Chappell: "Narcissus and Echo" reprinted by permission of Louisiana State University Press from *Source: Poems by Fred Chappell*. Copyright © 1985 by Fred Chappell.

Dorothi Charles: "Concrete Cat" reprinted by permission of the author.

Kelly Cherry: "Advice to a Friend Who Paints" from *Lovers and Agnostics* by Kelly Cherry. Reprinted by permission of the author.

John Ciardi: "Most Like an Arch This Marriage," copyright © 1958 by John Ciardi. Reprinted from *Collected Poems* by John Ciardi. Reprinted by permission from the University of Arkansas Press.

Lucille Clifton: "Homage to my hips" first published in *Two-headed Woman*, copyright © 1980 by The University of Massachusetts Press, published by The University of Massachusetts Press. Now appears in *Good Woman: Poems and a Memoir 1969-1980*, copyright © 1987 by Lucille Clifton, published by BOA Editions Ltd. Reprinted by permission of Curtis Brown, Ltd.

Judith Ortiz Cofer: "Quinceañera" is reprinted with permission from the publisher of *Terms of Survival* (Houston: Arte Publico Press-University of Houston, 1987).

William Cole: "On my boat on Lake Cayuga" reprinted by permission.

Billy Collins: "The Names" was read at a special joint session of Congress held in New York City, September 9, 2002. "Care and Feeding" first appeared in *Five Points*, March 2003. Both poems are reprinted by permission of the author. "Embrace" from *The Apple That Astonished Paris*. Copyright © 1988 by Billy Collins. Reprinted by permission of the University of Arkansas Press.

Wendy Cope: "Lonely Hearts" and "A Nursery Rhyme (as it might have been written by William Wordsworth)" from *Making Cocoa for Kingsley Amis*. © Wendy Cope 1986. Reprinted by permission of Faber and Faber Ltd. "Variations on Belloc's 'Fatigue'" from *Serious Concerns* by Wendy Cope. Reprinted by permission of Faber and Faber and Peters, Fraser & Dunlop.

Robert Creeley: "Oh No" from *The Collected Poems of Robert Creeley, 1945–1975*. Copyright © 1983 by The Regents of the University of California. Reprinted by permission of the University of California Press.

H. Fairchild. Copyright © 2003 by B. H. Fairchild. Used by permission of W. W. Norton & Company.

Judith Farr: Excerpt from pages 241–244 of *The Passion of Emily Dickinson* by Judith Farr, reprinted by permission of the publisher. Cambridge, Mass.: Harvard University Press, Copyright © 1992 by the President and Fellows of Harvard College.

Gene Fehler: "If Richard Lovelace Became a Free Agent" reprinted by permission of the author.

Leslie Fiedler: "The Relationship of Poet and Poem" from *No! in Thunder* by Leslie A. Fiedler. Copyright 1960 by Leslie A. Fiedler. Reprinted by permission of Stein & Day, a division of Madison Books, Lanham, MD 20763.

Stanley Fish: Excerpt from *Is There a Text in This Class?* by Stanley Fish. Cambridge Mass: Harvard University Press. Copyright © 1980 by the President and Fellows of Harvard College. Reprinted by permission of the publisher.

Adelle Foley: "Learning to Shave (Father Teaching Son)," copyright © 2001 by Adelle Foley. Reprinted by permission.

Carolyn Forche: "The Colonel" from *The Country Between Us* by Carolyn Forche. Copyright © 1981 by Carolyn Forche. Originally appeared in Women's International Resource Exchange. Reprinted by permission of HarperCollins Publishers, Inc.

Sigmund Freud: "The Destiny of Oedipus" from *The Collected Papers, Volume 5* by Sigmund Freud, translated and edited by James Strachey. Published by Basic Books, Inc. by arrangement with The Hogarth Press, Ltd. and the Institute of Psycho-Analysis, London. Reprinted by permission of Basic Books, a member of Perseus Books, L.L.C. and by permission of Random House Group Ltd.

Robert Frost: "The Silken Tent," "The Secret Sits," "Desert Places," "Acquainted with the Night," "Fire and Ice," "Design," "Stopping by Woods on a Snowy Evening" from *The Poetry of Robert Frost*, edited by Edward Connery Lathem. Copyright 1922, 1923, © 1969 by Henry Holt and Company, copyright 1936, 1951 by Robert Frost, © 1964 by Lesley Frost Ballantine. "In White" the earlier version of "Design" first appeared in *The Dimensions of Robert Frost* by Reginald L. Cook, © 1958 by Reginald L. Cook. Reprinted by permission of Henry Holt and Company, LLC.

Northrup Frye: "Mythic Archetypes" from *Anatomy of Criticism*. Copyright © 1957, renewed 1985 by Princeton University Press. Reprinted by permission of Princeton University Press.

Alice Fulton: "What I Like" from *Dance Script with Electric Ballerina: Poems*. Copyright © 1983 by Alice Fulton. Used with permission of the poet and the University of Illinois Press.

Shirley Geok-lin Lim: "Learning to Love America" from *What the Fortune Teller Didn't Say*. Copyright © 1998 by Shirley Geok-lin Lim. Reprinted with the permission of West End Press, Albuquerque, NM.

Sandra Gilbert and Susan Gubar: "Editor's Introduction to Emily Dickinson" from *The Norton Anthology of Literature by Women: The Tradition in English* by Sandra M. Gilbert and Susan Gubar. Copyright © 1985 by Sandra M. Gilbert aand Susan Gubar. Used by permission of W. W. Norton & Company, Inc.

Allen Ginsberg: "A Supermarket in California" from *Collected Poems 1947–1980* by Allen Ginsberg. Copyright © 1955 by Allen Ginsberg. Reprinted by permission of HarperCollins Publishers, Inc.

Dana Gioia: "California Hills in August," copyright © 1986 by Dana Gioia. Reprinted from *Daily Horoscope*. "Entrance (After Rilke)," copyright © 2001 by Dana Gioia. Reprinted from *Interrogations at Noon*. Both poems reprinted with the permission of Graywolf Press, Saint Paul, Minnesota.

Heather Glen: Excerpt from *Vision and Disenchantment: Blake's "Songs" and Wordsworth's "Lyrical Ballads"* reprinted by permission of Cambridge University Press.

Louise Glück "Mock Orange" from *The First Four Books of Poems* by Louise Glück. Copyright 1968, 1971, 1973, 1973, 1974, 1975, 1976, 1977, 1978, 1979, 1980, 1985, 1995 by Louise Glück. Ecco Press. Reprinted by permission of HarperCollins Inc.

Robert Graves: "Down, Wanton, Down!" and "Counting the Beats" from *Complete Poems* by Robert Graves. Excerpt from *The Crowning Privilege* by Robert Graves copyright © 1955 by Robert Graves, renewed. Reprinted by permission of Carcanet Press Limited.

Emily Grosholz: "Listening" from *Eden*, p. 73, © 1992. Reprinted with permission of The Johns Hopkins University Press.

Ronald Gross: "Yield" reprinted with permission of Simon & Schuster from *Pop Poems* by Ronald Gross. Copyright © 1967 by Ronald Gross. Copyright renewed © 1995 by Ronald Gross.

Arthur Guiterman: "On the Vanity of Earthly Greatness," copyright © 1936 by E. P. Dutton & Co. Reprinted from *Gaily the Troubadour* by permission of Louise H. Sclove.

Thom Gunn: "The Man With Night Sweats" from *Collected Poems* by Thom Gunn. Copyright © 1994 by Thom Gunn. Reprinted by permission of Farrar, Straus and Giroux LLC and Faber and Faber Ltd.

Lee Gurga: "Visitor's Room" from *Fresh Scent*, edited by Randy M. Brooks. Reprinted by permission of the author and the publisher, Brooks Books.

R. S. Gwynn: "Scenes from the Playroom" reprinted from *The Drive-In: Poems* by R. S. Gwynn by permission of the University of Missouri Press. Copyright © 1986 by the Curators of the University of Missouri.

Ha Jin: "Missed Time" by Ha Jin originally appeared in *Poetry*, July 2000. Copyright © 2000 by The Modern Poetry Association. Reprinted by permission of the editor of Poetry and Ha Jin.

John Haines: "Winter News" from *Winter News*. Copyright © 1966 by John Haines. Reprinted by permission of Wesleyan University Press.

Donald Hall: "Names of Horses" from *Old and New Poems* by Donald Hall. Copyright © 1990 by Donald Hall. Reprinted by permission of Houghton Mifflin Company. All rights reserved. Originally published in the *New Yorker*.

Penny Harter: "broken bowl" from *In the Broken Curve* by Penny Harter. Copyright © 1984 by Penny Harter. Reprinted by permission of Burnt Lake Press.

Geoffrey H. Hartman: "On Wordsworth's 'A Slumber Did My Spirit Seal'" from "Elation in Hegel and Wordsworth" in *The Unremarkable Wordsworth* by Geoffrey Hartman. Copyright © 1987 by The University of Minnesota. Reprinted by permission of the University of Minnesota Press.

Robert Hayden: "Those Winter Sundays," copyright © 1966 by Robert Hayden, "The Whipping," copyright © 1966 by Robert Hayden from *Collected Poems of Robert Hayden*, Frederick Glaysher, editor. Used by permission of Liveright Publishing Corporation.

Seamus Heaney: "Digging" and "Mother of the Groom" from *Poems 1965–1975* by Seamus Heaney. Copyright © 1980 by Seamus Heaney. Reprinted by permission of Farrar, Straus and Giroux and Faber and Faber Ltd.

Anthony Hecht: "Adam" from *Collected Earlier Poems* by Anthony Hecht, copyright © 1990 by Anthony E. Hecht. Used by permission of Alfred A. Knopf, a division of Random House, Inc.

Geoffrey Hill: "Merlin" from *New & Collected Poems, 1952–1992* by Geoffrey Hill. Copyright © 1994 by Geoffrey Hill. Previously published in *Somewhere is Such a Kingdom* (1975). Reprinted by permission of Houghton Mifflin Company and the Marvell Press. All rights reserved.

H. L. Hix: "I Love the World, As does Any Dancer" from *Rational Numbers, Poems* by H. L. Hix. By permission of Truman State University Press, 2000.

Jonathan Holden: "The Names of the Rapids," copyright © 1985 by Jonathan Holden..

John Hollander: "Swan and Shadow" from *Types of Shape* by John Hollander. Copyright © 1969 by John Hollander. Reprinted by permission of the author.

A. D. Hope: "Imperial Adam" by A. D. Hope from *Collected Poems*. © 1968 A. D. Hope. Reprinted by permission of Collins/Angus & Robertson Publishers.

Horace: "Ode XI" from *The Odes of Horace* by Horace, translated by James Michie. Copyright © 1965 by James Michie. Used by permission of Viking Penguin, a division of Penguin Putnam Inc.

Andrew Hudgins: "Elegy for My Father, Who Is Not Dead" from *The Never-Ending* by Andrew Hudgins. Copyright © 1991 by Andrew Hudgins. Reprinted by permission of Houghton Mifflin Company. All rights reserved.

Langston Hughes: "The Weary Blues," "I, Too," "Song for a Dark Girl," "Ballad of the Landlord," "Subway Rush Hour," "Dream Boogie," "Harlem ("Dream Deferred"), "Theme for English B," "Desire," "End," "Island," "Litany," "Prayer," "Dream Variations," "Mother to Son," "The Negro Speaks of Rivers," "Sliver" from *The Collected Poems of Langston Hughes* by Langston Hughes, copyright © 1994 by The Estate of Langston Hughes. Used by permission of Alfred A. Knopf, a division of Random House, Inc. Excerpt from "When the Negro Was in Vogue" from *The Big Sea* by Langston Hughes. Copyright © 1940 by Langston Hughes. Copyright renewed 1968 by Arna Bontemps and George Houston Bass. Reprinted by permission of Hill and Wang, a division of Farrar, Straus and Giroux, LLC. "The Negro Artist and the Racial Mountain," copyright 1926 by Langston Hughes. First printed in *The Nation*, June 23, 1926. Reprinted by permission of Harold Ober Associates, Inc.

Ted Hughes: "Hawk Roosting" from *Lupercal* by Ted Hughes, 1960. Reprinted by permission of Faber and Faber Ltd.

Kobayashi Issa: "only one guy" translated by Cid Corman from *One Man's Moon: Fifty Haiku* (Gnomon Press, 1984). Reprinted by permission of the publisher and the author. "Cricket" translated by Robert Bly. Reprinted from *Ten Poems by Issa*, English versions by Robert Bly, Floating Island, 1992. Copyright 1972, 1992 by Robert Bly. Reprinted with permission.

Mark Jarman: "Unholy Sonnet: After the Praying" reprinted by permission of the author.

Randall Jarrell: "The Death of the Ball Turret Gunner" from *The Complete Poems by Randall Jarrell*. Copyright © 1969, renewed 1997 by

Mary von S. Jarrell. Reprinted by permission of Farrar, Straus and Giroux LLC.

Robinson Jeffers: "Hands" and "The Beaks of Eagles" from *The Collected Poetry of Robinson Jeffers, Volume 2, 1928–1938*, edited by Tim Hunt. Reprinted with the permission of the publishers, Stanford University Press www.sup.org. Copyright 1938, renewed 1966 by Donnan Jeffers and Garth Jeffers. "To the Stone-cutters" copyright 1924 and renewed 1952 by Robinson Jeffers from *Selected Poetry of Robinson Jeffers* by Robinson Jeffers. Used by permission of Random House, Inc.

Onwuchekwa Jemie: "A Dream Deferred" from *Langston Hughes: An Introduction to Poetry* by Onwuchekwa Jemie. Copyright © 1976 by Onwuchekwa Jemie. Published by Columbia University Press.

Thomas H. Johnson: "The Discovery of Emily Dickinson's Manuscripts" reprinted by permission of the publishers and the Trustees of Amherst College from *The Poems of Emily Dickinson*, Thomas H. Johnson, ed., Cambridge, Mass.: The Belknap Press of Harvard University Press. Copyright © 1951, 1955, 1979 by the President and Fellows of Harvard College.

C. G. Jung: "The Collective Unconscious and Archetypes" by C. G. Jung, translated by R. F. C. Hull from *The Collected Works of C. G. Jung*.

Donald Justice: "Men at Forty" and "Counting the Mad" from *New and Selected Poems* by Donald Justice, copyright © 1995 by Donald Justice. Used by permission of Alfred A. Knopf, a division of Random House, Inc.

Alfred Kazin: Excerpt from *An American Procession* by Alfred Kazin, copyright © 1984 by Alfred Kazin. Used by permission of Alfred A. Knopf, a division of Random House, Inc.

Weldon Kees: "For My Daughter" reprinted from *The Collected Poems of Weldon Kees*, edited by Donald Justice, by permission of the University of Nebraska Press. Copyright 1975 by the University of Nebraska Press.

Hugh Kenner: "Imagism" from *The Pound Era* by Hugh Kenner. Copyright © 1971 by Hugh Kenner. Reprinted by permission of the University of California Press.

Jane Kenyon: "The Suitor" from *From Room to Room*. © 1978 by Jane Kenyon. Reprinted courtesy of Alice James Books, 33 Richdale Avenue, Cambridge, MA 02138.

Omar Khayyam: "Rubai" translated by Dick Davis. Reprinted by permission. "Rubai" translated by Robert Graves and Omar Ali-Shah from *The Rubiaayt of Omar Khayyam*. Reprinted by permission of Carcanet Press.

Hugh Kingsmill: "What, still alive at twenty-two?" from *The Best of Hugh Kingsmill*. Reprinted by permission of Victor Gollancz Ltd.

Etheridge Knight: "Making jazz swing in" is from *The Essential Etheridge Knight* by Etheridge Knight © 1986. Reprinted by permission of the University of Pittsburgh Press.

Yusef Komunyakaa: "Facing It" from *Dien Kai Dau*. Copyright © 1988 by Yusef Komunyakaa. Reprinted by permission of Wesleyan University Press.

Ted Kooser: "Carrie" from *Sure Signs: New and Selected Poems* by Ted Kooser. © 1980 by Ted Kooser. Reprinted by permission of the University of Pittsburgh Press.

Robert Langbaum: "On Robert Browning's 'My Last Duchess'" from *The Poetry of Experience* by Robert Langbaum. Copyright © 1957, 1986 by Robert Langbaum. Reprinted by permission of the author.

Philip Larkin: "Aubade," "Home is so Sad," and "Poetry of Departures" from *Collected Poems* by Philip Larkin, edited by Anthony Twait. Copyright © 1988, 1989 by the Estate of Philip Larkin. Reprinted by permission of Farrar, Straus and Giroux and the Marvell Press.

D. H. Lawrence: "Bavarian Gentians" by D. H. Lawrence from *The Complete Poems of D. H. Lawrence*, edited by V. de Sola Pinto and F. W. Roberts. Copyright © 1964, 1971 by Angelo Ravagli and C. M. Weekley, Executors of the Estate of Frieda Lawrence Ravagli. Used by permission of Viking Penguin, a Division of Penguin (USA).

Irving Layton: "The Bull Calf" from *A Red Carpet for the Sun* (McClelland & Stewart). Reprinted by permission of the author.

Brad Leithauser Brad: "A Venus Flytrap" from *Hundreds of Fireflies* by Brad Leithauser. Copyright © 1981 by Brad Leithauser. Used by permission of Alfred A. Knopf, a division of Random House, Inc.

John Lennon and Paul McCartney: "Eleanor Rigby," words and music by John Lennon and Paul McCartney. Copyright © 1966 Sony/ATV Tunes LLC (Renewed). All rights administered by Sony/ATV Music Publishing, 8 Music Square West, Nashville, TN 37203. All rights reserved. Used by permission.

Denise Levertov: "Leaving Forever" from *Poems 1960–1967*, copyright © 1966 by Denise Levertov. "Ancient Stairway" from *This Great Unknowing: Last Poems*, copyright © 1998 by The Denise Levertov Literary Trust, Paul A. Lacey and Valerie Trueblood Rapport, Co-Trustees. Reprinted by permission of New Directions Publishing Corp.

Phillis Levin: "Brief Bio" from *The Afterimage*. Reprinted by permission of Copper Beach Press.

Philip Levine: "They Feed They Lion" from *They Feed They Lion and the Names of the Lost* by Philip Levine, copyright © 1968, 1969,

1970, 1971, 1972 by Philip Levine. *The Names of the Lost*, copyright © 1976 by Philip Levine. Used by permission of Alfred A. Knopf, a division of Random House, Inc.

Li Po: "Drinking Alone by Moonlight" by Li Po from *Liu, The Art of Chinese Poetry*. Reprinted by permission of the University of Chicago Press and Routledge.

Adrian Louis: "Looking for Judas" from *Vortex of Indian Fevers*. Evanston: TriQuarterly Books/Northwestern University Press, 1995, p. 25. Reprinted by permission of Northwestern University Press.

Robert Lowell: "Skunk Hour" from *Life Studies* by Robert Lowell. Copyright © 1959 by Robert Lowell. Copyright renewed © 1987 by Harriet Lowell, Sheridan Lowell and Caroline Lowell. Reprinted by permission of Farrar, Straus and Giroux, LLC.

Archibald MacLeish: "Ars Poetica" from *Collected Poems 1917–1982* by Archibald MacLeish. Copyright © 1985 by The Estate of Archibald MacLeish. Reprinted by permission of Houghton Mifflin Company. All rights reserved.

Louis MacNeice: "Plain Speaking" from *Collected Poems of Louis MacNeice*, edited by E. R. Dodds. Reprinted by permission of Faber and Faber Ltd.

Charles Martin: "Taken Up" from *Room for Error* (University of Georgia Press, 1978). Reprinted by permission of the author.

David Mason: "Song of the Powers" from *The Country I Remember*. Reprinted by permission of the author and Story Line Press.

Sukio Matsushita: "Rain shower from mountain," "Cosmos in bloom" from *May Sky: There is Always Tomorrow*. Translated by Violet Kazue de Cristoforo. Sun & Moon Press. Reprinted by permission.

Paul McCartney: "Creating 'Eleanor Rigby'" from *The Beatles, In Their Own Words* by Miles. Used by permission of the publisher, Omnibus Press, 8/9 Frith Street, London W1V 5TZ.

Robert McDowell: "At Home with Dollface" from *On Foot, In Flames* by Robert McDowell, © 2002. Reprinted by permission of the University of Pittsburgh Press.

Rod McKuen: "Thoughts on Capital Punishment" from *Stanyan Street and Other Sorrows* by Rod McKuen, copyright 1954, 1960, 1961, 1962, 1963, 1964, 1965, 1966 by Rod McKuen. Used by permission of Random House, Inc.

Wallace McRae: "Reincarnation" from *Cowboy Curmudgeon and Other Poems*. Reprinted by permission of the author.

Samuel Menashe: "The Shrine Whose Shape I Am" from *Collected Poems* by Samuel Menashe. Copyright © 1986 by Samuel Menashe.

Reprinted by permission of the National Poetry Foundation.

James Merril: "Kite Poem" from *Collected Poems* by James Merrill and J. D. McClatchy and Stephen Yenser, editors, copyright © 2001 by the Literary Estate of James Merrill at Washington University. Used by permission of Alfred A. Knopf, a division of Random House, Inc.

Stephanie Merrim: "Endgames: Sor Juana Ines de la Cruz" from *Early Modern Women's Writing and Sor Juana Ines de la Cruz*. Reprinted by permission of Vanderbilt University Press.

W. S. Merwin: "For the Anniversary of My Death," copyright © 1967 by W. S. Merwin from *Poems, Selections, The Second Four Books of Poems*. Reprinted with the permission of The Wylie Agency, Inc.

Josephine Miles: "Civilian" from *Collected Poems, 1930–1983*. Copyright © 1983 by Josephine Miles. Used with permission of the University of Illinois Press.

Edna St. Vincent Millay: "Counting-out Rhyme" from *Collected Poems*, HarperCollins Publishers, Inc. Copyright © 1928, 1955 by Edna St. Vincent Millay and Norma Millay Ellis. All rights reserved. Reprinted by permission of Elizabeth Barnett, literary executor.

Brett C. Millier: "On Elizabeth Bishop's 'One Art,'" copyright © 1993 by Brett C. Millier. Used by permission of the author. A fuller treatment of the subject appears in *Elizabeth Bishop: Life and the Memory of It* by Brett C. Millier (University of California Press, 1993). Lines from the first draft of "One Art" are quoted by permission of the Special Collections of the Vassar College Libraries and Elizabeth Bishop's literary executor, Alice H. Methfessell.

Joseph Moldenhauer: "'To His Coy Mistress' and the Renaissance Tradition" from "The Voices of Seduction in 'To His Coy Mistress.'" Reprinted by permission of Joseph Moldenhauer.

N. Scott Momaday: "Simile" from *Angle of Geese and Other Poems* by Scott Momaday. Reprinted by permission of David R. Godine, Publisher, Inc. Copyright © 1972 by Scott Momaday.

Emir Rodríguez Monegal: "Borges and Paz" from the *Perpetual Present: The Poetry and Prose of Octavio Paz*, edited by Ivar Ivask. Reprinted by permission of the University of Oklahoma Press.

Marianne Moore: "Silence" is reprinted with permission of Scribner, an imprint of Simon & Schuster Adult Publishing Group from *The Collected Poems of Marianne Moore*. Copyright 1935 by Marianne Moore. Copyright renewed © 1963 by Marianne Moore and T. S. Eliot.

Frederick Morgan: "The Master" from *Poems: New and Selected*. Copyright © 1987 by Frederick Morgan. Used with permission of the poet and the University of Illinois Press.

Howard Moss: "Shall I Compare Thee to a Summer's Day?" from *A Swim off the Rocks*. Copyright © 1976 by Howard Moss. Reprinted by permission of Richard Evans.

Marilyn Nelson: "A Strange Beautiful Woman" reprinted by permission of Louisiana State University Press from *The Fields of Praise* by Marilyn Nelson. Copyright © 1997 by Marilyn Nelson.

Howard Nemerov: "The War in the Air" from *Trying Conclusions* by Howard Nemerov. Reprinted by permission of Margaret Nemerov.

Pablo Neruda: "Muchos Somos" ("We Are Many") from *Estravagario* by Pablo Neruda. Translated by Alastair Reid. Translation copyright © 1974 by Alastair Reid. Reprinted by permission of Farrar, Straus and Giroux LLC. "Sonnet V" from *100 Love Sonnets: Cien Sonetos de Amor* by Pablo Neruda, translated by Stephen Tapscott. Copyright © Pablo Neruda 1959 and Fundacion Pablo Neruda, copyright © 1986 by the University of Texas Press. Reprinted by permission of the University of Texas Press. "Towards the Splendid City," © The Nobel Foundation 1971. Reprinted by permission.

Lorine Niedecker: "Sorrow Moves in Wide Waves" from *Lorine Niedecker: Collected Works*, edited by Jenny Lynn Pemberthy. Copyright © 2002 by the Regents of the University of California. Reprinted by permission of the University of California Press. "Popcorn-can cover" from *From This Condensery: The Complete Writings of Lorine Niedecker*, edited by Robert J. Bertolf. Copyright © Cid Corman, Literary Executor of the Lorine Niedecker Estate. Reprinted by permission.

John Frederick Nims: "Contemplation" reprinted by permission.

Sharon Olds: "Rites of Passage" and "The One Girl at the Boys' Party" from *The Dead and the Living* by Sharon Olds, copyright © 1987 by Sharon Olds. Used by permission of Alfred A. Knopf, a division of Random House, Inc.

Olga Orozco: "La Realidad y el Deseo" ("Reality and Desire") translated by Stephen Tapscott, from *Museo Salvaje*. Copyright © Stephen Tapscott. Reprinted by permission.

Neiji Ozawa: "War forced us from California" and "The war" from *May Sky: There Is Always Tomorrow: An Anthology of Japanese American Concentration Camp Kaiko Haiku*, compiled, translated, and prefaced by Violet Kazue de Cristoforo. Copyright © 1997 by Violet Kazue de Cristoforo. Reprinted by permission of Sun & Moon Press.

José Emilio Pacheco: "Alta Traición" ("High Treason") translated by Alastair Reid, from *Don't Ask Me How the Time Goes By*. Reprinted by permission of Columbia University Press.

Dorothy Parker: "Résumé," copyright 1926, 1928, renewed 1954, © 1956 by Dorothy Parker from *The Portable Dorothy Parker* by Dorothy Parker. Used by permission of Viking Penguin, a division of Penguin USA.

Linda Pastan: "Ethics" from *Waiting for My Life* by Linda Pastan. Copyright © 1981 by Linda Pastan. Used by permission of W. W. Norton & Company, Inc.

Octavio Paz: "With Our Eyes Shut" by Octavio Paz, translated by Eliot Weinberger, from *Collected Poems 1957–1987*, copyright © 1986 by Octavio Paz and Eliot Weinberger. "Certainty" by Octavio Paz, translated by Charles Tomlinson, from *Collected Poems 1957–1987*, copyright © 1968 by Octavio Paz and Charles Tomlinson. Reprinted by permission of New Directions Publishing Corp. "In Search of the Present" © The Nobel Foundation 1990. Reprinted by permission.

Robert Phillips: "Running on Empty" from *Personal Accounts: New and Selected Poems 1966–1986* (Princeton: Ontario Review Press, 1986). Copyright © 1981, 1986 by Robert Phillips. Reprinted by permission.

Darryl Pinckney: "Black Identity in Langston Hughes" from "Suitcase in Harlem" by Darryl Pinckney in the *New York Review of Books*, February 16, 1989. Reprinted with permission from the *New York Review of Books*. Copyright © 1989 by NYREV, Inc.

Robert Pinsky: "ABC" from *Jersey Rain* by Robert Pinsky. Copyright © 2000 by Robert Pinsky. Reprinted by permission of Farrar, Straus and Giroux LLC.

Sylvia Plath: "Metaphors" from *Crossing the Water* by Sylvia Plath. Copyright © 1960 by Ted Hughes. "Lady Lazarus" and "Daddy" from *Ariel* by Sylvia Plath. Copyright © 1963 by Ted Hughes. Reprinted by permission of HarperCollins Publishers, Inc. and Faber and Faber Ltd.

Craig Raine: "A Martian Sends a Postcard Home" from *A Martian Sends a Postcard Home* by Craig Raine. Reprinted by permission of David Godwin Associates.

Arnold Rampersad: "Hughes as an Experimentalist" from *African American Writers*, edited by Smith, Bacchler & Litz. Reprinted by permission of The Gale Group.

Dudley Randall: "A Different Image" from *Cities Burning* (Broadside Press) Copyright © 1966 by Dudley Randall. Reprinted by permission of Broadside Press. "Ballad of Birmingham" from *Cities Burning*. Reprinted by permission of the author.

John Crowe Ransom: "Piazza Piece" from *Selected Poems*, Third Edition, Revised and Enlarged by John Crowe Ransom, copyright 1924, 1927 by Alfred A. Knopf, Inc. and renewed 1952, 1955 by John Crowe Ransom. Used by permission of Alfred A. Knopf, a division of Random House, Inc.

Henry Reed: "Naming of Parts" from *A Map of Verona* by Henry Reed. © 1946 The executor of the Estate of Henry Reed. Reprinted by permission of John Tydeman.

James Reeves: "Rough Weather" reprinted by permission of The Estate of the Late James Reeves.

Alastair Reid: "High Treason," "Speaking a Foreign Language" and excerpt from "Neruda and Borges" reprinted by permission. © 1996 Alastair Reid. Originally in the *New Yorker*. All rights reserved.

Adrienne Rich: "Aunt Jennifer's Tigers," copyright © 2002, 1951 by Adrienne Rich, "Living in Sin," copyright © 2002, 1955 by Adrienne Rich, "Power," Copyright © 2002 by Adrienne Rich. From *The Fact of a Doorframe: Selected Poems 1950–2001* by Adrienne Rich, copyright © 1978 by W. W. Norton & Company, Inc. "Women," Copyright © 1993 by Adrienne Rich. From *Collected Early Poems: 1950–1970* by Adrienne Rich, copyright © 1969 by W. W. Norton & Company, Inc. Used by permission of the author and W. W. Norton & Company, Inc.

John Ridland: "The Lazy Man's Haiku" Reprinted by permission of the author.

Ranier Maria Rilke "Entrance (After Rilke)," copyright © 2001 by Dana Gioia. Reprinted from *Interrogations at Noon* with the permission of Graywolf Press, Saint Paul, Minnesota.

Theodore Roethke: "My Papa's Waltz," copyright 1942 by Hearst Magazines, Inc., "Root Cellar," copyright 1943 by Modern Poetry Association, Inc., "Elegy for Jane," copyright 1950 by Theodore Roethke, from *The Collected Poems of Theodore Roethke* by Theodore Roethke. Used by permission of Doubleday, a division of Random House, Inc.

Wendy Rose: "For the White Poets Who Would Be Indian" from *Bone Dance: New and Selected Poems 1965–1993. Sun Tracks*, Vol. 27. © 1994 by University of Arizona Press.

Clare Rossini: "Final Love Note" from *Winter Morning with Crow* by Clare Rossini. Reprinted by permission of the University of Akron Press.

Run D.M.C.: "Peter Piper" by Joseph W. Simmons and Darryl M. McDaniels © 1986 Rabasse Music Ltd. And Rush Groove Music (ASCAP). All rights administered by WB Music Corp. (ASCAP) All Rights Reserved. Used by permission. Warner Bros. Publications U.S. Inc., Miami, FL 33014.

Kay Ryan: "Turtle" from *Flamingo Watching*. Reprinted by permission of Copper Beach Press. "Blandeur" from *Say Uncle* by Kay Ryan. Copyright © 2000 by Kay Ryan. Used by permission of Grove/Atlantic, Inc.

Benjamin Alire Saenz: "To the Desert" from *Dark and Perfect Angels* by Benjamin Alire Saenz, 1995. Used by permission of the publisher, Cinco Puntos Press.

Mary Jo Salter: "Welcome to Hiroshima" from *Henry Purcell in Japan* by Mary Jo Salter, copyright © 1984 by Mary Jo Salter. Used by permission of Alfred A. Knopf, a division of Random House, Inc.

Carole Satyamurti: "I Shall Paint My Nails Red" © 1990 by Carole Satyamurti. Reprinted by permission of Bloodaxe Books Ltd.

Gjertrud Schnackenberg: "Supernatural Love" from *Supernatural Love: Poems 1976–1992*, copyright © 2000 by Gjertrud Schnackenberg. Reprinted by permission of Farrar, Straus and Giroux, LLC.

Robert Scholes: "How Do We Make a Poem?" excerpt from *Semiotics and Interpretation* by Robert Scholes. Copyright © 1982 by Yale University. Reprinted by permission of Yale University Press.

Anne Sexton: "Her Kind" from *To Bedlam and Part Way Back* by Anne Sexton. Copyright © 1960 by Anne Sexton, © renewed 1988 by Linda G. Sexton. "Cinderella" from *Transformations* by Anne Sexton. Copyright © 1971 by Anne Sexton. Letter, from *Anne Sexton: A Self Portrait in Letters*, edited by Linda Gray Sexton and Lois Ames. Copyright © 1977 by Linda Gray Sexton and Loring Conant, Jr., executors of the will of Anne Sexton. All reprinted by permission of Houghton Mifflin Company. All rights reserved.

Elaine Showalter: Excerpt from "Toward a Feminist Criticism," copyright © 1979 by Elaine Showalter. From Elaine Showalter, ed., *Feminist Criticism: Essays on Women, Literature, and Theory* (Pantheon, 1985). Reprinted by permission of the author.

Charles Simic: "Fork" from *Somewhere Among Us a Stone is Taking Notes*, first published in *Kayak* 1969, from *Charles Simic: Selected Early Poems*, published by George Braziller.

Louis Simpson: "American Poetry" from *A Poetry Collection*. Reprinted by permission of the author and Story Line Press.

David R. Slavitt: "Titanic" reprinted by permission of Louisiana State University Press from *Big Nose: Poems* by David R. Slavitt. Copyright © 1983 by David R. Slavitt.

Stevie Smith: "Not Waving But Drowning" and "This Englishwoman" by Stevie Smith from *Collected Poems of Stevie Smith*, copyright © 1972 by Stevie Smith. Reprinted by permission of New Directions Publishing Corp.

William Jay Smith: "American Primitive" from *The World Below the Window: Poems 1937–1997*, pp. 91 © 1998. Reprinted with permission of The Johns Hopkins University Press.

Gary Snyder: "Piute Creek" from *Riprap & Cold Mountain Poems*. Reprinted by permission.

Cathy Song: "Stamp Collecting" from *Frameless Windows, Squares of Light: Poems* by Cathy Song. Copyright © 1988 by Cathy Song. Used by permission of W. W. Norton & Company, Inc.

Sor Juana: Excerpt reprinted by permission of the publisher from *A Sor Juana Anthology*, translated by Alan S. Trueblood, pp. 224–225, Cambridge, Mass.: Harvard University Press, copyright © 1988 by the President and Fellows of Harvard College. "Asegura la Confianza de que Oculturö de Todo un Secreto" (She Promises to Hold a Secret in Confidence) and "Presente En qu el Cario Hace Regalo la Llaneza" (A Simple Gift Made Rich by Affection) both translated by Diane Thiel. Reprinted by permission.

William Stafford: "Farm on the Great Plains," "Traveling Through the Dark," "Ask Me," copyright © 1959, 1962, 1977, 1988 by the Estate of William Stafford. Reprinted from *The Way It Is: New & Selected Poems* with the permission of Graywolf Press, Saint Paul, Minnesota. "At the Un-National Monument Along the Canadian Border" reprinted by permission of the author.

A. E. Stallings: "Sine Qua Non" first appeared in *Poetry*, October–November 2002. Copyright © 2002 by The Poetry Foundation. Reprinted by permission of the Editor of *Poetry* and the author. "A New Year's Toast" (translation of Horace *Odes*, Book 1, Ode XI) by A. E. Stallings. First appeared in *Light*. Reprinted by permission of the author.

Jon Stallworthy: "An Evening Walk" from *Rounding the Horn* reprinted by permission of Carcanet Press Limited.

Timothy Steele: "Epitaph" from *Uncertainties and Rest* by Timothy Steele. Copyright © 1979. "Summer" from *Sapphics Against Anger and Other Poems* Random House, 1986. Copyright © 1986 by Timothy Steele. Reprinted by permission of the author.

Anne Stevenson: "Sous-Entendu" and "The Victory" from *The Collected Poems 1955–1985* (Bloodaxe Books, 2000). Reprinted by permission of the publisher.

Michael Stillman: "In Memoriam John Coltrane" from *Occident*, Fall, 1971. Copyright © 1976 by Michael Stillman. Reprinted by permission of the author.

Ruth Stone: "Second Hand Coat" from *The Iowa Review*, Volume 12: 2/3, Spring/Summer 1981. Reprinted by permission of the author.

Alfonsina Storni: "Peso Ancestral" from *Obras completas*, copyright 1964 by Ed. Aguilar. Translated by Diane Thiel. Reprinted by permission.

Sara Teasdale: "The Flight" reprinted with the permission of Scribner, an imprint of Simon & Schuster Adult Publishing group, from *The Collected Poems of Sara Teasdale* by Sara Teasdale. Copyright © 1926 by The Macmillan Company; copyright renewed © 1954 by Mamie T. Wheless.

Cornelius J. Ter Maat: "Etienne de Silhouette" reprinted by permission of the author.

Diane Thiel: "Memento Mori in Middle School" from *Echolocations*. Copyright © 2000. Reprinted by permission of the author and Story Line Press.

Dylan Thomas: "Fern Hill," copyright © 1945 by The Trustees for the Copyrights of Dylan Thomas and "Do Not Go Gentle Into That Good Night," copyright © 1952 by Dylan Thomas. Both from *The Poems of Dylan Thomas*. Reprinted by permission of New Directions Publishing Corp. and David Higham Associates.

Peter Townsend: Excerpt from "Langston Hughes and Jazz" from *Jazz in American Culture* by Peter Townsend. Copyright © 2000. Reprinted by permission of Edinburgh University Press.

Natasha Trethewey: "White Lies," copyright © 2000 by Natasha Trethewey. Reprinted from *Domestic Work* with the permission of Graywolf Press, Saint Paul, Minnesota.

John Updike: "Recital" from *Telephone Poles & Other Poems* by John Updike, copyright © 1959 by John Updike. "Ex-Basketball Player" from *The Carpentered Hen and Other Tame Creatures* by John Updike, copyright © 1982 by John Updike. Used by permission of Alfred A. Knopf, a division of Random House, Inc.

Amy Uyematsu: "The Ten Million Flames of Los Angeles" from *Nights of Fire, Nights of Rain*. Reprinted by permission of the author and Story Line Press.

César Vallejo: "Anger" by Thomas Merton, original by César Vallejo from *The Collected Poems of Thomas Merton*, copyright © 1948 by New Directions Publishing Corporation, 1977 by The Trustees of the Merton Legacy Trust. Reprinted by permission of New Directions Publishing Corp.

Hakuro Wada: "Even the croaking of the frogs" from *May Sky: There is Always Tomorrow*, translated by Violet Kazue de Cristoforo. Reprinted by permission of the publisher.

CORBIS; 496: Brown Brothers; 499: Ted Russell; 504: By courtesy of the National Portrait Gallery, London; 506: Fay Godwin/Network Photographers/CORBIS SABA; 515: Brown Brothers; 517: AP/Wide World Photos; 519: Dorothy Alexander; 521: Gail and Bonnie Roub; 523: © Nancy Crampton; 524: Dorothy Alexander; 526: Bettmann/CORBIS; 532: Willie Williams, courtesy Broadside Press; 536: Bettmann/CORBIS; 537: Photograph by Imogen Cunningham © 1978 The Imogen Cunningham Trust; 538: Jerry Bauer; 540: By courtesy of the National Portrait Gallery, London; 547: Reprinted from School Figures, by Cathy Song, © 1994, by permission of the University of Pittsburgh Press; 549: Bettmann/CORBIS; 554: By courtesy of the National Portrait Gallery, London; 559: Amy Uyematsu, courtesy Story Line Press; 561: Bettmann/ CORBIS; 563: Gabriel Harrison/Library of Congress; 566: Courtesy of New Directions; 567: By courtesy of the National Portrait Gallery, London; 571: The Royal Photographic Society

Index of First Lines of Poetry

The largest stock of armaments allows me, 41
The lies I could tell, 28
The Lightning is a yellow Fork, 261
The midge spins out to safety, 626
The Negro beach jumped to the twitch, 469
The old woman across the way, 383
The piercing chill I feel, 94
the poor, 314
The poorest countries, 547
The readers of the *Boston Evening Transcript*, 260
There are, 426
There are no stars tonight, 464
There ought to be capital punishment for cars, 376
There's a certain Slant of light, 403
There's never an end to dust, 272
There were three ravens sat on a tree, 443.
The sea is calm tonight, 445
these hips are big hips, 254
The shrine whose shape I am, 314
The skylark and the jay sang loud and long, 338
The Soul selects her own Society, 404
The splendor falls on castle walls, 173
The thing could barely stand. Yet taken, 508
The time you won your town the race, 498
The tusks that clashed in mighty brawls, 382
The war—this year, 104
The whiskey on your breath, 22
The wind stood up and gave a shout, 129
The winter evening settles down, 96
The women on my mother's side were known, 310
The world is charged with the grandeur of God, 179
The world is too much with us; late and soon, 282
They flee from me that sometime did me sekë, 570
They say that Richard Cory owns, 147
They say the wells, 109
Thirty days hath September, 5
Thirty days in jail with my back turned to the wall, 153
This Englishwoman is so refined, 228
This *Humanist* whom no beliefs constrained, 228
This is my letter to the World, 406
This is the field where the battle did not happen, 44
This living hand, now warm and capable, 214
This one was put in a jacket, 501
This page, discreetly, will convey, 348
This strange thing must have crept, 100
Thou ill-formed offspring of my feeble brain, 23
Thou still unravished bride of quietness, 501
Three Summers since I chose a maid, 514
Tired of earth, they dwindled on their hill, 292
Today we have naming of parts. Yesterday, 533
To fling my arms wide, 422

Tongi-ye may-e la'l kh'aham o divani, 335
To see the world in a grain of sand, 124
To share with you this rough, divisive weather, 176
Traveling through the dark I found a deer, 376
Treason doth never prosper; what's the reason?, 227
True Ease in Writing comes from Art, not Chance, 166
Tú me dijiste: no lloró mi padre, 362
Tu ne quaesieris—scire nefas—quem mihi, quem tibi, 332
Turning and turning in the widening gyre, 286
'Twas brillig, and the slithy toves, 75
Two roads diverged in a yellow wood, 266
Tyger! Tyger! burning bright, 453

Visitor's Room—, 104
Voluptuous in plenty, summer is, 226

War forced us from California, 104
Wave of sorrow, 426
Way Down South in Dixie, 424
We are two eagles, 270
Weary with toil, I haste me to my bed, 541
Weathered gray, the wooden walls, 510
We dance round in a ring and suppose, 136
We four lads from Liverpool are, 337
Welcome to Hiroshina is what you first see, stepping off the train, 538
We lie back to back. Curtains, 135
Well, son, I'll tell you, 421
Wer du auch seist: Am Abend tritt hinaus, 329
We real cool. We, 193
We're trying to strike a match in a matchbook, 106
Western wind, when wilt thou blow, 445
We stood by a pond that winter day, 263
We were very tired, we were very merry, 515
What, still alive at twenty-two, 338
What did we say to each other, 124
What does reincarnation mean?, 377
Whatever it is, it must have, 543
What happens to a dream deferred?, 428
What lips my lips have kissed, and where, and why, 223
What passing-bells for these who die as cattle?, 524
What she remembers, 491
What thoughts I have of you tonight, Walt Whitman, 482
What you have heard is true, 248
When, in disgrace with Fortune and men's eyes, 540
Whenas in silks my Julia goes, 65
Whenever Richard Cory went down town, 146
When first we met we did not guess, 232
When fishes flew and forests walked, 461
When God at first made man, 132
When Han Kan was summoned, 518

Index of Authors and Titles

Each page number immediately following a writer's name indicates a quotation from or reference to that writer. A number in **bold** refers you to the page on which you will find the author's biography. n following a page number indicates an entry in a note.

To the Student

As publishers, we realize that one way to improve education is to improve textbooks. We also realize that you, as students, largely determine the success or failure of textbooks. Although the instructor assigns them, the student buys and uses them. If enough of you don't like a book and make your feelings known, the chances are your instructor will not assign it again.

Usually only instructors are asked about the quality of a text; their opinions alone are considered as revisions are planned or as new books are developed. Now, we would like to ask you about X. J. Kennedy and Dana Gioia's *An Introduction to Poetry*, Eleventh Edition: how you liked or disliked it; why it was interesting or dull; if it taught you anything. Please fill in this form and return it to us at: Longman Publishers, Literature Editor, 1185 Avenue of the Americas, New York, NY 10036.

School: _____

Instructor's name: _____

Title of course: _____

1. Did you find this book too easy? _____ too difficult? _____ about right? _____

2. Which chapters did you find the most interesting? _____
_____

3. Which chapters did you find least interesting? _____
_____

4. Which poems do you like most? _____
_____
_____
_____

Do you particularly dislike any of the poems? _____
_____
_____
_____

5. Are the chapters "Writing About Literature," "Writing About a Poem," and "Writing a Research Paper" very useful? _____ somewhat useful? _____ of no help? _____
   Comments? _____
   _____

6. Have you used the Companion Website to this book?
   Yes _____   No _____
   Any comments on the Website? _____
   _____
   _____

7. Do you intend to keep this book for your personal library?
   Yes _____   No _____

8. Any other comments or suggestions: _____
   _____
   _____
   _____

9. May we quote you in our efforts to promote this book?
   Yes _____   No _____

Date: _____

Signature (optional): _____

Address (optional): _____

INDEX OF LITERARY TERMS

The page numbers below indicate where each term is discussed in the body of the anthology. A page number in **bold** indicates an entry in the Glossary of Literary Terms which begins on page 693. n following a page number indicates an entry in a note.

(continued)

INDEX OF LITERARY TERMS

(continued)

An Introduction to POETRY

ELEVENTH EDITION

X.J. Kennedy and Dana Gioia

In *An Introduction to Poetry*, two distinguished poets and teachers—X.J. Gioia—bring to students the joyful and liberating experience of reading poetry. The book's fresh, commonsense approach helps to demystify poetry for those with limited exposure to it. For those who already enjoy poetry, here is a feast.

An Introduction to Poetry has been newly revised with the help of instructors and students. The eleventh edition includes the following features:

- *More than 500 poems* represent a diverse mix of classic favorites and exciting contemporary works.

- *A new and unique Casebook on Latin American Poetry* recognizes the important role Spanish-language poetry plays in the literature of the Americas. All poems in the casebook are given in their native Spanish and in English translation.

- *Two critical casebooks* feature Emily Dickinson and Langston Hughes.

- *A Writer's Perspective* section in each chapter showcases a poet discussing his or her own work.

- *Writing Critically* sections at the end of each chapter offer insightful and accessible advice for writing about literature.

- *Three chapters* provide detailed guidance for writing a...

- *A new chapter,* "Writing a Research Paper," provid... ...vice on such topics as getting started, evaluating Internet sources, plagiarism... ...enting sources.

- *Six student papers* give students realistic ... ...ow to write about poetry.

- *The Kennedy/Gioia Companion Website* ...igman.com/kennedy) offers a wide range of extended biographies and critical archi... ...r 18 poets.

From the ballad poets of the Middle Ages to the rap poets of today, from Shakespeare and Donne to Dickinson and Frost, Kennedy and Gioia show poetry in all its richness and range. Through their own love for the subject, they encourage students to discover poems that can speak to them personally and for life.

PEARSON
Longman

VISIT US ON THE WEB
AT WWW.ABLONGMAN.COM

ISBN 0-321-20939-7

90000

9 780321 209399